Understanding
Biological
Psychology

Basic Psychology

This series offers those new to the study of psychology comprehensive, systematic and accessible introductions to the core areas of the subject. Written by specialists in their fields, they are designed to convey something of the flavour and excitement of psychological research today.

Understanding Children's Development
Fourth Edition
PETER K. SMITH, HELEN COWIE AND MARK BLADES

Understanding Cognition
PETER J. HAMPSON AND PETER E. MORRIS

Understanding Abnormal Psychology
NEIL FRUDE

Understanding Biological Psychology
PHILIP J. CORR

Understanding Biological Psychology

Philip J. Corr

Department of Psychology
University of Wales Swansea

Blackwell
Publishing

BLACKWELL PUBLISHING
350 Main Street, Malden, MA 02148-5020, USA
9600 Garsington Road, Oxford OX4 2DQ, UK
550 Swanston Street, Carlton, Victoria 3053, Australia

First published 2006 by Blackwell Publishing Ltd

Library of Congress Cataloging-in-Publication Data

Corr, Philip J.
    Understanding biological psychology / Philip J. Corr.
        p. cm. – (Basic psychology)
    Includes bibliographical references and index.
    ISBN-13: 978-0-631-21953-8 (hardcover : alk. paper)
    ISBN-10: 0-631-21953-6 (hardcover : alk. paper)
    ISBN-13: 978-0-631-21954-5 (pbk. : alk. paper)
    ISBN-10: 0-631-21954-4 (pbk. : alk. paper)
    1. Psychobiology.   I. Title.   II. Series: Basic psychology (Oxford, England)
QP360.C6677 2006
612.8–dc22

                                                        2005033633

A catalogue record for this title is available from the British Library.

Set in 10.5/12.5pt Dante
by Graphicraft Limited, Hong Kong

For further information on
Blackwell Publishing, visit our website:
www.blackwellpublishing.com

Contents

Preface

Biological psychology has entered an exciting era. Rapid advances are being made in our understanding of the biological basis of the mind, and whole new areas of investigation are being opened up by technological innovation (for example, the Human Genome Project). These advances are destined to transform our understanding of psychology and promise to lead to many practical benefits, notably innovative therapeutic approaches in medicine and psychiatry. This is indeed an exciting time to be studying biological psychology; it is certainly an exciting time to be writing about it.

As a result of this rapid scientific progress, however, biological psychology is becoming increasingly complex (there are between 20,000 and 30,000 scientific articles on the brain published each year). This complexity poses a challenge to the student, who is bombarded with an array of new concepts, processes, systems and experimental findings, many of which come with their own obscure nomenclature. Biological psychology can, indeed, seem daunting. In this book the presentation of material, while not disguising this complexity, focuses on the central themes running through the subject and how these themes relate to some of the major areas of interest to the psychologist.

Biological processes are at the heart of our own experiences, as well as being at the heart of psychology: they form the foundations of every thought, feeling and action we have, and they are implicated in all experimental effects reported in psychology journals. For example, there can be no cognition or social behaviour without the mediation of the brain. In clinical neurology, all too easily it is seen that brain damage (resulting from tumour, stroke, etc.) robs patients of certain aspects of their minds (e.g., long-term memory), and certain pathological brain processes (e.g., senile dementia) rob patients of their sense of self and identity. The *extent* to which brain processes must be considered in psychological theories of normal behaviour is, of course, open to debate – at times, heated debate – and quite rightly so, as no one approach in psychology can claim supremacy.

The main theme of this book concerns *understanding* biological psychology, by which is meant not the learning of long lists of facts and figures about brain structure and function (although some learning in this respect is unavoidable), but rather the appreciation of the central role that biological processes play in psychology. Thus, the aim of this book is to cover the core aspects of the biological perspective in psychology from a conceptual viewpoint, which, it is hoped, will give a better perspective over the whole psychological landscape. This book surveys not only what is currently known, but also what is knowable and will be known in the not too distant future (e.g., the molecular basis of major psychiatric disorders); this will involve acknowledging the lack of empirical findings and theoretical agreement, but also the recognition that innovative techniques are pushing forward the boundaries of our knowledge (e.g., gene sequencing techniques). This Janus-faced approach is core to the scientific perspective: looking back to the past and published research and looking to the future with all its prospects and problems.

As noted by the Nobel Prize winning chemist, Harry Kroto (2002), the key to understanding complex phenomena is the recognition of the importance of framing the research problem clearly in the first place: first, it is important to know what we do not really understand; and second, the crucial questions in need of answer must be clarified. Some mysteries in psychology (e.g., consciousness) consist not so much in our inability to provide appropriate tools of investigation but rather in our inability to frame the crucial research questions in a sufficiently precise manner. Confucius was way ahead of us in recognizing this problem: 'I seek not the answer, but to understand the question.'

The book is divided into three main Parts: 'Foundations', 'Approaches' and 'Applications'. Part I covers a number of fundamental aspects of biological psychology; Part II surveys the main methodologies used and, by way of illustration, describes the types of careers open to the biologically inspired psychologist; and Part III provides a presentation of a sample of some of the implications of biological psychology in psychopathology, personality and cognition.

This book is primarily aimed at undergraduate psychology students, but is also appropriate for postgraduate students without a formal background in psychology or biological aspects of psychology – some of the chapters, especially those in Part II ('Approaches') will be useful to psychology postgraduate students, and the chapters in Part III ('Applications') to clinical and health psychology students.

Understanding Psychology

What is meant by *understanding*? This involves more than merely learning theories and findings and being able to recall these in sufficient detail to pass assessment tests. Understanding is to know the reasons for the adoption of a research approach and to appreciate the intellectual excitement and the human passions that go to make up a scientific discipline. The learning of specific theories and findings is, needless to say, important, but appreciating *why* these theories and findings are considered important is a necessary precondition to *understanding* their true significance.

As noted by the famous neuropsychologist Donald Hebb (1949, p. xi), 'the task of the psychologist, the task of understanding behavior and reducing the vagaries of human thought to a mechanical process of cause and effect, is a more difficult one than of any other scientist'. In addition to the sheer complexity of psychological phenomena, understanding psychology is more difficult than understanding other disciplines (e.g., physics or chemistry) for a number of reasons. First, its object of study is familiar to us all: we all have first-hand experience of what it is like to have a human mind and we have common-sense ideas about our own and others' behaviour, motives, intentions, etc. These naive ideas often stand in the way of our appreciating and accepting scientific findings. Second, psychology is a fragmented discipline. This fragmentation can lead to fragmented understanding. As any student quickly learns, undergraduate degree programmes in psychology typically comprise a number of separate courses (Cognition, Social Psychology, Biological Psychology, Individual Differences, Clinical Psychology, Occupational Psychology, etc.). Upon entering the library, one quickly sees that textbooks and academic journals are also divided along these lines. The undergraduate student may be forgiven for thinking that psychology is little more than a collection of relatively separate – indeed, sometimes seemingly incompatible – sub-disciplines. This fragmented structure of psychology is unfortunate because it promotes the false idea that psychology is not a unified discipline. As Toates (2001, p. xi) stated,

> the fragmentation of psychology is to be regretted and . . . the future lies in reinforcing bridges rather than blowing them up.

This book endorses Toates' conclusion wholeheartedly. Accordingly, one of the aims of this book is to show the essential overlaps between the biological approach to psychology and other areas of psychology that are usually seen as being rather separate (e.g., personality and computation/consciousness). In particular, this book tries to show what biological psychology is *for*. Thus, the emphasis of the text will be more on biological *psychology*, rather than *biological* psychology.

Although biological psychology is a discipline in its own right – as usually described in most biological or physiological psychology texts – it is perhaps best understood by the psychology student from the perspective of its applications to core topics in psychology. What is emotion? Why do people differ in their behaviour? Are some people especially prone to schizophrenia? Are some people more prone to addiction than others? Is anxiety beneficial? What is the function of being conscious of the external world? Indeed, is the world perceived really 'out there'?

Learning to Learn Psychology

To *understand* one first has to *learn*. But what is the best way to learn about a new and highly complex topic such as biological psychology? The typical organization of undergraduate psychology programmes tacitly endorses the view that psychology is best learned by first acquiring (via *episodic* learning) the basic knowledge of the different courses that go to make up the psychology syllabus. Then, as the undergraduate moves from the first level to higher levels of the degree programme, it is assumed that a deeper *semantic* form of knowledge develops – very often though it is not made explicit how this deeper knowledge develops. The psychology of learning informs us that an important feature of knowledge acquisition is 'learning to learn' – intellectually limbering up – that is, to have first acquired a conceptual framework in which the separate elements of theories and data may be accommodated. In the language of cognitive psychology, a *schema* is developed which serves to guide and organize further knowledge acquisition.

```
SSSS
S      S
S      S
SSSS
S
S
S
```

Figure 0.1 This example of a Navon figure shows whole (P) and part (s) features. Information processing is biased in favour of analysis of the global (P) feature, as shown by interference (e.g., slowed reaction times) when processing local features (s). (For further discussion see Navon, 1977.)

It is known from social and cognitive psychology that human beings search for holistic meaning in new environments, especially where information is novel and apparently unstructured. Look at the 'P' in figure 0.1. What do you first see? Most people perceive the holistic 'P' first, and only then the 's' parts that make up the holistic pattern (Navon, 1977). This perception reflects our preference for *whole* rather than *parts* analysis. Likewise in the learning of psychology: understanding the holistic framework of psychology is useful for assimilating individual aspects of psychology. Motivation research informs us that having a conceptual overview promotes positive affective reactions and approach behaviour in new environments – two important elements in the effective *learning* of any new area of knowledge.

As noted by Bain (2004), outstanding academics know that learning has little meaning unless it has an influence on how we think and feel and our behaviour, building new mental models and challenging preconceptions and 'self-evident truths'. Learning is most productive when we are *engaged* in issues; and such engagement make the rote learning of names, dates, theories, etc., much easier – indeed, when learning is occurring such rote learning starts to seem effortless. Also, learning occurs best when we are trying to solve a puzzle that we find important and intriguing. For this reason, many puzzles are discussed in this book. If the answers are not always clear-cut then this is a reflection of the state of the literature; it is also an opportunity to develop our own critical perspective on the issues discussed and to build our own unique mental models of biological psychology. With an appropriate conceptual and motivational framework in place let us endorse Albert Einstein's advice,

> Never regard study as a duty, but as an enviable opportunity to learn.

Learning and understanding are not easy, and a sign that true learning is taking place is feeling that the material *is* difficult to grasp. Thus, a mild feeling of intellectual struggle should be seen as a positive sign of the learning process, even though the results of learning may take some time to become fully manifest – there is an inevitable time lag (reflecting a process of 'incubation') between the initial acquisition of information and later stages of learning, which are occupied by ease of recall and understanding. That is why learning is as much a motivational process as an intellectual one: sticking with the task, especially when the going gets tough, is the key to success.

Literature Coverage of the Book

All textbooks aim to be comprehensive in their coverage of the relevant literature – at least they used to have this aim. But today the field of biological psychology is simply too enormous for this aim to be realistic: in order to include most of the important findings in this area many more volumes than the present one would be needed. Important also is the fact that biological psychology is continually progressing, and it is not uncommon now to see significant new findings being published week-on-week: if this book aimed at comprehensiveness then it would be out of date before the ink dried on the page! This book should be a *starting* point to reading the latest scientific research: online library resources, the world-wide web and journal publishers' resource – for example, the *Nature* family of journals at www.nature.com – should be regularly checked: if nothing else, this proactive approach makes learning easier, more informative and more fun.

The aim of this textbook is to provide the fundamental conceptual elements – these do not change so rapidly – and use *illustrative examples* from the literature. I recommend that instructors use additional journal references to tailor the book to their specific course of instruction. The chapters in Part I ('Foundations') can be viewed as a stand-alone text; those in Part II ('Approaches') will be gradually developing; but those in Part III ('Applications') will be undergoing much more rapid development, and will require monitoring of the research literature. Separating 'Approaches' from 'Applications' reflects these different rates of change.

In order to help you structure your reading, 'Learning Objectives' are given at the beginning of each chapter. In addition, 'Ask Yourself' questions are provided after each major section, which are designed to stimulate you to think critically about the material you have just read. Lastly, at the end of each chapter are 'Learning Questions', which provide the opportunity to assess your newly acquired knowledge and understanding.

However, it is important that *you* construct *your* own pathway through this book. The best way to *get into* a topic is to start with the familiar. You may want to have a cursory read of some of the chapters that take your immediate interest before reading more systematically. It is sensible, though, to read chapter 1 (the Introduction) first, in order to get a conceptual overview of biological psychology. However, *you* should choose how to travel through this book; it will then be *your* unique understanding of biological psychology. Whatever your route, remember that biological psychology is about *you*, and the more you know about the biological processes of the mind, the more you will know about what makes you the way you are. Bon voyage.

Acknowledgements

A debt of gratitude is due to the many people involved in the planning, preparation and production of this book; their expertise, generosity and patience have helped shape the book in a multitude of ways.

Professor Peter Smith (Series Editor of the Blackwell 'Understanding' psychology books), of Goldsmiths College (University of London), originally suggested that I write a book proposal. Although some time has now passed, I hope he has not had reason to doubt his choice of author. Two anonymous referees offered unstinting advice, informed and informative criticism, and guidance from the original proposal to the final draft. I was especially grateful for their tolerance of the proposed structure and the emphasis placed on biological *psychology*. The final structure and content owe much to their wise counsel.

Blackwell Commissioning Editors, first Martin Davies and then Sarah Bird, provided constant support and encouragement throughout the writing process, despite deadlines rushing past, often with little sign of progress. Their editorial assistants, Lindsay Howarth and William Maddox, provided the right balance of support and good-humoured admonishment to get the book finished – during the later stages, William kept me on my toes. The production staff at Blackwell deserve acknowledgement, especially Joanna Pyke, who coordinated final production.

A number of colleagues generously read portions of the book. Dr Ulrich Ettinger (McGill University, Canada) and Dr Veena Kumari (Institute of Psychiatry, London) read several chapters. Mr Adam Perkins (Goldsmiths College) read many of the earlier chapters and helped with the compilation of references. Dr Peter Chadwick offered his own unique perspective on the experience of schizophrenia. Professor Max Velmans (Goldsmiths College) commented on philosophical, including consciousness, issues. Dr Susan Blackmore provided a valuable critique of the final cognition and consciousness chapter. Dr Alan Pickering (Goldsmiths College), Professor Neil MacNaughton (University of Otago, New Zealand) and Professor Phil Reed (University of Wales Swansea) read the learning and neural plasticity chapter. Presentation of statistical and molecular genetics (including the whole of chapter 2) was read by Professor Robert Plomin (Institute of Psychiatry, London), whose feedback was both reassuring and invaluable in clarifying current knowledge in this important, though complex, field. Professor Richard Dawkins (University of Oxford) provided information on Darwin's knowledge of Mendel's breeding experiments. I am indebted to the late Professor Jeffrey Gray (Institute of Psychiatry, London), who allowed me to see a pre-publication draft of his 2004 consciousness book, which inspired the final chapter, and for engaging in an email debate concerning his theory of consciousness – his wider scientific influence on my thinking and research is obvious throughout the book.

A very special 'thank you' to Dr Frederick Toates (Open University), who read the entire manuscript and provided line-by-line feedback. His reading went 'beyond the call of duty' of a textbook reviewer, and I was indeed fortunate that he was so generous in sharing his knowledge and experience as the author of a major biological psychology textbook already firmly established in the market. More errors would have remained without Dr Toates' contribution.

I am also grateful to Goldsmiths College (University of London), my former employer, for first providing a Hoggart Research Fellowship and Research Leave (2003–4), and then, after I was appointed to the University of Wales Swansea, for appointing me to a Visiting Fellowship (2004) that enabled completion of the book during the transition between appointments.

The author and publisher are grateful to the following for permission to reproduce material:

Figure 2.8: C. Patterson, figure 5.2, from *Evolution*. London: Natural History Museum, 1999. Copyright © 1999 by The Natural History Museum, London. Reprinted by permission of The Natural History Museum.

Figure 2.12: C. Patterson, figure 4.8, from *Evolution*. London: Natural History Museum, 1999. Copyright © 1999 by The Natural History Museum, London. Reprinted by permission of The Natural History Museum.

Figure 2.13: M. Ridley, table 2.1, from *Evolution*, 3rd ed. Oxford: Blackwell Publishing, 2003. Copyright © 2003 by M. Ridley. Reprinted by permission of Blackwell Publishing Ltd.

Figure 2.21: Edward O. Wilson, figure 5.9, p. 119, from *Sociobiology: The New Synthesis*. Cambridge, MA: The Belknap Press of Harvard University Press, 1975. Copyright © 1975, 2000 by the President and Fellows of Harvard College. Reprinted by permission of Harvard University Press.

Figure 3.7: H. Gleitman, from Wilder Penfield & Theodore Rasmussen, *The Cerebral Cortex of Man*. Macmillan, 1950. Copyright © 1950 by Macmillan. Reprinted by permission of The Gale Group.

Figure 4.1: J. P. J. Pinel, adapted from figure 3.5 in *Biopsychology*, 4th ed. Boston, MA: Allyn & Bacon, 2000. Copyright © 2000 by Pearson Education. Adapted by permission of the publisher.

Figure 4.5: S. M. Stahl, adapted from figures 4.15 to 4.17, from *Essential Psychopharmacology: Neuroscientific Basis and Practical Application*, 2nd ed. New York: Cambridge University Press, 2000. Copyright © 2000 by S. M. Stahl. Adapted by permission of the author and Cambridge University Press.

Figure 5.1: Frederic H. Martini, Michael J. Timmons and Robert B. Tallitsch, figure 18.3, p. 470, from *Human Anatomy*, 5th ed. Glenview, IL: Pearson, 2006. Copyright © 2006 by Frederick H. Martini, Inc. and Michael J. Timmons. Adapted by permission of Pearson Education, Inc.

Figure 5.2: F. Toates, adapted from *Biological Psychology: An Integrative Approach*. Harlow: Pearson. Copyright © 2001 by Pearson Education. Adapted by permission of the publisher.

Figure 5.3: Dan R. Kenshalo, figure 10.7, from *The Skin Senses*. Springfield, IL: Charles C. Thomas Publisher Ltd., 1968. Copyright © 1968 by Charles C. Thomas Publisher Ltd. Reprinted by permission of the publisher.

Figure 5.4: N. R. Carlson, figure 7.25, from *Physiology of Behavior*, 8th ed. London: Allyn & Bacon, 2004. Copyright © 2004 by Pearson Education. Reprinted by permission of the publisher.

Figure 5.8: Frederic H. Martini, Michael J. Timmons and Robert B. Tallitsch, adapted from figure 18.8, p. 475, in *Human Anatomy*, 5th ed. Glenview, IL: Pearson, 2001. Copyright © 2006 by Frederick H. Martini, Inc. and Michael J. Timmons. Adapted by permission of Pearson Education, Inc.

Figure 5.9: N. R. Carlson, adapted from figure 7.33, in *Physiology of Behavior*, 8th ed. London: Allyn & Bacon, 2004. Copyright © 2004 by Pearson Education. Adapted by permission of the publisher.

Figure 5.13: N. R. Carlson, figure 7.9, from *Physiology of Behavior*, 8th ed. London: Allyn & Bacon, 2004. Copyright © 2004 by Pearson Education. Reprinted by permission of the publisher.

Figure 5.18: N. R. Carlson, adapted from figure 6.6, p. 167, in *Physiology of Behavior*, 8th ed. London: Allyn & Bacon, 2004. Copyright © 2004 by Pearson Education. Adapted by permission of the publisher.

Figure 5.19: H. J. A. Dartnell, J. K. Bowmaker and J. D. Mollon, figure in 'Human visual pigments: Microspectrophotometric results from the eyes of seven persons', p. 220, from *Proceedings of the Royal Society in London, B*. London: The Royal Society, 1983. Copyright © 1983 by The Royal Society. Reprinted by permission of The Royal Society.

Figure 5.22: F. H. Martini, M. J. Timmons and M. P. McKinley, figure 18.25, p. 492, from *Human Anatomy*, 3rd ed. Upper Saddle River, NJ: Prentice Hall, 2000. Copyright © 2000 by Frederick H. Martini, Inc. and Michael J. Timmons. Reprinted by permission of Pearson Education, Inc.

Figure 5.28: N. R. Carlson, adapted from figure 6.20, from *Physiology of Behavior*, 2nd ed. Boston: Allyn & Bacon, 1981. Copyright © 1981 by Pearson Education. Adapted by permission of the publisher.

Figure 6.7: N. R. Carlson, adapted from figures 10.2 and 10.4, from *Physiology of Behavior*, 6th ed. London: Allyn & Bacon, 1998. Copyright © 1998 by Pearson Education. Adapted by permission of the publisher.

Figure 6.9: A. J. Vander et al., adapted from figure 19.1, *Human Physiology*. New York: McGraw-Hill, 1994. Copyright © 1994 by McGraw-Hill. Adapted by permission of The McGraw-Hill Companies.

Figure 7.13: S. Exner, from *Entwurf zu einer physiologischen Erklärung der psychischen Erscheinungen*. Leipzig & Vienna: Franz Deuticke, 1894; figure, p. 164.

Figure 7.23: N. R. Carlson, adapted from figure 14.8, from *Physiology of Behavior*, 6th ed. London: Allyn & Bacon, 1998. Copyright © 1998 by Pearson Education. Adapted by permission of the publisher.

Figure 7.24: N. R. Carlson, adapted from figure 14.5, from *Physiology of Behavior*, 6th ed. London: Allyn & Bacon, 1998. Copyright © 1998 by Pearson Education. Adapted by permission of the publisher.

Figure 7.25: N. R. Carlson, adapted from figures 14.10 and 14.7, from *Physiology of Behavior*, 6th ed. London: Allyn & Bacon, 1998. Copyright © 1998 by Pearson Education. Adapted by permission of the publisher.

Figure 8.2: Barbara Wilson, figure 19.1 (redrawn), from *Case Studies in Neuropsychological Rehabilitation*. New York: Oxford University Press, 1998. Copyright © 1998 by Oxford University Press, Inc. Reprinted by permission of the publisher.

Figure 8.4: J. P. J. Pinel, adapted from figure 16.6, from *Biopsychology*. London: Allyn & Bacon, 1990. Copyright © 1990 by Pearson Education. Adapted by permission of the publisher.

Figure 8.5: Arthur L. Benton, K. de S. Hamsher, N. R. Varney and O. Spreen, 'figure,' from *Contributions to Neuropsychological Assessment: A Clinical Manual*, 2. New York: Oxford University Press, 1983. Copyright © 1983, 1994 by Oxford University Press, Inc. Used by permission of Oxford University Press, Inc.

Figure 8.6: R. M. Reitan and D. Wolfson, 'figure: Trail Making Test,' from *The Halstead–Reitan Neuropsychological Test Battery: Theory and Clinical Interpretation*, 2. Tucson, AZ: Neuropsychology Press, 1993. Copyright © 1993 by R. M. Reiten.

Figure 9.1: G. D. Wilson, figure 8 in 'Personality, time of day and arousal', pp. 153–68 from *Personality and Individual Differences* 11. Elsevier Science, 1990. Copyright © 1990 by Personality and Individual Differences. Reprinted by permission of Elsevier.

Figure 9.2: M. Dawson, A. Schell and D. Filion, figure 10.4 in 'The electrodermal system', pp. 295–324 from John T. Cacioppo and L. G. Tassinary, *Principles of Psychophysiology: Physical, Social, and Inferential Elements*. Cambridge: Cambridge University Press, 1990. Copyright © 1990 by Cambridge University Press. Reprinted by permission of the publisher.

Figure 9.3: J. Papillo and D. Schapiro, figure 14.4 in 'The cardiovascular system', pp. 456–512 from John T. Cacioppo and L. G. Tassinary, *Principles of Psychophysiology: Physical, Social, and Inferential Elements*. Cambridge: Cambridge University Press, 1990. Copyright © 1990 by Cambridge University Press. Reprinted by permission of the publisher.

Figure 9.4: J. Cacioppo, L. Tassinary and A. Fridlund, figure 11.5 in 'The skeleto-motor system', pp. 325–84 from John T. Cacioppo and L. G. Tassinary, *Principles of*

Psychophysiology: Physical, Social, and Inferential Elements. Cambridge: Cambridge University Press, 1990. Copyright © 1990 by Cambridge University Press. Reprinted by permission of the publisher.

Figure 10.1: W. J. Ray, figure 12.2 in 'The electrocortical system', pp. 385–412 from John T. Cacioppo and L. G. Tassinary, *Principles of Psychophysiology: Physical, Social, and Inferential Elements*. Cambridge: Cambridge University Press, 1990. Copyright © 1990 by Cambridge University Press. Reprinted by permission of the publisher.

Figure 10.2: W. J. Ray, adapted from figure 12.1 in 'The electrocortical system', pp. 385–412 from John T. Cacioppo and L. G. Tassinary, *Principles of Psychophysiology: Physical, Social, and Inferential Elements*. Cambridge: Cambridge University Press, 1990. Copyright © 1990 by Cambridge University Press. Adapted by permission of the publisher.

Figure 10.3: M. Coles, G. Gratton and M. Fabiani, figure 13.2 in 'Event-related brain potentials', pp. 413–55 from John T. Cacioppo and L. G. Tassinary, *Principles of Psychophysiology: Physical, Social, and Inferential Elements*. Cambridge: Cambridge University Press, 1990. Copyright © 1990 by Cambridge University Press. Reprinted by permission of the publisher.

Figure 11.1: N. R. Carlson, figure 5.20, from *Physiology of Behavior*, 6th ed. London: Allyn & Bacon, 1998. Copyright © 1998 by Pearson Education. Reprinted by permission of the publisher.

Figure 11.2: N. R. Carlson, adapted from figure 5.27, from *Physiology of Behavior*, 6th ed. London: Allyn & Bacon, 1998. Copyright © 1998 by Pearson Education. Adapted by permission of the publisher.

Figure 11.3: N. R. Carlson, adapted from figure 5.30, from *Physiology of Behavior*, 6th ed. London: Allyn & Bacon, 1998. Copyright © 1998 by Pearson Education. Adapted by permission of the publisher.

Figure 11.4: N. R. Carlson, figure 5.6, from *Physiology of Behavior*, 6th ed. London: Allyn & Bacon, 1998. Copyright © 1998 by Pearson Education. Reprinted by permission of the publisher.

Figure 13.1: R. Plomin, J. C. DeFries, G. E. McClearn and P. McGuffin, figure 3.9, from *Behavioral Genetics*, 4th ed. New York: Worth, 2001. Copyright © 1980, 1990, 1997, 2001 by W. H. Freeman and Company. Reprinted by permission of W. H. Freeman & Company/Worth Publishers.

Figure 13.9: S. H. Friend and R. B. Stoughton, based on detail from 'How arrays work' in 'The magic of microrays', pp. 44–53 from *Scientific American*, Feb. 2002. Copyright © 2002 by Jared Schneidman. Adapted by permission of the author.

Figure 14.2: Y. I. Sheline, figure 1 in 'Neuroimaging studies of mood disorder effects on the brain', pp. 338–52 from *Biological Psychiatry* 54, 2003. Copyright © 2003 by Society of Biological Psychiatry. Reprinted by permission of the Society of Biological Psychiatry and Elsevier.

Figure 15.4: G. Matthews, I. J. Deary and M. C. Whiteman, figure 9.7, from *Personality Traits*, 2nd ed. Cambridge: Cambridge University Press, 2003. Copyright © 2003 by Cambridge University Press. Reprinted by permission of the publisher and authors.

Figure 16.2: I. I. Gottesman and T. D. Gould, figure 2 in 'The endophenotype concept in psychiatry: Etymology and strategic intentions', pp. 636–45 from *American Journal of Psychiatry* 160, 2003. Copyright © 2003 by American Psychiatric Association. Reprinted with permission from the American Journal of Psychiatry.

Figure 16.5: A. Shaner, G. Miller and J. Mintz, based on figure 1 in 'Schizophrenia as one extreme of a sexually selected fitness indicator', pp. 101–9 from *Schizophrenia Research* 70, 2004. Copyright © 2004 by Elsevier BV. Adapted by permission of Elsevier.

Figure 17.4: J. A. Gray and N. McNaughton, adapted from figure 1.8, p. 30, in *The Neuropsychology of Anxiety: An Enquiry into the Functions of the Septo-Hippocampal System*, 2nd ed. Oxford: Oxford University Press, 2000. Copyright © 2000 by J. A. Gray and N. McNaughton. Adapted by permission of Oxford University Press.

Figure 17.5: D. C. Blanchard and R. J. Blanchard, figure, pp. 188–99 from N. McNaughton and G. Andrews, *Anxiety*. Dunedin: Otago University Press, 1990. Copyright © 1990 by Otago University Press. Reprinted by permission of the publisher.

Figure 17.7: J. A. Gray and N. McNaughton, adapted from figure 5.1, from *The Neuropsychology of Anxiety: An Enquiry into the Functions of the Septo-Hippocampal System*, 2nd ed. Oxford: Oxford University Press, 2000. Copyright © 2000 by J. A. Gray and N. McNaughton. Adapted by permission of Oxford University Press.

Figure 17.8: J. A. Gray and N. McNaughton, figure 2.3, from *The Neuropsychology of Anxiety: An Enquiry into the Functions of the Septo-Hippocampal System*, 2nd ed. Oxford: Oxford University Press, 2000. Copyright © 2000 by J. A. Gray and N. McNaughton. Adapted by permission of Oxford University Press.

Figure 18.4: J. M. Wolfe, figure 2 in 'Cognitive neuroscience. How do you pay attention?', pp. 813–15 from *Nature* 400, 1999. Copyright © 1999 by J. M. Wolfe. Reprinted by permission of the author and Nature.

Figure 18.5: F. Toates, adapted from figure 1 in 'The interaction of cognitive and stimulus–response processes in the control of behaviour', pp. 59–83 from *Neuroscience and Biobehavioral Reviews* 22, 1997. Copyright © 1997 by Neuroscience and Biobehavioral Reviews. Adapted by permission of Elsevier.

chapter 1

Introduction

Learning Objectives

To be able to:

1. Discuss conceptual issues in biological psychology.
2. Describe Donald Hebb's neuropsychological approach to conceptual and real nervous systems.
3. Compare and contrast philosophical approaches to the mind–body problem.
4. Describe what is meant by 'reductionism' and evaluate its role in science.
5. Explain why and how Albert Einstein's brain was analysed.

Every thought, every emotion and every desire you have ever had, or will ever have, is a product of your brain. Understanding the brain, therefore, is of fundamental importance to understanding the mind – and understanding *you*. But what does it mean to say that the mind is a 'product' of the brain? Is this statement the same as saying that the mind can be *reduced* to the brain, or that the brain *causes* the mind? Answers to such questions have traditionally been given by philosophers; but now empirical science is starting to provide answers: data are fast replacing speculation.

This chapter provides an introduction to some of the central themes that run through this book, providing an intellectual route map to the many theories, approaches, applications and data that will be encountered on our journey through biological psychology. To *understand* we must first *think*, and to think we must have in mind a general framework to help organize new ideas within a coherent whole. Webster (2003) provides a lively discussion, using illustrative examples taken from everyday life (e.g., the cannabis debate), to demonstrate the type of issues that need to be considered when thinking about biological issues.

▣ Thinking about Biological Psychology

Biological psychology, in common with all branches of psychology, is enmeshed in a complex philosophical and scientific fabric. So what is the best way to *understand* biological psychology? In order to guide reading of subsequent chapters, the following discussion should be helpful.

Software/mind and hardware/brain distinction

One useful distinction in mind–brain relations is that between software and hardware. It has been tempting throughout the history of psychology to liken psychological processes to communication technology. Back in the 1940s the brain was likened to a telephone exchange. Today, the brain/mind is likened to a digital computer, which makes a sharp distinction between hardware and software. The brain may be seen as hardware (i.e., the processing units comparable to the central processing unit (CPU) of a computer), and the mind as software. Language is a good example. Following Noam Chomsky's seminal work in the 1950s, it is now assumed that we are born with an innate *capacity* to learn a language (a universal grammatical structure which underlies all languages). However, different communities speak different languages; that is, they acquire different software (words, pronunciation, etc.) via exposure to language environments (i.e., learning). Although this distinction is easy to break down (see chapter 18), it nevertheless is a useful *method of thought*.

Necessary and sufficient conditions

It is useful to think of brain–behaviour relations in terms of two types of conditions: *necessary* and *sufficient* conditions. First, *necessary* conditions are required for behaviour to be shown. In the case of language acquisition, a brain with the capacity to acquire language is required. However, possessing the capacity is not the same as acquiring language. Second, the *sufficient* condition of exposure to a language environment is needed for a specific language to be learned. It is thus useful to view the hardware of the brain as conferring psychological *potential*; but it is the interaction of the brain and the environment that leads to the realization of this potential.

Processes and output

Much of the activity of the brain is not accessible to the conscious mind. For example, when we utter a sentence we are aware of the final sentence – often only after we have spoken it – but not the processes that led to its construction. This example highlights something fundamental about the brain–mind; that is, brain processes do not correspond directly to the psychological contents that dominate conscious awareness. It is believed that we are largely unaware of the *process* of cognition, and aware only of its *outputs* expressed in a 'high-level language' which differs from the more basic neural code used in the computation (processing) of the brain–mind. The distinction between high-level and low-level processes may be understood by reference to how digital computers use these different level processes.

At the time of writing I am typing this sentence into a word-processing computer program (Microsoft Word) and the letters/words you are now reading appear on my computer screen in pretty much the same way as they appear on the page of your book. But my computer does not understand a word of what I have written, and nor need it. However, if I now click on the pull-down menu named *file* and click on *save* the computer obeys my command. But it does not know what *save* means; so how does it actually save my document?

Digital computers only process the following type of information:

01010010101010000010101010101010101010101010101010101010100000010111101001010101000
10100010101110100101010100001110010101010100101010101010101010101010010101000000101010
010101010111010010010010010010010100000010011101010010101010010

These 0s and 1s correspond to 'on' and 'off' states on the silicon chip that processes information: they are the *machine code*. Well, how does my machine know how to *save*? This end is achieved by a program, itself composed of 0's and 1's, which *translates* the symbols I have typed into machine code that the computer processor can compute. Once it has processed this information, it then presents the output, via a *retranslation* program, back into the symbols I understand: the letters/words on my screen. When the data of 0's and 1's get corrupted, or the (re)translation program fails to work, then what I see on my screen is, to me, nonsense output. As an analogy, if you are bilingual, then you have different 'higher-level' languages: they may look and sound different, but when translated into a common code (say a third language) they become the same.

A few years ago before the appearance of the Windows operating system and pull-down menus, these machine processes were more evident. Either it was necessary to program the computer in the machine code of 0s and 1s (a long and tedious task), or it was necessary to use some high-level language (e.g., Pascal) to write instructions that resembled English that the computer's central processor could understand after translation. Now, the computer is turned on and the icon clicked and, hey presto, things happen. In the same way, things seem to happen in our brain–mind; but this effortless processing conceals hidden layers of computational complexity: it is true in the case of the desk-top computer and it is true in the case of the brain–mind.

Cause and effect

In common with other sciences, biological psychology focuses on the fundamental importance of separating *cause* and *effect*. This focus stands in contrast to some areas of psychology, and the social sciences in general, which are more often concerned with accounting for *associations* between different types of data. For example, much of social psychology is concerned with explaining observational data; and differential psychology is largely concerned with describing the covariation observed in personality and intelligence variables.

Often there is no interest in causal relations – indeed, in some areas of psychology, there is a belief that psychological phenomena *cannot* be reduced to biological constructs and processes. In other areas of psychology (e.g., cognitive psychology), there is not a concern with the underlying biological reality, but rather with developing theories at a given level of explanation (e.g., computational theories). Biological psychology attempts to reduce data to the simplest level, formalized in cause–effect relations and couched in reductionist terms.

Phylogenetic continuity

Biological psychology makes use of observations and experiments on many different animals; in contrast, almost all other branches of psychology study only one animal: *Homo sapiens*. This choice of species results from a number of factors. First, we may simply be interested in human beings (e.g., in social interaction research); or we might want to study a feature of this species (e.g., language). Second, although less clearly articulated, there is a widespread belief in psychology that research on non-human animals cannot yield useful information about our species. This belief is almost certainly false and is perhaps an intellectual leftover of *dualism* – i.e., the belief that the mind and body are separate (see below).[1] Coupled with this belief is the idea that human beings are *qualitatively* different from other species. Also, it is often falsely believed that the experimental tools used to study non-human animals (e.g., conditioning experiments; see chapter 7) have little implication for the study of the complex human mind. In addition, it is often thought that higher cognitive functions, especially our language capacity, set us sufficiently apart from non-human animals to make any comparison meaningless. We see in chapter 2 that Darwinian evolution and genetics place human beings on a *phylogenetic continuum* with other animals; they do not set us apart any more than they set a bird and a whale apart. In fact, what Darwinian theory does is to rob us of our species arrogance – in the grand scheme of the natural world, we are no better and no worse than any other species.

Social vs. biological perspectives

It is somewhat unfortunate that social and biological perspectives are often seen as separate – indeed, they are often seen as opposing, mutually incompatible approaches. However, biological research has much to say about issues that have until recently been thought of as essentially social in nature; and social research has important implications for the manner in which the brain and behaviour are related – there is now an emerging 'neuroscience of social behaviour' (e.g., Easton & Emery, 2005). Most of the important effects of the brain on behaviour depend upon environmental input; and this input is important for how the mind structures the social environment. For example, although there may be genetic influences on aggression, the types of stimuli that activate aggressive responses are environmental, and meaning and interpretation attached to these stimuli can be restructured (learned), thus altering actual behaviour. Therefore, brain-based aggression is only a *potential* (the necessary condition); the social environment, and our cognitive interpretation of it, is the *potentiator* (the sufficient condition). This line of reasoning has proved remarkably successful in cognitive behaviour therapy, which restructures the thinking of patients suffering from clinical conditions (e.g., depression). Often, the more we learn about genetics and neurophysiology, the more importance needs to attach to environmental and social factors (Hebb, 1949).

Theory acceptance

Achieving a real understanding and appreciation of theory is not easy. Some theories lend themselves to more immediate acceptance than others. Therefore, we must be careful not to base our appreciation upon personal credulity. A good example of this process is Charles Darwin's theory of evolution (chapter 2). In the late 1850s, after 30 years of suppressing the desire to publish his theory of natural selection, Darwin learned in a letter from his collaborator, Alfred Russell Wallace (1823–1913), that Wallace had also developed a theory of evolution based upon the principle of natural selection. This letter forced Darwin to rush into print the now famous *On the Origin of Species* (1859). However, a year prior to this publication, in 1858, joint papers by Darwin and Wallace were read at the Linnean Society. The public announcement of one of the most important theories in science was met with little enthusiasm. Indeed, Thomas Bell, President of the Linnean Society, in his presidential address to the society in the same year, opined, 'The year which has passed has not, indeed, been marked by any of those striking discoveries which at once revolutionize, so to speak, the department of science on which they bear.' As the philosopher of science Browne (2002, p. 42) commented, 'Accurate enough in the short term, Bell's remark was destined to become known as one of the most unfortunate misjudgements in the history of science.'

Thus, a wise person may want to reflect upon theory and its supporting evidence before arriving at too hasty a conclusion. Otherwise, as Einstein remarked,

> Whoever undertakes to set himself up as judge in the field of truth and knowledge is shipwrecked by the laughter of the Gods.

Scientific problems and mysteries

A useful distinction is sometimes made in science between *problems* and *mysteries*. *Problems* are scientific questions still in need of answers (e.g., how the cortex processes colours); and the type of research needed is fairly obvious. On the other hand, *mysteries* refer to scientific issues that are important but difficult to conceptualize; and it is by no means obvious how they can be addressed. One good example of a mystery in psychology is the phenomenon of consciousness (e.g., the *experience* of colour). Part of the problem is being unable to frame the problem precisely enough; this problem framing issue is found through all science and biological psychology, but it is most obvious in the case of so-called mysteries. There are considerable debates in the consciousness literature and although it is suspected that consciousness is a function of the brain there are no *accepted* criteria by which its qualities can be empirically investigated (this problem is related to the different definitions of consciousness that exist; see chapter 18). Of course, just because this cannot be done at present does not imply that it will never be achieved: 'Our failure to solve a problem so far does not make it insoluble' (Hebb, 1949, p. xiii). The history of science consists in puzzling mysteries being turned into humble problems by the application of the scientific method. (For a discussion of the scientific method in relation to biological psychology go to: www.blackwellpublishing.com/corr/.)

> **ASK YOURSELF**
> What is unique about the biological perspective in psychology?

A Hebbian Approach: Conceptual and Real Nervous Systems

The theoretical orientation of this book owes much to the seminal thinking of the neuropsychologist, Donald Hebb (1949, 1955), who did much to influence the development of whole areas of psychology. His influence is evident throughout this book, either in terms of his own work (e.g., neural plasticity in chapter 7) or in others' work (e.g., the neuropsychological approach of Jeffrey Gray, in chapters 17 and 18). This approach has a number of distinctive features. First, the neuropsychology Hebb advanced is encapsulated in the following quote (Hebb, 1949, p. xiii):

> Modern psychology takes completely for granted that behavior and neural function are perfectly correlated, that one is completely caused by the other. There is no separate soul or life force to stick a finger into the brain now and then and make neural cells do what they would not otherwise. Actually, of course, this is a working assumption only – as long as there are unexplained aspects of behavior . . . the working assumption is a necessary one, and there is no real evidence opposed to it.

The neurosciences are complex, which poses a challenge to achieving even a superficial understanding of their main theories and findings. A way is needed to cut through the thicket of this complexity in order to focus on the overarching issues of importance. Hebb proposed that one way to achieve this clarity is to distinguish between two types of nervous system: the *conceptual nervous system* (cns) and the *central nervous system* (CNS). This *neuropsychological* approach was defined by Hebb (1949, p. vii) as the attempt

> to bring together a number of different lines of research, in a general theory of behaviour that attempts to bridge the gap between neurophysiology and psychology, as well as that between laboratory psychology and the problems of the clinic.

The conceptual nervous system is a set of postulated processes that carry out information processing and have a psychological frame of reference. It is built from behavioural data, and comprises theories concerning the structure of intervening processes between stimuli and responses. Hebb (1955) argued that research should go from the conceptual nervous system (cns, comprising psychological data) to the central nervous system (CNS, comprising neural processes). The cns is the behavioural scaffold around which neuropsychological theories are built (Gray, 1975). The value of this approach can be

Figure 1.1   Donald Hebb. (Courtesy of the McGill University archives.)

seen in the nature–nurture debate. Hebb (1953) pointed out that behaviour is determined jointly by heredity and the environment, in much the same way that a field is defined not by *either* its length or width, but by *both*. (See figure 1.1.)

Hebb (1949) inspired a whole generation of scientists by his joint psychological and physiological perspective on psychology; and his important contribution came from his view that psychological problems are physiological problems, and vice versa; and that most scientific progress will be made by pursuing a truly interdisciplinary approach. As Hebb (1949, p. xii, italics added) stated,

> There is a considerable overlap between the problems of psychology and those of neuro-physiology, hence the possibility (or *necessity*) of reciprocal assistance.

Throughout this book there will be much of a physiological nature, but there will also be much of a psychological nature (e.g., learning theory and neural networks in chapter 7) – the inclusion of such psychological theories and methods is not common in works on biological psychology, but a *Hebbian approach* requires their inclusion: a true neuropsychology demands both 'neuro' and 'psychological' perspectives.[2]

ASK YOURSELF
Will it be possible one day to account for all psychological processes in terms of neural events?

◼︎☐ Philosophy of Mind

Now, before specific topics of biological psychology are discussed, it is important first to appreciate some of the major debates in the philosophy of mind – i.e., that branch of philosophy concerned with conceptualizing the human mind and how it relates to the brain/body. The themes that have dominated discussion of the philosophy of mind summarize some of the major issues that continue to influence scientific thinking and research today. Therefore, to understand biological psychology, which encompasses the mind as well as the brain, it is useful to have, at the very least, a general sketch of the major themes in this area of philosophy.

You may prefer to skip over this section and return to it at the end of the book. I suggest, however, that you read it now. If you feel this material is difficult and obscure, then at least you have achieved one important understanding of philosophy: according to the famous philosopher Bertrand Russell,

> Science is what you know. Philosophy is what you don't know.

Everyone is confused about philosophy, especially philosophers. It might be said that the only people who understand philosophy are those who know that they do not fully understand it. Let us consider some of the major theoretical positions on mind–body relations.

Dualism

The famous French philosopher René Descartes (1596–1650) contended that the mind and brain/body are essentially separate entities. According to this position, both entities could exist without the other, but they typically interact to create psychological experience: ideas in the mind need to affect the brain/body in order for action to occur (via the operation of the muscles); likewise, a cut to the skin (a body event) leads to pain felt in the conscious mind. In the acquisition of knowledge, the body provides the means to acquire sensory information, the mind the analytic tools to understand this information. The influence of this theory cannot be overestimated. Although Descartes's conclusion may be criticized, there is no doubt that he asked fundamental questions about mind–brain relations.

In one important sense, Descartes was right. Simply knowing the neurophysiology of the brain will not be sufficient to understand the *psychological* functions of mind, but arguably it will be a *necessary* condition for such understanding. Not only is it necessary to know how brains are built, but also crucially it is necessary to know how they carry out their functions (computational, or cognitive processing). The idea that the mind and body/brain are *truly* separate entities is not openly entertained by most psychologists; however, it is explicitly accepted by some philosophers. None the less, dualism is apparent in the working assumptions of many psychologists, who continue to treat the brain (i.e., physical/objective stuff) and the mind (i.e., experience/subjective stuff) as separate – at least in terms of how they can be conceptualized as research problems (see chapter 18).

There are a number of philosophical positions relating to the mind and brain/body debate, as follows.

Monism

This philosophical position argues that the mind and body/brain are identical and composed of some common stuff (what this stuff comprises differs between theories). Monism takes three forms (Velmans, 2000), given in descending order of importance to biological psychology.

1. The mind is nothing more than a particular aspect of the body (physicalism). This approach, now dominant in biological psychology, argues that the mind is nothing more than a product of the physical reality of the body and the functions it serves. For example, being aware (conscious) serves the function of monitoring the success/failure of behaviours, providing useful feedback to modify further actions (see chapter 18). This position is also known as 'identity theory'.
2. Body and mind may be different aspects of a more fundamental reality that is neither mental nor physical (called *dual-aspect theory*, or *neutral monism*).
3. The body may be nothing more than the mind (*idealism*). At the extreme, Bishop George Berkeley believed that the objective world does not exist and what we perceive is entirely in the mind, which in turn is part of the mind of God. This theory has fallen out of favour in modern-day psychology.

Identity theory

The most widely accepted view among scientists concerning mind–body/brain relations is some form of identity theory. This theory argues that every mental event is identical to a corresponding brain event; according to this position, it is not possible to have a mental event without a preceding brain event – thus when the brain is dead, the mind can no longer exist.

Material reductionism

Identity theory comes in two major variants: the view that mental states are nothing more than physical states of the brain (physicalism, e.g., Crick, 1994), and the view that mental states are nothing more than the way physical systems such as the brain function (functionalism, e.g., Dennett, 1991).

Emergent interactionism

Sperry (1969, 1970) attempted to bridge the gap between brain processes and conscious experience. He argued that (a) consciousness is an emergent property of neural networks in the brain; and (b) the activity of individual nerve cells can only be understood by appreciating their place in the neural network. Thus, Sperry argued that it is the *organization* of neurons that gives rise to the mind. Sperry's approach offers a good argument for viewing biological psychology as an integrative discipline in the social and biological sciences. The essence of this approach is that different levels of explanation are required to explain functions at the molecular, chemical, neuroanatomical, neuropsychological, cognitive/behavioural and social levels of psychology. Sperry's position is also known as 'property dualism' because it argues that the mind is a special kind of non-physical property which emerges when the physical brain attains a given level of complexity (this form of dualism should be contrasted with Descartes's 'substance dualism', which contends that minds and brains are essentially separate entities).

Emergent interactionism of the kind advocated by Sperry should be distinguished from the more humble variety of interactionism advocated by Crick (1994) and others; namely that complex systems can be understood by knowledge of (a) component parts and (b) the ways in which they interact to determine final behaviour: there is nothing more to 'emerge' from this interaction, the final product is inherent in the individual parts (even the wetness of water is inherent in the combination of gases that produce water, albeit in a non-obvious way). According to this view, the total is no more than the sum of parts – the individual parts are more complex than often assumed. That is, knowledge of the sum of parts and how they combine together is sufficient to explain the final product of interaction. It is often said that the wetness of water is not inherent in the gases that make up water, but this argument confuses the physical nature of gas from our experience of it.

As is now evident, these different philosophical positions share much in common and most contain some important grains of truth. The typical biological psychologist would endorse the following conclusions. (a) The brain and mind require different levels of explanations and different forms of analytical tools. (b) The mind is a consequence of the brain, and both mind and brain exist as a single unitary, indivisible system. (c) The mind comprises complex processes that are formed by large neural networks in the brain. (d) Localization of function in the brain is only a first step to understanding the true complexity of the organization of the brain. (e) Ultimately, understanding of the brain and mind will be achieved by an integrated theory that allows brain processes to be translated into mind processes, and vice versa.

ASK YOURSELF
Are philosophical debates little more than idle speculation in lieu of scientific data?

Reductionism

The most popular of the biological psychologist's theoretical tools is *reductionism*. Reductionism takes two forms: (a) *methodological reductionism*, and (b) *theoretical reductionism*. Although (a) and (b) are closely related, they are not identical. If one endorses theoretical reductionism, then this necessarily implies methodological reductionism; however, methodological reductionism does not necessarily imply theoretical reductionism: it could be chosen as the best available research approach.

Theoretical reductionism argues that higher-order complexity is best understood by breaking down processes into their lower-order basic units. This approach is central to biological psychology, where behaviour is analysed in terms of DNA, neurotransmitters, neurons, etc. But theoretical reductionism in psychology is constantly under challenge. It is often argued that a 'holistic' approach is needed to understand the great complexity of the interplay of the brain and mind and that reductionism is doomed to failure. Thus, according to this argument, reducing psychology to genetics and the physiology of the brain and body is naive, at best. Biological psychologists defend their position robustly. The following quotes give a flavour of the thinking of some of the leaders in the neurosciences, and reflect some of the passion with which they hold their positions. For example, Churchland and Sejnowski (1992, p. 2) put the situation succinctly:

> emergent properties are high-level effects that depend on lower-level phenomena in some systematic way. Turning the hypothesis around to its negative version, it is highly improbable that emergent properties cannot be explained by low-level properties.

Similarly, Dennett (2003, p. 16) argued that the mind is nothing more than the brain and is, therefore, the subject matter of the naturalist:

> Look. It's too late in the day to hold any other view other than this. Each of us is a collection of some 100 trillion little cells, little robotic cells that team together and sometimes form alliances and sometimes compete. Now, the organisation of these little cells is what we are. And somehow all the wonderful things that we can do – our culture, our art, our consciousness, our free will – have to be composeable out of these raw materials without any wonder tissue, without any mysterious new stuff.

ASK YOURSELF
Do there exist 'holistic' psychological processes that could never be explained in reductionist terms?

A Darwinian Perspective

Charles Darwin did much to map out the scientific problems and research strategies for ethologists, who study animal behaviour, as well as for psychology in general. In the chapters that follow the importance of Darwin's ideas will become evident; and this will form the basis of much of the discussion in this book, which assumes a fundamental role for Darwinian evolution by natural selection – indeed, this is the core concept running through the whole book, as it is the core concept running through the whole of biology. For the present, the following comment of the famous ethologist Konrad Lorenz (1965, p. xii) should be noted:

> Darwin was fully aware of a fact which though simple in itself, is so fundamental to biological behaviour study . . . This fact, which is still ignored by many psychologists, is quite simply that behaviour patterns are just as conservatively and reliably characters of species as are other forms of bones, teeth, or any other bodily structures. Similarities in inherited behaviour unite the members of a species, of a genus, and of even the largest taxonomic units in exactly the same way in which bodily characters do so.

Lorenz (1965, pp. xii–xiii) goes on to stress a related point of considerable importance for psychology:

> That behaviour patterns have an evolution exactly like that of organs is a fact which entails the recognition of another: that they also have the same sort of heredity. In other words, the adaptation of the behaviour patterns of an organism to its environment is achieved in exactly the same manner as that of its organs, that is to say on the basis of information which the species has gained in the course of its evolution by the age-old method of mutation and selection. This is true not only for the relatively rigid patterns of form or behaviour, but also for the complicated mechanisms of adaptive modification, which are generally subsumed under the concept of learning.

> **ASK YOURSELF**
> What are the implications for psychology of taking Darwinian processes seriously?

▢▢ The Day-to-Day Business of Science: Einstein's Brain

Some of the philosophical themes of brain–mind that have permeated intellectual thought throughout the ages have now been presented. But before embarking on our exploration of biological psychology it may be helpful to have an insight into the day-to-day business of science. How scientists *do* science is largely misunderstood by the general public and misrepresented by the popular media. As James Watson (1968, p. xi), who co-discovered the structure of DNA with Francis Crick (see chapter 2), notes,

> science seldom proceeds in a straightforward logical manner imagined by outsiders. Instead, its steps forward (and sometimes backward) are often very human events in which personalities and cultural traditions play major roles.

In chapter 3, the post-mortem analysis of Albert Einstein's brain is discussed in an attempt to understand his remarkable abilities. (See figure 1.2.) This literature provides us with an example of how scientific ideas and research are initiated – often a series of chance events lead to the production of a new idea. The first analysis of Einstein's brain was performed by Diamond et al. (1985).[3] Diamond subsequently described the events that led to this analysis.

1. *A passing comment.* One day in the laboratory, a world renowned professor of neuro-anatomy mentioned to Diamond that, contrary to theory at the time, he thought the inferior parietal cortex was more highly evolved than the frontal cortex. Because the number of glial (support) cells increase up the phylogenetic ladder, then the more highly evolved areas in the brain should have more glial cells per neurons than less developed areas (see chapter 3).
2. *Experimental inspiration.* Diamond knew that experimental evidence showed that the brains of rats reared under environmentally enriched conditions have more glial cells than those reared under impoverished conditions (see chapter 7).
3. *Picture on the wall.* One day a graduate student gave Diamond a photograph taken from the journal *Science* which showed Einstein's brain in a box. This photograph was pinned up on the wall, serving as a daily reminder to Diamond of Einstein's brain.

Figure 1.2   Albert Einstein, 1951. (© Bettmann / CORBIS.)

4. *A lazy day at the office*. Not all days at the office are action-packed. On this particular day, Diamond was at a loose end, with nothing much to do but think. She wondered whether she could obtain pieces of Einstein's brain for a histological analysis (for the results, see chapter 3; for description of the method, see chapter 11).
5. *Making contact*. Having tracked down Dr Harvey (who stored Einstein's brain), Diamond called him, but without success; she persisted though, and contacted him every 6 months with a view to getting samples of the brain. After 3 years (and considerable patience!), Dr Harvey sent the samples.
6. *Einstein's brain through the post*. Finally through the post arrived four sugarcube-size pieces of Einstein's brain. It was fortunate that Einstein's brain had been preserved in the first place; it was also fortunate that Dr Harvey provided Diamond with brain pieces that were suitable for the type of histological analysis she wanted to perform.

In the main, scientists are not white-coated, emotionless drones; most are passionate, creative, energetic individuals, fascinated by their research problems and unable to stop thinking (even dreaming) about them. It is not unknown for scientific thinking to occur with the aid of alcohol in cheery surroundings (e.g., the *Eagle* public house in Cambridge, in the case of Watson and Crick's work on the structure of DNA; see Watson, 1968). The white-coated 'egghead' image of the scientist so beloved of the popular media is not an adequate portrayal of real working scientists: the world of science contains some of the most creative, imaginative and inspirational individuals in society.

> **ASK YOURSELF**
> What does the analysis of Einstein's brain tell us about the scientific process?

▢ Overview of the Book

The book is divided into three parts, 'Foundations', 'Approaches' and 'Applications'. These three parts are designed to clarify three important areas of biological psychology – in practice, they are often related, but they are conceptually distinct enough to allow their separation for the purpose of clarity of understanding.

Part I (Foundations) deals with some of the foundation topics in biological psychology. Chapter 2 deals with evolution and genetics, which form the bedrock of biology in general and biological psychology in particular. Chapter 3 deals with the structure of the nervous system and the psychological functions carried out by the various structures. Chapter 4 summarizes what is known about neurons and neurotransmission, including drug action and addiction. Chapter 5 summarizes what is known about sensory and motor systems. Chapter 6 covers the functions of the neuroendocrine system, focusing on sex/gender development, stress reactions and the immune system. Chapter 7 summarizes behavioural approaches to learning, artificial neural networks, which formally model learning processes, and neurophysiological mechanism of plasticity that underlie learning.

Part II (Approaches) presents the principal methods of investigation used in biological psychology, including the more recent methods of molecular genetic analysis and neuroimaging. Chapter 8 covers the main procedures in neuropsychological investigation and assessment. Chapter 9 surveys the various techniques used in psychophysiology. Chapter 10 presents neuroimaging techniques, including EEG/ERP and the various forms of brain scanning currently in use. Chapter 11 outlines more traditional methods of direct (invasive) brain techniques used in non-human animals, and occasionally in human beings for therapeutic purposes. Chapter 12 covers psychopharmacology research used in the discovery of drugs and as a tool in investigating neuronal processes. Chapter 13 deals with the analysis of genes in the postgenomic era of the sequencing of the human genome.

Part III (Applications) surveys a number of select areas of interest to the psychologist. Chapters 14–16 cover some of the major psychiatric conditions (depression, anxiety and schizophrenia), taking examples from the literature to illustrate the uses to which the various approaches surveyed in Part II are put. Chapter 17 summarizes the biological bases of normal and abnormal expressions of personality, serving to show the vulnerability factors to the clinical conditions covered in chapters 14–16. Chapter 18 considers the applications of biological psychology to cognition, comprising computation and consciousness – the latter phenomenon now is starting to show signs of being transformed from a philosophical mystery to a tractable scientific problem. These topics are considered in some detail: only this way can we get a proper scientific understanding of these topics.

Listed in 'Further Reading' below are books that offer insight into biological psychology from more general and popular perspectives, including personal accounts of scientific endeavours. They may be read alongside the technical books to provide a broader perspective on the biological approach to understanding the human brain–mind. Probably the best piece of advice we can be given concerning what to read is: read the author's own theory in their own words. That's where to find the vitality of theory – secondhand, reheated, summaries, although convenient to the student and lecturer alike – lose much of the flavour of the author's original words. Textbooks are a good place to start the journey of understanding, but a poor place to end.

Learning Questions

1. How does consideration of conceptual issues help us understand bio-logical psychology?
2. In what ways are conceptual and real nervous systems complementary approaches?
3. What is the relevance of philosophical theories of mind–brain relations?
4. How can a reductionist approach explain the emergence of complex, higher-level psychological processes?
5. What do the circumstances that led to the analysis of Albert Einstein's brain reveal about the everyday business of scientific research?

NOTES

1   The French philosopher René Descartes believed that animals are merely machines, and the body of human beings is also a machine; but the intervention of the Creator gave human beings a mind/soul which gave the authority of intellect and *reason* over brute instincts. According to this view, it is a hopeless task to try to understand the human mind/soul by studying mindless/soulless non-human animals. Today, many psychologists would view this position as untenable: the belief that non-human animals have no mind is contrary to evidence and based on an unsubstantiated assumption. However, there *is* a lingering feeling among many people that human beings are somehow fundamentally unique and special, and not simply another product (albeit a highly evolved one) of evolution by natural selection: this is anthrocentrism.

2   As we discuss in relation to theories of consciousness (chapter 18), we must be wary of labelling things 'physiological' and 'psychological', as this dichotomy suggests that they belong to separate (dualistic) realms. Hebb's terms – 'conceptual nervous system' for 'psychological' processes and 'real nervous system' for physiological processes – are more apt in avoiding a dualistic way of thinking.

3   In order to avoid littering the text with authors – some papers have an author list longer than an international football squad – the names of three or fewer authors are given in full, and those with more authors are truncated after the first author to 'et al.'.

FURTHER READING

Darwin, C. (1887/1993). *The Autobiography of Charles Darwin.* London: Norton.

Dawkins, R. (1976). *The Selfish Gene.* Oxford: Oxford University Press.

Dawkins, R. (2003). *A Devil's Chaplain.* London: Weidenfeld.

Greenfield, S. (2001). *Brain Story: Unlocking our Inner World of Emotions, Memories, Ideas, and Desires.* New York: Dorling Kindersley.

LeDoux, J. (2002). *Synaptic Self.* London: Penguin.

Pinker, S. (1997). *How the Mind Works.* London. Norton.

Watson, J. D. (1968). *The Double Helix: A Personal Account of the Discovery of the Structure of DNA.* London: Touchstone.

Watson, J. D. (2003). *DNA: The Secret of Life.* New York: Knopf.

Webster, S. (2003). *Thinking about Biology.* Cambridge: Cambridge University Press.

Foundations

In keeping with the general theme of this book, understanding in terms of conceptual (theoretical) and real (empirical) processes is emphasized. In our tour of the foundations of biological psychology, it will be appreciated that theoretical issues drive empirical research strategies, and how, in turn, findings from empirical investigation influence theoretical refinement and development. For example, Darwin's theory of evolution by natural selection contained many theoretical assumptions that had to wait many years for empirical support from biological research in general and genetics in particular; today Darwin's theory is being used to generate new hypotheses in psychology. This interplay of theory and data has also been important in understanding the basic processing unit in the central nervous system: the neuron has been modelled in mathematics and computers (*computational neuroscience*) for many years, and this formalism has influenced investigation of the actual brain, which, in turn, has led to more biologically realistic assumptions in formal mathematical models.

Chapter 2 (Evolution and Genetics) summarizes one of the greatest achievements of all science, that of evolutionary theory and the science of genetics. It is instructive to trace the development of Charles Darwin's ideas on evolution and the rationale of his *mechanism* of evolution, namely natural selection. Here may be sensed something of the intellectual atmosphere of the time and the problems faced by Darwin (e.g., how selected characteristics were actually inherited). Next, Mendelian genetics is covered, which solved the puzzle of inheritance, and then the discovery of the structure of DNA, from the original work of Watson and Crick to the cracking of the genetic code (i.e., how genes code for amino acids and proteins). A number of genetic diseases are presented in the context of mutation processes. In the latter part of the chapter evolutionary thinking in social behaviour and psychology is covered, through the development of *sociobiology* to *evolutionary psychology* – a science that Darwin predicted some 150 years ago. Along the way the validity of the selfish-gene notion is considered, as is the evolutionary basis of altruism, cooperation and spite. Theoretical biological theory (e.g., altruism) and empirical research (e.g., DNA) are presented as separate though highly complementary approaches to understanding biological problems. The material covered in this chapter informs our discussion of the whole of biological psychology. The distinction between *distal* (i.e., ultimate evolutionary functions relating to gene replication) and *proximate* (physiological and psychological mechanisms) factors is explained.

Chapter 3 (Brain Structure and Function) sketches the structure of the central nervous system (CNS: brain and spinal cord) and the peripheral nervous system (PNS: somatic and autonomic nervous systems). The main parts of the brain and some of its important functions (e.g., language) are surveyed. Lastly, a discussion of Albert Einstein's brain addresses the issue of the neural basis of his genius (function).

Chapter 4 (Neurons and Neurotransmission) builds on the material covered in chapter 3, specifically focusing on the structure and function of the neuron, the biochemical nature of the nerve signal, and the neuron-to-neuron neurotransmission by neurotransmitters. The nature of receptors and how neurotransmitters serve as a means of communication, as well as a means by which neurons communicate molecular information (i.e., how genes are turned on and off to regulate the functioning of the neuron), are discussed. Also covered are the ways in which common drugs exert their effects, and the cellular basis of addiction.

Chapter 5 (Sensory and Motor Systems) covers the principal senses: touch/pain, taste, smell, hearing and vision. These proximate systems serve the ultimate functions of genes: that is, to sense the local environment and organize responses appropriate to internal goal states (e.g., feeding, mating and defence). These sensory processes add to the knowledge gained in chapter 3 of the relationship between the structure of the nervous system and its functions. This chapter highlights one important aspect of function: much of what we experience psychologically cannot yet be understood solely by reference to the action of physical events in the world, or by (current) knowledge of the physiology of receptors and neural pathways. The basics of the motor system, focusing on control processes that link external stimuli with internal goal states and overt action/movement, are covered.

Chapter 6 (The Neuroendocrine System) surveys the major systems of communication within the body by way of hormones secreted from endocrine glands and acting on sites around the body (including the brain). How hormones provide a means of the brain influencing the rest of the body is discussed. The role of hormones in *organizational* effects on sexual development (e.g., masculinization of the body and brain) and *activational* effects on sexual desire and behaviour is summarized. The regulatory functions of hormones are also surveyed (e.g., availability of glucose to the body and brain). How hormones are central to the stress reaction and how they affect the efficiency of the immune system are outlined. This chapter highlights the interaction of different systems in the body. It also shows that many modern-day illnesses are the result of activation of systems that may have been adaptive in the past during the time they evolved, but which today are inappropriate and damaging (e.g., chronic stress and immune impairment). Such findings serve to highlight that evolution by natural selection is a blind process without consideration for our happiness and genes are 'selfish' in their propensity to make copies of themselves (replication) despite the costs imposed on us as individuals (e.g., the genes controlling HIV viruses have evolved to promote their own interests – i.e., successful replication).

Chapter 7 (Learning and Neural Plasticity) addresses the proximate processes of behavioural (learning) and neurophysiological (plasticity) processes involved in adjusting behaviour as the result of experience in local environments that are novel and constantly changing. The temptation will be avoided to set in opposition biology and learning, instead seeing learning as a fundamental process of biological psychology. Following standard practice, the various historical approaches to learning are summarized, including habituation, Pavlovian conditioning and instrumental learning. Then the conceptual understanding of the neural processes, including Hebb's cell-assembly ideas and computational work in artificial neural networks (which preceded a full understanding of the real neuron), is outlined. Lastly, a survey is provided of what is known about how learning is instantiated in the brain in the form of new local neural connections (i.e., neural plasticity).

chapter 2

Evolution and Genetics

Learning Objectives

To be able to:

1. Explain Darwin's theory of evolution by natural selection.
2. Describe the main principles in classical (Mendelian) genetics.
3. Outline the structure of DNA and how it relates to the 'genetic code'.
4. Provide examples of mutations in genetic disorders.
5. Critically evaluate current evolutionary thinking in terms of genetic and non-genetic relatedness.

In common with all life forms, we are the product of many millions of years of evolution – the outcome of the struggle for existence fought by thousands upon thousands of generations of ancestors. The results of their struggles and successes are coded in our genes – the chemical sequences of DNA, contained in every cell in the body, that define life and make each of us unique. Our thoughts, emotions and behaviours have also been shaped by the past struggles; therefore a proper appreciation of evolution and genetics is essential in order to understand psychology. This chapter provides a summary of this literature, and sets the scene for subsequent chapters that consider the implications of evolution and genetics for normal and abnormal behaviour. An excellent introduction to psychological genetics is provided by Plomin et al. (2001).

To understand the biological nature of life, it is necessary first to understand the evolution of biological organisms and then the nature of inheritance (i.e., *genetics*, a term first coined by William Bateson in 1902) and how it is instantiated in the body (the molecular processes of DNA). The ingenuity of Nature's solution to life is truly awe-inspiring. Only in recent years have we been in a position to reflect upon our origins, the biological basis of life, and our prospects for the future. Few other topics in psychology, or science in general, are more important.

Evolution

The theory of evolution was developed before the time of Charles Darwin, but it was Darwin who provided the mechanism for evolution: why some characteristics were selected and passed on to future generations, while other characteristics (and whole species) went extinct. Let us start with a survey of some pre-Darwinian ideas on evolution.

Pre-Darwin evolution ideas

Publication in 1859 of *The Origin of Species* changed the world of biology and changed our view of our place in that world. As Copernicus displaced the Earth from the centre of the universe, Darwin (1809–82) displaced humankind from the centre of the natural world. We were soon to learn that, like the lowly single-cell amoeba, human beings evolved by natural selection and therefore deserved no God-given right to claim superiority over the animal kingdom. Darwin started an intellectual revolution that not only continues to this day but which is having an increasing impact on theory and research in the biological and psychological sciences.

The idea that animals evolved over long geological time was not discovered by Darwin; it had been suggested for centuries before (Darwin acknowledged 30 previous thinkers in *Origin of Species*). Darwin's grandfather, Erasmus Darwin, produced, in 1794, one such theory in *Zoonomia*, which discussed the struggle for existence (a concept to become central to Darwin's theory) and competition for females (coined by Darwin as *sexual selection*). The most respected theory of evolution was proposed by J. B. Lamarck (1744–1829) in *Philosophie Zoologique* (1809). Lamarck's theory of evolution (or 'transformation', as it was known at that time) was the inheritance of *acquired* characteristics. Not unreasonably at the time, Lamarck argued that, as animals have to compete for survival, their organs would enlarge and change shape (i.e., adapt) to the local demands of the environment; importantly for his theory, these acquired changes would, by some unknown means, be passed on to future generations. The obvious example seems to be the giraffe, whose long neck evolved by its stretching to reach leaves in tall trees; in a similar manner, manual labourers were thought to pass on their (acquired) strong hands and arms to their offspring. Prima facie a nice theory but, as discussed below, untrue.

The *Vestiges of the Natural History of Creation* (1844), published anonymously but later revealed to have been written by the publisher Robert Chambers (1802–71), also argued for evolution, resting the case on the fossil record. Chambers also pointed to rudimentary and vestigial organs, such as the human coccyx (tail) and appendix (evolutionary relics of former structures whose functions have been lost). Rather fancifully, Chambers proposed that new species appeared from spontaneous 'monstrous' births, some of which proved successful (e.g., a goose might give birth to a frog!). This idea may have been stimulated by his own abnormal physical feature: he had six fingers on each hand. Chambers' idea was ridiculed for obvious reasons; this instilled in Darwin a sense of caution in rushing into print with his theory of evolution.

Even before Darwin embarked on his famous voyage on HMS *Beagle*, between 1831 and 1836, the problem of evolution was apparent; shortly after his return from the *Beagle*

Figure 2.1 Charles Darwin, 1840, watercolour by G. Richmond. (Photo akg-images.)

voyage, the solution to this problem was clear. Darwin's genius was to show *how* evolution occurred, not *that* it occurred. He was helped in the development of his theory by his reading and research in geology (he studied coral reefs, volcanoes and icebergs), for which he was well known (along with his extensive work on barnacles) before the publication of his ground-breaking theory. On the *Beagle* he studied Sir Charles Lyell's *Principles of Geology*. Darwin's reflection on the gradual changes to the Earth's surface may well have set the cognitive template for the idea that species too changed – if whole mountains and continents could change over the millennia then maybe so could animal and plant life. The personal and professional life of Darwin is described in Desmond and Moore (1991).[1]

Darwin's theory is the most important one in biology, and one of the most important theories in the whole of history (many would argue *the* most important theory). According to the American philosopher Daniel Dennett (1996), it is the best idea that anyone ever had, even ahead of Newton's and Einstein's ideas. It is necessary to devote time to understanding Darwin's arguments in order to appreciate the theory's implications for human psychology. From the first edition of *The Origin of Species*, Darwin realized the implications of his theory for psychology, stating in his chapter 'Recapitulation and Conclusion':[2]

> In the distant future I see open fields for far more important researches. Psychology will be based on a new foundation, that of the necessary acquirement of each mental power and capability by gradation. Light will be thrown on the origin of man and his history.

The Origin of Species, which is still as highly readable today as it was nearly 150 years ago, requires the reader to follow a simple, though extended, line of reasoning, illustrated by a wealth of evidence collected by Darwin and others. It is mercifully free of jargon, has no mathematical notation, and contains no obscure, esoteric or tortuous lines of reasoning. The philosopher John Stuart Mill summarized the reaction of many on encountering the book: 'Nothing can be at first sight more implausible than this theory, and yet after beginning by thinking it impossible one arrives at something like an actual belief in it.' It was also a rather simple, if ingenious, argument, as T. H. Huxley's reaction epitomizes: 'How extremely stupid not to have thought of that.'

ASK YOURSELF
If Darwin's theory of evolution by natural selection was so obvious why was it not discovered by previous evolutionists?

Today, as then, there is simply no *viable* alternative theory to explain the origins and nature of living things; however, today, unlike then, there is an overwhelming corpus of data to support Darwin's theory and a mechanism of inheritance in the form of knowledge of genetics and DNA.

Charles Darwin: Transmutation and Selection

Before discussing Darwin's theory of evolution, it is necessary first to deal with a problem of terminology. The terms used by Darwin's theory, *evolution* by *natural selection*, are open to misunderstanding and confusion.

Only in the last editions of *Origin of Species* did Darwin use the term *evolution*; in the earlier editions he preferred *transmutation*, meaning the transformation of one variety into another. The word *evolution* tends to imply an improvement – for example, it may be said that a theory is *evolving*, invariably meaning it is getting better by improvement; rarely is 'evolution' used to refer to something getting worse. But, for Darwin, species *changed*, they neither improved nor worsened (human intelligence may be seen as an improvement over that of chimpanzees, but this is a different meaning from Darwin's use of the term). In his copy of the *Vestiges*, Darwin noted, 'Never use the words higher and lower. I believe in no law of necessary development.'

Next, *natural selection* was prone to misunderstanding. In *Origin of Species*, natural selection was Nature's version of domestic selection, that is, the everyday business of dog breeders, pigeon fanciers and the cattle industry. Darwin devoted chapter 1 to the incontrovertible fact that 'variation under domestication' is easily achieved by selective breeding of favoured traits (the domestic dog being the best example of how such variety is latent in the wolf and which through deliberate breeding produces highly differentiated varieties). Darwin then went on to argue that if such changes (transmutations) can be achieved by human beings, then think of what changes must be achieved by the fierce selection pressures of Nature over millions of years (it is known from recent experience that, in any one year, as many as half of a population can be killed by a bacterium or virus). Thus, *natural selection* (i.e., Nature's selection) is simply an extension of the argument of domestic breeding. However, to some people, selection implied a selector. Unlike domestic breeding, Nature does not *purposefully* select: Nature's mechanism is a *blind*[3] – unthinking and uncaring – process of favouring those characteristics that led to greater survival and, crucially, greater reproductive success, the latter being the key to evolution.[4] Darwin was to admit that 'Natural Preservation' (part of the full title of *Origin of Species*) might have been preferable to natural selection: in writing to his lifelong mentor, Sir Charles Lyell, Darwin's appalling handwriting rendered 'Natural Preservation' as 'Natural Persecution' – this was only to be the start of the misunderstanding of Darwin's ideas.

Darwin's theory of natural selection

The evidence in favour of the mutability of species, as opposed to their fixity (or immutability), was suggested by a number of observations. First are the similarities of animals (e.g., humans and chimpanzees). Second is the fossil record, which shows that bones from older geological strata are not the same as bones from more recent strata, pointing to a change over time. Third is the embryological development of different species which share a number of common features (species often resemble each other during pre-natal development; post-natally there are also similarities, e.g., compare the faces of a newborn chimp and human being). Such evidence could not provide decisive proof, but it is highly suggestive of a gradual process of transmutation of one species into another.

Accepting that evolution occurs, then *how* does it occur? Darwin was not impressed by Lamarck's mechanism of the inheritance of acquired characteristics, for this seemed to demand the replacement of one mystery by another. (However, for a number of reasons, Darwin did not totally reject Lamarck's mechanism as a supplementary mechanism to natural selection.) It was apparent to Darwin, as it had been to others, that the various characteristics of species seemed to serve important purposes. The function of the giraffe's neck is obvious in an environment where the best leaves are high up in the trees. Darwin was concerned not only with how species change, but also how they acquire specific useful characteristics: *adaptations*.

During his travels on the *Beagle*, Darwin saw the wide variety of species and the subtle differences both within and between species. For example, in the Galapagos Islands, each island had a different variety of finch; indeed, their differences were so great that they were actually different species of finch, although they must have all had a common ancestor. Darwin reasoned that the descendants of the common ancestor diverged over the years after inhabiting different islands (the local ecological conditions of the sea prevented populations of finches from hopping from one island to another).

Darwin's process of evolution is *natural selection*.[5] In chapter 4 of *Origin of Species* Darwin stated,

> preservation of favourable variations and the rejection of injurious variations, I call Natural Selection.

Natural selection requires three essential conditions: (a) variation, (b) selection and (c) inheritance. First, there must be variation, or differences, between individuals for evolution to operate: if there are no differences, then there can be no (systematic) differential success in terms of reproduction. Next, there must be selection of preferred characteristics; that is, individuals with some heritable variants leave more offspring because those attributes help with the tasks of (a) survival (*viability*) and (b) reproduction (*fecundity*). Third, there must be some means by which favoured characteristics that have led to differential reproduction can be passed on to the next generation. Assuming some mechanism of inheritance, differential reproductive success is the crucial aspect of evolution. It was this mechanism of inheritance that was to baffle Darwin; its solution would come in the form of Mendelian genetics (see below).

The argument for the 'Struggle for Existence' (chapter 3 of *Origin of Species*) rested on the assumption that the potential population of any species vastly outstrips the environment's means of support. If all animals that were born both lived and reproduced, then within a short space of time there would not even be standing room on the Earth! The notion of overpopulation was inspired by the work of the political philosopher Thomas Malthus, who in 1798 published a highly influential book, *An Essay on the Principle of Population*. The struggle for survival occurs: (a) between individuals within a species; (b) between species; and (c) with the environment. It is this struggle which gives rise to reproductive success based upon the inheritance of preserved characteristics.

The essence of natural selection is captured in Darwin's famous quote (chapter 4 of *Origin of Species*):

> It may be said that natural selection is daily and hourly scrutinising, throughout the world, every variation, even the slightest; rejecting that which is bad, preserving and adding up all that is good; silently and insensibly working, whenever and wherever opportunity offers, at the improvement of each organic being in relation to its organic and inorganic conditions of life. We see nothing of these slow changes in progress, until the hand of time has marked the long lapses of the ages, and then so imperfect is our view into long past geological ages, that we only see what the forms of life are now different from what they formerly were.

In everyday life, it is easy to overlook this potential for overpopulation. For example, in woodlands we might see an appropriate number of birds per number of trees and wonder at the foresight of Nature to achieve this balance. What we do not see are the vast numbers of births that quickly lead to death by other animals (often their own siblings) or harsh climate. It was this line of reasoning that led Darwin to emphasize the struggle for existence. As Darwin (1859) stated in the Introduction to *Origin of Species*,

> As many more individuals of each species are born than can possibly survive; and as, consequently, there is a frequently recurring struggle for existence, it follows that any being, it vary however slightly in any manner profitable to itself, under the complex and sometimes varying conditions of life, will have a better chance of surviving, and thus be *naturally selected*.

However, Darwin's view of natural selection was not crude, but a subtle description of the forces of the preservation of favoured characteristics. In chapter 3 of *Origin of Species*, Darwin defines the 'struggle for existence':

I use the term Struggle for Existence in a large and metaphorical sense, including the depend-ence of one being on another, and including (which is more important) not only the life of the individual, but success in leaving progeny. The mistletoe is dependent on the apple and a few other trees, but can only in a far-fetched sense be said to struggle with these trees, for if too many of these parasites grow on the same tree, it will languish and die.

Thus, natural selection can lead to the interdependence of species and cooperation, today called *biological symbiosis*. This interdependence is discussed below in the context of altruism and cooperation.

The success of the theory of natural selection led Konrad Lorenz (1965, p. x) to state,

I would go as far to assert that any, even the most strikingly unbelievable, forms of structure and behaviour can be understood, at least in principle, as the outcome of the selection pressure exerted by their particular survival function. We are always ready to ask the question 'What for?'

Sexual selection

In *Origin of Species*, later to be fully developed in *The Descent of Man* (1871), Darwin was to propose the concept of *sexual selection*: the selection of and access to sexual partners. This process was suggested as the means by which each sex evolved different charac-teristics (e.g., weight/strength and beards in men). In fact any dimorphism (i.e., differ-ences between the sexes) could have evolved by sexual selection. There are two sides to the sexual selection coin. Not only do men compete with each other for access to females, as well as evolving characteristics that are especially appealing to the female (e.g., the ornate plumage of the male peacock), so too females compete for access to the fittest males and have evolved mechanisms for fertilization by preferred males. For example, in some species, females eject the sperm of sub-dominant males after multiple copula-tions with different partners (Pizzari & Birkhead, 2000); in human beings, the female orgasm appears to serve the function of facilitating the sperm of preferred males along the reproductive tract (the associated emotion is Nature's solution to evolving a proximal mechanism to respond favourably to males that are a 'turn-on'; i.e., those in possession of favoured characteristics – in technical and common parlance, those who are 'fit'). Darwin tended to see natural selection as to do with life and death struggles, sexual selection with reproduction. Today, sexual selection is seen as a variety of natural selection. However, these two kinds of selection can act in concert or separately, so may be seen as different sources of selection.

At this point in our discussion of evolution, you may be wondering whether it is really possible that such incredibly complex life forms, such as mammals, could have evolved *purely by chance* (i.e., Nature's selection of haphazard variations in phenotypes). In addressing this important question, several points are relevant. First, evolution occurred over many millions of years: there is no good reason for assuming that adaptations did not occur over this immense time span – the earliest member of the human family, the hominid *Sahelanthropus tchadensis*, so far discovered is between 6 and 7 million years old (Brunet et al., 2002); and *Homo erectus* (meaning 'upright'), thought to be our closest relative (it had a large brain and probably used tools), appeared around 1.8 million years ago (Asfaw et al., 2002). Second, severe environmental conditions may have imposed harsh selection pressures such that new mutations came to dominate over a relatively short period of time ('short' cannot be less than tens of thousands of years). Third, each new adaptation does not start from scratch, but is built on pre-existing structure (i.e., *pre-adaptations*); this fact might lead to an exponential growth in evolved functions, producing multiplier effects in adaptations (Wilson, 1975). Also, some 'master genes' seem to have the power to exert disproportionately large effects, which can lead to rapid evolution.

The evolution of the human eye is a good example of these processes. As demonstrated by Dawkins (1986) in *The Blind Watchmaker*, the eye did not develop all at once, fully formed. It started as a light-sensitive patch of skin that could extract visual information from the environment; the chance mutation that led to this light-sensitive skin conferred selection advantages in terms of the organism's ability to navigate the world (to avoid predation, and find food and partners for reproduction). It can be imagined that with each improvement in the skin's sensitivity to light there were additional survival and/or reproduction advantages that produced more offspring in subsequent generation with genes that coded for light-sensitive skin. Over the vast expanse of time, the highly developed (but not perfect) human eye evolved. Although it may seem that it must have been designed by a very clever engineer, there is no reason to think that it did not evolve by natural selection – indeed, the imperfections and occasional absurdities found in nature would suggest that, if such a creator existed, they were either incompetent or possessed of a warped sense of humour!

Darwin's problem of inheritance

It was clear to Darwin that Nature's selection of adaptive characteristics must be transmitted to offspring by some physiological means. Darwin (1868) proposed the theory of *pangenesis*, which he believed solved the problem of the mechanism of inheritance. This theory argued that every tissue, cell and living part of an organism ('units of the body') produced small 'gemmules' (granules or germs) that carried inheritable features, which were passed on to the next generation in the sex process. Gemmules were said to exist for eyes, feet, hands, etc., with each gemmule containing information only about its parent cell or organ. But, if it is assumed that evolution is composed of small variations, then surely these variations would be blended away, and differential reproduction of adaptive individuals would not result in favoured characteristics being passed on to future generations. He did suggest that the gemmules in his theory of pangenesis were particulate, so therefore not prone to this paint-pot blending-away effect. However, the problem of particulate inheritance continued to trouble Darwin, and partly for this reason he did not reject the role of Lamarckian inheritance of acquired characteristics.[6]

Also, in chapter 5 of *Origin of Species*, Darwin wrote,

> On the whole, I think we may conclude that habit, use and disuse have, in some cases, played a considerable part in the modification of the constitution and of the structure of various organs; but that the effects its use and disuse have often been largely combined with and sometimes overmastered by, the natural selection of innate differences.

It is now known this conclusion is wrong. However, although it is much derided today, Lamarck's theory was perfectly sensible given the state of knowledge at that time. As shown below, the *central dogma* of molecular biology is that the environment cannot systematically alter genetic information sufficient for Lamarckian inheritance: the genotype–phenotype road is one-way. It is very difficult to conceive of a mechanism that would allow the phenotype (e.g., strong muscles acquired by hard manual labour) to change the genotype (genes) in any way that would support the transmission of these acquired characteristics.

The solution to Darwin's blending problem was contained in the publication of Mendel's (1866)[7] theory of genetics (five years before *The Descent of Man*). What Mendel showed was that phenotypes (expressions of genes) of parents are blended in offspring, not the units of inheritance, the genes, which remained unchanged by sexual reproduction.[8] (The distinction between the 'genotype' and 'phenotype' was made by Wilhelm Johanssen in 1909; see Gottesman & Gould, 2003.) The entirety of genes is the *genotype* (also called gene complex, or genome); the *phenotype* is the final form, or expression, of the genotype on physical, psychological and behavioural processes.

> **ASK YOURSELF**
> Do there exist any psychological characteristics that seem to defy explanation by Darwin's theory of evolution by natural selection?

Mendelian (Classical) Genetics: The New Synthesis

Mendel's paper went largely unread and certainly unappreciated until its rediscovery in the early 1900s; its theoretical implications were established with the statistical genetics work of Sir Ronald Fisher (1890–1962), J. B. S. Haldane (1892–1964) and Sewell Wright (1889–1988). Their work is now referred to as the *New Synthesis* of neo-Darwinian theory.

Mendelian (gene) particulates

The Austrian monk Gregor Mendel (1822–84) conducted a series of systematic experiments on the garden pea (*Pisum sativum*). He first found varieties with clear-cut differences in features, such as flower colour (white vs. purple), seed colour (green vs. yellow) and form of seed (round vs. wrinkled). He then crossed these varieties and observed which characteristics (phenotypes) bred true and which did not – that is, which parent generation passed on their phenotype (e.g., white flowers) and which did not. Some phenotypes bred true, others produced one or other characteristic on a probabilistic basis. Mendel's results revealed a number of important things. First, the important distinction between *genotype* and *phenotype* must be made, because the phenotype is not a simple expression of the genes (i.e., the genotype) – in other words, offspring (observed) characteristics are not always identical to parental (observed) characteristics (e.g., colour of flower). Second, some genes are 'dominant', always breeding true; others are 'recessive', only revealing themselves under certain conditions (see below). Mendel concluded that the unit of inheritance was a 'particulate', a discrete package of information that was not blended by reproduction but was passed on in its original form – the fact that phenotypes can

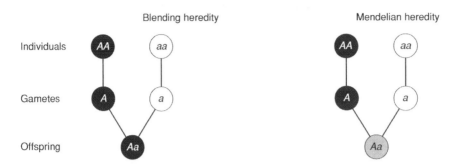

Blending heredity   Mendelian heredity

Individuals

Gametes

Offspring

Figure 2.2 Mendelian heritability compared with the blending theory of heritability. The parental alleles for black (A) and white (a) are preserved in Mendelian transmission but combined into grey with blending transmission. Mendelian transmission leads to genes being passed on to future generations unaltered (save mutations), whereas with blending genes are altered in each subsequent generation.

'jump' generations is evidence for the particulate nature of genes. Figure 2.2 shows how Mendelian inheritance differs from the blending theory.

There are two laws pertaining to Mendel's work. First is the *law of segregation*, stating that there are two elements of heredity for a single character. These two elements segregate, or separate cleanly during inheritance, so that the offspring receive one of the two elements. Second is the *law of independent assortment*, which states that the inheritance of two traits is independent.

Mendelian ratios

Mendelian ratios express the proportion of different phenotypes expected in the offspring of parents of particular combinations of genotypes (figure 2.3). As can be seen, combinations of dominant and recessive genes provide statistical distributions of the likely

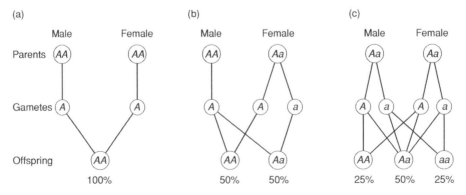

Figure 2.3 Mendelian ratios for (a) AA × AA cross; (b) AA × Aa cross; and (c) Aa × Aa cross.

phenotype. This type of analysis is important in the case of genetic disorders that follow a Mendelian pattern of inheritance.

Basic genetics

Every cell in the body contains a complete set of genes, the only exception being the sex cells (male sperm, female ova; these are *gametes*). The entire genome is the *genotype* and the *phenotype* is the final form, or expression, of the genotype. Phenotypes change as a result of exposure to the environment, genotypes cannot (but see the section on Mutations). Development is the process where genes interact with the environment to mould the final phenotype. Throughout life genes continue to play an important part, regulating every aspect of the body.

Genes are found on chromosomes, which are located in the nucleus of cells (see figure 2.4). In human beings, there are 23 pairs of chromosomes (other animals have more or less: dogs, 19; mice, 20; flies, 4; carp 52); on each pair of chromosomes, and at the same locus (plural, *loci*), there is a different version of a specific gene. These versions of a gene are called *alleles*: these are the unit of inheritance – genes that come in different varieties (i.e., alleles) are termed 'polymorphic' (meaning 'many forms'). In broad terms a gene (allele) may be defined as a segment of DNA that has specific functional effects (e.g., eye colour). If both chromosomes have the same allele then the individual is said to be 'homozygous' for the gene; if the two chromosomes have different alleles then the individual is said to be 'heterozygous' for the gene. Twenty-three chromosomes come from each parent, and 22 of the chromosomes are *matching* or *homologous*: these are the same whether they come from the mother or the father; but the 23rd chromosome is different. This sex chromosome comes in two forms: X and Y.[9] Females inherit XX, males XY. These two chromosomes (usually) determine the final phenotype – however, various conditions prevent these chromosomes from leading to the predicted outcomes (see chapter 6).

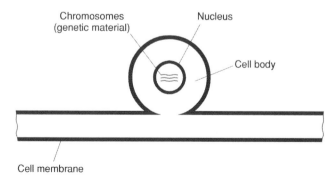

Figure 2.4 Prototype cell, nucleus and DNA. The genetic material (genes on 23 pairs of chromosomes) is located in the nucleus of the cell body. This genetic material is responsible for the functioning of the cell, and in the case of neurons in the brain it is especially important in the regulation of neurotransmitters (chemical messengers) as well as cell growth involved in neuronal connections.

When stained and viewed under a light microscope, chromosomes reveal a pattern of light and dark bands, which reflect regional variations in the amount of the four base pairs (see figure 2.5). These differences in regional variation allow the chromosomes to be identified – an analysis called *karyotype*.

Having two sets of chromosomes, and therefore two versions of each gene, is known as *diploidy* ('diplo' means two or double; 'oid' means like or resembling) (see figure 2.6). Gametes (sex cells) are *haploid* ('haplo' means single), containing only a single chromosome.

Dominant and recessive genes

Mendel's work was influential in distinguishing between different types of genes, with differing effects. Genes may be *dominant* (denoted by a capital letter, *A*), or recessive (denoted by a lower-case letter, *a*). If a dominant gene (*A*) is present in at least one of the two chromosomes then its phenotype will be expressed; for the phenotype of a recessive gene to be expressed, genes on both chromosomes must be recessive (i.e., *aa*) – in this case, the individual is homozygous for the gene.

Many pathological phenotypes are caused by recessive genes (e.g., sickle-cell anaemia; see below). Recessive genes will not be expressed in the presence of a dominant gene, which usually has a higher frequency in the population; therefore recessive genes can escape selection pressure and be passed on to future generations. Dominant genes that express their pathological (lethal) phenotype early in life quickly go extinct: the affected individual does not reproduce and pass on the gene.

Sex cells (gametes) and reproduction

Cells in our body are continuously dividing and the 46 chromosomes replicating – this is the process of *mitosis*. The major exception is the manufacture of sex cells: *gametes* (from *gamein*, 'to marry'). Knowledge of how sex cells divide solves another of Darwin's problems: the origin of variety in offspring. Unlike other types of cells, gametes contain only 23 chromosomes, not 46. The father's 23rd chromosome can be X or Y; the mother's is always X; therefore, it is the father's gamete which determines the sex of offspring (figure 2.7).

The sex-determining region of the Y chromosome (SRY gene) is located near the structure's tip (sometimes it is broken off during sperm production and added to one of the X chromosomes in the XX offspring; this accident of nature leads to offspring who look like males (e.g., genitalia), and are males in all respects, save their absence of a normal male Y chromosome). The SRY gene contains fewer than 1,000 base pairs, and codes for 204 amino acids (see below) – in other words, it is a relatively simple gene, but with important consequences. SRY acts as a molecular switch that directs other genes, and it is the sole gene necessary for the production of the testis. It is activated about 4 weeks after conception, and 'In its brief moment of glory it sends billions of babies on a masculine journey' (Jones, 2003, p. 6). The SRY gene is discussed further in chapter 6.

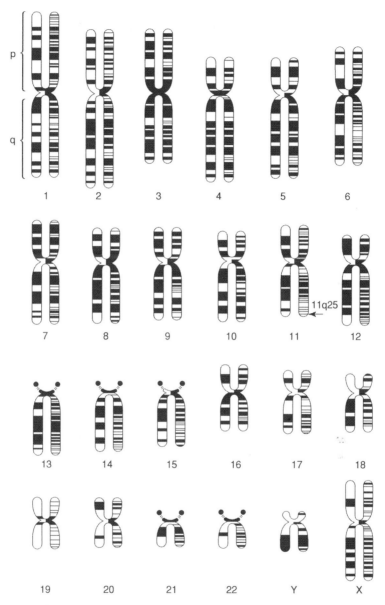

Figure 2.5 46 chromosomes. There are 23 pairs of chromosomes in the cell of the body (except the sex cell, where there are only 23 single chromosomes). The banding pattern reflects sequences on the DNA strand. Each chromosome is twisted with its partner, at the centre, as shown. Genes are identified by their location on the strand (p = upper half; q = bottom half), and their position on the strand. For example, the 11q25 gene (implicated in sickle-cell anaemia) is shown on chromosome 11. The 23rd chromosome is responsible for sex determination: the male Y is much smaller than the female X. Chromosomes are dyed to reveal their specific patterns and thus can be identified – a process known as karyotyping.

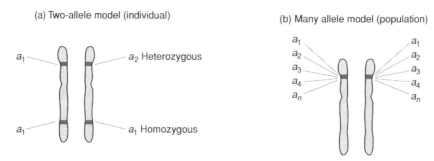

(a) Two-allele model (individual)

a_1 — a_2 Heterozygous

a_1 — a_1 Homozygous

(b) Many allele model (population)

a_1 a_1
a_2 a_2
a_3 a_3
a_4 a_4
a_n a_n

Figure 2.6 Homozygous and heterozygous alleles. For any given gene (which is always found at the same location on both chromosomes), the alleles (i.e., versions) of the gene may be the same (i.e., homozygous) or different (i.e., heterozygous). There can only be two versions of the gene in any individual because there are only two strands of each chromosome (a), but there may be many alleles distributed throughout the population (b).

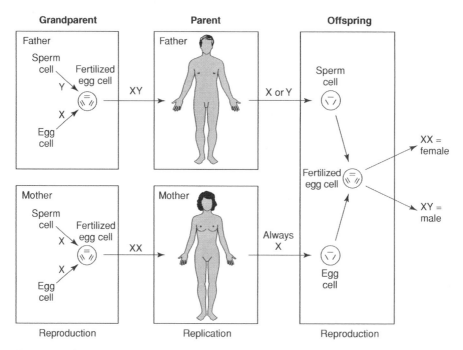

Grandparent

Father

Sperm cell — Fertilized egg cell
Y
XY
X
Egg cell

Mother

Sperm cell — Fertilized egg cell
X
XX
X
Egg cell

Reproduction

Parent

Father

X or Y

Mother

Always X

Replication

Offspring

Sperm cell

Fertilized egg cell

XX = female

XY = male

Egg cell

Reproduction

Figure 2.7 The reproduction–replication cycle. Sex cells (ovaries and sperm) contain 23 chromosomes. The 23rd chromosome from the mother is always X, the chromosome from the father may be X or Y (the father's chromosome determines the sex of the offspring). All 23 chromosomes are passed from the mother and father, which produces the 23 pairs of chromosomes in the offspring.

Crossing over

During the manufacture of gametes, chromosomes are broken apart and intermixed (the integrity of the separate genes is, of course, retained); therefore, each single chromosome in the gamete (with the exception of the X/Y sex chromosome) is a combination of the original two chromosomes. This outcome is achieved in the following way. Before manufacture of gametes, pairs of chromosomes line up with each other and exchange alleles – this process is known as *crossing over* (figure 2.8).

Thus, the chromosomes passed on by each parent are truly unique. Calculating the number of possible alleles (30,000 to 40,000) multiplied by 23 chromosomes yields an astronomical number of possible phenotypes. This recombination of alleles in each generation helps to explain the variety of phenotypes seen in offspring.

Let us take a simplified example of the division and recombination of alleles in the formation of gametes (figure 2.9). In the centre circle there are two pairs of chromosomes (*a* and *b*) with two alleles for a gene on each chromosome (a1, a2, b1, b2). How many different gamete combinations may be formed from this simple example? This principle can be demonstrated with reference to a simplified height/fat gene (perhaps a good example given the significant progress that has been made in the understanding of the genetics of body mass; Barsh, Farooqi & O'Rahilly, 2000). The possible outcomes are shown in figure 2.9.

With only two alleles on two chromosomes, there are four phenotypes. But given that there are some 40,000 genes in the human genome, imagine how many phenotypes are possible. The number runs into the trillions. Furthermore, when it is considered that genes often interact with each other, and often are not fully dominant or recessive, then it is possible to appreciate that the number of possible phenotypic combinations far exceeds the number of human beings who have ever lived: truly, we are all unique. This process of crossing over provides the variation that allows evolution to work. Added to this variation is further variation from mutations (see below).

Genetic imprinting

In many species, including human beings, there is evidence for the existence of what is known as 'genetic imprinting'. This is a mode of inheritance whereby only one parental allele is expressed, while the other is silenced. Some genes get thus marked or 'imprinted' according to their origins, and this effect can influence developmental processes. This process may also help to balance the conflicting tendencies of maternal and paternal genomes (e.g., from the viewpoint of the father there is a strong interest in building a larger baby; but the mother does not want too large a baby).

There has been extensive study in the mouse of one imprinted gene (IGF2) that makes a growth hormone, similar to insulin, which plays a role in the development of the cells in the early embryo and the placenta. When the hormone becomes active in the placenta it increases the amount of the nutrients that can be passed from mother to child. It is no surprise that this gene is paternal. Inactivation ('knocking-out') of this gene

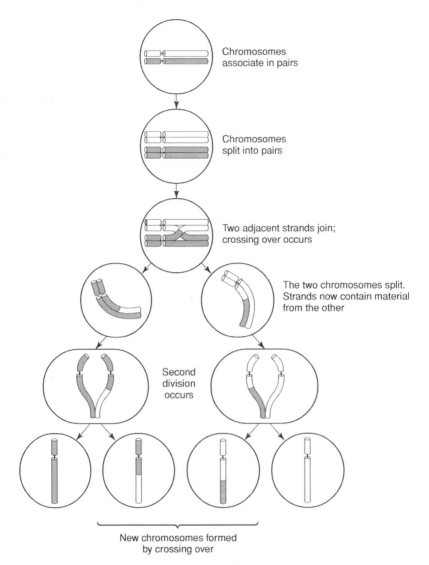

Chromosomes
associate in pairs

Chromosomes
split into pairs

Two adjacent strands join;
crossing over occurs

The two chromosomes split.
Strands now contain material
from the other

Second
division
occurs

New chromosomes formed
by crossing over

Figure 2.8 Crossing over of alleles. During the production of gametes (sex cells), crossing over of segments of DNA occurs between pairs of chromosomes. The final single chromosome passed to offspring is thus a combination of the parents' two versions of each of the 23 pairs of chromosomes. This process produces considerable variety in the genes transmitted.

leads to mouse pups being 40 per cent smaller. Maternal genes appear to work in the opposite direction: the mother switches on a gene for a receptor whose role is to mop up excess protein produced by the paternal IGF2 – in effect, her genes are counteracting the effect of the paternal IGF2, reducing the amount of nutrients getting across the placenta. Mice that lack the maternal gene are 16 per cent larger than normal mice.

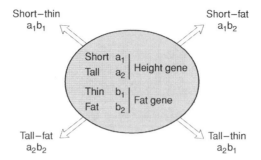

Figure 2.9 Height/fat genes. With two alleles of two genes distributed across two chromosomes there are four possible gene combinations. Assuming a gene value of 1 codes for a low score and 2 a high score, then we have the following combinations: (1) a_1, b_1 = short–thin; (2) a_1, b_2 = short–fat; (c) a_2, b_1 = tall–thin; and (d) a_2, b_2 = tall–fat. This is a gross oversimplification of the true complexity of body size, but it illustrates the combination of separate alleles that give a 'genetic disposition' to the development of actual body size (i.e., the phenotype).

The most suggestive evidence of imprinting on psychological development is found in Turner's syndrome, which is an uncommon genetic disorder that afflicts 1 in 2,000 girls born each year. Turner's syndrome is caused by a missing X chromosome: their single X chromosome can be inherited from the mother or father, so instead of being XX such females are X0. These girls have difficulty learning social skills, and they tend to be disruptive, impulsive, aggressive and generally antisocial: they butt into conversations, misread people's facial expressions and they are often very insensitive. Skuse et al. (1997) found that girls who inherited their X chromosome from their mother are more disruptive and have greater problems adjusting. Thus it seems that the paternal X chromosome acts as a brake on behaviour – as boys get their X from the maternal line, they tend to be less well behaved. It appears that mothers make their sons into men. (See also Bishop et al., 2000.)

Why sex?

Why do we reproduce sexually, mixing our own genes with those of other members of the species? Not all organisms reproduce sexually; some organisms clone themselves via asexual meiosis. In the discussion below it will be shown that the *selfish gene* hypothesis (Dawkins, 1976) might well have favoured asexual reproduction. Also, there is a cost to sexual reproduction: it leads to a greater variety of errors (mutations). According to the logic of Darwinian thinking, there must be an advantage to sexual reproduction. What might this advantage be?

With asexual reproduction (replication), there is usually no variety from one generation to the next (mutations are the only source of variation). This situation is fine if the genes that are being passed on all confer a sufficient level of survival and reproductive value (*fitness*). Let us imagine that this highly desirable (albeit improbable) state of affairs was achieved. Should this state of affairs be expected to continue? The answer is 'no'. It is known that mutations happen often (indeed, very frequently: mistakes are made in the transcription of DNA sequences in the formation of gametes; see below); and it is known that most mutations either have no effect on fitness or reduce fitness (mistakes rarely lead to improvements – although they do occasionally). Thus, our imaginary asexual animal that reached a perfect state of genetic fitness would quickly go extinct because *all* mutations would be passed on to *all* offspring, and these damaging mutations would accumulate over the series of generations. Imagine a mutation that made offspring infertile!

By virtue of the rearrangement of genetic material in each generation achieved by sexual reproduction, some offspring will get damaged genes (via errors in cell division), or will inherit a poor genotype, but other offspring will get fitness-enhancing genes, thus increasing chances of survival and reproduction. Thus, sexual reproduction is a good way to hedge reproductive bets on an uncertain future environment. Such flexibility is especially important in the struggle against the evolution of parasitic viruses, which need host bodies to replicate (often in the process destroying the host body; e.g., the HIV viruses).

Genes, immunity and sexual attraction

An example of the type of proximate mechanism that develops to avoid the effects of defective genes is shown in the case of mate choice based upon immune-system compatibility. The *major histocompatibility complex* (MHC) is a polymorphic set of genes (i.e., containing different alleles of the same gene) that play an important role in the functioning of the immune system (in vertebrates, including human beings). MHC genes produce proteins which identify foreign pathogens (e.g., they are responsible for the typical rejection of transplanted organs and thus need to be suppressed after transplantation) – these genes show great inter-individual variability and for this reason make it difficult to find suitable bone marrow donors.

Several studies have shown that, in mice and human beings, there is a preference for sexual partners who have a dissimilar MHC genotype: this can be detected in the pheromones of partners (Wedekind et al., 1995). The idea is that offspring are heterozygous for this/these gene(s) and therefore have more robust immune systems. For example, women prefer the smell of shirts containing the sweat of males with dissimilar MHC genes. In one study, preference for perfume ingredients was correlated with MHC genotypes (Milinski & Wedekind, 2001). Participants were first genotyped for their MHC polymorphism and then exposed to different scents and asked (a) whether they would like to smell like the scent, or (b) whether they would like their partners to smell like the scent. The results showed that there was a consistent pattern of preference for scents for one's self which was predicted by the participants' MHC polymorphism. The implications of this study are that scents are used to amplify body odours to advertise immunogenetics.

ASK YOURSELF
How would Darwin have modified his theory of evolution if he had known about classical genetics?

▮▯ DNA: The Molecule of Life

The publication in 1953 by James Watson (b. 1928) and Francis Crick (1916–2004) of the molecular basis of the gene represents one of the most important breakthroughs in biology. (See figure 2.10.) The delineation of the structure of the deoxyribonucleic (DNA)[10] molecule spawned a new science of molecular biology and, now with the human genome decoded, promises to revolutionize biological science and medicine. Along with Maurice Wilkins, Watson and Crick were awarded the Nobel Prize in 1962 (the other important name in this story is Rosalind Franklin, who collected the X-ray images that allowed Watson and Crick to guess the structure of the DNA molecule; she died of cancer, possibly due to her X-ray work, before the award of the Nobel Prize, which is not awarded to the dead; Maddox, 2002).[11] DNA has been around for thousands of millions of years; the oldest sample discovered was 425 million years old.

A gene may be defined as a segment of the DNA molecule that is (a) inheritable in Mendelian terms, and (b) functional in terms of producing a specific phenotypic trait. DNA and its supporting proteins form the chromosome. The Human Genome Project and a private biotechnology company, Celera Genomics (Venter et al., 2001) published drafts of the 3 billion base sequences of the human genome[12] – it covers some 750,000 pages of A4, and would take up 270 feet of library shelving (fortunately, it is

Figure 2.10 Francis Crick (right) and James Watson admiring their original model of the structure of DNA shortly after its discovery in Cambridge, UK, in 1953. (Photo © A. Barrington Brown / Science Photo Library.)

freely available on the Internet and computer disk).[13] Both research groups estimate the number of genes to be somewhere between 26,000 and 40,000, an estimate that is much lower than previously thought and only twice as many as that of the humble fruit fly (approximately 13,600), and roughly the same number as for mice and worms. According to Chinese scientists, rice has more than 46,000 genes!

The 50th anniversary of the discovery of the structure of DNA was celebrated by a number of short articles in *Nature Genetics* (Crow, 2003; Slobodkin, 2003; Mawer, 2003) and summary articles in *Nature* (24 April 2003), in which Watson and Crick's (1953) paper was published.

The DNA molecule consists of a sequence of units; each unit is called a nucleotide, which consists of a phosphate and sugar group with a base attached. The full DNA molecule consists of two paired complementary strands, twisted around each other like a free-standing spiral staircase, each made up of sequences of nucleotides. The rails of the staircase comprise alternating sugar and phosphate groups, held chemically bonded together by base pairs. The two strands form a double helix (figure 2.11.) This DNA structure made sense chemically and biologically, Watson and Crick (1953, p. 737) announced, in one of the understatements of all time:

> It has not escaped our notice that the specific pairing we have postulated immediately suggests a possible copying mechanism for the genetic material.

The total length of DNA is made up of genes (also known as *cistrons*), which are composed of two parts: (a) *introns* are sequences of active code; and (b) *exons* are non-coding sequences, which can be much longer than the coding sequences. The beginning and end of a gene are signalled by distinct base sequences, which provide a kind of punctuation in the DNA message. Most DNA base sequences do not code for genes (i.e., genes code for amino acid sequences); the estimate of active base pairs varies, from 2 to 5 per cent. Thus many, perhaps most, base pairs are so-called 'junk DNA',[14] which consists of large parts of DNA that do not seem to code for proteins.

Proteins

A single gene may contain thousands of base pairs on the DNA molecule; the sequences of these base pairs code for the synthesis of specific proteins.[15] Proteins form the basis of the nervous system and produce all other cells (e.g., *keratin* forms the hair of mammals and the feathers in birds; and collagen forms the framework of our bones and teeth), as well as acting as transporters (e.g., haemoglobin, the red protein which carries oxygen in our blood) and serving important functions in metabolic processes, catalysed by a battery of proteins called enzymes. Although the DNA code is identical in each cell in the body, within a particular cell only a subset of genes is *expressed* in the form of protein synthesis.

Proteins are made up of sequences of amino acids. It is the three-dimensional shape of amino acid sequences that defines the function of the protein. Each amino acid behaves chemically in distinct ways, such that different sequences of amino acids result in pro-

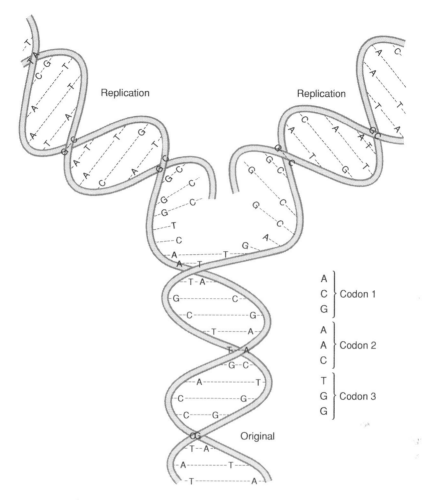

Figure 2.11   DNA base-pair structure. The bases inside the double-stranded backbone contain the DNA sequence. The backbone is composed of sugar phosphate. The four nitrogenous bases of DNA share a special relation: adenine (A) always pairs with thymine (T), and cytosine (C) always pairs with guanine (G). When the double helix is 'unzipped' the second strand can be reconstructed, leading to replication. A gene is a sequence of bases on the DNA molecule, located at a specific location, which contains information sufficient for the production of proteins.

teins with different properties. For example, haemoglobin has a sequence of 144 amino acids and insulin has a different sequence of 51 amino acids. As is shown below, the 'genetic code' specifies the relationship between the sequence of base pairs on the DNA molecule and the production of the sequence of amino acids that form the proteins of the body. Each cell in our bodies may contain 10,000 different types of protein.

The genetic code

The discovery of the coding relationship between DNA and proteins was fully described by the mid-1960s, less than 20 years after the initial discovery of the structure of DNA. The search for this code is well described by Watson (2003), who details the people and the science involved in this search.

DNA base pairs and amino acids

The sequence of nucleotides in a gene specifies the sequence of amino acids in the protein. There are four types of nucleotide in DNA; they differ only in the base part of the nucleotide unit. The sugar and phosphate group is the same in all four: adenine (A), cytosine (C), guanine (G) and thymine (T).

A and G belong to a chemical group called purines; C and T are pyrimidines. In the double helix, an A in one strand always pairs with a T in the other; and C and G always pair. Thus, if the nucleotides of one strand are known, then the sequence of the second strand will also be known. This pairing of base pairs is essential for gene replication, which entails the double helix being unzipped and reconstructed during cell division (figure 2.12). For example, if the sequence on strand is AGGCTCCTA then the complementary strand is TCCGAGGAT.

A three-letter (triplet) sequence (called a *codon*) codes for one amino acid, but there are 64 possible variations on these four bases, triplet codes. In fact, there are not 64 amino acids; there are only 20 amino acids and one 'stop' triplet, thus only 21 triple coding statements are required. As there cannot be a one-to-one triple to amino acid code, most

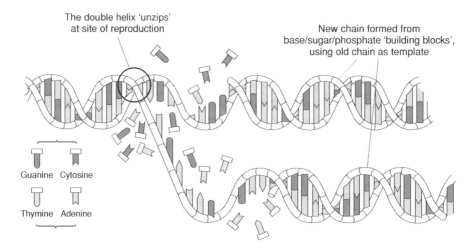

Figure 2.12 DNA unzipping. Replication of DNA is achieved by complementary base pairing after separation of the two sugar-phosphate backbones that comprise the double helix.

		Second letter				
		A	G	T	C	
First letter	A	AAA Phenylalanine AAG Phenylalanine AAT Leucine AAC Leucine	AGA Serine AGG Serine AGT Serine AGC Serine	ATA Tyrosine ATG Tyrosine ATT Stop ATC Stop	ACA Cysteine ACG Cysteine ACT Stop ACC Tryptophan	A G T C
	G	GAA Leucine GAG Leucine GAT Leucine GAC Leucine	GGA Proline GGG Proline GGT Proline GGC Proline	GTA Histidine GTG Histidine GTT Glutamine GTC Glutamine	GCA Arginine GCG Arginine GCT Arginine GCC Arginine	A G T C
	T	TAA Isoleucine TAG Isoleucine TAT Isoleucine TAC Methionine	TGA Threonine TGG Threonine TGT Threonine TGC Threonine	TTA Asparagine TTG Asparagine TTT Lysine TTC Lysine	TCA Serine TCG Serine TCT Arginine TCC Arginine	A G T C
	C	CAA Valine CAG Valine CAT Valine CAC Valine	CGA Alanine CGG Alanine CGT Alanine CGC Alanine	CTA Aspartic acid CTG Aspartic acid CTT Glutamic acid CTC Glutamic acid	CCA Glycine CCG Glycine CCT Glycine CCC Glycine	A G T C

(Third letter column at right: A, G, T, C for each block)

Figure 2.13 Base-pair amino acid code. The 'genetic code' is the relationship between three bases (codons) and 20 amino acids: chains of amino acids compile proteins. The 64 possible triplet combinations are reduced to 20 amino acids and a stop sequence by redundancy in the third letter (e.g., GC = arginine, irrespective of the third letter).

of the 64 messages in the triplet code are redundant, and several triplets have the same meaning (figure 2.13).

Transcription and translation of DNA

How does the DNA code get translated into the production of proteins? In the first stage, an intermediate molecule called messenger ribonucleic acid (mRNA) is transcribed from DNA (this process is termed *transcription*). mRNA has a similar structure to DNA, except that it is single-stranded and a base called *uracil* (U) is present instead of thymine (T). (The genetic code is expressed in terms of codons in the mRNA.) This transcription process is shown in figure 2.14.

Transcription takes place in the nucleus of the cell. After the mRNA molecule has been assembled on the gene it then leaves the nucleus and travels to one of the structures in the cytoplasm, called the *ribosome*. The ribosome is the site of the second main stage in protein production: it is where the amino acid sequence is read off from the mRNA sequence and the protein is assembled. As different cells are specialized for different functions, different segments of the DNA sequence (genes) are expressed. The mRNA molecule passes through the ribosome rather like recording tape through the head of a tape recorder: this is the process of *translation*. The newly synthesized molecule of mRNA reproduces the entire sequence of the gene, including the introns, and is then processed or 'matured' by snipping out the introns and slicing together the coding sequence. The actual translation is achieved by yet another kind of RNA, called *transfer RNA* (tRNA).

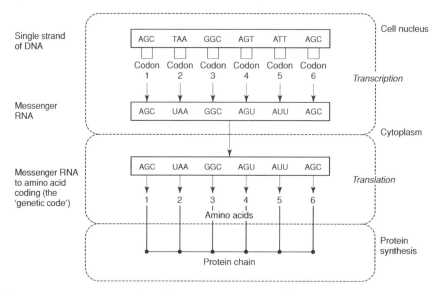

Figure 2.14 Transcription and translation are the processes that lead from DNA to the production of proteins. First, messenger ribonucleic acid (mRNA) is transcribed from DNA (this is *transcription*) in the nucleus of the cell; and then this mRNA, which has a similar structure to DNA except that it is single-stranded and a base called *uracil* (U) is present instead of thymine (T), leaves the nucleus and travels to one of the structures in the cytoplasm, the *ribosome*, which is the site of the second main stage in protein production: this is where the amino acid sequence is read off from the mRNA sequence and the protein is assembled.

Amino acid protein structure

ASK YOURSELF
Why was the discovery of the structure of DNA so important?

Different proteins have different numbers of amino acids (some 100 to 300). For example, insulin has 51 amino acids. A 300 amino acid protein needs roughly 1,000 nucleotide bases (i.e., 300 times 3, plus another 100 for the 'promoter signal' which precedes a gene sequence). The structure of myoglobin is shown in figure 2.15.

▢ Mutations: The Mistakes of Life

We are the product of errors in DNA; however, more often than not mistakes in DNA replication are either of no consequence or deleterious. Sexual reproduction is a tricky business: cell division, during the construction of gametes, with the dividing and combining of DNA segments (crossing-over), is prone to mistakes of various kinds. In

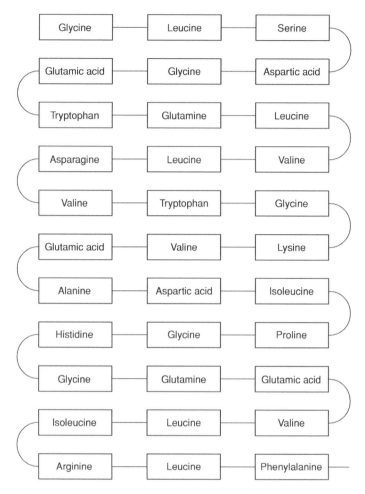

Figure 2.15 Structure of myoglobin (with DNA sequence). The human haemoglobin protein comprises 33 amino acids.

addition, exposure to environmental radiation is thought to lead to mutations – only mutations in sperm and ova can be passed on to further generations. For example, during 1949–89, the Soviet Union tested 470 nuclear weapons at one site in Kazakhstan; double the number of mutations in sperm and eggs have been reported in residents in this affected region.

Mutations may be of two kinds: (a) changes in the coding of small sections of DNA with individual genes (*point mutations*); or (b) large-scale change in chromosomes (*chromosome mutations*) – the examples given below are based on Patterson (1999), who provides an excellent introduction to evolution and genetics.

Point mutations

Consider the four triplet sequences that may be found at the end of a gene-coding sequence:

CAT TAG GAT ACT

Assuming that the first letter is the start of a triplet, these bases will form a sequence of four triplets which, after transcription and translation, will specify the following amino acid chain: valine, isoleucine and leucine, and a stop sign. Now suppose that during gamete manufacture the first base pair in this sequence is eliminated. The message now reads:

ATT AGG ATA CT

What would be the effect of this point mutation? The first triplet now becomes a stop sign (see figure 2.13); therefore the remainder of the code will not be translated and the enzyme molecule will lack its last three amino acids. This type of mutation is known as *deletion*.

Another type of change in the base pairs can come from *insertion*. Say G now appears at the beginning of the sequence. This produces:

GCA TTA GGA TAC T

This sequence now specifies arginine, asparagine, proline and methionine, and there is no stop signal, so the following DNA will also be translated and added to the enzyme molecule.

Single deletion or insertion of a base has profound effects; but if all bases of a codon are changed then there is less of an impact because only one amino acid would be changed (perhaps one out of many hundreds). Deletions or insertions of base pairs in numbers other than three or multiples of three are called *frameshift* mutations.[16]

Another common type of mutation is *substitution*, in which one base pair is replaced by a different one. Suppose the first of the two Gs in the middle of the sequence is replaced by a T, so that the triplet TAG is changed to TAT. The code shows that both triplets specify isoleucine, so such a mutation would have no effect (such mutations are *silent* or *synonymous*). However, most substitutions will have the effect of changing one amino acid (*missense* mutations) – this change may or may not affect the functioning of the protein. Substitutions that change a triplet into a stop signal (*nonsense* mutation) are especially influential, as they stop the further formation of the amino acid change and thereby radically alter the protein (a stop signal could be changed into an amino acid, lengthening the amino acid chain).

Chromosome mutations

Mutations to chromosomes involve large-scale changes. Point mutations change the coding sequence; chromosome mutations rearrange the sequence. This particularly occurs in meiosis, during crossing over. They are mainly errors or mispairing in crossing over. There are different varieties of chromosome mutations.

a) Inversions: a section of a chromosome maintains its position, but is turned around, end to end.
b) Translocation: sections of the chromosome are exchanged between non-homologous chromosomes.

There are other chromosome mutations: *deletions and duplications* (crossing over is unequal, with one chromosome getting more than it loses, so a gene is duplicated on one chromosome and lost to the other); *fusions* (two chromosomes join together, reducing the number of chromosomes by one); and *fragmentations* (a chromosome splits into two, producing an additional chromosome) (figure 2.16).

Mutations may have no effect, damaging effects, or may lie hidden to be passed on to future generations when they may express themselves (e.g., recessive gene). However, occasionally this error may code for a phenotype that increases the adaptive advantage of the animal. This mutant animal should now have a better chance to survive and reproduce and thus pass on the gene. Over the time course of animal evolution these errors have conferred adaptive advantage and resulted in new species, including human beings.

It is important to appreciate that there is no grand design or plan: evolution works by capitalizing upon transcription errors in DNA which happen *purely by chance* to confer, sometimes, a survival and reproduction advantage. Human beings, like all other animals, are the result of error and serendipity. Many mutations (especially in non-coding, intron, base pairs) will have no selective advantage or disadvantage; in these cases, the frequency of the mutation in subsequent generations will fluctuate by chance; it is, however, conceivable that such innocent base sequences could become part of a more active gene sequence in further mutations of that portion of the chromosome; an example of a *pre-adaptation* at the gene level.

Recent research is pointing to evidence that small genetic mutations can lead to large changes in the phenotype. It has already been mentioned that new adaptations may build upon existing characteristics or existing DNA code (i.e., pre-adaptation). Now research is showing that 'major genes', which control other genes, can lead to rather large physical changes. One class of 38 genes known as a homeobox (*Hox*) seems to switch other genes on and off during an organism's development as an embryo. In the brine shrimp, suppression of this gene leads to a 15 per cent decrease in limb development. Such research is starting to provide a clue as to how evolution can produce large changes in species – this is sometimes known as 'punctuated evolution'. The locus of genes is sometimes related to their expression in the body (Kmita et al., 2002), pointing to some form of mapping between gene loci and their morphological expression.

Replication of DNA is essentially a 'selfish' process: DNA does not purposefully code for anything, and it does not care what it codes for – if it codes for anything at all. Nature has selected DNA sequences that produced phenotype vehicles (bodies) that reproduced and thus replicated the gene.

The gene is no more purposeful than water running downhill as a consequence of gravity. DNA sequences that code for phenotypes that did not reproduce, or reproduced

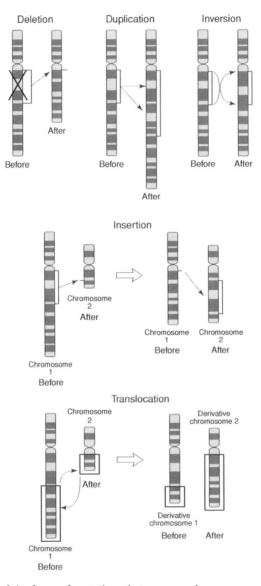

Figure 2.16 Some of the forms of mutations that occur on chromosomes.

at a lower rate than other sequences, simply disappeared from the gene pool: they went extinct. As Dawkins (1976, p. ix) states, 'We are survival machines – robot vehicles blindly programmed to preserve the selfish molecules known as genes.'

In recent years, one of the best examples of the evolution of species, based upon random mutations, is the hospital 'superbug': due to the harsh environment of hospitals

(i.e., use of disinfection, antibiotics, etc.) bacteria have been subject to severe selection pressures; those that have survived this
environment now have resistance to many of the commonly
used antibiotics, causing significant problems for the patients'
bodies they invade in order to replicate.

Genetic Disorders

A large number of genetic disorders – about 5,000 single-gene disorders, most of which
are very rare – have now been identified. Many common physical disorders, including
heart disease and cancer, have an important genetic contributor; and it is now known
that psychological and psychiatric conditions have a genetic component. The genetic and
environment interaction in such diseases is often complex, but the importance of genetic
effects in a number of well-delineated disorders can be demonstrated: (a) phenylketonuria
(PKU), (b) Huntington's disease (HD), (c) haemophilia, (d) neurofibromatosis, (e) sickle-
cell anaemia, and (f) Down's syndrome. (It is helpful to include physical disorders to
show the different forms genetic mutation can take, as well as to highlight why some
deleterious mutations are maintained in the population and how the damaging effects
of these mutations may be circumvented.)

Phenylketonuria (PKU)

Phenylketonuria (PKU) is a severe mental retardation disorder, affecting around 1 in 10,000
births. Mutation in the PAH gene leads to a metabolic problem caused by the absence
or inactivity of a particular enzyme, phenylalanine hydroxylase. This enzyme converts
phenylalanine (one of the 20 amino acids that make up proteins) to tyrosine; when this
conversion is blocked, phenylalanine levels increase in the blood and can be detected
in urine. High levels of phenylalanine in the blood depress the levels of other amino
acids, depriving the nervous system of other required nutrients. The parents of PKU
individuals do not usually suffer from the condition; but the pattern of inheritance
shows a strong genetic basis. As you may have guessed, it turned out that PKU could
be traced to the influence of a recessive gene (allele). The PKU gene was found to
be on chromosome 12. Although it is a single-gene, recessive disorder, the molecular
genetics of PKU are not simple: the PAH gene shows more than 100 mutations, some
of which produce a milder form of retardation. The mode of inheritance is shown in
figure 2.17.

PKU is perhaps the best example of how a purely genetic disorder does not imply
the inability to alter its course of action. Fortunately, the effects of this unpleasant
genetic disorder can be stopped in its tracks by environmental (dietary) intervention, by
reducing the amount of phenylalanine eaten in foods (some foods are especially high in
this substance). As a result, today, many people with PKU do not show the expressed
phenotype.

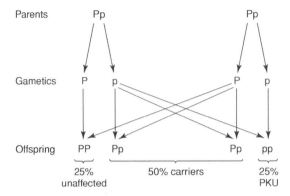

Parents   Pp   Pp

Gametics   P   p   P   p

Offspring   PP   Pp   Pp   pp

25% unaffected   50% carriers   25% PKU

Figure 2.17 The PKU inheritance pattern. The pattern of inheritance of phenylketonuria (PKU) is complex but it is known to be a recessive disorder, which means that offspring must possess both liability genes (Pp) – the high percentage of 'carriers' (Pp), who do not express the disorder, allows this gene to escape selection pressure.

Haemophilia

This condition is the result of a mutation in one of the genes producing the proteins necessary for the clotting of blood. This genetic disorder shows a particular pattern of inheritance: it is *sex-linked*. The mutated gene is carried on the X chromosome and is recessive. The gene has no effect in females (XX), as one of the Xs will counteract the effect of the other (in rare cases, both Xs are recessive, in which case the female would express the phenotype). But in male offspring (XY), there is a 50 per cent chance that they will inherit the faulty X chromosome. If it is inherited by the male, then this recessive gene behaves like a dominant gene because there is not an alternative allele of the gene (the male has only one X, and the gene is not found on the much shorter Y chromosome). In this case half the offspring would be expected to carry the gene, but only male carriers would show the disorder (figure 2.18).

Huntington's disease (HD)

Huntington's disease is a terminal degenerative brain disease that typically occurs between the ages of 30 to 50, found in 4 to 7 per 100,000 of the population. It too has a straightforward genetic basis. Unlike *haemophilia*, its genetic basis does not involve recessive alleles (figure 2.19). HD has been linked to a DNA marker near the tip of chromosome 4; the DNA sequence of the gene was finally characterized in 1993. It is caused by a dominant allele – more specifically, the allele on chromosome 4 has more than 40 repeats of CAG (the normal version of the allele has between 11 and 34 repeats – these repeats can accumulate over generations and the greater the number of repeats, the earlier the onset of the disorder). (CAG codes for the amino acid glutamine and results in a protein

When the father has haemophilia and the mother is unaffected

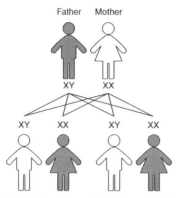

None of the sons will have haemophilia. All of the daughters will carry the haemophilia gene.

When the mother carries the haemophilia gene and the father is unaffected

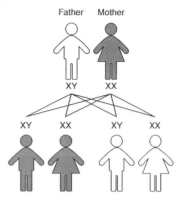

There is a 50% chance at each birth that a son will have haemophilia. There is a 50% chance at each birth that a daughter will carry the haemophilia gene.

Figure 2.18 The haemophilia inheritance pattern. Haemophilia is an example of sex-linked transmission. The affected gene is on the X chromosome. As only the mother passes on her X chromosome to the son (the father passes only his Y chromosome), and as a healthy X chromosome counteracts the deleterious effects of the affected X chromosome in the daughter, only (XY) sons are affected by this disorder.

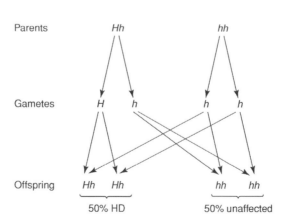

Figure 2.19 The Huntington's disease (HD) inheritance pattern shows a strong dominant effect of the liability gene. Dominance (*H*) means that the gene is not modified by the environment and possession of the genotype leads to development of the phenotype – the presence of a recessive gene (*h*) on the alternate chromosome is insufficient to counteract effects of the dominant gene.

with an expanded number of glutamines; this produces a toxic effect in the protein.) This dominant allele evaded extinction by expressing its effects after the peak years of reproduction. If one parent has the dominant allele then there is a 50 per cent chance that the offspring will be affected. Those affected show movement disorders, personality changes and forgetfulness. The American folk singer Woody Guthrie died of this disorder. Premorbid personality features include anxiety, depression, apathy, hallucinations, obsessions and compulsions.

Sickle-cell anaemia

Sickle-cell anaemia is a life-threatening disorder, with its highest frequency in central/west Africa, the eastern Mediterranean and India. There are some 500 known variants of human haemoglobin, most of which have no obvious ill-effects. However, the haemoglobin-S variant produces sickle-cell anaemia. In afflicted individuals, the red blood cells are sickle or spindle shaped, not disc shaped as in normal blood. There is only a single amino acid difference in the chain of haemoglobin in afflicted individuals: valine appears instead of glutamic acid at position 6. Thus, it is caused by a *point mutation* in DNA – a substitution of A for T in the middle of the triplet. Substitution of valine for glutamic acid alters the electric charge of the haemoglobin molecule, and because of this when the blood is deoxygenated the molecules tend to bond together in long fibres, which cause a cascade of resulting medical complications.

The inheritance pattern shows this mutant gene to be recessive; the disorder is apparent only in those who are homozygotic for the gene (i.e., have inherited the mutation from both parents). Heterozygotic individuals may show some effects, but they usually lead normal lives. The gene lives on chromosome 11, on the short arm (p) at a region called 11p15.5. In Africa, the proportion of heterozygotes is as high as 40 per cent in some regions. These regions have the most severe form of malaria. Malaria is caused by minute, single-celled parasites, introduced into the blood by the bite of a mosquito, which then replicates by asexual reproduction. They feed by breaking down haemoglobin. People with the mutated gene are less vulnerable to malaria because infected cells tend to 'sickle' or collapse together, interfering with the development of the parasite. Therefore, in high malaria areas, sickle-cell heterozygotes are better adapted than either sickle-cell homozygotes (who suffer from the sickle-cell anaemia) or the normal homozygote (who may die from malaria). For this reason, the faulty gene is maintained in the population.

Neurofibromatosis

This disorder causes skin, neurological and orthopaedic problems, which, in severe cases, can lead to cognitive problems (e.g., learning difficulties and cognitive distraction) as well as tumours (the manifestation of this disorder is very variable in individuals). It is prevalent in about 1 in 3,000 births. The disorder is caused by a mutation in or a deletion of the NF1 gene that codes for neurofibromin, which serves as a tumour-suppressing factor; half of cases reflect a mutation in the gene. This is a dominant gene disorder; the faulty NF1 gene is located on the long arm of chromosome 17. This gene is highly *penetrant*: almost all individuals with an NF1 gene mutation will show some of the clinical signs of the disorder. Like other genetic influences on mental retardation there is a high mutation rate for this gene (approximately 50 per cent of cases are the result of a mutation).

This disorder shows that disruption of the correct amino acid sequence to build the neurofibromin can lead to variety of physical and psychological effects. The patho-physiology of the disorder involves the development of minute tumours, which can impair functioning of neural pathways (e.g., the optic nerve).

Down's syndrome

Down's syndrome is not caused by a specific gene/allele, but by an abnormality in the number of chromosomes inherited. It has already been noted that the combination of male (sperm) and female (ovum) gametes produces 46 chromosomes, 23 from each parent. Well, in this disorder this process is disrupted, and the offspring inherits three chromosomes, not two, at chromosome number 21. Down's children have a character-istic phenotype: short stature, small round head, learning difficulties and generally a very congenial personality – Down's is the most common cause of mental retardation. The incidence is about 1 in 700 births, and its probability increases with the age of the mother.

These genetic disorders illustrate that even relatively small changes in base sequences or whole chromosomes can have very large effects on phenotypes.

> **ASK YOURSELF**
> What do mutations reveal about the evolutionary process?

Current Evolutionary Thinking

In the past 40 years there has been a new wave of thinking in evolutionary biology that has particular significance for psychology. This research has focused on the gene's-eye view of adaptation, and has led to theories of kin selection, the concept of the selfish gene, and the idea that psychological processes are the result of the natural selection of adaptations. These three areas are addressed in turn.

Inclusive fitness

When animal behaviour is closely studied it is evident that much of the behaviour seen is what might be called selfish behaviour – such behaviour can be understood easily in terms of the Darwinian struggle for existence. But, especially in mammals, one also observes behaviour that appears to fly in the face of Darwin's theory: selfless, altruistic and coop-erative behaviour. Apart from the case of biologically related kin, it is known that Nature cannot favour genes that code for the reproductive success of other people's genes – simple mathematics rules out this effect. Darwin (1859, ch. 4) recognized this problem when he considered *cooperation* between species (the same rationale holds for cooperation *within* a species),

> What natural selection cannot do, is to modify the structure of one species, without giving it any advantage, for the good of another species.

This problem in Darwin's theory was solved by William Hamilton (1963, 1964a,b), in the early 1960s, while studying for his Ph.D. at the London School of Economics. Hamilton is perhaps the most important theoretical biologist of the last 40 years. Buss (1999, p. 12) notes, 'Hamilton's theory sparked a revolution that transformed the entire field of biology.' As we will discuss below, his theoretical work shaped a revolution in psychology, the full implications of which are still being worked out.

Before discussing this new wave of thinking, it may be asked, now that so much is known about the molecular structure and functions of DNA, whether theoretical biology is still needed. The answer is that it is indeed still required because there are many evolutionary problems (distal questions) that cannot be answered by molecular analysis alone. As noted by Hamilton (1996, p. 12),

> I admitted the DNA story to concern life's most fundamental executive code. But, to me, this wasn't the same as reading life's real plan. I was convinced that none of the DNA stuff was going to help me understand the puzzles raised by my reading of Fisher and Haldane or to fill the gaps they had left.

Before discussing Hamilton's theory, it is necessary to first discuss the notion of *fitness*. Fitness may be defined as the ability of an organism to leave a greater proportion of its genes in succeeding generations than other individuals. It may achieve this aim by *individual fitness* (i.e., differential reproductive success) or *inclusive fitness* (i.e., increasing the survival and reproduction chances of genetically related individuals). The notion of *inclusive fitness* is the key to the new thinking in biology. According to Hamilton, what is selected by Nature is the individual gene (DNA sequence), not the individual organism. As individual genes are distributed in the population, according to inclusive fitness theory, individuals can achieve reproductive fitness by enhancing the chances of survival and reproduction of not only themselves but genetically related others.

Kin selection

The major means by which inclusive fitness may be enhanced is to promote the interests of genetically related kin. Thus, inclusive fitness can be viewed as the sum of individual reproductive success (classical fitness) plus the effects the individual's actions have on the reproductive success of his/her genetic relatives.

In survival or resource-limited environments, when an individual performs an altruistic act towards a relative, the inclusive fitness is the individual's fitness (which has been lowered by the act) plus the incremental fitness enjoyed by that proportion of the relative's hereditary constitution that is shared with the altruistic individual. The pro-

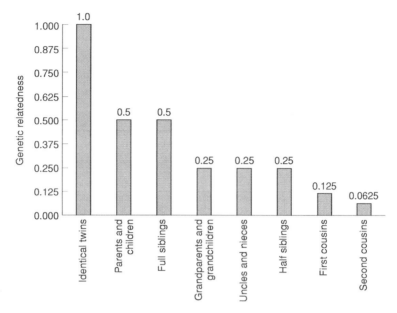

Figure 2.20   Genetic relatedness. According to Hamilton's theory, inclusive fitness is a function of genetic relatedness, which is defined as the sharing of those genes that show *variation* in the population.

portion of shared heredity is the fraction of genes held by common descent by the two relatives and is measured by the coefficient of relationship, *r* (see figure 2.20).

The logic of altruism also applies to selfishness and spite. Altruism is defined as self-sacrifice for the benefit of genetically related individuals; selfishness, increasing one's own fitness by lowering another's; and spite is the lowering of someone else's fitness without an increase to one's own fitness (there may even be a decrease) (Wilson, 1975; figure 2.21). These behaviours do not necessarily involve biological kin. Hamilton's key result is as follows. A genetically based act of altruism, selfishness or spite will evolve if the average inclusive fitness of individuals within networks displaying it is greater than the inclusive fitness of individuals in otherwise comparable networks that do not display it.

Inclusive fitness predicts that altruism would be selectively applied to relatives according to the probability that they contain a copy of the gene for kin-induced altruism, in other words their coefficient of relatedness (*r*). Hamilton's rule, as it has come to be called, is thus:

$$K > 1/r$$

where *K* is the ratio of gain in fitness to loss in fitness. Thus, in the brother-to-brother case, $1/r$ must be at least $= 2$ (in genetic terms, two brothers equal one altruistic individual). Thus, in a life-and-death act of altruism, a person would not act altruistically unless the benefit was greater than two brothers. As genetic relatedness declines, so too does altruism.

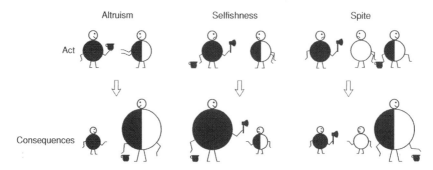

Figure 2.21 The basic conditions required for the evolution of altruism, selfishness and spite by means of kin selection. In this example, the family is reduced to an individual and a brother – the proportion of genes shared by common descent ($r = 0.5$) is shown in shading. An environmental resource is shown by the vessel; harmful behaviour is shown by an axe. *Altruism*: the altruist reduces their own genetic fitness but raises that of their brother/sister to the extent that the shared genes are increased in the next generation. *Selfishness*: the selfish individual reduces the fitness of their brother/sister but increases their own to an extent that more than compensates. *Spite*: the spiteful individual reduces the fitness of an unrelated competitor (the unshaded figure) while reducing his own fitness (or, at least, not improving it) – however, the act increases the fitness of the brother/sister to a degree that more than compensates.

Hamilton's fundamental work was published in a highly readable three-page article that was to transform our understanding of social behaviour. At the time of publication (1963, 1964), altruism had been interpreted as acting for the good of the species – this is the Group Selection hypothesis (Wynne Edwards, 1962; this hypothesis is thought relevant only under special ecological conditions). However, the reality of such truly selfless behaviour is extinction: it leaves too many chances for individuals to cheat (i.e., to freeload), reaping the benefits and incurring little cost. The genes of such cheats would quickly dominate and drive out the selfless individuals from the gene pool.

A recent study demonstrated that human beings trust others that look like themselves. DeBruine (2002) devised an ingenious experiment in which participants were engaged in bargaining with others; the unseen opponent's picture was displayed on a computer screen. Unbeknown to the participants, the opponent's picture was computer morphed to resemble their own face. The results showed that participants were more likely to cooperate, be generous and act unselfishly with an opponent whose face resembled their own. Such findings may help to explain why we tend to have friends and sexual partners who are similar to us (*assortative mating*), yet it is necessary to avoid 'incest' (inbreeding that increases the chances of recessive genes being expressed).[17]

One theory, *genetic similarity theory*, argues that not only do kin favour each other but they can also detect genetic similarity in others with whom they prefer to cooperate (Rushton, Russell & Wells, 1984). There is evidence, for example, that chimpanzees can recognize kin (Parr & de Waal, 1999). One suggestion is that human beings use proximal indicators of genetic similarity. For example, Oates and Wilson (2002) found that electronic mail requests for information were responded to more by those who shared the sender's name; people do seem especially interested in others who share their first and last names. Such findings may indicate that kin selection extends beyond the close genetic family unit and operates in the wider population.

Reciprocal altruism (reciprocity)

You may be wondering why human beings, in common with other animals, also show altruism to non-related conspecifics. In recent years, such altruism and cooperation have been the subject of intensive theoretical analysis. Trivers (1971) published his theory of *reciprocal altruism* (which Hamilton – who died a few years back of a tropical disease during a biology field trip investigating the origins of HIV – preferred to call *reciprocity* to distinguish it from genetically based altruism). Such cooperation is not common in nature; very few species engage in any reciprocity (i.e., selflessness) beyond kin selection. However, for human beings, and some higher primates, reciprocal altruism is widespread and theoretically important.

The process of reciprocal altruism – 'I'll scratch your back if you scratch mine', in common parlance – evolves under certain conditions. Importantly, the helped must return the favour at some point in the future (it is shown below that apparently altruistic behaviour, such as giving to charity, does not always entail payback from the recipient, but it usually entails payback of some form – e.g., making conspecifics aware of their altruistic nature).[18] Given the time delay, this means that the helper must be able to remember the altruistic act and identify the recipient of the act. In addition, it is necessary to have a psychological mechanism that allows cheaters to be detected, otherwise cooperation could be a cheater's charter, resulting in the runaway selection of cheating genes and thus an end to reciprocal altruism. Cheating is common in nature; it is even found among humble bacteria (Velicer, Kroos & Lenski, 2000). There is some evidence that reasoning about cheating is different from other forms of reasoning (Stone et al., 2002), suggesting it may have evolved as a specific adaptation to counteract the potential costs associated with reciprocal altruism.

In order for complex psychological mechanisms to have evolved to support reciprocal altruism, other processes – which are now used for other purposes – would be highly valuable. For example, the cognitive ability (intelligence) to remember, recognize, calculate, etc. would have obvious benefits, as would the development of a 'theory of mind', which would allow each party in the exchange to guess the intentional states of the other (will he/she return the favour?), as well as predict the emotional (empathetic) and likely behavioural consequences of cheating.

Cooperation

In everyday life, reciprocal altruism works because the costs to the individual are comparatively small, but the long-term benefits of a successful cooperative relationship are high (a 'win–win' strategy). Formal computer modelling of the best strategy to adopt in such a situation is 'tit for tat': on the first move, cooperate and then mirror the actions of your partner (Axelrod & Hamilton, 1981): this is the best 'evolutionarily stable strategy' that cannot be invaded by a better strategy. This strategy, of course, only works if the first act is not a matter of life and death.

Cooperation often occurs in a social context, so the one-on-one exchange discussed above needs to be expanded. Cooperation can develop without reciprocity. The 'indirect reciprocity hypothesis' states that benevolence to one agent increases the chance of receiving help from others (Riola, Cohen & Axelrod, 2001). For example, in human society, the giving of money to charity is often a public event, or declared in some manner (e.g., having a credit card issued on behalf of the charity; the wearing of stickers; appearance on charity fund-raising stunts on television). It is thought that this promotion of an altruistic image can encourage altruistic acts by others, leading to a net gain in resources; as Nowak and Sigmund (1998, p. 573) state, 'Cooperation pays because it confers the image of a valuable community member to the cooperating individual.'

In the social context, one deterrent to cheating (i.e., not reciprocating) is the prospect of punishment. Fehr and Gachter (2002) showed that the altruistic punishment of cheaters is important in maintaining cooperation (indeed, people are willing to pay – i.e., incur a cost to themselves (spite) – to punish cheaters); without the prospect of such punishment, altruism breaks down. Negative emotions are the proximate mechanism behind such punishment. If one party involved in the exchange feels that they have been cheated, then negative emotions of anger and hate ensue, often leading to behavioural reactions (aggression) – in this context, it is interesting to note that aggression is often accompanied by *moralistic* outrage: acts of aggression are very often accompanied by some form of 'they deserved it' justification. This outrage is usually conveyed to other people (e.g., 'gossip'), who are warned of the behaviour of the cheater.

Selfish-gene theory

What does natural selection select? In terms of the unit of inheritance, it is the gene – that flint-like sequence of DNA that is transmitted via the gametes. It is true that cultural selection works on the phenotypic expression of genes, but phenotypes are not transmitted, while genotypes are (for this reason many genetic disorders escape the natural selection of the phenotype by being recessive: not expressed in the phenotype in each generation).

This 'gene's-eye view' of evolution implies, according to Richard Dawkins (1976), that we are merely gene-replication machines. In other words, our bodies (Dawkins' robotic replication machines) are slaves to successful (e.g. selfish) DNA. The genes in our bodies have survived for millions of years and will survive for many more – our feeble bodies will be cast off by the life cycle in the years to come, at which point our genes would have manufactured other bodies (individual and inclusive offspring). Dawkins' views are built upon firm foundations of evolutionary theory and are, in a technical sense, impeccable (genes must be 'selfish' in a pure replication sense); however, as shown below, the *implications* of selfish-gene theory are open to more doubt.

Well, what is meant by 'selfish' genes? In a similar way to confusions caused by the phrases 'evolution' and 'natural selection', the selfish-gene notion is open to misunderstanding. First, it should be noted that the 'selfish' gene is no more selfish than it is happy or disappointed – it is nothing other than a sequence of triple base pairs on the DNA molecule. What is meant is that genes build bodies not for our purpose but for their own purely selfish 'aim' of replication: genes that coded for replicates survived, those that did not went extinct. The consequence of this product of evolution is that genes encourage us to replicate and to behave 'selfishly': this is the proximate mechanism that subserves the distal goal of gene replication. It is important to be careful and precise about the meaning of 'selfish'.

What is meant by 'selfish' is not necessarily selfish behaviour (at least in the sense that it is usually meant); selfish genes can promote altruism or cooperation *if* these strategies serve their aim of replication. It is thus a mistake to confuse selfish genes with selfish behaviour. Selfish-gene theory states that all genes are selfish in that they have a high frequency in the population because they survived – that is, they coded for phenotypes that led to successful, differential reproduction: their vehicles (animals) were better able to survive and reproduce. 'Successful' genes may be a better way of putting it than 'selfish'. Selfish genes code for phenotypes (behaviour) that have proved successful in the past. They make no decision in this respect: they simply code for amino acid sequences that make proteins that make bodies and minds that 'want' to replicate. It is possible that much of the so-called junk DNA in the genome (that is, non-coding base-pair sequences) is truly selfish: replicating for the sake of replication.

A number of observations have inspired the hypothesis that competition between males has led to the selection of specific genes that code for certain types of selfish behaviour and emotions.[19] For example, intriguing work on competition between sperm suggests that competitive pressures (sexual selection) between men led to the evolution of different types of sperm: some are involved in fertilization; others seem devoted to attacking the sperm of other (non-genetically related) men (so-called *kamikaze* sperm). Such sperm are engaging in a form of kin selection. This finding suggests that, during evolutionary history, females were regularly carrying more than one man's sperm at the same time (sperm is viable for up to 5 days) (Baker & Bellis, 1995). The morphology of the penis of some higher mammals (e.g., *Homo sapiens*) may also serve to scrape previously deposited sperm from the vagina.

It has been reported that the wood mouse has evolved a fascinating solution to the problem of sperm competition: sperm team up to speed their way to the egg. These teams help faster swimming sperm reach the egg first, despite incurring a cost to their own chances of fertilization. Cooperating sperm form a train, connected together by hooks on their heads that link to the tails of other sperm; their speed is 50 per cent faster than that of lone sperms. Also, these sperm may cooperate, with those at the front of the train acting as the pathfinders that change the mucus in the reproductive tract to ease the passage of the other sperm (Moore et al., 2002). This strategy in the wood mouse is sensible because females of this species are 'promiscuous', mating with multiple males during the same time period. It is thus in the interests of sperm from the same genome to evolve strategies to defeat sperm from other genomes. Also, in some species, non-fertile sperm seem to be involved in delaying female re-mating (Cook & Wedell, 1999). From such observations, it is inferred that common emotions, such as sexual jealousy, serve a similar selfish function to sperm competition.

> **ASK YOURSELF**
> Are selfish minds a logical consequence of selfish genes?

Sociobiology and Evolutionary Psychology

Since the 1970s there has been renewed interest in the implications of evolutionary thinking for human psychology, and today the field of evolutionary psychology is large and expanding, but also hotly contested.

Sociobiology

Perhaps the boldest – certainly the most controversial – statement of the genetic basis of individual organisms and societies came in the form of E. O. Wilson's (1975) *Sociobiology: The New Synthesis*. The book provoked a storm of protest in sociology and social anthropology (e.g., Sahlins, 1976). Wilson (1975, p. 3) claimed that,

> In the process of natural selection, then, any device that can insert a higher proportion of certain genes into subsequent generations will come to characterize the species. One class of such devices promotes prolonged individual survival. Another promotes superior mating performance and care of resulting offspring. As more complex social behaviour by the organism is added to the genes' techniques for replicating themselves, altruism becomes increasingly prevalent and eventually appears in exaggerated forms.

The structure and function of society is seen to serve these 'exaggerated forms'. Wilson's sociobiology is an attempt to put population genetics at the heart of sociology and social anthropology; this position contrasts with notions of a *tabula rasa* ('blank slate') at birth on which the environment carves its design (for a robust critique of this position, see Pinker, 2002). Wilson's model conceives of a co-evolution of species and society. In the case of human beings, he considers among other societal forms the emergence of barter, division of labour, role playing, communication, culture, ritual and religion, ethics, aesthetics, territoriality and tribalism, and warfare.

The *New Synthesis* is neo-Darwinain evolutionary theory, in which social phenomena are weighted for adaptive significance. A few years later, Lumsden and Wilson (1981) put forward a theory of *gene-culture co-evolution*: an interaction in which culture is generated and shaped by biological imperatives while biological traits are simultaneously altered by genetic evolution in response to cultural innovation. They proposed the idea of a sequence of 'epigenetic rules', which are genetically determined procedures that direct the assembly of the mind, including screening of stimuli by peripheral sensory filters, cellular organizing processes, and deeper processes directing cognition. These rules comprise the restraints that the genes place on the development: the *tabula* never was *rasa*.

The units of cultural information are called *culturgenes*; these serve genetic fitness, both individual and inclusive fitness. Culturgenes affect such things as face recognition, non-verbal communication, mother–infant bonds, fears and phobias, incest avoidance and decision-making. The 'gene-culture landscape' is thus restricted by genetics and evolutionary imperatives.

Evolutionary psychology (EP)

Evolutionary psychology (EP) is an offspring and extension of sociobiology. It focuses on psychological adaptations, addressing four questions (Buss, 1999). (1) *Why* is the mind designed the way it is? (i.e., what causal processes created, fashioned or shaped the human mind into its current form?; this is the *distal* question). (2) *How* is the mind organized and what are its mechanisms or component parts, and how are they organized? (3) *What* are the *functions* of the component parts and their organized structure? (4) *How* does input from the current environment, especially the social environment, interact with the design of the human mind to produce observable behaviour? (The latter questions are called *proximal*.) (Evolutionary psychology is further discussed in chapter 18.)

EP attempts to explain current patterns of behaviour in terms of the solutions to recurrent problems encountered in ancestral Pleistocene environments. The fact that often our behaviour is inappropriate (e.g., having a 'sweet tooth') is traced back to environmental conditions that prevailed many hundreds of thousands of years ago. EP has been applied to a large number of psychological functions, and is continuing to excite much thinking and research (Crawford & Krebs, 1998; Pinker, 1997) and controversy (Rose, 1997; Rose, Lewontin & Kamin, 1984). Barkow, Cosmides & Tooby (1992, p. 3) expressed their view of EP:

> It unites modern evolutionary biology with the cognitive revolution in a way that has the potential to draw together all of the disparate branches of psychology into a single organized system of knowledge.

Of general relevance to EP is observational research on the social behaviour of primates. In recent years, much of the political game-playing seen, *par excellence*, in human beings has been observed in these phylogenetically related species. It is here that we start to see the evolution of truly complex forms of cognition underlying social behaviour, including (what is loosely called) social intelligence. Primate cognition seems to have arisen in response, not to the demands of the physical environment (e.g., the need to forage), but to the demands of complex social life. De Waal (1982, 2005) refers to primate 'politics' in such social behaviour; and Byrne and Whiten (1988) talk of 'Machiavellian intelligence' (involved in the behavioural strategies used to manipulate conspecifics, often by 'cooperating' with them; see Tomasello, 2000). The importance of this work resides in its power to reveal the evolutionary continuity between human beings and other animals in cognition and complex behaviour.

Proponents of EP do not see it as simply another approach to psychology; they see it as forming the fundamental biological basis on which all psychological processes are based – a way of thinking about psychology. According to this view, it is not appropriate to consider behaviours in isolation from their biological basis. Thus, animals are not anxious, fearful, jealous, envious, hateful, loving, selfish and selfless for no reason: there are evolutionary (distal) forces behind the shaping of these (proximal) psychological states. EP has been successfully applied, among other things, to parent–offspring

ASK YOURSELF
Are criticisms of sociobiology and evolutionary psychology an example of confusing the messenger with the message?

conflict and parental investment (Trivers, 1985). Alcock (2001) provides a recent appraisal of sociobiology and EP.

⬚ Evolving Ideas

It is too easy to dismiss evolutionary theory and assume that the mind is a complex computer freed from its evolutionary past. Arguably, to understand evolutionary theory is to appreciate that such *total* freedom is not possible. However, the extent of the influence of evolution on our current psychology is still unknown and hotly debated. You and I *feel* independent, but are we? How would we know?

It is possible that psychological processes that evolved for one purpose (e.g., detection of cheaters in cooperative exchanges; see chapter 18) have been recruited to other purposes. Higher cognitive functions are used routinely to detect cheaters, and to make the best plans for our future; but they can be used for purposes that have no obvious evolutionary function. At a certain level of complexity, *emergent* psychological processes may be found which build upon more basic adaptations. These properties may free the mind to some extent from the basic biological instincts. However, simply to ignore or discount the importance of our evolutionary past would seem ill-advised.

In psychology there is considerable debate about the functional specificity of genes. At the one extreme, genes are said to make brains that enable flexible learning; at the other extreme, genes are said to code for specific psychological functions and 'hard-wired' adaptive functions (these functions are often referred to as modules, which have distinct functions and evolutionary/genetic foundations; see chapter 18). In the middle are variants of these two extreme positions, arguing that the functional specificity of genes interacts with proximal environmental factors, producing relatively flexible patterns of behaviour. It is not known which position is closest to the truth: it is likely that all are true to some extent for different functions.

Learning Questions

1. How does evolution by natural selection attempt to explain the existence of life by blind chance?
2. How did the discovery of classical (Mendelian) genetics solve one of Darwin's major problems of evolution?
3. What is the 'genetic code' and how does it convert DNA sequences into proteins?
4. What are the various forms of mutation seen in physical and psychological disorders?
5. What is the 'selfish gene' and how can it produce altruism and co-operation even in unrelated individuals?

NOTES

1   Our usual image of Darwin is of a long-bearded, old Victorian gentleman (which he was in later life), who was conventional in customs and behaviour (which he also was); however, there is another side to him that was less conventional: he disliked his school, which focused on Latin and Greek, which he considered a waste of his and everyone else's time; he detested his medical studies at Edinburgh University, involving, as they did at the time, rather inhumane procedures; and when he dropped out of Edinburgh and went to Cambridge to read theology he barely scraped a pass degree, seemingly benefiting only from learning about improbable theories of creation which conflicted with his extensive knowledge of the natural world (especially geology). His father despaired that he would ever find a productive occupation, considering him an idle, sports-loving time-waster. The voyage of the *Beagle* was to change his idle ways. In reality, his father 'did not understand him', not realizing that Darwin was preoccupied with teaching himself the wonders of the natural world. Thus, one of the world's greatest thinkers was considered less than promising as a school-boy and then an unimpressive university student: the path of genius does not always run smoothly!

2   The *Origin of Species* went through several revisions, and has been reproduced many times. The quotations used here are from the first edition (which contains a clearer account of Darwin's theory; subsequent editions attempted to placate critics). As page numbers differ between reproductions, in order to avoid confusion, the chapters in which quotes may be found are given.

3   It is important to note that, although the mechanism of natural selection is 'blind', it does follow a rigid algorithm of selection, based on the survival and reproduction of phenotypes best fitted to the environment. In relation to this point, although in one sense adaptations are the product of 'chance', the chance is in the availability of the phenotypes to be selected, not in the mechanism of selection.

4   Darwin's view of Nature was unsentimental. In a letter to Hooker in 1856, he wrote: 'What a book a Devil's Chaplain might write on the clumsy, wasteful, blundering low and horridly cruel works of nature' – of course, Nature is neither kind nor cruel, as it is simply an indifferent algorithm of differential survival and reproduction (see Dawkins, 2003). The *process* of evolution may be clumsy and blundering, but its products are the opposite.

5   As noted in chapter 1, Wallace arrived, by the late 1850s, at a theory of evolution by natural selection. However, unlike Darwin, who viewed evolution as a blind process (nature 'selects' in the same way that gravity 'pushes' water downhill), Wallace held to the belief that evolution had a purpose (i.e., a teleology), which was to remove from Nature the unfit in order to arrive at perfect forms. Wallace was a lifelong believer in spiritualism and a philosophical dualist who, unlike Darwin, contended that the human mind was not the product of natural selection but the creation of a supernatural power (Shermer, 2002). This utopian vision of human development stood in stark contrast to Darwin's view of natural selection as the 'survival of the fittest'. Therefore, it is not only possible but necessary to differentiate Darwin's and Wallace's views on natural selection.

6   The idea of pangenesis goes back to the Greek philosopher/physician Hippocrates. In order to explain the process of inheritance Darwin modified this theory to assume that 'gemmules' were modified throughout life and could be passed on to offspring; and then natural selection could work on these 'acquired' inherited characteristics. The irony was that Darwin was forced to defend his theory of natural selection by recourse to a Lamarckian process of acquired characteristics. (Watson, 2003, provides an excellent introduction to the history, science and future of genetics.)

7   There is no evidence that Darwin owned a copy of Mendel's scientific paper; neither collections at Down House, where Darwin lived, nor Cambridge University Library (which has a collection of Darwin's books and papers) has any record of this paper. Darwin did know of Mendel's work, as it was referred to in two books owned by Darwin (these books discussed Mendel's work, but did not call attention to its theoretical importance). However, as Dr Andrew Sclater, of the Manuscripts Room of the Cambridge University Library, noted, 'having knowledge of Mendel's work . . . was not tantamount to understanding the Mendelian basis of modern genetics . . . the scientific community was extremely slow in realizing the importance of Mendel's work, probably because he himself was not capable of fully explaining the difference between his clear-cut findings with peas and his less easily interpreted results from crosses in other genera.' I thank Professor Richard Dawkins of the University of Oxford for clarifying this matter.

8   As noted by Watson (2003), Mendel was an unlikely hero of science: he was a failed parish priest, who responded to his pastoral duties with a 'nervous breakdown'; he failed (twice) the exam needed to teach, and never got beyond the grade of substitute teacher.

9   The Y chromosome – the 'male badge of identity' – is small, with only 60 million base pairs out of the total 3 or so billion of the entire human genome (Jones, 2003). It has approximately only 70 coding genes – there are ten times as many on the X chromosome.

10 It was known before Crick and Watson that DNA might form the hereditary basis of life. Avery, in the 1940s, showed that hereditary traits could be passed from one bacterial cell to another by purified DNA molecules. Given that DNA is found in all cells in the body, this suggested the hypothesis that DNA, rather than complex proteins, carried the information of life. In fact, the first evidence that DNA might be the basis of life was gathered in 1928 by Griffith, who was a scientist at the British Ministry of Health (see Watson, 2003). However, the structure of DNA was not known.

11 Watson (1968) published his account of the discovery of the structure of DNA. Typical of Watson, his account is lively, stimulating and candid (to the point of indiscretion). This book shows the complex interplay of chance, passions and people that interact in scientific progress.

12 All people, apart from monozygotic twins, differ in their base sequences (approximately one out of every 1,000 base sequences, totalling some 3 million base differences); but the majority of the code is identical in the human species, hence we speak of 'the' human genome. Although these base sequence differences are small, they have important effects on the phenotype. However, the search for systematic base sequence differences that give rise to stable traits is a difficult and important task, especially for individual differences research (Plomin, 2002).

13 In fact, the announcement of the sequencing of the human genome was somewhat premature, as only a rough draft was available at the date of publication. Joint public announcements were made by the US President, Bill Clinton, and the British Prime Minister, Tony Blair: the public unity of the two teams racing to publish the first draft belied the fierce and acrimonious competition that existed between them (see Sulston & Ferry, 2002; Watson, 2003).

14 There is a lot of interest now in the possibility that non-exonic sequences are important; therefore 'junk' DNA may turn out, after all, to be useful (Professor Robert Plomin, personal communication, June 2004).

15 To be more precise, a gene does not simply code for one protein; it is more accurate to say that a gene (cistron) encodes a *polypeptide* (a polypeptide is a chain of amino acids), which may or may not produce a protein (some proteins requires several polypeptides, and thus the action of several genes).

16   It was the observation that the insertion or deletion of a single base pair results in harmful 'frameshift' effects that led to the discovery of the triplet code (see Watson, 2003). Consider the following letter code: JIM ATE THE FAT CAT. Now imagine the first 'base-pair' T is deleted; the sentence then reads: JIM AET HEF ATC AT (meaningless gibberish); with two base-pair deletions (or insertions), similar gibberish results; but with three consequential base-pair changes, much of the sentence remains (although its meaning has now changed): JIM THE FAT CAT. Thus, when three base pairs are changed, sensible proteins are assembled (it was Francis Crick and colleagues who discovered the triplet code). Thus a single or double deletion/insertion changes every single amino acid beyond the deletion/insertion point, often leading to a catastrophic effect. However, a triplet deletion/insertion will delete/add one amino acid, which may not disrupt the polypeptide or protein and thus the biological action of the gene.

17   There are anecdotal stories of long-lost brothers and sisters being reunited after many years and finding each other sexually attractive. If confirmed by rigorous research, then this observation would suggest that we tend to be attracted to conspecifics with similar phenotypes (and hence genotypes), which is inhibited by being brought up together.

18   As one reviewer of this book told me: 'I do not suppose that the African kid I helped in response to Bob Geldof 20 years ago is certain to help me' (in the 'Live Aid' famine-relief concert). It is interesting how often we advertise our charity-giving, spreading the message that we are 'selfless' and, by inference, can be trusted. Individuals who are 'well thought of' in a community receive preferential treatment. These motives and behaviours are usually not conscious; but the conscious–non-conscious distinction is irrelevant in this regard. (Of course, these deeper biological motives should not detract from the good that is done by these 'altruistic' acts – in an important sense, our ability to cooperate owes much to the intrinsic selfishness of these underlying biological motives.)

19   The differential reproduction of males and females can be very large. The record for the largest number of babies born to one mother is 69 (a Russian peasant woman, Madame Vassilyev, who gave birth 27 times between 1725 and 1765). In contrast, the Emperor of Morocco, Moulay Ismail the Bloodthirsty (1672–1727), is reputed to have fathered 888 babies – we hardly need to guess the secret of his (genetic) success!

FURTHER READING

Alcock, J. (2001). *The Triumph of Sociobiology*. Oxford: Oxford University Press.
Plomin, R., DeFries, J. C., McClearn, G. E. & McGuffin, P. (2001). *Behavioral Genetics*. New York: Worth.
Ridley, M. (2003). *Evolution*. Oxford: Blackwell.

chapter 3

Brain Structure and Function

Learning Objectives

To be able to:

1. Distinguish neurons and glial cells and describe their functions.
2. Describe the structure of the peripheral and central nervous systems.
3. Outline the main regions and structures in the brain.
4. Present the main factors in the development of the brain.
5. Explain what is meant by lateralization of function and describe how functions are assessed.

Chapter 2 discussed how evolutionary and genetic factors exert two types of influence on behaviour: evolution exerts a *distal* (ultimate) influence, mediated by Nature's selection pressures; and genetics exerts a *proximal* (local) influence, mediated by the structure and function of the nervous system (principally the brain).

Understanding the structure and function of the brain is one of the important challenges facing science today. This scientific challenge has fundamental implications (a) for our understanding of the nature of the psychological processes that go to make up the *self*, as well as (b) for our understanding of a range of pathological conditions, for example neurodegenerative diseases (e.g., Parkinson's disease, dementia and stroke). Much of the excitement in neuroscience is driven by the desire to develop effective interventions to prolong and enrich human life. For example, stem-cell research promises to provide a means by which damaged nerves in the brain can regenerate (see chapter 11). Much of neuroscientific work is, literally, a matter of life and death!

What is known about the human nervous system? It is known that the brain has a well-defined anatomical structure, arranged as a hierarchy of different neural circuits and centres that are responsible for specific psychological functions. It is also known that the brain is in constant communication with the rest of the body, via the spinal cord (together comprising the *central nervous systems*, CNS); and that there are neural pathways distributed throughout the body that carry out the orders of the CNS, as well as being responsible for vital functions such as respiration and digestion (i.e., the *peripheral nervous system*, PNS). It is also known that the brain can send instructions to other organs in the body by the release of chemical messengers into the bloodstream called hormones (see chapter 6). Lastly, it is known that there are specialized organs for receiving information from the environment as well as specialized organs for executing the demands of the CNS (see chapter 5). These systems work in a similar way to an orchestra, with the brain being the overall conductor and the peripheral systems being the dedicated musicians: when they work harmoniously together, the overall effect is effortless, smooth coordination; when they fail, disease results.

Quite apart from the marvellous psychological achievements of the nervous system, the neurophysiology of this system has its own charm. This is nowhere more apparent than in the basic processing unit in the nervous system: the nerve cell, called the *neuron* (or *neurone*). It is the interplay of billions of these neural processes that allows us to think, feel, love, hate, hope and despair.

Although it is tempting to start our discussion with a (necessarily) detailed description of the neuron, in keeping with our principles of *understanding* biological psychology, let us start at the higher levels of brain organization and function and then work downwards to the precise details of how individual neurons work (see chapter 4).

The Nervous System

The nervous system is composed of two major parts: (a) the *central nervous system* (CNS; the brain and spinal cord), which is contained in bone (skull and spinal column); and (b) the *peripheral nervous system* (PNS; all nervous structures outside the CNS), found outside these bony structures. Figure 3.1 shows the whole nervous system, and its division into the CNS and the PNS.

It is customary to speak of *afferent* and *efferent* nerves and systems. The bundles of nerve fibres that conduct excitation to the CNS are known as *afferent* nerves (from the Latin, *affere*, 'to bring to'); the bundles of fibres that travel to the effector systems are called *efferent nerves* (from the Latin, *effere*, 'to bring forth').

Types of receptor neurons

Before discussing the branches of the nervous system, let us first consider *receptors*. *Receptor cells* are sensitive to external energy (e.g., pressure, light, sound); and *transduce* physical energy into electrical patterns of activity that are recognized by other neurons in the nervous system. The cell bodies of some receptors (e.g., tactile receptors) are found next to the spinal cord, located in clusters called *ganglia*. In some systems (e.g., skin pressure), the same cell undertakes the job of both *transduction* and *transmission*. However, more often transduction and transmission are jobs carried out by different cells.

Interneurons (also called *association neurons*) are intermediate neurons, in the brain or spinal cord, between incoming (*afferent*) and outgoing (*efferent*) neurons that organize and control afferent nerve impulses to create efferent effects (some sensorimotor systems are very simple and do not contain interneurons). *Motor neurons* receive efferent impulses

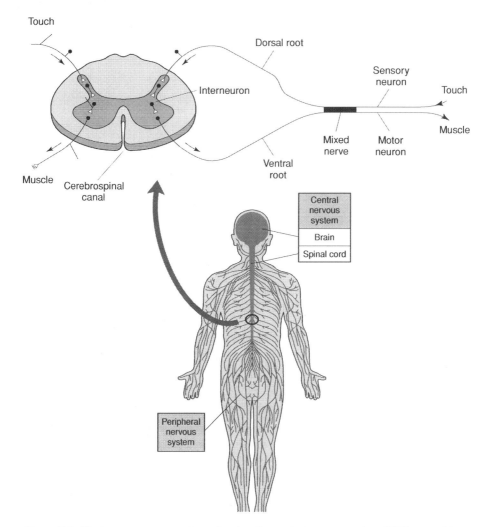

Figure 3.1 The human nervous system, showing the central nervous system (CNS), comprising the brain and spinal cord, and the peripheral nervous system (PNS), comprising nervous pathways outside the brain and spinal cord. The sensory and motor pathways to and from the spinal cord are shown.

from other neurons (often *interneurons*) and activate the skeletal musculature and glands. Upon firing, a motor neuron releases a chemical substance (*neurotransmitter*), which causes the muscle fibres to contract. These systems are covered in detail in the next chapter.

It is estimated that there are some 100 billion neurons in the CNS, each with as many as 1,000 to 10,000 connections with other neurons. The dense interconnections of these neurons are truly astonishing. However, they compose only some 10 per cent of cells in the brain, the others being support cells of various types. Raise your hand and touch your face now: you have just activated the whole sequence of neuronal and chemical events in one effortless motion, and activated millions of neurons in the process. The complexity of these processes is not fully appreciated until they malfunction.

The largest structure in the brain is the cerebral cortex, which is contained within a thin layer only a few millimetres thick. In order for this expanded space to fit within the brain, the cortex folds in on itself, resulting in a series of ridges and groves that create the characteristic wrinkled appearance of the brain.

Sketch of a neuron

In the next chapter the details of the structure, processes and functions of the neuron are presented. But for the purpose of this chapter only a sketch of the neuron is required. The job of the neuron is to transmit information in the form of a nerve signal. The neuron is composed of a cell body (*soma*) which contains DNA and the molecular machinery of the cell. Two processes are attached to the soma: (a) dendrites receive information (i.e., they are stimulated by other neurons); and (b) axons transmit the nerve signal from the dendrite, via the soma, to the *terminal buttons*, where chemicals (neurotransmitters) are released; these chemicals then stimulate the dendrites of the next neuron (although, depending on the neuron, they also stimulate the cell bodies and axons). The whole nervous system is made up of pathways of such neurons. Axons can be short (a few millimetres) or long (e.g., from the cerebral cortex to the spinal cord).

The network of neuronal connections might be likened to a messenger travelling through a chain of islands, each separated by sea, to deliver an important command. Within each island there is a single railway line, going from one end of the island to the other; in the middle of the line is found a maintenance depot where workers can be seen repairing tracks and rolling stock, and transporting materials along the line. Let us travel on this imaginary system. Our journey starts when we arrive by sea on one of the islands (at a 'dendritic port'); then we get on a train, composed of chemicals and electrical charge, called a 'nerve signal', and soon we find ourselves speeding down the line; as we travel along the line we spot the maintenance depot in the distance, and as we get closer we see its name – 'nucleus' – where we notice that much repair and maintenance of the line is being organized according to a standard operating procedures manual written in a strange code of As, Ts, Gs, Cs; we pass through this depot and find ourselves travelling down a long stretch of line, called the 'axon'. Then when we arrive at the station, where the trains rest against the buffers, we alight at the 'terminal buttons'; once ejected from our train carriage we are forced to take another ship (all ships are called the *Neurotransmitter*) across the sea (like all the other seas, this one is also called the 'synapse'); and soon we find ourselves docking at another dendritic port and our journey continues. In no time at all, our message has jumped from island to island, finally reaching its destination, where its journey ends. This is the daily grind of neurons and neurotransmission (figure 3.2).

Support cells

Neurons and populations of neurons (neural pathways) can only function with the help of supporting cells. One important class of cells are *glial cells* (or *neuroglia*, meaning 'nerve

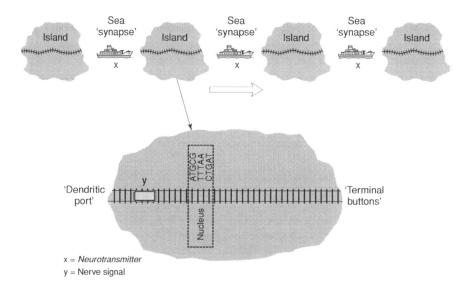

x = *Neurotransmitter*
y = Nerve signal

Figure 3.2 Sketch of an imaginary neuronal journey. The journey of a nerve signal that passes along the neuron and jumps to the next neuron is illustrated by a chain of islands. The nerve signal travels along the tracks (called the 'axon') and travels over the seas ('synapse') in a ship called *Neurotransmitter*. The ship docks at the 'dendritic port' and the onward journey continues within the island, until it ends at the 'terminal buttons', where the next sea trip begins. In the middle of the islands is a maintenance depot (the cell 'nucleus') which operates according to a manual written in a four-letter code (A, C, T, G).

glue', literally); there are many more of this type of cell than neurons (perhaps trillions). They serve a number of important functions: (a) they act as guide-wires for growing neurons and provide the scaffolding for mature neurons; (b) they insulate neurons from one another; (c) they regulate the energy entering neurons (e.g., from the blood) and the waste that comes out; (d) they remove dead and damaged cells from the nervous system; (e) they produce growth and trophic factors, playing a key role in regeneration and neural plasticity; and (f) they play a crucial role in immunological responses to various infections and toxic agents. Importantly, they also provide the myelin sheath that speeds up the rate of nerve signal (see chapter 4). In contrast to neurons,[1] glial cells grow and change after birth, and they seem especially important in accounting for the neural growth effects of enriched environments (the growth potential of neurons is more limited, but structural changes are seen, as in the case of neural plasticity; see chapter 7).

Three types of glial cell exist: (a) *astrocytes* absorb chemicals released by neurons and return them to neurons or release them into the blood (*radial glial* cells, a type of astrocyte, guide the migration of neurons and the growth of axons and dendrites during development); (b) *oligodendrocytes* provide neurons with their protective myelin sheath; and (c) *microglia* 'eat' dead cells and brain debris. Damage to these cells can impair the functioning of otherwise intact neurons.

The peripheral nervous system (PNS)

The CNS would be of little use if it could not communicate with the organs and glands in the rest of the body. As well as conveying information to the CNS, the PNS carries out the commands of the CNS, as well as regulating some vital bodily functions in its own right. The PNS has two divisions: (a) the *somatic nervous system (SNS)*; and (b) the *autonomic nervous system (ANS)*. The SNS is responsible for interacting with the external environment; that is, information from the sensory receptors (in skin, muscles and joints) to the CNS, and for sending motor signals from the CNS to muscles and glands. The ANS is responsible for interacting with the internal environment, regulating basic processes of the body (e.g., such as the heart, blood vessels, digestive system and genital organs). Figure 3.3 shows some of the major jobs carried out by the PNS, and from where in the spinal cord these instructions are issued.

Some sensory nerves do not go via the spinal cord: above the neck, information transfer between the body and the brain is via 12 pairs of *cranial nerves* (e.g., the optic nerves, which convey visual information from the eye to the brain; and the oculomotor nerves, which control eye movements).

The ANS is divided into *sympathetic* (fight–flight) and *parasympathetic* (rest–digest) branches, which exert opposite effects (by the release of different types of neurotransmitter). In times of emergency, the sympathetic branch dominates and inhibits the parasympathetic branch. This results in increased heart rate and increased blood flow to the muscles (to ready them for fight or flight). In times of quiet, the parasympathetic system dominates, resulting in lower heart rate and blood being diverted from the skeletal muscles to the gut to assist digestion (figure 3.4).

The CNS may activate the ANS directly (e.g., when threat is detected). Under these aversive conditions, the brain will also activate the neuroendocrine system, which will be responsible for releasing hormones into the bloodstream (see chapter 6). For example, the brain response to stress triggers the release of corticosteroids from the adrenal glands. When they reach their targets, they have a number of stress-related effects: increased heart rate; blood vessels open (dilate) to allow more blood to skeletal muscles; and energy is recruited from stores within the body.

Central nervous system (CNS)

The CNS is composed of the spinal cord and the brain, as follows.

Spinal cord

The spinal cord contains 31 pairs of spinal nerves; these are 'mixed' nerves because each contains both sensory and motor axons. Outside the spinal cord these nerves separate: all sensory axons pass into the *dorsal root ganglion*, where their cell bodies are located, and then into the spinal cord itself; and all motor axons pass into the *ventral roots* after they leave the spinal cord, before uniting with the sensory axons to form the mixed nerves.

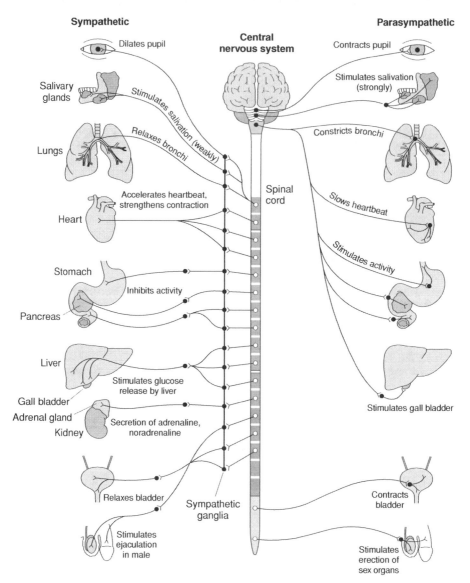

Figure 3.3 PNS functions. The main functions carried out by the sympathetic and parasympathetic branches of the peripheral nervous system (PNS).

Interneurons are contained in the spinal cord, which unite sensory and motor neurons. The spinal cord transmits afferent (sensory) impulses to the brain and efferent (motor) impulses from the brain to the organs; in addition, the spinal cord governs simple reflexes (e.g., withdrawal reflex).

The bundles of nerve fibres that run up and down the spinal cord are very sensitive to damage. In the case of a broken back, these fibres can become either damaged or severed,

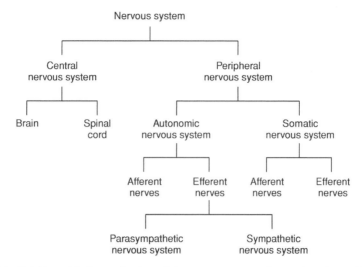

Figure 3.4 The hierarchical organization of the nervous system. (Note: there is considerable interaction between these systems, not shown.)

and as a result the efferent impulses travelling from the cell body never reach the effector organ (e.g., leg muscles); often the impulse never reaches the motor neurons in the spinal cord. In fact, most patients (some 11,000 in the USA alone each year) do not suffer severance of the spinal cord; instead, the injury consists of initial compression that damages the cord, causing it to swell in the spinal column. This swelling causes the lesion to spread up and down the spinal cord, producing tissue damage along the way (the higher up the spinal cord, the more damage will be suffered). The hope in neuroscience now is to develop technologies to discourage this post-trauma damage (which happens within hours and days of the initial trauma); and there is also hope in the form of stem-cell technology of encouraging nerve cells to regenerate (see chapter 11).

Brain

The brain is where higher psychological functions are found. There are several different ways of looking at the brain. Let us start at the general level, then move down to the detail.

First a few statistics. The human brain weighs between 1,300 and 1,400 grams (approx. 3 lbs). This size compares with a rhesus monkey brain of 420 g, a cat brain of 30 g and a rat brain of 2 g; however, the brain of the elephant is more than four times bigger (6,000 g). Clearly size is not everything! Although the human brain is only 2 per cent of total body weight, it consumes 20 per cent of available oxygen and energy in the blood – this is 10 times as much for its size as any other organ. The brain needs a regular supply of energy as it has no storage capacity and must run continuously all day and all year around.

In neuroscience it is customary to use a number of terms to refer to the position and direction of brain structures; these are necessary because if we were to say 'to the left

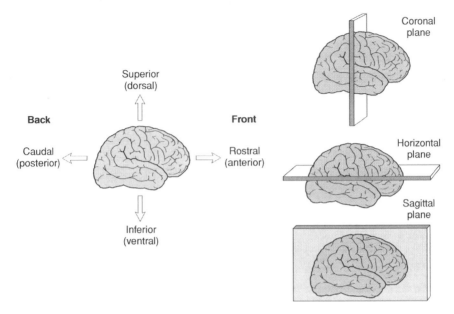

Figure 3.5 Directions of brain and axes. Structures in the brain are labelled according to their position, and planes (or slices) of the brain are labelled according to which of the three planes are cut.

of structure x', then this would not make sense unless we knew the orientation of the brain, and it is not convenient to hold the brain in one orientation. As the brain is a three-dimensional structure, any particular structure can be located by knowing three planes (or axes). Planes of the brain are also named to ease identification. These terms are shown on figure 3.5.

Structure of the brain

Now that the basic concepts are known, let us turn to detailed anatomy of the brain. Figure 3.6 shows the major divisions and landmarks, with some of the major processing centres.

From a horizontal plane, the brain is bilaterally symmetrical (the two halves of the brain look much the same); from this view the *cerebrum* dominates the appearance of the brain. The cerebrum consists of clefts (called *sulci*; singular: *sulcus*; also known as *fissures*); and the ridges formed along the sulci are *gyri* (singular: *gyrus*). These two halves of the brain are connected together by the *corpus callosum* (as well as by other structures). In the centre of the brain are the *ventricles*; these spaces are filled with cerebrospinal fluid (CSF).

The brain may be divided into three sections: (a) the hindbrain, (b) the midbrain, and (c) the forebrain. These divisions are characterized by (a) their evolutionary development (phylogeny), and (b) their functions.

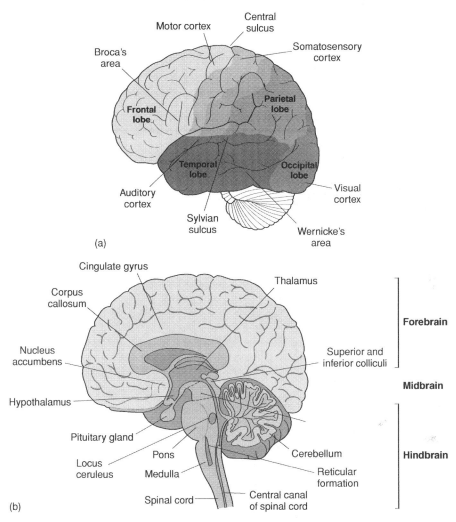

Figure 3.6 Anatomical landmarks of the brain. The major regions of the brain are shown in (a), along with some of the important structures within these regions corresponding to the hindbrain, midbrain and forebrain (b).

Hindbrain (rhombencephalon)

The hindbrain is essentially a continuation of the spinal cord. There are a number of important structures here involved in basic physiological functions. (a) The *medulla oblongata* is that part of the brain stem closest to the spinal cord; it controls such vital functions as the heartbeat, circulation and respiration and acts as a relay station for afferent and efferent impulses. Its destruction results in immediate death. (b) The *pons* acts as a relay station carrying impulses from various parts of the cerebral cortex to the cerebellum;

it is also involved in the reflexes controlling breathing. (c) The *reticular formation* runs through the middle of the hindbrain, and enters the midbrain; it receives sensory impulses (concerning sound) from higher brain centres and then passes these back up to the thalamus (this formation is vital for arousal and sleep). (d) The *locus ceruleus* contains relatively few neurons (approximately 30,000), but it sends out fibres extensively to other parts of the brain (this system is involved in states of vigilance). (e) The *cerebellum* consists of two deeply convoluted and separate hemispheres that control bodily balance and muscular coordination, including smooth eye movements. It also seems involved in the integration of movements (e.g., speech). This structure contains some 30 billion neurons that integrate information from the muscles, joints and tendons, leading to skilled automatic movements.

Midbrain (mesencephalon)

Above the hindbrain is the midbrain, which is a relatively small section of the brain. It contains neural centres that control motor reactions and auditory and visual functions. (a) The roof of the midbrain is the tectum, and the structures on either side are the *superior colliculus* and *inferior colliculus* (see chapter 5). Under the tectum is (b) the *tegmentum*, with parts of the reticular formation and the nuclei of some of the cranial nerves. (c) The *substantia nigra* is involved in smooth bodily movements; damage to this structure leads to Parkinson's disease. (d) The *ventral tegmental area* (VTA) is important in incentive motivation (i.e., motivation to an appetitive stimulus, e.g., food, sex).

Forebrain (prosencephalon)

The forebrain is the highest level of organization, containing those structures responsible for higher-order psychological functions: (a) *thalamus*, (b) *hypothalamus*, (c) *pituitary gland*, (d) *basal ganglia*, and (e) *limbic* system, and (f) two *cerebral hemispheres* (also called the *telencephalon*).

The thalamus and hypothalamus form the *diencephalon*. The *thalamus* is a collection of various centres (nuclei) that serve as reception centres for the cerebral hemispheres. Neurons from the eyes, ears, skin and motor centres pass to the thalamus; after processing, it then sends information to the cerebral hemispheres. One of these nuclei is the *lateral geniculate nucleus*, which receives visual signals from the eye, via the optic nerve.

The *hypothalamus* is composed of a number of distinct nuclei. It is situated below the anterior thalamus (*hypo* = 'below'). It has widespread connections with the rest of the forebrain and midbrain. It is involved in basic physiological processes, for example, eating, drinking, maintenance of temperature and sexual activity. It also exerts some of its effects via the neuroendocrine system: it stimulates the release of hormones from the *pituitary gland* (the source of eight hormones). One area of the hypothalamus, the *suprachiasmatic nuclei*, is responsible for the biological clock, working on a 24-hour cycle.

The *basal ganglia* comprise a group of subcortical structures (the *caudate nucleus*, the *putamen* and the *globus pallidus*). The basal ganglia have many subdivisions, each of which exchanges information with a different part of the cortex.

The *limbic system*, which comprises a collection of structures located near the centre of the cerebral hemispheres, is involved in emotional and motivational processes, as well as learning and memory. This system comprises the *hippocampus*, which is involved in memory, goal processes and emotion; the *fornix* (which is a major axon tract linking the two lobes of the cortex); and the *amygdala* (Latin: 'almond'), involved in the generation of emotional arousal, especially but not exclusively fear.

The two *cerebral hemispheres* (also called *lobes*) are both divided into four major divisions: (a) *frontal*, (b) *parietal*, (c) *occipital* and (d) *temporal*. The thin outer layer of the brain is the *cerebral cortex* (in Latin, *cortex* means bark, as the bark on a tree).

Cerebral cortex

The *cerebral cortex* is approximately 3 mm thick (if it were stretched out), and is composed of a densely packed network of nerve fibres capable of highly complex interconnections. Although this structure is thin, it comprises a large proportion of the entire human brain because it is deeply folded and convoluted (like screwing up a large sheet of paper to fit it into a smaller space). This newest part of the brain is either absent or underdeveloped in lower animals, but quite well developed in primates. It is thought that this structure is responsible for our cognitive processing, allowing planning, mental simulations, imagination and intelligence.

The cerebral cortex is composed of two separate hemispheres, each of which has *relatively* specialized sensory and motor functions relating (mostly) to the contralateral (opposite) side of the body. At the cerebral cortex is seen a layer of grey matter (cell bodies), and their axons extend inward from the cortex – this forms the white matter of the cerebral hemispheres. The two hemispheres communicate via the *corpus callosum* and the smaller *anterior commissure*.

Cerebral lobes

Let us take a closer look at the four cerebral lobes. The convolutions observed here increase the amount of cortex that can be fitted into a limited space – it is thus an adaptive solution to the problem of increasing processing capacity without first waiting for the total size of the skull to increase. The large furrows seen are known as *fissures* – these divide the lobes. (The central fissure and the lateral fissures serve as useful landmarks to demarcate the lobes. The smaller furrows are known as *sulci*, and the ridges between fissures and sulci are called *gyri*.) The midline fissure that separates the two hemispheres is called the *longitudinal fissure*.

Most (approximately 90 per cent) of the cerebral cortex is new (i.e., it is *neocortex*), that is, of relatively recent evolution. The cortex is numbered I to VI, starting at the surface and working down, in columns, inwards. In these layers there are two very different types of neurons: (a) *pyramidal* (cell bodies are pyramid-shaped) neurons have a large dendritic tress, which extends from the top of the pyramid to the cortex surface, and a long axon; and (b) *stellate* (star-shaped) neurons, which are interneurons, with short axons. The six layers of the cortex contain different combinations of these two types of neuron. These columns of neurons form circuits that perform a specific function.

The *frontal lobe* comprises a large part of the cerebral cortex, and is involved in higher-order cognitive processes (e.g., planning and inhibition of prepotent responses). This lobe extends from the central sulcus to the anterior surface of the brain; it contains the motor cortex, in the precentral gyrus, which is responsible for coordinating motor movements (see chapter 5), and the prefrontal cortex, which is responsible for the coordination of information from all sensory systems – it does not itself receive sensory input directly.

The *parietal lobe* is found between the central sulcus and the occipital lobe. This area is charged with somatosensory processing (e.g., touch). The *postcentral gyrus* contains the primary somatosensory cortex, where skin sensation is processed. There are four bands of cells running parallel to the central sulcus, and each band relates to different parts of the body. This region processes different representations of the sensory states of different parts of the body.

The *occipital lobe* is located at the back of the head (i.e., the posterior). It receives fibres from the thalamus that convey visual information. The *primary visual cortex* (or *striate cortex*) is found at the most posterior part of this lobe, and damage to this region causes cortical blindness (this topic is discussed in chapter 5). The *temporal lobe* is found near the temples; it is the primary area for the processing of auditory information (superior temporal gyrus), and it is vital for the comprehension and production of language. It also subserves other functions, including complex visual processing (e.g., face recognition). Temporal lobe epilepsy is sometimes associated with auditory and visual hallucinations.

Projection areas

The cerebral lobes contain a number of structures that are responsible for receiving sensory information; they also serve the function of dispatch centres for motor commands: (a) *sensory projection areas* receive information from the various senses; and (b) *motor projection areas* send commands that ultimately get executed at muscles. Sensory and motor areas of the body are mapped (i.e., projected) onto specific areas of the cortex. The *somatosensory cortex* is found in the parietal lobe next to the central fissure, the *motor cortex* in the frontal lobe next to the central fissure. Similar projection areas are found for vision and hearing, located in the occipital and temporal lobes, respectively.

The projection areas of the brain comprise about one-quarter of the total brain volume; the remaining areas of the cerebral cortex are *association areas*. These areas are involved in higher complex functions such as planning, thinking and speaking. The frontal lobes are especially important in this regard. They are involved in planning and complex cognitive processes. Damage to the frontal lobes impairs the ability to plan ahead, leading to behavioural impulsiveness.

Ventricles

The brain is bathed in fluid – cerebrospinal fluid. This fluid protects the brain from shock and it also serves to suspend the brain so the pressure on the base of the brain is lessened. The brain contains a number of empty spaces – interconnected chambers called *ventricles*. The anatomy of these ventricles need not concern us. Cerebrospinal fluid is extracted from the blood, under continuous production, and the half-life is a mere 3 hours.

Hydrocephalus ('water on the brain') may result from an obstruction in the flow of CSF; this build-up in pressure can lead to damage to surrounding tissue.

Energy supply

Chapter 10 reviews how neuroimaging techniques rely on the measurement of oxygen and glucose in the brain. These new sophisticated techniques to image the working brain capitalize on the fact that the brain's main source of energy comes from the simple sugar, glucose. Oxygen is required for this metabolic process, therefore neurons consume a relatively large amount of oxygen. Any disruption in the glucose or oxygen supply can destroy neurons. This destruction is seen in Korsakoff's syndrome, which is a severe form of memory impairment seen in chronic alcoholics who have a deficiency in their diet of *thiamine* (vitamin B_1), which is necessary for the use of glucose in the brain.

Blood–brain barrier

The brain is a sensitive organ and is especially prone to poisoning by toxins and infection by viruses and bacteria. In most of the body's cells, infection leads to attack by the immune system (see chapter 6) via the release of *natural killer cells*. However, when these killer cells attack the virus they also destroy the cell: this process would be a disaster in the brain, where neurons are finite in number and (usually) do not regenerate. Nature's solution to this problem is a barrier between the blood supply to the brain (which could carry toxins) and neural tissue: this is the blood–brain barrier. This barrier works so well that it often prevents medical drugs from entering the brain (e.g., the precursor to dopamine, L-dopa, which is used to control the symptoms in Parkinson's disease – in this case other drugs are given which prevent the destruction of L-dopa before it enters the brain).

All large and electrically charged molecules are prevented from entering the brain; but some uncharged molecules can cross (e.g., oxygen and carbon dioxide). The blood–brain barrier achieves its task with the aid of a special type of cell in the wall of capillaries (*endothelial cells*). These cells are tightly joined together, so stopping larger molecules from passing. Drugs such as heroin, nicotine and cannabinod (the active ingredient in marijuana), which are soluble in fats, do cross the barrier by being dissolved in the fatty substance of the capillary walls. Because the barrier works so well, there is the need for an *active transport system* that pumps important chemicals into the brain (e.g., glucose and amino acids) – these chemicals would otherwise fail to enter the brain.

> **ASK YOURSELF**
> Are there any obvious 'design' flaws in the human brain?

▭ Neurodevelopment

You may have started to wonder how the complexity of the adult brain develops from the humble beginnings as a small collection of cells. The picture of the development of the central nervous system is complex, and largely still not understood. However, developments in molecular genetics arising from the Human Genome Project are starting to make important new inroads into this landscape of ignorance. This area of research is especially important for understanding normal psychological development, as well as the development of psychiatric conditions: it is thought that neurodevelopmental processes play an important aetiological (causal) role in many abnormal psychological conditions (examples are given in Part III). Let us start with what is known about developmental processes.

The formation of the body, including the nervous systems, is the result of *maturation*: given an adequate environment, these structures and processes develop according to the genome – of course, the environment is important, but there would be no environmental effects without this blue-print. It is amazing to think that you and I started life little more than the size of a punctuation mark on this page.

After only a few hours the fertilized ovum (egg) starts dividing: it has now started its journey of development, which will take many years to complete. The resulting divisions upon divisions (exponential growth) produce the immense complexity in the structure and function of the mature nervous system. At two weeks of gestation the first signs of the development of the nervous system are evident: the embryo starts to thicken, finally forming the *neural tube* around day 23. This neural tube is made up of stem cells (see chapter 11; these undifferentiated cells have the potential to make any tissue in the body); in the case of the nervous system, these all-purpose cells make neurons and supporting (glial) cells. The length of the neural tube forms the rostal–causal axis of the spinal cord and brain. The inside of the tube will eventually become the fluid-filled ventricles in the brain, and the stem cells on the inner surface of the tube will eventually comprise the different regions of the brain and spinal cord. At this time three distinct regions of swelling in the neural tube can be seen – these are the three interconnected chambers: these chambers are destined to become the hindbrain, midbrain and forebrain. Later in the developmental process the distinctive gyri and sulci that segregate brain areas may be seen.

It is still largely a mystery how cell stems develop into specific neural processes and areas; however, there is some understanding of how this remarkable feat is achieved. By the time of birth the brain weighs around 350 grams; but more growth is seen in the first year with brain weight increasing to 1,000 grams – not far off the weight of the adult brain (approx. 1,400 grams).

Neural development is not just about growth but also about loss and organization: at the age of three years, synaptic density is at its highest; but from this age synaptic links are pruned to form effective systems of neurotransmission. A number of processes are entailed in the maturation of the adult nervous system (Toates, 2001).

1. *Neurogenesis*, or *proliferation*. This process consists of cell division among the stem cells in the neural tube; this produces neurons and glial cells – unlike glial cells, neurons are thought not to divide and reproduce themselves (there are some exceptions to this rule, and now neurons can be encouraged to grow from undifferentiated stem cells – see chapter 13). However, compared with glial cells, diseased neurons are very difficult to replace – as with lost innocence, once gone neurons are difficult to replace.

2. *Migration*. Neurons must move from their place of origin in the neural tube to their target location in the nervous systems. This is a major problem for the developing nervous system, especially given the long distances nerve fibres (axons) have to travel. For example, axons need to travel from the cerebral cortex to the spinal cord, and from the spinal cord to muscles all over the body. One of the major scientific prob-

lems facing developmental embryologists is to work out the process underlying cell migration: how do cells 'know' where to go to form synaptic connections with neurons that are often some distance away? It seems that some supporting cells (specifically *radial glial cells*, a type of glial cell) act as guide-wires for migrating cells (specifically the axons that travel from the cell nucleus to the next cell). In addition, cells may chemically attract other cells – acting as a chemical allure for their co-existence (other chemicals may also serve to repel unwanted neural matches).

3. *Differentiation.* In the beginning all cells look alike, but neurons need to be differentiated to take on their distinctive characteristics; the result is different types of neurons in different locations in the brain (i.e., there are a variety of types of axons, dendrites, terminal buttons, etc.). Then some axons myelineate, adding a fatty coat around the axon fibre (myelin is important for neural conduction; see chapter 4). The major source of influence here is gene expression: genes must know when to turn on and off their effects, otherwise chaos would ensue – chaos does sometimes ensue, resulting in brain abnormalities.

4. *Synaptogenesis.* Neurons are functional to the extent that they communicate with other neurons, and the way this is achieved is to form synaptic connections. The formation of synapses is, of course, fundamental to effective neurotransmission (see Kalat, 1998).

5. *Cell death/murder.* There is an excess of neuronal material in the developing brain, and useless neurons (i.e., neurons that are not functionally effective in forming meaningful connections with other neurons) either die away or are actively killed. Many neurons do die. Edelman (1987) has likened this process to that of natural selection: weak neurons go to the wall; fitter neurons survive and make effective connections.[2] *Neurotrophic factors* exist which are secreted by target cells (i.e., postsynaptic cells) and taken up by travelling cells, which allow the cell to prosper. It is as if the target cell is talking to the presynaptic cell, in the form of a chemical message, which says, 'I'll be your friend. Don't kill yourself' (Kalat, 1998). A nerve growth factor has already been identified. Less successful cells are subject to *programmed cell death* – this suicide, known as *apoptosis*, results in the pruning of useless neurons in the form of housekeeping to maintain an effective nervous system. It is thought that specific genes activate a process of cell suicide.

   There are other forms of neurotrophin in the brain (*trophin* is ancient Greek for nourishment); they serve important functions: they encourage axons to survive during early development rather than commit suicide (apoptosis); different neurotrophins affect different neurons, leading to differentiation of structure and function; in later development, neurotrophins are activated by a neuron or hormone, resulting in the axonal branching; and neurotrophins help to repair damage to connected neurons by promoting the re-establishment of functional neuronal links.

6. *Synaptic reorganization.* In reaction to the environment and experience, neural plasticity (chapter 7) ensures that effective connections are made between neurons that serve functional roles. The extent to which wiring together is coded within the genome or is the result of exposure to regularities in the environment (learning) is still unclear: it is likely that genetic disposition and experience are *both* necessary for effective organization (the neuronal organization of the visual cortex is known to be dependent upon sensory input – people who have gained sight after blindness from birth find the visual environment very strange and discomfiting, even to the extent that some would have preferred to remain blind).

Our genome plays a central role in the assembly of our nervous systems, but this assembly is incomplete. Experience (i.e., exposure to regularities in the environment that have produced a semi-permanent change in the nervous system) too is necessary. The effect of the environment on brain differences is evident in the differences observed in rats reared in impoverished and enriched environments (see chapter 7).

All too often assaults and injury to the developing brain lead to permanent and irreversible pattern abnormalities. Given the enormous complexity of brain development, entailing the interplay of genetic, chemical and environmental factors, it is truly awe-inspiring to realize that most of us develop a reasonably normal brain. However, not everyone is so lucky. Chapter 2 has already summarized some of the effects of genetic mutations (e.g., PKU; there are some 200 known mutations that lead to neurodevelopmental disorder; Thapar et al., 1994); but there are also a number of neurodevelopmental abnormalities that result largely from non-genetic reasons.

Most of us assault our brains with a variety of everyday chemicals (e.g., alcohol, nicotine, caffeine); and some of us even play a neural form of Russian roulette by using potent psychoactive drugs (e.g., cocaine). In all such cases we may develop an addiction, and even develop severe brain conditions (e.g., Korsakoff's syndrome in the case of alcoholism); in the latter case, we may trigger off a genetic disposition to psychosis or neurotoxicity, resulting in depression and perhaps even dementia (this is especially suspected in the case of Ecstasy, which is known to be neurotoxic). However, in the main, our brains are remarkably robust to our everyday chemical assaults. Not so the developing brain.

A particularly marked neurodevelopmental abnormality is *fetal alcohol syndrome*. This condition is caused by excessive alcohol intake in the pregnant mother. The condition is characterized by decreased alertness, hyperactivity, mental retardation, motor problems, and various physical abnormalities, such as a defective heart and irregularities in facial features. In these children, the dendrites that form connections with other cells tend to be short and few in number. Other children may be similarly affected, but may not show irregularities in facial features. How much alcohol is safe during pregnancy? The answer depends on the stage of neural development: it may be the case that *any* intake of alcohol is potentially dangerous. There does seem to be a correlation between amount of alcohol intake during pregnancy and behavioural problems (e.g., hyperactivity and impaired school performance) – a finding that should encourage all pregnant women to avoid alcohol for the duration of pregnancy (for a fuller account, see Kalat, 1998).

> **ASK YOURSELF**
> Why isn't the human brain pre-wired from birth?

Structure–Function Relations

The following chapters explore the neurophysiological basis of a range of normal and abnormal behaviours. The present chapter looks at some well-known structure–function relationships. But before embarking on this journey, a word of warning is needed. It is all too tempting to imagine that a psychological function (e.g., word comprehension) is 'localized' in a single structure. However, most psychological functions (even apparently simple ones) involve the activation of a large network of neural interconnections, not the activation of a single neural site.

The billions of neurons in the brain are organized into assemblies of specialized functional systems (e.g., visual system, motor system, olfactory system, motivational

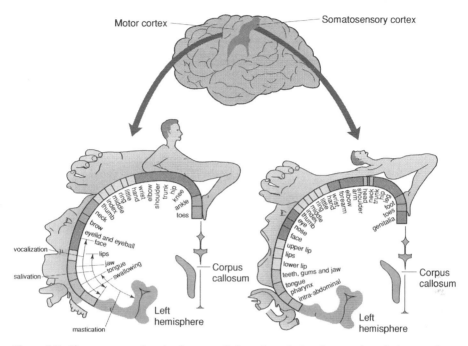

Figure 3.7   The sensory and motor homunculi show the relative degree of cortical processing devoted to different parts of the body. The degree of cortical specialization can be modified by experience and may differ between people (e.g., cortical processing devoted to fingers in violin and non-violin players).

system). Often, especially in the case of complex psychological processes, a particular neural system in the brain may be involved in very different psychological functions. For example, the hippocampus (an important structure in the limbic system) seems to be involved in a range of psychological functions, including memory, learning, anxiety and resolution of goal conflict.

There is a mapping of sensory and motor functions in the cerebral hemispheres. As is shown in figure 3.7, those parts of the body that require greater sensory processing (e.g., fingers) get more cortical space than other areas that are grosser in their operation (e.g., knees). These are the sensory and motor homunculi (Latin: 'little men').

The somatosensory cortex (also known as the *postcentral gyrus*) of the parietal lobe processes information from the skin, joints and muscles. Neural transmission via the PNS enters the spinal cord and then the thalamus of the brain before being sent to the somatosensory cortex for processing. The primary motor cortex (also known as the *precentral gyrus*) sends information from the cortex to the motor systems in the body.

Lateralization and specialization of function

Most parts of the brain are symmetrical, and this symmetry extends to function in the case of sensory and motor systems. In this regard, an important feature of the brain is that (most) sensory and motor neurons cross over as they enter and leave the brain (see chapter 5). Thus, the right brain controls the left-hand side of the body; the left brain controls the right-hand side of the body. For example, visual input from the right visual field is passed to the left hemisphere for processing, and input from the left visual field is passed to the right hemisphere. This arrangement is known as *contralateral* processing. Not all sensory systems are contralateral. Hearing, for example, does not fully cross over (so-called *ipsilateral* processing), but passes to both hemispheres (*bilateral* processing).

However, in the case of the association areas, where higher-order functions are processed, this symmetry is lost. The most marked difference is the dominance of the left hemisphere, which is specialized for language functions; and the right hemisphere is specialized for non-verbal visuospatial information processing. It should be stressed that not everyone is left-hemisphere dominant, and the relationship between hemisphere dominance and handedness is not totally straightforward.

The neurosurgeon Wilder Penfield, during the 1940s and 1950s, performed a number of classic experiments in which he electrically stimulated various parts of the human brain and observed the effects (these experiments were performed on patients before surgery – the brain does not contain pain receptors so patients feel no discomfort; a local anaesthetic is applied to the skin and scalp). As shown in figure 3.8, Penfield placed sterile pieces of paper, with numbers on them, to indicate which area of the cortex elicited which function.

The rationale for this approach was that before an epileptic attack many patients report experiencing a strange sensation, called an 'aura' (e.g., a specific smell); Penfield reasoned that if he could provoke this sensation by electrical stimulation then he might be able to locate the source of the abnormal electrical discharge and, in order to reduce symptoms, remove or destroy it. This technique proved clinically successful; but, more importantly for neuroscience, he discovered that stimulation on any part of the cerebral cortex elicited a response. For example, in the temporal lobe, highly specific memories were triggered (for one patient, stimulation brought forth a familiar song so clearly that she thought it was being played in the operating theatre). Penfield's pioneering work revealed that for each part of the motor cortex, there was a corresponding part of the body that moved when stimulated, with each hemisphere controlling the other side of the body. Penfield developed a map of the cortical surface of the brain that is now known as the sensory and motor homunculus.

As an example of the applications of Penfield's method, an orgasmic aura was studied in 22 epileptic patients (Janszky et al., 2002). Electrical stimulation of the non-dominant right hemisphere, in an area thought to be the amygdala, elicited this orgasmic aura, suggesting that this centre of emotional arousal may also be involved in sexual pleasure. In support of this conclusion, activation of the right amygdala has been observed during orgasm; and orgasmic aura can be induced by electrical stimulation of the right amygdala (Janszky et al., 2002). Research findings are often serendipitous.

Electrical stimulation studies have also started to address some of the deeper questions of humankind. For example, recent work has shown that stimulation of the temporal cortex can even elicit spiritual experience and the feeling of being at one with the cosmos and God (Persinger, 2001); in addition, there are greater temporal lobe signs and symptoms (reflecting greater activation in this brain area) in those who hold 'exotic' beliefs (e.g., paranormal experiences) (Persinger & Fisher, 1990).

The brain comprises two halves (i.e., *hemispheres*). These hemispheres can be shown to be relatively independent and, under the right conditions, can even be shown to have

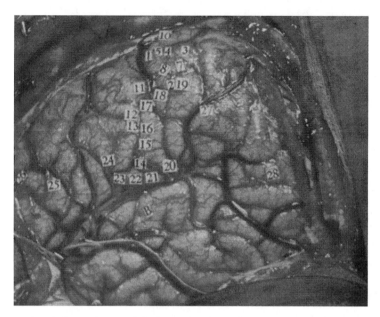

Figure 3.8 Electrical stimulation of the living brain. The exposed brain of a neurosurgical patient undergoing exploratory investigation to localize functional parts of the brain (e.g., speech centres). When cancerous tissue is removed from the brain, this procedure is routinely used to minimize impairment of functions. (From W. Penfield, *Speech and Brain Mechanisms* © 1959 Princeton University Press, 1987 renewed PUP. Reprinted by permission of Princeton University Press.)

opposing behavioural tendencies. Certainly, they subserve different functions. This asymmetry of function is known as *lateralization*. Handedness, language and spatial processing are strongly lateralized. Language disorders are localized to the left hemisphere, and this is sometimes known as the dominant hemisphere; however, the right hemisphere has its own functions.

In the 1960s, Roger Sperry and Michael Gazzaniga studied patients who had undergone surgery to sever the corpus callosum for the alleviation of intractable epilepsy (so-called 'split-brain' patients). The most obvious psychological outcome of this surgery was that, when objects were flashed to their right hemispheres, they could not identify them; but when they were flashed to their dominant hemisphere (usually left), they could. From this series of studies, the right hemisphere showed superior spatial skills, as seen by its preferential ability to solve spatial puzzles or draw geometric diagrams with the left hand (right hemisphere). In 1981, Sperry won the Nobel Prize for his pioneering work. Chapter 8 returns to split-brain studies.

Complex language is rare in the animal kingdom; although it may not be restricted to human beings, there can be little doubt that it is more highly developed in us than in any other species. There has been intensive neuropsychological interest in this topic. It is especially instructive in showing the specialization of the brain. Early evidence for localization of function came from the post-mortem brains of patients who had suffered a stroke ('brain attack') and who had shown specific psychological deficits. Two import-ant names in this regard are the French physician Paul Broca (1860s) and the German neurologist Carl Wernicke (1870s). Broca identified a region in the left frontal cortex as the site responsible for organizing speech production. Broca's ('expressive') aphasia is associated with slow and impaired speech – these patients have no problem in understanding speech though. In Wernicke's ('comprehension') aphasia, patients have difficulty in understanding speech; they produce fluent speech that is devoid of meaning. Wernicke identified the posterior part of the superior temporal gyrus as being the location of this deficit. Despite the problems associated with post-mortem studies, Broca's and Wernicke's conclusions have been confirmed by more sophisticated tools in neuropsychology (e.g., functional neuroimaging; see chapter 10).

There is a general lateralization in many functions, although many functions are found in both hemispheres. Typically, the left hemisphere is specialized for language whereas the right hemisphere is specialized for geometric patterns, visuospatial ability, music and emotion. However, many functions are not lateralized, and lateralization seems to be the exception, not the rule. Also, where lateralization is found, absolute differences are not important, only statistically significant biases in favour of one hemisphere. Let us take what is the most lateralized of all functions: language. There are still language functions in the right hemisphere, as assessed by behavioural measures and neuroimaging studies.

ASK YOURSELF
Does research suggest that 'spiritual' experiences are nothing more than an overactive temporal cortex?

▢ The Brain of a Genius: Albert Einstein

Albert Einstein is widely recognized as being one of the greatest scientists ever to have lived. He is recognized as a genius in mathematics and physics, famous for his general theory of relativity. At the age of 76, on 18 April 1955, he died. Fortunately, before cremation, his brain was saved for research purposes (figure 3.9). Is it possible to identify features of Einstein's brain that mark him out as a genius? Admittedly, these brain features are crude. But did his brain differ in gross anatomical terms from the typical human brain?

Einstein's brain went missing until the mid-1970s, when a journalist tracked it down: it was in the care of Dr Thomas S. Harvey, the pathologist at Princeton Hospital who removed Einstein's brain in the first place. Fortunately, it had been *fixed* in formaldehyde to preserve the nerve cells (see chapter 11). There have now been three scientific articles analysing Einstein's brain.

Diamond et al. (1985) were interested in the neuron : glial ratios (both astrocytes and oligodendrocytes) in the cerebral cortex. They reasoned that higher-order psychological functions have a higher ratio of glial cells to neurons, so they hypothesized that Einstein's brain might show a bias in favour of these support cells. Their analysis showed that, in some areas of his brain (especially the left inferior parietal area), there were more glial cells for each neuron. The inferior parietal area is an association area, responsible for analysing information; this association area is one of the last parts of the cortex to myelinate. Lesions in this area produce deficits in writing, spelling and calculation. Perhaps Einstein's mathematical genius may be explained by his neurons having received more nutritional or structural support from the glial cells, thus enhancing the efficiency of his neural pathways. An environmental effect should also be considered, as rats reared in an enriched environment also possess more glial cells per neuron.

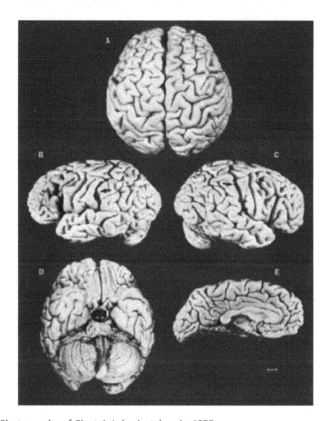

Figure 3.9   Photographs of Einstein's brain taken in 1955.

Anderson and Harvey (1996) took the analysis of Einstein's brain one step further by studying the neuronal density, neuron size and numbers of neurons in the cerebral cortex. They found that his brain weighed 1,230 grams (less than the average brain of 1,400 grams). Not only was the cortex thinner than in the control group, but he had a greater neuronal density: that is, there was a greater concentration of neurons in a smaller space.

Witelson, Kigar and Harvey (1999) conducted a detailed analysis of the gross anatomy of Einstein's brain. Their analysis was guided theoretically by current knowledge of the cortical localization of cognitive functions. Specifically, the manipulation of three-dimensional spatial images and the mathematical representation of abstract concepts were essential cognitive elements in the development of Einstein's theory of relativity. Einstein himself played down the role of words in his thinking, stressing instead images and visuospatial processes.

Einstein's brain differed in that it seemed to have an unusual pattern of sulci (grooves) on the right and left parietal lobes (these lobes may be important in mathematical ability). It also had a much shorter lateral sulcus. His brain was also 15 per cent wider than the average brain. According to the authors, these gross anatomical differences suggest that extensive development of the parietal lobes occurred early in development. These features may have facilitated the type of mathematical reasoning for which Einstein was to become famous.

These results are interesting indeed, but they need to be treated with some caution. In such studies there is always the problem of identifying an appropriate comparison (control group). In addition, it is not known whether other mathematical geniuses share the peculiar patterns of Einstein's brain: maybe the differences observed were unrelated to his genius. Nowadays, it is possible to address this latter issue more precisely with functional imaging: a group of mathematical geniuses would be required to perform a mathematical task while their brains are being scanned; the pattern of neural activation observed would then be compared with an appropriately selected comparison (control) group matched for such factors as age, general intelligence and gender.

ASK YOURSELF
What does the analysis of Einstein's brain tell us about the relationship between structure and functions?

Throughout the following chapters many examples of structure–function relations will be encountered, first in terms of research approaches to addressing research questions (Part II: Approaches), and then in relation to some of the major psychiatric conditions (Part III: Applications).

Learning Questions

1. In what ways do glial cells play an important role in neurotransmission?
2. Is the peripheral nervous system simply a slave of the central nervous system?
3. To what extent are functions localized in brain regions?
4. By which mechanisms do neurodevelopmental problems lead to abnormal adult brains?
5. Is it true that psychological functions are lateralized, with each hemisphere having its own unique realm of responsibility?

NOTES

1 Until recently it was thought that neurons do not grow after birth; however, this view is being revised and there is now a greater appreciation of the plasticity in neuronal processes, including the growth of new neurons.
2 This is an analogy only: if anything, neuronal development is more Lamarckian than Darwinian in that neurons are guided by chemical factors, and their changed connections are passed on to 'future' generations of neurons – more precisely, dendritic and synaptic connections. Mutations in genes always occur randomly; synaptic connections do not.

FURTHER READING

Haines, D. E. (2002). *Fundamental Neuroscience*. London: Churchill Livingstone.
Pinel, J. P. J. (2000). *Biopsychology*. London: Allyn & Bacon.
Toates, F. (2001). *Biological Psychology: An Integrative Approach*. Harlow: Pearson.

chapter 4

Neurons and Neurotransmission

Learning Objectives

To be able to:

1. Outline the structure of a neuron and describe the function of each part.
2. Describe the process of a nerve signal along the neuron.
3. Explain how neurons communicate across the synaptic cleft.
4. Present the key-and-lock model of neurotransmitter–receptor actions.
5. Describe the action of drugs and explain the process of dependence/addiction.

Now that a good understanding of the structure and gross functions of the nervous system has been achieved, it is time to turn to the basic processing unit in the nervous system – the neuron – and its form of communication – neurotransmission. Although the neurophysiology of the neuron entails the learning of a number of new concepts, its basic properties are simple and easily understood. It is hoped that, after digesting the contents of this chapter, the reading of psychopharmacology articles will be much easier and unfamiliar terms (e.g., allosteric interactions) will not appear so daunting. Understanding the neurophysiology of the neuron is important in another sense: that of understanding our psychological nature. As Crick (1994, p. 3) stated,

> 'You', your joys and your sorrows, your memories and your ambitions, your sense of personal identity and free will, are in fact no more than the behaviour of a vast assembly of nerve cells and their associated molecules . . . You're nothing but a pack of neurons.[1]

Therefore, to understand one's own mind, as well as that of others, it is necessary to understand the neuron. Let us make a start.

It is estimated that a one-year-old child has about 100 billion (10^{11}) neurons. It was previously thought that no new neurons are formed throughout the child's life, and each day sees the loss of some 200,000 neurons; however, this dogma is starting to be challenged. In any event, with increasing age comes complexity of interconnections (each neuron may have connections with some 10,000 other neurons). The neuron is a specialized cell whose job is the transfer of information; more precisely, to transmit electrochemical signals (i.e., *action potentials*) from one neuron to another.

The conceptual neuron

In chapter 3 the neuron was likened to a railway system crossing a chain of islands. More realistically the neuron could be likened to an electrical wire: at one end of the wire is a switch which is activated by another neuron; this switch triggers a signal along the wire (electrical current), which produces some effect (e.g., turns on a light; in the neural case, it activates other neurons or activates glands and muscles). Like a house light switch, the neuron is either on or off (a neuron does not have a dimmer control). With a few additional points of information (most importantly, neurons can either excite or inhibit other neurons), it is possible to dispense with the neurophysiology of the neuron entirely and pursue a purely *computational* (information-processing) account. This strategy is essentially what those working in the area of neural networks do (chapter 7). However, abandoning the *real* nervous system in preference for a *conceptual* nervous system has inherent dangers.

Many neuropsychologists see great advantage in combining the two types of nervous system – that is, combining the *conceptual nervous system* and the *real nervous system* (see chapter 1). This joint research strategy is especially important in the formulation and testing of new theories: assuming each strategy is correctly specified, the conceptual nervous system must be compatible with the real nervous system, and vice versa. Attacking a research problem from both perspectives strengthens conclusions drawn from each separately, while exposing errors arising from a discrepancy between these approaches.

Structure of the Neuron

Our discussion of the neuron focuses on the *typical* neuron. However, neurons come in many different varieties. For example, some neurons do not have an axon; others have terminal buttons that synapse on other terminal buttons; some neurons synapse on axons (i.e., an *axoaxonic* synapse), others on the cell bodies (i.e., an *axosomatic* synapse; the more usual dendrite synapse is known as an *axodendritic* synapse); and some neurons communicate via electrical, not chemical, means. However, understanding these basic principles allows us to comprehend more advanced texts in neuroscience (for an excellent intermediate introduction to psychopharmacology, see Stahl, 2000; Carlson, 2000, gives a more basic introduction to this topic). The structure of a typical neuron is shown in figure 4.1.

Cell body (soma)

The body of the cell consists of a nucleus ('nut'), which is the powerhouse: it contains the nucleolus (which manufactures *ribosomes*, involved in protein synthesis) and chromosomes

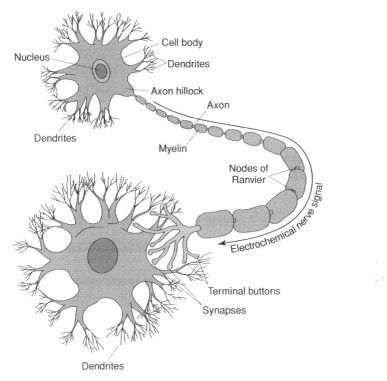

Figure 4.1 Schematic diagram of a typical neuron, showing all the major processes involved in neurotransmission.

(the genetic material; DNA). When the nucleolus is active, portions of the chromosomes (genes) create another complex molecule, called *messenger ribonucleic acid* (mRNA; see chapters 2 and 13). This mRNA contains a copy of the genetic information stored at that location; it then leaves the membrane and attaches to ribosomes, where it causes the production of proteins. These proteins are important in cell structure and functioning; in particular they serve as enzymes, which direct the chemical processes of a cell – enzymes are special protein molecules that act as a catalyst: they cause a chemical reaction to occur without being part of the final action. Cells have the potential to produce a large number of compounds. The ones that are produced are caused by these specific enzymes. The main function of the cell body is to perform the maintenance needed to keep the neuron functional (e.g., converting nutrients into energy).

Here is described one of the most common types of neurons (for a description of other types, see Toates, 2001). The one part of the cell body that is involved in the generation of an action potential is the *axon hillock*: the neuron fires when the aggregate input is greater than the axon hillock's threshold value. The cell body is also responsible for initiating the production of cellular material (e.g., vesicles; and mitochondria, which turn oxygen and glucose into energy).

Dendrites

Dendrites are tree-like structures, often densely branched (dendrites: Greek for tree; singular: 'dendron'). They are the 'listening' part of the cell: they receive inputs signals from other neurons. This dendritic tree can be in contact with as many as 100,000 other neurons. The strength of stimulation received by the dendrites is summed together by two processes: (a) *spatial summation*, which can add together several weak input signals from a local population of contacting neurons (i.e., small amounts of neurotransmitters released from a group of axonal terminal buttons) into a single large one (this simultaneous activation combines to send a strong signal to the axon hillock); and (b) *temporal summation*, which can convert a series of rapid weak input signals from a single neuron (resulting from successive release of a neurotransmitter over a period of time – in the order of milliseconds) to produce one larger input signal. The aggregate input signal is then passed to the cell body (soma) and axon hillock: then the neuron either fires or not. The grey appearance of the brain is the result of the dense collection of cell bodies and dendrites.

The input signal travels from dendrites (and also sometimes from the soma, which can receive input signals directly) as a *graded potential* (i.e., its strength is in proportion to activation by the stimulation of neurotransmitters released presynaptically): only at the axon hillock does the action potential take on its all-or-none characteristic.

Axon

The structure of the axon is similar to an electrical wire; it may extend over very long distances (e.g., from the cerebral cortex to lower regions of the spinal cord) and extend into several branches. It carries the action potential arising at the axon hillock to the terminal endings (*buttons*; also known as *boutons*).

Many axons are covered by a sheath of fatty tissue (i.e., the *myelin sheath*; provided by oligodendrocytes; Schwann cells serve a similar function in the PNS). This sheath serves several functions. First, it protects the axon from other cells, ensuring that the electrical signal does not stray to nearby cells; and, second, it serves to increase the velocity of the action potential (an unmyelinated axon requires 100 times the volume of a myelinated axon to conduct an action potential at the same velocity). As at least 10 per cent of the brain volume is made up of myelineated axons, the brain would have to be 10 times larger to function without myelin. A loss of myelin has profound consequences (e.g., multiple sclerosis). The sheath is not continuous; instead it comprises a number of elongated segments. The gaps in the sheath are known as *nodes of Ranvier*; these gaps allow energy to enter the axon to boost the electrical signal. The white matter of the brain comprises bundles of axons, each coated with a sheath of myelin (which appears as a white fatty substance).

Axons are vulnerable to injury when the brain mass moves as a result of rotational forces (e.g., during a blow to the head during the sport of boxing). Axons typically stretch across different layers of different densities in the brain; as these densities move at different speeds, rapid acceleration or deceleration creates a sliding effect of these layers, leading to the possibility of axonal damage ('brain damage'). Outside the brain, in the spinal cord, axons are vulnerable to severance and compression; these effects can result in paralysis (i.e., the axons cannot travel to their muscle/gland targets and thus execute their message).

Terminal buttons

Terminal buttons are the 'talking' end of the neuron. They release chemicals[2] (called *neurotransmitters*) that flow into the gap between neurons (the *synaptic cleft*) to talk to the dendrites (as well as sometimes the soma and axon) on neighbouring neurons. The next neuron then passes the signal on to other neurons or to effector organs.

Neurons are very small – cell bodies vary from 5 to 100 microns in diameter (1 micron = 1/1,000 millimetres; i.e., 1,000 microns equal 1 mm). Dendrites are a few hundred microns long. In contrast, the axon can be exceedingly long (e.g., from the head to the base of the spinal cord; and from the spinal cord to the feet and hands).

Synaptic cleft

Neurons communicate with each other by *inter*cellular signalling. This process is achieved by the release of a neurotransmitter across the synaptic cleft (gap; 'synapse' derives from Greek: 'syn', meaning together, and 'haptein', meaning to clasp); that is, between the terminal button of the sending (presynaptic) neuron and the receiving (postsynaptic) neuron (this extracellular space is tiny, 30 to 50 nanometres). The neurotransmitter travels across the gap and 'talks' to the neighbouring cell. Usually the postsynaptic neuron is 'listening', but by a variety of pharmacological means it can be made deaf. Neurotransmitters can have excitatory effects (i.e., increasing the probability that the postsynaptic, receiving, neuron fires) or inhibitory effects (i.e., decreasing the probability that it fires); they can also have modulatory effects (i.e., modifying the functioning of synaptic transmission) – these effects are considered below.

The chemical and physical features of each synapse determine the strength and polarity of the new input signal (the electrical potential does not cross this gap, only the neurotransmitter released at the terminal buttons). The nature of the synapse is responsible for the great flexibility of the brain; but also it is a very vulnerable point in neural information processing. For example, changing the chemical substance in the synaptic cleft can change the inhibitory or excitatory nature of the chemical message. Drugs have important effects on the production and destruction of these critical chemicals (see below). Biological weapons exploit the nature of the synapse. The deadly nerve gas *sarin* kills because it neutralizes one chemical, *acetylcholinesterase*, that normally regulates the neurotransmitter, *acetylcholine*: its lethal effect results from the fact that, as a consequence of this chemical action at the synapse, when neurons fire they keep triggering neighbouring neurons, and control of muscles is no longer possible (suffocation results).

Vesicles

The presynaptic terminals contain vesicles ('little vessels') filled with chemical molecules (i.e., neurotransmitters). When the action potential reaches the terminal buttons, a

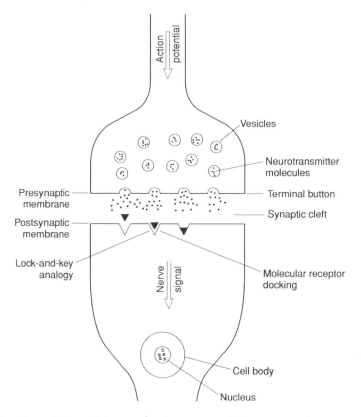

Figure 4.2 Schematic view of the process of neurotransmission. Storage of neurotransmitter molecules in vesicles, their rupture at the presynaptic membrane, their release into the synaptic cleft, and their activation of receptors on the postsynaptic membrane, which leads to the molecules entering the postsynaptic cell to produce either fast nerve conduction or slower molecular processes.

chemical signal forces the vesicles to fuse with the presynaptic membrane of the cell and then to burst open and spill their neurotransmitter into the synaptic cleft. Once the vesicle releases its neurotransmitter, and if this occupies a sufficient number of receptors, then the molecules on the postsynaptic membrane are activated (figure 4.2).

Autoreceptors are molecular receptors in the presynaptic membrane that monitor the number of neurotransmitter molecules in the synaptic cleft; once detected, autoreceptors decrease the rate of synthesis of fresh neurotransmitter molecules; they can also inhibit the release of more neurotransmitter, and they also reclaim the excess of molecules in the synaptic cleft – a process known as *re-uptake* (some drugs designed to improve mood are so-called *re-uptake inhibitors* because they allow greater transmitter availability to the postsynaptic neuron by blocking the recovery by the presynaptic neuron of the released neurotransmitter). The vesicle is re-formed and filled with neurotransmitter ready for release once again. A second, though less common, way in which neurotransmitters are removed from the synaptic cleft is *enzymatic degradation*: neurotransmitters are broken apart by enzymes (chemicals that stimulate or inhibit other chemical reactions). For example, acetylcholine is one of the few neurotransmitters which uses enzymatic degradation as the main mechanism of synaptic deactivation. This neurotransmitter is broken down by the enzyme *acetylcholinesterase* (as noted above, sarin gas works by preventing this breakdown). Other methods of eliminating excess neurotransmitters from the synaptic cleft are: (a) *diffusion*, where the neurotransmitter drifts away out of the cleft; and (b) removal by glial (astrocyte) cells.

> **ASK YOURSELF**
> What are the functional advantages of having so many neurons in the brain?

Intracellular Signalling

Neurons transmit information within the cell (i.e., from dendrites to terminal buttons) in the form of electrochemical impulses; that is, there is an electrical component and a chemical component. Together these two components produce the nerve impulse of the neuron. The interaction of these electrical and chemical processes is perhaps the least easy neuronal process to comprehend. Therefore, for clarity, let us consider each in turn.

Electrical impulse

Information is transmitted from dendrites to terminal buttons in the form of electrical signals, or impulses. Within the neuron, there are two main forms of transmission: (a) from the dendrite to the axon hillock; and (b) from the axon hillock to the terminal button. As seen below, the nature of these electrical signals is different.

Resting potential (polarization)

When the neuron is at rest (i.e., not firing), there is a difference in the electrical potential measured between the inside and outside of the axon. The inside of the axon (and the rest of the neuron) is negatively charged; the outside is relatively positively charged. This resting potential is about −70 millivolts. In this resting state the cell membrane is said to be *polarized* (the inside and outside of the axon have been likened to the positive and negative electrical poles of a battery). This polarization is shown in figure 4.3.

Action potential (depolarization)

When the typical neuron is activated (i.e., when the dendrites are chemically activated by the neurotransmitter released by another neuron), a sequence of electrical and chemical changes is set in train. This activation reduces the electrical potential difference across the membrane of the axon. A critical strength of the electrical potential is required (approximately −55 millivolts in human beings). Once the strength of the

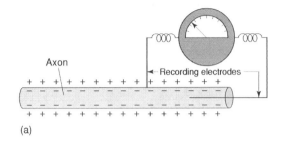

Axon

Recording electrodes

(a)

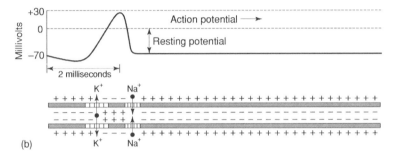

(b)

Figure 4.3 Voltmeter and action potential. The electrical signal can be measured by placing one electrode inside the axon and the other on the outside: this difference is the voltage (a). The positivity and negativity of the inside and outside of the membrane change as potassium leaves the membrane and sodium enters the membrane: this is responsible for the propagation of the action potential (b).

stimulus is strong enough – known as the *threshold of response* – then an all-or-none response occurs (starting at the axon hillock).

Now, when this all-or-none response occurs, instead of the electrical potential gradually increasing in proportion to the strength of the input signal (which occurs from the dendrites to the action hillock), it collapses, and the potential on the inside of the cell now switches from being negative to being positive. This nerve flare lasts very briefly (about 1 millisecond). The neuron then returns to its resting potential state. This wave of electrical excitation travels down the axon: this is achieved by each segment of the axon exciting the segment next to it; the segment then depolarizes; and excites the next segment, and so on until the action potential reaches the terminal buttons and the neurotransmitter is released into the synaptic cleft and the whole process starts afresh in other neurons. The depolarization wave travels fast (some 50 metres per second).

All-or-none law

The axon fires or does not fire depending on the critical threshold of response reached. This action (depolarized) potential is not affected by the strength of the stimulus above this threshold. This is the all-or-none law of action potentials: rather like a digital switch in a computer, they either happen or they do not, and when they occur their speed and strength are always the same. The all-or-none law implies that the input signal does not provide the energy for an action potential.

However, stimulus intensity does have an effect on the firing of the neuron. Although it does not affect the strength of a response, it does affect the rate of firing. This is the *impulse frequency* of the response. Some neurons can fire 1,000 times per second. In addition, different neurons have different thresholds of response. Thus a faint sound activates a relatively small number of neurons, and thus is perceived as a faint sound; a much louder sound activates a larger population of neurons and thus is perceived to be louder. By this route, stimulus intensity leads to greater activity in populations of neurons and is thus experienced psychologically as being of a higher intensity. Some neurons have a very low threshold of response. For example, neurons responsible for processing innate fear stimuli (e.g., snakes) are likely to be especially active even when the physical energy coming from the feared object is no stronger than that coming from a cup of tea. This example shows the importance of neurons that are involved in cognitive appraisal of stimuli defined in purely physical terms.

Chemical propagation of electrical impulse

So far it has been shown that the electrical potential changes as the action potential propagates down the axon to the terminal buttons. But how is this propagation achieved? An interaction of both electrical and chemical factors explains this effect.

The neuronal membrane is porous, allowing some chemicals to enter and exit the cell while stopping the passage of others (technically called 'selective permeability'). This effect is achieved by protein molecules embedded in the neuronal membrane, which provides channels for what are termed 'ions'. Many molecules have either a positive or negative electrical charge: these are ions.[3] Now some ion channels are always open, others open only when activated. Some chemicals within the neuronal membrane (intracellular) and some outside the membrane in the extracellular fluid that surrounds the cell are electrically charged. Specifically, potassium ions (K^+) are more common within the cell, sodium ions (Na^+) more common outside the cell. (K comes from the Latin name for potassium, *kalium*, Na from the Latin word *natrium*.) The net effect is a negatively charged interior of the cell and positively charged exterior.

Now, at resting potential, there is a higher concentration of positively charged sodium ions (Na^+) on the outside of the neuron. This difference is the result of the action of a pump which actively transports (a) sodium ions out of the cell (the *sodium pump*), and (b) potassium ions into the cell (the *potassium pump*) – in a ratio of 3 sodium per 2 potassium (joint effects of these separate pumps is sometimes referred to as the *sodium–potassium pump*). This ratio difference in electrically charged particles gives rise to the voltage (potential) difference across the membrane of −70 millivolts: this charge comes about because positively charged molecules outside the membrane are attracted to negatively charged ones inside the membrane (the membrane keeps out these positively charged molecules). This electrical difference provides the source of electrical energy for the action potential to occur. Now, what happens when the neuron's dendrites are excited?

In addition to these sodium–potassium pumps, which work at resting potential, the neuron's membrane also has special sodium ion gates which spring open when they receive an electrical potential of a critical voltage; potassium ion gates are much slower acting. These ion gates are usually closed to sodium ions, which would otherwise gush into the cell. When the neuron is excited, and the input stimulus reaches the critical threshold, these ion gates spring open, sodium ions rush in, producing an excess of positively charged particles inside the neuron. These give rise to the positive potential inside the membrane (i.e., a brief +30 millivolt potential difference). Soon afterwards these ionic gates close, and other positively charged (potassium, K^+) ions are moved out as a result of their own concentration gradient, and the potential once again returns to its resting state. It is now ready to fire again if a sufficiently strong signal is received from the dendrites and cell body. In fact, when the neuron returns to rest the electrical charge across the membrane overshoots the resting potential of −70 millivolts because the potassium channels stay open too long, an overshoot known as *hyperpolarization* – this is an imperfect design of the neuron's action. Thus, the faster acting sodium ion channels start the action potential and the slower acting potassium stop it. Upon completion, the ion channels then close and the axon returns to its resting potential of −70 millivolts.

The action potential travels along the axon for the following reason. The cell membrane has so-called 'cable properties'. A small electrical current flows along the membrane just in front of the action potential; this small current is sufficient to cause the electrically sensitive gated sodium ion channels to open and thus initiates the next phase of the action potential wave. In neurons without a myelin sheath, this process is quite slow because each part of the membrane has to be activated (a maximum of 2 metres per second). In a myelinated neuron, this maximum speed increases to something closer to 120 metres per second. This increase in speed is achieved because the action potential now has only to jump the gaps between the myelin sheaths (nodes of Ranvier) and not traverse the whole axon. The myelin sheath stops ion flows in the covered regions of the axon, and by this process the current flow is not so easily dissipated (rather like wrapping tape around a leaking hose: this would allow water to flow faster). The action potential thus 'jumps' from one node of Ranvier to the next (technically known as 'saltatory conduction', from the Latin *saltare*, to jump).

Ion gates and vesicles

Ion gates are also involved in the release of vesicles from the terminal buttons. Once the action potential reaches the presynaptic terminal, a third type of ion channel (i.e., a calcium double-positively charged, Ca^{2+}, ion channel) is activated (sodium and potassium ion channels in the axons were the first two types). Ca^{2+} rushes into the presynaptic terminal, causing the vesicles to fuse with the presynaptic membrane, releasing the neurotransmitter into the synaptic cleft. On the postsynaptic neuron, specialized receptor molecules are activated; this activation either opens or closes ion gates in the membrane, depending on whether the effects are excitatory or inhibitory. These ion gates send the graded signal from the dendrites to the axon hillock, where a further action potential then either happens or not.

ASK YOURSELF
What is the importance of 'graded potential' in intracellular signalling?

■☐ Intercellular Signalling

Communication *between* neurons is usually by the release of chemicals (i.e., neurotransmitters) from the terminal buttons of the 'sending' neuron, across the gap between the neurons (i.e., the synaptic cleft), that lock onto receptors on the dendrites of the 'receiving' neurons.

Excitatory and inhibitory postsynaptic potentials

Before going into the details of neurotransmission, a general feature of neurotransmitters should be noted: they either *excite* or *inhibit* neural activity in the postsynaptic neuron. As can be seen, excitation and inhibition are a function of (a) type of neurotransmitter and (b) type of receptor (a single neurotransmitter may activate a number of different receptors).

Postsynaptic excitatory neurotransmitters open chemically sensitive channels to positively charged Na^+ and K^+ ions: this leads to the simultaneous movement of Na^+ ions into the neuron and K^+ ions out of it (in essentially the same manner as the exchange that takes place during an action potential). As in the case of axon transmission, now because more Na^+ is drawn into the neuron than K^+ is removed, an electrochemical signal (i.e., the excitatory postsynaptic potential; EPSP) is produced. In contrast, an inhibitory postsynaptic potential (IPSP) occurs as a result of inhibitory transmitters opening chemically sensitive channels to two types of ions: one positive (K^+) and the other negative (chloride, Cl^-): this process results in the simultaneous movement of positively charged K^+ ions out of the neuron and the negatively charged Cl^- ions into the neuron. As a result of this exchange, the inside of the neuron becomes more negatively charged and thus less likely to fire (i.e., the cell becomes more polarized). The probability that a neuron fires is thus determined by the algebraic summation of EPSPs and IPSPs. IPSPs serve very important functions in regulating psychological functions. For example, in order for one neural circuit to work effectively it may be necessary to inhibit the action of other circuits that may have opposing effects. As you may already have guessed, the actual electrochemical processes involved in neuronal transmission are much more complex than this simple account suggests.

Fast-onset vs. slow-onset signals

Neurotransmitters do not all lead to the same type of postsynaptic signal. It is necessary to contrast those neurotransmitters that exert a fast onset with those that exert a slow onset. Fast-onset signals initiate an action potential within milliseconds of the receptor being occupied by the neurotransmitter. The neurotransmitters *glutamate* (one of the main excitatory chemicals) and *gamma-aminobutyric acid* (GABA; one of the main inhibitory chemicals) are both fast-onset acting. Neurotransmitters with fast-onset properties work by activating ion gates in the postsynaptic membrane (as discussed above).

In contrast to fast-onset signals, some neurotransmitters use slow-onset signalling – these effects can take anywhere between hundreds of milliseconds to several seconds.

Often these neurotransmitters are known as *neuromodulators* (see below): these signals have a longer lasting effect on postsynaptic excitability and have the ability to influence the actions of other neurotransmitters – they set the general tone of the neuron's excitability. However, the effects of slow-onset neurotransmitters are not limited to neuro-modulatory functions: they can also affect the postsynaptic membrane directly. Slow-acting neurotransmitters may take seconds to exert their effects, but they are capable of setting in train a biochemical cascade that can last for days. Slow-onset neurotransmitters fall into the class known as monoamines (e.g., norepinephrine and serotonin) and neuro-peptides (these neurotransmitters are discussed below).

Receptor subtypes

A specific neurotransmitter does not bind to only one receptor molecule type. In fact, most neurotransmitters bind to more than one type of receptor, and a variety of receptor subtypes exist for most neurotransmitters. This receptor variety serves the function of allowing a single neurotransmitter to have many different effects: the intracellular effects of a neurotransmitter are determined by the properties of the receptor molecule. For most neurotransmitters, a number of receptor subtypes have been identified and characterized (i.e., described). A lock-and-key analogy is often used to describe the neurotransmitter–receptor complex (see below); but more accurately most neurotrans-mitters serve as master keys that are able to unlock different receptor types.

Allosteric interactions

To understand fully the process of neurotransmission it is necessary to know a little about the *interplay* of different types of receptors: often neurotransmitters do not influence the postsynaptic membrane in isolation. It has already been shown how many slow-onset neurotransmitters serve to modulate the effects of faster-onset neurotransmitters (i.e., they *modulate* fast-onset activity). Another way in which neurotransmitters work together is via allosteric interactions: these refer to the joint effects of different types of receptor (often one receptor modulates the action of another receptor). Sometimes the interact-ing receptor binding sites may be located on the same receptor molecule; in other cases, the binding sites may be neighbouring receptors of a different class.

Allosteric interactions can boost or retard neurotransmission. In the case of a positive allosteric interaction, the effect of activation of one receptor type facilitates the activa-tion of a different receptor type; a negative allosteric interaction refers to an inhibitory effect of one receptor type on activation of a different receptor type. If the primary recep-tor is not bound then the allosteric receptor has no effect; thus the function of the allosteric receptor is to modulate the effects of the primary receptor. Allosteric interaction is an important concept because numerous drugs, including benzodiazepine, barbiturates and anticonvulsants, are mediated by positive allosteric interactions at molecular sites around the GABA receptor and the chloride channel (figure 4.4).

Negative allosteric modulation is seen in the case of antidepressants: these act as neuro-transmitter re-uptake blockers for the neurotransmitters norepinephrine and serotonin. Shortly after norepinephrine and serotonin bind to their receptor sites, they are normally

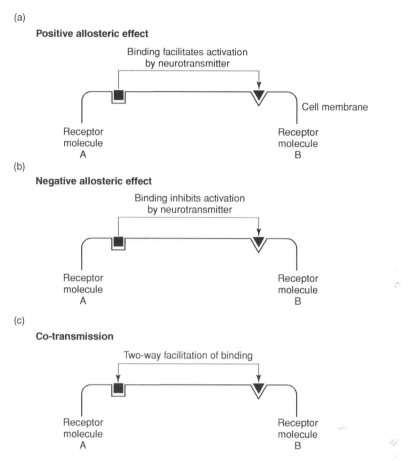

Figure 4.4 Examples of allosteric interactions. On some receptor complexes, the activation of one receptor type (A) has the power to influence the sensitivity to a second receptor type (B). (a) In the case of a positive allosteric effect, neurotransmitter binding to A facilitates the operation of receptor type B. (b) In the case of a negative allosteric effect, binding to A inhibits the operation of B. In other receptor complexes, activation of either type of receptor facilitates the operation of the other receptor. (c) Co-transmission refers not to allosteric effects but to additive effects of binding.

transported back to the presynaptic neuron. Re-uptake inhibitors bind to an allosteric site close to the neurotransmitter transporter, with the effect that the neurotransmitter in the synapse is no longer able to bind there; the net effect is a blocking of synaptic re-uptake of the neurotransmitter and thus more of the molecule is left in the synapse cleft to stimulate the postsynaptic membrane.

A variation of allosteric interactions is *co-transmission*: this process refers to the *additive* effects of two transmitters at the same receptor. However, unlike allosteric interactions, it is not necessary for one transmitter to be present for the other transmitter to activate the receptor. This co-transmission sometimes involves a monoamine coupled with a neuropeptide. The neuron thus has a 'polypharmacy' of its own (Stahl, 2000). Drugs may need to target more than one neurotransmitter to be effective.

Support (glial) cells revisited

As shown in chapter 3, the function of glial cells tends to put them in a subservient role to the neuron. However, some research has suggested that glial cells may be more important in neurotransmission than typically thought.

Araque et al. (1999) summarize findings suggesting that glial cells participate in the regulation of synaptic transmission, and they propose a tripartite theory of synaptic transmission which argues that, in addition to presynaptic and postsynaptic effects, glial cells serve a third role of neurotransmitter regulation. As seen in chapter 3, Albert Einstein's brain was distinguished in terms of the number of glial cells present. Astrocytes may be especially important in neurotransmission. As Araque et al. (1999) note, 'Astroctyes . . . as well as Schwann cells . . . all show Ca^{2+}-dependent glutamate release' (p. 209). This release is known to affect Ca^{2+} processes within the neuron (see above); and it may also affect synaptic transmission (although it is known that they 'listen' to neuronal transmission, it is not yet known whether they 'talk back'). This is an exciting new area of neural research that is starting to pose new questions about neural transmission.

> **ASK YOURSELF**
> What are the functional advantages of having so many different types of neurotransmitters and receptor types?

▢▢ Neurotransmitters

Neurotransmitters are chemical substances (molecules) that upon release from the presynaptic membrane transverse the synaptic cleft and stimulate postsynaptic receptor molecules. There are thought to be at least 100 neurotransmitters in the CNS. The action of neurotransmitters on the postsynaptic membrane receptor molecules has been likened to a lock and key – recall, though, that because there are different receptor subtypes, neurotransmitters often serve as master keys (in contrast, drugs may activate only one receptor subtype). This analogy highlights the fact that transmitter molecules (i.e., the key) can only affect the postsynaptic membrane if their shape fits into the shape (i.e., the lock) of the receptor molecule.

In addition to this key–lock fit notion, in order to exert excitatory and inhibitory effects the key must be able to turn in the lock. You can think of this process in the same way as your front door key working: the key must fit the lock, but you must turn it to activate the locking mechanism and open the door. If the stem of your key breaks off in your lock then you will not be able to use another key to open the door. This analogy will be important when discussion turns to pharmacological drugs that serve this very purpose: that is, to block postsynaptic receptor molecules to disable neurotransmitters from activating the postsynaptic cell.

Neurotransmitters were discovered in the early 1920s. In one classic experiment, two frogs' hearts were used. One heart was still connected to the vagus nerve (which exerts control over the heart beat) and placed in a saline solution in a chamber; this chamber was connected to a second chamber, which contained a second heart which was not connected to the vagus nerve. Electrical stimulation of the vagus nerve slowed down the first heart, and, crucially, it also slowed down the second heart. This observation led to the conclusion that the vagus nerve released a chemical that travelled through the saline solution to activate the second heart. The Austrian scientist Otto Loewi, who performed this seminal experiment in 1921, christened this chemical 'Vagusstoff' – it is now known by its common name, acetlycholine (see below); he won the Nobel Prize in 1936. Loewi (1953) recounted how the idea of this experiment occurred to him:

> In the night of Easter Saturday, 1921, I awoke, turned on the light, and jotted down a few notes on a tiny slip of paper. Then I fell asleep again. It occurred to me at six o'clock in the morning that during the night I had written down something most important, but I was unable to decipher the scrawl. That Sunday was the most desperate day in my whole scientific life. During the next night, however, I awoke again, at three o'clock, and I remembered what it was. This time I did not take any risk; I got up immediately, went to the laboratory, made the experiment on the frog's heart, described above, and at five o'clock the chemical transmission of nervous impulse was conclusively proved.

What makes a chemical a neurotransmitter? There are many chemicals in the brain that do not serve as neurotransmitters. There are a number of criteria that are used to identify a chemical as a neurotransmitter: (a) the chemical must be produced in the neuron; (b) when a neuron is stimulated, it must release the chemical; (c) when the chemical is released it must act on the postsynaptic receptors to cause an effect; (d) after release, it must be inactivated, by one of several processes (e.g., re-uptake); and (e) when the chemical is experimentally applied to the postsynaptic receptor it should have the same effect as when released by the neuron.

Neurotransmitter release: size matters

Neurotransmitters are complex molecules. One of their important characteristics is their size: some are small, others are large. Small molecules come in several types, but large molecules are called *peptides* (or *neuropeptides* – these are chains of 10 or fewer amino acids, that is, they are short proteins; see chapter 2).

The process of neurotransmitter release (called *exocytosis*) differs for small and large neurotransmitter molecules. At rest, vesicles containing small molecule neurotransmitters lie close to the presynaptic membrane, which is rich in calcium channels. When an action potential reaches the terminal buttons, the voltage-activated calcium channels spring open and Ca^{2+} ions enter the button: this causes the vesicles to fuse with the presynaptic membrane and then to spill their contents into the synaptic cleft.

However, the exocytosis of small molecule neurotransmitters differs from that of large molecule neurotransmitters (neuropeptides) in one important respect: molecule neurotransmitters are typically released in a pulse each time an action potential triggers a momentary influx of Ca^{2+} ions, but large molecule neuropeptide neurotransmitters are typically released gradually in response to increases in the level of intracellular Ca^{2+} ions.

Ionotropic receptors and metabotropic receptors

Let us now deepen our understanding of how receptors work. Neurotransmitter molecules binding to a postsynaptic receptor can have one of two effects: (a) *ionotropic receptors* are receptors associated with neurotransmitter-activated ion channels (as discussed above); (b) *metabotropic receptors* are proteins associated with *signal proteins* and G *proteins*. These two processes are related to the speed and consequences of neurotransmitter activation.

In the case of an ionotropic receptor, once the neurotransmitter has occupied the postsynaptic receptor, the ion channels spring open immediately, and this leads to the classic postsynaptic potential. In the case of metabotropic receptors, however, their actions are slower to develop, longer lasting and more diffuse. In fact, there exist many different types of metabotropic receptors, but each is attached to a signal protein that wends its way back and forth through the postsynaptic membrane. The action of metabotropic receptors is of two kinds: (a) a G protein may move along the membrane and bind at a nearby ion channel and cause an EPSP or IPSP; or (b) it may trigger the synthesis of a *second messenger* (the first messenger is the neurotransmitter itself) – this second messenger moves through the cytoplasm of the cell and, among other actions (e.g., causing metabolic activities), it enters the nucleus of the soma and binds to DNA, which results in gene expression. These two routes of action show how fast-onset and slow-onset neurotransmitter effects work. It is the nature of the receptor subtype rather than the neurotransmitter that is important in determining which effect is observed.

Two important second messengers are *cyclic adenosine monophosphate* (cAMP) and *phosphatidyl inositol* (PI). cAMP interacts with important regulatory enzymes called *protein kinases*, which upon activation stimulate transcription factors in the nucleus of the cell (a process known as *phosphorylation*).

Small molecule neurotransmitters (e.g., serotonin) tend to activate either ionotropic or metabotropic receptors that act directly on ion channels; but large molecule neurotransmitters (i.e., neuropeptides) tend to work via metabotropic receptors producing secondary messengers. Thus, the function of small molecule neurotransmitters appears to be the transmission of rapid, brief excitatory or inhibitory signals; and the function of neuropeptide neurotransmitters appears to be the transmission of slow, diffuse, long-lasting signals.

Neurotransmitter types

Here are detailed the various types of neurotransmitter molecules found in the nervous system. There exist four classes of small molecule neurotransmitters: (a) amino acids; (b) monoamines; (c) soluble gases; and (d) acetylcholine; and one class of large molecule neurotransmitters, *neuropeptides*. Although most neurotransmitters produce either excitation or inhibition, a few can produce either effect depending on the specific subtype of receptor activated.

Amino acids

Most fast-acting receptors are sensitive to amino acids – as discussed in chapter 2, amino acids are the building blocks of proteins. There are four main amino acid neurotransmitters: glutamate, aspartate, glycine and gamma-aminobutyric acid (GABA). The first three amino acids are found in food; GABA is synthesized by a simple modification of glutamate. Glutamate is the most common excitatory neurotransmitter in the mammalian CNS, acting by means of opening ion channels. GABA is the most common inhibitory neurotransmitter, acting by means of closing ion channels. These two neurotransmitters are probably the most important in the central nervous system: they are found throughout the brain and they are responsible for excitatory and inhibitory potentials. They are found in even simple animals, suggesting that they evolved before other neurotransmitters.

Monoamines

Monoamines – which form another class of small molecule neurotransmitters – are synthesized from a single amino acid. They are slightly larger than amino acids, and their actions tend to be longer lasting and more diffuse. These neurotransmitters are mainly found in neurons whose cell bodies are located in the brainstem. The four main monoamine neurotransmitters are dopamine, norepinephrine, epinephrine and serotonin.

Monoamines are divided into two groups: *catecholamines* and *indolamines*. Dopamine, norepinephrine and epinephrine are catecholamines; serotonin (also called 5-hydroxytryptamine, 5-HT) is an indolamine. Neurons that release norepinephrine are called *noradrenergic*; those that release epinephrine, *adrenergic* (epinephrine and norepinephrine are also known as adrenaline and noradrenaline, respectively).

Norepinephrine-releasing cells are concentrated in the *locus ceruleus*, which mediates general arousal. The number of neurons is small but it exerts a widespread influence because its terminals 'bathe' groups of neurons rather than being released at specific synapses.

Dopamine (DA) is involved in emotional and cognitive processes, including the pleasure-regulating areas of the brain; it is widespread in the limbic system, which includes the cingulate gyrus, the hippocampus and the amygdala. Pathologically high levels of dopamine and dopamine receptors have been found in the limbic system of schizophrenics (assessed post-mortem); and drugs used to reduce the symptoms of schizophrenia, such as chlorpromazine and haloperidol, bind to dopamine receptors and block their effects. The drug amphetamine acts by releasing dopamine, and it can exaggerate existing symptoms and has been known to initiate full-blown psychosis; in addition, normal volunteers given amphetamine perform on cognitive tasks in a similar manner to schizophrenic patients (for a discussion of this literature, see chapter 16).

Soluble gases

Another class of small molecule neurotransmitters is soluble gases, especially nitric oxide and carbon monoxide. These gases do not exert effects like the other neurotransmitters: they pass easily through cell membranes because they are soluble in lipids (fats), and once inside the postsynaptic membrane they stimulate the production of a second messenger (these gases are difficult to study because they exist for only a few seconds). Nitric oxide in particular may serve an important role in providing retrograde transmission – that is, providing feedback signals from the postsynaptic membrane to the presynaptic membrane. Unlike other neurotransmitters they are not stored in synaptic vesicles.

Acetylcholine

Acetylcholine (ACh) is another small molecule neurotransmitter. It is the neuro-transmitter at neuromuscular junctions, found at many of the synapses in the ANS, and at synapses in several parts of the CNS. Neurons that release ACh are said to be *cholinergic*.

Neuropeptides

Some 50 or more neuropeptides have been identified. These large molecule neuro-transmitters include the endorphins (*endogenous morphine*), which are opioids (i.e., opium-like molecules). Endorphins were first suspected when it was discovered that a number of opiate drugs (e.g., opium, morphine and heroin) bind to receptors in the brain – it was concluded that there would not be receptors in the brain for substances that the body itself did not produce. It is now known that there exist different types of endorphins and receptor subtypes. Endorphins activate neural systems that produce analgesia and that mediate the experience of pleasure. Neuropeptides are often called neuromodulators – however, not all neuropeptides are neuromodulators.

Unlike other neurotransmitters, neuropeptides are synthesized not near the terminal buttons but in the cell body itself, where the molecular machinery of DNA–RNA is located. Synthesis of a specific neuropeptide begins with the *pre-propeptide gene* in the nucleus and this gene is transcribed into primary RNA for the assembly of this protein. The pre-propeptide is transported to the axonal terminal, where an enzyme converts it into a neuropeptide ready for release and action as a neurotransmitter. Another unique feature of neuropeptides is the relative absence of re-uptake from the synaptic cleft – this fits in well with their putative role as a neuromodulator.

Neuromodulators

Neuromodulators are molecules that need not stimulate the postsynaptic receptor directly; rather they serve to adjust the sensitivity of populations of cells to the excitat-ory and inhibitory signal of fast-onset neurotransmitters. In other words, they seem not to have *direct* effects on excitatory or inhibitory actions; they seem to exert *indirect* effects on the environment of popula-tions of neurons. Populations of neurons may be said to be *bathed* in a neuromodulator. Neuromodulators play an import-ant role in the regulation of psychological functions.

ASK YOURSELF
What roles do genes play in the neuron-to-neuron communication?

▢▢ Psychopharmacology of Disease

With our newly acquired knowledge of the information concerning neurotransmission, let us now turn to the neuronal processes involved in neurodevelopment and in the development of disease processes (for an excellent summary of this complex literature, see Stahl, 2000).

Neurodevelopment

It is suspected that many disorders have a neurodevelopmental basis. There is a long and tortuous route from the stem cells found on the surface of the embryonic neural tube to the fully developed and fully functioning mature brain (i.e., *neurogenesis*). Neurons must migrate to the correct location in the brain and then make functional connections by using supporting (glial) cells as guide-wires; they must be sensitive to neurotropic growth factors; synaptic connections between neurons must be formed (*synaptogenesis*); neurons must be pruned in order for neurotransmission to be most effective; neurons and support cells need to be maintained; and all the highly complex cellular and molecular machinery of neurons must be operating properly. At each stage genetic effects could compromise mental integrity (e.g., in Down's syndrome; Arai et al., 2002).

Any abnormality in the developmental pathway may seriously compromise the integrity of the brain and can form the foundations of neurological and psychiatric disease. Epilepsy and mental retardation are just two classes of disorder that result from neurodevelopment problems; more subtle disorders also result at this stage of development, including the large range of specific learning disorders (e.g., dyslexia). The fetal environment is especially sensitive: exposure to toxins, alcohol, radiation and infection can all compromise the growing fetus (e.g., Pearce, 2003), and there is also evidence that exposure to natural environmental disasters (e.g., earthquakes) can lead to psychiatric problems in later life. These effects could be mediated by a range of factors, especially during the second trimester: infection, malnutrition, stress-induced hormonal influences or physical trauma (for a review, see Koenig, Kirkpatrick & Lee, 2002; Wong & Van Tol, 2003).

As noted by Koenig, Kirkpatrick and Lee (2002), a common mechanism may be a stress response during a restricted period of gestation, which may interact with a specific genetic predisposition – an example of a gene–environment interaction (see chapter 13) – to produce schizophrenia. Results from animals exposed to prenatal stress support the hypothesis that exposure to high glucocorticoid levels and/or other components of the stress response increases this risk. This hypothesis has been supported in psychotic patients whose mothers were exposed to severe flooding during the second trimester (Selten et al., 1997).

Drugs are also important in influencing neuronal plasticity, especially during the development of the nervous system. For example, an allele may lead to the underproduction of an enzyme necessary for growth factors; drugs could be developed to help this process along, by either leading to the greater production of the enzyme (via activation at DNA) or allowing the enzyme to work longer by retarding its degradation. Almost at every level in the cellular and molecular machinery, drugs could be effective.

Apoptosis

It is all too common to see the healthy mature brain degenerate in later life due to a range of pathological cellular factors. Such forms of dementia can result from the death of neurons and the degradation of synapses. Other neural degeneration is the direct result of poisoning by toxins and a lack of oxygen due to stroke. In the case of the dementia, one pathological process is important: *apoptosis*. Apoptosis is the natural process of cell death, necessary to prune useless cells from the developing brain and maintain the effective working of the mature brain. However, in dementia (e.g., Alzheimer's disease), apoptosis is inappropriately triggered, causing the death of healthy and necessary neurons. It is suspected that such degeneration of healthy neurons occurs in a range of psychiatric conditions – this is suggested by the chronic and degenerating nature of many such disorders. For example, there is the phenomenon of 'kindling' in some affective disorders and addictive conditions (Post et al., 1984). This phenomenon refers to the increased sensitivity of the brain to eliciting stimuli over the course of the illness, and is part of the developing pathophysiology of the disease. It is to be hoped that, once the cellular and molecular mechanisms are elucidated, drug therapies can be developed which interfere with these pathological processes either to slow the decline or even to restore healthy brain functioning (Rivas-Vazquez et al., 2004).

It may be possible by understanding the normal development of the brain to gain insights into the pathological processes underlying neurodegeneration – in the same way that the pathological processes of cancer are understood by understanding the mechanisms of normal cell growth. For example, the neurotropic factors so essential in the developing brain to make neural connections may be encouraged in the degenerating brain: this may restore to good health neurons that are starting to decay. There was a long-held dogma in neuroscience that neurons could not regenerate in the mature CNS (i.e., neurogenesis), but this belief is being challenged by research that suggests the growth of neurons may be possible in the mammalian brain (Zhao et al., 2003). Thus, there is a vital link between neurodevelopmental science and neurodegenerative science: in a sense, they are the opposite sides of the same coin (chapter 11 explores how stem cells are now used for neural repair in the mature brain).

In the context of drug research, genes that lead to pathological cellular processes are being hunted; once identified, either (a) their activation can be modulated; or (b) their products (e.g., enzymes) can be inactivated. In much the same way, it should also be possible to develop drugs that either (a) activate genes that lead to normal cellular functioning; or (b) enhance the effects of their gene products.

Toxic effects of neurotransmitter excitation: glutamate

Another way in which neurons and neural connections may become impaired is by the action of neurotransmitters. Glutamate is the principal excitatory neurotransmitter in the brain. The level of glutamate in the synapse can have a profound effect on post-synaptic dendrites.

Glutamate activates ion channels that lead to the postsynaptic membrane taking in calcium. An excess of glutamate at the postsynaptic receptor leads to too much calcium being absorbed, and this can result in excitatory symptoms, such as panic, seizures, mania and even psychosis. It is known that the rate and quantity of neurotransmitters have effects upon cellular processes above and beyond merely causing an action potential. In particular, too much calcium triggers the production of intracellular enzymes and this can lead to the production of toxic *free radicals*: these radicals roam around the cell destroying its components (especially dendrites). Given enough time, this riot of free radicals triggers the excitotoxic process of apoptosis (cell death). By this route, repeated episodes

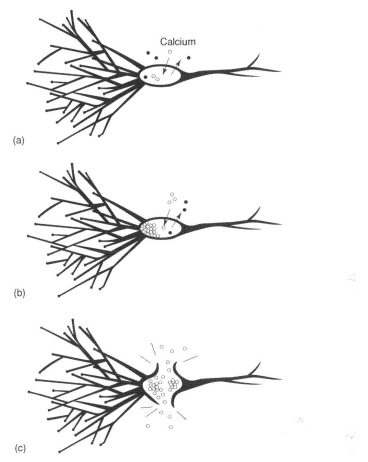

Figure 4.5 Glutamate overexcitation effects. Neuronal excitability is regulated by calcium ions, which are continuously entering and leaving the neurons through ion channels. The normal process of calcium movement is shown in (a). However, if the ion channels are opened too frequently by excitation by glutamate, this can start to damage the neuron (b); and with hyperexcitation of the neuron, the influx of calcium ions can destroy the neuron, which then degenerates (c) – this is the process of excitotoxicity.

of overexcitatory processing (e.g., in mania) can lead to damaging chronicity (see figure 4.5).

Long-term cognitive impairments have been reported in bipolar patients (who experience swings of major depression and mania; see chapter 14), consisting of a disruption of verbal learning, executive functioning (involving higher-level planning) and motor coordination; the effect of number of episodes was shown by the negative correlation with executive functioning: the more episodes, the poorer the executive functions (Zubieta et al., 2001).

> **ASK YOURSELF**
> What type of interventions could be used to retard or halt neurodegenerative processes?

Drugs

Drugs are chemical substances that have the capacity to alter the action of neurons; they usually work by influencing the action of neurotransmitters. One widely accepted definition of a drug is 'an exogenous chemical not necessary for normal cellular functioning that significantly alters the functions of certain cells of the body when taken in relatively low doses' (Carlson, 1998, p. 87). This definition lays stress on the chemical being 'exogenous' (i.e., produced outside the body) – but does not include everyday nutrients, such as proteins, fats and minerals. A drug need not be synthetic (i.e., manufactured), as many drugs are found naturally in nature (e.g., opium in poppies). Also, a low dose must be sufficient for a biological effect to be observed – large quantities of almost any substance would affect the nervous system.

Drugs have effects because there are receptor molecules on neurons that are sensitive to the chemical structure of the drug. This observation suggests that drugs must resemble naturally occurring endogenous neurotransmitters. For example, the brain makes its own morphine (i.e., beta endorphin) and its own marijuana (i.e., anandamide); it may also make its own antidepressants, its own anxiolytics and its own hallucinogens. Drug effects are usually known before the ligand (neurotransmitter) and receptors have been identified. For example, the effects of morphine were known long before the discovery of beta endorphin; marijuana before the discovery of cannabinoid receptors and anandamide; the benzodiazepines diazepam (Valium) and alprazolam (Xanax) before the discovery of benzodiazepine receptors; and the antidepressants amitriptyline (Elavil) and fluoxetine (Prozac) before the discovery of the serotonin transporter site. In fact, the psychoactive properties of drugs were known long before it was even known that there were chemicals in the brain.

Agonists and antagonists

Drugs have a number of distinctive effects. *Agonists* are drugs that enhance a neurotransmitter's activity; *antagonists* are drugs that impair a neurotransmitter's activity. Drugs exert their effects in a variety of ways. For example, many drugs operate by increasing or decreasing the quantity of neurotransmitter available. Some agonists work by blocking the *re-uptake* of neurotransmitter from the synaptic cleft, making available more neurotransmitter to activate the postsynaptic neuron; other agonists work by increasing the availability of a *precursor*, which is an enzyme required for the neurotransmitter's chemical manufacture in the neuron. Antagonist drugs work by having the opposite effects to agonist drugs: by increasing re-uptake; by increasing clean-up enzymes; and by decreasing precursors that assemble the neurotransmitter. Other drugs work directly on the postsynaptic receptor molecules: agonists mimic the action of the neurotransmitter; antagonists occupy the receptor molecules and thereby prevent neurotransmitters from binding with the receptor and activating the neuron.

Now let us look more closely at the effects of drugs on neurotransmission.

All neurotransmitters stimulate receptors, leading either to excitatory or inhibitory postsynaptic potentials: these are thus *agonists*. In contrast, drugs exert a range of effects,

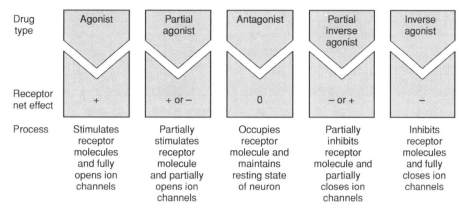

Drug type	Agonist	Partial agonist	Antagonist	Partial inverse agonist	Inverse agonist
Receptor net effect	+	+ or −	0	− or +	−
Process	Stimulates receptor molecules and fully opens ion channels	Partially stimulates receptor molecule and partially opens ion channels	Occupies receptor molecule and maintains resting state of neuron	Partially inhibits receptor molecule and partially closes ion channels	Inhibits receptor molecules and fully closes ion channels

Figure 4.6 The spectrum of agonists and antagonists. Drugs that facilitate receptor molecule excitability are *agonists* (as are naturally occurring neurotransmitters) and drugs that inhibit them are *antagonists*. Agonists fully open the ion channel to facilitate neurotransmission, while antagonists occupy the receptor molecule and block the effects of neurotransmitters, thus retaining the resting state of the neuron. Partial agonists activate the receptor molecule, but their *net* effect may be either facilitatory or inhibitory: if they block the action of naturally occurring neurotransmitter, then their net effect may be inhibitory, but if they replace the action of an abnormally low level of neurotransmitter, then their net effect would be facilitatory (the same is true of partial inverse agonists). Inverse agonists actively inhibit the excitability of the neuron by blocking ion channels: unlike antagonists, they do not merely bind to and block receptor molecules. Partial inverse agonists partly inhibit the neuron by closing ion channels.

Inverse agonists are the opposite of agonists, not antagonists – antagonists are blockers and can block any of the other effects in the spectrum. To use the example of anxiety: an agonist may induce anxiety; an inverse agonist would reduce anxiety – a partial agonist would induce *some* anxiety; a partial inverse agonist would reduce *some* anxiety – but an antagonist would neither increase nor decrease anxiety by itself: it can only block the effects of full/partial agonists and inverse agonists.

sometimes called a *spectrum* of effects (figure 4.6). Some drugs stimulate receptors in the same manner as natural neurotransmitters (i.e., the drug molecule binds to the receptor): they are thus *agonists*. Other drugs block the actions of a natural neurotransmitter, by occupying the receptor site and stopping neurotransmitter molecules from activating the receptor; they are thus *antagonists*. An important point is that antagonists only have an effect in the presence of an agonist – that is, they have no intrinsic action of their own. There are also partial agonists and antagonists. Full agonists are usually the natural neurotransmitters themselves.

A full agonist fully activates the cell; a partial agonist only partially activates the cell. But a complication to this neat scheme is that a partial agonist can act either as a net agonist or as a net antagonist depending on the amount of naturally occurring neurotransmitter (full agonist) in the system. With the absence of a full neurotransmitter agonist, a partial agonist will be a net agonist: it excites the postsynaptic membrane beyond the naturally existing (low) level. However, when a full neurotransmitter agonist is present,

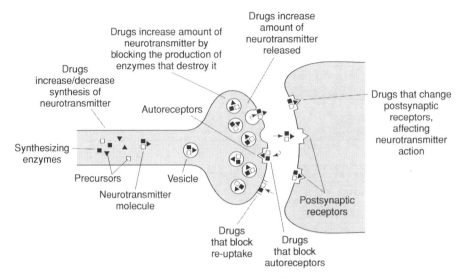

Figure 4.7 Mechanisms by which drugs affect the rate of neurotransmission.

then the same partial agonist becomes a net antagonist: as it occupies the receptors, it prevents the full agonist effects of the natural neurotransmitter. Thus a partial agonist can both boost and block neurotransmitter activity, depending on levels of the natural neurotransmitter already in the system. These effects are important in understanding why drugs have different effects in different people – indeed, it helps us to understand the paradoxical effects of some agonists (e.g., amphetamine).

There is a class of drugs that have the opposite effect of agonists, called *inverse agonists*. These drugs bind to the receptor in a way that has the opposite effects of an agonist: it causes the receptor to close the ion channel. The difference between an antagonist (which does not have any effect on its own) and an inverse agonist (which does have an effect) is important. The inverse agonist itself is blocked by an antagonist. The spectrum of drug effects is mediated via a variety of mechanisms, summarized in figure 4.7.

Drugs and genes

When considering the possible mechanisms of drug effects, it is helpful to extend thinking beyond agonist/antagonist effects on nerve conductance and to consider how the drug may influence the complex biochemical and molecular machinery within the neuron's nucleus. However, most currently available psychotropic drugs influence the processes that control chemical neurotransmission at the level of the neurotransmitter (e.g., blocking re-uptake) or of their enzymes (e.g., preventing or facilitating the production of receptors). With knowledge gleaned from the Human Genome Project, the target for research is increasingly turning to the development of drugs that impact on the different components of the biochemical cascade involved in the expression of presynaptic and postsynaptic genes. To know how to turn on and off specific genes by drugs, a well-developed pharmacogenetics is required that allows us to map genomic differences onto individual differences in reactions to different drugs (see below).

Drugs and gene expression

How do drugs influence gene expression? Chapter 2 noted that the majority of genes have two separate regions: a coding region and a regulatory region. The coding region provides the template for RNA, and DNA is transcribed into RNA with the help of the enzyme RNA polymerase. The regulatory region of the gene activates RNA polymerase, thus leading to the transcription of the gene into polypeptides and proteins.

There exist a number of immediate early genes (known as *early response genes*), such as cJun and cFos, that are the first to be transcribed directly following binding by the neurotransmitter: these genes are expressed within 15 minutes of being activated – however, their effects are short-lived, lasting for about 20 minutes to 1 hour. The effect of these early-onset genes is to activate *late-onset genes*. These late-onset genes are the ultimate regulators of the postsynaptic neuron: their gene products comprise the important proteins that constitute the cell (i.e., enzymes, receptors, transcription factors, growth factors, structural proteins). The precise nature of gene expression is influenced by a number of factors: (a) the specific neurotransmitter; (b) frequency of postsynaptic binding; and (c) the combined effects (additive or interactive/allosteric) of several neurotransmitters. It is possible to measure these gene products, for example in measuring the brain regions activated by a performance task (see chapter 10).

Neurotransmitters affect gene expression, which, in turn, affects the regulation of receptor numbers. By this route, the effects of the neurotransmitter come full circle: neurotransmitter action to gene expression to receptor numbers to neurotransmitter action. The biochemical environment of the neuron can be finely balanced – in psychiatric conditions and abuse of drugs, this fine balance is disturbed. The process that leads to a reduction in the number of receptors is known as *down-regulation* (or desensitization); the process that leads to an increase in the number of receptors is known as *up-regulation* (or sensitization) (see figure 4.8). It is obvious that the *number* of receptors on both the presynaptic and postsynaptic membrane have a profound effect on neurotransmission.

Sometimes the overproduction of receptors leads to disease. For example, if receptors are blocked by a drug for a certain period of time, up-regulation may occur. Such an outcome is seen in *tardive dyskinesia*, which is a motor disorder seen in patients who have been maintained on dopamine-blocking antipsychotic drugs (Llorca et al., 2002). With abuse of psychostimulants (e.g., cocaine), there may be down-regulation (i.e., fewer receptors), resulting in adverse effects upon withdrawal from the drug – one of the maintaining factors of addiction is the urge to take the drug to alleviate these unpleasant withdrawal symptoms. 'Kicking the habit' requires a period of abstinence during which time receptors up-regulate to functional levels. The genetic component to addiction may well consist in the ease with which receptors down-regulate and up-regulate: a system that rapidly down- or up-regulates in response to a drug may be especially vulnerable to addiction (Turchan et al., 1999).

ASK YOURSELF
How does the action of drugs help us identify (unknown) endogenous neurotransmitters?

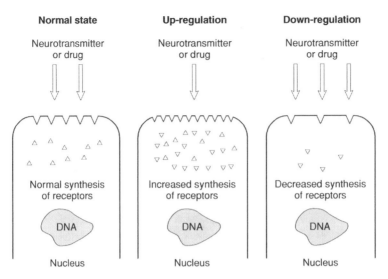

Figure 4.8 Up-regulation and down-regulation. Intracellular enzymes activated by slow-action naturally occurring neurotransmitters (ligands) and drugs can stimulate DNA transcription of factors leading to the increase in synthesis of receptors: this is *up-regulation*. A similar process can lead to the decrease in receptor synthesis: this is *down-regulation*. These processes may be important in the action of antidepressants (see chapter 14). This is one way genetic effects are found in neurotransmitter functioning.

Addiction

By virtue of the fact that the mind is the product of the brain, it is possible to alter the mind – the way we think, feel and act – by interfering directly with neurotransmission: by ingesting psychoactive drugs. Drugs can have positive reinforcing properties: they produce a pleasurable state. In addition, they can have negative reinforcing properties: they reduce negative emotions. Both of these mechanisms have the potential to lead to a state of dependence, commonly known as 'addiction'.

Pharmacology of addiction (dependence)

Often the stimulation of receptors leads to them being down-regulated – that is, the number of receptors diminishes. This is a process of homeostasis, designed to maintain a consistent level of stimulation. The brain assumes that the greater receptor occupancy, due to the drug, is a result of changes to the internal processes of the brain and sensibly makes fine adjustments. All is well at this point – but rarely is all well in the long term when receptors are artificially stimulated, and thereby modified in their regulation of the internal environment: as the brain is changed then so too is the mind.

These changes are most clearly seen when the drug is no longer taken; this produces a marked disturbance in the neurotransmission system and the brain takes action to remedy this imbalance – but this takes time. In the meantime the individual is in a deficient chemical state. The organism has already learned that taking the drug has psychoactive effects; therefore, it 'knows' (but not necessarily consciously) that taking the drug again removes this negative state. A process is thus set in train in which the individual behaves in a way to get and consume the drug and this, in turn, reinforces (i.e., strengthens) the drug-taking behaviour. Before long this drug-getting/taking behaviour may be the only thing important in the person's life: they are 'addicted'. Craving and motivation to get the drug are the main signs of addiction. This is drug 'dependence': the efficient running of the brain is dependent on administration of the drug.

It is known that certain chemical substances, such as nicotine, alcohol and cocaine, have psychological effects because there are receptors in the brain that are sensitive (i.e., can be excited or inhibited) to them. Many drugs subvert the normal cycle of motivation–behaviour–satisfaction. Indeed, rats literally work themselves to death in order to self-administer electrical stimulation to brain circuits activated by cocaine and other drugs (see chapter 11). Motivational brain processes have developed by Darwinian processes to lead to behaviours that enhance the individual's fitness. Drugs lead to direct central stimulation, cutting out of the cycle the normal processes of behaviour and satisfaction. In consequence, drug addiction is usually associated with a loss of day-to-day motivation, which has significant occupational, domestic, academic and social pernicious effects.

Addiction vs. dependence

What is called 'addiction' is often, strictly speaking, 'dependence' (necessitating continued administration of the drug(s) to prevent the appearance of the withdrawal syndrome). Addiction proper requires a number of necessary conditions: repetitive behaviours that (a) do not serve a normal physiological or psychological need, and (b) are not constrained by conventional social norms. Life becomes dominated by thoughts and actions directed towards getting and taking the drug – if the drug is not available then adverse psychological states are experienced, leading to craving. In addition to these necessary conditions, there are a number of sufficient conditions: (a) self- or other-injurious outcomes (e.g., smoking and drinking); (2) the desire on the part of the addict to reduce or stop the behaviour; and (3) an inability to reduce or stop the action, even though the individual has this desire. In addiction there is a high incidence of relapse following treatment (Stahl, 2000). More loosely, 'abuse' is a form of self-administration of any drug in a culturally disapproved manner that causes adverse consequences. From a pharmacological viewpoint, 'dependence' is the correct term to use; if this view is broadened to include the adverse effects of dependence on behaviour, then 'addiction' captures the psychological and social consequences of dependence.

Psychopharmacology

A number of processes are seen in chemical dependence.

1. *Tolerance*: With repeated administration, a given dose of a drug produces a decreased effect, or, conversely, increasingly larger doses must be administered to obtain the effects observed with the original use.

2. *Cross-tolerance and cross-dependence*: This is the ability of one drug to suppress the effects produced by another drug and to maintain the physically dependent state. This process is responsible for the poly drug use seen in many dependent individuals.

3. *Withdrawal*: Physiological and psychological reactions are seen in response to the abrupt cessation of a dependence-producing drug; and the unpleasant effects serve as a form of aversive reinforcement for the drug-taking behaviour (their elimination is a powerful form of negative reinforcement).

4. *Relapse*: This is the reoccurrence of the dependent drug-taking behaviour following a cessation programme.

5. *Rebound*: This is the exaggerated expression of the original condition (e.g., medical or psychological problem) sometimes experienced by patients after cessation of an effective treatment – it is not the same as withdrawal, and is mediated by different mechanisms. For this reason patients are advised to reduce their dose gradually when coming off medication rather than stopping suddenly.

There are individual differences in these processes: some people seem more susceptible to dependence than others; and this is probably due to the ease with which neuroadaptation to the chemical substance takes place – it is also a result of the dose and frequency of use, which might be influenced by other factors (e.g., social expectation).

Let us now look at the pharmacological action of some of the commonly abused drugs.

Stimulants: cocaine and amphetamine

Cocaine

Cocaine is an anaesthetic and a potent inhibitor of monoamine transporters that re-uptake molecules from the synaptic cleft; it thus serves as an agonist, influencing especially dopamine, but also norepinephrine and 5-HT. It produces a state of euphoria, loss of appetite and insomnia. It is a highly addictive drug because: (a) it leads to pleasurable experience; and (b) its repeated use down-regulates the normal levels of dopamine and norepinephrine. At high doses a range of unpleasant effects are observed: restlessness, emotional instability, tremor, anxiety, panic, paranoia and hallucinations.[4]

Repeated administration of cocaine may produce complex adaptations of the dopamine system, including tolerance or reverse tolerance (sensitization). Cocaine psychosis is virtually indistinguishable from paranoid schizophrenia (see chapter 16), which is interesting given that the mesolimbic dopamine system has been implicated in both drug dependence and schizophrenia (see chapter 16) – treatment with antipsychotics, which block postsynaptic dopamine D_2 receptors, relieves the symptoms of cocaine intoxication, supporting this connection with schizophrenia.

Amphetamine

Amphetamines also act as agonists at both dopamine and norepinephrine sites, leading to the increase in chemical release from the presynaptic neurons. Due to its effects of norepinephrine, as well as dopamine, amphetamine increases alertness and arousal (hence its name, 'speed'). The clinical effects of amphetamine are similar to those of cocaine, although the euphoria is less intense but may last longer. Signs of intoxication, toxicity, overdose, sensitization and acute paranoid psychosis, and withdrawal symptoms, are similar to those of cocaine.

Nicotine

Nicotine acts directly on nicotinic cholinergic (acetylcholine) receptors. The reinforcing actions of nicotine are very similar to those of cocaine and amphetamine, since dopaminergic cells in the mesolimbic pathway receive direct nicotinic cholinergic input: this mediates the reward experienced by smokers, including elevation of mood, enhancement of cognition and decrease of appetite. However, the pharmacological and behavioural actions of nicotine appear to be much more subtle than those of cocaine. Cocaine blocks the dopamine transporter and causes a flood of dopamine to act on the postsynaptic dopamine receptor; in contrast, nicotine shuts down the nicotinic receptor shortly after binding to it (with this shut-down receptor, neither nicotine nor acetylcholine can stimulate the nicotinic receptor). Thus, dopaminergic stimulation of mesolimbic dopamine receptors stops for a short period: it is this turning off of pleasure-inducing dopamine that leads to the repetitive behaviour of inhaling. Unlike cocaine, which gives a single immediate 'rush' of euphoria, etc., nicotine leads to multiple 'mini-rushes'.

The profound dependence and withdrawal of nicotine may, in part, be due to the up-regulation of cholinergic receptors: when nicotine is no longer used, these receptors are in a deficit state, leading to unpleasant withdrawal effects.

Hallucinogens

Hallucinogens produce a state of intoxication known as a 'trip'; this is associated with changes in sensory experiences, including visual illusions and hallucinations and enhanced awareness of external stimuli, as well as enhanced awareness of internal thoughts and stimuli. Hallucinations are produced with a clear level of consciousness and a lack of confusion.

The Oxford University psychologist Gordon Claridge reported his experience of LSD in the 1960s. He noted that as long as he sat perfectly still the world appeared to remain the same size; but once he stood up he had the impression that he was up against the ceiling, very tall, while his assistant become very small; and the music he was listening to became too painful to hear and very frightening (see Greenfield, 2001).

Hallucinogens are *psychedelic* and *psychotomimetic*. 'Psychedelic' is used for the subjective experience, the mind-altered state, which includes a feeling of being in unison with the cosmos, often including a spiritual/religious experience. It was thought by some people that this drug provides the keys to 'the doors of perception' – it has clearly been the inspiration of many artistic and literary works (the Beatles' 'Lucy in the Sky with Diamonds' (LSD) being the most famous song with an explicit reference). Certainly, hallucinogen intoxication includes some interesting perceptual aberrations: visual 'trails' in which the image smears into streaks as it moves across a trail; the subjective slowing of time; the sense that colours are heard and sounds are seen; and intensification of sound perception. The fear of 'going mad', impaired judgement, anxiety, nausea, racing heart (i.e., tachycardia), increased blood pressure and raised temperature are some of the less desirable effects.

It may be the doors to perception, but the same key opens doors to less pleasant rooms: it is 'psychotomimetic', which refers to its ability to produce a state that mimics psychosis – however, the resemblance between a 'trip' and psychosis is superficial: stimulants such as cocaine and amphetamine mimic psychosis much better (Stahl, 2000). Also, some 'trips' can be bad, involving terrifying scenes – these trips can occur spontaneously some time after cessation of the drug, suggesting that the brain has undergone profound changes.

Common hallucinogens include two major classes of agents: the classic hallucinogens that resemble 5-HT, and include LSD (*d*-lysergic acid diethylamide), while the second class resemble norepinephrine and dopamine, are related to amphetamine and include mescaline. More recently, 'designer drugs' have been developed, such as MDMA (3,4-methylenedioxymethamphetamine): these drugs produce subjective states referred to as 'ecstasy', hence the common name of MDMA. The effects of MDMA include euphoria, disorientation, confusion, enhanced sociability and a sense of increased empathy and personal insight. MDMA seems to be a powerful releaser of 5-HT and it and several drugs structurally related to it may even destroy 5-HT axon terminals.

Phencyclidine

Phencyclidine (PCP) produces a unique psychotomimetic hallucinatory experience. It is structurally related to ketamine, which is still used as an anaesthetic, which causes mild hallucinatory experiences – it is one of the popular 'club drugs', sometimes called 'Special K'. High doses can cause catatonia, hallucinations, delusions, paranoia, disorientation and a lack of judgement. PCP acts to decrease the flux of calcium into the neuron by blocking ion channels.

Marijuana and endocannabinoids

Various forms of cannabis are ingested in order to deliver their psychoactive substances, cannabinoids. These cannabis substances interact with the brain's own cannabinoid receptors to trigger dopamine release from the mesolimbic dopamine system. There are two known cannabinoid receptors: the CB1 receptors may mediate not just marijuana's reinforcing properties but also those of alcohol (the CB2 receptors are found in the immune system). There is also an endogenous cannabinoid system (the brain's own marijuana) capable of activating these cannabinoid receptors functionally.

Marijuana has both stimulant and sedative properties; in usual intoxicating doses it produces a sense of well-being, relaxation and friendliness, loss of temporal awareness, slowing of thought processes, impairment of short-term memory and a feeling of achieving special insights. At high doses it induces panic, toxic delirium and, rarely, psychosis – increasingly, marijuana use is seen as one of the major challenges facing psychiatric services: a disproportionately high number of young schizophrenia patients abuse marijuana (see chapter 16), and given its ability to affect the mesolimbic dopamine system – the same system that is involved in the acute symptoms of schizophrenia – this association is unsurprising.

These acute effects can be serious; but more subtle long-term effects are seen that can lead to a significant impairment in the normal personal and social behaviours that lead to quality of life. Long-term use leads to *amotivational syndrome*, characterized by the emergence of decreased drive and ambition (nothing seems to really matter any more), and this is associated with socially and occupationally impairing syndromes, including shortened attention span, poor judgement, easy distractibility, impaired communication skills, introversion and diminished interpersonal skills. There may also be a loss of insight and feelings of depersonalization. What is happening in this syndrome is that the taking of the drug and its effects on neurotransmission substitute for the usual circle of motivation–behaviour–pleasure–motivation. Marijuana short-circuits this chain of neuropsychological events.

Whether marijuana leads to physiological dependence is still debated. In experimental animals cannabinoid antagonists lead to withdrawal, indicating that not only tolerance, which has been demonstrated, but dependence develops. In reality, most long-term users have difficulty stopping using marijuana, if only for 'psychological' reasons: they now have to face the world with a clear head.

Opiates

Opiates act on a variety of receptors. The brain makes its own endogenous opiate-like substances (i.e., endorphins and enkephalins). Exogenous opiates exist in the form of painkillers, such as codeine and morphine, or drugs of abuse such as heroin. Such drugs produce an intense euphoria, sometimes called a 'rush', followed by a sense of tranquillity. As an opiate antagonist, naloxone reverses the acute effects of opiates.

Chronic use of opiates leads to tolerance and dependence. Adaptation of opiate receptors occurs readily after chronic opiate administration; people need to take a higher dose to achieve the same degree of pain relief or euphoria. Withdrawal consists of a feeling of dysphoria, craving for another dose of the opiate, irritability, and signs of autonomic hyperactivity, such as tachycardia, tremor and sweating. Naloxone can produce these withdrawal symptoms in dependent people.

Alcohol

One of the most popular drugs of use and abuse, alcohol, affects a wide range of neurotransmitter systems. Alcohol seems to act not only by enhancing inhibitory neurotransmission at $GABA_A$ receptors, but also by reducing excitatory neurotransmission at the NMDA subtype of glutamate receptors (see chapter 7). Thus, alcohol enhances inhibition and reduces excitation: this explains its CNS depressant effects.

Its reinforcing effects are mediated by the effects that its changes in GABA and glutamate have on dopamine release in the mesolimbic dopamine pathway. Also, it seems to release both opiates and cannabinoids in the reward system: blocking cannabinoid receptors in animals reduces craving for alcohol in alcohol-dependent animals; and blocking opiate receptors with naltrexone in alcohol-dependent animals decreases craving and thereby increases abstinence rates – this opiate blockade takes the pleasure out of drinking (naltrexone is used in the early stages of abstinence).

Mesolimbic dopamine pathway and reward

The final common pathway of reinforcement and reward in the brain is hypothesized to be the mesolimbic dopamine pathway – this is sometime called the 'pleasure centre'. There are many natural ways to trigger mesolimbic dopamine neurons to release dopamine, ranging from intellectual accomplishments to sexual orgasm. There are many naturally occurring chemicals that activate this pathway: morphine/heroin (related to brain endorphins) to the brain's own marijuana (related to brain anandamide), to the brain's own nicotine (related to brain acetylcholine), to the brain's own cocaine and amphetamine (related to brain dopamine).

Because there appears to be an optimal range in which dopamine receptor stimulation by the mesolimbic dopamine system is reinforcing, the risk of becoming a substance of abuse may depend on the number of receptors a person possesses. With only a relatively small number of receptors, the initial taking of the drug may not cause much of an effect; but the drug becomes more and more rewarding as the dose increases. In contrast, in people with many receptors, the taking of the drug is aversive and they will shy away from taking it again. One might postulate that, in those with few substance receptors, their own internal reward system is not working too well in the first place: this might predispose them to keep trying drugs as a means of compensating for their own naturally decreased activation of reward circuits. In fact, in studies with alcoholics, cocaine abusers and amphetamine users, it has been shown that a weak initial response to a drug predicts a high risk for ultimate use, whereas a strong initial response predicts a low risk (Stahl, 2000).

> **ASK YOURSELF**
> How could we assess whether we are dependent and/or addicted to a drug?

Conclusion

This chapter has shown that knowledge of the neuron and neurotransmission is fundamental to an understanding of biological psychology in general and to clinical disorders in particular – many other applications are presented throughout this book. However, it should be borne in mind that biological *psychology* is concerned not only with the structure and mechanism of neurons (i.e., neurobiology) but with their *function*: how they mediate psychological processes, such as memory and learning, and how disruptions in basic cellular mechanisms exert profound influences upon these processes. As is emphasized throughout this book, in biological psychology it is necessary to keep one eye on the hardware component and the other eye on the software component: then, when these two images combine, an integrated biological psychology is achieved – a true understanding that avoids the pitfalls of a brainless mind and mindless brain.

Learning Questions

1. What functions are carried out by each part of a typical neuron?
2. Is the nerve signal electrical or chemical in nature, or some combination of the two?
3. Why are there so many different types of neurotransmitters?
4. In what ways do neurotransmitters influence postsynaptic neurons?
5. Why do drugs have the power to influence neuronal communication and how can this influence result in drug dependence/addiction?

NOTES

1   Crick is not saying that by knowing the functioning of an individual neuron we know the mind; rather, he is saying that the thing called 'the mind' is the product of the coordinated actions of millions of individual neurons, formed into functional systems. Crick's point is that, in accordance with reduction, if we want to understand the whole (i.e., the mind), we should first understand the parts (e.g., neural processes).

2   Chemicals are molecular compounds comprised of several elements. There are 92 elements in Nature (more can be constructed in the laboratory; the *periodic table* lists each of these elements). Every element is composed of atoms, and cannot be reduced to a more fundamental element; in contrast, a *compound* (as its name indicates) can be divided into smaller pieces (i.e., elements). Before the compound is finally broken down into elements, it is called a molecule. For example, a molecule of water is composed of two atoms of hydrogen and one atom of oxygen – hence H_2O. A molecule is thus the smallest piece of a compound that retains the properties of the compound. The nature of the chemical bonds in the DNA nucleotides and neurotransmitters is described in Kalat (1998).

3   Atoms are composed of protons, which have a positive charge, and neutrons, which have a neutral charge – these form the nucleus of the atom; electrons, which have a negative charge, orbit the nucleus. The difference between one element and another is their number of protons (this gives the *atomic number* of the element). When there is a difference between the number of protons and electrons, an electrical charge (potential) is generated. Ions are atoms with an electrical potential: positively charged ions are called *cations* (indicated +), and negatively charged atoms, *anions* (indicated −). Where protons and electrons equal each other, then there is no electrical charge and the element is not an ion.

4   It is interesting to note that Sigmund Freud, the founder of psychoanalysis, was dependent on cocaine for many years; it can only be guessed what influence this drug-induced state had on the formulation of his psychological theories: perhaps it led to a highly creative, optimistic and productive working life, but also to a loosening of associative thought (the very hallmark of the interpretation of dreams: the 'royal road to the unconscious').

FURTHER READING

Carlson, N. R. (2000). *Physiology of Behaviour*. London: Allyn & Bacon.

Kandel, E. R. (2000). *Principles of Neural Science*. London: McGraw-Hill.

Stahl, S. M. (2000). *Essential Psychopharmacology*. Cambridge: Cambridge University Press.

Sensory and Motor Systems

In common with all living creatures, our survival and reproductive success are dependent on acquiring accurate information about the external world and organizing appropriate responses (a) to reduce threat (e.g., fleeing from a predator), and (b) to capitalize upon available opportunities (e.g., act as predator to secure food, or find a mate). Sensory and motor systems serve as the proximate mechanisms by which all animals achieve these evolutionary goals.

Now, at first glance, it may seem that sensory systems are purely physiological and process stimuli from the external world in a straightforward way: we see a tree as it *actually* looks; we smell and touch its branches as they *actually* are; and we hear the sound of it falling as it *actually* sounds. This view of perception is, alas, wrong: seeing is more than sensing. Sensory and motor systems entail a high degree of *psychological* organization, processing and interpretation (i.e., *computation*, referring to the active construction of perception from the basic material of sensory stimuli – according to the *computational approach*, sensory stimuli themselves are inadequate for perception: they require interpretation and inference). To illustrate this point, it is possible to show, in non-visually impaired people, that blindness occurs to certain features of the visual environment when there is a discrepancy between the *actual* visual scene and the brain's *interpretation* of the visual scene (Bonneh, Cooperman & Sagi, 2001). Throughout this chapter examples of the importance of psychological interpretation are given.

The term *psychological* is used to refer to various computational processes: registration of stimuli, encoding, analysis, inferences and, finally, the organization of motor responses. The term *physical* is used to refer to the nature of the environmental information hitting our senses (light waves, air pressure, etc.). The brain has evolved to process stimuli in order to achieve a good *correspondence* between *physical* inputs and the *psychological* states that lead to the subjective perception of colour, sound, taste, etc. This good (but far from perfect) correspondence is nothing more, of course, than the result of natural selection: those organisms which had relatively poor *physical–psychological correspondence* failed to survive and reproduce: you and I are the lucky ones in this sensorimotor battle for survival.

At the outset, it is important to recognize that the science of sensory and motor systems is rather complex. To help our understanding, these various systems are presented in some detail but, it is to be hoped, in a way that does not allow the processes of the systems to detract from their important psychological functions. *Understanding* the psychological functions of systems should be helped, not hindered, by understanding their physiological processes. Along the way, it may be possible to understand some artistic mysteries, such as Mona Lisa's enigmatic smile.

The Senses

Sensory systems comprise vision, hearing, smell and taste; the somatosenses comprise a collection of systems concerned with senses in the body – the focus is on the somatosenses of touch and nociception (experienced as pain). Each system is responsible for: (a) detecting physical events in the world; (b) processing this information as it is transmitted to the brain; and (c) the psychological construction (computation) of perceptual *experience*.

Sometimes a distinction is made between 'sensory systems', which *detect* physical events, and 'perceptual systems', which *interpret* these events. This distinction is largely for convenience, and no clear-cut separation exists between detection and interpretation (e.g., interpretation can influence detection – this 'top-down' influence is seen in the context of pain).

The initial stage of sensing is done by *sensory receptors*. The physical events that carry information to these sensory receptors are light (vision), pressure waves (hearing), mechanical pressure (touch) and chemicals (taste and smell). These receptors reduce to: (a) *chemoreceptors*, sensitive to chemicals (taste and smell; and some specialized skin receptors); (b) *mechanoreceptors*, sensitive to mechanical events (touch and hearing); and (c) *photoreceptors*, sensitive to light (vision). The first stage of processing is common to all sensory systems: the sensory receptor performs a translation of physical events into electrical signals that the brain can interpret: this is the process of *sensory transduction*.

It is usually said, with justification, that vision is the most important of all the senses – it is probably the one we would least prefer to lose and it is involved in a large number of psychological functions. For these reasons it is the sensory system that is usually discussed first; only then are the other systems presented, often in considerably less detail.

As the most detailed – more is known about vision than any other – this sense is perhaps the most difficult system to understand. For this reason, and because it shares many features with the other sensory systems, vision is presented last, not first. Although this is not a typical decision in the organization of a chapter on the sensory system, it is hoped that we will be in a better position to understand this system once the basic properties of the other systems have been summarized.

ASK YOURSELF
In terms of everyday experience, how do the senses work together?

Somatosenses: Tactile (Touch and Pain)

The somatic sensory system is sensitive to stimuli in the tissue and organs of the body. There are several different somatosenses. For example, *kinaesthesia* provides information about the position of the body and has its receptors in joints, tendons and muscles – stretch receptors in skeletal muscles detect changes in muscle length; stretch receptors in tendons measure the force exerted by muscles; and receptors within joints between bones are sensitive to the magnitude and direction of limb movements. Another example concerns receptors in and around organs, leading to such sensations as stomach ache. In this section the tactile sense is described, which is concerned with the perception of the location, size and texture of mechanical objects that come into contact with the skin. The cutaneous (skin) senses include several submodalities, serving different functions.

The evolutionary function of the tactile sense is to enable the animal to identify different types of objects (e.g., snake or apple) and to avoid noxious stimuli; in addition, it is also necessary for the fine-grained motor controls (e.g., of fingers).

Receptor types

In the skin are located tips of *somatosensory neurons* that are sensitive to different qualities of tactile (cutaneous) stimulation: (a) pressure, (b) vibration, (c) heating and cooling and (d) tissue damage. (a) Pressure is caused by the mechanical deformation of the skin, giving information on force and hardness; (b) vibration is produced by rubbing over a textured surface (e.g., by finger), giving information on roughness; (c) temperature is caused by changes in the coolness or warmth of an object; and (d) tissue damage is caused by physical events that destroy tissue, mediated by *nociceptive neurons*. These neurons are sometimes collectively called *dorsal root ganglion* (DRG) *cells* because of the location of their cell bodies alongside the spinal cord (other neurons, for example, from the face, project above the neck, via the cranial nerves). Each class of DRG cells detects information which is transmitted to distinct brain regions for further processing: to the sensory homunculus (see chapter 3).

As shown in figure 5.1, there are different types of neuron tips: some are simple neurons (nociceptive neurons); in contrast, the hair follicle receptor consists of a neuron ending wrapped around the root of a hair, and it detects the deflection of the hair.

The tactile process of touch (pressure and vibration) results from the tip of the sensory receptor being bent, relative to the axon, by external pressure: this stimulation causes the membrane of the receptor neuron to depolarize, which may, if the threshold of excitation is reached, result in an action potential. A similar effect is seen in temperature receptors

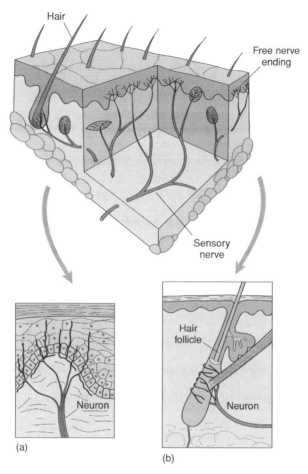

Figure 5.1 Pain and hair sensory receptors. There are different types of somatosensory receptors in the skin. Shown are (a) free-ending simple neuron, and (b) a hair follicle receptor with a neuron ending wrapped around the root of a hair.

(these are buried deeper in the skin). In the case of tissue damage and pain, a variety of stimuli can lead to an action potential being initiated, including intense mechanical stimulation. When cells are damaged they synthesize *prostaglandin* (a type of hormone first discovered in the prostate gland), which serves to sensitize free nerve endings to another chemical (histamine), which is also released by damaged cells. (Aspirin relieves pain because it interferes with the synthesis of prostaglandins.)

One important characteristic of tactile receptors is their sensitivity to *change* in stimulation. In fact, most receptors adapt rapidly and detect only changes. If somatosensory receptors did not adapt rapidly, then we would be aware of all stimuli touching our skin, which would result in a wasteful use of processing resources. However, some receptors (e.g., nociceptors in pain) adapt very slowly, if at all. In evolutionary terms, it is sensible to stop paying attention to the feel of your feet on the ground, but not to tissue damage, which, if ignored, might result in reduced genetic fitness.[1]

Fibre types

There are different nerve fibres connected to the different types of receptors in the skin, muscle and internal organs. These afferent fibres come in different sizes, which are related to the speed of their nerve conduction. In reducing order of size, the large fibre is A-alpha, concerned with proprioception (muscles); A-beta fibres convey information concerning touch; A-delta fibres convey information concerning pain and temperature; and C-nerve fibres convey information concerning pain, temperature and itch. The thicker the fibre, the faster its conduction. A-alpha, A-beta and A-delta fibres are myelinated; C-fibres are unmyelinated. We have all had the experience of hitting our leg on a hard surface: first we sense the touch (mediated by fast, large myelinated fibres), and only then, some time later, do we feel the pain, mediated by slower, unmyelinated fibres – the nerve signal travels slower than walking pace at 2 miles per hour. The signals in faster fibres travel anywhere between the speed of an Olympic sprinter and an aeroplane.

Receptor fields

Irrespective of its type, each receptor has its own receptive field: this is the area on the skin to which it is sensitive. The density of the branches of the receptor neuron is greatest at its centre and less towards the periphery (figure 5.2). The frequency of action potentials of individual receptor neurons, as well as the pattern of firing in relation to other sensory receptors, produces a neural representation that provides accurate information on the position on the skin of the object. The sensory homunculus (see chapter 3) shows that, at the somatosensory cortex, there is a receptor–cortex spatial mapping of the

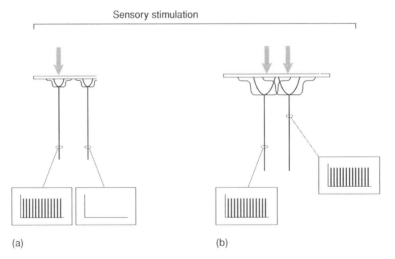

Figure 5.2 Density of receptor branches. Each receptor has its own receptive field: this is the area on the skin to which it is sensitive. The density of the branches of the receptor neuron is greatest at its centre, and less towards the periphery. Some neurons have a very restricted area of sensitivity (a), whereas other neurons are sensitive to stimulations over a larger area (b).

sensory surface of the body with processing within the cortex. If cortical neurons are individually stimulated, then this causes a sensation of touch on that part of the body that is mapped to that somatosensory neuron (examples of this phenomenon were given in chapter 3).

Receptive fields vary in size. Smaller receptive fields are associated with greater tactile acuity (e.g., finger tip and tongue); and there are more neurons in the somatosensory cortex to process this higher level of information. Acuity is measured by the ability to discriminate between one and two points of stimulation. The spatial distance at which discrimination is reliably above chance is the *two-point threshold*: that is, the shortest distance apart at which you can feel that two separate points are touching your skin. These thresholds vary greatly over the body: fingers have high acuity, the back low acuity – it is evident from the sensory homunculus that some parts of the body get more cortical processing. Stimulation of different parts of the receptive field thus provides information on the exact location of the stimulus; stimulation of the periphery of other receptors further adds information on the location of the stimulus. Figure 5.3 shows these different two-point thresholds.

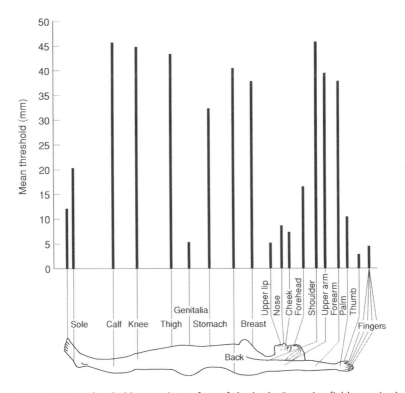

Figure 5.3   Two-point thresholds over the surface of the body. Receptive fields vary in size, with smaller receptive fields associated with greater tactile acuity. Acuity is measured by the ability to discriminate between one and two points of stimulation: the spatial distance at which discrimination is reliably above chance is the *two-point threshold*, defined as the shortest distance apart at which you can feel that two separate points are touching the skin. As shown, these thresholds vary greatly over the body. (Adapted from Toates, 2001.)

Somatosenses and the brain

Somatosensory receptor axons, from the skin, muscles or internal organs, enter the CNS via the spinal nerves; those receptors located in the face and head enter through the fifth cranial nerve. The cell bodies of the neurons are located in the *dorsal root ganglia* (DRG) and the *cranial nerve ganglia* (in the case of cranial nerves). Axons that transmit localized information (e.g., fine touch) ascend through the dorsal columns of the spinal cord to nuclei in the lower medulla; from there axons cross the brain and ascend to the *ventral posterior nuclei* of the thalamus (Carlson, 1998). Axons from the thalamus project to the *somatosensory cortex* (both primary and secondary) (figure 5.4). (Axons that transmit poorly localized information, such as pain or temperature, take a slightly different path to the ventral posterior nuclei of the thalamus (Carlson, 1998.)

The *secondary somatosensory cortex* differs from the *primary somatosensory cortex* in terms of the type of receptive fields, with neurons in the secondary somatosensory cortex responding to more complex features and less tied to specific sensory regions; some neurons respond to specific shapes, and it seems that input is compared with stored memories of the tactile features of objects.

The receptive fields of DRG neurons are composed of an excitatory region, defined by their tips in the skin. However, as information ascends in the somatosensory pathways, further processing occurs. Neurons in the medulla, whose activity depends upon activity in the DRG neurons, have receptive field properties that are more complex: stimulation of the centre of the receptor with no stimulation at neighbouring cells would produce the greatest ON excitatory input. Within the somatosensory pathway, there is lateral inhibition between cells. The pattern of information gained from ON/OFF processing is important in localizing the position of stimulation (figure 5.5).

Our discussion of the tactile senses has assumed that information flows from the cutaneous receptors in the skin, through the spinal cord, medulla and thalamus, and then on to the cortex for processing. This is a *bottom-up* account. Research now shows that *top-down* processing is also relevant: sensory information is detected and interpreted by means of comparison against representations in memory (e.g., reading Braille script). Top-down influences are especially important in pain.

Pain

On the face of it, pain should be the easiest of the somatosenses to understand in terms of bottom-up processes: we cut our finger, and nociceptive signals are sent to the spinal cord and brain which result in the experience of pain. As an appropriate response, we might flinch from the nociceptive stimulus (this spinal reflex occurs before the experience of pain), or we might take a more complex action (cortex-mediated). But this account of pain is too simplistic, and in some respects wrong.

Gate theory of pain

Melzack and Wall's (1965, 1984) influential theory of pain highlights the need to consider the interplay of physiological and psychological factors. Their 'gate theory of pain'

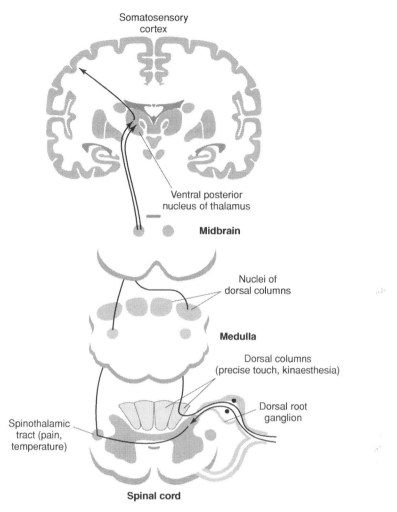

Figure 5.4 CNS pathways. Somatosensory receptor axons enter the CNS via the spinal nerves. The cell bodies of neurons are located in the *dorsal root ganglia* (DRG) and their axons ascend through the dorsal columns of the spinal cord to nuclei in the lower medulla; from the medulla, axons cross the brain, through the midbrain, and ascend to the *ventral posterior nuclei* of the thalamus, and from there to the somatosensory cortex.

postulates that sensory information does not travel in a simple pathway from the skin to spinal cord to brain; they postulate that there is a complex interaction of ascending bottom-up sensory pathways and descending top-down neural influences. Importantly, the brain has the power to influence the *experience* of pain. Several observations point to the influence of the top-down psychological control of pain. First, hypnosis can reduce pain (even eliminate it during surgery). Second, much chronic pain is *neuropathic*, that is, caused by a problem in the CNS (e.g., a compressed nerve in the spinal cord), which

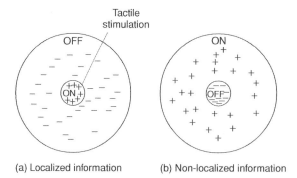

(a) Localized information   (b) Non-localized information

Figure 5.5 ON/OFF effects in the medulla. There is integration of information in the medulla from many sources of neuronal input. Neurons in the medulla, whose activity depends upon activity in the DRG neurons, have complex receptive fields: stimulation of the centre of the receptor with no stimulation at neighbouring cells produces greatest ON excitatory input (a); other cells show the opposite pattern (b). The pattern of information gained from ON/OFF processing is important in localizing the position of stimulation.

gives rise to the sensation of a peripheral pain. Third, pain is often experienced in limbs *after* they have been surgically removed (*phantom limb* pain) – such pain points to the importance of a neural representation (memory) that can be activated centrally without the involvement of the presence of pain stimuli or the action of pain (nociceptive) receptors. Psychological therapies for the management of chronic pain are now common practice. The gate theory of pain is shown in figure 5.6.

But why should the brain reduce the signal of tissue damage – would it not make more sense to intensify pain so as to motivate immediate defensive reactions? It may be speculated that, at the point of severe tissue damage (e.g., savage attack by predator), it would not be adaptive to experience a high degree of pain as this would tend to impair the appropriate fight–flight–freeze response mediated by the fear system (see chapter 17); in addition, an animal in pain might signal to the predator that it is badly hurt and thereby encourage further attack. Thus, the temporary suppression of pain may have an adaptive function. Only later, when out of harm's way, would the physiological effects of pain (e.g., rest, activation of immune system; see chapter 6) be adaptive. It is an astonishing fact that, in battle, soldiers sometimes only realize they have been badly injured some time after the initial trauma.

> **ASK YOURSELF**
> Why might the *experience* of sensation (e.g., pain) persist long after receptor activation?

The Taste System

Each day we experience many different tastes, and we often encounter new tastes. It is, therefore, surprising that these varied and rich taste experiences are processed from four basic primary tastes: *sweet, salt, sour* and *bitter* (recently, a fifth receptor type has been isolated for the taste of *umani*:[2] Chaudhari, Landin & Roper, 2000). These tastes are the

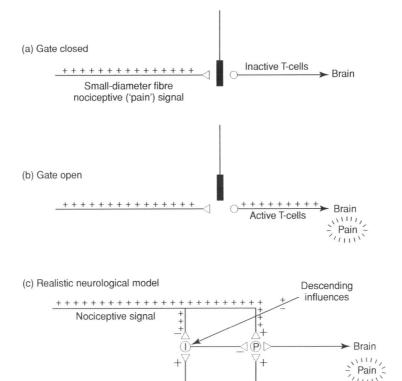

(a) Gate closed

Small-diameter fibre
nociceptive ('pain') signal

Inactive T-cells

Brain

(b) Gate open

Active T-cells

Brain

Pain

(c) Realistic neurological model

Nociceptive signal

Descending
influences

Brain

Pain

Large-diameter fibre

Figure 5.6   Gate control system. In the gate theory of pain, a 'gate' is used to refer to an inhibitory mechanism that blocks the passage of small-diameter fibre nociceptive ('pain') nerve signals (via transmission, T, cells) to the brain. The probability that a net pain signal will be sent to the brain is a product of: (1) the activity of small-diameter fibre (nociceptive) activation; (2) the activity of large-diameter fibre (non-pain sensory) activation; and (3) descending influences from the brain. With the gate 'closed', nociceptive nerve transmission is blocked (a); but with it open, nerve transmission (via T-cells) is permitted, leading to the experience of pain (b). A more neurologically realistic process is shown (c). Without stimulation, both large- and small-diameter fibres are inactive, and an inhibitory (–) signal is sent to the projection (P) neuron, which blocks T-cell activation (this is the 'resting state' of the system). With stimulation of large-diameter fibres, an inhibitory signal is also sent to the projection neuron, because these fibres excite this inhibitory neuron, and no pain is experienced. However, as shown here, when small-diameter fibres become active, they activate (+) the projection neuron, which then activates the T-cells; and, importantly, they also inhibit the inhibitory interneuron, which has the effect of removing the inhibitory influence on the projection neuron, which leads to its excitation and thus T-cell activation: the result is the experience of pain. There is also an important descending influence from the brain, which can either excite (+) or inhibit (–) the transmission of nociceptive ('pain') information.

psychological end products of the neural processing initiated by the different chemical receptors. Thus, we do not taste *sweetness* directly, but we infer this quality from a subclass of chemical molecules to which the sweet receptor is sensitive. This ability to experience many different tastes from only a small number of receptor types allows an economy of neural machinery. As with much else in the field of biological psychology, what we *experience* psychologically as highly complex is often the product of a relatively simple set of (adaptively clever) neural processes. The adaptive function of taste is to check the quality of food to be ingested.

Receptors

The four types of taste receptor are sensitive to chemical molecules (see figure 5.7). (a) *Sweet* is produced by sugars, which indicate the availability of nutrients essential for physiological functioning. (b) *Salt* is produced by sodium chloride (common table salt), as well as other types of salt, once again essential for physiological functioning. Both sweet and salt give rise to appetitive (approach) behaviour (i.e., we work to attain them when in a motivational state of depletion). In contrast to these pleasant tastes, sour and bitter elicit an avoidance response (i.e., we work to avoid tasting them[3]). (c) *Sour* is a common indication of food decay (during food decay, acids are produced), and we have evolved to experience a natural repulsion for foodstuffs producing this sensation. (d) *Bitter* is a common taste of poisonous plants (a product of alkaloids). It is obvious from an appreciation of evolution by natural selection why we should shy away from foodstuffs that produce these unpleasant tastes: those individuals whose genes did not code for an instinctive repulsion simply went extinct. Taste receptors have been isolated for salt, sour and umani; bitter and sweet receptors have yet to be described at the molecular level of analysis (Lindemann, 2001).

Most so-called bitter and sour foods are not pure tastes, and usually include either salt, sweet or umani molecules; therefore we do not avoid all food containing bitter and sour molecules. Bitter and sour tastes are used in cooking because they modify the perception of the other tastes, producing novel and pleasant tastes. However, in sufficient strength and in isolation from other modifying taste chemicals we are repulsed by bitter and sour.

Chemical molecules are dissolved in saliva and bind to receptors (contained in *taste buds*) on different parts of the tongue. In fact, the tongue, palate, pharynx and larynx all contain taste buds (approximately 10,000). Each type of taste receptor has a characteristic reactivity curve: although all receptors respond to all classes of chemical, they respond maximally only to one. Perception of taste involves the activation patterns of all types of receptor: this joint activation pattern is necessary to experience complex tastes. Imagine receptors that responded only to one chemical class (e.g., sweet). How would the brain know whether a small or large quantity of the chemical was present? Although one could think of other solutions to this problem, Nature's elegant solution is as follows: if a large quantity of sugar molecules activates the *sweet* receptor maximally and non-sweet receptors beyond a certain threshold, then the brain infers that a high quantity of sugar molecules is present (a low level would activate only the sweet receptor and not any of the other three receptor types).

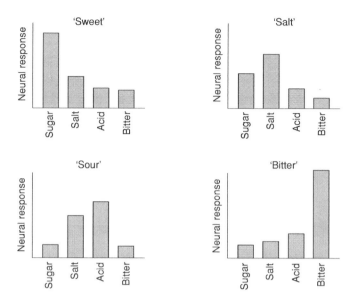

Figure 5.7   Taste bud reactivity. The different types of taste buds have differential responses to sugar, salt, acid and bitter taste-eliciting chemical substances. The experience of the taste is a product of brain processing and not an inherent property of the taste receptors, which only possess properties of differential sensitivity to certain classes of substances.

Thus, from the presence of a certain level of a chemical molecule (e.g., sugar), the brain receives information on: (a) degree of activation of sweet receptor; (b) degree of activation of the other receptor types; and (c) differential activation pattern of sugar of these other receptor types (each are differentially sensitive to the other subclasses of chemical molecules – see height of bars in figure 5.7). Thus, the brain receives a rich source of information from which it can compute the degree of activation of each subclass of molecule and the *pattern* of activation from all subclasses of molecules. Much of the art of cooking is to add ingredients to influence this complex pattern of information processing.

Tongue to brain

Taste receptors synapse with dendrites of sensory neurons that convey information to the brain. Taste receptors are activated when the chemical molecule binds with the specialized receptor in a lock-and-key manner (see chapter 3). Once the key (molecule) is in the lock (receptor), a change in the permeability of the membrane of the receptor occurs, leading to an action potential. Each type of taste receptor responds to different ions in the molecules; for example, salt opens sodium channels, leading to depolarization and neurotransmitter release. Action potentials travel via cranial nerves 7, 9 and 10 to the medulla (specifically, the *nucleus of the solitary tract*, NST); here the axons terminate and synapse with neurons whose axons travel to a specific region in the thalamus (the *ventral*

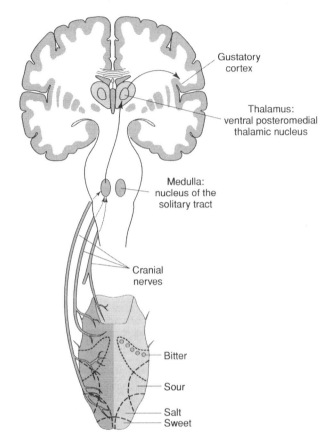

Figure 5.8 Receptor–medulla–thalamus–cortex pathway. Location of different types of taste buds on the tongue. Once taste buds are activated, nerve signals are transmitted along the cranial nerves to the medulla (the *nucleus of the solitary tract*, NST), where they synapse before travelling to a part of the thalamus called the *ventral posteromedial thalamic nucleus*, before their onward passage to the gustatory cortex for final processes.

posteromedial thalamic nucleus); from the thalamus information projects to the gustatory (taste) cortex. Neural projections also go to the amygdala and the hypothalamus, which subserve emotional activation and basic regulatory functions, respectively (figure 5.8).

The distribution of the taste-sensitive neurons in the nucleus of the solitary tract and the thalamus resembles that found on the surface of the tongue; however, at the cortex their distribution is less systematic, although there appear to be columns of neurons that respond to sweet and salty, and to sour and bitter. Taste processing is *synthetic* (as opposed to *analytical*), combining qualities of molecules to generate the complex experience of taste. At the level of cortical processing, much knowledge is still missing in our understanding of the psychological computation of taste.

ASK YOURSELF
How is the rich experience of taste generated by only a small number of receptor types?

▮▢ The Olfactory System: Smell

Smell is mediated by the *olfactory system*, which, in a similar manner to taste, is sensitive to (airborne) chemical molecules; but, unlike taste, olfactory stimuli and receptors do not break down into a few subclasses of chemical molecules and receptor types: there are hundreds of different types of receptors, each of which is specialized for a particular olfactory quality. The combined psychological experience of taste and smell is termed *flavour* – without the sense of smell, many foods would have little flavour (e.g., steak would taste like salty cardboard). Like the perception of taste, olfactory processing is *synthetic*, combining qualities of molecules to generate the complex experience of smell.

Receptors

Receptors in the nose operate on a lock-and-key principle. Olfactory receptors are sensitive to the shape of only certain chemical molecules: occupation of the lock (receptor) by the key (chemical molecule) triggers activity within the cell. There are 50 million *olfactory receptors* in the human nose. During the process of sniffing, the flow of air into the nasal cavity is increased and so too are the airborne molecules. Olfactory receptors both transduce chemical information and generate action potentials that convey information onwards to the brain for processing (figure 5.9). They are thus part of neurons.

Olfactory bulb

The olfactory bulb is located at the base of the brain, positioned on the end of a stalk-like olfactory tract. Each olfactory receptor neuron sends a single axon to the olfactory bulb; here it synapses at the *olfactory glomeruli*. There are approximately 10,000 glomeruli, each of which receives inputs from a bundle of some 2,000 axons. These axons travel to the rest of the brain through the olfactory tracts. Some of these axons terminate in the brain; others cross the brain and enter the other olfactory nerve and terminate in the contralateral olfactory bulb.

Nose to brain

From the *olfactory bulb* neurons convey information to various brain regions (e.g., olfactory cortex, amygdala and hypothalamus). (Olfaction is the only system with a direct link to the cortex, bypassing the thalamus.) Projections to the amygdala (the site of emotional arousal) provide fast information on the potential emotional significance of the molecules detected in the environment; projections to the hypothalamus are linked to motivation (e.g., feeding and sexual behaviour). Other projections to the orbitofrontal cortex link smell with conscious awareness. Olfactory tract axons travel directly to two other regions of the limbic cortex: the *pyriform cortex* and the *entorhinal cortex*. The entorhinal cortex sends information to the hippocampus, and the pyriform cortex to the hypothalamus and to the orbitofrontal cortex.

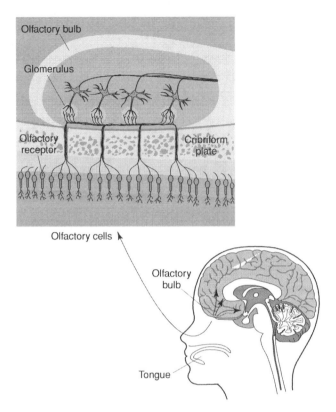

Figure 5.9 Nose, olfactory receptors/neurons and olfactory bulb. Molecules enter the nose and stimulate olfactory receptors whose axons travel to the olfactory bulb and on to various parts of the brain, including the olfactory cortex, amygdala, hypothalamus and the orbitofrontal cortex.

Even though there may be many different types of olfactory receptors, we experience many more smells due to the *synthetic* processing of information. This rich psychological experience is made possible by the fact that each odorant binds to more than one receptor: it binds to some receptors better than others (a similar process is found in taste and, as discussed below, vision). A given glomerulus receives information from only one type of receptor. The experience of a particular smell is thus a matter of a particular pattern of activity in glomeruli. Unlike the other senses, how the brain processes these complex patterns of information is still being worked out.

At a functional level, it may be desirable to assign particular importance to the sense of smell. The fact that there are many different types of receptors suggests that sensitivity to a wide range of chemical molecules was important in our evolutionary past. Unlike the senses of vision or audition, smells contain information that is not so time-constrained: we can only see or hear a predator if it is in our immediate environment. Smells, however, linger over longer time periods, and many animals mark their territory with excretions. Thus, smell provides information on the *probability* of the presence of predators, producing cautionary behaviour. For the rat, the ability to smell a cat, and start to prepare for action, is much more important than the ability to see or hear a cat attacking – then it will often be too late to escape.

Pheromones

In many species of animals and plants, pheromones serve as an important channel of communication. Pheromones are detected via the *vomeronasal system* (neurons from this system synapse at the olfactory bulb). Pheromones are airborne chemicals which have the capacity to alter physiological and psychological functions; they are usually not consciously perceived (but it is possible that consciously perceived smells also act as pheromones). These chemicals are used to excite sexual interest in many species, but in human beings the evidence for such a sexual function is largely absent. It is likely that, with further research, the role played by pheromones in a number of functions in human beings will be more appreciated (for example, there is evidence that pheromones influence the menstrual cycle; see chapter 6). There is some evidence that a baby's sweat contains pheromones that are preferred much more by males than females, possibly serving to act to reduce aggression in males and promote bonding.

> **ASK YOURSELF**
> What unique information about the environment comes from the sense of smell?

◼☐ The Auditory System: Hearing

The above discussion revealed that objects do not have a taste of their own: they merely give off chemical molecules that are interpreted psychologically as taste. The same is true of the sense of smell. But what about hearing: do objects make a sound that is simply detected? Does the falling tree in the forest make a sound irrespective of whether anyone is there to hear it?

The psychological perception of sound is the result of complex brain processing, involving the *interpretation* of physical events in the external world, namely air pressure waves. Thus, the falling trees causes pressure waves which reach the ears and which are then *processed* by the brain to produce the *experience* of sound. Sound thus comprises a *physical–psychological correspondence*. By instinct and learning, a neural representation (memory) of different types of air pressure changes (corresponding to the perceptual experience of sound) and their psychological significance is constructed.

Physical event: air pressure

The physical event of what finally is interpreted as sound consists in objects vibrating; this vibration causes the surrounding air alternately to condense and rarefy (pull apart), producing air pressure waves that travel about 700 miles per hour. It is these air pressure changes that stimulate the auditory system.

The concept of air pressure is best described with the aid of a tuning fork. When hit it vibrates, producing a wave of compression, creating a cycle of high and low pressures in the air (this wave can be shown on an oscilloscope). The wave has two important features (parameters): (a) *frequency* and (b) *amplitude*. The frequency is related to the wavelength (as frequency goes up, wavelength comes down) of these high and low air pressures – this is the period of time that the wave takes to complete one cycle. Frequency is expressed in number of cycles per second (expressed in hertz, Hz). A 50-hertz (50 Hz) wave completes 50 cycles in one second. This frequency sounds very different from a 1,000 Hz wave. The human ear is sensitive to frequencies between 30 and 20,000 Hz (other animals have different ranges of sensitivity). The second parameter is amplitude – this is the strength (magnitude) of the wave (with a tuning fork, magnitude can be increased by hitting it harder) (figure 5.10).

The three perceptual dimensions of sound are *pitch*, *loudness* and *timbre*. Pitch is determined by frequency; loudness is the intensity of the wave (i.e., the degree to which the condensations and rarefactions of air differ from each other); and timbre provides

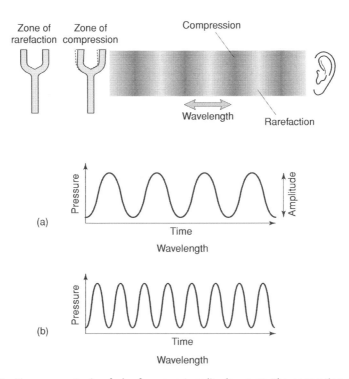

Figure 5.10 Air pressure, tuning forks, frequency/amplitude waves. The generation of sound (e.g., with a tuning fork) produces a change in air pressure and sound waves due to the disturbance of air molecules. The zones of rarefaction and compression produce the wavelength (or frequency) of sound (which is the number of rarefaction–compression cycles per second), which can range from low (a) to high (b). If the tuning folk is hit harder then the amplitude of the wave increases, but not the wavelength.

information about the nature of the particular sound (e.g., a dog's bark vs. a violin) – the particular mix of simpler waves determines timbre.

The problem of locating sound is solved in a number of ways. First, there are small differences in arrival times at the two ears; thus the closer the source of sound the earlier the activation of the action potentials in the nearest ear. Second, there are differences in intensity of sound received by the two ears: the head casts a *sonic shadow* leading to differences in intensity that provide important clues to source location.

Unlike taste, the olfactory system and (as shown below) the visual system, all of which use *synthetic* processing (i.e., putting together incoming information), the auditory system uses *analytical* processing: it takes complex waves and transforms them into a series of simpler waveforms. Therefore, the function of the auditory system is to decompose a complex waveform into more basic waveforms.

Outer and middle ears

Waveform analysis is achieved by processing in various parts of the ear. Transduction from pressure changes in the air to oscillations is achieved in the *tympanic membrane* ('eardrum'), which vibrates at the same frequency as the air pressure. Within the middle ear there are three bones (*auditory ossicles*), which are caused to oscillate by oscillations of the tympanic membrane. The bones communicate oscillations to a fluid-filled coiled structure termed the *cochlea* at the *oval window*. The membrane that forms the oval window vibrates back and forth in sympathy with the tympanic membrane. At the oval window, movements of a bone are transduced into pressure changes in the fluid that fills the cochlea (figure 5.11).

Let us look at these structures in more detail.

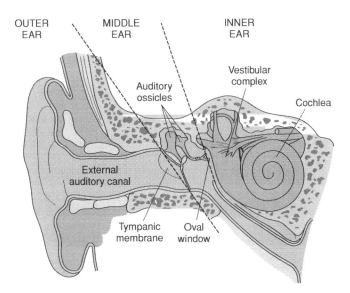

Figure 5.11 Division of the ear into outer, middle and inner ear, showing the main structures involved in the nerve conductance of air pressure.

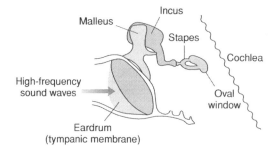

Figure 5.12 Structure of the ossicles. The tympanic membrane activates the three bones in the middle ear (the auditory ossicles), which then stimulate the cochlea.

Tympanic membrane ('eardrum')

The *tympanic membrane* vibrates at the same frequency as the air pressure and oscillates to *complex waves* (i.e., the combined waveform that hits the ear); this complex wave is composed of many simple waves, and it is the simple waves that are important in the further sensory processing from the eardrum: these simple waves can be extracted from the complex waveform. This is quite a remarkable feat. If you listen to an orchestra you will be able to detect the sounds of individual instruments; if only the complex wave was processed then this would not be possible – of course, the artistic beauty of an orchestra comes from the higher-order integration of these separate sounds to create a totality of sound (a *gestalt*). At this psychological level, it is possible to switch attention from this holistic processing of the gestalt to the partial processing of specific waveforms (instruments). This is the first stage of transduction.

Auditory ossicles

The tympanic membrane activates three bones in the middle ear; these ossicles are caused to move back and forth by oscillations of the tympanic membrane. At the oval window, the third ossicle communicates oscillations to a fluid-filled coiled structure termed the *cochlea* ('land snail') (figure 5.12).

Cochlea

When pressure waves at a particular frequency occur in the cochlea, the *basilar membrane* is caused to move back and forth at a particular location: this location depends on the frequency of the vibrations, a relationship termed *place code*. For high frequencies, displacements in the basilar membrane occur near the end which is secured (i.e., at the oval window); lower-frequency vibrations cause movements at points far from the oval window. Amplitude change in air pressure is represented by amplitude of displacement of the basilar membrane (figure 5.13).

Associated with the basilar membrane are sensory receptors, cells called 'hair cells', which form synaptic connections with neurons that project to the brain as part of the *auditory nerve* (eighth cranial nerve). When hair cells are mechanically stimulated during

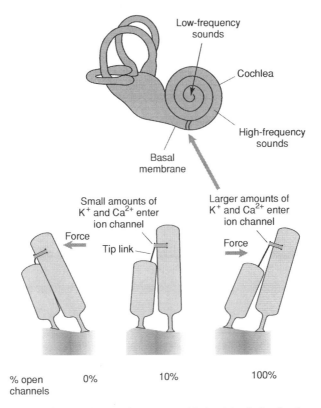

Figure 5.13 Structure of the cochlea and structure of hairs. Stimulation by the ossicles on the basal membrane activates the cochlea, which sends nerve signals to the brain. Auditory hair cells are moved by the sound pressure exerted at the basal membrane. Movement towards the tallest hair increases tension on the tip links, which open ion channels and increase the influx of potassium (K^+) and calcium (Ca^{2+}) ions; movement towards the shortest hair reduces tension at the tip, which results in the ion channels closing. Different regions of the basal membrane are sensitive to different ranges of pressure.

displacement of the basilar membrane, electrical changes occur in them and thereby action potentials are triggered in the associated neurons. These action potentials are transmitted along the auditory nerve to the brainstem.

Two types of auditory receptors, *inner auditory hair cells* and *outer auditory hair cells*, lie on the inside and outside of the cochlea coils, respectively. Hair cells contain *cilia*, which are fine, hair-like appendages arranged in rows according to height. The human cochlea contains 3,500 inner hair cells and 12,000 outer hair cells. The hair cells form synapses with dendrites of neurons whose axons bring auditory information to the brain.

The bending of the hair receptors causes action potentials. The resting potential of an auditory hair cell is −160 mV. With movement of the hairs, ion channels are opened and potassium (K^+) and calcium (Ca^{2+}) diffuse into the hair cell. As a result, the release

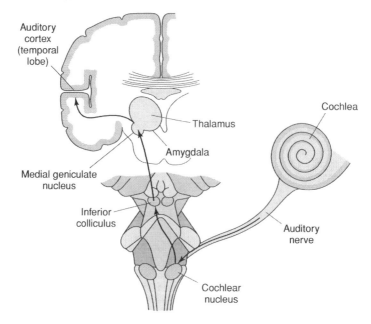

Figure 5.14 The classical route of auditory processing. (There is a secondary route from the thalamus to the amygdala, which is involved in coarse-grained, rapid responses.)

of neurotransmitters by the hair cell increases. Deafness is usually caused by the progressive degeneration of hair cells.

Ear to brain

A series of neurons conveys information in the auditory nerve to the cochlear nucleus, where a synapse occurs; information then ascends through various brain regions (inferior colliculus, medial geniculate nucleus of the thalamus) to the auditory cortex. There is a partial crossover of information (i.e., contralateral and ipsilateral processing; figure 5.14).

Intensity of pressure waves is coded by the rate at which action potentials occur in a particular neuron; particular neurons are responsive to particular sound frequencies, corresponding to particular basilar membrane locations (*tonotopic representation* – 'tonos' meaning tone; 'topos' meaning place; or *place code*). Intensity of air pressure, which is perceived psychologically as loudness, is coded in two ways: one is by the rate at which action potentials occur in particular neurons; the other is by the different threshold of activation of neurons (some neurons are only triggered by high-intensity sounds).

The route of the ears–thalamus–auditory cortex is called the *classical route*. However, in addition, there is a route from the thalamus to the amygdala, which is a crucial site of emotional processing. This route is quick and involved in defensive reaction, especially the rapid arousal of fear. The slower route through the auditory cortex and then to the amygdala also plays a role, providing a refined analysis of threat.

Complex computational processes are involved in the cortical analysis of sound, and learning is important in recognizing and effectively processing new sounds (e.g., listening to a new voice). This example of *perceptual learning* is necessary for feature extraction, which entails extracting for further analysis the salient aspects of the sound.

> **ASK YOURSELF**
> Can it *really* be true that a falling tree does not make a sound if no one is there to hear it?

The Visual System: Seeing

The above discussion of sensory systems is relevant to the visual system. For a start, what we see is not simply what is out there in the real world: as falling trees do not make a sound – at least not until the auditory system processes air pressure changes into perceived sound – blood is not really red, lemons are not really yellow and grass is not really green (and no greener in the other field). These psychological *experiences* are constructed out of sensory input, providing us with a good enough *physical–psychological correspondence* of the external world.

There is a vast amount of physical energy in the world of which we are blissfully unaware. This fact is especially true for the visual system. The wavelengths outside our sphere of sensitivity were unimportant in evolutionary terms, therefore there was no selection pressure on the adaptation of mechanisms sensitive to them. Radiation in the visual range comes from objects in our environment that have survival implications (e.g., predators and potential mates). The visual system is sensitive to the properties of light, detected in the eye by *photoreceptors*. Light is defined in terms of two parameters: (a) *wavelength* (or frequency) and (b) *amplitude*. These are the two physical dimensions that give rise to the psychological experience of vision.

Understanding vision is made somewhat difficult by how effortless it seems to us: typically, people look at an object and see what appears to be there. However, vision is not this straightforward, and what we 'see' is the final product of a high level of feature extraction, interpretation and analysis. For example, a wavelength of 650 nanometres (nm) leads to the perception of the colour red, but there is no 'redness' in this wavelength, and no redness in the objects that reflected this wavelength.

Light: physical dimensions

We are being consistently bombarded with electromagnetic radiation (e.g., from outer space and radio transmitters). This radiation varies in wavelength (defined in terms of nanometres, nm). We are insensitive to most of the electromagnetic spectrum: we are sensitive only to a small portion between approximately 380 and 760 nm (see figure 5.15). Light travels at a speed of 186,000 miles per second (300,000 kilometres) – which, we are told on the good authority of Einstein, is constant.

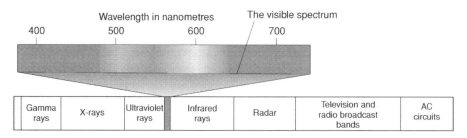

Figure 5.15 The electromagnetic spectrum, of which light comprises only a small part.

Light: psychological dimensions

The *perceived* colour of light is determined by three dimensions: *hue, saturation* and *brightness*. The wavelength of light determines *hue*; light can also vary in intensity, which corresponds to *brightness*; the purity of the light corresponds to *saturation*. If radiation contains all wavelengths then it produces a sensation of no hue (i.e., it would appear white).[4] Light waves are reflected off objects (their chemical composition determines which wavelengths are absorbed and which are reflected). An object perceived as black absorbs all frequencies and reflects none; an object perceived as white absorbs no frequencies and reflects back to the observer all frequencies.

The eye

Light enters the eye and the lens focuses it on the retina; due to the optics of the eye, this image is upside down and reversed left to right with respect to the external world. The brain does not receive this *analogue* image so this reversal does not matter; complex processing takes place that sends *digital* signals to the brain in the form of action potentials. In the retina are the photoreceptors that are sensitive to the wavelength and amplitude of light (figure 5.16).

The external world viewed by the eyes is termed the *visual field*. Light arising from the right half of the visual field arrives at the left half of each retina; light from the left visual field arrives at the right half of each retina. Neural pathways run from the left half of each eye to the left half of the brain; pathways from the right side of each eye run to the right side of the brain. This involves a crossover of half the pathway from each eye to the other side, at the optic chiasma (figure 5.17). Each visual field receives a slightly different image of the world, producing stereo vision (*stereopsis*) and three-dimensional perception[5] as a result of integration in the cortex, where neurons are sensitive to image disparity, which provides important information on depth, distance, etc. (this is similar to the differences in sound reaching the two ears, which give clues to location).

There are two types of photoreceptor: *rods* and *cones* (named because of their shapes). Rods are colour-blind; cones process colour information. Photoreceptors have different sensitivities to wavelengths; their activation changes their electrical activity (this is not action potential). Photoreceptors then pass wavelength information, via synapses, to other

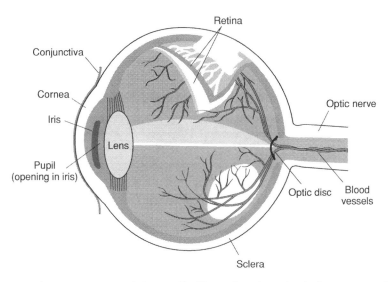

Figure 5.16 The gross anatomy of the eye (for illustration, the retina is shown torn and folded back).

Left side | Right side

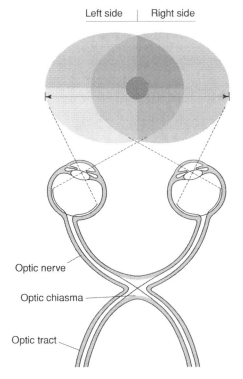

Figure 5.17 Visual fields and crossover of fibres. Stimuli entering the right visual field cross over to the left hemisphere, and stimuli entering the left visual field cross over to the right hemisphere. (Note that stimuli entering each eye go to *both* hemispheres.)

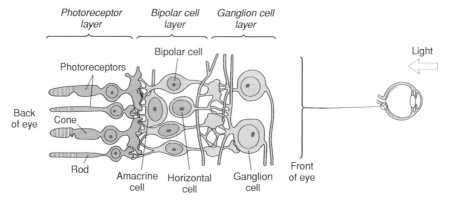

Figure 5.18 Retinal function. Light enters the dense layer of cells in the retina and is first processed by rods and cones at the back of the layer of cells. The retinal layers consists of (1) the ganglion layer, (2) the bipolar cell layer, and (3) the photoreceptor layer (rods and cones).

neurons, called *bipolar cells*. These bipolar cells then pass information, once again via a synapse, *to ganglion cells*, which then, after some local processing, pass information to the brain in the form of action potentials. Axons conveying information from the rods and cones are gathered together at the *optic disc*, and the *optic nerve* (a cranial nerve) comprises the millions of the axons of the ganglion cells. The eye is formally part of the brain and the optic nerve is a cranial nerve and not part of the peripheral nervous system (PNS; see chapter 3). It is this set of processes that is considered in detail in this section.

Retina

The human retina is made up of some 120 million rods and 6 million cones. Rods are concentrated on the periphery of the retina; cones are concentrated in the middle of the eye, the *fovea* (this contains only cones).

The retina consists of several layers of neurons: (a) the photoreceptor layer (contains rods and cones); (b) the bipolar cell layers; and (c) the ganglion layer (there are approximately 1 million ganglion cells). The rods and cones are at the *back* of the retina; before reaching them, light must first pass through the other two layers. In addition the retina contains horizontal cells and amacrine cells, both of which transmit information in a direction parallel to the surface of the retina, and thus combine messages from adjacent photoreceptors (figure 5.18).

At the fovea there is dense packing of cones and little convergence (i.e., the cone/ganglion ratio is low); in contrast, at the periphery many rods all feed into a single ganglion cell. Where there is little convergence (e.g., at the fovea), the ability to resolve fine detail is high (i.e., *acuity*). At the periphery of the retina, where convergence is high, acuity is poor; however, as a result of the pooling of outputs from many receptors, the ability to detect the presence or absence of weak light is good, that is, *sensitivity* is high (sensitivity is important in detecting the presence of weak stimuli, such as an approaching predator) – in fact, rods are so sensitive that they can detect a single photon.

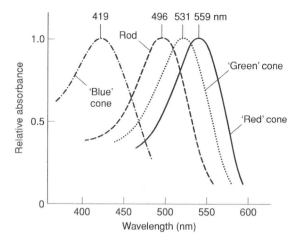

Figure 5.19   Absorption curves of rods and cones. Rods and cones in the photoreceptor layer are not simply sensitive to light of a given frequency; rather, they have different sensitivity curves, with maximal peaks of response. Activation of these separate sensitivity curves provides a rich source of information for the cortex and allows for the multitude of colours experienced.

Photoreceptors

How does light affect the photoreceptors (rods and cones)? The first step in the chain of events that leads to visual perception involves a special chemical called *photopigment*: There are special molecules embedded in the membrane of the receptors, and when a molecule is exposed to light it breaks down its constituents; this breakdown causes a change in the membrane potential of the photoreceptor. Photoreceptor sensitivity is thus caused by the absorption of chemicals contained within rods and cones. There are three types of cones, loosely termed 'blue', 'green' and 'red'. These terms relate to the wavelengths of light to which the cone is maximally sensitive – but they are also sensitive to the other two wavelengths (figure 5.19). Degeneration of photoreceptors leads to blindness.[6]

Photoreceptors provide input into both bipolar and horizontal cells. Photoreceptors and bipolar cells do not produce action potentials; instead their release of transmitter substance is regulated by the value of their membrane potential: depolarizations increase their release and hyperpolarizations decrease it. The hyperpolarization *reduces* the release of transmitter substance (*glutamate*) by the photoreceptor. Because the transmitter substance normally hyperpolarizes the dendrites of the bipolar cell, a *reduction* in its release causes the membrane of the bipolar cell to depolarize. Thus, light hyperpolarizes the photoreceptor and depolarizes the bipolar cell; and this depolarization causes the bipolar cell to release more transmitter substance, which depolarizes the membrane of the ganglion cell, causing it to increase its rate of firing (figure 5.20).

Ganglion cells

Information from the photoreceptors passes to the ganglion cells; it is the action potentials of these cells that are passed to the brain for higher-order processing. Individual

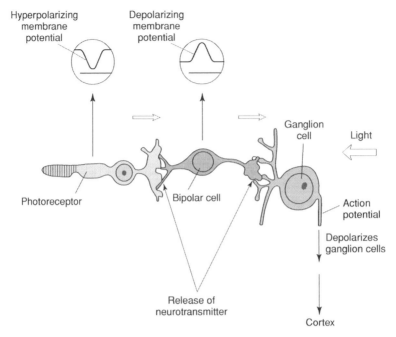

Figure 5.20 Hyperpolarization (photoreceptor) and depolarization (bipolar) cascade. Photoreceptors and bipolar cells release transmitter substance according to their membrane potential: depolarizations increase their release and hyperpolarizations decrease it. Because the transmitter substance normally hyperpolarizes the dendrites of the bipolar cell, a *reduction* in its release causes the membrane of the bipolar cell to depolarize, and this depolarization causes the bipolar cell to release more transmitter substance, which then depolarizes ganglion cells, causing an action potential.

ganglion cells are sensitive to a portion of the visual field. Single-cell recording (see chapter 11) can be used to determine which cells are sensitive to which areas of the visual field. Such experiments have uncovered that ganglion cells have an excitatory ON centre and an inhibitory OFF surround; other cells are the inverse. Stimulation of the OFF areas leads to a reduction in the background frequency of action potentials; stimulation of the ON centre leads to an increase in frequency of action potentials (figure 5.21).

A ganglion cell is maximally stimulated by any light which fills the ON area but does not touch the OFF area: thus, there is maximal excitation and minimal inhibition. A light that covers both the ON and OFF areas leads to little activation due to the cancelling out of the excitatory (ON) and inhibitory (OFF) inputs, producing zero response (the precise level of stimulation depends on the precise weights applied to the excitatory and inhibitory receptor fields). This type of processing allows feature detection. The ON/OFF characteristic of ganglion cells is known as *lateral inhibition*. Many receptors may contribute to the effect on a single ganglion cell, and areas of ganglion cells may overlap with other ganglion cells, providing complex information about the spatial distribution of light.

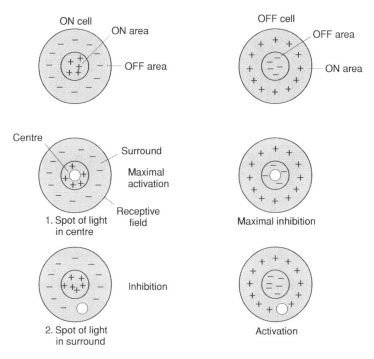

Figure 5.21 ON/OFF areas of ganglion cells. Ganglion cells are maximally stimulated by light which fills the ON area and which does not touch the OFF area: maximal excitation and minimum inhibition. Partial stimulation of the ON area is shown. A light covering both the ON and OFF areas leads to little activation due to the cancelling out of the excitatory (ON) and inhibitory (OFF) inputs: this is *lateral inhibition*.

Eye to brain

Impulses from ganglion cells go to various destinations: they ascend through the optic nerve to the (dorsal) *lateral geniculate nucleus* (LGN; a nucleus of the thalamus). The ganglion cells synapse in the LGN and information leaves this structure to arrive at the visual cortex, where LGN neurons synapse with neurons in the primary visual cortex (often called the *striate cortex*): at the cortex, information from both eyes becomes integrated. However, in human beings, some 100,000 ganglion cell axons provide information outside this cortical system; they travel to the *superior colliculus*, which seems to be the older system: it is unable to resolve the fine detail of complex patterns. Functions of the superior colliculus include that of controlling the eye muscles to direct gaze. Trevarthan (1968) refers to *ambient vision* as being mediated by the subcortical system, and *focal vision* as being mediated by the primary cortical system. The subcortical system localizes objects; the cortical system provides the fine-grained analysis (fibres also travel to other regions: hypothalamus, pineal gland and the reticular formation, as well as the suprachiasmatic nucleus, which is involved in keeping track of time regulated by light; figure 5.22).

There thus seem to be two systems that process visual information in parallel: (a) the *cortical system* (retina–LGN–cortex); and (b) the *subcortical system* (retina–superior colliculus). Let us now consider the cortical system in some detail.

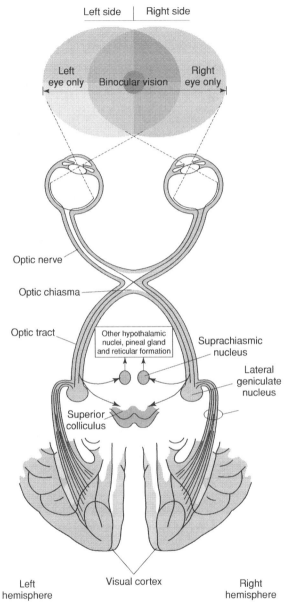

Left side | Right side

Left
eye only   Binocular vision   Right
eye only

Optic nerve

Optic chiasma

Optic tract

Other hypothalamic
nuclei, pineal gland
and reticular formation

Suprachiasmic
nucleus

Lateral
geniculate
nucleus

Superior
colliculus

Left
hemisphere

Visual cortex

Right
hemisphere

Figure 5.22 Cortical and subcortical visual pathways. Passage of information from eyes to brain, showing the various subcortical pathways.

Cortical system: retino-geniculo-cortical pathway

The optic nerves join at the base of the brain to form an X-shaped optic chiasma (cross). There axons from the ganglion cells cross through the chiasma and ascend to the dorsal LGN of the opposite side of the brain. In addition to this pathway, several other pathways are taken by fibres from the retina. One pathway to the hypothalamus synchronizes an animal's activity cycles to the 24-hour rhythms of day and night; other pathways coordinate eye movements and control the iris muscle and thus the size of the pupil.

Lateral geniculate nucleus (LGN)

The LGN contains six layers of neurons. The two inner layers contain relatively large cell bodies: this is the *magnocellular layer*; the two layers either side of these layers are the *parvocellular layers*. These two layers belong to two different systems: the *magno system* is concerned with transmitting information necessary for the perception of form, movement, depth and small differences in brightness; and the *parvo system* is concerned with transmitting information necessary for the perception of colour and fine details (Zeki, 1993; figure 5.23).

The magno system is particularly tuned for changes in the image; images that are visible with the help of only this system disappear within a few seconds of fixation (Livingstone & Hubel, 1995); thus, it is tuned for the detection of moving objects. The parvo system analyses fine detail, which can take time and exploits differences in wavelength. The magno system seems phylogenetically older.

At the primary visual cortex, segregation of parvo and magno systems remains intact, although some limited combination occurs (some cortical neurons respond to both types of input). Beyond the primary visual cortex, distinct cortical regions analyse particular qualities, such as form, colour and motion: this is the theory of *functional specialization* (Zeki, 1993).

Neurons in the LGN have receptive field properties similar to those of ganglion cells, but those of cortical cells are different. The receptive field of a cell anywhere in the visual system is defined by a stimulus of light at the retina. Typically, rather than concentric forms of ganglion cells, a cortical cell has a slit-shaped receptive field.

Primary visual cortex (striate cortex)

The striate cortex is composed of several layers of neurons, each containing the nuclei of cell bodies and dendritic trees. The striate cortex contains a map of the contralateral half of the visual field. When the responses of neurons in the visual cortex are examined, an orderly relationship between retina and cortex appears. Adjacent regions of retina are associated with adjacent neurons in the visual cortex: *topographical mapping* (this map is somewhat distorted, with approximately 25 per cent devoted to analysis of information from the fovea, which is only a small part of the entire visual field). Damage to a region of the primary visual cortex is associated with loss of vision in a particular area of the visual field, termed a *scotoma* (Zeki, 1993). The cortical pathways are shown in figure 5.24.

Hubel and Wiesel's (1962, 1977, 1979) work has been highly influential in determining the functions of the striate cortex (for which they both received the Nobel Prize in 1981). Most neurons are sensitive to orientation; some neurons respond best to a vertical line; others to a horizontal line; and some to diagonal lines. Some neurons, called *simple cells*, have an opponent component: a line of a particular orientation might excite the cell; a line of a different orientation might inhibit the cell. Another type of neuron,

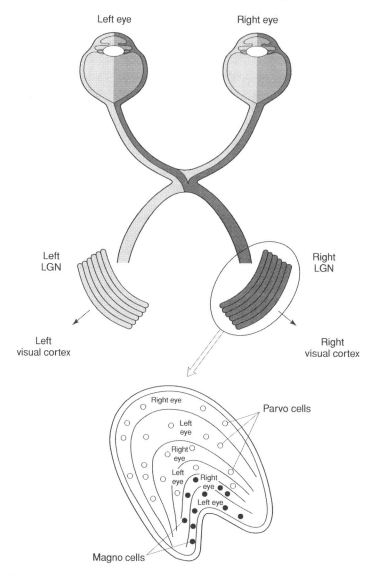

Figure 5.23 LGN magno/parvo divisions. The lateral geniculate nucleus (LGN) is composed of six layers of neurons. The two inner layers contain relatively large cell bodies: this is the phylogenetically older *magnocellular layer* (involved in information concerning form, movement and depth); the layers either side of these layers are the *parvocellular layers* (involved in information concerning fine detail and colour).

the *complex cell*, responds to a line of a particular orientation, not caring about its location on the retina, but does not show an inhibitory aspect (figure 5.25).

It is estimated that the striate cortex is divided into approximately 2,500 modules, each containing about 150,000 neurons, and each concerned with a particular feature extraction.

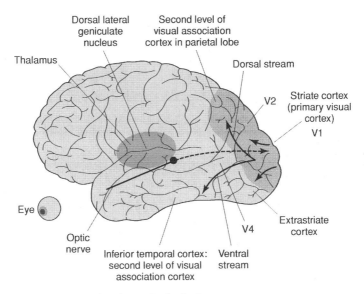

Figure 5.24   The major visual pathways in the brain.

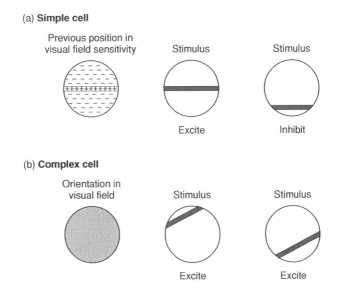

Figure 5.25   Orientation sensitivity. Neurons in the cortex are sensitive to the orientation of stimuli. (a) *Simple cells* have an opponent component: a line of a particular orientation might excite the cell; a line of a different orientation might inhibit the cell; and (b) *complex cells* respond to a line of a particular orientation, irrespective of its position.

The neurons in each module are devoted to the analysis of various stimuli in one very small portion of the visual field. The striate cortex is necessary for visual perception; but the perception of objects and of the totality of the visual scene takes place elsewhere. Each module of the striate cortex sees only what is happening in a tiny part of the visual field. Thus to perceive objects and entire visual scenes it is necessary to integrate information from these separate modules. This integration takes place in the visual association cortex.

Extrastriate cortex

Neurons in the striate cortex send axons to the *extrastriate cortex*. This cortex consists of several regions, each of which contains one or more independent maps of the visual field. Each region is specialized, containing neurons that respond to a particular feature, such as orientation, movement, spatial frequency, retinal disparity and colour. For example, the recognition of visual patterns and identification of particular objects takes place in the *inferior temporal cortex*. It is here that the analysis of colour and form is put together and perception of three-dimensional objects takes place. One of the regions of the extrastriate cortex (V5) contains neurons that respond to movement. Damage to this region disrupts the ability to perceive moving stimuli; area V5 receives input from the striate cortex, as well as from other areas of the extrastriate cortex.

Ventral and dorsal streams

In fact, there are two streams from the striate cortex, each specialized in function (Ungerleider & Mishkin, 1982). Both streams start in the striate cortex but they begin to diverge in the extrastriate cortex. One stream turns downwards, ending in the inferior temporal cortex (the occipitotemporal *ventral stream*); the other stream turns upwards, ending in the posterior parietal lobe (occipitoparietal *dorsal stream*). The ventral stream recognizes *what* an object is (object recognition); the dorsal stream, *where* an object is (spatial processing). However, there remains debate concerning the nature of these streams. In particular, Milner and Goodale (1995) argue for the existence of a third stream: the inferior parietal stream is thought to offer a visuospatial resource, which is used for object recognition under non-optimal circumstances (they assign to the dorsal stream the task of visually guided action). Ventral and dorsal streams are summarized in table 5.1.

Table 5.1 Characteristics of ventral and dorsal streams in visual processing

	Dorsal stream	Ventral stream
Input:	Mainly magno system	Magno and parvo systems
Function:	'Where' information	'What' information
Route:	Visual cortex to parietal cortex	Visual cortex to temporal cortex
Features:	Fast, coarse-grained, peripheral input	Slower, fine-grained, colour, fovea input

The dorsal stream is dominated by information derived from the magno system and has a relatively high sensitivity to information derived from the periphery of the retina: this is assumed to be involved in alerting functions, involving the direction of attention and eye movements – it might be thought of as a fast-action system. The ventral stream is dominated by the parvo system, but with considerable magno contribution: it is especially sensitive to events at the fovea, where resolution of detail is high – it might be thought of as a perception system. The ventral stream is slower than the faster dorsal stream, and seems to be more involved in controlled processing, whereas the dorsal stream seems to be involved in automatic processing.

At the primary visual cortex there remains some segregation but also some combination (i.e., functional specialization; Zeki, 1993). Visual cortex areas V1 and V2 are involved in early visual processing, mainly concerned with form and colour; area V3 is involved in processing information about an object's form but not its colour; V4 is concerned with colour processing and also line orientation; and V5 is involved in the processing of visual motion.

If the theory of functional specialization is correct – that is, visual processing occurs in different parts of the brain – then there should be brain-damaged patients who exhibit specific visual impairments. Such patients do exist: in *chromatopsia*, colour vision is intact, but nearly all other processes are impaired (this condition results from carbon monoxide poisoning); *akinetopsia* involves moving objects appearing invisible, even though the same object is visible when stationary (V5 is damaged in this condition).

Computational vision

At the cortical level of processing, considerable organization of perceptual input is found. This aspect of perception was popularized by the Gestalt psychologists of the early twentieth century (e.g., Koffka, 1935; Wertheimer, 1923). They argued that, in perception, the whole is greater than the sum of its parts, and they put forward a number of laws (figure 5.26).

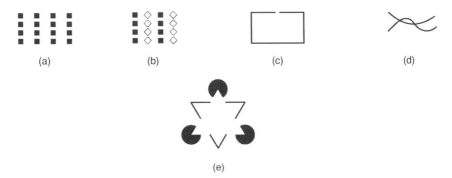

(a)   (b)   (c)   (d)

(e)

Figure 5.26 Some examples of gestalt laws: (a) law of proximity; (b) law of similarity; (c) law of closure; and (d) law of good continuation. The imposition of form on stimuli is shown in (e), where a triangle illusion is formed from non-triangular stimuli.

1. *Law of proximity*: parts of a visual display that are close together tend to be perceived as belonging together.
2. *Law of similarity*: when several stimuli are shown together there is a tendency to see the form in such a way that the similar terms are grouped together.
3. *Law of closure*: small missing parts of a figure are filled to complete it.
4. *Law of good continuation*: parts of a display are grouped together so as to involve the smallest number of interruptions of smooth lines.

In these examples, the strong organizational tendencies in visual perception are evident; also it is possible to view perceptual illusions that result from these organization tendencies (for some superb examples of contrast illusions, go to: www.purveslab.net).

More recent attempts to develop computational models of vision emphasize the multistage route to perception. One of the most influential models, which has inspired more recent models, was proposed by David Marr (who tragically died of cancer in his thirties). Marr's (1982) computational model of object recognition involves the construction of three increasingly detailed representations of the visual world. (a) The *primary sketch* is a two-dimensional representation that includes information about contours, edges and blobs (this information is obtained by making use of light intensity changes in the visual scene). (b) The *2-D sketch* is a representation using information from shading, binocular disparity, motion to form a description of the relative depth and orientation of visual surfaces. (c) The *3-D model* is an advance on the *2-D sketch*: it is 3-D, and is independent of the observer's viewpoint. Marr's influence came from his theoretical argument that visual object recognition (a form of visual processing) involves a *series* of processes intervening between the sensation of the object on the retina and its recognition in the cortex. The visual system builds up successive representations of the object, and at the highest level construction and interpretation (top-down processing) are important.

Mona Lisa's enigmatic smile

Is it possible to put our knowledge to work to understand a mystery that has intrigued and perplexed art lovers for centuries: Leonardo da Vinci's famous *Mona Lisa* seems to be smiling, at other times not. How can this be? Margaret Livingstone, a neurobiologist at Harvard University Medical School, noted that when you look at the mouth she is not smiling; but when you look elsewhere on the face (e.g., the eyes), she has a definite smile. Livingstone reasoned that our peripheral vision sees blurry images (especially involving shadows), whereas the fovea processes fine detail; in other words, peripheral vision is best at processing low-frequency information; the fovea, high-frequency information. When one looks away from the mouth, the low-frequency (blurred) smile becomes evident; but when the smile is looked at directly the fovea's processing of high-frequency information is insensitive to the blurred smile. Livingstone blurred the whole face so that only low-frequency information is available: the smile was evident wherever one looked. The genius of Leonardo da Vinci was to exploit the differences in peripheral and fovea processing to create such an intriguing artistic effect.

Colour perception

As already noted, three types of colour-sensitive photoreceptors (cones) exist in the retina. The processing that starts in these photoreceptors is called *trichromatic colour vision*. All hues (colours) are formed by these three receptor types. There are some 1 million short-wavelength ('blue') cones; over 4 million medium-wavelength ('green') cones; and over 2 million long-wavelength ('red') cones.

Cones

In 1802, Thomas Young confirmed the essentials of the theory that the eye detects different colours because it contains three types of receptors, each having its own sensitivity to wavelengths of light. Physiological studies have since confirmed Young's theory. The reason for several types of cones to detect colour is that a single type of receptor could not distinguish frequency/wavelength from intensity. Imagine a short wavelength of 420 nm was detected. Why could not cones report to the cortex that this short wavelength corresponds to the colour blue? Well, if this 420 nm were presented at an intensity of 100 units to a 'blue' receptor, let us argue it would generate action potentials at a frequency of 100 per second (i.e., 100 Hz). But now if the physical frequency/wavelength (e.g., 50 Hz) and intensity were changed, then frequency processed by the brain might stay at 100 Hz. Thus, the brain would not be informed of the differences in wavelength, only the product of the wavelength given a certain intensity. As with taste receptors, the solution to this problem is to have different types of receptors that are maximally sensitive to different wavelengths: it is the *differential* activation of the three types of cones that provides sensitive information to the brain concerning frequency/wavelength and intensity.

Ganglion cells

In 1890, Hering proposed the *opponent process theory*, which posits that there is a form of opposition between the complementary colours. According to this theory there are three processes, each of which can function in opposite directions: one process is responsible for the perception of red at one extreme and green at the other; the second process is responsible for the perception of blue and yellow; and the third produces black and white. DeValois and DeValois (1975) provided physiological evidence for this theory. They reported opponent cells in the LGN of monkeys. These cells showed increased responses to some wavelengths but decreased responses to others: specifically, red–green and yellow–blue. Other cells increased activity to all wavelengths, indicating a black–light opposition.

At the level of the retinal ganglion cells, the three-colour code gets translated into an opponent colour system: red opposes green; blue opposes yellow (figure 5.27). Thus, the retina contains two kinds of colour-sensitive ganglion cells: *red–green* and *yellow–blue*. Some colour-sensitive ganglion cells respond in a centre–surround fashion

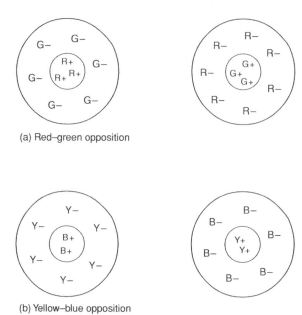

(a) Red–green opposition

(b) Yellow–blue opposition

Figure 5.27 Opponent colour ganglion cells. At retinal ganglion cells, the three-colour code is translated into an opponent colour system: (a) red opposes green, and (b) blue opposes yellow. Some colour-sensitive ganglion cells respond in a centre–surround fashion; other ganglion cells receive input from cones that do not respond differentially to different wavelengths but simply encode relative brightness in the centre and surround (i.e., 'black-and-white' detectors).

– e.g., a cell might be excited by red and inhibited by green in the centre of their receptive field, while showing the opposite pattern in the surrounding ring. Other ganglion cells that receive input from cones do not respond differentially to different wavelengths but simply encode relative brightness in the centre and surround: these are 'black-and-white' detectors.

As shown in figure 5.28, red light excites the 'red' cones, which causes the *excitation* of red–green ganglion cells, and red is seen; green light excites 'green' cones, which causes *inhibition* of red–green cells, and green is seen. Yellow is more complicated: because the wavelength that produces the sensation of yellow is intermediate between red and green, it stimulates both 'red' and 'green' cones about equally. Yellow–blue retinal cells are excited by both 'red' and 'green' cones, so their rate of firing increases. However, red–green ganglion cells are excited by red and inhibited by green, so their rate of firing does not change. The brain detects an increased firing rate from the axons of yellow–blue ganglion cells and interprets this firing pattern as yellow.

The capacity to discriminate red–green colours may be adaptive because it confers an advantage in the long-range detection of ripe fruits and young leaves (which appear red, and high protein, low toughness) against a background of mature (green) foliage (Dominy & Lucas, 2001).

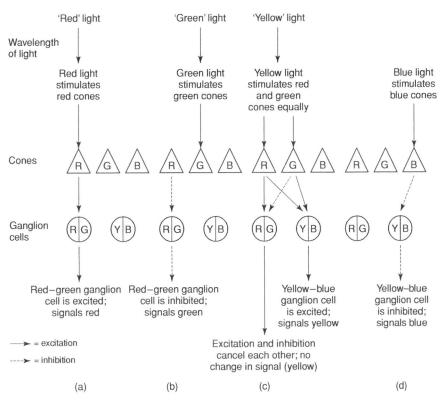

Wavelength of light

'Red' light   'Green' light   'Yellow' light

Red light stimulates red cones

Green light stimulates green cones

Yellow light stimulates red and green cones equally

Blue light stimulates blue cones

Cones

Ganglion cells

Red–green ganglion cell is excited; signals red

Red–green ganglion cell is inhibited; signals green

Yellow–blue ganglion cell is excited; signals yellow

Yellow–blue ganglion cell is inhibited; signals blue

⟶ = excitation

----➤ = inhibition

Excitation and inhibition cancel each other; no change in signal (yellow)

(a)   (b)   (c)   (d)

Figure 5.28 Simplified opponent-processing effects. Colour-coding in the retina follows the following (simplified) pattern. (a) Light corresponding to 'red' causes excitation (unbroken line) of red–green ganglion cells. (b) Light corresponding to 'green' causes inhibition (broken line) of red–green ganglion cells. (c) Light corresponding to yellow stimulates both red and green cones equally, but does not affect blue cones; the stimulation of red and green cones causes excitation of a yellow–blue ganglion cell, but excitation and inhibition of red–green cones, which cancel out, leaving red–green ganglion cells active. (d) Light corresponding to blue stimulates the 'blue' cone, which causes inhibition of yellow–blue ganglion cells. (Adapted from Carlson, 1998.)

After-images

The existence of *after-images* suggests that cone (colour) receptors are in opposition to each other: fixate on a point of colour for a minute and then stare at a white surface. What do you see? You should see a negative after-image, opposite in brightness and complementary in colour (the after-image of blue is yellow, green is red). The most important cause of an after-image is adaptation in the rate of firing of retinal ganglion cells: when the ganglion cells are excited or inhibited for a prolonged period of time they later show a *rebound effect* (they fire at a faster or slower rate than normal); receptors too adapt, which would add to this effect. The after-image is the alternate hue in the ganglion opponent process: yellow–blue, red–green.

Colour blindness

Deficiencies in these receptor types lead to various forms of colour blindness. The existence of the different forms of colour blindness confirms the trichromatic theory. Genetic defects appear in one or more of the 'blue', 'green' and 'red' cones. Two examples of colour blindness result from a defective gene on the X-chromosome (therefore males suffer more from these disorders; see chapter 2). *Protanopia* involves the confusion of red and green. Affected individuals see the world in shades of yellow and blue (red and green look yellowish to them). As their acuity is intact it seems that their 'red' cones are filled with 'green' cone photopigment. The other conditions involve an inadequacy of 'blue', 'green' or 'red' photopigment.

> **ASK YOURSELF**
> To what extent is vision an illusory construction of the brain?

Our tour of the sensory systems is now complete. Next is discussion of motor systems of movement and action.

Motor Systems

It is useful to draw a distinction between *movement* and *action*. Movement denotes the physical (neuromuscular) change of the body. For example, in dancing there are many different movements, but all aimed at one single, coordinated action (*action* denotes what is being achieved by the varied movements). Movement is initiated by a combination of external stimuli and internal triggers (e.g., proprioceptive feedback from sensors in the joints) and internally set goals. Some movements are triggered exclusively by external events (e.g., hearing a clap of thunder); these might be called *reactions*. Other movements are spontaneous and triggered by internal states (e.g., putting on the kettle when thirsty): coordinated movements are termed *action*.

Conceptual issues

Motor control systems are organized hierarchically. At the lowest level, sensors in the muscles make tiny adjustments so as to maintain balance and posture; these reflexes are organized at the level of the spinal cord and are relatively autonomous reactions designed to deal rapidly with challenges. Systems higher up the hierarchy require conscious awareness to guide fine-grained movements. In general terms, movement control entails monitoring: (a) plans/goals; (b) motor outputs; and (c) the difference between them. Disparity triggers action by negative feedback. Conscious awareness and control is slow and can easily become overloaded with information. One solution to this problem is to delegate to other levels, such as reflexes, but to monitor their success or failure (figure 5.29).

A *control theory* approach to movement assumes that the brain sets goals to be met by the body, corresponding to positions in space. The CNS measures the difference between actual position and the goal, and guides behaviour towards the goal by making adjustments in response to negative (error) feedback. Some actions may require guidance from other people: they provide the negative feedback (e.g., learning to drive a car). Other actions are learned automatically (e.g., riding a bicycle) – in this instance, the body itself

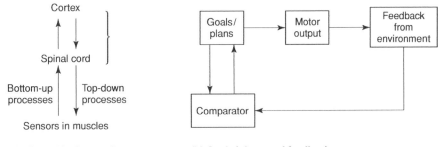

(a) **Hierarchical control**   (b) **Goals/plans and feedback**

Figure 5.29 Muscular control and feedback system. The motor system is organized hierarchically: (a) at the lowest level, sensors in the muscles make adjustments to maintain balance, posture, etc. – these reflexes are organized at the spinal cord. There is a two-way interaction up and down the hierarchy. (b) Once a motor movement is carried out, feedback from the environment (e.g., catching a ball) goes to a comparator, which compares the goals/plans of the system with feedback; adjustments to the motor plan are made on the basis of negative feedback.

is providing the error information for the brain and adjustments to the motor control systems are made. Many movements require some degree of conscious control when first performed (so-called conscious, attentional or controlled processing); but, with practice, most movements become (largely) error-free ('second nature') and can be performed with little conscious awareness.

A second type of error correction information, *feedforward*, is also important: these are anticipatory movements before receiving negative feedback (e.g., leaning into a strong wind – you may be on your back if you wait for negative feedback to tell you that your posture is wrong). In more complex models of feedforward, the nervous system forms dynamic cognitive models and extrapolates to future scenarios (e.g., the behavioural interactions between two animals, predator chasing prey). Feedforward emphasizes that we usually operate on the future environment, not the past (defined in terms of milliseconds) (figure 5.30).

Skeletal muscles

Motor movements are achieved by skeletal muscles, which are responsible for moving the skeleton. Most of these muscles are attached to bones, via tendons (strong bands of connective tissue). The synapse between the terminal button of an efferent neuron and the membrane of a muscle fibre is the *neuromuscular junction*. When an axon fires, *acetylcholine* is released by the terminal buttons and produces a depolarization of the postsynaptic membrane. This potential is much larger than that seen between neurons in the CNS. This depolarization of the muscle fibre opens gates of voltage-dependent calcium channels, permitting calcium ions to enter the membrane. This event triggers the muscle contraction. Movement occurs by changing the extent of shortening (*contraction*) of skeletal muscles; this shortening increases the force that the muscle exerts.

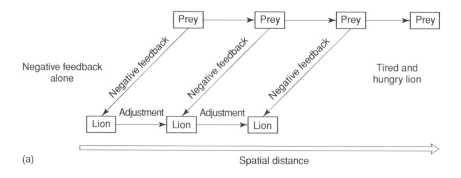

(a)

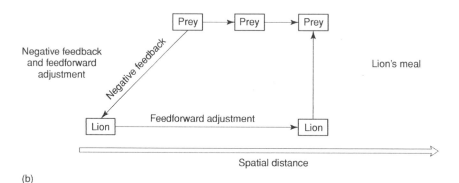

(b)

Figure 5.30 *Feedforward* is a control process that permits anticipatory movements before receiving the negative feedback signal. Working on negative feedback alone will always result in inadequate motor adjustments because of the passage of time (a). But feedforward takes into account this factor and anticipates the likely effect on the environment of time-corrected motor adjustments (b).

Strength of contraction of a muscle is achieved by (a) increasing the frequency of action potentials in motor neurons and (b) increasing the number of motor units that are simultaneously activated. The cell bodies of motor neurons are located in the *ventral horn* of the spinal cord (see chapter 3). In some cases the muscle is a distance from the part of the body it moves and the tendon is long (e.g., muscles that move the fingers are in the forearm).

Brain control of movements

A number of key areas of the brain are involved in motor control. Output signals are produced that are conducted either via the cranial nerves (e.g., to eyes) or via the spinal cord. At the motor cortex, of which there are several areas, the task is one of strategy; the next layer is concerned with tactics and is found in the primary motor cortex, subcortical brain regions and the cerebellum. At the bottom of the hierarchy is the process of execution, embodied within motor neurons with cell bodies in the spinal cord. At the lower level, the options become less open-ended and more constrained, and based upon locally available information in the muscles. Feedback is also sent up the hierarchy concerning what has been achieved and which strategies and tactics may need to be altered.

Figure 5.31 shows the location of the primary motor cortex on the precentral gyrus, other cortical areas, the premotor area and the supplementary motor area.

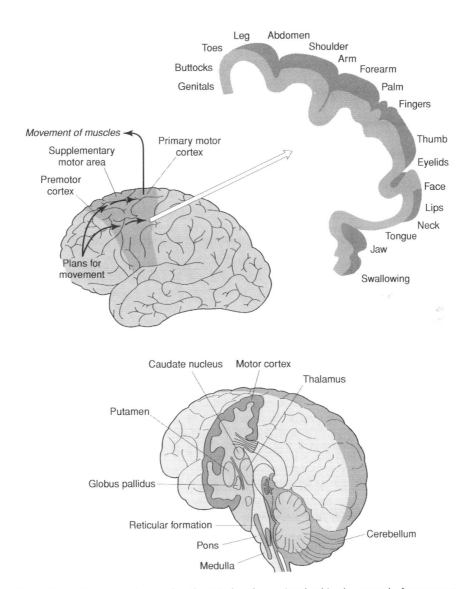

Figure 5.31   The main subcortical and cortical pathways involved in the control of movement.

Premotor cortex

The premotor cortex is concerned with planning and strategy: planning of movement and selection of possible motor programmes, which are then translated into tactics (i.e., implemented) by the primary motor cortex. The premotor area derives inputs from other regions of the cortex, concerned with extracting perceptual information (e.g., occipital, temporal and parietal). Thus, planning is based upon current information on the body and the external world (sensory–motor integration).

Primary motor cortex

The motor homunculus (see chapter 3) shows the responsibility that parts of the primary motor cortex have for regions of the body. The relationship between cortical motor areas and muscles has some plasticity, reflecting the experience of using muscles. The primary motor cortex does not encode specific muscular movements; these are computed by lower centres. Activation of neurons located in the primary motor cortex causes movements of particular parts of the body; thus, it shows *somatotopic organization* (*soma*, body; *topes*, place). If this specific area of the motor cortex is stimulated, then the body part on the opposite side of the body responds; if there is damage to this area, then control is lost over that specific body part.

The principal cortical input to the primary motor cortex is the frontal association cortex: the supplementary motor area and premotor cortex – both of these structures receive input from parietal and temporal lobes and both send axons to the primary motor cortex. Planning of most complex behaviours takes place in the prefrontal cortex.

Other areas can initiate movements. For example, the *prefrontal* cortex can initiate 'willed' actions, which are voluntary and not prompted by external stimuli. When this structure is damaged, the patient is more stimulus-bound, being unable to will actions and withhold prepotent responses. This structure may be especially important in controlled, voluntary actions; with automatic behaviour, this structure becomes less important.

Supplementary motor cortex

Activation of the supplementary motor area is at a maximum at the start of training and decreases with skill acquisition; associated with voluntary movements there is a wave of electric activity recorded at the motor cortex, termed a *motor potential*: this occurs about 55 ms before the muscles start to activate. This structure appears to get the motor system ready for action. Just across the central sulcus from the primary motor area is the somatosensory cortex, concerned with processing tactile information. There are specific projections from regions of the somatosensory cortex to corresponding regions of the primary motor cortex.

The cortex collaborates with the basal ganglia and cerebellum, as follows.

The basal ganglia

A group of subcortical nuclei, termed the basal ganglia, are involved in the control of movement. They are situated to each side of the brain's midline and include among other structures the caudate nucleus, putamen and globus pallidus. Together the caudate nucleus and putamen are the *striatum*.

Through the thalamus, the basal ganglia outputs convey information particularly to areas of cortex concerned with motor control. Damage to this structure is associated with disturbances to movement. Motivation and reward-related inputs can bias movement selection to take account of current priorities.

In the striatum, dopaminergic (DA) neurons project from the midbrain, originating in the substantia nigra (there are also other dopamine systems involved; e.g., the mesolimbic dopamine system). The rich input to the basal ganglia from all cortical regions, especially the prefrontal cortex, suggests an important role for these interacting regions in planning actions. The basal ganglia appears to have access to information on wishes, goals and feelings. It is often called the 'motor programming system'. A major output from the basal ganglia projects, via the thalamus, to areas of cortex associated with both the preparation (e.g., supplementary motor area) and execution of motor action (e.g., to the brainstem).

The basal ganglia deliver instructions based on a readout of ongoing activity in the sensorimotor cortex to premotor areas in such a way as to set up the correct motor programmes required for the next motor action. Based on the prediction of the next move, the basal ganglia appear to be able to select motor programmes and hold them 'offline' in the supplementary motor area in readiness for the appropriate trigger to place them online at the primary motor cortex. The basal ganglia compute get-ready information based upon scene-setting cues that are not themselves direct triggers but which specify conditions under which direct stimuli can trigger 'go now'. In performing a skilled action, the basal ganglia are activated during sequences of activity.

Disruption of dopamine (DA) in the basal ganglia profoundly affects movements. The basis of Parkinson's disease (PD) is degeneration of DA neurons within cell bodies in the substantia nigra; in turn DA signals in the basal ganglia are disrupted. Upstream the supplementary motor area is inhibited, leading to a retardation in movement.

The cerebellum

The cerebellum is concerned with predicting information; it appears not to have an executive role. Its electrical stimulation causes neither sensation nor a motor response. It is involved in the smooth performance of behaviour, once the action has started. It plays a role in skills learning by comparing the actual state of the body and muscles with the goals set and progress towards meeting them. The control exerted by the cerebellum is unlike that of the cortex: one side of the cerebellum controls the same side of the body.

The cerebellum gets information from the motor cortex and information on posture and movement. It projects via the thalamus to the cortex (primary motor area) and, among other structures, to the spinal cord. Highlighting the importance of this structure, it contains 50 billion neurons.

The cerebellum links negative feedback and feedforward; with experience of a task, it allows the weight of control to shift to feedforward. At the start of learning it monitors performance, control being in negative feedback mode, but with practice feedforward comes to dominate. The cerebellum forms representations of the motor actions and their consequences in reaching goals.

If the cerebellum is damaged it results in a loss of feedforward, which forces patients to rely on slower negative feedback. Patients have difficulty in performing behaviour with experience and executing smooth and accurate goal-directed actions (*ataxia*).

The brainstem

Some organization of posture and movement occurs here. Some species-typical patterns (e.g., licking and swallowing) are organized in nuclei here. Influences outside the brainstem (e.g., the hypothalamus) modulate these systems, making them more or less likely to gain expression in behaviour.

Sensation and Experience

Now the major systems and processes in sensory and motor systems have been covered; but it should be evident that this presentation has managed only to provide a sketch of this vast literature. It should be noted that these systems work effortlessly together – the presentation treated each system separately, but this was for the sake of exposition.

It is known that, in the reality of the brain, at the higher cortical levels there is considerable integration of systems, and all work together in a coordinated fashion: an animal detects prey with a combination of sound, vision and smell; we enjoy a good meal as much with our eyes as with our tongue and nose; we are amused by ventriloquism because

> **ASK YOURSELF**
> To what extent are perception and action part of the same process?

our brain is fooled into believing the voice is coming from a puppet because we can *see* the puppet's mouth moving; and we watch our favourite movie stars in the cinema not in the least disturbed by the fact that their voices are coming from speakers many metres away from their mouths.

To illustrate sensorimotor integration, in one study, monkeys were trained to look left, centre or right, and then they heard a sound. In a third of the neurons from the inferior colliculus, the same sound produced a different rate of firing depending on eye gaze. The authors reported being 'astonished', because the inferior colliculus is not usually thought to be involved in the coordination of hearing and vision (Groh et al., 2001). No doubt, future research will continue investigation of *cross-modal* processes, and will start to explain such everyday examples of cross-modal priming.

Another important issue that has arisen from our discussion of sensorimotor systems is the psychological nature of the *experience* of sensation. For example, why a wavelength of 490 nm should be perceived as blue or why four or five taste receptors give rise to the many different tastes we experience daily remains obscure. These types of issues are at the heart of the problems of consciousness (see chapter 18).

Our survey of sensorimotor systems highlights the need to consider the hardware features of the sensory organs and the brain as well as the software features encompassing the complex computational processing required to transform raw sensory data into a conscious percept. Here it is possible to see the importance of the dynamic interplay of bottom-up data processing and top-down conceptual processing; this dual form of processing is fundamental to many psychological processes. Perception solely relies neither on raw sensory data nor on higher-level computational processes (e.g., categorization):

perceptual experiences are a combination of both processes – as discussed in chapter 18, their point of intersection may be important in conscious awareness.

Learning Questions

1. How do the various forms of physical energy get converted in sensory nerve signals?
2. How are the physical properties of stimulation coded in the brain?
3. Explain what is meant by 'physical–psychological correspondence' and explain why this is a puzzle?
4. What do illusions reveal about the nature of visual perception?
5. Why is 'feedforward' considered important in the planning of motor actions?

NOTES

1   Would life without pain be better? Some individuals are born with a condition known *as congenital insensitivity to pain*. They tend to suffer a number of accidents, which highlights the function of pain. One such individual, a high-functioning university student, had bitten off the tip of her tongue as a young child; suffered severe burns from resting against a hot radiator; and had joints and spine damaged as a result of not making the appropriate compensatory action (e.g., changing posture). This individual died at the age of 29, in large part as a result of her insensitivity to pain (Melzack & Wall, 1984). Pain thus serves an important function: its unpleasant nature serves to motivate us to take appropriate action to remove/reduce the source of tissue damage.

2   The taste of *umani* (a Japanese name) is caused by the breakdown (e.g. by cooking) of glutamic acid, one of the 20 common amino acids, which produces monosodium glutamate, which, when added to food (as is done commonly in Japanese and Chinese cooking), enhances the perceived tastes and flavours (tasted on its own it is not particularly pleasant) – English-language equivalent words are 'savoury', 'deliciousness' and 'meaty'. This ability of monosodium glutamate to enhance taste/flavour was recognized as long ago as 1907, when a Japanese scientist, Kikunae Ikeda, encouraged a commercial company to market it in 1909 as a universal food enhancer. As glutamic acid is the most abundant amino acid in animal protein, the evolution of the umani taste receptor is easy to discern.

3   Some 10–15 per cent of the population are 'supertasters': they have an unusually large number of taste buds, and thus they live in a 'neon taste world' in which all tastes seem stronger. This supersensitivity can have a downside, including more burn from oral irritants like chilli peppers, more intense oral pain and a greater tendency to avoid some bitter-tasting vegetables that contain anti-cancer agents (Bartoshuk, 2000).

4   The light spectrum has been known for thousands of years, going back to at least the time of Aristotle: the spectrum could be seen in the sky as well as produced by glass acting as a prism. Until the 1600s, it was assumed that coloured light was not composed of different lights, and what was seen as a spectrum was the result of distortion caused by being passed through a prism. In the 1660s, Isaac Newton proposed, on the basis of his work in optics, a radically new theory, which he confirmed with a 'critical experiment'. He argued that white light was, in fact, composed of a number of different colours, which could be seen with the aid of a

prism. His critical experiment showed that if a restricted range of light produced by a prism (e.g., green light) was put through a *second* prism (i.e. refracted) then this green light was *not* distorted but remained resistant to further changes. This simple, but ingenious, experiment showed that white light is composed of a spectrum of different colours; and that the light spectrum is not an artefact of the distorting effects of prisms.

5 The phenomenon of stereopsis is used in film-making in the creation of three-dimensional films (IMAX technology). The film camera uses two reels of film that capture, like the eyes, two images of the visual scene. These two images are then projected separately using different polarizing filters. Cinema-goers wear glasses which have the same polarized lenses and thus each eye gets a different image. This visual disparity fools the brain into inferring a three-dimensional perspective. Cinema-goers are immersed 'in' a film of their own brain's making. By a similar process of vision disparity integration, we are immersed 'in' our visual environments (although here usually the brain is making valid inferences using depth cues, such as size, perspective and shading).

6 It is now possible to replace the retina with a prosthetic to help patients with, for example, *retinitis pigmentosa* (a hereditary condition in which the retina gradually deteriorates). Recently an Artificial Silicon Retina™ (developed by Optobionics Corporation) has been developed which restores eyesight in patients with retinal degenerative conditions. This chip is smaller than the head of a pin (2 mm in diameter) and about half the thickness of paper (i.e., a thousandth of an inch); it contains 3,500 microscopic solar cells, which serve the roles of rods and cones, each with an electrode designed to stimulate remaining retinal cells from underneath the retina (the underlying cell network remains healthy in these patients). By converting light into tiny electrochemical signals, it is hoped that these photoreceptors will stimulate the remaining photoreceptors and send impulses to the brain that will be interpreted.

FURTHER READING

Bruce, V., Green, P. R. & Georgeson, M. A. (1996). *Visual Perception: Physiology, Psychology and Ecology*. Hove: Psychology Press.

Decety, J. (ed.) (1999). *Perception and Action: Recent Advances in Cognitive Neuropsychology* (a special issue of the *Journal of Cognitive Neuropsychology*). London: Taylor & Francis.

Farah, M. J. (2000). *The Cognitive Neuroscience of Vision*. Oxford: Blackwell.

chapter 6 | The Neuroendocrine System

Learning Objectives

To be able to:

1. Distinguish between glands, endocrines/hormones and target cells, and explain their modes of action.
2. Summarize the main endocrine glands and hormones.
3. Discuss the role of hormones in sexual differentiation and activation.
4. Explain the role that hormones play in the stress reaction.
5. Outline the main sources of interaction of endocrine and immune systems and discuss their effect on illness.

The *neuroendocrine system* consists of a number of chemical communication systems distributed throughout the body, using *hormones* in the blood as the main source of information transmission. It is responsible for a large number of fundamental developmental and activation functions; and, importantly for the understanding of biological psychology, its activity exerts significant effects upon brain and, therefore, mind functioning. This system is not separate from the central and peripheral nervous systems; all three act in an integrated manner.

The neuroendocrine system consists of: (a) hormones of the body; (b) the glands/cells that secrete them; and (c) their physiological and psychological effects. In our discussion, first the basic principles of the neuroendocrine system are covered; and then the principal glands and hormones are summarized. After this introduction, the hormonal effects in three important areas are presented: (a) sexual and gender development; (b) stress reactions; and (c) health, focusing on hormonal effects on the immune system. Those endocrine systems (e.g., those involved in heart regulation) that are responsible for the routine maintenance of the body are not discussed in detail; the focus is on those systems that have significant psychological effects.

By the end of this chapter, it should be possible to answer some fundamental questions in biological psychology. (a) Why are we male or female? (b) Is it possible for a genetic (XY) male to develop into a female? (c) Do hormones activate our sexual desires and behaviour? (d) What happens in our bodies when we are faced by stressors (e.g., at examination time)? (e) Do hormones affect psychiatric disorders (e.g., depression)? (f) What are the effects of hormonal events on the immune system and the probability of developing physical disease?

Basic Principles

Hormones of the neuroendocrine system are defined as chemicals secreted into the blood at one location (from *glands*) and carried to another location (*target cells*) where they exert their effects (this is known as endocrine *action*). However, two other distribution channels for the action of hormones may be defined: *paracrine action*, where the hormone acts locally by diffusing from its source to target cells in the local neighbourhood (*neurohormones* use this action); and *autocrine action*, where the hormone acts on the same cell that produced it (e.g., *growth factor*) (figure 6.1).

Hormones come into contact with nearly all cells in the body, but they target only a limited number of these, that is, those *target cells* containing the specific receptors for hormonal molecules – the lock-and-key analogy already used for the action of neurotransmitters on postsynaptic receptors (chapter 4) is applicable to the action of hormones on target cells, as are the concepts of agonist actions (stimulating the target cells) and antagonist actions (inhibiting the target cells).

Hormones are secreted from glands (and sometimes neurons), but not all glands excrete hormones. There are two types of glands in the body: (a) *exocrine glands*, which release their chemicals into ducts that carry them to their target cells, mostly on the surface of the body (e.g., sweat glands); and (b) *endocrine glands* (ductless glands), which release their chemicals (hormones) directly into the blood system. For this reason, organs whose primary purpose is to release hormones are called *endocrine glands* (sometimes called *classical* hormone glands). However, other organs (e.g., stomach, intestine, heart) also release hormones into the bloodstream (but this is not their primary purpose); these organs are part of the *diffuse endocrine system*. Virtually all hormones are released in pulses (over minutes to hours), or bursts, rather than as continuous secretions (figure 6.2). Longer-term endocrine rhythms are also evident (most being those hormones associated with the menstrual cycle).

Types of hormones

Many hormones have been chemically characterized (defined); others are assumed to exist because of their observed actions, but have not yet been isolated (these putative

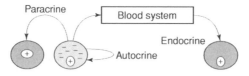

Figure 6.1   Three main types of hormone–receptor action.

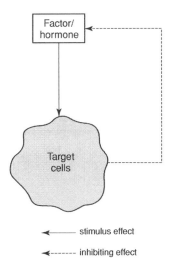

Figure 6.2 Schematic example of releasing factors and hormones and forms of feedback. The gland releases the factor/hormone to the target cell, and then there is a negative feedback signal to the releasing gland to stop (or reduce) further release of the factor/hormone.

hormones are called *factors* to distinguish them from hormones that have been chemically defined). Most hormones fall into three major classes: (a) *Amino acid-derived hormones* are synthesized in a few simple steps from amino acid molecules; there are two types: *thyroid hormones* (produced in the thyroid gland) and catecholamines (e.g., noradrenaline and dopamine; produced in the *adrenal medulla*). (b) *Peptide hormones* and *protein hormones* are chains of amino acids (peptide hormones have shorter chains; protein hormones, longer chains). (c) *Steroid hormones* are synthesized from cholesterol (a fat molecule; e.g., cortisol and corticosterone, released by the adrenal cortex); the sex hormones testosterone and oestrogen are examples of steroid hormones.

Hormone receptors

Hormones bind to specific receptors at target cells. It is this binding process that activates the target cells and sets in train the molecular events that comprise hormonal action. Hormone receptors fall into two broad types: (a) *surface receptors*; and (b) *intracellular receptors*.

Surface receptors

In this mode of hormone molecule–receptor binding, the receptor is located on the surface of the cell. Activation of the receptor leads to the production of a *secondary messenger* (the first messenger is the hormone itself), which has the effect of changing the activity of other molecules (enzymes) within the cells. The activation of these enzymes then activates molecular processes in the cell to produce the action/effects of the hormone. This mode of action is used by the following classes of hormones: (a) protein, (b) peptide and (c) amino acid-derived.

Intracellular receptors

Some classes of hormones bind to receptors within (*intra-*) the cell, acting to alter the *transcription* of the DNA of responsive genes (see chapter 2). The hormone–receptor complex binds to promoter regions of responsive DNA sequences and either stimulates or inhibits the expression of genes. This gene expression then alters the concentration of proteins within the cell and thus the action of the cell. Steroid hormones, which play a major role in sexual development and behaviour, are the major class to use this mode of action (however, it appears that not all steroid hormones exert their effects by binding to nuclear receptors that lead to gene expression; Grazzini et al., 1998).

Hormone concentrations

The physiological effects of hormones depend upon their concentration in the blood and other regions of extracellular fluid. Three factors determine blood concentration levels. (a) *Rate of production*: the synthesis and secretion of hormones are regulated by *negative feedback* and *positive feedback* loops, which instruct the producing/secreting gland either to inhibit activity (negative feedback) or facilitate activity (positive feedback). (b) *Rate of delivery*: the flow of the blood determines how much hormone reaches the target cells. (c) *Rate of survival*: hormones degrade and are metabolized, finally to be excreted from the body. Some hormones have a short half-life (i.e., the time it takes for the potency of the hormone to drop by one-half of its peak effect); other hormones stay in the blood for longer and thus have longer-lasting endocrine effects.

Agonist and antagonist hormones

In the same way as neurotransmitters, hormones can act as either *agonists* or *antagonists*. Agonists are molecules that bind to the receptor and produce the postreceptor events; antagonists are molecules that bind to the receptor but do not produce the postreceptor events, and block the binding of agonists (i.e., blocking the locking mechanism so other molecular (hormonal) keys will not work). Many hormones come in pairs, exerting opposite effects on the target cells. For example, *insulin* and *glucagon* have opposite effects on the liver's control of glucose levels in the blood: insulin lowers this level; glucagon raises it. Balance within accepted bounds depends upon feedback loops that stop further production of the hormone (negative feedback) or encourage it (positive feedback). By this means, balance and homeostasis are achieved.

Hormone–neurotransmitter differences

A hormone may travel the whole length of the body (although some are carried by local blood vessels in specific brain regions). Hormonal action is much broader than that of a neurotransmitter, which involves chemical transmission of information across the synaptic cleft (see chapters 3 and 4). Compared with neurotransmitters, hormones are more diffuse in space (the body) and time. Therefore, hormones serve only as a means of general transmission of information; they cannot code specific information. In addition, hormones often affect multiple sites of action, unlike a neurotransmitter, which interacts with a local and limited number of neurons. In general, hormones tend to regulate slow activities in the body, such as growth and sexual development, as well as determining the environment of the body sufficient to meet anticipated challenges (e.g., fleeing from a predator; preparing the sex organs for reproduction; conserving blood glucose to maintain effective brain functioning).

Although important differences exist between the mode of release and action, neurotransmitters and hormones share a number of common features. Some hormones are *local hormones* that are released into regional blood vessels in the brain, influencing neurons in much the same way as neurotransmitters: these *neurohormones* are important in exerting general modulatory effects, bathing neuronal circuits in specific hormones (Deutch & Roth, 1999). The clear distinction between hormones and neurotransmitters also breaks down when considering certain chemical (e.g., adrenaline and noradrenaline) that serve as both neurotransmitters and hormones. Although hormones may modulate neuronal transmission – perhaps by acting as an amplifier control – they do not seem to act as specific chemical messengers at the synaptic cleft.

In general terms, it is possible to distinguish hormones and neurotransmitters by their mode of release and distance of travel. A chemical substance is serving as a hormone: (a) when it is released at some distance from its target cell; and (b) when it uses the blood as its means of transport. In contrast, neurotransmitters (a) are released by a neuron and bind to receptors of adjacent cells; and (b) have a well-defined onset and end of their action.

> **ASK YOURSELF**
> What are the clear-cut distinctions between the actions of hormones and neurotransmitters?

Neuroendocrine Glands

The position of the glands in the body and their major functions are shown in figure 6.3.

Pituitary gland

The *pituitary gland* is attached to the base of the hypothalamus by a thin stalk that contains neurons, blood vessels and connective tissue. (See figure 6.4.) This pea-sized structure consists of two distinct glands/lobes: (a) the *anterior pituitary*, which secretes *growth hormones*, *gonadotrophins*, *prolactin*, *thyroid-stimulating hormone* (TSH) and *adrenocorticotropic hormone* (ACTH) (see below); and (b) the *posterior pituitary*, which regulates the secretion of the hormones *oxytocin* and *arginine vasopressin*.

The *anterior* and *posterior pituitary* have separate embryological origins, emphasizing the separateness of these two lobes. Release of hormones by the anterior pituitary is under strict control of the neurosecretory neurons of the hypothalamus (these hormones are called *releasing hormones*).

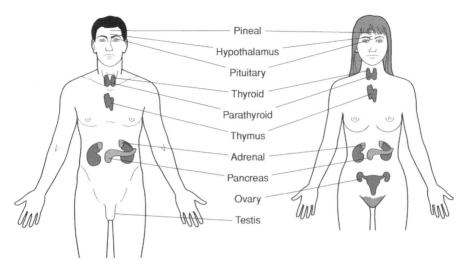

Figure 6.3 Endocrine glands: position of the glands in the body and their major functions.

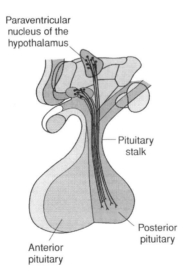

Figure 6.4 Physiology of the paraventricular nucleus (PVN) of the hypothalamus, where the cell bodies of corticotropin-releasing factor (CRF) are located.

The *anterior pituitary* is composed of glandular tissue which synthesizes protein hormones, although the hypothalamus controls their release (see figure 6.5); the hypothalamus secretes releasing hormones, which flow through the blood to the anterior pituitary, where they stimulate or inhibit the release of hormones, which then flow to other glands to exert their action. The anterior pituitary is often called the *master gland* because most of its

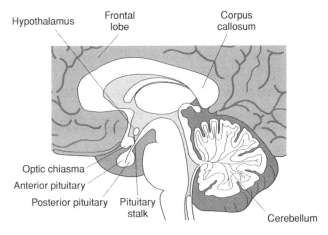

Figure 6.5 The position of the hypothalamus and pituitary gland.

Organ	Hormone	Functions
Hypothalamus	Various releasing hormones	Stimulates or inhibits release of various hormones by pituitary.
Anterior pituitary	Thyroid-stimulating hormone (TSH)	Stimulates thyroid gland.
	Luteinizing hormone (LH)	Increases production of progesterone (female) and testosterone (male); stimulates ovulation.
	Follicle-stimulating hormone (FSH)	Increases production of oestrogen and maturation of ovum (female) and sperm production (male).
	ACTH	Increases secretion of steroid hormones by adrenal gland.
	Prolactin	Increase milk production.
	β-Endorphin	Pain reduction.
Posterior pituitary	Oxytocin	Controls uterine contractions, milk release, certain aspects of parental behaviour, and sexual pleasure
	Vasopressin	Constricts blood vessels; raises blood pressure.

Figure 6.6 The hormones and widespread functions of the hypothalamus and the pituitary gland.

hormones are *tropic hormones* whose primary purpose is to influence the release of hormones from other glands: its secretions control the timing and amount of hormone secretion by other glands, such as the thyroid, adrenal glands and ovaries/testes. Among these functions, it secretes a hormone that tells the kidneys to decrease the amount of water excreted in the urine, a useful mechanism when the body is short of water (figure 6.6).

The *posterior pituitary* is composed of neural tissue and can be considered an extension of the hypothalamus (i.e., axons of hypothalamic neurons that extend downward as a large bundle behind the anterior pituitary). It also forms the pituitary stalk, which gives the appearance that the anterior pituitary is hanging from the hypothalamus. Neurons in the hypothalamus synthesize the hormones *oxytocin* and *vasopressin*, plus smaller amounts of various other peptides. Hypothalamic cells then transport these hormones down their axons to their terminals in the posterior pituitary.

The hypothalamus regulates a wide variety of physiological processes, including maintenance of body temperature, water balance, sleeping and feeding. Its functions are largely mediated by the pituitary gland, which responds to releasing hormones secreted by the hypothalamus (there is a separate releasing factor for each hormone secreted by the pituitary). The action of the hypothalamus is seen in the release of the thyroid hormones.

Thyroid

This butterfly-shaped gland, found at the base of the neck, secretes two thyroid hormones: (a) *thyroxine* and (b) *triiodothyronine*. These hormones control the rate of all metabolic processes and influence growth and development. Attached to the thyroid are four very small glands called the *parathyroids*; they release *parathyroid hormone* and *calcitonin*, which regulate the level of calcium in the blood.

Growth and activity of the thyroid are controlled (a) by the hypothalamus, which secretes thyroid-releasing hormone (TRH; also called *thyrotropin*), which binds to anterior pituitary cells called *thyrotrophs*, which (b) stimulates the anterior pituitary to secrete *thyroid-stimulating hormone* (TSH). TSH travels in the blood to cells in the thyroid gland, stimulating synthesis and secretion of the thyroid hormones, which affect (maybe all) cells in the body. Now, when blood concentrations of thyroid hormones reach a certain level, TRH-secreting neurons in the hypothalamus are inhibited, and this inhibits release of TSH from the anterior pituitary and thus reduces the release of the thyroid hormones themselves. The *hypothalamus–pituitary–thyroid* (HPT) *axis* is an example of the action of a *negative feedback mechanism*. When blood levels of the thyroid hormones then fall below a certain level, this hypothalamic inhibition is released, and the hypothalamus once more secretes TRH and the HPT axis is activated.

Pancreas

The pancreas is located next to the small intestine. It serves two functions: (a) it secretes digestive enzymes into the small intestine; and (b) it secretes hormones for the regulation of blood sugar levels (the discussion is concerned only with the second function).

The pancreas is composed of many small clusters of cells called *islets* (there are approximately one million islets in human beings). Pancreatic islets house three major cell types, each of which produces a different hormone: (a) *alpha cells* secrete *glucagon* (which has the opposite effect to insulin; i.e., it has the effect of increasing blood glucose levels, ensuring sufficient glucose is available for the brain); (b) *beta cells* produce *insulin*; and (c) *delta cells* produce *somatostatin* (involved in growth and development). Insulin is vital for the glucose homeostasis in the blood; a dysfunction in the production of insulin leads to the disease *diabetes mellitus* (see below).

Adrenal gland

These triangular-shaped glands are located next to the kidneys. As discussed below, they are important in mediating reactions to stress, via the *hypothalamus–pituitary–adrenal* (HPA) *axis*. The adrenal gland is composed of two distinct regions: (a) *medulla* (secreting adrenaline and noradrenaline); and (b) *cortex* (excreting steroid hormones, including glucocorticoids and androgens). The medulla and cortex are functionally separate glands, and have different embryological origins.

The *adrenal medulla* synthesizes and secretes adrenaline and noradrenaline, which have the same effects as release from the neuron terminals of the sympathetic branch of the autonomic nervous system, although the effects of these hormones are more long lasting. The physiological effects of the secretion of these two hormones are initiated by the receptors to which they bind on the surface of target cells. Essentially their physiological response is concerned with dealing with stress: increased heart beat; constriction of blood vessels (increasing blood pressure); increased metabolic rate; dilatation of pupils; cessation of non-essential processes (e.g., digestion and motor activity); and increased sugar output of the liver.

The *adrenal cortex* is a site for the manufacture of many steroid hormones, including sex hormones, especially androgens; the production of corticosteroids is especially important (see below).

Pineal gland

This gland, located in the centre of the brain, is connected to nerves from the eyes, and is stimulated by light. This *photoneuroendocrine system* is influenced by retinal photoreceptors that project to the *suprachiasmatic nucleus*, which is the site of the endogenous circadian clock. The gland produces *melatonin* (also produced elsewhere in the body; e.g., in the gut) at night when it is dark, secreting more of this hormone in the darkness of winter. Melatonin promotes sleep, depresses the activity of the gonads, and has effects on the thyroid and adrenal cortex.

Sex glands: ovaries and testes

The testes and ovaries serve two functions: (a) the production of the reproductive elements of sperm (testes) and follicles (ovaries) (*gametogenic* functions); and (b) sex-steroid hormones. The female *ovaries* secrete oestrogens, which are responsible for female characteristics and involved in sexual behaviour; another hormone (progesterone) prepares the uterus for implantation of an embryo. The male *testes* are responsible for the production of testosterone (along with the adrenal gland), which, in turn, is responsible for male characteristics and sexual arousal. The action of these two hormones is discussed in more detail below. In the male foetus, the gonads differentiate into testes early in gestation, and by week 8 are producing appreciable quantities of testosterone, along with other androgens (figure 6.7).

> **ASK YOURSELF**
> In relation to the central nervous system, are endocrine glands servant or master?

▢ Neuroendocrine Hormones

This section summarizes the action of the major hormones; then in the sections to follow, the action of some of the more important hormones are discussed in further detail.

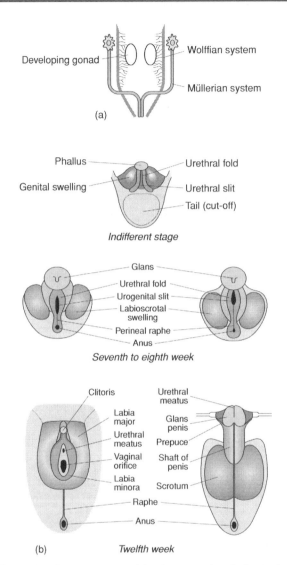

Figure 6.7 Wolffian and Müllerian systems and development of genitalia. At six weeks the human foetus has the bases of Wolffian (male) and Müllerian (female) reproductive ducts: this is the indifferent, undifferentiated, stage (a). From the seventh to eighth weeks, under the influence of testicular testosterone, the male Wolffian system develops, and the testicular Müllerian-inhibiting substance causes the Müllerian system to degenerate; in the absence of testosterone, the Müllerian system develops into reproductive ducts and the male Wolffian system fails to develop. By the twelfth week, the female and male reproductive systems are developed (b).

Insulin

Insulin is a protein hormone that is secreted from the pancreas. It exerts an influence upon a large number of cells of the body that use glucose (a sugar) as fuel for energy. When the glucose level in the blood rises (e.g., after eating a chocolate bar) a control system detects this concentration and triggers the release of insulin. Insulin promotes glucose uptake in cells (neurons are the major exception: they do not depend on insulin for glucose uptake). Low levels of glucose lead to a reduction in insulin and insulin-dependent cells do not take up glucose. As the brain uses only glucose for fuel, this reduction in the body's uptake of glucose is important: it leaves the glucose remaining for exclusive use by the brain.

Injection of glucose directly into the bloodstream or the ingestion of food leads to an increase in insulin release. However, the mere sight or smell of food also leads to insulin release: this *glucose anticipation insulin effect* is adaptive because anticipation of glucose allows the body to start metabolizing glucose in order that food-related glucose levels neither rise nor fall too far. The pancreatic insulin system allows the body to maintain constant blood concentrations of glucose despite the varying frequency and content of meals – without this system, skipping breakfast could lead to coma and death!

Adrenocorticotropic hormone (ACTH)

Adrenocorticotropic hormone (ACTH) is secreted by the anterior pituitary in response to *corticotropin-releasing hormone* (CRH) from the hypothalamus; CRH is released in response to various forms of stress (see below). ACTH (also called *corticotropin*) stimulates the adrenal cortex, leading to the secretion of *glucocorticoids*, such as cortisol. CRH is itself inhibited by glucocorticoids, which act via a negative feedback mechanism. The release of ACTH stimulates the outer layer of the adrenal gland (the *adrenal cortex*) to secrete corticosteroids (the main one in humans is cortisol; there are other types of corticosteroids). Release of corticosteroids elevates blood sugar and enhances metabolism. These outcomes are important in terms of emergency when the body is made ready for a state of rapid response. As discussed below, this system mediates long-term stress, which can lead to a number of diseases.

Among its other functions, ACTH is involved in the expectation that sleep comes to an end at a specific time: there is a marked increase in the concentration of this hormone one hour before awakening (Born et al., 1999). Thus, ACTH appears to arouse the body for action – this release may occur too early in depressed patients, who often experience early waking.

A common test of the response of the adrenal gland to ACTH is the 'dexamethasone suppression test', in which the chemical dexamethasone – which is a synthetic steroid similar to cortisol – is given and levels of cortisol are measured. Cortisol levels should decrease in response to the administration of this chemical, because it mimics its action, which in normal individuals is to suppress the release of ACTH from the pituitary gland and thus stimulation of the adrenal gland and the secretion of cortisol. This test identifies people who produce too much cortisol, which is a significant health risk.

Glucocorticoids

Cortisol is the most important of the glucocorticoids in human beings; these are involved in glucose metabolism, maintaining a constant level of glucose in the blood.

Glucocorticoids are secreted in response to a single stimulator: the *adrenocorticotropic hormone* (ACTH; see above) from the anterior pituitary.

Arginine vasopressin

Arginine vasopressin (AVP), produced by the posterior pituitary, is a hormone that regulates body fluids; on account of this role, AVP is often called an antidiuretic hormone (ADH). As the body is composed of some 60 per cent water, regulation of body fluid is vital. AVP is synthesized in neurons in the brain and transported along their axons to terminals at the posterior pituitary gland, where it is stored. When the body is deficient in water this is detected by neurons, which then excite AVP-producing neurons. Activation of AVP-containing neurons causes them to release AVP into the blood, which transports it to the kidneys, where it inhibits the production of urine. When there is excess of water in the body, the secretion of AVP is inhibited and the kidneys excrete more urine. Deficiency of AVP results in *diabetes insipidus*, which entails large volumes of urine being secreted. In addition to these basic regulatory functions, this hormone has also been implicated in pair bonding and attachment.

Oxytocin

Oxytocin is produced by neurosecretory cells of the hypothalamus and transported to the posterior pituitary gland (in the same manner as AVP); it is also secreted within the brain and the testes and ovaries. It is responsible for: ejection of milk from the breast; stimulation of muscle contraction at birth (it is released during childbirth when the foetus stimulates the cervix and vagina, enhancing the contraction of the muscles); and it establishes maternal behaviour (e.g., its injection into virgin or non-pregnant rats leads to maternal behaviour; antagonizing the action of the hormone leads to a failure of the mother to accept her pups). The body releases enormous amounts of oxytocin during orgasm (3 to 5 times the normal level in the blood), in both males and females, leading to the 'afterglow' of orgasm. Like vasopressin, it is important in pair bonding and attachment.

Oxytocin is sensitive to touch and physical contact, and is one of the hormones involved in romantic love. It can be thought of as an unconditioned stimulus (UCS), which reinforces the conditioned stimulus (CS; e.g., a particular person) associated with its release. There is a cycle established such that the release of oxytocin leads to reciprocal touching, which reinforces further touching. This happens in pair bonding between mother and baby, as well as between lovers.

In the case of sexual behaviour, the release of oxytocin increases sexual desire and receptivity; it leads to the increase in testosterone, which increases sex drive in males and females. In females, it stimulates the release of oestrogen and prepares the vagina for penetration. Oxytocin also increases the sensitivity of the penis and nipples and makes orgasms stronger; further stimulation of these organs then leads to a further increase.

The effects of oxytocin are largely dependent on oestrogen; and the effects of oxytocin rise as oestrogen levels rise. For this reason, it seems that females are more affected by

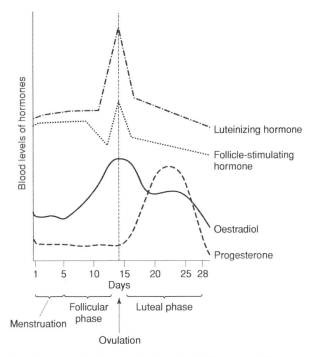

Figure 6.8 Levels of hormone during menstrual cycle. At the start of the menstrual cycle the anterior pituitary releases *follicle-stimulating hormone* (FSH), which promotes the growth of a follicle in the ovary. The follicle nurtures the *ovum* (egg cell) and leads to the production of oestrogen. Towards the middle of the cycle, the follicle becomes more sensitive to FSH (even though the concentration of FSH in the blood is in decline). As a result, the follicle produces increasing amounts of one type of oestrogen, oestradiol, which leads to increased release of FSH and a surge in the release of luteinizing hormone (LH) from the anterior pituitary: FSH and LH cause the follicle to release the hormone progesterone, which prepares the uterus for the implantation of a fertilized ovum at the middle of the cycle, when conception is possible.

touch than men, and this sensitivity differs over the menstrual cycle, with greatest sensitivity at mid-cycle ovulation. It also appears that oxytocin impairs memory, so a hug or sexual activity after an argument might reduce thinking about a prior argument and even cause one to forget about some of the distress caused.

Experimental studies support the role of oxytocin in sexual and maternal behaviour. Oxytocin (a) facilitates maternal behaviour in oestrogen-primed female rats; (b) in virgin rats induces full maternal behaviour within minutes of injection; and (c) injection of an oxytocin antagonist (which blocks the effects of oxytocin) suppresses the onset of maternal behaviour in postpartum rats. However, these effects are not seen after several days of maternal behaviour, indicating that oxytocin is involved in the onset rather than the maintenance of maternal attachment (Leckman, Mayes & Cohen, 2002).

Somatotrophin and somatostatin

Growth hormone (GH) is synthesized and secreted by cells called *somatotrophs* in the anterior pituitary. The major function of this growth hormone is to stimulate the liver and other tissue (e.g., pancreas) to secrete IGF-1 (i.e., *insulin-like growth factor 1*), which, in turn, stimulates the production of cartilage cells, resulting in bone growth. The secretion of this hormone is highest during the years of development; its impairment leads to short stature ('dwarfism'). GH is controlled by two hormones released from the hypothalamus: growth hormone-releasing hormone (*somatotrophin*) promotes its release, and *somatostatin* inhibits it. In addition to its clinical use in children of short stature, growth hormones are widely used in agriculture to accelerate growth of cattle and enhance the production of milk in dairy cattle.

Melatonin

This hormone is released by the pineal gland and is controlled by light-sensitive receptors. Melatonin secretion is tied to the 24-hour circadian rhythm. Passengers travelling across time zones often take melatonin tablets in order to 'reset their biological clocks' (i.e., to phase-shift their circadian rhythm to match the night/day phase of the new time zone). Within 2 hours of taking melatonin, sleep is induced (unless taken late in the evening when the pineal is secreting its own melatonin).

Seasonal affective disorder (SAD; a type of depression) is related to the production of too much melatonin. In northern hemisphere countries with little sunlight at certain times of the year, the prevalence of SAD is high. SAD patients are given *phototherapy*, which consists of sitting in front of a bright light for several hours each day to inhibit the production of melatonin.

Gonadotrophins

This class of hormone is secreted from cells in the anterior pituitary called *gonadotrophs*; they stimulate the production of the testes and ovaries (i.e., the gonads; see below); they are essential for reproduction, but not the maintenance of life. Pituitary gonadotrophins include *luteinizing hormone* (LH) and *follicle-stimulating hormone* (FSH). The regulator of LH and FSH is secretion of gonadotrophin-releasing hormone (GnRH) from the hypothalamus. Negative feedback from the gonads inhibits further synthesis and secretion of LH and FSH (figure 6.9).

Luteinizing hormone (LH): in both sexes, LH stimulates the secretion of sex steroids from the gonads (testosterone from the testes; oestrogen from the ovaries). In addition, in females, large quantities of LH are responsible for the production of mature follicles in the ovaries during the preovulatory phase of the menstrual cycle; during ovulation these follicles travel down the fallopian tubes, where fertilization takes place before the fertilized egg is embedded in the wall of the uterus (i.e., the womb). *Follicle-stimulating hormone* (FSH) stimulates the maturation of ovarian follicles; and it is also responsible for sperm production.

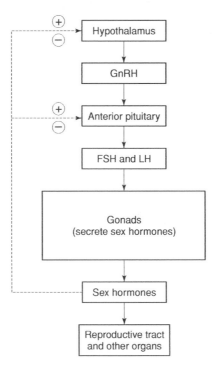

Figure 6.9 Hypothalamus–pituitary–gonads system. *Gonadotrophins* stimulate the testes and ovaries and the pituitary. Gonadotrophins comprise *luteinizing hormone* (LH) and *follicle-stimulating hormone* (FSH), the regulator of which is secretion of gonadotrophin-releasing hormone (GnRH) from the hypothalamus. Negative feedback from the gonads inhibits further synthesis and secretion of LH and FSH.

Prolactin

This hormone is secreted by the *lactotrophs* in the anterior pituitary gland; it is also secreted by other cells in the body, including immune cells, the brain and the pregnant uterus. It stimulates growth of the mammary gland and the production of milk in mammals (i.e., lactation) and stimulates the ovaries to secrete the hormone *progesterone*. However, its effects go beyond these functions. For example, some types of immune cells synthesize and secrete prolactin, suggesting that prolactin may act as an autocrine (i.e., acting on neighbouring cells) or paracrine (i.e., acting on itself) modulator of immune activity. Unlike most other hormones released from the anterior pituitary, which are stimulated by releasing factors from the hypothalamus, the hypothalamus suppresses prolactin secretion (dopamine serves this function by binding to prolactin-producing lactotrophs in the anterior pituitary): when this hypothalamic suppression is released, then prolactin is synthesized and secreted by the anterior pituitary. In addition, other hormones, including *thyroid-releasing hormone* (TRH), also suppress prolactin release; oestrogen has the opposite effect, especially during the period of late pregnancy when the breast needs to be prepared for milk production.

Sex hormones

The gonads do not just create sperm and egg cells, they also release hormones. The two main classes of gonadal hormones are *androgens* and *oestrogens*; testosterone is the most common androgen, and oestradiol the most common oestrogen. The testes and ovaries produce *both* hormones, although in very different amounts: compared with men, women produce a trifling amount of testosterone, just enough for normal ovulation (although it is sufficient to enhance sexual activity); adult men produce 20 times more (approximately 7 mg per day). These steroid hormones are also synthesized and released from the adrenal gland.

Androgens are called 'male hormones' because their level is so much higher in men than in women. Oestrogens are often referred to as 'female hormones' because their level is 10 times higher in women. The ovaries and testes release a class of hormones called *progestins*, the most common of which is progesterone, which in females prepares the uterus (e.g., by decreasing uterine sensitivity to oxytocin) and breasts for pregnancy. In males, oestrogen is present in low concentrations in the blood, but in very high concentration in semen (in fact higher than the serum concentration in females). This finding has led to the suggestion that this hormone plays an important part in male fertility (Hess et al., 1997).

Testosterone

Testosterone is secreted in the bodies of both males and females. It is secreted from the testes and adrenal gland in the male; in females, from the adrenal gland only. Its secretion is controlled by other hormones (i.e., *gonadotrophins*) that are secreted into the bloodstream at the pituitary gland. Testosterone plays a role in sexual motivation and behaviour and seems to be important in dominance hierarchies (e.g., defeat of a male primate leads to a decline in this hormone, which biases the male's behaviour away from challenging for dominance – this might be the sensible short-term strategy given the previous defeat). In the case of sexual behaviour, testosterone levels are highest between the ages of 15 and 25 years, when sexual motivation is at its typical peak.

As noted above, androgens and oestrogens are steroid hormones, and as such exert their action within the molecular machinery of the cell, leading to gene expression. Now, some of the genes that these sex hormones activate are *sex-limited genes* because their effects are much stronger in one sex than in the other. For example, oestrogen activates the genes responsible for breast development in women, and androgens activate the genes responsible for the growth of facial hair in men. Androgens stimulate the growth of pubic hair in both sexes. Thus, the XY differences between males and females accounts for the different effects of androgens and oestrogens: if this were not the case, then their effects would be the same in both sexes (albeit to varying degrees, depending on their concentrations in the blood). It is therefore not surprising that sex hormones are steroids that bind to intracellular receptors capable of DNA transcription (see above).

After removal of the testes or ovaries in the rat, sexual behaviour declines in proportion to the blood concentration of the sex hormones. Testosterone restores sexuality in castrated males; oestrogen activates sexual behaviour is females. In the vast majority of species, males compete for access to females (i.e., sexual selection; see chapter 2);

aggression is a common way to win such access. Increased levels of testosterone are associated with increased aggression. Thus, sex hormones are fundamental to the key component of fitness: differential reproduction.

In summarizing the major effects of hormones, it should be remembered that they work in a synergistic manner; it is too simplistic to associate one hormone with one effect or a few isolated effects: the action of one hormone often depends upon the actions of other hormones, and may have multiple effects (Nature favours adaptations that serve more than one purpose: this makes efficient uses of resources and allows newly evolved functions to build upon *pre-adaptations*; see chapter 2). For example, *corticotrophin-releasing factor* (CRF), *vasopressin*, *oxytocin* and *adrenocorticotropic hormone* (ACTH) all seem to have effects on fear and anxiety, as well as on learning and memory (Croiset, Nijsen & Kamphuis, 2000).

ASK YOURSELF
To what extent are we slaves to our hormones?

The Menstrual Cycle

The female reproductive system is characterized by its periodicity, the *oestrous cycle*, which is typically 28 days. This cycle is the outcome of the interactions of ovaries, anterior pituitary and hypothalamus. The cycle starts with the secretion of *gonadotropin-releasing hormone* (GnRH) from neurons in the hypothalamus; the feedback effect of oestrogen at the anterior pituitary, and possibly also the hypothalamus, is associated with excitatory and inhibitory effects (see figure 6.8, above). Positive feedback is seen as a surge in luteinizing hormone (LH) preceding ovulation (in the male there is only negative feedback at the anterior pituitary).

At the beginning of the menstrual cycle, the anterior pituitary releases *follicle-stimulating hormone* (FSH), which promotes the growth of a follicle in the ovary; this follicle nurtures the *ovum* (egg cell) and leads to the production of oestrogen. Towards the middle of the cycle, the follicle builds up more and more receptors to FSH; so even though the actual concentration of FSH in the blood is decreasing, its effects on the follicle increase. As a result, the follicle produces increasing amounts of one type of oestrogen, oestradiol. This leads to increased release of FSH, as well as a sudden surge in the release of luteinizing hormone (LH) from the anterior pituitary. FSH and LH cause the follicle to release the hormone progesterone, which prepares the uterus for the implantation of a fertilized ovum. Progesterone also inhibits the further release of LH. At the end of the menstrual cycle, the levels of LH and FSH, oestradiol and progesterone all decline. If the ovum is fertilized then the level of oestradiol and progesterone increase gradually throughout pregnancy; if the egg is not fertilized, the lining of the uterus is cast off (through menstruation) and the cycle begins again.

Contraceptive and birth pills work by disrupting the feedback cycle between the ovaries and the pituitary. The *combination pill* contains both oestrogen and progesterone; it works in several ways: high levels of oestrogen beginning shortly after the end of the menstrual period suppress the release of FSH, thereby preventing the development of the follicle and the release of the ovum. Progesterone blocks the secretion of LH, thus further ensuring that the ovum is not released. Unlike women who show increased sexual fantasizing, masturbation and initiation of sexual behaviour at mid-cycle (the *periovulatory period*) – that is, the point of highest oestrogen concentration in the blood and greatest fertility – women on the contraceptive pill show no increase at this period (Adams, Gold & Burt, 1978), suggesting that oestrogen is important in maintaining sexual motivation and behaviour.

Women who live together tend to synchronize their menstrual cycles (McClintock, 1999; Weller, 1998); the taking of the contraceptive pill abolishes this effect, suggesting human beings, like most other mammals, are sensitive to pheromones (i.e., airborne chemical signals, not consciously detected, that can affect physiology and behaviour; Wyatt, 2003). To test whether pheromones are responsible for this synchronization, young women were exposed to the underarm secretions of donor women. Most of the exposed women synchronized their cycles to the donor's (Preti et al., 1986; Russell, Switz & Thompson, 1980). In addition, Stern and McClintock (1998) found that odourless compounds from the armpits of women, taken at different phases of their menstrual cycle, affected the release of LH (accelerated and delayed depending on donor's phase of cycle).

Most mammals use pheromones in sexual attraction. The effects of pheromones depend on activity of the *vomeronasal* organ (a set of receptors located near the olfactory receptors). It is a prominent structure in most mammals, and is easily seen in the human foetus, but in adult humans it is very small (Monti-Bloch et al., 1994). There is, as yet, little evidence that pheromones are used in human beings in sexual attraction. However, a few studies do suggest a sexual role. For example, male underarm secretion, when applied (for six hours and masked by fragrance) to females, alters the length and timing of the menstrual cycle and affects mood (increasing relaxation and reducing tension). Pheromones may impact upon several components of fertility: endocrine responses (primer effects), behaviour (releaser effects), information (signaller effects) or mood (modulator effects). But why should this phenomenon exist? An evolutionary perspective might argue that it would be an advantage in hunter–gatherer societies for women to be fertile around the same time in the presence of men, because groups of men spent a considerable proportion of time away hunting.

In other mammals, the effects of pheromones are widespread. For example, male elephants constantly monitor the urine of their female harem to determine which ones are in 'heat' (i.e., sexually receptive and fertile) – the vomeronasal organ is in the roof of the elephant's mouth. In the urine is a pheromone that activates a hard-wired circuit in the brain that leads to an instant erection (Rasmussen et al., 1996).

ASK YOURSELF
What might be the evolutionary advantages of synchronized ovulation?

Sex and Gender

Hormones play a fundamental role: (a) in the foetal *organization* of the sex organs; and (b) during puberty, in the development of *secondary sexual characteristics* (e.g., pubic hair, breast enlargement, voice breaking). They also play an important role in the *activation* of sexual desire, motivation and behaviour during adulthood.

Organizational effects

Organizational effects refer to permanent change in the structure (i.e., morphology) of both the sex organs and the central nervous system as a result of exposure to hormones. These changes occur at *critical periods* during gestation (in the case of human beings, about the third and fourth months), during which time primitive sexual structures are most sensitive to hormonal influence.

Gonads

In all mammals during very early development, the gonads are identical in genetic male (XY) and female (XX) foetuses – this is the undifferentiated 'sexually indifferent stage'. Differentiation is the process of the formation of the male or female reproductive system from the undifferentiated structures: *Müllerian ducts* and *Wolffian ducts* (see figure 6.7 above). These primitive structures degenerate or develop to form male testes or female ova,[1] and the external genitalia. What determines the developmental route is the presence of testosterone: exposure to this hormone leads to development along the male line; in the absence of exposure to the hormone, the primitive ducts develop along the female line.

The mechanism by which testosterone is produced in XY males is the presence of the Y chromosome, which contains genes that lead to the ducts developing into early testes; the production of these testes then leads to the production of testosterone and the further growth of the testes, and thus to the production of more testosterone: this is the process of *gonadogenesis.*

Testosterone also causes the primitive Wolffian ducts to develop into *seminal vesicles* (sacs that store semen) and *vas deferens* (a duct from the testes to the penis). A peptide hormone, *Müllerian inhibiting hormone* (MIH), released from the testes, causes the Müllerian ducts to degenerate; at the same time the testes secrete testosterone, which stimulates the development of the Wolffian duct system to form the male sexual organs. In contrast, females develop along a default developmental path to form the female sexual genitalia made from the primitive Müllerian ducts and Wolffian ducts: her Wolffian ducts degenerate and her primitive Müllerian ducts develop into female structures (uterus and vagina). Ovarian (oestrogen) hormones seem not to be involved in early sexual development; without the effects of testosterone (secreted by the testes) the default sex is female.

Turner's syndrome is found in women with only one X chromosome (so-called X0; see chapter 2). These women do not develop ovaries and therefore adequate levels of oestrogens, which require two X chromosomes; however, they do develop female internal sexual organs and external genitalia. This syndrome seems to show that oestrogens are not required for female sex organs to develop. Therefore, it seems that androgens cause males; the absence of sex hormones leads to the formation of the female phenotype.

Therefore, it is the production of testosterone during the critical periods of development that determines maleness (presence of testosterone) and femaleness (absence of testosterone) in terms of genitalia, internal reproductive organs and psychological characteristics. X and Y chromosomes bias development in favour of one of the two versions of sex. In experimental animals it can be shown that, if genetically female rats are exposed to testosterone during these early critical periods, then they develop male sexual organs. As discussed below, in human beings natural experiments occur in which some individuals develop, both morphologically and psychologically, along male *and* female lines.

Androgens (principally testosterone) pass the cell membrane of certain cells (including neurons) and attach to receptors in the nucleus (as do most steroid hormones); these androgens are then converted into oestradiol (the principal type of oestrogen), which then alters the expression of genes within cells. By this means genetic effects are expressed to form morphic, physiological and psychological sexual characteristics. It is interesting that the final effect of testosterone is mediated by the so-called 'female hormone', oestrogen. (The fact that oestrogen in females does not lead to this same outcome is due to the presence of an inhibiting molecule, *alpha-fetoprotein*; see below.)

After playing this fundamental role in the organization of the reproductive system, including the brain structures that mediate sex-typical motivation and behaviour, the effects of sex hormones lie dormant until the period of puberty, when there is a further input from gonadal hormones to sexual development. Boys experience their voices 'breaking' and secondary sexual characteristics forming (e.g., pubic hair); girls begin their menstrual cycle, and fat is laid down on the thighs, buttocks and breasts. Puberty is initiated by the hypothalamus, which releases *luteinizing-releasing hormone* (LRH) at a rate of one burst per hour (these bursts seem to be triggered by body weight). This releasing hormone stimulates the pituitary to secrete *luteinizing hormone* (LH) and *follicle-stimulating hormone* (FSH), which in turn stimulates the gonads to release oestradiol in females and testosterone in males.

Sex-determining genes

Genes on the X and Y chromosomes play a major role in sexual differentiation. Two major genes are involved in this process: the SRY male-making gene and the DAX1 female-making gene.

SRY male-making gene

One clue to sex-determining genes came from the study of XX men – that is, men with the female XX chromosomes (the first indication that they are genetically female often comes with the discovery that they are sterile). In these men, it appears that a tiny part of their father's Y chromosome had become attached to the X chromosome – it is this paternal X that is passed on to the son. A search was made for the male-determining gene on the Y chromosome, which was absent in XX men. This research revealed a 250 base pair sequence – a tiny gene – christened the SRY (see Cookson, 1994) and located on the short arm (top half) of the Y chromosome. Around the sixth week of foetal life, it is this gene that causes the undifferentiated tissue to develop into testes – without this activation, the tissue develops along default female lines. It is remarkable that a gene with so few base pairs (many genes are composed of, often many, thousands of base pairs) could have such a profound effect on sex determination.

An XY offspring may have the SRY gene missing from the Y chromosome (or the gene may be inactive), hence this chromosomally XY boy develops into a girl. In all respects the child appears to be a girl, but menstruation does not occur, and then the problem is identified.

DAX1 female-making gene

The absence of the SRY gene, or its inactivation, leads to the default development of female genitalia. Another gene is important too: DAX1 is located on the X chromosome and acts at the same point in the developmental pathway as SRY – in normal males SRY wins out, and sexual tissue develops along male lines. However, if the DAX1 gene duplicates, then it causes the individual who is genetically male (i.e., XX) to develop physically as a female. It seems that the function of DAX1 is to ensure that secondary male genes are turned off (it is an anti-male gene) – in too strong a dose (due to duplication), it beats the SRY gene and turns off male-making processes. The 'female' often finds out the truth when they fail to menstruate at puberty. There are also chromosomal XX females who develop as males, because of the activation of SRY and the inaction of DAX1. Thus, SRY and DAX1 interactions can account for the genetic basis of sex reversal syndromes – technically known as a 'dose-sensitive sex reversal' (Swain et al., 1998; also see Meeks, Weiss & Jameson, 2003).

The central nervous system

In addition to the organizational effects of early exposure to testosterone on the development of the gonads and sexual reproductive anatomy, the central nervous system also undergoes organization along sex-specific lines. The most obvious effect of this sex-specific organization is on the hypothalamus (which controls the anterior pituitary, the *master gland*), which, in the female, is responsible for cyclic patterns of hormone release from puberty to menopause (i.e., the menstrual cycle). The male hypothalamus is incapable of generating this cyclic release of hormones – the same is also true of genetic (XX) females exposed to high levels of testosterone during their critical period of development, who have developed along male lines.

An example of this hormone-related sexual dimorphism is found in the medial pre-optic area (MPOA) of the hypothalamus. The MPOA – a *sexually dimorphic nucleus* – is typically larger in males than females, and its stimulation in males causes male-typical behaviour, and in females, female-typical behaviour. Destruction of the MPOA results in impaired sexual motivation in most species. Dopamine and noradrenaline are important neurotransmitters in sexual behaviour. Neurons in the MPOA increase the release of dopamine during sexual behaviour; sexual behaviour also increases dopamine release in the nucleus accumbens, an important structure in the brain involved in reinforcement and motivational processes.

Exposure to androgens in the sexually developing foetus causes a process of *masculinization*. In the rat, exposure to testosterone sensitizes the male rat to rough-and-tumble play (Fitch & Denenberg, 1998), that is, masculinization of play mechanisms. Male rats that inherit insensitivity to androgens show a female-like pattern of play.

Masculinization and feminization

Psychological differentiation occurs along two axes in the brain: (a) *masculinization* and (b) *feminization*. In the male, testosterone has two effects on the central nervous system: (a) masculinizing and (b) defeminizing (corresponding to the male phenotype). In the absence of testosterone, two effects occur: (a) demasculinization and (b) feminization (corresponding to the female phenotype). These two axes produce four possible categories (types): (a) masculinization–defeminization (typical male development); (b) demasculinization–feminization (typical female development); (c) masculinization–feminization (atypical male development) and (d) demasculinization–defeminization (atypical female development). Oestrogens may be involved in the feminization of the female brain during development (Fitch & Denenberg, 1998). The development of these *gender* types depends upon exposure to testosterone at different stages of foetal development.

The effects of testosterone are mediated by the oestrogen oestradiol, which exerts masculinizing effects on sexual behaviour (it is thus somewhat misleading to talk of oestrogen as a 'female hormone'). In the female, testosterone (which is present in low concentrations) does not have this masculinizing effect because *alpha-fetoprotein*, which is not present in adults, binds with oestrogen and blocks it from leaving the bloodstream and entering the cells that are developing during the critical period: if this blocking effect did not happen (as sometimes it does not) then oestrogen produced in females would lead to masculinization (in rare clinical cases, this protein is defective, leading to masculinization of the female's brain). The precise effects of oestradiol depend upon the stage of development.

Masculinization and *feminization* can be studied experimentally in the rat, where rigorous control over important variables is possible. From such studies, exposure to testosterone during critical periods leads to the biasing of sex-specific behaviours. For example, phenotypal males and females denied access to testosterone develop female-typical behaviour; females exposed to androgens during early development form male-typical behaviours. A masculinized, but not defeminized, rat would develop a strong potential to show both forms of sex-specific behaviours, *mounting* and adopting the female *receptive* position. It is tempting to see this process underlying human male homosexuality, but too little is known at present to allow firm conclusions in this regard.

Psychological differences also develop during this critical period. For example, female monkeys exposed to testosterone during their sensitive period engage in more rough-and-tumble play than other females; are more aggressive; and make more threatening facial gestures (Goy, Bercovitch & McBrair, 1988). Female rats exposed to a single treatment of testosterone on the day of birth show reduced female-typical sexual behaviour and increased male-typical sexual behaviour in adulthood (Goy & McEwen, 1980). Human females who had been exposed to elevated androgen levels during prenatal development (because of a gene that causes inadequate cortisol production and an excess production of androgens in the adrenal gland; *congenital adrenal hyperplasia*, CAH[2]) tend to spend more time than other girls playing with 'boys' toys', such as cars, and were more likely to choose other boys as their preferred playmate (Berenbaum & Hines, 1992). It seems that 'This relationship between prenatal androgen and childhood gender role behaviour is the best-established link between the early hormone environment and human psychosexual development' (Hines et al., 2002). (Although such statements may be interpreted as reflecting sex stereotypes, it is the case that, on average, boys and girls have very different preferences for and modes of play.) However, in contrast to other species, the relationship between hormones and behaviour in human beings is highly complex, involving other factors (e.g., socialization), and is not a simple function of hormonal influence (Kalat, 1998).

Exposure to abnormal levels of androgens, as the result of some congenital defect, during critical periods does seem sufficient to affect psychosexual development in girls. But are such influences found in the normal range of androgen levels, or are these hormonal effects found only at the pathological extreme of androgen functioning? Research findings bear directly on these questions: (a) effects of testosterone on the development of male-typical behaviour in females is dose-dependent (i.e., higher levels of testosterone produce more male-typical behaviour); and (b) female rats are more behaviourally masculinized by proximity to males *in utero* by virtue of being exposed to their higher levels of testosterone (see Goy & McEwen, 1980). Hines et al. (2002) found that, in human females at 3.5 years of age, prenatal exposure to testosterone did relate to psychological masculinization (i.e., child's frequency of play with respect to a variety of sex-typical toys, games and activities), showing that effects previously found in lower animals extend to human beings. Whether this testosterone effect is a result of androgen passing from the mother to the foetus, or whether both the mother and the child have a similar genetic effect on the production of testosterone, is unclear.

Activation effects

Androgens (especially testosterone) play a role in both male and female reproduction. The hormonal axis, common to males and females, is the *hypothalamic–pituitary–gonadal* (HPG) *axis*. It consists in the secretion of *gonadotropin-releasing hormone* (GnRH) from neurons in the hypothalamus. Sexually related external stimuli are able to influence secretion in this axis. Action potentials in the neurons that synthesize and store GnRH are the trigger for its release, and it travels only a short distance in a special blood vessel before it triggers the release of *follicle-stimulating hormone* (FSH) and *luteinizing hormone* (LH) at the anterior pituitary gland. At the anterior pituitary gland, FSH and LH are secreted into the general bloodstream and exert their effects at the gonads, to cause excretion of sex hormones. Because of their effects on the gonads, FSH and LH are sometimes termed 'gonadotrophins'. As a result of FSH/LH at the gonads, androgens in the male and oestrogens in the female are secreted into the general bloodstream and exert various effects throughout the body.

During foetal life and shortly thereafter, secretion of GnRH, FSH and LH and the sex hormones is high, corresponding to the period of differentiation. At puberty there is once again a sharp rise in activity in this axis. This reaches a stable level in males, but in females there is oscillation in the axis corresponding to the menstrual cycle (there are changes in the responsiveness of the anterior pituitary to GnRH and of the ovaries to FSH and LH over the 28-day period). In both sexes, impairment of the pituitary results in a loss in sexual drive; sex drive tends to be reduced in men with a reduction in testosterone.

Unlike the dominant effect of testosterone on sexual motivation in the male, there is no comparable dominant hormone in the female; both oestrogen and androgens are involved. Oestrogens bind to receptors in various regions of the brain associated with sexual arousal (e.g., hypothalamus, amygdala and septum). As in males, androgens play the principal role in human female sexual desire and motivation. Androgens are secreted from the adrenal gland (androgens are produced in both sexes in the adrenal gland; in males they are also produced in the testes). The role of androgens in female sexuality may explain why sexual desire and motivation do not cease after the menopause, when oestrogen levels drop significantly. At menopause, the ovaries (which produce about 95 per cent of oestrogen) show a loss of sensitivity to FSH and LH and thus a reduction in the production and release of oestrogen.

Increased levels of testosterone and oestrogen have effects in the brain which are not directly related to sexual behaviour. For example, they increase production of dopamine and serotonin receptors in the nucleus accumbens, the prefrontal cortex and the olfactory cortex; these receptors are known to be associated with emotion, reinforcement and mood. A decline in oestrogen would, therefore, lead to decreased activity at these receptors and thus emotional changes. The decline in oestrogen just before menstruation, just after giving birth and during the menopause may be responsible for mood changes often seen during these periods.

Organizational effects vs. activation effects

In discussing the *organizational effects* and *activation effects* of hormones, it was noted that the former involve long-term structural changes while the latter involve short-term activation of sexual motivation and behaviour. However, the distinction between these two types of effects is not complete, and should be thought of as one of degree rather than kind. For example, neural systems are plastic (see chapter 7) and subject to change by activating hormones – such neural systems are said to be 'permanently transient' (Fitch & Denenberg, 1998). Also, sexual organs can undergo structural changes during adulthood. For example body builders in search of the 'body perfect' who use steroids are liable to develop smaller testes and sometimes experience breast enlargement: these structural effects are due to a negative feedback mechanism that instructs the brain not to stimulate the testes to produce testosterone. The brain, in particular, might best be seen as a semi-permanent structure that is undergoing continuous restructuring.

Sexual orientation

Sexual orientation concerns the relationship between sexual stimuli and motivation. If heterosexuality has a hormonal basis, then does homosexuality? There does not appear to be a testosterone difference in heterosexual and homosexual males, although there is some evidence for greater testosterone in homosexual females. However, as shown, hormones exert complex effects, and their effects interact with a host of psychological factors.

There is some evidence that the third interstitial nucleus of the anterior hypothalamus is smaller in homosexual males; it is also smaller in females (irrespective of orientation) (LeVay, 1991). Also, the suprachiasmatic nucleus of the hypothalamus is 1.7 times larger in homosexual men compared with heterosexual ones (cell numbers are 2.1 times larger;

Swaab & Hofman, 1990). However, no difference in this structure is found between the sexes. Such research is still at an early stage of development, and it will be necessary to await the outcome of this work before firm conclusions are possible. However, it is conceivable that sexual orientation is a result of atypical masculinization and feminization processes during early development – if this theory is true, then homosexuality is just as 'natural' as heterosexuality.

> **ASK YOURSELF**
> Can our sexual orientation and behaviour ever escape hormonal constraints?

Sex Development Abnormalities

It is known that chromosomal sex (i.e., XX vs. XY) does not *determine* phenotypal gender (although it does bias it very strongly in one direction) – the path of true gender does not always run smoothly. Without the release of specific hormones at critical stages in development, we can find chromosomal sex and phenotypal gender to be different. These developmental abnormalities throw important light on the nature of hormonal influences on the organization and activation of sexual behaviour.

Intersex

Testosterone masculinizes the formation of the genitals and the hypothalamus during sensitive periods of development. Exposure of males and females to too much or too little testosterone can lead to partial masculinization of the genetic female (e.g., overproduction of testosterone from the adrenal gland) and feminization of the male (relative insensitivity to testosterone). Various atypical hormonal environments can lead to *hermaphroditism*, i.e., individuals whose genitals do not correspond to genetic sex. In rare instances, both female and male genitals may be present (*true hermaphroditism*); one gonad may be a testis, the other an ovary (*lateral hermaphroditism*), or one or both gonads may be a combination of the two (an *ovotestis*). More commonly, development is intermediate between full male and female phenotype (*pseudohermaphroditism*; or *intersex*). These effects are obvious in the case of morphology (e.g., external genitalia); they may be less obvious in the case of psychological intersexism, but no less important. A number of hormonal-related conditions have been well described in the clinical literature.

Androgen insensitivity syndrome

Some women who have experienced difficulty in conceiving receive the shock of their lives when they go for a medical examination. It sometimes (albeit rarely) turns out that women who in all outward appearance and in motivation and behaviour are female are, in fact, chromosomally male (XY). A genetic mutation prevents the development of functioning androgen receptors, and this prevents the masculinization of the body and mind – there is a defect in the androgen receptor gene on the X chromosome (this is an 'X-linked recessive effect'). The primitive gonads of a genetic male foetus with androgen insensitivity syndrome become testes and secrete both *anti-Müllerian hormone* and androgens; but the absence of functioning androgen receptors prevents the development of the male sexual organs. However, the anti-Müllerian hormone still has its defeminizing effect, with the result that the female internal sexual organs (uterus, fallopian tube, etc.) fail to form (the vagina is usually shallow).

A second disorder, *persistent Müllerian duct syndrome*, results from defective receptors for Müllerian inhibiting hormone. When this syndrome occurs in genetic males, androgens have their masculinizing effects but defeminization does not occur. Thus, the person is born with *both* sets of internal sexual organs.

Delayed penis development

Delayed penis development is a condition seen in the Dominican Republic. This genetic condition, known as *guevedoce* (colloquially, 'balls at twelve'), prevents the growth of the penis until puberty (it does not affect other forms of masculinization); children with this disorder are raised as females. What happens at puberty when they grow a penis? Would their socialization lead to the development of a female identity? The answer to this nature–nurture questions is plain: in most cases, a male identity is adopted and a heterosexual orientation (although a smaller number of individuals prefer to remain in the female role).

Damage to penis

Accidental removal of the penis offers another instance that allows us to examine the nature–nurture issue of sexual identity, and in particular the *gender neutrality hypothesis*, which contends that before the age of 3 years gender identity is not fixed, but after this age gender is 'locked in'. Circumcision (i.e., the removal of the male baby's foreskin) sometimes does not go according to plan. In one high-profile case, too high a level of electricity was used to remove the foreskin, with the result that it damaged the penis beyond repair. The interesting aspect of this unfortunate event was that this baby was one of a monozygotic (identical) pair. The physicians and parents decided to raise the damaged son as a female – little Bruce Reimer was renamed Brenda – which is usual in such cases, as it is easier to remove male genitalia than to create them. By the age of 10 Brenda sensed something was wrong and felt herself to be really a boy: she was an unhappy and lonely child, and preferred playing with boy's toys; even tried urinating in a standing position; and by the age of 14, when the truth was revealed, Brenda insisted that she live as a boy. Brenda changed his name to David, and by the age of 25 he was married and had adopted his older wife's children. David said, 'I was never happy being Brenda, never!', and 'I would rather cut my throat than go back to being a girl.' Despite penis reconstruction surgery, David remained depressed throughout his life. On 4 May 2004, then 38 years old, he drove to a parking lot, placed a shotgun against his head and ended his misery.

The case of Brenda was widely quoted by the influential gender reassignment scientist John Money (Money & Ehrhardt, 1972, 1975). For many years Brenda was cited as living proof of the truth of the *gender neutrality hypothesis*. Money knew that Brenda was unhappy – he had received a psychiatrist's report to this effect – and that Brenda had decided to revert to being a male, yet he did not publish these facts until David 'went public' to reveal the truth about his gender identity. For many years, the case of Brenda was standard orthodoxy in the gender reassignment community. The scientific community was disappointed by this realization; but Money continued to argue that Brenda's case did not disprove the gender neutrality hypothesis. He argued that the peculiar circumstances surrounding Brenda's case were responsible for the failure of this case of gender reassignment (e.g., living with a male twin).

These examples show that early hormonal influences are fundamental to the development of female and male psychology and, although chromosomes bias gender development in one direction or the other, it is the early hormonal environment that determines gender.

> **ASK YOURSELF**
> Is the gender neutrality hypothesis totally wrong?

▦ Hormones and Stress

Hormones are important in the body's reaction to stress and have been implicated in a number of psychiatric conditions (e.g., depression). An external force is known as a *stressor*, and the internal reaction of the body as a *strain*. A strain occurs when the internal coping mechanism is unable to deal adaptively with the external stressor. For example, a brittle rubber band snaps with little external stress; a more robust one needs a much greater stress to break it. The same effect is seen in human beings: some individuals show suboptimal performance at relatively low levels of stressors; other individuals require much greater levels before their performance is markedly impaired.

The word *stress* is commonly used to refer to the internal physiological and psychological reactions to some perceived external force. It is known that, within normal bounds, external stressors do not exist in isolation from the psychological reaction to them; rather, our *perception* of such stressors plays a large role in the effects of stressors (i.e., *personal efficacy* and *control*). Individual differences (such as neuroticism, intelligence, perceived control), prior experience (such as traumatic experiences) and changes in hormonal and neurotransmitter levels all influence the level of stress. Cognitive-behavioural therapy (CBT; the preferred psychological treatment for stress-related conditions) involves the attempt to change the patient's perceptions of their efficacy and control over everyday stress-inducing negative events.

Irrespective of the psychological process by which stress is generated, common hormonal effects are seen. Hormonal reaction to actual or perceived stress (psychologically this difference may not be important) are adaptive strategies to the threats faced by our ancestors during the Pleistocene period (over 100,000 years ago), when it is thought *Homo sapiens* evolved the psychological mechanisms in use today (see chapter 2). The difference in environmental challenges faced by our Pleistocene ancestors and human beings in the modern environment may be one of the main reasons why hormonal responses to stressors today often lead to disease processes – this theme is discussed below in relation to hormonal effects on the immune system.

Stress-related hormonal reactions have evolved to deal with brief periods of threat that require rapid mobilization of the body to achieve a fight, flight or freeze response. Brief threats become long-term stressors if the aversive stimulus cannot be easily avoided (e.g., being in debt; caring for a relative with a chronic illness; work environments which entail high demand but low control). Stress is associated with activity throughout the autonomic nervous system (ANS); the sympathetic (SNS) branch of the ANS is activated during emergencies, triggering bodily reactions (i.e., increased heartbeat): this branch releases catecholamines: (a) noradrenaline from the sympathetic neurons; and (b) adrenaline and noradrenaline from the *adrenal medulla*.

Hypothalamic–pituitary–adrenal (HPA) axis

Stressors activate not only the SNS branch of the ANS, but also the *hypothalamic–pituitary –adrenal* (HPA) *axis* (figure 6.10). When an aversive stimulus – comprising uncertainty, threat, challenge and the need for action – is encountered, hypothalamic neurons release *corticotropin-releasing hormone* (CRF); at the anterior pituitary gland, occupation of receptors by CRF releases *adrenocorticotropic hormone* (ACTH), which travels in the blood to stimulate the outer layer of the adrenal gland (the adrenal cortex); this in turn secretes *corticosteroids* into the blood (especially cortisol in human beings). Release of corticosteroids elevates blood sugar and enhances metabolism, readying the body for swift action. The most robust endocrine dysfunction seen in psychopathology is hyperactivity of the HPA axis, resulting from hyperactive hypothalamic CRF-releasing neurons.

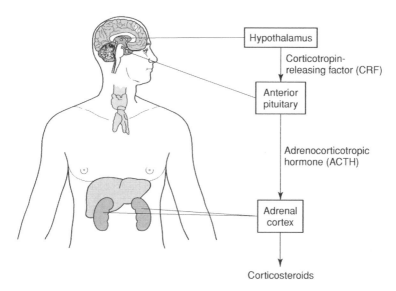

Figure 6.10 The HPA axis. The *hypothalamic–pituitary–adrenal* (HPA) *axis* is reactive in response to stressful events, consisting of uncertainty, threat, challenge and the need for action. The hypothalamus releases *corticotropin-releasing factor* (CRF); and at the anterior pituitary gland, occupation of receptors by CRF releases *adrenocorticotropic hormone* (ACTH), which travels in the blood to stimulate the adrenal cortex, which, in turn, secretes *corticosteroids* into the blood (especially cortisol in human beings).

Corticotropin-releasing hormone (CRH)-containing neurons, with cell bodies in the paraventricular nucleus (PVN) of the hypothalamus, receive inputs from various regions (e.g., other hypothalamic regions, brainstem, hippocampus and the amygdala). The HPA axis – the 'get ready for action' system – cascade of hormonal effects is initiated by the perception and appraisal of threat, especially that entailing lack of control and frustration. It is often activated by psychological factors (e.g., worrying about a pending examination). However, activation of the HPA axis is not itself pathological, and does not occur only in times of stress. It is also activated upon presentation of an appetitive (i.e., pleasant) stimulus that may need a readiness response.

Along with the effects of CRH in the HPA axis, CRH-containing neurons terminate in various parts of the brain, apparently acting as a neurotransmitter. CRF neurons innervate a brainstem structure called the *locus ceruleus*, the *amygdala* and the *hippocampus*, and appear to be widespread throughout the brain, especially in those structures concerned with autonomic control; corticosteroids also target components of the limbic system, particularly the hippocampus, which is involved in emotions, especially anxiety. One theory holds that this HPA axis overactivity leads to disturbances in serotonin functioning, which is one of the neurobiological abnormalities most consistently associated with suicide (Lopez et al., 1997).

The HPA axis ensures an increased fuel supply, sustaining a high and steady rate of coping with stress, as opposed to the sudden bursts of fight-and-flight activity associated with the SNS. As cortisol directs energy towards increasing blood sugar and metabolism, HPA axis activity produces a shift away from the synthesis of proteins, including the proteins necessary for the immune system (see below). If negative feedback is working properly then when the stressor is terminated there is a shutdown of the HPA axis. However, in modern environments, this system may be continuously activated, leading to pathological effects. Continuous activation of the HPA axis is damaging to health because it leads to abnormally high release of glucose and lipids (fats) in the bloodstream, mobilizing the body for rapid action. Fatty substances in the bloodstream when left unmetabolized (i.e., turned to energy) lead to 'furring' of the artery walls and to circulatory complications (e.g., *arteriosclerosis*).

In primates, lower-ranking males have higher levels of cortisol than high-ranking males. Sapolsky (1989) studied the olive baboon (*Papio anubis*) and concluded that events in the lives of the low-ranking males triggered the HPA axis, namely, lack of predictability and control, frustration, and being the victim of aggression. Dominant males who are in an unstable hierarchy also experience increased corticosteroid release. If primates are experimentally deprived of their dominance in the hierarchy then they too suffer a stress reaction.

In human beings, Type 1 personality, *coronary-prone* individuals, who are defined by high drive *and* aggression/frustration, may be prone to HPA axis overactivity. Paralleling the increased cortisol effects of displaced baboons, middle managers, as compared with junior and senior managers, are most prone to coronary problems and a host of other diseases, suggesting that their higher levels of frustration and lack of control, mediated by the HPA axis, are responsible for their comparatively poor health.

Prenatal stress may also be related to developmental delays and behavioural abnormalities in children; in adulthood, it may also be associated with schizophrenia, a reduction in cerebral asymmetry and anomalies in brain morphology. Experimental studies with prenatally stressed rats model these dysfunctions: behavioural depression; learned helplessness; impaired functioning of the HPA axis in response to stress; and demasculinization and feminization of sexual behaviour (Weinstock, 2001) – this latter effect may parallel the finding that, in human beings, prenatal trauma biases males in favour of homosexuality.

The HPA axis is clearly an important adaptation, serving fundamental functions. However, its operating principles were not evolved by natural selection to cope with current environment triggers and, as a consequence, it can become overactive, leading to physical problems as well as psychological problems.

Hormones, the Immune System and Illness

Hormones have the power to influence the immune system and thus exert important effects on the susceptibility to illness. The *germ theory* of disease contends that organic dysfunctions and infections lead to pathological states; in contrast, the *psychosomatic theory* argues that psychological factors can be the primary cause of disease. Both theories are true: infection with some bacteria, irrespective of psychological state, produces illness and death; and perception of stressors can also lead to serious, and sometimes fatal, illness (if you believe in voodoo magic and have been told that you have been cursed, then this stress may well lead to your death – you may literally be scared to death!). Less exotic disease processes involve the *interaction* of organic/infectious and psychological factors. This interaction is nowhere more apparent than in the effects of stress, which can inhibit or facilitate the pathological effects of purely physiological factors.

Stress is associated with a range of diseases (e.g., hypertension, leading to increased risk of stroke), gastric ulcers and greater susceptibility to infection. In particular, a rise in corticosteroid levels in response to stress can impair the functioning of the immune system. It is well known that at times of stress (e.g., examinations) people are more prone to catch a range of illnesses (e.g., the common cold, sore throat). The immune system can be markedly impaired by chronic activity in the HPA axis, and interactions occur between the neuroendocrine, the immune and the central nervous systems (*psychoneuroimmunology* is the branch of science that deals with these interactive effects).

The immune system

The immune system is responsible for the body's defence against *pathogens* (i.e., harmful microorganisms, bacteria and viruses), as well as cancerous cells. Many millions of cells (termed white cells or *leukocytes*) compose the immune system (leukocytes are produced in bone marrow and then migrate to the thymus gland, the spleen and the peripheral lymph nodes, which store and nurture them until a pathogen is detected). Each cell has on its surface certain proteins called antigens (antibody-generator molecules); when the leukocyte finds a cell with antigens different from the body, it attempts to destroy it.

In launching this attack, *cytokines* are released from cells of the immune system; these chemicals influence the nervous system (Konsman, Parnet & Dantzer, 2002). The *cytokine interleukin-1* (IL-1) plays an important role, conveying information to the brain. Injection of IL-1 leads to a reaction of fever, withdrawal from social contact, reduction of exploration, fatigue and reduced appetite (adaptive reactions to physiological compromise), jointly called 'sickness behaviour'. Also, on the walls of immune cells are receptors that are sensitive to neurotransmitters and hormones released by the nervous system. The sympathetic nervous system has the capacity to activate the organs (containing leukocytes) that constitute part of the immune system. The leukocytes contain receptors for the transmitter released by these neurons, suggesting that the nervous system can excite or inhibit the release of leukocytes. This set of interactions may be an adaptation that allowed the preparation of immune reactions to likely invasion of pathogens (e.g., eating potentially contaminated meat). The evolution of the systems of detection and elimination of pathogens must be one of the oldest of all adaptations. Interleukin-1 also provides an excitatory input to the HPA axis; as this is a product of the immune system, infection might be thought of as a stressor.

Stress reactions

During acute emergency states (the classical fight–flight–freeze response), immune activity is increased (e.g., Willemsen et al., 2000). For example, subclinical anxiety can boost the immune system, although this might be a transient effect before down-regulation of the system (Koh, 1998). This is an adaptive response to imminent infection (e.g., from a predator-inflicted wound). However, as shown in a meta-analysis of 300 studies, long-term stress leads to depressed immune reactions (Segerstrom & Miller, 2004). Helplessness-associated stress seems especially powerful in impairing the immune system. Assuming that this increased and decreased activity confers an adaptive advantage, immune system suppression during long-term stress might serve the function of avoiding the immune system attacking not only foreign invaders but the body itself (i.e., autoimmune disorder). It is possible to imagine alleles that code for certain levels of immune system activity under high stress. Those individuals possessing alleles for high activity, sustained over a long period may have been at a disadvantage due to the autoimmune disorders that compromised their viability (survival) and fecundity (reproductive fitness).

One index of immune function integrity that is easily measured in saliva in human beings is secretory immunoglobulin A (sIgA; Phalipon et al., 2002; Robert-Guroff, 2000). sIgA is the dominant immunoglobulin that bathes mucosal surfaces (e.g., respiratory, intestines, mouth) and is the first line of defence against pathogenic microorganisms, viruses and bacteria (see chapter 9). A lower than normal level of sIgA is a risk factor for upper respiratory infections. Stress and high emotionality are known to reduce levels of sIgA (e.g., academic stress; Jemmot & Magloire, 1988); and academic-induced (examination) stress on sIgA levels persists for, at least, several weeks after the offset of the stressor (Deinzer et al., 2000).

Natural killer cells are blood cells that attach to certain types of tumour cells. When exposed to examination stress, natural killer cells are activated especially in emotionally stable individuals, but decreased in emotionally unstable individuals (Borella et al., 1999). The impact of personality is an important moderator of the effects of stress on immune functioning (Daruna, 1996). The production of *endorphins* (i.e., pain-reducing morphine-like molecules; *endogenous morphine*) also suppresses the immune system; these are released in times of stress, but also at other times (e.g., during vigorous exercise).

Another example of the interaction of hormones and the immune system is seen during pregnancy. A foetus's major organs are developing between 6 and 14 weeks after conception. At this time, the mother's immune system is relatively underactive – a necessity at this time to allow the foetus to establish itself in the uterus without attack as a pathogen. During this period, women are especially vulnerable to bacteria and viruses. It is perhaps not surprising, therefore, that during this time mothers are regularly sick and develop strong aversions to certain foodstuffs (e.g., meat, fish and eggs, all potential sources of infection) and sometimes a strong preference for others.

> **ASK YOURSELF**
> Should we be less concerned about actual stressors and more concerned about the body's reactions to them?

Integrating Systems

It is known that important interrelations exist between the brain, the peripheral nervous system, the neuroendocrine system and the immune system. In relation to the central nervous system and neuroendocrine system, there is an intricate pattern of causes and effects, which calls our attention to their interdependence (figure 6.11). There is also an interplay of what it is often tempting to call *physiological* and *psychological* factors. To be sure, some processes are purely 'physiological' in origin: defective receptor molecules will not activate cellular processes despite all the psychological will in the world; so, too, a perfectly working *hypothalamic–pituitary–adrenal* (HPA) axis can be activated and exert long-term disease-generating effects by pure psychological means alone (e.g., excessive anxiety) – of course, this 'psychological' factor is a physiological process in a different system (in this case, the limbic system): there can be no such thing as a *purely* psychological (non-physiological) factor. As shown in the case of the organizational and activating effects of sex steroids, the very way individuals *think* about sexual matters (e.g., sexual orientation to sexually attractive stimuli) is heavily influenced by the hormonal molecules that they were exposed to during early foetal development.

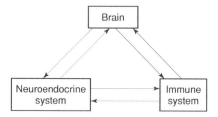

Figure 6.11 Interaction of brain, endocrine and immune systems. For example, activation of the HPA axis and the release of corticosteroids impact upon brain circuits involved in such psychological functions as anxiety; and then these changed brain functions impact upon perceptions of threat and activate the HPA axis. At the same time, immune system functioning is changing, which in turn impacts upon peripheral and central nervous system functioning. These complex interactions counsel caution in interpreting the effect of any one system in isolation.

The interaction of the nervous system and the neuroendocrine system is iterative: activation of the HPA axis and the release of corticosteroids impact upon brain circuits involved in such psychological functions as anxiety; and then these changed brain functions impact upon perceptions of threat and activate the HPA axis. At the same time, immune system functioning is changing, which in turn impacts upon peripheral and central nervous system functioning. These complex interactions counsel caution in interpreting the effect of any one system in isolation.

Seen in the light of evolutionary theory about adaptations (chapter 2), all the systems of the body are aimed at achieving the same general goals of survival and reproduction; the local environment of the body has led to the evolution of specific adaptations (i.e., bodily processes) to meet these challenges. The fact that these systems work in close harmony is to be expected.

Study of the neuroendocrine system is making important advances in our understanding of a whole range of behaviours and processes, many of which are pathological. For example, recent advances in understanding the control functions of the neuroendocrine system is shedding new light on and promising therapeutic breakthroughs in common problems (e.g., obesity; Schwartz & Morton, 2002; Schwartz et al., 2000). It is likely that future research will show the increasing importance of hormonal influences on psychological functions, specifically psychopathologies (e.g., depression and anxiety: the hippocampus contains receptors for hormones of gonadal origin; and ovarian hormones affect serotonin gene expression in this brain region; Birzniece et al., 2002).

This research will be greatly facilitated by the revolution currently taking place in medical genetics, which will reveal the molecular processes underlying normal and abnormal processes. Until the day arrives when these processes are fully understood and they can be controlled for our benefit, you and I live within a psychophysiological environment in which the daily pulses of hormones influence to a large extent, among a great many other things, our sexual desires, our reactions to stressors, our vulnerability to infection, even the way we think, and the disease processes that will finally lead to our shuffling off this mortal coil.

Learning Questions

1. In what ways are hormones and neurotransmitters the same and different?
2. What are the crucial neuroendocrine factors in the making of boys and girls?
3. Do abnormalities in early exposure to hormones reveal anything about the development of sex and gender?
4. If stress reactions are adaptive then why do they often lead to longer-term physiological disease?
5. Do the neuroendocrine, immunological and central nervous systems reflect a single integrated system?

NOTES

1   The ovum is one of the largest cells in the body, and over the course of 30 or so years a woman may release just 400 ova (a woman has some 300,000 at puberty, but these die with ageing).

2   A problem with interpreting the effects of CAH on masculinization is that this condition masculinizes the external genitalia, which are usually surgically feminized during infancy. However, it is possible that the appearance of the genitalia could change the parents' perception of their child and bias their child's development along masculine lines; in addition, there is the experience of the illness itself, sometimes involving further hospitalization, which needs to be taken into account when interpreting these putative hormonal effects (Hines et al., 2002).

FURTHER READING

Becker, J. B., Breedlove, S. M., Crews, D. & McCarthy, M. M. (eds.) (2002). *Behavioral Endocrinology*. Cambridge, MA: MIT Press.

Buckingham, J. C., Gillies, G. E. & Cowell, A.-M. (eds.) (1997). *Stress, Stress Hormones and the Immune System*. London: Wiley.

Schulkin, J. (1998). *The Neuroendocrine Regulation of Behavior*. Cambridge: Cambridge University Press.

chapter 7
Learning and Neural Plasticity

Learning Objectives

To be able to:

1. Describe the different types of learning and the procedures for measuring them.
2. Discuss the influence of Hebb's theory for the neural analysis of learning.
3. Describe the neural network approach, outlining its strengths and weaknesses.
4. Explain what is meant by neural plasticity and sketch its neuronal basis.
5. Discuss the benefits of combining behavioural computer simulations and neural approaches to learning.

The brain's capacity to learn from experience is a major achievement of evolution – arguably, the *most* important achievement. Not only must the brain produce an accurate model of the gross physical features of the external world (see chapters 5 and 18), it must also encode the regularities that make the world predictable. Learning may be seen as the proximate mechanism underlying adaptive responses to a changing local environment, where innate responses are no longer appropriate. However, learning and evolution should be viewed on a single continuum: both involve the strengthening of connections – one within a generation (learning) and the other over generations (adaptations).

Learning is often placed on the 'nurture' side of the nature–nurture account and is frequently contrasted with biology (genetics and physiology). This dichotomous mode of thinking is not helpful and is, in certain respects, misleading as to the true relationship of so-called nature and nurture. In some areas of psychology there has always been a close link between learning and physiology – as two aspects of the same fundamental neuropsychology (see chapter 1). This chapter highlights the ways in which learning is a fundamental part of biological psychology.

Learning is required for developmental pathways. For example, the visual system comes pre-wired for vision, but the development of vision requires exposure to the visual environment, which in turn entails learning processes (e.g., perceptual learning; see chapter 5). For learning to be possible, neural systems need to be *plastic*, that is, to be able to produce the short-term and long-term changes in the biochemistry and structure of neurons (e.g., synapse formation) that represent a latent change in the reactivity of the system (retrieval then involves activity in these populations of neurons). The last part of this chapter presents what is known about how neural processes *instantiate* learning processes: neural plasticity.

Learning and Genes

It has been estimated that there are 1,000 million neural connections in a piece of brain the size of a grain of sand. But there are only a small number of genes (let us be liberal and accept the upper estimate of 50,000 – even if there were hundred of thousands of genes, the argument that follows is still valid). Even if every one of these 50,000 genes were involved in wiring the brain (which is far from being true), then each gene would need to hold the blueprint for arranging 1 billion neural connections. This outcome is simply inconceivable. Thus, for hard-wiring, there seems to be a gene shortage. One solution to this problem has been for genes to set up a chemical gradient in order to determine the general wiring of the system – this is a fundamental process of brain development and maturation. A second solution has been to produce a system capable of learning, especially in novel and changing environments. Thus, genes produce a spectrum of adaptability (learning) and pre-adaptation (innate potential set up during development).

In relating biological processes to learning it is appropriate to ask to what extent genetics and physiology impose constraints on (a) the *structure* and (b) the *contents* of learning. In relation to the structure of learning, it seems that learning systems have a number of constraints. For example, stimuli that one is continuously and repeatedly exposed to without any consequence (i.e., they are not predictive of a salient event) are more difficult to condition than novel stimuli (this is a phenomenon known as *latent inhibition*; see below). This particular constraint on learning makes perfect sense in evolutionary terms: there are limited attentional resources to process stimuli; therefore it makes sense not to pay attention to stimuli that are unimportant. In relation to the content of learning, it is easier to learn associations involving some stimuli rather than others. For example, it is easier to condition individuals to pictures of snakes and spiders than to more dangerous stimuli, such as electric sockets (this phenomenon is known as *biological preparedness*). More speculatively, adaptive learning systems may have evolved that reflect important events in our evolutionary past (e.g., potential dangerous stimuli involving our children; stimuli concerning cheating and deception; and stimuli associated with reproduction, e.g., opposite-sex partners – for a lively discussion of these possible evolutionary foundations of the mind, see Pinker, 1997, 2002[1]). Learning the appropriate courtship ritual in one's local environment is clearly beneficial to successful reproduction (for further examples of the biological constraints on learning, see Alcock, 2001). The (proximate) neurophysiological basis of such effects probably involves activation of the emotion circuits in the brain that guide and strengthen learning connections.

ASK YOURSELF
In evolutionary terms are there any disadvantages to learning?

In recent years, there has been great interest in unifying psychological, or computational, approaches to learning with neurophysiological approaches. In keeping with the distinction between the *conceptual nervous system* and the *central nervous system* (Hebb, 1955; see chapter 1), this chapter covers three interlocking approaches to understanding learning: (a) behavioural approaches; (b) artificial neural networks; and (c) neural plasticity.

Behavioural Approaches to Learning

The history of psychology has been dominated by attempts to understand the fundamental behavioural laws of learning. Indeed, whole areas of psychology have been devoted to this topic, and claims have been made that the study of behaviour and learning is the *only* legitimate approach to psychology – radical behaviourism being the most public declaration of this position (Watson, 1914; Skinner, 1938).

The aim of this section is to summarize the major behavioural approaches to learning and to describe their principles and laws. These principles/laws are important in subsequent chapters when experimental findings relating to specific behavioural/learning paradigms (e.g., latent inhibition in relation to schizophrenia) are discussed.

Definition of learning

Learning refers to a change in behaviour as a direct result of experience (not maturation or a transient state of the organism). Learning is inferred from measures of performance, usually in some form of objectively defined behaviour. However, learning is not always manifest in behaviour. For example, consider the phenomenon of *latent learning*. In this type of learning, performance may reflect learning only under certain conditions. For example, if a rat is exposed to a water maze and left to explore it, then it may not show any evidence of learning until it is motivated (e.g., by food); then its swimming speed is much faster than a naive rat's, providing clear evidence of behaviour facilitation due to prior experience (learning). Sensory preconditioning is another example of a form of learning that is not necessarily manifest in behaviour (see below). Other forms of learning – habituation and sensitization – that reflect a change in behaviour as a result of exposure to the environment, but do not entail an association of stimuli, are also evident.

Thus, the definition of learning may be refined to refer to the process or procedure by which an animal either (a) changes behaviour, or (b) changes the *potential* for behaviour. Given that learning has occurred, the term *memory* may be used to refer (a) to the change in the nervous system that underlies changes in actual and potential behaviour; and (b) to the process of recall of learning and its expression in behaviour.

Types of learning

The history of the psychology of learning is characterized by distinctions between a rather large number of processes (e.g., classical vs. instrumental learning). A major debate has centred on whether these apparently different learning processes reflect: (a) the

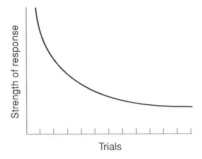

Figure 7.1 Habituation curve. Habituation is observed as the weakening of a response to a stimulus with repeated and non-reinforced trials. The figure shows an idealized habituation curve – the shape of actual curves depends on the nature of the stimulus and individual differences of experimental participants.

fundamental nature of learning in the brain; or (b) the peculiarities of the experimental method used to produce and measure learning. This is an important issue, because if it can be shown from behavioural experiments that different forms of learning occur then it *must* be the case that there are different learning systems in the brain (that is, different functions have different neural processes).

In the study of these forms of learning, behavioural research has adopted the assumption that complex forms of learning are built from simpler forms – much as a complex chemical compound is composed of simpler atoms. This assumption has motivated the study of three simple forms of learning: (a) non-associative (e.g., habituation); (b) associative (e.g., Pavlovian conditioning); and (c) response–outcome (e.g., instrumental learning).

Habituation

The simplest form of learning is *habituation*, which is *non-associative* because it does not entail the learning of the relationship between stimuli. Habituation may be defined as the weakening of the strength of a response as a result of the stimulus that elicits the response being repeatedly presented *without consequence* (i.e., reinforcement).

For example, if an 80 dB(A), 50-ms tone were presented to a human volunteer in a psychology experiment and some response (e.g., skin conductance or evoked potentials in the brain) were measured, then a very large response would be observed on first presentation of the tone; but, after a few more presentations, this response would become very weak and finally it would disappear. Under these circumstances, the brain has learned that the tone is of no importance (consequence), and therefore needs no further attention (figure 7.1).

In fact, it is not necessary to go to a psychology laboratory to observe this simple form of learning. We are habituating to stimuli on a moment-by-moment basis. If this were not the case, then we would be sensitive to all stimuli in our ambient environment: every sound of a car passing, every closing of the door, every ringing of the telephone would elicit a large reaction. We learn rapidly that such sounds have little significance in themselves, so we do not continue paying them much attention. Imagine a world in which you responded to every visual and auditory stimulus as if it held great significance. The world you just imagined may not be too far from the world experienced by schizophrenia patients (see chapter 16).

To illustrate this point, consider the behaviour of harbour seals (Deecke, Slater & Ford, 2002). Harbour seals respond strongly to the calls of mammal-eating killer whales and unfamiliar fish-eating killer whales, but not to the familiar calls of the local fish-eating population. This finding shows that the behaviour of harbour seals is not built-in, but changes as a function of local conditions (which can be highly variable and changing over time). Predation is a major force in shaping the behaviour of animals. Successful species have thus evolved mechanisms to recognize and discriminate harmful and harmless animals.

Characteristics of habituation

There are a number of important points concerning habituation. The first is that it is used only for stimuli that elicit a response in an innate manner (i.e., the ability of the stimulus to elicit the response does not depend upon learning; e.g., Pavlovian conditioning). In standard conditioning terms, this stimulus is an *unconditioned stimulus* and the habituated response is an *unconditioned response*. The weakening of a *learned* (i.e., *conditioned*) response falls under other headings in behavioural psychology (e.g., *extinction* and *conditioned inhibition*). It was emphasized above that the stimulus that elicits the response must be presented *without consequence*. This is a necessary and important qualifier because, if the stimulus is biologically important (or has acquired biological significance through conditioning), then habituation is not observed.

Another important point is that, if the stimulus is aversive (i.e., noxious, such as an electric shock), then the response does not habituate; indeed, an opposite response is observed, namely *sensitization*. This process refers to an *increase* in a response to repeated presentation. Habituation and sensitization are found across the phylogenetic scale, from the lowest animals to human beings. As discussed below, both measures have been extensively studied to reveal the processes underlying neural plasticity.

The major adaptive function of habituation is that it narrows the range of stimuli to which the organism is sensitive; it is especially important in the *orienting response* (i.e., a response elicited by novel stimuli, usually involving the turning of the head towards the eliciting stimulus). If a stimulus has no biologically important aspects, then it would be disruptive physiologically (e.g., by sweating) and cognitively (e.g., attracting attention) to continue to respond to it. The context in which the stimulus is presented is important; if the habituated stimulus is presented in a different context, then the response is likely to reappear. Habituation allows us to focus on the important and to ignore the unimportant in relevant environments: a rather clever adaptation of evolution.

Habituation has often been the response of choice in behavioural experiments because, although it is basic, it is *plastic*, being influenced by a number of psychological factors (e.g., expectations). For example, 200 tones presented over a 5-minute period produce a different habituation effect from the same tones presented over a 24-hour period, the first procedure leading only to *short-term habituation* (lasting minutes/hours), the second to *long-term habituation* (lasting days/weeks). The habituation method can be used to measure such psychological processes as temporal (time) processing (e.g., does a newborn baby remember the presentation of a stimulus over a period of 24 hours?).

ASK YOURSELF
What might be some of the problems associated with impaired habituation?

Associative learning

Associative learning has generated an enormous research literature and has spawned a number of theories of the underlying learning processes. In this section, Pavlovian conditioning (also known as *classical conditioning*) is reviewed.

Associative learning consists in the observation that if two stimuli are paired systematically then each stimulus takes on the eliciting properties of the other stimulus. This is a fundamental – perhaps *the* fundamental – process of learning: some theorists believe it underlies all forms of learning. Associative learning is especially important in learning the regularities of the world: that is, the way stimuli go together (Shanks, 1995). This form of learning can also be applied to instrumental learning, which contains an associative component.

Pavlovian conditioning

The rigorous experimental study of associative learning was initiated by the Russian physiologist Ivan Petrovich Pavlov (1849–1936). He chanced upon the phenomenon of associative learning, and many of its components, by accident, through his work on the physiology of the digestive system, for which he won the Nobel Prize in 1904 (figure 7.2).

Pavlovian conditioning consists of the following basic properties. Dogs salivate when they see, smell and taste meat (as indeed do most of us; this is the *unconditioned response*, UCR, to the *unconditioned stimulus*, UCS) – these are 'unconditioned' because no learning is required. Pavlov was fortunate to have been studying digestion because of the easily measured physiological response. What he observed was as follows: sometimes his dogs

Figure 7.2   Ivan Pavlov with one of his experimental dogs. (Photo © Novosti / Science Photo Library.)

would salivate *before* they were exposed to the meat. This response was odd and un-expected, and it might be imagined something of a nuisance for Pavlov's study of the digestion system. Pavlov was intrigued by this strange response and spent the rest of his career studying its laws and implications. What Pavlov observed was the *anticipation* of the meat by stimuli that had become associated with the meat (e.g., the attendant coming into the room, the sound of food dishes). That is, stimuli served to 'signal' the presentation of food.

Pavlov established that, if an initially neutral stimulus was presented at about the same time as the presentation of the food (the UCS), then this neutral stimulus would take over some of the eliciting powers of the UCS: this stimulus is termed the *conditioned stimulus* (CS). After a number of pairings of the CS–UCS, the CS presented alone has the power to elicit the UCR (e.g., salivation). This CS-elicited response is the *conditioned response* (CR). In other words, the power of the CS to elicit a response is *conditional* upon its relationship to the UCS (i.e., the meat). ('Conditioned' was incorrectly translated from the original Russian work; 'conditional' is closer to the semantic and psychological meaning of Pavlov's original Russian term.) Pavlov's move from the study of the *unconditioned* to the *conditioned* response represented his move from physiological to psychological study (Gray, 1979). A real sense of the scientific flavour of this work can be found in Pavlov (1927).

It was originally thought that what happened during the course of Pavlovian conditioning was a form of *stimulus substitution*: previously only the UCS elicited the UCR, but after conditioning the CS had the power to elicit the UCR. However, this theory proved difficult to sustain. Response *multiplication* was then suggested to reflect the fact that the CR is often very different from the UCR (i.e., the CS acquires the ability to elicit a larger class of responses than before conditioning occurred). Today, the stimulus(S)–response(R) link has been supplemented with an internal process: S–0–R. The '0' represents central states of the brain/mind.

Let us consider an example to illustrate the problem with the response substitution theory. If we were exposed to an unpleasant UCS (e.g., electric shock), our UCR would consist of a jumping, withdrawal reflex. Now, if we conditioned this UCS shock to a CS (e.g., light), what should we expect when the light CS alone is presented? Well, before the conditioning phase, the to-be-conditioned CS (light) would elicit little more than an orienting response, which would quickly habituate; but, after conditioning, the light would elicit a CR. The crucial question is: is the CR the same as the UCR? The clear answer is 'No'. In fact, presentation of an unpleasant (aversive) CS elicits behavioural immobility (which resembles freezing), and an increase in arousal, attention and vigilance – virtually the opposite behavioural response pattern to the UCR! These passive avoidance responses are appropriate to the CS: look, listen and learn how to avoid the aversive UCS (shock) signalled by the CS (figure 7.3).

Although Pavlov's learning procedure seems rudimentary, its importance in psychology can hardly be overestimated. As an example of this influence, during the 1960–1980 period, when the 'cognitive revolution' was redefining psychology and challenging the 'mindless' behaviourism that dominated psychology for most of the century, learning theories were downgraded in relevance and importance. But from the 1980s to the present time, associative ideas have enjoyed a resurgence of interest. For example, they form the basic argument for neural network models of behaviour and cognition. In addition,

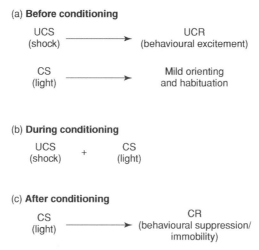

(a) **Before conditioning**

UCS
(shock) → UCR
(behavioural excitement)

CS
(light) → Mild orienting
and habituation

(b) **During conditioning**

UCS
(shock) + CS
(light)

(c) **After conditioning**

CS
(light) → CR
(behavioural suppression/
immobility)

Figure 7.3 Example of associative learning. (a) Before conditioning the *unconditioned stimulus* (UCS; electric shock) elicits behavioural excitement (i.e., an *unconditioned response*; UCR); the *to-be-conditioned stimulus* (to-be-CR; light) elicits only a mild orienting response. (b) During conditioning, presentation of the CS is paired with presentation of the UCS. (c) Now, after training, when the CS is presented alone, it elicits a new response (i.e., behavioural immobility and enhanced information processing; CR). Importantly, the CR does not always resemble the UCR: this is an example of response multiplication.

many of the best lines of evidence for the importance of cognitive factors and central states of emotion (e.g., fear and anxiety) come from learning paradigms inspired by the work of Pavlov. Much of neuroscience research uses basic Pavlovian procedures – if Pavlov were to visit a neuroscience laboratory today he would feel very much at ease with the type of behavioural experiments found there.

Sensory preconditioning

In this procedure, two stimuli (e.g., light and a tone) are presented together. These stimuli need not have any biological significance, nor need they elicit any response. The basic observation is that if two neutral stimuli are repeatedly presented together then they become *associated* (i.e., linked). How is it known that they become associated? Let us assume that the light and tone were paired in the 'preconditioning' phase. Now a light is used as a CS in a Pavlovian conditioning procedure. It is established that this light CS elicits a CR. Now what happens if the tone is presented (remember this has not been conditioned to the UCS)? It would be observed that the tone has the power to elicit the CR, even though it has never been conditioned to the UCS. The two stimuli have become associated merely by being placed in a temporal relationship (Brogden, 1939).

It is easy to see how sensory preconditioning can widen the range of stimuli that could elicit a CR. For example, we may have had a bad experience with a dog as a child (such as being bitten). The sensory association of dogs with other animals may have led to a

(a) **Paired presentation** (before conditioning)

Light   +   Tone

No significant
response

(b) **During conditioning**

CS   +   UCS
(light)   (shock)

(c) **After conditioning**

CS ———————→ CR
(light)   (behavioural suppression/
               immobility)

(d) **Crucial sensory preconditioning test**

CS ———————→ CR
(tone)   (behavioural suppression/
               immobility)

Figure 7.4 Example of sensory preconditioning. (a) A light and tone presented together over a number of trials do not produce any significant response. (b) During a conditioning phase, the light is used as a *conditioned stimulus* (CS), which (c) after a sufficient number of conditioning trials leads to the CS producing a *conditioned response* (CR; in this instance behavioural suppression/immobility). But now (d) when the tone is presented – which has not been associated with the *unconditioned stimulus* (UCS) – it elicits the CR, demonstrating that in the preconditioning phase the behaviourally silent light and tone are associated.

generalization of our fear. What sensory preconditioning confirms is that associative learning does not need to be reinforced, either by being associated with an unconditioned response (e.g., salivation) or by the presence of reward and punishment: mere temporal *contiguity* is sufficient for learning to occur (figure 7.4).

In order to understand the applications of Pavlovian conditioning, especially to psychopathological conditions, such as fear and anxiety, it is necessary to know some more about the *acquisition* and *extinction* of CRs.

Acquisition of conditioned response

In the above discussion, it was rather loosely stated that Pavlovian conditioning occurs when the CS is presented *at about the same time* as the UCS. In fact, the ordering of the CS/UCS is important. There are three types of CS/UCS temporal ordering. (a) *Forward conditioning* is the most effective: this entails the CS onset being presented just before the UCS onset (usually seconds). (b) *Backward conditioning* is least effective: this entails the CS onset coming on after the UCS onset. (c) *Simultaneous conditioning* entails the simultaneous onset of the UCS and CS (figure 7.5).

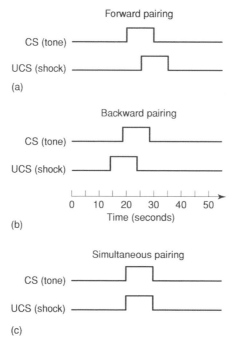

Figure 7.5 Types of CS–UCS pairings. The temporal pairing of the unconditioned stimulus (UCS) and conditioned stimulus (CS) takes one of three forms: (a) *forward conditioning*; (b) *backward conditioning*; and (c) *simultaneous conditioning*.

Two factors are important in CS/UCS pairing: (a) the longer the interval, the weaker the association; and (b) CS onset before UCS is much more effective than UCS onset before CS onset. Both factors suggest that what is important about the CS is that it *predicts* the UCS. This pairing *reinforces* the association of the two stimuli. When a CS is presented without the UCS, these trials are known as *non-reinforced* (this is seen during *extinction*, and also in differential conditioning, where one type of CS is paired (denoted CS+), the other unpaired (denoted CS–) (an example of differential fear conditioning is given in chapter 15). The CR may be measured in a number of ways: (a) *probability*, (b) *amplitude* and (c) *latency* of the CR (figure 7.6).

Generalization. This process is crucial in associative learning. For example, if a tone were used as a CS of a given frequency, then the maximal CR would be seen to this frequency; however, a CR (though weaker) to tones either side of this frequency would also be observed. The generalization *gradient* is shown in figure 7.7. Generalization allows flexibility in behaviour: response is elicited by a *class* of stimuli, and not just the particular CS that formed the initial conditioning.

Second-order conditioning. Once the CS is firmly established then it can be paired with another CS, a process known as second-order conditioning (the logic of this procedure can be extended to higher-order conditioning). Thus, stimuli may be chained together such that they elicit a response even though most of these stimuli have not been paired

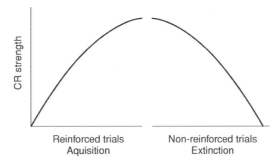

Figure 7.6 Idealized acquisition and extinction curves. Pairing the *conditioned stimulus* (CS) with an *unconditioned stimulus* (UCS) *reinforces* the association of the two stimuli, and the strength of the *conditioned response* (CR) increases during *acquisition* trials; but when the CS is presented alone (non-reinforced), then CR strength decreases during *extinction* trials.

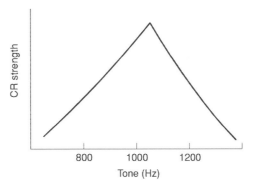

Figure 7.7 Generalization curve. *Generalization* refers to a *conditioned response* (CR) to stimuli on the same sensory dimension as the CS. For example, if the CS is a 1,000 Hz tone, then a weaker CR will be observed to tones (e.g., 800 and 1,200 H$_z$) falling either side of this value.

with the original UCS. Thus, it is not always clear what was the original UCS that set in train the chain of conditioned associations.

In human beings, a good example of this process is the evaluative nature of money: this is a CS, as it cannot be directly consumed and it is only of value as long as it leads to the acquisition of a primary reinforcer (i.e., UCS) – in times of monetary collapse, it is devalued and even worthless. Yet, in our daily life, it is of no little psychological importance. Money is also a high-order CS because its value to us resides not only in its ability to purchase food and shelter but also in its power to attain status and respect and help us maintain learned behaviours that themselves are not directly tied to UCSs. This higher-order matrix of CSs forms an important part of society and culture and our personal psychological worlds.

Extinction

As the CS/UCS link is established by pairing, so too it can be weakened and finally broken by non-pairing. The process of *extinction* refers to the decline in the strength of the CR as a consequence of the CS being presented unpaired with the UCS (i.e., the CS is *non-reinforced*; see figure 7.6). Extinction sometimes does not occur, and this can lead to the maintenance of neurotic disorders (e.g., phobias; see chapter 15).

However, extinction is not as simple as it may at first appear. In particular, it does not consist in the breaking of CS/UCS bonds in a straightforward manner. This fact is seen in the phenomenon of *spontaneous recovery*: an apparently extinguished CR can be reinstated to its full strength under a number of special conditions. For example, after a rest interval (e.g., the following morning in the case of Pavlov's dogs), the CR is often seen on first presentation of the CS (it then quickly wanes). The theoretical basis of this effect is unclear. It might be that extinction sets up a new Pavlovian conditioned association: that is, the CS predicts nothing of importance and thus becomes an *inhibitory stimulus*. When excitatory conditioning is stronger than inhibitory conditioning, spontaneous recovery of the CR is sometimes observed.

Latent inhibition

Another example of inhibition is seen in the phenomenon of *latent inhibition*: the mere presentation of a stimulus (e.g., an apparently random noise; to-be-CS) leads to it being actively inhibited, such that, when it is then used as a CS, it is much harder to form the CS/UCS association. This inhibition is not simply due to habituation, but to an active process of inhibition that draws attention away from the stimulus (Lubow, 1989; see chapter 8).

Biological preparedness

It is the case that some stimuli are more easily conditioned than others (e.g., spiders/snakes vs. flowers/mushrooms; see chapter 15). For example, laboratory-reared rhesus monkeys seeing a snake for the first time do not show fear, but their wild counterparts show great fear. What accounts for this difference? It seems that these monkeys condition extremely quickly to snakes when they see a conspecific showing a fear reaction – this fear reaction is strong and permanent. Now, if the monkey sees the terrified face of a conspecific and, by a trick with mirrors, is led to believe that the conspecific is terrified by seeing flowers, then does this learning too lead to a permanent fear reaction to flowers? The answer is that the monkey does not develop such a reaction. Therefore, some stimuli (snakes and spiders in particular) become easily associated with a negative event (e.g., terrified look on a conspecific's face – which induces a fear reaction in the monkey); other stimuli (e.g., flowers and mushrooms) simply do not. It is thus concluded that some stimuli are 'prepared' by evolution for fear conditioning.[2]

This finding suggests that temporal contiguity is not a sufficient explanation for associative learning. Also short CS–UCS temporal gaps are not always necessary for a strong association to be made. For example, if you tried a new type of seafood last night and today you were ill, you would probably think that the seafood caused the illness and you would shy away from this food in future (perhaps for ever). What is important about the seafood is its salience and novelty – the fact that you had also eaten bread, potatoes, etc. the day before does not enter your mind as the cause of your illness (these mundane foods have undergone latent inhibition over the course of your lifetime). *Cognition mediation* closes this temporal gap and makes the association possible.

Kamin blocking

The phenomenon of blocking also shows that there is more to associative learning than the temporal co-occurrence of stimuli (i.e., continuity; Kamin, 1968). To demonstrate blocking two groups are required. (a) The control group undergoes associative conditioning with a compound CS (e.g., light and tone), and after training either stimulus alone is sufficient to elicit the CR. (b) The experimental group is first conditioned to one of these stimuli (e.g., light), and only then goes through the same conditioning procedure as the control group with the compound (light + tone) stimulus. Blocking is observed in the experimental group: once they have conditioned to the light, their conditioning to the compound (light + tone) stimulus is retarded (i.e., the light conditioning blocks the tone conditioning). This effect has attracted considerable theoretical attention because it seems to say something important about the process underlying associative conditioning. Specifically, it disconfirms the continuity principle – temporal association is not sufficient to support conditioning – and instead suggests that the important principle is *predictive power*. This blocking effect is interesting because it shows the limitations of learning, perhaps pointing to biological constraints. In Nature, being able to predict important biological events has a clear advantage; but blocking shows that this facility may impair learning when stimulus conditions change. This effect may suggest why it is difficult to change our mind once we have acquired a certain belief about the world, even when we are confronted by contradictory evidence.

ASK YOURSELF
Why is classical conditioning considered to be such a fundamental learning process?

Instrumental learning

Instrumental learning is a form of trial-and-error learning in which responses are shaped by 'reinforcement'. This approach to learning was initiated by Thorndike (1898, 1911) and pioneered by B. F. Skinner (1938, 1953, 1957, 1966, 1971, 1984). Skinner attempted to develop a technology that could account for the environmental control of behaviour as well as proving a means to change behaviour in society (e.g., token economies used in prisons: prisoners' behaviour shaped by linking responses to specific consequences). Skinner's idea of a utopian society based upon instrumental learning principles is described in his 1948 novel, *Walden Two*. Skinner's psychology was ambitious and wide-ranging, purporting to account for individual and collective behaviour, and providing a technology to 'socially engineer' society.

Now, unlike Pavlovian learning, in which the subject has no control over the presentation of stimuli, in instrumental learning the presentation of stimuli is contingent (i.e., dependent) upon responses – for example, a food reward being dependent on a particular

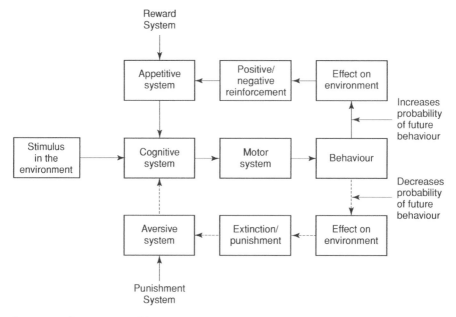

Figure 7.8 The instrumental learning process. Appetitive stimuli (i.e., rewarding and relieving non-punishment), mediated by the Reward System, increase the probability of behaviour contingent upon the presentation of adequate stimuli; and aversive stimuli (i.e., punishing and frustrative non-reward), mediated by the Punishment System, decrease the probability of behaviour contingent upon the presentation of adequate stimuli.

response. When the animal is allowed freely to respond then the instrumental response is known as an *operant*. It is emitted freely by the animal and it 'operates' on the environment: the environment feeds back to the behaviour of the animal in the form of salient consequences (e.g., reward and punishment). Like Pavlovian conditioning, the instrumental response is strengthened with increasing number of reinforcements; and if behaviour is not accompanied by reinforcement then it undergoes a process of extinction. It is 'instrumental' in the sense that behaviour changes environmental consequences – more precisely, different behaviours lead to different consequences.

In a general sense, reinforcement provides a form of feedback from the environment. This feedback is not neutral, though, because it has the power to influence subsequent behaviour. Thorndike's Law of Effect states that animals emit behaviours that lead to favourable environmental outcomes, and eliminate behaviours that lead to unfavourable outcomes. Experimental contingencies can be established experimentally such that successive approximations to a desired response are reinforced, and thus highly complex behaviours may be conditioned, a process known as 'shaping' behaviour. The effectiveness of this behavioural technology has been demonstrated in the training of dogs to pilot spacecraft, and is seen in the training of animals for entertainment.

Reinforcement

Unfortunately, 'reinforcement' and 'reinforcing stimuli' have different meanings in the various approaches to learning. These differences need to be clarified in order to avoid confusion. In the strict form of Skinnerian behaviourism, the term *reinforcement* is reserved for environmental consequences, contingent upon behaviour, which increase the probability of the future emission of that behaviour. The process of 'reinforcement' can be defined in terms of the 'operation' and 'outcome' of the experimental set-up. The 'operation' refers to the application or removal of a stimulus; the 'outcome' refers to the behavioural effects of the application/removal of a stimulus. A stimulus acts as 'reinforcement' if its application or removal increases the probability and/or strength of behaviour. There are two forms of reinforcement.

1. Positive reinforcement = application of a stimulus that leads to *increased* probability or strength of behaviour (e.g., food delivered following a particular response);
2. Negative reinforcement = removal of a stimulus that leads to *increased* probability or strength of behaviour (e.g., removal of shock following particular response).

In addition, in Skinnerian terminology, there are two operations that have behavioural consequences:

3. Extinction = removal of a stimulus that leads to *decreased* probability or strength of behaviour (e.g., non-delivery of food following a response when the delivery previously was contingent upon that response);
4. Punishment = application of a stimulus that leads to *decreased* probability or strength of behaviour (e.g., delivery of a shock following a particular response).

In Skinnerian psychology, there is also a contingency known as 'negative punishment', which is the non-delivery of a punishment contingent on a particular response (below, this type of response is called 'relieving non-punishment').

More generally, following Pavlov's definition, 'reinforcement' is used to refer to *anything* that reinforces (e.g., strengthens) connections (either between stimuli or between stimulus and response). In this more general sense, a reinforcer can lead to *conditioned inhibition*, reflecting a strengthening of connections but a *reduction* in the probability or strength of behaviour – though these terms play no part in the Skinnerian conception of reinforcement and behaviour, where such terms as 'inhibition' are eschewed in favour of stimuli and responses that can be directly observed and manipulated (see above).

Likewise, the removal of a positive or a negative reinforcer leads to experimental extinction of whatever behaviour, or inhibition of behaviour, was current. This non-Skinnerian, broader definition of extinction refers to the weakening of *any* form of association: the type of behaviour shown is irrelevant.

It should be borne in mind that Skinnerian psychology avoids such hedonically valenced terms as 'aversive' and 'appetitive', and focuses only on the experimental operations that lead to measurable behavioural outcomes. To the Skinnerian psychologist, the inference of internal (causal) states, such as emotion, are seen as unnecessary at best and muddled fictions at worst. For example, 'punishment' refers to the application of a stimulus that reduces behaviour; the idea that punishment leads to a negative emotional state, which *then* leads to the reduction in behaviour, is not entertained: internal states independent of the operation of a stimulus have no causal status in Skinnerian psychology.

Throughout this book, and consistent with a wider behavioural and neuropsychological literature, such internal-state terms are employed, often liberally and in a causally efficacious way. 'Reinforcement' is here used to refer to any class of stimuli that have the power to alter (any) behaviour (or its potential) in a systematic way (in any direction). This definition is needed to account for types of reinforcement that are not easily accounted for in Skinnerian terms.

For example, the termination or omission of a stimulus that previously had positive ('rewarding') reinforcing properties is a significant psychological event. Indeed the resulting behaviour, in many respects, resembles punished behaviour (it does not resemble the behaviour seen under extinction); more precisely, omission of reward elicits the same behaviour as a punisher (e.g., animals faced with extinction will try to escape the situation or attack other animals). Importantly, the central state that motivates this punishment-like response may be assumed to be 'frustrative non-reward'. In stark contrast to Skinnerian reinforcement and behaviour conceptions, the causal chain of influence contains an intervening variable: removal of (expected) appetitive stimulus [leads to] central state of 'frustrative non-reward' [leads to] punishment-like behaviour.

In a similar fashion, if an animal is trained to expect punishment, but then unexpectedly punishment is not presented, it behaves as if it had been presented with a positive ('rewarding') reinforcer. The causal chain is thus: removal of (expected) aversive stimulus [leads to] central state of 'relieving non-punishment' [leads to] reward-like behaviour.

Moving away from behavioural data to examining the effect of drugs on behaviour further supports these associations: (a) drugs that impair responses to punishing stimuli also tend to impair responses to frustrating stimuli; and (b) drugs that impair responses to rewarding stimuli also tend to impair responses to relieving non-punishing stimuli (see Gray, 1975, 1987). Thus, the delivery of punishment, as well as the termination or omission of expected reward, may be thought of as types of *aversive* stimuli (i.e., things that the animal would work to decrease); and the delivery of reward, as well as the termination or omission of punishment, may be thought of as types of *appetitive* stimuli (i.e., things that the animal would work to increase).

It is difficult, but not impossible, to account for such real behavioural effects without inferring 'expectation' of pleasant and unpleasant outcomes on the animal's behalf (even the humble laboratory rat) – such expectation is also observed in purely association effects, as seen in sensory preconditioning (see above). As emphasized throughout this book, central states are important (e.g., emotion), and these are not treated as 'explanatory fictions': they are seen as central motivators of behaviour activated by environmental stimuli that can be shown to have adaptive significance in terms of survival and fecundity.

Reinforcement schedules

Training on an operant schedule entails providing positive reinforcement for desired behaviours and negative reinforcement (usually the withholding of reward) for un-

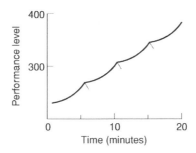

Figure 7.9   Examples of fixed interval (FI) behaviour. The scheduling of reinforcement has a major influence on the rate and pattern of behaviour and learning. On a fixed interval schedule (e.g., FI5 is reinforcement every 5 minutes), there is a characteristic scalloped shape, with performance greatest just before the expected delivery of reinforcement and least just after reinforcement (adapted from Ferster & Skinner, 1957).

desirable behaviours. A process known as *successive approximation* is used to reinforce behaviours that increasingly approximate the final desired behaviour. Through a process of selective *shaping*, lower animals (and us) can be trained to perform complex behaviours – in human beings, this reinforcement technology is used in different types of training programmes.

The sequencing of positive and negative reinforcement (i.e., *schedules of reinforcement*) has important effects on the build-up and extinction of instrumental responses (Ferster & Skinner, 1957). Reinforcement can be based on work rate (i.e., ratio schedule) or time elapsed (i.e., interval schedule). In addition to ratio and interval schedules, reinforcement can be continuous (i.e., delivered after each response) or intermittent/partial (i.e., delivered after every *n*th response). Reinforcement can also be fixed (i.e., predictable) or variable (i.e., containing a random ratio/interval factor).

A *fixed ratio* schedule delivers reinforcement after a set number of responses (e.g., FR20, after every 20th response); a *variable ratio* schedule after a certain number of responses (e.g., VR20 has a mean of 20, but on each trial the precise number of responses varies). A *fixed interval* schedule delivers reinforcement the first time a response is made after the passage of a fixed period of time (FI20, every 20 seconds); a *variable interval* after a period of time which varies on each trial around a mean value (e.g., VI20). Different schedules of reinforcement produce characteristic patterns of behaviour during acquisition. For example, on a fixed-interval schedule, immediately following a reward, response rate declines and then starts to increase as the time nears the schedule time (figure 7.9). A combination of reinforcement schedules can be used to maximize work rate in a given position.

Skinner is responsible for developing a whole technology of changing behaviour by manipulating reinforcement schedules; and, in case it is thought that such changes are peculiar to experimental pigeons and rats, most human beings are motivated by one form of reinforcement schedule or another (piecework, performance-related pay, etc.). Some form of partial schedule (on which reinforcement is made every *n*th response), which

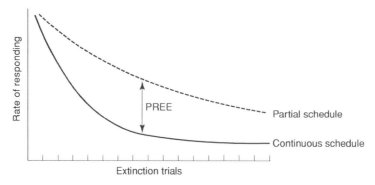

Figure 7.10 Partial reinforcement extinction effect (PREE). Experimental animals trained on a continuous schedule, on which there was a reinforcement on each trial, show more rapid extinction than animals trained on a partial schedule (e.g., 50% of trials).

has a random (unpredictable) element, usually produces the highest work rate: this fact is capitalized on by gaming machine operators who know that human beings are more likely to play machines where reward is intermittent and where there is perceived to be some element of control (however illusory in practice) – despite the identical outcome, simply receiving a small reward every nth response, irrespective of choice made, is demotivating to gamblers, who often show superstitious behaviour (e.g., they think they have worked out how to beat the machine), which is itself reinforced by intermittent schedules of reinforcement. (If you think that the principles of behaviourism are not relevant to human cognition, then consider the prevalence of gambling in society – and then think about the similarities of gambling principles, based on reinforcement schedules, and those operating in everyday life: e.g., occupational behaviour.)

In terms of extinction, the major findings are that partial schedules lead to slower extinction: this is known as the *partial reinforcement extinction effect* (PREE; figure 7.10). A similar effect is found with the use of variable rather than fixed schedules, an effect that may be termed the *variable reinforcement extinction effect*. The theoretical basis of these effects is still debated. It may be that the subject on a continuous or fixed schedule is more sensitive to non-reinforcement during extinction: if it always occurred or occurred on a regular fixed basis, then its non-occurrence is salient. Another interpretation relates to *conditioned frustration* (i.e., Pavlovian conditioning of the innate state of frustration): during partial schedules, the subject is exposed to non-reward, which it finds frustrating. Stimuli (CSs) in the animal's environment then get classically conditioned to this negative emotional state, with the result that, during extinction, conditioned frustration maintains responding and retards extinction (it could do this by increasing arousal, which is known to increase the probability of on-going behaviour).

ASK YOURSELF
What are the advantages of adopting a 'schedules of reinforcement' behaviourist perspective?

Similarity of Pavlovian and instrumental conditioning

What is learned in Pavlovian and instrumental paradigms is the association between two events: CS/UCS in the case of Pavlovian conditioning; instrumental response and consequence (reinforcement) in the case of instrumental learning. Temporal *contiguity* and *contingency* seem necessary conditions for these associations to be formed. In both cases, one stimulus comes to signal (or predict) another. The CS predicts the UCS; the response predicts the reinforcement (in our everyday lives, we know, with a certain probability, that if we behave in way *x* then consequence *y* follows). In other words, events must go together (contiguity) and this relationship must have some predictive value (contingency).

Whether these two approaches to learning represent different behavioural expressions of the same underlying learning process is still debated. However, there exists behavioural evidence that Pavlovian and instrumental learning rely upon different learning processes (Gray, 1975); and, discussed in a later section, there is evidence from neural plasticity research to support this 'two-process model of learning' (Mowrer, 1960).

However, in both forms of learning, the importance of a *mental (internal) representation* of the causal relationship between either the CS/UCS or response (operant) and outcome (reinforcement) can be clearly seen in the case of *vicarious* or *imitation* learning. Much of our behaviour is learned by observing others. In this type of learning, responses are not simply emitted: we watch others behaving and being reinforced and learn from this experience. This form of learning may be understood in terms of the *cognitive* association of events. This cognitive perspective contrasts with the *radical behaviourist* perspective in that the latter insists that the key to learning is the association of stimuli with motor responses: if there is no obvious response, then what is there to learn? It is now known that an overt response is not needed for learning to occur (e.g., sensory preconditioning).

> **ASK YOURSELF**
> Do classical conditioning and instrumental conditioning differ only in terms of how stimuli and responses are arranged?

Other forms of learning

Pavlovian and instrumental processes have dominated the psychology of learning. However, other forms of learning exist. For example, *perceptual learning* involves learning the relationship between sensory stimuli, thereby facilitating perception. Look at the drawing in figure 7.11. What do you see? If you have seen this image before, then your answer comes easily; if not, then it takes a while for your brain to work out the object in the image. You should see a Dalmatian dog in the snow (head in centre of image, body to the right). Once you have perceived this image your cognitive processing has been permanently altered (and so too has your brain). Thus, we learn to see the world ('perceptual learning'): it is not simply waiting there to be seen.

Motor learning involves the acquisition of skilled behaviours and habits. In the last 20 years, a major distinction has arisen between *declarative/explicit* and *procedural/implicit* learning and memory. Declarative/explicit learning and memory involve the acquisition

Figure 7.11 Dalmatian dog. *Perceptual learning* involves learning the relationship between sensory stimuli, an important process in perception. What do you see in this image? Once you have seen the dog, then it is difficult *not* to see it the next time the image is viewed.

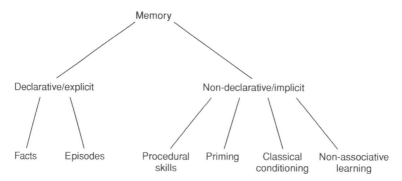

Figure 7.12 The division of memory into declarative/explicit (conscious) and non-declarative/implicit (non-conscious) systems.

of knowledge of which there is conscious awareness: it is possible to remember the learning event and what has been learned. In contrast, procedural/implicit learning and memory can occur without conscious awareness of the learned material, and sometimes even without awareness of the learning event (figure 7.12).

Much of the research on Pavlovian and instrumental learning has been purely behavioural, without recourse to neurophysiological concepts. Now, at about the same time as the experimental study of learning was taking off in earnest, important discoveries were being made in neurophysiology that influenced a different way of thinking about learning and psychological processes. Especially important in this regard was the discovery of the neuron as a discrete processing unit in the brain – this is credited to Ramon y Cajal, who with Camilo Golgi won a Nobel Prize in 1906. Once the neuron had been identified it was natural to think in terms of a network of neuronal inter-connections. The most influential psychologist in proposing links between psychological and physiological explanations was Donald Hebb (1949): his influence can be seen in neural networks and neurophysiology. Before turning to neural networks and neural plasticity, the next section considers the central contribution of Hebb.

> **ASK YOURSELF**
> Can you think of any examples of learning that do not fit the learning processes discussed above?

Hebb's Theory

Donald Hebb's (1949) *The Organization of Behaviour: A Neuropsychological Theory* called attention to the promising work of the first formal mathematical expression of the neuron proposed by McCulloch and Pitts (1943) – in fact, this was the first neural network model, designed by an interdisciplinary collaboration of a senior psychiatrist/neurophysiologist (McCulloch) and a young mathematician (Pitts). Hebb was to state presciently, 'Undoubtedly there is great potential value in such work . . .' (p. xii). It was to be another 40 years for the full potential of this work to be appreciated. Before the full realization of neural network ideas in the 1980s, neurophysiological research was inspired by Hebb's two highly influential postulations concerning: (a) the cell assembly; and (b) synaptic strengthening.

Cell assembly

An active neural circuit, or *cell assembly*, is a closed reverberatory loop. A cell assembly fires in a fixed sequence, and the firing in this closed loop allows neural activation to persist across a short period of time: a *reverberatory circuit*. Hebb (1949) stated,

> It is proposed first that a repeated stimulation of specific receptors will lead slowly to the formation of an 'assembly' of association-area cells which can act briefly as a closed system after stimulation has ceased; this prolongs the time during which structural changes of learning can occur and constitutes the simplest instance of a representative process. (p. 60)

This is the neural process underlying thinking and attentional focus.

> The assumption, in brief, is that a growth process accompanying synaptic activity makes the synapse more readily traversed . . . An intimate relationship is postulated between reverberatory action and structural changes at the synapse, implying a dual trace mechanism. (pp. 60, 61)

Thus, in order for this short-term processing to become a long-term memory, some structural changes must take place between neurons: 'cells that fire together wire together'.

Synaptic strengthening

Hebb's second postulate states that the strength of connections between neurons increases in proportion to the degree of correlation between their activity. In Hebb's own words,

> Let us assume then that the persistence or repetition of a reverberatory activity (or 'trace') tends to induce lasting cellular changes that add to its stability. The assumption can be precisely stated as follows: When an axon of cell A is near enough to excite a cell B and repeatedly or persistently takes part in firing it, some growth process or metabolic change takes place in one or both cells such that A's efficiency, as one of the cells firing B, is increased. (Hebb, 1949, p. 62)

A synapse that increases in effectiveness because of simultaneous activity in the presynaptic and postsynaptic neurons is called a *Hebbian synapse* (this process has now been confirmed by studies of *long-term potentiation*; see the 'Neural Plasticity' section below).

Hebb (1949) went on to suggest a possible neurophysiological process for structural change: 'the most probable suggestion concerning the way in which one cell could become more capable of firing another is that synaptic knobs develop and increase the area of contact' (p. 62), such that 'When one cell repeatedly assists in firing another, the axon of the first cell develops synaptic knobs (or enlarges them if they already exist) in contact . . . with the second cell' (p. 63).

ASK YOURSELF
How does Hebb's theory relate to classical and instrumental conditioning?

As noted in the following section, there is evidence for this specific suggestion. With Hebb's insights in mind, let us move on to considering how learning is represented in (a) the artificial brain (neural networks) and (b) the real brain (neural plasticity).

Artifical Neural Networks

One useful way of thinking about the relationship between learning and the functions of neurons and neuronal networks is in terms of artificial neural networks implemented in computers to model and simulate likely brain processes. Artificial neural networks are computer simulations of psychological functions inspired by knowledge of the workings of the real brain, especially the workings of the *real* neuron (see chapter 3); as such they are an example of the *conceptual nervous system* (Hebb, 1955); they are (to use McCulloch and Pitt's phrase) 'neuro-logical' models. These computer models are variously called *connectionist architectures*, *parallel distributed processing*, *neurocomputing* and *soft computing*. (For an introduction to connectionism in cognitive psychology, see Ellis & Humphreys, 1999; Harnish, 2002.)

Neural networks are fundamentally different to conventional computers, which use a list of fixed instructions for carrying out specific functions. In contrast, neural networks are designed to allow the system to learn and change its input–output associations on the basis of some learning rule (see below).

Work on neural networks has been motivated by the recognition that the human brain computes in an entirely different way from the conventional digital computer. The brain is a highly complex, non-linear and parallel computer, working at a high speed; it also has the capacity to organize its structural parts (i.e., neurons and their interconnections). Psychological functions are highly complex mathematically, entailing non-linear transformations which either are unknown or cannot be easily modelled. Neural networks are especially useful when modelling such complex processes.

Another strength of neural networks over conventional computer models is that degraded input does not destroy the functional capabilities of the system. Rather like human brain damage, neural networks are still able to work, albeit less effectively, when the network is 'lesioned'. Also, rather like the real nervous system, the system can reorganize after damage. In other words, it can *relearn*.

Neural networks are now used for a wide variety of functions, many of which have nothing to do with attempts to understand the workings of the biological brain; for example, face recognition, predicting stock-market movements and modelling engine dynamics. This discussion concerns only those networks relating to the biological brain. Good introductory texts on neural networks include Carling (1992), Aleksander and Morton (1995), Rojas (1996) and Haykin (1999).

Some of the earliest thinking on the formal arrangement of neurons to form psychologically meaningful circuits may be traced to Sigmund Exner, who, in 1894, published a monograph, *Project for Physiological Explanations of Mental Phenomena*, which contained a number of drawings of neural networks (figure 7.13).

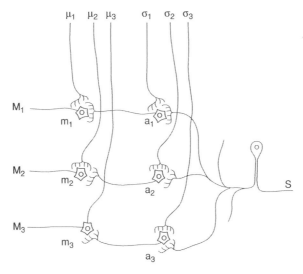

Figure 7.13 Exner's 1894 neural net. An early neural network by Sigmund Exner (1894), which purports to model the choice reaction-time studies. Sensory (*S*) input travels to sensory cells (a_1, a_2, a_3), and then to motor output cells (m_1, m_2, m_3). Processing at sensory (σ_1, σ_2, σ_3) and motor (μ_1, μ_2, μ_3) cells can be 'primed' by the 'organs of consciousness'.

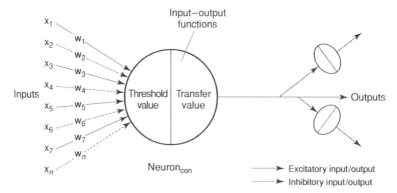

Figure 7.14 A simple artificial neuron (neuron$_{con}$). A processing element comprises a set of different excitatory and inhibitory inputs (x_1 to x_n), each of which has a different weight (i.e., influence; w_1 to w_n), which enter the processing element, where two functions are found: (a) the *threshold value* is the sum (input value multiplied by weight) of all the weights of all inputs (i.e., $\Sigma(x_1w_1 + x_2w_2 + x_nw_n)$), and the neuron is active if the weighted value of inputs exceeds the threshold value; and (b) the *transfer value* specifies how summed input is transferred to output (e.g., linear function). A neural network consists of networks of such processing elements. This element is the foundation of all neural network models.

At about the same time, another Sigmund, this time Freud, also flirted with the possibility of neural connections as an explanation of psychological phenomena. However, his promising *Project for a Scientific Psychology* (1895) was rapidly abandoned in favour of his fantasy theory (Stein & Ludik, 1998). The first development of a formal neural network model was by McCulloch and Pitts (1943). After a period of disillusionment with neural network models in the 1960s and 1970s, the 1980s saw a resurgence of interest, and today such models are commonplace in *cognitive neuroscience*. The challenge of bringing together knowledge of the neurophysiology of the real nervous system and neural networks is now being met by the emerging field of *computational neuroscience*.

Although there are significant differences in the construction and operation of neural networks, modern-day neural networks contain a number of characteristic features: (a) local processing in artificial neurons (processing elements, PEs); (b) massively parallel processing, consisting of rich connections between PEs; (c) the ability to learn from experience through training; and (d) storage of knowledge in the form of memories.

Processing element (PE; neuron*$_{con}$*)

The processing element (conceptual or artificial neuron) forms the basic processing unit of neural networks (figure 7.14; the conceptual neuron is denoted neuron$_{con}$). First, input to the neuron$_{con}$ has a *weight* (i.e., the amount of influence) – comparable to a synaptic strength. Second, the weighted influence can be either excitatory or inhibitory. Third, the neuron$_{con}$ can have a number of inputs, in much the same way that the real neuron can have as many as 10,000 inputs. Fourth, each neuron$_{con}$ has a *threshold value*: if the sum of all the weights of all inputs is greater than this threshold value then the neuron$_{con}$ is active (recall that the threshold of response is determined in the real neuron at the axon hillock).

The neuron$_{con}$ has a *transfer value*, which specifies how a quantity of input is transferred into output to other neurons$_{con}$: the *firing rule* determines whether a neuron should fire for any given input; and the *learning law* specifies how weights are adjusted to reflect learning in the system. This learning law may be based on a number of different *learning rules*.

Learning rules

A number of learning rules are available to guide the internal construction of neural networks. These rules are mathematical algorithms used to determine the weights of inputs.

Hebb's Rule. This is the oldest and best-known rule, introduced by Donald Hebb (1949). This rule states: if a neuron receives an input from another neuron, and if both are highly active and have the same sign (either excitatory or inhibitory), then the weight between the neurons is strengthened.

Hopfield Rule. This rule is similar to Hebb's Rule; it states: if the desired output and the input are both active or both inactive, increment the connection weight by the *learning rate*, otherwise decrement the weight by the learning rate (i.e., a predetermined constant).

Delta Rule. This is another variation of Hebb's Rule, and is widely used in neural networks. This rule continuously changes the strengths of the input connections to reduce the difference (the delta) between the desired output value and the actual output of a neuron.

Kohonen's Rule. This rule was inspired by learning in biological systems. In this system, neurons compete for the opportunity to learn, or to update their weights. The procedure works by the processing neuron$_{con}$ with the largest output being declared the winner, and this winning neuron$_{con}$ has the capability to inhibit its competitors.

Input and output layers

Let us illustrate how a simple neural network may work with an example of pattern recognition. The problem faced by this simple network is: is it light or dark? One neuron$_{con}$ can be used for each possible state (light or dark; neuron$_{dark}$, neuron$_{light}$). This *input layer* could be a 2×2 grid of pixels. Assuming that the input is 'light', then the neuron$_{light}$ would be most active, and thus is the output of the network. This processing may be represented mathematically. Let us give each input a value of 1 for 'light' and −1 for 'dark'; when the input is 'light' then the total input value is 4 (i.e., Σ $p1$, $p2$, $p3$, $p4$ – where pn is one of the 2×2 inputs); if it had been 'dark', then the value would be −4; a value if 0 would indicate some intermediate input between 'dark' and 'light' (figure 7.15).

This simple neural network contains some important features. First is the *input layer*: neurons$_{con}$ are sensitive to the input signal (e.g., the lightness/darkness of a computer image would be read as the corresponding binary code). Second is the *output layer*:

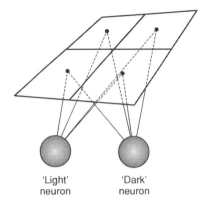

Figure 7.15 2 × 2 light/dark input layer. The 2 × 2 input grid layer is sensitive to inputs that correspond to light–dark (dark has an input value of –1; light an input value of +1; intermediate values from –1 to +1). When the input is 'light' the input value is 4 (4 × 1); when dark, –4 (4 × –1).

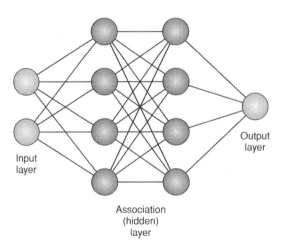

Figure 7.16 Input, association and output layers. Most neural networks contain (a) an input layer; (b) an output layer; and (c) an association layer, which is a hidden layer that abstracts higher-order functions and forms internal representations of the underlying structure of the input/output pattern (this layer can be scrutinized by statistical analysis to determine its structure).

neurons$_{con}$ produce outputs (that are pre-specified) that, after appropriate training, correspond to the input. Often there are intermediate *association layers* between input and output layers: in complex systems, these are used to abstract higher-order functions, to infer complex relations and to form *internal representations* of the underlying structure of input/output pattern (figure 7.16).

Let us consider a more complex problem using light/dark neurons$_{con}$: to recognize the letter T (figure 7.17). The input array could comprise a 5 × 7 grid; a set of neurons$_{con}$ (in this case 26, one for each letter of the alphabet) would share this 35-pixel input space.

(a) **Start of training**

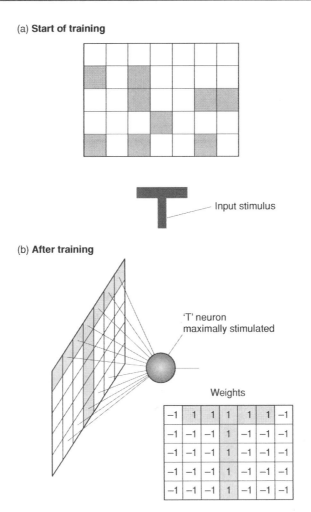

Input stimulus

(b) **After training**

'T' neuron
maximally stimulated

Weights

−1	1	1	1	1	1	−1
−1	−1	−1	1	−1	−1	−1
−1	−1	−1	1	−1	−1	−1
−1	−1	−1	1	−1	−1	−1
−1	−1	−1	1	−1	−1	−1

Figure 7.17   Neural network T. This example shows a 5 × 7 output grid and a set of 26 input neurons (only one is shown) that correspond to the letters of the alphabet; these neurons represent a 35-pixel input space. At the start of training there is only a random correspondence between input and output (panel (a)); but, as training progresses, the system learns that the output of a specific input pattern of light and dark corresponds to the letter T (panel (b)). This is achieved by input weights changing until the neurons$_{con}$ converge on the correct T set (i.e., there is maximal activation of T neuron and inaction of all other neurons (neurons$_{A-Z}$).

At the beginning of training, there would be little correspondence between input and output (panel a), but as training progresses, the system would come to learn that the corresponding output of a specific input pattern of light and dark that corresponds to the letter T (panel b). To achieve this end, the weightings between neurons$_{con}$ could change randomly until they eventually converge on the correct set to allow the output to correspond to the input. At each random change of weightings, the approximation of the neural model against the standard input would be assessed: if the random changes worsen the fit of the model, then the change is undone, and a new random change is tried. All 26 neurons$_{con}$ would compete for activation, but only one (i.e., the T neuron$_{con}$) would win out by being most active, this being the neuron$_{con}$ weighted inputs that correspond to the letter T.

In this specific case, training would take the following form. (a) The desired output pattern is drawn. (b) A neuron$_{con}$ is selected that should learn this pattern. (c) For each active pixel, 1 is added to the weight of each link between the pixel and the neuron$_{con}$. (d) For inactive pixels, 1 is subtracted from the weight of each link between the inactive pixel and the neurons$_{con}$. Thus, after training, presentation of the letter T would maximally activate the T neuron$_{con}$, and this is the output. This procedure is an example of *supervised training*.

One solution to this weighting problem is the *back-propagation* algorithm: this compares the result that was expected with the result that was obtained. This information is then used systematically to change the weights throughout the neural network. This method is more highly efficient than trial and error. An important feature of this method is that it can be used to train networks where only a portion of the data is available – that is, it can make inferences to reach the final solution.

Psychological processes

The above examples are useful for understanding how neural networks work, but for psychological purposes they are too simple. Psychological problems are complex – even apparently simple ones – and require interactions, often considerably complex ones, between a large number of neurons$_{con}$. Under these conditions, the system is allowed to develop its own network of neurons$_{con}$ in order to achieve a correspondence between input and (specified) output. This procedure is an example of *unsupervised training*, or self-organization. Another form of training is *reinforcement training*, in which the network is corrected as it achieves its internal self-organization. *Learning rules* are applied in order to allow a system to settle upon a stable solution. The precise way in which the system achieves its outputs is not clear, and for this reason further analysis of the system may be needed. With five association layers, the final network might look something like that shown in figure 7.18.

One problem in constructing a psychologically viable network concerns the degree of input–output fit. If neurons$_{con}$ are too well specified (*over-fitted*), then they train quickly and perform flawlessly on the trained set of inputs–outputs; but they may be so rigid that they are unable to process novel or degraded input, and thus do not show the processing flexibility that is characteristic of the real brain. On the other hand, they may be ill-specified (*under-fitted*), and thus perform poorly on the trained set. There is clearly a balance to be achieved between under- and over-fitting the model.

Neural networks and associative learning

As a concrete example, let us return to Pavlovian conditioning. It would be possible to develop a neural network model to simulate the processes involved in associative learning.

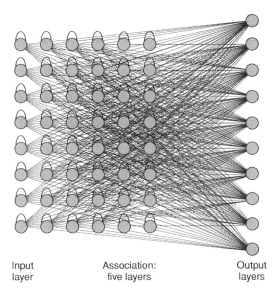

Input   Association: Output
layer   five layers   layers

Figure 7.18   Network: input, five association layers, output.

This model could start with a number of inputs: for example, type of UCS, magnitude of UCS, type of CSs, prior associative strength of CSs, number of trials, drive (e.g., hunger) of subject. These data would represent the *input layer*. Next, the model could specify behavioural responses: for example, trials of CR, strength of CR, learning and generalization curve, extinction rates. This would be the *output layer*. Then the system could be trained using data from actual behavioural studies. Then the network could form an *internal representation*, via the association layers, to provide a correspondence between input and output. The adequacy of the model could be tested by inputting new variable values that have known (behavioural) output values. Assuming that an adequate internal representation of the relation between inputs and outputs has been achieved, then two further things are possible. The first is to enter new values (e.g., imaginary experiments) and observe the outputs. This could lead to new knowledge. Second, the network could be interrogated and the structure of the association layer (via statistical analysis) ascertained in order to determine the causal structure underlying associative conditioning. It is hoped that by such analysis of the network's interconnections real insights may be gained into the workings of the real nervous system.

> **ASK YOURSELF**
> How are neural networks used to test old hypotheses and generate new ones?

Neural Plasticity

Neural plasticity refers to the brain's capacity to change and reorganize in response to changing input from internal or external sources. Plasticity informs us that the development and continued reorganization of the brain are not dictated solely by the action of genes: if plasticity did not exist, then every neuron would have to be coded individually. Genes code for generality rather than specificity, thus facilitating adaptive changes in response to the local environment, leading to greater flexibility of behaviour. The capacity for neural change ensures that each individual's brain is truly unique.

What neuronal changes correspond to learning? In other words, what is the brain machinery that makes learning and memory possible? Much of the work aimed at addressing this question has adopted Hebb's (1949) theory that short-term memory consists of a *reverberatory circuit* (see above), which after some period of time of operation is *consolidated* into long-term memory by permanent structural changes in the brain (i.e., biochemical and neuronal alterations).

There is ample evidence that changes in the brain can be observed following stimulation and learning. For example, rats reared in an enriched environment (i.e., 'toys' in the home cage that are novel and allow exploration and activity), compared with rats reared in an impoverished environment (i.e., dim light, quiet cage), have a number of brain differences: thicker cortex, better capillary blood supply, more glial cells and more protein content (Rosenzweig & Bennett, 1996). Turner and Greenough (1985) reported increases in the size of postsynaptic densities (thought to reflect the size of the active zone of the synapse) in the brains of rats that had spent time in a complex environment. Greenough, Juraska and Volkmar (1979) found larger dendritic fields in the visual cortex of animals exposed to a series of mazes. In one ingenious experiment, Chang and Greenough (1982) divided the rats' cerebral hemispheres, by cutting the corpus callosum, allowing visual information to reach only one hemisphere. The results showed that changes in dendritic fields were seen only in the hemisphere that received the enriched visual information. This experiment ruled out the possibility that the previous reports could have been due to increased exercise, or some other irrelevant effect.

Therefore, there are widespread structural changes in the brain as a result of sensory stimulation. In human beings too, continual stimulation of the brain seems to lead to an enhancement in brain size. For example, it has been found that extensive use of the cognitive facility of spatial mapping – found in London taxi drivers, who are extensively trained on learning the street names/routes in London, UK – has the physiological effect of increasing the size of the hippocampus (a crucial structure involved in memory); in addition, size differences are correlated with years of experience (Maguire et al., 2000).

Aplysia californica: *the sea hare*

The science of neural plasticity owes much to the humble sea hare, *Aplysia californica* (a marine invertebrate related to the common slug; figure 7.19). *Aplysia* has been the creature of choice for the study of neuronal changes in learning for a number of reasons: (a) it has a very simple central nervous system made up of about 20,000 cells; (b) its neurons are large (up to 1 mm in diameter); (c) there are few inter-individual differences in neuronal pathways; and (d) it exhibits an innate gill-withdrawal reflex that can be modified in simple or associative learning paradigms. The most impressive work on neural plasticity is Kandel's (e.g., 1991), for which he was awarded a Nobel Prize in 2000.

Habituation, sensitization and *Pavlovian conditioning* have been studied in *Aplysia*. The neuronal basis of these three types of learning is outlined below.

(a)

(b)

Figure 7.19 Picture and diagram of *Aplysia californica* (a marine invertebrate related to the common slug), which is the size of a human hand (a). The main body parts involved in experimental studies of learning are depicted in (b). Touching the siphon causes the gill to withdraw. (Photo © Marty Snyderman Image Quest Marine.)

Habituation

When its siphon, mantle or gill is touched, *Aplysia* withdraws the gill vigorously. But with repeated touching (sensory stimulation) the gill-withdrawal reflex becomes progressively less vigorous, and finally disappears. This is exactly what should be expected from the discussion of habituation. Habituation in *Aplysia* lasts 2 to 3 hours following a single stimulus habituation session.

Castellucci and Kandel (1974) measured the excitatory postsynaptic potentials (EPSP) from a motor neuron during habituation. As habituation progressed, the size of the EPSP decreased. But how does this effect occur? The basic finding is that habituation in the *Aplysia* is associated with a decline in the number of action potentials that are elicited in the gill motor neurons by each touch of the siphon. However, the responsiveness of the motor neurons to the transmitter released by the sensory neurons does not decline during habituation; it is thus concluded that the progressive decline in the number of motor neuron action potentials results from a decline in the release of neurotransmitter from the sensory neurons (figure 7.20).

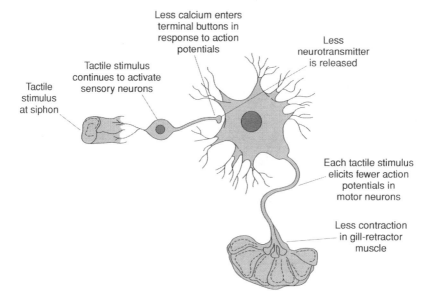

Figure 7.20 Habituation process in *Aplysia*. After repeated touching of the siphon, the gill-withdrawal response habituates. In this form of habituation the sensory neuron and motor neuron remain active (e.g., if directly stimulated). Habituation occurs due to decreased neurotransmitter release at the sensory–motor neurons synapse (itself a result of less calcium entering the terminal button of the sensory neuron).

What causes the siphon's sensory neurons to reduce the release of neurotransmitter? The number of sensory neuron action potentials *does not* decline with habituation; what causes the decline in the amount of neurotransmitter released is that fewer calcium ions enter the terminal button and thus fewer vesicles are activated (see chapter 3). This basic model of habituation has been extended to account for *sensitization* and *Pavlovian conditioning* (Hawkins & Kandel, 1984).

Sensitization

Sensitization in *Aplysia* occurs when a noxious stimulus causes a relatively weak gill-withdrawal reflex to be strengthened ('weak' in this context refers to the strength of the gill-withdrawal reflex in response to a siphon touch compared with a noxious stimulus, e.g., electrical stimulation). This process involves a change at the same neural locus as habituation, but in sensitization there is an *enhancement* of neurotransmitter release by the sensory neurons on their target cells. Electrical shock to the tail causes sensory neurons to increase their release of neurotransmitter onto the gill motor neurons. A process of *presynaptic facilitation* occurs: sensory fibres from the *Aplysia*'s tail synapse on facilitatory serotonergic (i.e., serotonin-releasing) interneurons, which, in turn, synapse on the buttons of the siphon sensory neurons (figure 7.21). Thus, with each touch of the siphon, there is increased influx of calcium ions and thus greater neurotransmitter release.

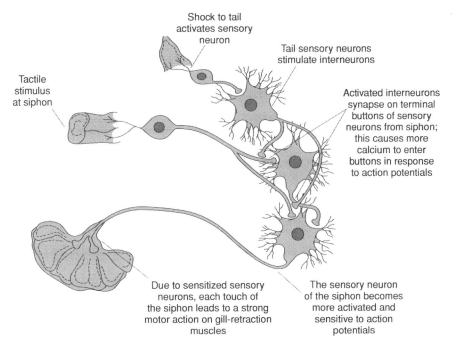

Shock to tail
activates sensory
neuron

Tail sensory neurons
stimulate interneurons

Tactile
stimulus
at siphon

Activated interneurons
synapse on terminal
buttons of sensory
neurons from siphon;
this causes more
calcium to enter
buttons in response
to action potentials

Due to sensitized sensory
neurons, each touch of
the siphon leads to a strong
motor action on gill-retraction
muscles

The sensory neuron
of the siphon becomes
more activated and
sensitive to action
potentials

Figure 7.21   Sensitization process in *Aplysia*. In the case of sensitization in *Aplysia*, a similar (though opposite) process to habituation works. A shock to the tail activates the tail's sensory neurons, which then facilitate interneurons that synapse on the buttons of sensory neurons from the siphon, which causes an increased influx of calcium, and thus the release of greater quantities of neurotransmitter from the siphon's sensory neurons. The result is increased action potentials in the gill's motor neurons, and thus a greater gill-withdrawal response when the siphon is touched.

Pavlovian conditioning

Associative learning has been studied in the *Aplysia*. If the touch to the siphon (CS) – which produces a weak gill-withdrawal reflex – is *paired* with a shock to the tail (UCS), then the light touch to the siphon (CS) begins to elicit a strong gill-withdrawal reflex similar to that elicited by a tail shock. At this point, you may be wondering how this procedure differs from sensitization. It does in the crucial aspect that is known to be important in Pavlovian conditioning: *temporal contiguity*.

As a consequence of this Pavlovian pairing of CS and UCS, now when the siphon is weakly stimulated (i.e., presentation of the CS), more neurotransmitter is produced and a stronger gill-withdrawal reflex occurs. As in the case of sensitization, once again this is a process of *presynaptic facilitation*: the sensory neuron (the *presynaptic neuron*) is made more effective, or facilitated, by means of the activation of the facilitator interneurons (figure 7.22).

The primary difference between Pavlovian conditioning and sensitization, therefore, is the temporal coincidence of the activity of the facilitating and facilitated pathways. As a

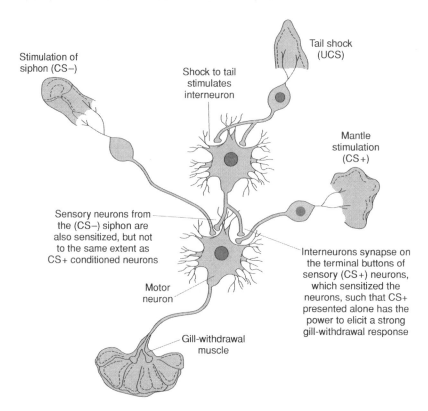

Figure 7.22 Pavlovian process in *Aplysia*. Pavlovian conditioning in the *Aplysia* is an extension of the process of sensitization. First a shock to the tail (i.e., the unconditioned stimulus; UCS) stimulates the neuron on which tail sensory neurons synapse, and this causes increased release at the interneuron's terminal buttons. This process sensitizes, in a general way, the motor neuron to activation by siphon stimulation (CS–); however, stimulation of the mantle, which is paired with shock to the tail (i.e., CS+), has a large effect on the terminal buttons of the mantle's sensory neuron on which the interneuron synapses. As a result, the next CS+ leads to the release of a greater amount of neurotransmitter, and thus the conditioned response (CR) is observed.

result, Kandel calls the process *activity-dependent presynaptic facilitation* (this may be defined as the 'enhancement of synaptic transmission whose induction depends on the presynaptic neuron being active during the enhancement-inducing presynaptic input'; Pinel, 2000).

In sensitization, a shock to the tail acts on siphon sensory neurons to bring about presynaptic facilitation. In Pavlovian conditioning, presynaptic facilitation is dependent upon the temporal pairing of CS (siphon) pathway activity and UCS (tail) pathway activity. The CS pathway is active just prior to activation of the UCS pathway, thereby enhancing presynaptic facilitation of the siphon sensory neuron (Hawkins & Kandel, 1984).

It would seem that the effects of reinforcement, made contingent upon a response (instrumental learning), are dependent upon this process of *activity-dependent presynaptic facilitation*. In this specific instance, facilitation would come from 'reinforcement centres' in the brain, which would send fibres to the pathways that mediate the link between stimuli and responses. For example, in a human experimental context, this process may consist of the delivery of reinforcement (e.g., money) con-sequent upon the pressing of a button on a computer keyboard (the response) each time A is presented (the stimulus). In general terms, this process supports Hebb's (1949) claim that 'cells that fire together wire together'.

> **ASK YOURSELF**
> What have been the advant-ages of studying *Aplysia californica*?

◼️◻️ Long-term Potentiation (LTP) and Long-term Depression (LTD)

Long-term potentiation (LTP)

Long-term potentiation (LTP), first reported in the seminal work of Bliss and Lomo (1973), is an important experimental model of learning and memory at the cellular level of analysis (Okulski, Hess & Kaczmarek, 2002). Study of the hippocampus has revealed much of what is known about LTP, although LTP is observed at synapses in many brain structures (e.g., prefrontal cortex, motor cortex, visual cortex, thalamus and amygdala). LTP represents long-term structural changes in synaptic connections that correspond to learning and memory – more precisely, the *Hebb synapse* – comprising a long-term increase in the magnitude of excitatory postsynaptic potentials.

LTP consists of at least two phases, each corresponding to different molecular mechanisms. First, the 'early phase of LTP' (E-LTP) does not involve protein syntheses, but depends on neuronal activity; and second, the enduring phase, lasting 3–4 hours, termed the 'late phase of LTP' (L-LTP), is dependent on protein synthesis – this phase of memory consolidation can be blocked with drugs that interfere with protein synthesis (e.g., *anisomycin*; see Okulski, Hess & Kaczmarek, 2002).

The details of how LTP in the hippocampus is induced and measured are shown in figure 7.23. (a) A stimulating electrode is placed among the axons that project to the dentate gyrus; (b) a recording electrode is placed in the dentate gyrus; (c) a single pulse of electrical stimulation is delivered and then the resulting excitatory postsynaptic potentials (EPSP; see chapter 3) are recorded in the dentate gyrus; (d) the size of the first EPSP shows the size of the synaptic connections before LTP occurs; (e) LTP is now induced by stimulating the axons with a burst of approximately 100 pulses, delivered within a space of a few seconds. Now, if the axons that travel to the dentate gyrus are stimulated by a *single* electrical pulse, it can be seen that the EPSP burst is now greater than it was before the induction of LTP.

This procedure can be extended to associative learning (e.g., Kelso & Brown, 1986). Here, strong electrical stimulation of the neuron (similar to a UCS) is paired with a weaker stimulation (similar to a CS). After a sufficient number of rapid bursts of the strong stimulus, the weaker stimulus now acquires the ability to activate the postsynaptic neuron (see figure 7.24).

Thus, the process of learning and formation of memory entails patterns of neural activity that cause alterations in the strength of synaptic connections within the brain;

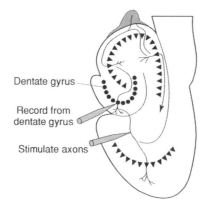

Figure 7.23 Hippocampus and electrodes. The procedural details of measuring long-term potentiation (LTP) in the hippocampus: (a) a stimulating electrode activates axons that project to the dentate gyrus; (b) a recording electrode is placed in the dentate gyrus; (c) a single pulse of electrical stimulation is delivered, and then the resulting excitatory postsynaptic potentials are recorded in the dentate gyrus; (d) the size of the first EPSP shows the size of the synaptic connections before LTP occurs; and (e) LTP is now induced by stimulating the axons with a burst of approximately 100 pulses, delivered within a space of a few seconds.

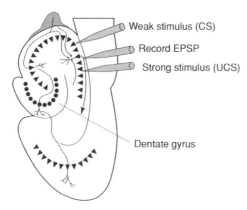

Figure 7.24 Schematic representation of LTP in associative learning. The simple case of LTP can be extended to associative learning: strong electrical stimulation of the neuron (similar to a UCS) is paired with a weaker stimulation (similar to a CS); and after a sufficient number of rapid bursts of the strong stimulus, the weaker stimulus now acquires the ability strongly to activate the postsynaptic neuron.

reactivation of these altered connections constitutes the experience of memory for these events (Martin & Morris, 2002). It is easy to see the similarity of this process with artificial neural networks, which operate along similar lines: training leads to stronger connections between some neurons and, by default, relatively weaker connections between other neurons. If the series of pulses is delivered at a slow rate, then LTP does not occur; in fact, under these conditions, an opposite effect may be observed: *long-term depression* (LTD).

Long-term depression (LTD)

Low-frequency stimulation of a neuron can lead to a decrease in synaptic strength, an effect known as *long-term depression* (LTD); this is an opposite effect to LTP, but is still involved in learning. LTD may be defined as a decrease in the excitability of a postsynaptic membrane to a synaptic input caused by stimulation of presynaptic terminal buttons. One role for LTD may be to break LTP. The brain has billions of neurons, and, although this number is large, it is not infinite. New neural circuits need to be formed, and old circuits that have outlived their usefulness need to be weakened. LTD plays a crucial role in this neural reorganization.

Dudek and Bear (1992) stimulated neurons in hippocampal tissue with 900 pulses, delivered at between 1 and 50 Hz (i.e., cycles per second). Frequencies above 10 Hz led to LTP, but frequencies below 10 Hz led to LTD. LTD has been found to occur under a number of conditions. For example, LTD is observed when synaptic inputs are activated at the same time that the postsynaptic membrane is either weakly depolarized or hyperpolarized. As high-frequency stimulation is more likely to activate the postsynaptic membrane (by temporal summation), this is more likely to lead to depolarization and thus increase the chances of joint activation of the two neurons – it is as if neurons in this reverberatory circuit are all 'singing from the same hymn sheet'.

Mechanisms of action of LTP and LTD

What causes the increase in synaptic strength during LTP? There are a number of logical possibilities. They could be produced: (a) presynaptically by increased release of neurotransmitter; (b) postsynaptically by increased number of receptor molecules; (c) by increased ability of receptors to activate changes in the permeability of the postsynaptic membrane; (d) by increased communication between the postsynaptic membrane and the rest of the neuron; and (e) by increased number of synapses, entailing both pre- and postsynaptic alterations. Experimental evidence is available to support all of these possibilities (Carlson, 2000).

Research has focused on postsynaptic sensitivity. Experiments have demonstrated that synaptic strengthening takes place when molecules of the neurotransmitter bind with postsynaptic receptors located in the dendritic spine that is in a state of depolarization (figure 7.25). For example, if depolarized neurons in the hippocampus are stimulated by another neuron, then the synaptic connection between these neurons is strengthened (Kelso, Ganong & Brown, 1986). It is crucial that depolarization of the (sending) neuron occurs *at the same time* as depolarization of the (receiving) neuron. This is the fundamental nature of LTP: to repeat, the postsynaptic dendrites must be in a state of depolarization in order for the neuronal changes that underlie LTP to occur. It should be noted at this point that this dendritic depolarization is not the same as depolarization of the axon (a result of all dendritic impulses being summed at the axon hillock; see chapter 3).

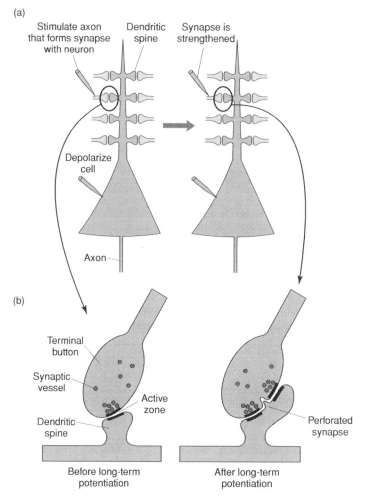

Figure 7.25   Synaptic strengthening of synapses (before/after LTP). Synaptic strengthening takes place when molecules of the neurotransmitter bind with postsynaptic receptors located in the dendritic spine that is in a state of depolarization. It is crucial that depolarization of the (sending) neuron occurs *at the same time* as depolarization of the (receiving) neuron: this is fundamental to LTP (a). The nature of the structure alterations between synaptic connections is shown (b).

Let us now turn to the molecular machinery that underlies the strengthening of synaptic connections (i.e., the *Hebb synapse*).

NMDA receptors

LTP depends on certain changes at glutamate synapses. There are three major types of glutamate receptors. The one that concerns us is the *NMDA glutamate receptor,* which can be stimulated by the chemical NMDA (*N*-methyl-D-aspartate); other glutamate

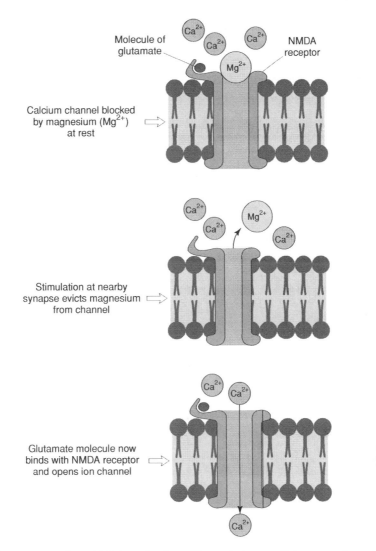

Figure 7.26 NMDA and non-NMDA mechanisms. Glutamate is an excitatory neurotransmitter at non-NMDA receptors, opening ion channels for sodium to enter the neuron, thus causing depolarizations in the dendrites. At the NMDA receptors, the ion channels of the NMDA molecule are blocked by magnesium ions (Mg^{2+}), which do not pass through the channel. Activation of NMDA receptors requires both glutamate and the removal of magnesium ions by activation of nearby non-NMDA glutamate receptors.

receptors also exist (i.e., non-NMDA receptors). At non-NMDA receptors, glutamate is an excitatory neurotransmitter, opening ion channels for sodium to enter the neuron and thus causing depolarizations in the dendrites. At the NMDA receptors, glutamate produces neither excitatory nor inhibitory effects. The reason for this unresponsiveness to glutamate is that the ion channels of the NMDA molecule are blocked by magnesium ions (Mg^{2+}), which do not pass through the channel (figure 7.26).

The activation of NMDA receptors requires both glutamate (or the drug, NMDA) and the removal of magnesium ions. The standard position is that the only way to activate the NMDA receptor is first to activate the nearby non-NMDA glutamate receptors repeatedly, thereby depolarizing the dendrite; however, depolarization of the neuron is now known to be sufficient to achieve the same end. This depolarization repels the magnesium ions (Mg^{2+}; ejected by electrostatic forces) and enables glutamate to open the NMDA channels, through which both sodium and calcium ions enter. The entry of calcium induces the expression of certain, otherwise inactive, genes; and these genes produce proteins that alter the structure of the dendrites and increase the future responsiveness of the active non-NMDA receptors (Kalat, 1998). LTP thus requires *joint* events: (a) activation of the synapse; and (b) depolarization of the postsynaptic neuron. This means that the ion channel controlled by the NMDA receptor is both a neurotransmitter and voltage-dependent channel. Although the precise mechanism of LTP is not known, research shows that, during LTP, the postsynaptic neuron releases a *retrograde transmitter*, which travels from the postsynaptic membrane to the presynaptic membrane (possibly nitric oxide); this then signals the presynaptic neuron to release more of its neurotransmitter.

To summarize, when glutamate stimulates non-NMDA receptors, the resulting depolarization enables glutamate to also stimulate nearby NMDA receptors; then stimulation of the NMDA receptors feeds back to potentiate the non-NMDA receptors. This short-term potential leads to LTP when structural changes accompany these effects. Structural change underlying LTP is suggested by the finding that maintenance of LTP does not depend on NMDA receptors. These structural changes may affect non-NMDA receptors. Support for this NMDA model comes from studies showing that, when these NMDA receptors' channels are blocked by drugs, then the establishment of LTP is abolished, but existing LTP is unaffected (Brown et al., 1989).

Structural synaptic changes

As the dendritic spine and terminal button elongate, two active zones appear (Hosokawa et al., 1995). Studies have shown that, as LTP develops, the number of such features ('perforated synapses') increases. Permanent LTP appears to involve a further process of *protein synthesis*. LTP is thus dependent on postsynaptic activation by NMDA receptors by the entry of calcium ions. These calcium ions activate some special calcium-dependent enzymes known as *protein kinases*. These enzymes set in train a chemical process that results in high concentrations of proteins, which can result in postsynaptic thickening. Structural changes may involve a growth in dendritic spines and reorientation to be in more precise contact with the presynaptic membrane (Hosokawa et al., 1995).

LTP and learning

If a weak synapse is active (e.g., in response to a CS), then this does not activate the non-NMDA postsynaptic motor neuron receptors; their dendrites do not depolarize, and thus the necessary conditions for LTP do not exist. However, if the activity of a strong synapse (e.g., UCS), also located on the CS presynaptic neuron, causes the motor neuron to fire (UCR), then a dendritic spike depolarizes the postsynaptic membrane enough for calcium ions to enter the membrane, thus permitting the weak synapse (CS) to form a structural connection with the motor system's neurons: an associative link. Martin and

Morris (2002) provide a review of neural plasticity in relation to learning and memory formation.

LTP and memory drugs

An understanding of LTP may lead to drugs ('cognitive enhancers') that can help people with memory impairments. LTP depends on entry of calcium ions into postsynaptic neurons; in old age these calcium channels become 'leaky', resulting in higher than normal resting levels of calcium within neurons. This excess interferes with learning: a sufficient amount of calcium is needed at the right moment (i.e., during learning), but not at other times. Injection of magnesium, which blocks the glutamate NMDA receptor, enhances learning and memory in older mammals. In the future, specific drugs to enhance learning and memory should be available to soften the cognitive decline associated with old age.

> **ASK YOURSELF**
> What might be the beneficial applications of knowledge of the neural mechanisms of learning and memory?

▭ Unifying Learning Perspectives

An interdisciplinary consideration of the perspectives afforded by behavioural, neural network and neural plasticity research provides us with a powerful way of thinking about and understanding learning. For example, there has been considerable debate concerning the nature of Pavlovian conditioning: does it depend upon stimulus substitution or response multiplication; and is this type of learning dependent on the existence of a well-defined unconditioned response? A neural network approach calls attention to the *internal representation*, or mapping, of inputs and outputs, and the complex interconnections of processing units (neurons), which are related by weights. This perspective diverts our attention away from the behavioural focus on the stimulus and response ends of learning, and draws attention to internal states of mediation.

An appreciation of the neural activity involved in learning, entailing activity-dependent presynaptic facilitation (ADPF), long-term potentiation (LTP) and long-term depression (LTD), draws our attention to the machinery that is needed to *instantiate* learning in the brain. Thus, what may look like instrumental learning may well depend on pure association (not requiring any response; as seen in *sensory preconditioning*), and may not be immediately evident in behaviour; alternatively, what may seem like Pavlovian conditioning may well involve a reinforcement component, in the instrumental sense of this term. In these two cases, consideration of ADPF (involved in reinforcement-based learning) and LTP/LTD (involved in associative learning) may allow us, at the neuronal level, truly to distinguish between different types of learning. Such information is crucial for modelling these processes in artificial neural networks.

The future will surely see a still greater integration of behavioural experiments, neural networks and neurophysiology, all designed better to understand the workings of the human brain and its unrivalled power to benefit from experience. Although there are formidable problems still to be solved, to be sure there are considerable scientific benefits to be derived from this joint consideration of the *conceptual nervous system* and the *central nervous system* in learning.

Learning Questions

1. What are the main differences between habituation, classical and instrumental conditioning procedures?
2. Why is Hebb's account of learning and memory so influential?
3. What is the scientific value of neural networks in understanding the operation of the real neurons?
4. What does the humble *Aplysia californica* reveal about the process of neuronal connections during learning?
5. What roles do 'long-term potentiation' and 'long-term depression' play in neural plasticity?

NOTES

1 Pinker (1997) provides an example of an imaginary stimulus that, if it had existed in our evolutionary history, would now scare us witless: a contraceptive tree (eating the leaf of such a tree would render one sterile)! No such tree existed, and our minds now do not fear contraceptive devices; indeed, such devices are welcomed – yet we fear the irrational (i.e., stimuli that, in reality, now have no chance to harm us, e.g., household spiders and the dark). Given the differential rates of reproduction that result from the use of contraceptives, we might one day evolve a dislike similar to that we feel for snakes and spiders.

2 We might compare 'preparedness' to exposing an image on a photographic film. After exposure the image is present but invisible; the film must first be developed before the image is seen. It is as if the fear of snakes has been imprinted on the film and a brief learning event is all that is required for the behavioural fear reactions to be fully developed.

FURTHER READING

Ellis, R. & Humphreys, G. (1999). *Connectionist Psychology: A Text with Readings*. Hove: Psychology Press.

Kalat, J. W. (1998). *Biological Psychology*. London: Brooks/Cole.

Mackintosh, N. (1994). *Animal Learning and Cognition*. London: Academic Press.

Approaches

Advances in scientific knowledge in the neurosciences are, in large part, made possible by technological innovation. This fact is nowhere more apparent than in *cognitive neuroscience*, which has emerged on the back of research opportunities opened up by neuroimaging. The technological innovations accompanying the Human Genome Project are having a similar effect in the molecular studies of psychological processes. To understand biological psychology it is necessary to have a good appreciation of the techniques available to scientists.

Part II aims to provide a comprehensive overview of the range of technical approaches used in biological psychology. In this survey, technical issues are not divorced from theoretical ones; for this reason, the theoretical contexts in which these techniques are employed are presented; and some of the applications of these techniques in current research are surveyed.

As in Part I, the six chapters are organized for convenience and clarity. However, leading-edge research today is increasingly combining different technological tools. For example, now it is common to see genetics, neuroimaging and neuropharmacological approaches being used in single studies. Future research in biological psychology is sure to see an even greater integration of technological approaches.

These chapters also provide a summary of the types of career possibilities open to students who aspire to research work in biological psychology; the range of techniques reviewed is fairly exhaustive, containing all the principal approaches. Fortunately, there are now many postgraduate programmes for training in these techniques, for those who want to develop careers, specifically, in university research, pharmaceutical clinical trials and the biotechnology industry. Of course, knowledge of these techniques is also important for those working within the practitioner-scientist model (e.g., clinical psychologists).

Chapter 8 ('Neuropsychology') surveys some of the classical and newer methods used in the attempt to link physiology to psychology. Clinical neuropsychology is contrasted with experimental neuropsychology, and the natures of single and double dissociations are described. The following specific areas are covered: brain injury; cognitive deficits (e.g., aphasia, agnosia and amnesia); hemispheric specialization; split-brain patients; transcranial magnetic stimulation (TMS, as a new tool to lesion temporarily the human cortex); neuropsychological tests of brain functions; and experimental tasks to measure specific psychological functions (e.g., latent inhibition; see chapter 7).

Chapter 9 ('Psychophysiology') covers a broad range of tools used to infer psychological functions from surface recording of the body. After discussing measurement issues (reliability and validity), a number of specific psychophysiological systems are defined: the electrodermal (sweating) system; the cardiac (heart) system; electromyography (EMG; electrical activity in muscle); the ocular (eye movement) system; and, lastly, measurement of immunological responses. In discussing these systems, examples are given, covering: classical conditioning; measurement of facial expressions; the detection of truth and lies; measurement of emotional reactivity, as well as information processing deficits seen in psychopathological conditions (e.g., schizophrenia).

Chapter 10 ('Neuroimaging') includes discussion of electrophysiological (EEG and ERPs) measurement from the scalp – these techniques span psychophysiology and neuroimaging proper – and the various types of neuroimaging techniques available: magnetoencephalograms, which measure magnetic fields from the scalp; computerized tomography (CT), which provides an X-ray of the brain; positron emission tomography (PET), which measures metabolic activity in the brain; magnetic resonance imaging (MRI), which provides highly detailed anatomical images of the brain and shows areas of activation during the performance of psychological tasks. Several other types of neuroimaging techniques are also summarized. Both the research issues and problems of interpretation are discussed.

Chapter 11 ('Neurophysiology') surveys the range of direct (invasive) techniques used in experimental animal research and occasionally in human beings for clinical purposes. These techniques include: recording and stimulation (chemical and electrical) techniques; lesion research; tracing techniques; therapeutic interventions in human beings (including lesions and electrical stimulation); and the procedures used in brain surgery (stereotaxic procedures), as well as those used in the analysis of brain tissue. Lastly, stem-cell technology is outlined and its potential for treating neurodegenerative diseases (e.g., Parkinson's disease) discussed; and the exciting development of brain prostheses to replace damaged neural systems in the human brain is reviewed.

Chapter 12 ('Psychopharmacology') builds upon chapter 4 ('Neurons and Neurotransmission') in outlining the techniques used to understand the mode of action of neurotransmitters and drugs on the central nervous system. Different types of psychopharmacological research are outlined; the process of drug discovery and development, focusing on clinical trials in human beings, is described; how drugs are handled by the body (pharmacokinetics) and how they exert their effects (pharmacodynamics) are outlined; and the importance of considering genetic differences in reactions to drugs (i.e., psychopharmacogenetics), including emerging ethical concerns in this area of research, is presented.

Chapter 13 ('Psychogenomics') explores the implications of the Human Genome Project for biological psychology, describing the procedures used in quantitative (statistical) genetics – which attempts to partition phenotype variance into genetic and non-genetic (environmental) components, using twin and adoption studies – and qualitative (molecular) genetics – which focuses on the expression of DNA to produce the polypeptides and proteins which compose our bodies. The definition of heritability and its misunderstandings are discussed; gene–gene effects and gene–environment correlations are delineated, as is analysis of environmental influences using statistical genetic methodologies. Lastly, the ways in which *both* quantitative and qualitative genetic methodologies are being used to uncover the genetic basis of behaviour, both normal and abnormal, are discussed.

Ethical Principles and Procedures

It is appropriate here to summarize some of the general ethical issues that relate to research in psychology; more specific issues are raised in the following chapters. The British Psychological Society (BPS) and the American Psychological Association (APA), along with most other scientific bodies regulating psychological research, require that research in human and non-human animals is conducted in an ethical fashion.[1] In the case of studies involving human participants, it is usual for research to be considered by a local ethics committee, who consider any ethical issues entailed by the research (the ethics committee usually consists of scientists, lay members and other professionals; the same is true of research using animals; see chapter 11). In the case of patients in hospital, as well as children and other vulnerable groups of people (e.g., learning-disabled adults), *all* studies must be approved by the local ethics committee; but, in the case of non-contentious experiments in university teaching departments, sometimes ethical issues are the responsibility of a senior researcher, who oversees the work of junior members of staff and students.

A number of ethical issues are important: (a) fully explaining the procedures and likely consequences before obtaining informed consent from the participant; (b) ensuring confidentiality of data; (c) the researcher behaving in an appropriately professional manner; (d) avoiding unnecessary deception, and, if this is essential, then ensuring that the participant is warned in advance that information is being withheld, but that everything is explained at the end of the experiment (at which time the participant may be given the opportunity to withdraw their data from further use); (e) a full, accurate and appropriate debriefing at the end of the session to ensure that the participant feels at ease and understands what happened to them; (f) explaining any potential risk or adverse effects in advance (under these circumstances it is usual to allow the participant to terminate the experiment at any stage without penalty); and (g) participants should not be induced financially to take part in experiments which may have an adverse outcome (e.g., in a psychopharmacology study). The overriding importance is to ensure that the participant knows enough to make an informed choice concerning their participation. Ethical guidelines should not deter good research; but it should promote good practice. Often ethical obstacles can be overcome by redesigning the experiment or using different measures or procedures.

In each of the chapters in Part II there are specific sets of ethical problems, and, accordingly, different solutions. For example, participants in a large-scale genetics study (chapter 13: 'Psychogenomics') should be informed how their DNA is to be used – after all, it is still their DNA and their permission should be given before using it; participants given drugs should be fully informed of possible adverse side effects (chapter 12: 'Psychopharmacology'); neurological patients should be informed if their data are to be included in a study, and not taken purely for their own clinical assessment (chapter 8:

'Neuropsychology'); participants should be warned about the unpleasant nature of slides used in a affective startle modulation experiment (chapter 9: 'Psychophysiology'); patients and volunteers should be warned of the possible (albeit remote) dangers of chemical labelling used in some neuroimaging procedures (chapter 10: 'Neuroimaging'); and a consensus must be reached on the desirability of conducting an invasive animal experiment to address a specific scientific problem (chapter 11: 'Neurophysiology'). All ethical problems should be carefully considered before experiments are permitted to go ahead: the final decision must weigh the likely benefits of research against the likely (or probable) harm inflicted on research participants.

The Nuffield Council on Bioethics considers the ethical issues arising from development in medicine and biology.[2] Their reports cover many of the ethical issues pertaining to the type of research summarized in this book: genetic screening, genetics in psychiatry, stem-cell therapy, genetics of human behaviour and ethical issues arsing out of pharmacogenetics (i.e., using genetic strategies in drug development research).

NOTES

1   BPS ethical guidelines may be found at: www.bps.org.uk; APA guidelines at: www.apa.org
2   Go to www.nuffieldbioethics.org

Neuropsychology

Learning Objectives

To be able to:

1. Describe the main sources of damage to the brain and the associated cognitive deficits.
2. Explain the 'split-brain' procedure and what it tells us about brain specialization.
3. Discuss the rationale of neuropsychological assessment and outline the main tests.
4. Describe the use of transcranial magnetic stimulation (TMS) to induce experimental 'lesions'.
5. Explain what is meant by single and double dissociations and why they are important.

Neuropsychology is concerned with the relationship between physiological structures and processes and psychological functions. This is a broad definition and encompasses most areas of biological psychology involving structure–function relations, including those in non-human animals. The chapter focuses on one important part of neuropsychology, namely the clinical study of structure and function: *clinical neuropsychology*. However, also covered here are purely experimental approaches that are now being used to elucidate structure–function relations: *experimental neuropsychology*. (In other chapters other investigative approaches are covered, such as neuroimaging and neurophysiology, which fall under the broader definition of neuropsychology.) These neuropsychological techniques are put to good use in Part III ('Applications'), where further examples are given of how they are used to gain insight into a range of normal and abnormal behaviours.

Traditionally, the study of brain structure and psychological function has relied upon congenital deficits, accidents, strokes, etc. This type of study has been successful, although problematic, leading among other things to the discovery of the speech areas of the brain. It was not until Wilder Penfield's pioneering electrical stimulation of the cortex in awake patients that a more direct approach could be adapted to mapping functions in the brain (see chapter 3). Until recently, it would have been true to say that electrically stimulating the brain of normal psychology volunteers was clearly neither possible nor desirable, but even this state of affairs has changed: now techniques are available that can temporarily excite or inhibit brain activity in order to study cognitive functions (e.g., transcranial magnetic stimulation; TMS).

This chapter summarizes some of the older literature, which reveals fascinating insights into the neurophysiological basis of psychological functions (e.g., 'split-brain' patients); also surveyed are some emerging technologies that are opening up new and exciting approaches to neuropsychological problems in experimental (i.e., normal) individuals. The first half of this chapter focuses on changes to the structure and processing of the brain, while the second half focuses on the measurement of psychological functions used in clinical and experimental neuropsychology.

Brain Injury

Historically, neuropsychology has had to rely upon brain damage to reveal patterns of cognitive deficits that would give clues to the association of brain regions and psychological performance. Such brain damage results from a variety of sources (Wilson, 1999):

1. Traumatic head injury, resulting from road traffic accidents, falls, accidents or military missiles/gunshot;
2. Cerebral vascular accident (stroke);
3. Viral infection of the brain (e.g., encephalitis);
4. Hypoxic (oxygen-deficit) brain damage following myocardial infarction (heart attack), carbon monoxide poisoning (e.g., suicide attempts) or an anaesthetic accident;
5. Wernicke–Korsakoff syndrome as a result of alcoholism and inadequate nutrition;
6. Brain tumour (including unavoidable damage during surgery for tumour removal);
7. Degenerative disease (e.g., Alzheimer's disease and Huntington's disease);
8. Surgery that deliberately lesions part of the brain in order to control such neuropathologies as epilepsy (e.g., cutting the corpus callosum to prevent electrical discharges travelling from one hemisphere to the other; see 'split-brain' studies below).

Wilson (1999) provides a detailed description of these causes of neuropsychological damage, illustrates the use of neuropsychological tests (see below) and provides illustrative case studies.

For obvious practical and ethical reasons it is not possible experimentally to lesion the brain of human volunteers (although it is now possible electrically to stimulate the cortex using transcranial magnetic stimulation, TMS); and experimental research involving brain lesioning techniques has necessarily depended upon non-human animals (chapter 11).

Research which relies upon accidental or deliberate brain damage (as in the case of battlefield trauma) has a number of problems. First, the injury is unlikely to be localized to one specific structure in the brain; second, the very act of being seriously wounded is bound to entail a range of psychological effects which are independent of the injury (e.g., depression and anger/aggression); and, third, until recently, it was not possible to assess the nature of the damage until after death, which might have been many years after the initial trauma (in this intervening time neural reorganization and plasticity might have altered the brain). Now, of course, it is commonplace to take a structural scan of the brain to isolate the region of damage (see chapter 11), but the first two problems still complicate interpretation.

Accidental brain damage

Each year many thousands of people suffer brain damage due to a variety of accidents, ranging from falling over and hitting the head on hard objects and road traffic accidents, to ingesting toxic substances (and non-accidents such as physical assault).

A peculiar fame: Phineas Gage

One of the most famous cases of accidental brain damage concerns a 25-year-old construction foreman working on the railway in Vermont, USA. In September 1848, Phineas Gage was loading explosives with a tamping rod (3 feet, 7 inches long, and 1 1/4 inches in diameter[1] at one end, tapering to 1/4 inch at the other end, weighing about 13 lbs) in order to blast rock: the rod he was using to push in the explosives set them off, and the explosion sent the rod through his left cheek, passing through his left frontal lobe, and exiting at the top of his head, finally landing some 25 yards away (figure 8.1). In fact, although he was knocked over by the blast, after a short while he was able to walk and talk (apparently asking the doctor whether he could return to work!). Remarkably, he survived this accident. As noted by the *Boston Post* (14 September 1848) the following day, 'The most singular circumstance connected with this melancholy affair is, that he was alive at two o'clock this afternoon, and in full possession of his reason, and free from pain.' Ten weeks after the accident, Phineas was at home recovering.

In the middle of 1849, Phineas returned to work. However, family, friends and colleagues noticed a change in his personality: before the trauma, he was sensitive, intelligent and respectful, being the mining contractor's most efficient foreman; now he was rude, profane, impatient, unable to settle on any plans for the future, and showing little regard for his fellow workers – because of his behaviour, he was not re-employed by the contractors. He lived until 1860; and in 1867 his body was exhumed and his skull removed (Macmillan, 2000a,b). This was one of the early cases showing that frontal lobe damage can lead to disinhibited, impulsive and reckless behaviour; the damage seems to be located at the ventromedial region of the frontal lobes on both sides (Damasio et al., 1994) – speech and motor areas were spared.

There are several noteworthy features of this case. First, it was the first case which pointed to the relationship between brain damage to the frontal lobes and personality, and, in general, one of the best examples of the relationship between brain and behaviour. Second, it also had an influence on the development of brain surgery: Gage's injury suggested that psychological functions are localized (the first brain surgery for a tumour was in 1885). In 1894, the first *psychosurgery* was performed (i.e., surgical

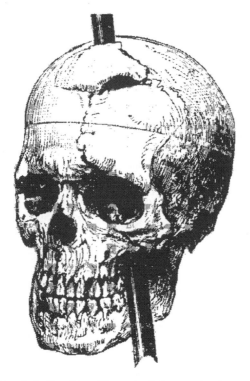

Figure 8.1 Phineas Gage's skull and bar. The path of the tamping bar as it entered Gage's cheekbone and exited the ventromedial region of the frontal lobes. (Illustration from *Massachusetts Medical Journal*, 1868.)

disconnection or removal of brain tissue to alleviate psychological/psychiatric symptoms): this patient reported becoming dull in thinking, generally lazy and slow in mental activity, and unable to express his ideas clearly. The surgeons made explicit reference to the 'American crowbar case' (i.e., Gage), which provided the theoretical grounds for the collection of further cases showing symptoms related to damage in specific brain areas.

For many years psychological symptoms were used as a diagnostic sign for brain tumours. Surgeons often removed the whole lobe, as the tumour was not sufficiently differentiated from the surrounding tissue. This procedure led to the further discovery that there were often few effects on patients' behaviour. Such observations encouraged the view that frontal lesions could be used to alleviate psychological/psychiatric symptoms.

ASK YOURSELF
What are the main limitations of inferring structure–function relations from clinical neuropsychological cases?

Phineas Gage is remarkable because his trauma was anatomically extensive, but his cognitive deficits were relatively minor (his emotional life, though, was greatly changed). However, in most cases of head injury there are notable cognitive consequences.

▣ Cognitive Deficits

Traditional clinical neuropsychology has identified a number of specific deficits that show the high specificity of cognitive impairments.

1. *Aphasia*: brain damage that results in a deficit in communication, ranging from the inability to construct a sentence (Broca's aphasia) to the inability to comprehend speech (Wernicke's aphasia).
2. *Visual neglect*: this type of damage results in information from one hemisphere being ignored (such patients may not be aware of one-half of their visual environment).
3. *Agnosia*: this deficit consists in the patient's inability to recognize familiar objects.
4. *Amnesia*: this memory deficit can affect memories of events before the brain damage (*retrograde amnesia*) or after the damage (*anterograde amnesia*).

Visual agnosia

Visual agnosia ('failure to know') refers to the inability to perceive or identify common objects (e.g., a chair), even though its details can be detected and patients can draw the object (Humphreys & Riddoch, 1987). There are different forms of this condition.

Prosopagnosia is the inability to recognize particular faces (*prosopon* means face): such patients cannot say to whom the face belongs (even a close relative; they can remember these people and identify them from additional information such as the sound of their voice). This disorder has led to the hypothesis that facial recognition is mediated by special circuits in the brain devoted to the specific analysis of facial features – from a Darwinian perspective, this adaptation would be especially important in holding in memory cooperative and cheating members of one's own species (see chapter 2).

There have been cases of patients who have experienced loss of colour sensation on one side of their visual field. At autopsy, such patients are found to have discrete lesions in their occipital lobe outside the primary visual cortex, involved in colour perception (Zeki, 1993). Such cases point to the high degree of cortical specialization.

Blindsight

Blindsight is a particularly intriguing condition, consisting in patients reporting being (consciously) blind, yet they show evidence of the ability to use visual information: that is, when they are given a performance task, they score above chance, showing that visual information is being processed. Spared visual performance in blindsight patients may be subserved by those neurons that pass from the *lateral geniculate nucleus* (LGN) to cortical regions other than the visual cortex, e.g., the *superior colliculus* (Zeki, 1993; see chapter 5).

In the case of D.B.[2] (Weiskrantz, 1986), in 1973 he received surgery to remove from his right visual cortex abnormal tissue that was causing severe headaches. This rendered him blind in his left visual field. However, D.B. retained the capacity to locate objects at an accuracy much better than chance. So, although he was subjectively blind, he did possess some residual visual processing that facilitated performance.

In another case, D.F., in 1988, suffered carbon monoxide poisoning, which damaged regions of the prestriate cortex. This disrupted ventral stream visual ('what') processing, but not dorsal stream ('where') processing (see chapter 5). D.F. was impaired in identifying geometric objects, but could initiate action based on these objects.

As early as the 1930s, it was known that removal of the visual cortex did not abolish performance dependent upon the processing of light. For example, monkeys whose bilateral striate cortex was removed were rendered 'blind', but they could still acquire a classically conditioned eye-blink response (which depends on the processing of a light CS); and they could also show this conditioned response even if it had been conditioned prior to lesioning (Weiskrantz, 2003). Thus, the visual cortex is not necessary for the processing of light – but, of course, it *is* for the extraction of visual features. It also seems important in the subjective state of consciousness.

Visual neglect

As discussed by Wilson (1999), visual neglect is a neuropsychological condition in which the patient ignores one side of their body, as if were not there. This unilateral (i.e., one-sided) neglect is commonly associated (in around 40 per cent of patients) with right-hemisphere strokes; the symptoms are heterogeneous and often short-lived. (Left-hemisphere strokes are less often associated with unilateral neglect, and when it occurs it tends to be less severe.) Patients with this condition fail to report, respond to or orient to objects in the space contralateral to the cerebral lesion; they behave as if one side of space has lost its meaning. As a result they may collide with objects, ignore food on one side of the plate, and attend to only one side of their body (e.g., when washing). Neuropsychological assessment is achieved with tests of reading, writing and drawing.

Clinical case: Dolly

This neuropsychological deficit is illustrated by the case of a 62-year-old woman, Dolly, who awoke one morning to find that her left arm and leg seemed not to be working, and she could not make sense of the hands and numbers on the alarm clock (Wilson, 1999). A computerized tomography scan (CT scan; see chapter 10) confirmed that Dolly had had a stroke in the night, and she was diagnosed as having, among other things, 'unilateral neglect' of the left side of her body. Her left inattention was marked: for example, she would sit at the extreme right of the table; when she stood up, she would turn to the right to leave the room even though the door to exit was to the left; and she frequently misjudged distances, especially when leaving or entering a room, when she would bump into the left side of the doorway. Dolly had poor insight into her problems and seemed unconcerned about the difficulties they presented, almost as if the left side of her body did not exist – we can only appreciate this situation if we imagine for one moment that, in fact, we have *three* arms and legs and have forgotten about the third. When asked to draw a clock, Dolly produced the drawing shown in figure 8.2.

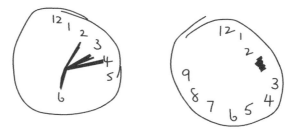

Figure 8.2 Dolly's clock drawings. The drawing of a clock by a 62-year-old woman, Dolly, with unilateral neglect of the left side of her body. The drawing shows her marked inattention to the left side of her visual field, which was also evident in her everyday behaviour. (From Wilson, 1999; used with permission.)

Rehabilitation strategies produced a marked improvement in Dolly's behaviour, and she returned home to be cared for by her husband; however, she suffered another stroke and died.

Amnesia

Patient H.M. is psychology's most famous neuropsychological patient (Milner, 1966). This patient fell off his bicycle when he was 9, injuring his head. He then started having epileptic attacks. At adulthood, H.M. received surgery to treat the epilepsy. Tissue from the medial temporal lobe (including the hippocampus) was removed bilaterally (i.e., from both sides). Following this operation, H.M. was able to recall information acquired early in his life, his personality was largely unaffected, and there was no marked decline in general cognitive ability (intelligence). But H.M. developed severe *anterograde amnesia*: he is unable to remember events that occurred after the operation (i.e., he has a failure to update new memories – he can reread the same newspaper article time after time without any sense of familiarity). H.M. revolutionized the study of memory, shifting attention from the search for the location of old memories to studies of the formation of new memories (figure 8.3).

H.M.'s condition gave rise to the hypothesis that the hippocampus is necessary for the processing of new memories. However, he does have normal working memory, as

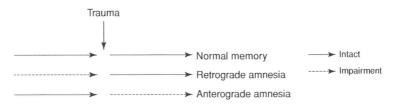

Figure 8.3 Patterns of memory loss associated with retrograde and anterograde amnesia.

he can carry on a normal conversation (this requires some level of retention of what has been said), therefore the problem seems to be the encoding or consolidation of memory.[3] H.M. can even remember digits for 15 minutes (he apparently uses verbal rehearsal to achieve this end). He shows intact procedural learning and memory (e.g., skills such as mirror writing), but his declarative learning/memory is severely disrupted. Baddeley (1986) cites H.M. as the best evidence for the distinction between short-term memory (STM – memories rehearsed from seconds to minutes) and long-term memory (LTM – consolidated memories that are semi-permanent, lasting years).

In amnesia cases, there seems to be a failure of certain contents of STM to enter LTM, or a failure of certain contents of LTM to become accessible to conscious recall. This latter possibility might explain why procedural learning and memory are intact in amnesia: as they do not depend upon conscious recall, they may be less disrupted. Cues at retrieval can aid the performance of amnesics. For example, words presented cannot be free-recalled, but if a fragment of the word is given for completion then performance is much improved (e.g., H O _ _ _, the stem of H O U S E): this form of *priming* seems to clearly indicate that the material was encoded, but that the patient has special problems with retrieval.

Retrograde amnesia consists of a severe memory dysfunction for memories acquired prior to the traumatic event; new memories can be formed though. This form of amnesia is evident in Korsakoff's syndrome, named after Sergei Korsakoff (1854–1900), who discussed a number of cases of amnesia. This degenerative disorder results from chronic alcoholism coupled with malnutrition (specifically thiamine, B_1, deficiency).

Clinical case: Clive Wearing

The case of Clive Wearing is one of the best-known and most informative examples of profound amnesia (Wilson, 1999). Until the age of 46 years, Clive was an outstanding musician, a gifted academic and one of the world's leading experts on Renaissance music. He sang daily at Westminster Cathedral and by all accounts worked 7 days a week, rarely taking breaks and working long into the night. Then an illness destroyed virtually all of his memory. While his wife was lecturing, and Clive was resting in bed with suspected influenza, he rose from bed, left the house, hailed a taxi but could not remember his address; the taxi driver took him to a police station, where his identity was established and his wife contacted.

Upon returning home, Clive could not remember his apartment, and his behaviour in the hours that followed convinced his wife that he was seriously ill. He was admitted to hospital, where a diagnosis of herpes simplex virus encephalitis (HSVC) was made. A computerized tomography (CT) scan showed an area of low density, particularly in the left temporal lobe, extending into the inferior and posterior frontal lobe and into the right medial temporal lobe – more specifically, there was *marked* impairment in the hippocampus, which is known to be involved in memory formation. In the days following this incident, Clive's mood in hospital was somewhat euphoric and he seemed unconcerned about his condition – his wife noted that 'he was too confused to be confused' (this is one saving grace of some, but not all, neuropsychological deficits, especially in the dementias). However, this state quickly disappeared and, for several months, Clive would sit and cry for most of the day.

Clive's profound amnesia of (virtually) all past and present events – retrograde and anterograde amnesia – produced the experience that he had just woken or become conscious – he would make this statement every few minutes. Clive also has object recognition problems, being unable to recognize everyday objects (i.e., aphasia), although he knew which food products he preferred. At times, he also tried to work out why he had suffered this illness, thinking at times that someone was trying to 'shut him up' because he had uncovered an international conspiracy. He regularly confabulated, generating *post hoc* explanations as to why he did things (e.g., thinking that he was employed by the hospital in which he was a patient). In later years, Clive developed auditory hallucinations, consisting of hearing a tape of himself playing in the distance. Clive has been in this state ever since.

Clive's case is an extreme example of memory impairment; few other patients have such profound and enduring memory loss. He does have intact immediate (short-term or working) memory, but all information is lost after a few minutes and he denies that he was ever shown test material before. However, his memory has improved slightly over the years, seemingly as a result of rehabilitation strategies (e.g., he can name four musicians in a 60-second period – but not the one musician, Lassus, who was the subject of his lifetime academic work. One intriguing cognitive sparing is his musical skills, which remain largely unaffected – although his performance has declined, to the untrained ear he is as skilful and competent as ever. This observation is another demonstration of the dissociation of procedural (e.g., habits) and declarative (e.g., episodic) memory (see chapter 7).

Synaesthesia

Synaesthesia is an intriguing phenomenon consisting of the subjective experience of a sensory input in the 'wrong' modality. This may involve many different combinations of senses, but the most common is 'word–colour synaesthesia', or 'coloured hearing'. When the synaesthete hears or sees a word they also experience a colour or multicoloured pattern. These synaesthetes (the majority of whom happen to be female) are perfectly normal in all other respects: they are not fantasists or experiencing a psychotic state, and their condition does not impair their everyday life (indeed, it may actually enhance it).

Nunn et al. (2002) used functional magnetic resonance imaging (fMRI; see chapter 10) to explore the neural correlates of synaesthesia. They used this technique to detect brain regions activated by simply hearing spoken words. Participants listened to alternating blocks of words and (control) tones, each lasting 30 seconds. In non-synaesthete controls, activation caused by spoken words occurred in the auditory cortex and language areas, as expected; this pattern was also observed in the word–colour synaesthete, who *in addition* showed activation in the visual system, namely area V4, which is known as a colour processing centre (see chapter 5). These data confirm that the synaesthete's experience is perceptual in nature; a result of a mis-wiring in the brains of synaesthetes that causes the 'sparking-over' of word to colour processing (see Gray, 2004). These data also support the claim that perceptual experiences are constructed in the brain and are only (at best) indirectly related to the states of affairs in the 'real world' that cause them to be constructed (see chapters 5 and 18).

ASK YOURSELF
To what extent do clinical neuropsychological cases offer scientific insights that are simply not available by any other means?

☐ Hemisphere Specialization

One way to study structure–function relations of the two hemispheres is experimentally to split their processing. Split hemispheric processing can be assessed by presenting a stimulus to one hemisphere very briefly and measuring the reaction time (RT) of each hemisphere in turn: RT differences are then used as an index of the processing efficiency of each hemisphere. For example, the experimental participant may be required to name, by making a response (e.g., pressing button *A* for correctly spelled words and button *B* for non-words); this elicits a faster RT from the left hemisphere (i.e. right visual field).

Underlying such experimental studies of hemispheric processing is the assumption that each hemisphere is specialized and that this functional specialization results in faster RTs, as compared with the alternate hemisphere – of course, if enough time were allowed for the response, then hemispheric differences would disappear due to hemispheric transfer of information (via *corpus callosum*).

Split-brain patients: two brains, two minds

Let us imagine that it were possible to prevent the hemispheric transfer of information: this would truly separate processing in the two hemispheres. This is exactly what is done in *split-brain patients*.

The first split-brain operations were performed in the 1950s, initially on cats and later monkeys; finally, the procedure was sufficiently perfected to be used on human beings (in 1961) for the alleviation of symptoms of severe epilepsy (to prevent the seizure travelling to the other hemisphere). The operation, known as *commissurotomy*, involves the cutting of the fibres (the *corpus callosum*) that connect the two hemispheres. Some of the most important – certainly the most spectacular – findings relating to structure–brain functions come from observations on split-brain patients.

Roger Sperry is now famous for his initial split-brain investigations; Michael Gazzaniga (1970; Gazzaniga & LeDoux, 1978), who was Sperry's doctoral student, has extended these split-brain investigations. Such patients provide a unique opportunity to study cortical specialization because information can be presented to one hemisphere only. The left brain is relatively easy to investigate because it can speak; the non-speaking right hemisphere is less easy to study and must rely upon performance measures.

Perhaps the most surprising thing about split-brain patients is how normally they behave: unless you knew, you would probably not guess from their behaviour that their brains were split in two. However, patients sometimes report a number of peculiar things which suggest that not only is their brain split, but so too is their mind.

After the operation, patients sometimes report that their left hand (i.e., right hemisphere) has a 'mind of its own'. For example, patients may find themselves putting down a book held in their left hand, even if they had been reading it with great interest. This conflict occurs because the right hemisphere cannot read, therefore it finds holding the book boring, so it switches to a more interesting motor programme. A patient may go to make a cup of tea, only to find the left hand (right hemisphere) reaching for the coffee jar: in extreme instances the assistance of someone else is required to remove the object from the left hand. At other times, the left hand may make obscene gestures, embarrassing the left hemisphere.[4] This is the phenomenon of 'alien hand'. It is tempting to extend this observation to the everyday indecisions we all face.

In the intact brain there must be inhibitory mechanisms that suppress the wishes of one hemisphere in order to focus attention and behaviour on to a single goal: this achieves hemispheric integration. Even in split-brain patients there is integration of behaviour, but this comes from two sources: (a) *subcortical integration*; and (b) *cross-cueing*.

Subcortical integration

Only the fibres at the level of the cortex are severed; other smaller commissures and subcortical routes remain intact. These small connections allow, among other things, inter-hemispheric *negative priming*: slowed reaction times to a target previously ignored in the contralateral visual field. Negative priming is thought to reflect an inhibitory attentional mechanism: if a stimulus is ignored then it is more difficult – that is, reaction times are slower – to name the stimulus when it becomes a salient target in the next phase of the experiment.

Cross-cueing

The two separate brains, minds and consciousnesses work together because they share information by behavioural cues. For example, in experimental settings, the left hand may stroke the teeth of a comb so that it could be heard by the left hemisphere and interpreted as a 'comb'. Or the left hemisphere may shake the head when the right hemisphere is making a mistake when the stimulus (e.g., colour) is projected only to the right hemisphere. In everyday life, objects in environments can be seen, touched, tasted, smelled, etc. by both hemispheres.

Thus, in order to tease out the true nature of the functional (cortical) specialization in split-brain patients, special experimental procedures are needed.

Split-brain testing procedures

The basic experimental set-up is shown in figure 8.4. This set-up allows the experimenter to project visual stimuli to the right or left half of the screen (i.e., to the left and right hemispheres, respectively) and to place objects within reach of either the left or right hand. The patient is required to focus on a fixation point in the centre of the screen and the object is flashed up very briefly (too quickly for a shift of gaze to the object).

Sperry's work is famous for showing that by splitting the brain the mind is also split. However, some caution needs to be exercised when extrapolating from split-brain studies to normal cortical specialization. The most important caveat concerns the *normal integration* of information. It may be assumed that what is shared between the hemispheres is *processed* information (i.e., the outputs of information processing); however, it is probably more commonly the case that the two hemispheres share *underprocessed* information, with the final processed output being a combination of the interplay of the two hemispheres. This limitation to one side, the relative independence of the two hemispheres is impressive, including their separate volition and intention of purpose.[5]

> **ASK YOURSELF**
> What does the apparent unity of the mind in split-brain patients imply about the subjective experience of brain processes?

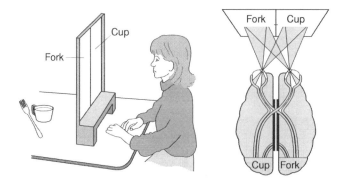

Figure 8.4 Split-brain testing procedure. The basic split-brain experimental procedure, which allows the experimenter to project visual stimuli to the right or left half of the screen (i.e., to the left and right hemispheres, respectively) and to place objects within reach of either the left or right hand. Measures of response latency (in the case of visually presented information) and accuracy (in the case of tactile information) are used to infer hemisphere specialization.

Neuropsychological Tests

Clinical neuropsychology makes extensive use of diagnostic tests that assess psychological functions: these are *neuropsychological tests*. According to Lezak (1995, p. 7), 'Clinical neuropsychology is an applied science concerned with the behavioural expression of brain dysfunction.' This section summarizes some of these tests (Lezak, 1995, provides a standard and comprehensive text on neuropsychological assessment). Wilson (1999) provides examples of how neuropsychological tests are used in clinical practice.

Assessment of functions

Neuropsychological tests are used to describe the functional strengths and weaknesses of patients. Screening and diagnosis of brain damage and behavioural disturbance are high during times of war, and the need for accurate diagnosis has provided a strong impetus to the development of neuropsychological tests. Only once an accurate diagnosis is made is it possible to design rehabilitation programmes to help patients adjust to their impairments.

Neuropsychological tests are also used to assess *premorbid functioning* – a useful yardstick against which to assess the extent of psychological impairment due to brain damage. Although neuropsychological tests were, and still are, widely used to ascertain the nature, location and extent of brain damage, advances in neuroimaging technology (chapter 10) are rapidly providing more precise estimates of brain damage; however, this new technology does not help the assessment of the current *functional* level of the patient, and for this reason classic neuropsychological tests will for the foreseeable future continue to play an important role in neuropsychology. Tests can also help to differentiate patients presenting with neurological and psychological problems. For example, a patient presenting with depression and impaired cognitive functioning could be suffering from clinical depression or a tumour in the frontal lobe.

Neuropsychology is concerned with three dimensions of behaviour (Lezak, 1995): (a) *cognition*, involving information processing; (b) *emotionality*, involving emotions, moods, motivations; and (c) *executive functions*, involving the integration and expression of cognitive functions. The vast majority of neuropsychological tests have been concerned only with cognitive functions, but, increasingly, executive functions have been emphasized in a number of key developmental disorders (e.g., autism). Lezak likens these three dimensions of behaviour to the length, height and width dimensions that define a physical object.

Cognitive functions

Cognitive functions may be divided into four separate processes: (a) *receptive functions*, entailing the detection, acquisition and classification of stimuli; (b) *learning and memory*, entailing the modification of behaviour and retention of acquired information; (c) *thinking*, entailing the organization and active processing of symbolic information; and (d) *expressive functions*, entailing the communication of psychological products (e.g., decision-making). Final *behaviour* is seen as the outcome of these functions. Specific cognitive impairments are linked to each of these functions. For example, *agnosia* is related to receptive functions; *amnesia* to memory; poor *problem-solving* to thinking; and *apraxia* (impairment of voluntary actions) and *aphasia* (impairment in speech) to expressive functions.

Personality or emotional changes

Personality or *emotional changes* often accompany brain damage. Phineas Gage (see above) provides a good example of these changes. A range of emotional changes is observed: emotional dulling, disinhibition, reduced or increased anxiety, mild euphoria, decreased social sensitivity, and depression. It is often difficult to know whether these changes are a *direct* result of the brain damage or an *indirect* result of the experience of loss, frustration and an altered way of life.

Executive functions

Executive functions are required to integrate cognitive functions, and to enable a person successfully to engage in purposive and independent living. Impairments in executive functions tend to affect global areas of functioning, affecting all behaviour. For example, lack of self-control, self-direction and independence is a hallmark of this disorder; and such patients have difficulty in switching attention and modifying behaviour to reflect changing environmental contingencies (e.g., continuing to carry on with a topic of conversation when the listener is showing clear signs of disinterest). Behaviours that are less easy to identify are: impaired capacity to initiate activity; decreased or absent motivation (*anergia*); and deficits in sequencing actions to meet end goals.

Types of neuropsychological tests

There are a large number – indeed a bewildering number – of separate neuropsychological tests (Lezak, 1995), which differ greatly in their content and procedures, and a much smaller number of test batteries, which aim to provide a comprehensive assessment of psychological functioning. Here are summarized only a small number of tests: these should be sufficient to get a good sense of the type of functions they assess.

Finger localization

The finger localization test (Benton, 1959) is used to assess finger agnosia. Patients with this disorder have impaired finger recognition, identification, naming and orientation. When it involves only one hand it is usually caused by a sensory deficit resulting from brain damage contralateral to the affected hand. The test for assessing finger agnosia is in three parts. In Part A, the patient is required to identify their fingers when the examiner touches the tip of the fingers in turn. In Part B, the hand is shielded from the patient's sight, using a curtained box in which the hand is placed, and once again the examiner touches the tip of each finger. In Part C, two fingers are touched at a time. The number of errors made in each of these three parts is taken as an index of (a) the existence of finger agnosia, and (b) the severity of the disorder.

Visual form discrimination

The visual form discrimination test (Benton et al., 1983) is a multiple-choice test of visual recognition. There are 16 items consisting of a target set of stimuli and 4 stimuli sets below the target, only one of which is a correct match (the other stimulus sets are similar but not identical). This is an easy task for normal people, but brain-damaged patients make errors, indicating that they have a problem with sensory processing or the relatively simple cognitive processes involved in matching (figure 8.5).

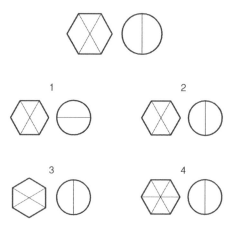

Figure 8.5 Visual Form Discrimination stimulus set: a multiple-choice test of visual recognition – consists of 16 items consisting of a target set of stimuli and 4 stimuli sets below the target, only one of which is a correct match. This test is sensitive to some forms of brain damage, indicating a problem with sensory processing or simple cognitive processes involved in matching.

Digit span test

The digit span test (Wechsler, 1945) is very widely used to assess encoding as well as serving as a measure of verbal working memory; it also requires intact auditory attention. It is the most common method for measuring span of immediate verbal recall (it is also incorporated in many of the major batteries of general intelligence). The examiner verbally presents digits at a rate of one per second. The *digit-forward test* requires the patient to repeat the digits they have just heard in the correct order; the *digit-backward test* requires the patient to reverse the order of presentation in their recall. The number of digits increases from three by one until the patient consecutively fails two trials of the same digit length span. Scoring is made for the digit span length.

Brown–Peterson technique

The Brown–Peterson technique (Peterson & Peterson, 1959) is a classic test of short-term memory and working memory (see Baddeley, 1986). This is a distractor task in which the distractor is used to prevent the rehearsal of material held in the short-term memory store. Patients are presented with the stimulus material and then they are required to count backwards from a given number until they are told to stop counting. For example, the stimulus material may be 'T J V X U', and the examiner then gives a number (e.g., '234') from which the patient counts backwards. Stimuli may be presented *sequentially* (i.e., one at a time) or *simultaneously* (i.e., all at once, such as on a single card). Recall is usually perfect or near perfect in normal people presented with a short string of letters, and typically recall declines as a function of time counting. This is one of the most sensitive tests to head injury, Alzheimer's disease, Huntington's disease and Korsakoff disease.

Paced auditory serial addition test (PASAT)

The PASAT (Gronwall, 1977) requires the patient to add 60 pairs of digits (each digit is added to the digit immediately preceding it – e.g., if the examiner presented '2, 8, 6, 1, 9', the correct answer is '10, 14, 7, 10'). The digits are presented by tape, as a precise rate of delivery is important to standardize the test (there are four speeds of delivery, corresponding to increasing level of difficulty). Performance is calculated in terms of percentage of correct responses. The PASAT is very sensitive to deficits in information processing, and is used as a sensitive test of recovery from short-term head trauma (e.g., concussion). However, the test is stressful,[6] which may complicate the interpretation of performance as reflecting a purely cognitive deficit.

Trail-making test

This test, developed by US Army psychologists, consists of visual, conceptual and visuo-motor tracking. It is given in two parts: In Part A, the patient draws lines to connect consecutively numbered circles; in Part B they connect the same number of consecutively numbered and lettered circles (figure 8.6). The patient is told to do the task as fast as they can. The test can be scored for time taken and number of errors. This is a test

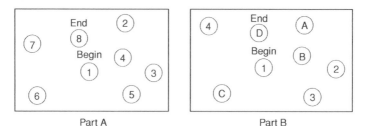

Figure 8.6 The trail-making test consists of visual, conceptual and visuomotor tracking. It is given in two parts: In Part A, the patient draws lines to connect consecutively numbered circles; in Part B they connect the same number of consecutively numbered and lettered circles. The test is scored for time taken and number of errors, and is sensitive to attention and motor speed (impaired, for example, in dementia).

of visual scanning with a strong motor component. The test is sensitive to attention and motor speed, and it easily detects brain damage, including progressive dementia. It seems especially sensitive to damage to the frontal lobes.

Peabody picture vocabulary test

The Peabody picture vocabulary test (Dunn & Dunn, 1981) is a measure of non-verbal vocabulary, allowing the patient to signal that they recognize a spoken or printed word by pointing to one of a set of pictures that allows assessment of recognition vocabulary. This test permits a rapid assessment of intellectual level in patients who, for a variety of reasons, cannot speak. The test consists of 175 picture plates, each with four pictures, with one plate for each word. The pictures/words are arranged in order of difficulty, and span all age groups. The patient's score is compared against normative data collected on age-relevant samples. Vocabulary is often used as a measure of premorbid intelligence (i.e., estimated intelligence of patient before trauma or degeneration), because vocabulary is more often spared than other cognitive functions.

National adult reading test (NART)

The NART (Nelson & O'Connell, 1978) is widely used in patients to assess premorbid intelligence; it is also sometimes used in non-brain-injured people to get a quick measure of general cognitive ability, although other, more appropriate, measures are available for this purpose. The test is based on the observation that vocabulary correlates highly with general cognitive level. The test measures pronunciation that indicates premorbid familiarity with the word (if you had never seen the irregular word YACHT before how would you pronounce it?). Thus, the test allows patients to reveal their knowledge of familiar but phonetically irregular words (irregular words are used because demented patients are often able correctly to pronounce unfamiliar but *regular* words). The NART comprises 50 phonetically irregular words. Care must be exercised in interpretation because test scores correlate not only with general intelligence, but also education and social class.

Block design

The block design test (Wechsler, 1955) is a visuospatial construction test in which the patient is presented with red and white blocks. Each block has two white and two red sides, and two half-red, half-white sides with the colours divided along the diagonal. The task is to use the blocks to construct replicas of two block constructions made by the examiner. Increasing levels of difficulty can be achieved in the designs of the blocks. This is an important test in *performance* IQ and is remarkably preserved, and sometimes actually enhanced, in neurodevelopmental disorders (e.g., autism; one theory being that the lack of 'central coherence' allows the segmentation of the block design into its separate parts, which makes the task easier than it is for normal people, who have a bias towards processing the gestalt, holism, of the design, thus obscuring the separate parts). One advantage of the test is that it is not sensitive to education: it is thus a 'culture-free' test of one important aspect of cognitive ability.

Raven's progressive matrices (RPM)

The RPM (Raven, 1960) is one of the best measures of fluid general intelligence. It measures learning and abstract reasoning, using matrices that are presented in a progressive order from the simple to the complex. The test consists of a series of visual matrices, each of which has a piece missing. The task of the test-taker is to select from a number of candidate answers the correct one.

The standard form of this test contains 60 items that take about 40 minutes to complete; an advanced version is available to test higher IQ individuals, as well as a coloured version for children and cognitively retarded adults. The test provides a measure of visuospatial processing (pattern matching on the easy items; vulnerable to right-hemisphere lesions) as well as higher-order abstract reasoning for the more complex items (analogical reasoning; vulnerable to left-hemisphere lesions). The nature of the patient's errors may be inspected to indicate the precise nature of their reasoning deficit (e.g., by performing a simplified abstraction by attending to only one dimension of the matrix).

Wisconsin card sorting test (WCST)

The WCST (Berg, 1948) is a widely used test that measures concept formation and abstraction, although it is also used as a measure of *executive functioning* (i.e., the cognitive ability to sequence and organize cognitive processes, including attention). This task requires patients to sort cards according to shape, colour and the number of objects they contain; patients have to match cards to one of four key cards, but are not told the matching principle. After each trial, patients are told if their response was correct or not. The matching rule changes after 10 correct responses.

In one version of the test, the patient is given a pack of 60 cards on which are presented one to four symbols (triangle, star, cross or circle, in red, green, yellow or blue). The patient then sorts the cards and the examiner then states whether they are correct or not according to some rule (e.g., the principle of sorting by colour). After a run of 10 correct cards the rule changes (unbeknown to the patient). The test continues until the patient has made six runs of 10 correct placements, or has placed 64 cards in one

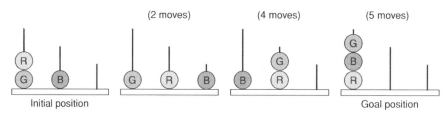

Figure 8.7 The Tower of London task is a measure of executive functioning requiring the patient to plan ahead to the consequences of their next move. The patient must move the three coloured rings from their initial position to the goal position in the fewest possible moves, and level of difficulty can be manipulated from easy to difficult.

category, or verbally reports the rule to the examiner, or is obviously unable to perform the task.

Frontal lobe involvement has been implicated in the performance of this test. There are two frontal lobe executive functions that are impaired on this test: (a) the ability to inhibit inappropriate responses; and (b) the ability to maintain a response set. The WCST is used as a test of *perseverance*, defined as a continuing class of response previously labelled incorrect. Successful completion of this test requires patients: (a) to attain a concept (rule); (b) to maintain the concept for a number of consecutive trials; and (c) to switch the concept when the rule has changed.

Tower of London task

The Tower of London task (Shallice, 1982) is a measure of executive functioning and requires that the patient look ahead to the consequences of their next move. It is an excellent test of planning. The aim is to move the three coloured rings from their initial position to the goal position in the fewest possible moves (figure 8.7). Level of difficulty is manipulated by the number and complexity of subgoals.

The *Tower of Hanoi* version of this task is more complex: it does not use the same size rings; instead the stimuli have to be rearranged according to wooden blocks or rings of varying sizes. The procedure is, however, the same as the Tower of London. All are on the same stick: the smaller blocks/rings must always be on top of the larger blocks/rings. The *Tower of Toronto* adds a further layer of complexity. In addition to adding a fourth ring (all rings are the same size), the rings have different colours (white, yellow, red, black). The patient's task is to keep the lighter-coloured rings on top of the darker ones.

Neuropsychological test batteries

For a comprehensive assessment of functions it is usual to use a neuropsychological test battery, which assesses a range of functions in a standardized format. Two of the most widely used test batteries are (a) the *Luria–Nebraska neuropsychological battery*, and (b) the *Halstead–Reitan battery*.

Luria–Nebraska neuropsychological battery

The Luria–Nebraska neuropsychological battery (Golden, Purisch & Hammeke, 1985) is used to assess higher cortical functions in neuropsychiatric patient groups. The test uses unstructured qualitative techniques, and items were selected on the basis of whether they discriminated between normal individuals and a group of neurologically impaired patients.

This test uses the assessment techniques employed by the famous neuropsychologist, Luria; it is not the items themselves that are traced to Luria but rather the manner in which he used the items to test hypotheses concerning abilities and defects. Golden (1981) selected items based on whether they discriminated between normal people and damaged patients. Items were chosen to represent clinical scales that differentiated between these two samples: *motor functions, rhythm, tactile functions, visual functions, receptive speech, writing, reading, arithmetic, memory* and *intellectual processes.* Five summary scales are formed from these clinical scales: the *pathognomonic, right hemisphere, left hemisphere, profile elevation* and *impairment scales.* Other scales have been added to the battery over the years, including eight *localization* scales (four for each of the two hemispheres, divided into *frontal, sensorimotor, parietal-occipital* and *temporal* scales) and 28 *factor* scales (including such tests as simple phonetic reading and reading simple material).

Halstead–Reitan battery

The Halstead–Reitan Battery (Reitan & Wolfson, 1993) was developed to assess the presence of brain damage while offering a comprehensive account of the patient's psychological functioning. It was originally developed to differentiate between patients with frontal lobe damage and those with other forms of damage or with normal people. It is composed of seven tests (although not all are now used, e.g., *critical flicker fusion test*); some examples give an indication of the type of functions assessed. The *category test* requires patients to deduce the principle contained in sets of items. The *tactual performance test* requires patients to fit blocks of different shapes into a board containing holes of corresponding shape. The *finger oscillation/tapping test* consists of a tapping task. These separate tests provide seven scores, three (*total time, memory, location*) come from the *tactual performance test*; and the other four scores form a single index, the *impairment index,* which is used for gross diagnostic discriminations (running from 0, no scores in the impaired range, to 10, all scores in the impaired range).

The battery enables the clinician to infer the nature, location and extent of structural damage that may explain the pattern of impaired psychological functions. Impaired psychological functions are not always the result of structural changes in the brain; for example, depression is often accompanied by impaired memory. Each test purports to measure a specific cognitive function and the location of neurological deficits (Hom & Reitan, 1990). Patients' scores on these tests are compared with *normative data* collected from normal populations. From such data the mean and standard deviation of normal scores is known: patients' scores are compared against these data to indicate type and severity of deficit. The test is sometimes used to differentiate brain-damaged patients from those feigning brain damage (Lezak, 1995). This test is usually used in conjunction with other neuropsychological tests, including a full IQ test.

The next section outlines behavioural tasks that are not used directly for clinical neuropsychological assessment but which are used to measure important aspects of neuropsychological functioning in order to formulate theoretical models of normal and abnormal psychological processes.

Experimental (Behavioural) Tasks

The formulation of neuropsychological theories often uses purpose-built behavioural paradigms in order to measure specific psychological processes; in addition, psychophysiological tasks are used for a similar purpose (e.g., prepulse inhibition of the startle reflex; see chapter 9).[7] These tasks are often taken from standard behavioural paradigms used in behavioural psychology (*learning theory*). This section summarizes two such behavioural measures, namely, *latent inhibition* (LI) and the *Kamin blocking effect* (KBE) (chapter 16 also discusses these measures in relation to schizophrenia; also see chapter 7). In addition, the emotional Stroop task is outlined, which is widely used in experimental studies of clinical conditions to measure attentional interference.

Latent inhibition (LI)

Latent inhibition (LI) consists in the retardation of learning a CS–UCS association when the CS has been pre-exposed without consequence (i.e., reinforcement) (Lubow, 1989). It is a well-established phenomenon in the animal-learning literature (see chapter 7).

In a typical animal experiment, rats are trained to learn an association between a tone (CS) and a shock (UCS). One group of rats simply gets the CS–UCS training: they quickly learn to fear the tone (i.e., they know it predicts an unpleasant shock). Now, the second group of rats get the same CS–UCS training; however, unlike the first group, before the training they are exposed to the tone-CS without consequence (it is simply presented on its own). LI is evident in this second group because they find it harder to associate the CS–UCS pairing in the training phase (i.e., they need more training trials to reach the same criterion of fear).

According to *conditioned attention theory* (Lubow, 1989), this second, pre-exposed, group has formed a cognitive representation that the tone-CS feature of their environment is unimportant and their attention is directed away from it. When it subsequently becomes important, during the CS–UCS training phase, then they have (a) to first overcome this learned irrelevance (i.e., inhibitory processing), before (b) forming an excitatory CS–UCS association.

How is LI measured in animals? Often a *conditioned emotional suppression* paradigm is used. First the animals are trained to perform some reward-contingent instrumental response (e.g., pressing a lever for food). Then, after CS–UCS training, the CS is presented alone: this has the effect of suppressing instrumental behaviour (a conditioned aversive stimulus leads to a cessation of ongoing behaviour): the degree of suppression is used as the measure of LI (it is greater in the non-pre-exposed group).

Conditioned emotional suppression is typically not used in human studies (e.g., it would be ethically problematic when used with schizophrenia patients); other procedures are preferred. For example, Baruch, Hemsley and Gray (1988) used a between-groups design, in which one group of participants were pre-exposed and the other group were not pre-exposed. The task has two phases. In Phase 1, participants wear headphones, over which are played nonsense syllables. Participants are told to pick one of these syllables and to count how many times it occurs (this is the *masking task*, which is necessary for LI to be shown using this task). Now, the pre-exposed group also occasionally heard white noise presented over the headphones; the non-pre-exposed group do not hear this noise – they hear only the nonsense syllables. In Phase 2, the task changed: participants are told to watch a digital counter increment from 1, 2, 3, etc. They are told that they can predict when this counter is about to increment, and once they know the rule then they should tell the experimenter. In fact, what is predicting the counter increment is the white noise presented over the headphones (figure 8.8).

In this task, LI is seen as the slower association of the white noise (CS) and counter increment (UCS) in the group who has been pre-exposed to the white noise in Phase 1 (figure 8.9).

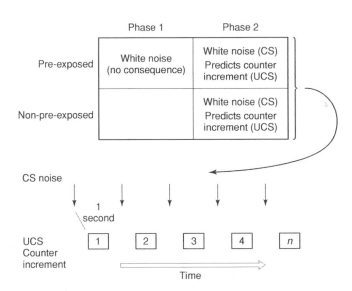

Figure 8.8   The Baruch, Hemsley and Gray (1988) latent inhibition (LI) procedure used with human experimental participants is a two-phase procedure. In Phase 1, half of participants are 'pre-exposed' to bursts of white noise, while the other half of participants do not hear the white noise (i.e., the 'non-pre-exposed' group). During this phase, both groups undertake a masking task of counting the occurrence of one nonsense syllable from a list tape recording of repeating nonsense syllables. During Phase 2, participants are told to listen to the headphones and try to work out what predicts the increment of a counter (starting at 1, 2, 3, 4 . . .) placed on the desk in front of the participant. As shown, what predicts the counter increment is white noise presented over the headphones.

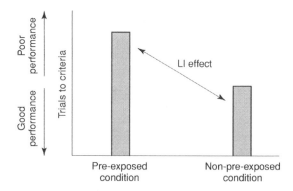

Figure 8.9 Typical LI data. Latent inhibition (LI) consists in the retardation of learning in the pre-exposed group (shown as more trials needed to reach an acceptable criterion of performance) compared with the non-pre-exposed group, indicating that passively listening to 'irrelevant' stimuli in Phase 1 of the experiment leads to inhibitory processing and the withdrawal of attentional resources from stimuli that previously had no significance.

Other versions of the human LI task are now available, some depending on reaction time to measure learning, and some which use a within-groups design, in which the same participants serve in the pre-exposed and non-pre-exposed conditions (of course, in this design there are two separate associations to be learned) (De La Casa & Lubow, 2001).

Kamin blocking effect (KBE)

The Kamin blocking effect (KBE; Kamin, 1968) is also well established in the animal-learning literature. It requires two groups. (a) The control group undergoes associative conditioning with a compound CS (e.g., light and tone), and after training either stimulus alone is sufficient to elicit the CR. (b) The experimental group are first conditioned to one of these stimuli (e.g., light), and only then go through the same conditioning procedure as the control group with the compound (light + tone) stimulus. Blocking is observed in the experimental group: once they have conditioned to the light, their conditioning to the compound (light + tone) stimulus is retarded (i.e., the light conditioning blocks the tone conditioning) (figure 8.10).

Both latent inhibition and the Kamin blocking effect are thought to rely upon attentional and/or inhibitory processes. For example, in the case of latent inhibition there is said to be a failure to inhibit the pre-exposed stimulus which is presented without reinforcement (consequence): most normal individuals quickly inhibit this stimulus and then find it difficult to associate it with the second stimulus in the test phase of the experiment. The idea is that LI depends on attention being drawn away from the unimportant stimulus, which produces inhibitory effects in performance. A similar process is thought to work in KBE: once the initial CS–UCS association has been made, then attention is drawn away from other stimuli – the introduction of the compound stimulus then has to compete for these attentional resources.

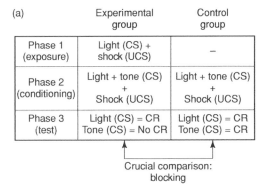

(a)

	Experimental group	Control group
Phase 1 (exposure)	Light (CS) + shock (UCS)	–
Phase 2 (conditioning)	Light + tone (CS) + Shock (UCS)	Light + tone (CS) + Shock (UCS)
Phase 3 (test)	Light (CS) = CR Tone (CS) = No CR	Light (CS) = CR Tone (CS) = CR

Crucial comparison: blocking

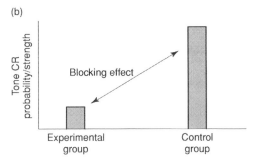

(b)

Figure 8.10   KBE procedure and typical data. The Kamin blocking effect (KBE) is shown as performance difference between two groups: (a) the control group undergo associative conditioning with a compound CS (e.g., light and tone), and after training either stimulus alone is sufficient to elicit the CR; and (b) the experimental group are first conditioned to one of these stimuli (e.g., light), and only then go through the same conditioning procedure as the control group with the compound (light + tone) stimulus (a). Blocking is observed in the experimental group: once they have conditioned to the light, their conditioning to the compound (light + tone) stimulus is retarded (i.e., the light conditioning blocks the tone conditioning) (b).

As discussed further in chapter 16, (a) schizophrenia patients, (b) people drawn from the normal population who score high on various psychometric measures of 'psychosis-proneness', and (c) normal individuals given the drug amphetamine show impaired LI. This effect is thought to represent a failure of inhibitory (attentional) processing because in the test phase of the task LI is shown by *better* (i.e., faster) learning. (This *better* learning is important because it is easy to find *impairments* in clinical groups, but much harder to find *facilitated* performance.)

The distinctive feature of such behavioural paradigms as LI and KBE is that they are *theoretically* motivated by theories and data from extensive work on non-human animals. They can be used to *model* psychological processes: that is, they attempt to measure the core elements of the psychological process under investigation. One powerful advantage they possess is that basic neurophysiological work (chapter 11) can be conducted to advance understanding of the underlying processes. This approach contrasts with most of the neuropsychological tests surveyed above: often these tests measure multiple processes, making it difficult to isolate the core deficit; and these tests are constructed in a way which makes it difficult to adapt a parallel line of neurophysiological work in non-human animals.

Modelling psychological processes by behavioural tasks when they are taken from the non-human literature is not without its problems. For, although there may be a superficial similarity between a human version of a non-human animal task, considerable research is needed to support the construct validity of the paradigm. For example, human latent inhibition employs procedures very different from typical animal situations: in the typical animal situation, LI is measured by the retardation in CS–UCS learning as indexed by suppression of an operant response; in human beings, by rate of learning. In addition, human LI tasks typically employ a masking task that conceals the true purpose of the experiment. One way to develop *construct validity* (see chapter 9) is to compare different forms of the task – for example, it would be possible to compare LI as measured by behavioural and psychophysiological means (e.g., pre-exposing a to-be-CS before a classical conditioning experiment).

The Stroop test

One of the most popular experimental paradigms in the whole of psychology is the Stroop task. This task requires the participant to name the colour of the ink in which a word is written. For example, the word GREEN might be written in red ink: the participant should responsd 'red'. The task measures distraction and attentional interference: the word GREEN distracts from the red colour and naming 'red' is slower than if the red ink spelled the word RED. This effect has been attributed to a response conflict, though failure of response inhibition or failure of selective attention are also possible explanations. Patients who fail this test tend to have difficulty concentrating.

In clinical psychology, this task has been modified to form the 'emotional Stroop task'. In this version, ink colours are once again used, but this time the words spell not colours but emotionally laden words, both positively (FLOWER, LOVE, HARMONY) and negatively (e.g., CANCER, SHAME, BLOOD, SPIDER); neutral words are also included for comparison purposes (BOOK, HOUSE, OCEAN). Specific clinical conditions show a marked interference effect on this task (e.g., anxiety; chapter 15). For example, the reaction times of social phobics to words congruent with their condition are significantly slowed down (e.g., EMBARRASSMENT) (Dalgleish, 1995).

> **ASK YOURSELF**
> In developing neuropsy-chological theories, what are the principal advantages of experimental measures over classical neuropsychological tests?

▭ Transcranial Magnetic Stimulation (TMS)

Today there is an exciting new technique in the neuropsychologist's toolkit which is capable of temporarily exciting and inhibiting the brain processing of normal volunteers by using a safe and non-invasive procedure: transcranial magnetic stimulation (TMS; Walsh

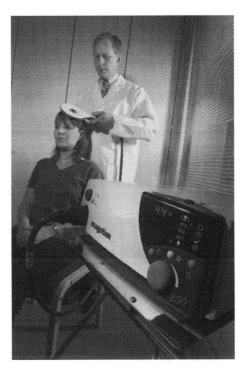

Figure 8.11 The transcranial magnetic stimulation (TMS) device. (Photo courtesy of the Magstim Company Ltd.)

& Pascual-Leone, 2003). It is now commonly used for cerebral mapping in conscious human beings (figure 8.11).

TMS uses a strong magnetic field to induce an electrical current within the brain. When TMS stimulates an area, there is a time lag before the area returns to normal functional capacity. For example, by stimulating with TMS, then asking the participant to perform a task, investigators are able to establish the particular cortical region necessary for a given cognitive operation. TMS is now being used with electrophysiology and neuroimaging (see chapter 10) to assess connectivity and excitability in the human cerebral cortex.

TMS uses pulses of magnetic fields. This procedure capitalizes on the fact that the skull is a good insulator, and attempts of the past to change electrical activity within the skull have required very high voltages, with little opportunity for fine control or focus of effects. However, magnetic fields pass through insulators with little difficulty, and can induce electrical current in neurons.

As presented in chapter 3, cell membranes sustain a potential difference between intra- and extracellular space of about −70 mV (the intracellular charge being more negative), and an action potential (depolarization) consists in the disruption of this resting potential. An externally applied electric field can be used to change the cell membrane potential, therefore stimulating (by depolarizing) the cell. Such a change in electrical potential is made possible with the use of magnetic fields: electromagnetic induction. Depending on the rate of pulses, TMS can either excite or inhibit the cortex. The principle on which TMS works is simple. Magnetic fields can induce electrical current: simply changing the field over time, any charge carriers (e.g., ions in the cells of the brain) are influenced to flow, creating an electrical current.

The first TMS, which delivered a pulse every 3 seconds, was developed as a diagnostic aid for neurologists. For example, the motor part of the brain can be stimulated, inducing a twitch of the thumb, which shows that the nerve pathways are intact: electromyographic (EMG; see chapter 9) electrodes can be placed on muscles to record their activation. TMS techniques now allow up to 50 stimuli per second (rapid-rate, or repetitive, TMS, or rTMS).

The magnetic fields used in TMS are produced by passing current through a hand-held coil, whose shape determines the properties of the size of the field. The coil is driven by a machine that switches the large current necessary in a very precise and controlled way, at rates up to 50 cycles per second. The coil is held against the head and the magnetic field passes through the skull and into the brain. Small induced currents then make brain areas below the coil more or less active, depending on the setting.

TMS and rTMS are able to influence many brain functions: movements, visual perception, memory, reaction time, speech and mood. The effects are temporary, lasting only a short time after the stimulation has been stopped. Thus far, TMS appears not to have any harmful effects – although there remains the possibility that it could induce a seizure on rare occasions (standardized testing procedures have been developed to minimize this possibility). TMS has been used as a therapeutic technique for depression (see chapter 14), although this research is still in its preliminary phase.

ASK YOURSELF
What can TMS *not* reveal about structure–function relations?

Single and Double Dissociations

The final part of this chapter tackles a basic logical issue that runs through neuropsychology: how to relate brain structure to psychological function (figure 8.12). Imagine we carried out a neuropsychological study and found that a lesion in brain area X was associated (correlated) with impaired psychological performance on function A, but not function B. We might conclude that area X is responsible for function A, but not B. This would be an example of a *single dissociation* of functions. We might conclude that function B is mediated by another (unknown) brain area. But wait a minute: there is the possibility that function B is related to area X (maybe function A is more difficult than function B and for this reason seems to be more impaired by a lesion in area X). In addition, if we found that damage to area X impairs functions A and B, then this might be due to a general effect on performance (e.g., by producing a lack of motivation). Either way, we are left in considerable doubt about the true relation between brain structure and function. The way out of this conundrum is to look for a *double dissociation* (a concept introduced by Teuber, 1955).

More formally, a *double dissociation* is found when it can be demonstrated that damage to brain region X_1 impairs only function Y_1; and damage to brain area X_2 impairs only Y_2 (X_1 does not impair Y_2; X_2 does not impair Y_1). Given this pattern of effects, we

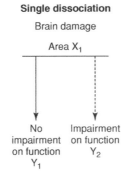

Single dissociation

Brain damage

Area X₁

No impairment on function Y₁

Impairment on function Y₂

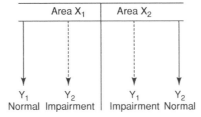

Double dissociation

Brain damage

Area X₁	Area X₂
Y₁ Normal Y₂ Impairment	Y₁ Impairment Y₂ Normal

Figure 8.12   Definitions of single dissociation and double dissociation.

can be confident that we are not dealing with a generalized effect with X_1 and X_2 impairing Y_1 to Y_n, or some other artefact (e.g., task difficulty). Therefore, a double dissociation indicates that: (a) the two functions that were selected have non-overlapping cognitive processes; and (b) the damaged brain areas selectively impair only one of these cognitive functions.

> **ASK YOURSELF**
> Why is double dissociation considered such a prized finding in neuropsychological research?

Conclusion

Selective brain damage provides a 'natural experiment' and an opportunity to relate brain structure to psychological function; and standardized batteries of neuropsychological tests provide the means to assess these functions and to identify deficits by comparison of patient scores with normative data taken from healthy and clinical groups. Such assessment is important in the diagnosis and identification of specific deficits, and especially important in the design of rehabilitation programmes. Behavioural tests can be used to probe functions, allowing specific neuropsychological research questions to be explored in the normal population (e.g., schizophrenia; see chapter 16). In addition to tests, new techniques are becoming available which allow experimental and temporary lesions of the cortex to explore functions (e.g., TMS). With the increasing availability of neuroimaging technology (see chapter 10), there is greater scope more precisely to associate specific neurological deficits with specific psychological deficits – this is another example of how different approaches are being combined to increase the reliability and precision of diagnosis and treatment. Part III includes examples of how these neuropsychological tests are used to study clinical disorders.

In interpreting neuropsychological data, caution must be exercised. As with other techniques (e.g., neuroimaging), the data are essentially correlational, and it is often difficult – sometimes impossible – to interpret them with any degree of confidence. For example, if damaged area x is associated with impaired function y, then this could be because the neural circuit that mediates function y (say area z) just happens to pass through area x – this is especially likely to be a problem when brain damage is diffuse, affecting more than one area or circuit. However, basic inferential statistics should be borne in mind: correlation does not imply causation. As discussed in chapter 11, the only way to get around this problem is to use a neurophysiological approach, where direct investigation of the brain allows the necessary experimental conditions that permit sound causal inferences – however, much of this type of invasive research is not possible with human beings. Despite these caveats, neuropsychological procedures provide important information on the effects of brain damage, which helps with the development of theoretical models of structure–function relations as well as with the design of clinically effective rehabilitation programmes.

Learning Questions

1. What does accidental brain damage reveal about structure–function relations that is not available by any other means?
2. How is it possible that patients with 'split brains' appear to behave as if they had an intact brain?
3. Has neuroimaging replaced the need for neuropsychological tests?
4. What do behavioural procedures (e.g., latent inhibition) contribute to neuropsychology?
5. What does double dissociation reveal about structure–function relations?

NOTES

1 The details surrounding this case are marred with mistakes. This started with the *Boston Post*, which reported that the circumference, not the diameter, was 1 1/4 inches at one end – we know the exact dimensions because the rod is now on display at the Medical School at Harvard University, USA, where his skull is also stored (however, his name was misspelt 'Phinehas'). Much that has been written about his life after the trauma is either fabricated or misinterpreted (Macmillan, 2000b).

2 It is customary to refer to famous neuropsychological patients by their initials in order to maintain their confidentiality.

3 An alternative view of the role of hippocampal damage is that of 'catastrophic hyperamnesia' (Gray & McNaughton, 2000): according to this view, memories are stored but the memory problem is one of retrieval. According to these authors, the hippocampus resolves conflicts

between candidate outputs. In anterograde amnesia, the damaged hippocampus does not properly resolve this conflict, therefore the patient is unable to recall stored information. The fact that this form of hippocampal damage does not impair procedural ('how to') memories is explained by the fact that such memories have no conflict components: they are simply a sequence of inputs–outputs.

4   A comic parody of this type of conflictual behaviour is seen in the film *Dr Strangelove*, in which Dr Strangelove has to use one hand to restrain the other from making a Nazi salute. This Peter Sellers character was not split-brained, but there was a relative independence of the two hemispheres, and thus the relative independence of the two minds, which was used to artistic effect in the film. In a less obvious way, we all have two minds, which appear to be a single mind because they usually work so seamlessly together.

5   Debates concerning the separation of minds in the brain have excited philosophers and psychologists for many hundreds of years; and have also found expression in the popular imagination through such novels as *Dr Jekyll and Mr Hyde* (a psychopharmacologically induced transformation of character) – this novel is thought to be based on a real-life, respectable Edinburgh city official who, at night, turned to crime to fuel his baser instincts.

6   It is common in research on the psychophysiology of stress to use mental arithmetic to induce stress (however, the PASAT is designed to minimize stress, although it is still present for many people even with the simplest arithmetic problems).

7   Although these behavioural and psychophysiological measures are not designed for use in clinical neuropsychological diagnosis, they are nevertheless sometimes used to indicate the presence of brain pathology (e.g., deficits on these tasks have been used by expert witnesses in court proceeding to support the claim that the defendant has impaired psychological functioning). For reasons discussed in Part III, assessments based on such measures of individual cases are probably not warranted.

FURTHER READING

Lezak, M. D. (1995). *Neuropsychological Assessment*. Oxford: Oxford University Press.

Whishaw, K., Kolb, B. & Whishaw, I. Q. (2003). *Fundamentals of Human Neuropsychology*. New York: W. H. Freeman.

Wilson, B. A. (1999). *Case Studies in Neuropsychological Rehabilitation*. Oxford: Oxford University Press.

Psychophysiology

Learning Objectives

To be able to:

1. Discuss the importance of measurement issues in the context of reliability and validity.
2. Describe the main peripheral nervous system indices of psychological functions.
3. Evaluate the role of psychophysiological procedures in classical conditioning and lie detection.
4. Explain how psychophysiology is used to test the integrity of brain systems in psychopathology.
5. Outline how psychoneuroimmunological assays are used to assess reactions to acute stress.

Biological studies of human beings have traditionally relied upon a toolbox of techniques that have attempted to infer psychological state from physiological measurement of the surface of the body: this is the field of *psychophysiology*. However, that toolbox has now been greatly expanded by the development of *neuroimaging* techniques, which allow us to see inside the brain, permitting the measurement of anatomical structures and analysis of their functions (see chapter 10). Although neuroimaging techniques have opened up a whole new arena for neuroscientific studies, they have not replaced traditional psychophysiological approaches, which offer relatively inexpensive, non-invasive and unique insights into a range of important psychological phenomena.

According to Cacioppo and Tassinary (1990, p. ix),

> Psychophysiology represents the scientific study of cognitive, emotional, and behavioral phenomena as related to and revealed through physiological principles and events.

This chapter surveys a number of these traditional psychophysiological techniques and their applications in answering important psychological questions. The focus is on the measurement of peripheral systems (with the exception of eye movements, which are formally controlled by the central nervous system) – the next chapter focuses on the direct measurement of brain activity.

Measurement Issues

Psychophysiology is interested in two types of cause-and-effect relationships. Sometimes psychological stimulation (e.g., time-pressure stress) is the causal factor (i.e., the *independent variable*, IV), and physiological response (e.g., heart rate) the effect (i.e., the *dependent variable*, DV). At other times, a physiological manipulation (e.g., drug) serves as the causal IV and the psychological response (e.g., attentional focus) is the effect DV. However, in both cases, it is important that outcome (DV) variables conform to a number of important measurement principles.

True score

In all sciences, but especially in the physiological and psychological sciences, *observed* responses (i.e., effects – the variables being measured) are composed of two major components: *true variance* and *error*. Thus,

$$O = T + e$$

where:

O = observed response (or observed variance)
T = true variance
e = error (which is the difference between O and T); error is assumed to be random, that is, it randomly fluctuates around the true score.

To illustrate this point, let us assume that your mean resting pulse rate is 70 beats per minute: this is your *true* pulse rate. Now, what reading would we get if we tested you on 10 occasions? We would not get, or expect to get, a run of ten 70s. In all likelihood, we would get something like the following run: 65, 72, 73, 71, 64, 70, 74, 72, 74, 74. (These data give a mean of 70.) On each day, your *observed* pulse rate is likely to be slightly different from your *true* pulse rate (which we could determine with a very large number of trials with complete accuracy), and this difference is *error*. Error can arise from a variety of sources: you may have felt upset on one day of testing; or you may have been fighting a bacterial infection; or the researcher may not have attached the recording device firmly enough. We live in an imperfect world and our psychophysiological measurements are also imperfect: imperfection in measurement is the norm when we take a sample of observations from a population of all possible observations. It is something we have to live with; however, we can estimate the accuracy of our estimates.

These principles are no different from those found in other areas of psychology, but in the case of psychophysiology they are especially important because often there is large variation (statistical error) resulting from: (a) the nature of the physiological systems;

and (b) the sensitivity of recording equipment. For example, skin conductance and heart rate responses are very sensitive to transient events in the environment, therefore a sufficient number of experimental trials are needed to ensure that the true variance is larger than the error variance. On the recording side, problems arise from participants moving, or coughing, and there is also the problem of non-specific changes in responses throughout the experiment – for example, there may be a gradual reduction in response due to acclimatization to the testing situation, quite irrespective of the specific experimental manipulations. For these reasons, rigorous experimental designs and appropriate statistical analyses are required for the collection and interpretation of psychophysiological data; and of course adequate training of researchers is needed.

Reliability

The concept and measurement of reliability relate to the extent to which observed measurements correspond to true score variance; the closer the match, the higher the coefficient of reliability. Reliability is thus a necessary condition of adequate measurement. The way to improve reliability is known: increase the number of samples taken – this is a general principle in psychology going under the heading of *aggregation of data* (Epstein, 1979). The reason why more readings increase reliability is simple: error variance is assumed to be random, fluctuating around the true score, therefore it has plus and minus signs, and over a longer series of measurements, these positive and negative deviations from the true score cancel out, leaving exposed the observed score that is close to the true score.

Reliability refers to the stability of measurement. A stable measurement is (a) repeatable, (b) dependable, and (c) homogeneous (i.e., individual readings are each measuring a large portion of the true variance). Two main subtypes of reliability are considered here. *Internal consistency* refers to the extent to which separate readings are measuring the true variance (e.g., readings that are intended to measure physiological arousal should all be highly correlated – whether or not they actually measure this arousal is a different question of validity). *Test–retest reliability* refers to stability of measurement over time (e.g., readings that seem reliably to measure physiological arousal on one occasion should also measure it on another occasion): correlating scores obtained on the two occasions provides the coefficient of test–retest reliability. If a measure cannot be shown to be reliable – that is, provide accurate measurement – then it cannot be valid.

Validity

Validity refers to the extent to which a measurement relates to the construct it purports to measure. In other words, the extent to which the observed scores measure *theoretical* true variance. For example, a physiological measure of arousal should relate to arousal and not to non-arousal processes. Validity breaks down into subtypes. (a) *Content validity* refers to experts' judgement of the validity of the physiological measure used to index some psychological function (this form of validity does not prove that measurement is valid but it is usually a good start to selecting candidate measures from among a much larger pool of measures). (b) *Criterion-related validity* refers to the ability of a physiological measure empirically to relate to psychological functions, either concurrently (i.e., *concurrent validity*) or in the future (i.e., *predictive validity*). (c) *Construct validity* comprises a network of theoretical concepts and empirical data that provide the theoretical foundations of the physiological measure: this is the most important form of validity, providing the scientific rationale for the use of the operational measure of a central psychological process.[1]

Psychophysiological Systems

With these important measurement issues in mind, let us now move on to surveying some of the widely used psychophysiological techniques.

The electrodermal system

Electrodermal activity (EDA) is one of the most widely used – some would say abused – physiological response systems in psychophysiology. It was discovered in the 1870s by Vigouroux, who measured resting (tonic) skin resistance levels in various patient groups; then in the 1880s, Fere found that by passing a small electrical current across two electrodes placed on the surface of the skin, a momentary decrease in skin resistance could be measured (Dawson, Schell & Filion, 1990). It is now common to use electrical *conductance* rather than *resistance* as the preferred method of measuring the changes in electrical passage between two electrodes: this is skin conductance level, SCL; phasic responses to stimuli are referred to as the skin conductance response (SCR). SCL and SCR depend upon the activation of the sweat glands, which are innervated by the sympathetic branch of the autonomic nervous system (ANS; see chapter 3). Skin conductance is measured by the placement of two electrodes on the same finger (e.g., index finger). (EDA used to be more commonly known as galvanic skin response, GSR.) SCL/SCR have been widely used in biological psychology because they have been associated with emotion, arousal and attention systems.

Skin conductance level (SCL)

As an example of the use of SCL, Wilson (1990) measured SCL of introverts and extroverts across the course of the day. One hundred and eleven participants carried a battery-powered skin conductance meter throughout the day, and each hour they recorded their SCL. This simple device was sufficient to show that introverts were more aroused during the early part of the day, extroverts during the later part of the day. The pattern of findings is shown in figure 9.1.

These data show one of the problems with SCL. It is correlated with age: older people tend to have fewer sweat glands (in this sample they also tended to be more introverted, necessitating a correction for age in order to show clearly the introvert–extrovert difference).

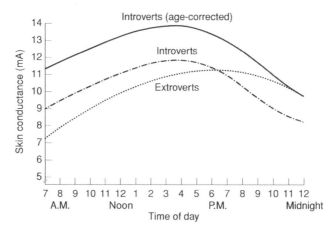

Figure 9.1 Time of day effects. Data from Wilson (1990) showing skin conductance level (SCL) over the course of the day in introverts and extroverts. These data show time of day effects, personality differences and age effects (i.e., older people tend to have fewer sweat glands – in the sample shown, they were also more introverted).

Skin conductance response (SCR)

The general levels of arousal, as measured by SCL, are not always of central interest. Often the researcher is interested in the skin conductance response (SCR) to specific and discrete stimuli. Blair (1999) tested the physiological responses of children (N = 42) with emotional and behavioural problems, who were at risk for developing psychopathy. These children were shown three types of slides (threatening, distressing and neutral). Slides were presented for 8 seconds, with a 10–20 second gap (the intertrial interval, ITI) between slides. SCRs were compared with baseline SCL measured prior to the onset of the slide. SCR magnitude was defined as the greatest departure from baseline occurring between 1 and 5 seconds after slide onset. In accordance with Blair's *violence inhibition mechanism* (VIM) theory of psychopathy – which argues that psychopaths are insensitive to the distress cues of others (e.g., crying and submission cues, which usually serve to attenuate or terminate further violence) – psychopathy-prone children did not show larger SCRs to distress slides (compared with neutral slides), but control children did. However, these psychopathy-prone children did show normal SCRs to threat slides, indicating that their deficit is specific to distress cues.

SCR parameters

Once the SCR has been measured then a decision is necessary concerning the best measure to summarize the response. SCR is complex, and although a simple measurement is often taken, as seen in Blair's (1999) study, other choices are possible. The nature of the SCR is shown in figure 9.2.

It may be decided to measure *response onset latency* (i.e., how long after the stimulus onset the response takes to start); *rise time latency* (i.e., the time it takes from stimulus

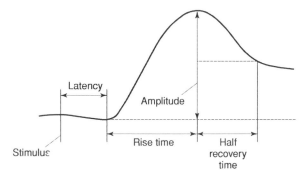

Figure 9.2 SCR parameters. The skin conductance response (SCR) is a complex wave made up of a number of components: (1) from the onset of the eliciting stimulus to the start of the response, *response onset latency*; (2) the time from stimulus onset to peak amplitude, *rise time latency*; (3) the maximal point reached, *peak amplitude*; and (4) the time it takes for the response to return to baseline value, *recovery time*, often measured in terms of *half-recovery time*. Although these components tend to be correlated, they often reflect separate processes and reflect the nature of the eliciting stimulus.

onset to peak amplitude); *peak amplitude*[2] (the highest point of the response); and *recovery time* (the time it takes to decline to some specified level). These measures provide different sources of information and are dependent on the nature of the stimulus presented. For example, a highly emotive stimulus may have a long recovery time, and this might be the best measure of the extent of processing (emotional people tend to take longer to recover from an emotion-inducing experience).

Interpretation of electrodermal data

There are several issues that need to be considered when using skin conductance recordings.

First, there are considerable individual differences in resting SCL, and considerable differences in SCR. One problem of SCL relates to the Law of Initial Value, which states that tonic (loosely defined as resting) levels of a response system influence phasic reactions of that system. Imagine a highly anxious patient who is in a chronically aroused state. If the researcher is interested in testing whether this patient is more reactive to the presentation of unpleasant stimuli, they might show this patient unpleasant slides and neutral (control) slides and then compare their SCRs to these slides with those a control group showed. Under these conditions, they might find that the anxious patient shows a *weaker* SCR to the unpleasant slides (as defined as the difference between pre-stimulus baseline and real amplitude). However, this unexpected outcome might be due to the fact that the initial values of the patient's SCL were so high that they could not be pushed much higher; in contrast, the SCLs of less anxious (control) participants had more potential to rise.

A similar effect is often found with highly aroused individuals who show a reduction in apparent arousal levels when given a physiological stimulant (e.g., caffeine). For example, Smith, Rypma and Wilson (1981) found that, using caffeine (vs. a placebo) to induce arousal, there was large basal and phasic arousal in introverts under placebo, and this finding was reversed under caffeine, where extroverts exhibited the greatest responsiveness, and introverts showed an actual reduction.

Second, SCLs often show a tidal drift throughout the testing session. When the experimental participant is first wired up, they are in a state of some arousal, and it takes time for them to habituate to the novel testing environment. Usually a quiet period of habituation (a *habituation session*) is given in order to stabilize the SCL. However, different individuals need different lengths of habituation to reach a given criterion of stability; and once the experiment begins proper, the presentation of stimuli produces a gradual upward drift. Therefore, it is sometimes difficult to establish a stable baseline SCL against which the response (SCR) is compared. This problem is especially acute in experiments that use aversive (unpleasant) stimuli (UCS) (e.g., loud noise) to study fear processes (e.g., classical conditioning of fear; see below).

Third, the SCR is a non-specific response: it is a measure of (emotional) arousal irrespective of the valence (pleasantness vs. unpleasantness) of the eliciting stimulus. If you now think of an unpleasant image, your SCR rises; if you think of a pleasant image, it rises too; and if you are confronted by a neutral, but novel, stimulus, it rises also. Therefore, the mere presence of an SCR does not say anything about the specific nature of the underlying psychological process: it merely indicates that a state of non-specific arousal/emotion has been generated. However, the SCR is a highly sensitive measure of emotional responding, and when used within a rigorous experimental design can provide highly powerful information on internal psychological processes (see below).

The financial cost of EDA equipment is modest, making it a widely available tool in psychophysiology, used to address a wide range of psychological processes. It is especially useful in investigations of the orienting response and habituation (see chapter 7).

> **ASK YOURSELF**
> Is the widespread use of electrodermal activity based more on practical convenience than on well-formulated principles?

Cardiac rhythm

The cardiovascular system moves blood around the various organs and tissue of the body and comprises the heart, the blood vessels and complex control mechanisms for regulating their functions. The beating of the heart is an electrochemical event, and electrical impulses generated by specialized cells within the heart (pacemaker cells) initiate the mechanical contraction of the heart muscle. The orderly transmission of electrical activity through the various portions of the heart gives rise to an electrical field that can be easily detected and measured by electrodes placed on the body surface. The *electrocardiogram* (ECG) is a graphical representation of the stereotypic pattern of electrical activity generated by the heart during each beat (figure 9.3).

The heart is made up of four chambers that function as two pumps in series. The right-side pump is composed of the right atrium and right ventricle; the left-side pump is composed of the left atrium and left ventricle. The heart beat is complex, comprising a number of different components that relate to the separate pumping chambers of the heart. The major components are: (a) the *P-wave*, corresponding to the depolarization

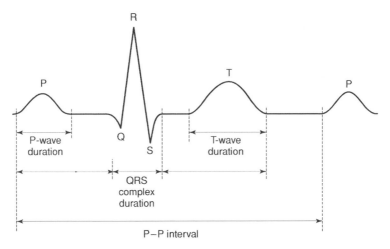

Figure 9.3 The *electrocardiogram* (ECG) response, showing the different components that correspond to the pumping of the heart.

of the atria; (b) the *QRS complex*, corresponding to the depolarization of the ventricles; and (c) the *T-wave*, corresponding to the repolarization of the ventricles. These components are crucial for detecting disease of the heart, but they are not commonly analysed in psychological studies of the heart, which tend to look at heart rate per time period.

The heart is innervated by both the sympathetic and the parasympathetic branches of the autonomic nervous system. Increased heart rate results from increased sympathetic activity and/or decreased parasympathetic actions; decreased heart rate results from increased parasympathetic activity and/or decreased sympathetic activity. Psychological factors that shift the sympathetic/parasympathetic balance alter heart rate. Thus, measures of heart rate may only be interpreted as reflecting the net result of the interaction of both divisions of the ANS.

As with skin conductance activity, heart rate (HR) equipment is relatively inexpensive to purchase and run, and for this reason is widely used in psychophysiology. However, as with skin conductance, interpretation of heart rate data must be made with caution, and a rigorous experimental design and appropriate statistical analysis are necessary to infer the psychological state underlying the response.

ASK YOURSELF
Why is the cardiac rhythm widely used in psychophysiological studies?

Skin conductance and heart rate measures in classical conditioning

One use to which both skin conductance measures (SCR) and heart rate (HR) have been put is in classical conditioning studies. SCR and HR are often used as the dependent (outcome) measures in human studies of the effects of UCS intensity and the preparedness of stimuli (see chapter 7). In a differential classical conditioning paradigm, individuals are presented with two types of conditioned stimuli: CS+ (paired with UCS) and CS− (unpaired with UCS). CSs can comprise prepared stimuli (snakes and spiders) or unprepared stimuli (flowers and mushrooms); the UCS can be either a mild shock or a loud noise. Classical conditioning predicts that participants form an association between the shock/noise UCS and CS for the paired stimuli (CS+) only; the unpaired stimulus (CS−) does not become conditioned and therefore does not show an SCR. SCR and HR are well suited to measuring this classical conditioning effect.

In a typical human experiment there are three phases. (a) During the *habituation phase*, the to-be-CSs are presented on their own and, after an initial orienting response, the SCR habituates and the SCL is stabilized. (b) During the *acquisition phase*, half of the stimuli are paired with the UCS (CS+), and the other half are not paired. Participants develop an anticipatory conditioned response (CR) to the CS+: i.e., they show SCR and HR effects upon presentation of the CS+ but before the UCS (which elicits the unconditioned response, UCR). The difference in SCR/HR to the CS+ and CS− is taken as the strength of conditioning. (c) During the *extinction phase*, where the CS+/UCS bond is broken (i.e., the UCS is no longer presented), there is a gradual decline in the CR until, in theory at least, the CR completely disappears – the time it takes to extinguish a CR is an important component in clinical models of anxiety (see chapter 15). Such classical conditioning paradigms illustrate the usefulness of SCRs and HR as operational measures of the degree of emotional activation generated by classically conditioned stimuli.

SCR and HR are also useful for detecting physiological responses elicited by stimuli presented below the threshold of conscious awareness. There is an important issue of awareness in human conditioning studies (see chapter 15); in this respect, the use of SCR and HR can provide information which is not available by either verbal self-report or by other behavioural or physiological methods.

> **ASK YOURSELF**
> Why is a rigorous experimental design so important in interpreting skin conductance and heart findings?

Electromyography

Animals interact with their environment through the skeletomotor system, and we have discussed in chapter 4 how the contraction of muscles is caused by electrical activity. This electrical activity can be measured by placing electrodes on the skin covering the muscle, a procedure known as *electromyography* (EMG). There are many applications of EMG to measure muscle activity and tension. This discussion of EMG focuses on the facial muscles and their significance for important psychological functions.

The face contains a large number of muscles (20) for the control of facial expressions and defensive reactions; shown in figure 9.4 is the electrode placement to detect different types of expressions. The face contains a rich source of information, much of which is not evident to the untrained observer; and even to the trained observer, much of its information may be lost without the use of EMG. Facial muscles are controlled by the seventh cranial nerve, and they interact to produce a very large number of facial expressions.

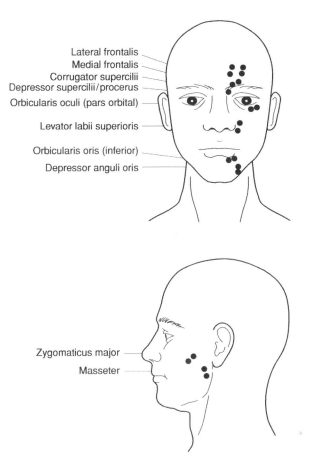

Lateral frontalis
Medial frontalis
Corrugator supercilii
Depressor supercilii/procerus
Orbicularis oculi (pars orbital)

Levator labii superioris

Orbicularis oris (inferior)
Depressor anguli oris

Zygomaticus major
Masseter

Figure 9.4 Facial muscles. Some of the major muscles that comprise the complex musculature of the face involved in the expression of emotion.

Facial emotions

The facial muscles have been shaped by natural selection to produce gestures that convey information about intentions and emotional states. Facial expressions do not need conscious awareness or control, and are even activated when stimuli are presented below the threshold of conscious awareness. EMG is highly sensitive to the electrical activation of facial muscles. As the examples presented below show, EMG can differentiate true and false facial expressions; and it can measure the muscle activity that mimics (i.e., mirror) the facial expressions of others (Dimberg & Ohman, 1996). After successful classical conditioning, using angry faces as the CS, a specific pattern of facial EMG is evident (this is the conditioned response, CR) – in the case of angry faces, more corrugator activity is observed.

Although it is possible to employ slow-frame video technology to measure facial expressions, EMG is more sensitive. For example, EMG may detect electrical activity in muscles that do not generate clearly defined facial expressions; and EMG can detect facial expressions presented for a very short period of time (i.e., milliseconds).

In general, increased *corrugator supercilii* activity accompanies negative emotion; and increased *zygomaticus major* activity accompanies positive emotion. Measurement of these muscles is particularly important in discriminating true and false facial expressions.

Truth and lies

Ekman (2001) is famous for his work on universal facial expressions, and he has developed procedures for detecting true and false expressions. It turns out that it is much easier to express true emotions than it is to fabricate false ones. In fact, concealed emotions, which are often masked by false emotions, 'leak': this leakage can be detected by EMG. In addition, false emotional expressions often look insincere because they do not contain the full set of muscle movements seen during a truthful expression. This insincerity results from the fact that some muscles are difficult to control voluntarily. For example, only about 10 per cent of people can deliberately pull the corners of their lips downwards without moving their chin muscle. But these movements appear without difficulty when sadness, sorrow or grief is felt. Another clue to lying is asymmetrical facial expressions. Let us now look at some true and false facial expressions.

The forehead is the chief locus for reliable muscle movements. In sadness (and also grief and distress) the inner corners of the eyebrow are pulled upward. This would not usually be present in a false display of these emotions, and it should appear when a person feels sad or distressed, despite attempts to conceal these feelings (however, a small number of people can control the eyebrow muscles).

In fear (and worry, apprehension and terror), the eyebrows are raised and pulled together; also, the upper eyebrow is raised and the lower eyelid tensed. These features usually disappear when fear is faked.

The simple action of the zygomaticus major muscles produces the felt smile; in contrast, the false smile does not contain this muscle action. The contempt smile involves a tightening of the muscles in and around the lip corners, producing a muscle bulge in and around the corners; the contempt smile is also shown by a unilateral version of this expression in which one lip corner is tightened and slightly raised (Ekman, 2001). Anger is accompanied by a narrowing of the lips, which is hard to suppress even when there is the attempt to conceal this emotional state (figure 9.5).

An interesting form of a concealed facial expression is a *microemotion*: this example of facial leakage consists of the complete array of the facial muscles underlying the true emotion flashed on and off in a quarter of a second. Its speed of delivery is difficult to detect. Ekman (2001) recounts the case of a depressed psychiatric patient who faked a happy expression in order to gain release from hospital in order that she could commit suicide. Careful analysis of her face showed a microemotion of distress for a fraction of a second, which revealed her true emotional state.

A second form of facial leakage is *squelched expressions*. This expression is observed during the early stages of an emotional expression, before the person is aware that they are leaking emotional information and before they deliberately conceal the expression. The smile is the most common mask, as it is easy to produce and is intended to produce a positive reaction in other people. The squelched expression usually lasts longer

Figure 9.5 Emotive faces. Facial expression (modelled by Paul Ekman) of different types of emotion, showing the subtle interplay of muscles involved in genuine and false expressions. (From Ekman, 2001; © 1993–2004 Paul Ekman.)

but is not as complete as the microemotion (Ekman, 2001). Careful use of EMG data, which can be analysed in terms of milliseconds, can be used to detect these types of true expressions, as well as detecting facial expressions that are false.

ASK YOURSELF
Why do we find it so difficult to conceal our lies?

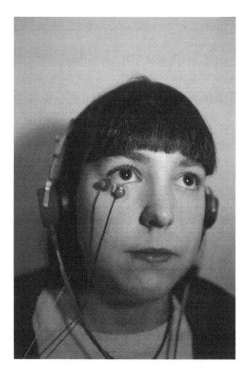

Figure 9.6 Apparatus used to measure eye-blink startle reflex in human beings. Two recording electrodes are placed on the orbicularis oculi (eye-blink) muscle (a third is placed either on the forehead or on the bone behind the ear, the mastoid, to form a ground). Acoustic startle stimuli are presented over headphones.

Startle reflex

EMG is widely used to measure the startle reflex. This reflex is a cross-species involuntary response to an abrupt, intense stimuli, consisting of a shock wave that travels from the head down the whole neuromuscular system (Landis & Hunt, 1939). In the rat, startle is measured by whole-body flinch; in human beings, it is easily and conveniently measured by the eye-blink reflex, measured electromyographically from the orbicularis oculi (eye-blink) muscle, which is innervated by the facial nerve (one advantage of the eye-blink response is its relative slow habituation). Figure 9.6 shows a participant in a typical startle reflex experiment.

The startle reflex is plastic, being modified by a number of experimental manipulations. This section looks at two such effects: (a) modulation by affective stimuli; and (b) modulation by prestimulation.

The startle circuit consists of the following: the startle probe (e.g., a loud noise) activates the cochlear nucleus, sending impulses to the lateral lemniscus and then on to the reticular formation; and the output path passes through spinal neurons to the reflex effectors. This is the *obligatory* circuit, driven by parameters of the input stimuli (e.g., intensity and frequency). Now, there is a second circuit that mediates the fear component of startle; this is the *secondary* circuit. It has been shown that, by applying an electrical stimulus with a microelectrode, augmentation of startle occurs only when the point of stimulation is earlier in the circuit than the nucleus reticularis pontis caudalis (Davis, 1990). The next question concerns the source of the augmenting stimulation.

There is evidence that the nuclei of the amygdala are important sites in this secondary, modulatory circuit. Several lines of evidence support this theory: (a) there is a direct connection from the amygdala nuclei to the key reticular site; (b) electrical stimulation of the amygdala enhances the startle reflex; (c) lesions of the amygdala abolish startle augmentation by a conditioned stimulus; and (d) electrical stimulation in human beings produces emotion-laden images.

There is now overwhelming evidence for the involvement of the amygdala, as well as other structures, in fear and anxiety. It receives projections from sensory and association areas, so is well equipped to deal with externally threatening stimuli as well as internally interpreted or generated stimuli. Affective modulation of the startle reflex is discussed further in chapter 15.

Modulation by affective stimuli

Numerous studies demonstrate that conditioned fear increases the magnitude of the startle reflex in animals (Davis, 1986); and it has long been known that fearful human beings are easily startled. Affective modulation of the startle reflex is now widely used in human psychophysiology to study emotional reactivity. In human beings, pleasant and unpleasant stimuli comprise static slides, depicting various types of images which have been validated on scales of *pleasantness–unpleasantness* and *arousal* (figure 9.7). One major advantage of the modulated startle technique over other psychophysiological procedures (e.g., electrodermal activity and heart rate) is its ability to index emotional valence: the directions of startle reactions are different in appetitive and aversive contexts (irrespective of level of arousal).

In a typical affective modulation of startle study, participants are presented with a number of loud noises (i.e., the startle probe; 115 dB(A)) for a brief period (50 ms). This probe elicits the startle reflex. Sometimes the startle probe is presented during the viewing of emotive slides, and at other times during the interval between slides. The presentation of startle probes cannot be precisely anticipated by the participant, therefore the response is not the result of classical conditioning.

The startle reflex is observed to increase in magnitude when the startle probe is presented during the viewing of unpleasant slides, as compared with neutral slides. This effect is commonly known as *fear-potentiated startle* – this process is the same one that is experienced when watching a horror film alone and/or when startled by an expected stimulus. Now, when probes are delivered during the viewing of pleasant slides, significant attenuation of the startle is observed, providing an independent measure of reactivity to pleasant events (i.e., Hamm et al., 1993). This is sometimes called *pleasure-attenuated startle*. (See figure 9.8.) Affective modulation of startle is seen to provide an objective measure of emotional reactivity (e.g., Cuthbert, Patrick & Lang, 1991; Cuthbert, Bradley & Lang, 1996).

Affective startle modulation has proven to be a useful tool to study the interrelation of normal traits of personality, emotion and emotion-related psychopathological conditions

Figure 9.7 Examples of the type of images used in affective modulation of the startle reflex. Actual images are available from the International Affective Picture System (IAPS; Lang, Ohman & Vaitl, 1988), which comprises a set of several hundred images depicting pleasant, unpleasant and neutral stimuli, rated and standardized in terms of valence, arousal and dominance.

(for a review, see Grillon & Baas, 2003). Anxious individuals, who are more sensitive to threats, may be expected to show greater potentiation of the startle reflex in the context of aversive stimuli, and this indeed is found; also anxious patients show greater fear potentiation, with psychopaths showing an absence. Fear-potentiated startle can be reduced by anti-anxiety drugs. Examples of affective modulation of the startle reflex are given in chapter 15.

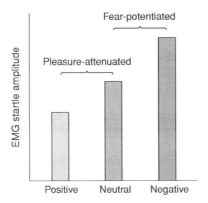

Figure 9.8 Affective startle modulation effects. Compared with the EMG response during the viewing of neutral slides, the response during the viewing of unpleasant slides is increased ('fear-potentiated startle'), while during the viewing of pleasant slides it is reduced ('pleasure-attenuated startle').

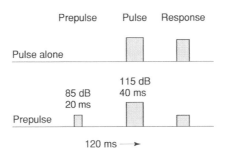

Figure 9.9 The procedure for measuring prepulse inhibition (PPI) of the human startle reflex. Two types of trials are used: (1) pulse-alone trials, consisting of a 115 dB(A) startle-eliciting stimulus; and (2) prepulse trials, consisting of a weaker (85 dB(A)) stimulus just 120 ms before the startle-eliciting stimulus. As shown, the startle reflex on prepulse trials is reduced compared with the pulse-alone trials. This percentage reduction is the main measure of PPI.

Modulation by prestimulation: prepulse inhibition (PPI)

Eye-blink EMG is also widely used to measure a quite different neuropsychological process, namely prepulse inhibition (PPI) of the startle reflex. PPI consists in the reduction in amplitude of the startle reflex when the startle-eliciting stimulus (i.e., the pulse) is preceded by a weak stimulus (i.e., the prepulse) at short lead intervals (<500 ms) – in fact, maximum PPI is observed at a lead interval of 120 ms (Graham, 1975) (figure 9.9).

PPI provides a simple operational measure of 'sensorimotor gating', which is thought to serve to prevent the interruption of ongoing perceptual and early sensory analysis (i.e., pre-attentive stimulus processing) during the time required to analyse new stimuli.

The general idea is that, at the start of stimulus processing, attentional resources are withdrawn from subsequent stimuli for a very brief period. If this protective process did not exist then the information-processing system would become overwhelmed with stimuli and be unable to extract important information from stimuli that bombard the senses (chapter 16 considers the role of this process in schizophrenia). PPI has attracted considerable research attention due to the fact that it is impaired across a range of clinical conditions (e.g., obsessive-compulsive disorder, Tourette syndrome and Huntington's disease), but most notably in schizophrenia (e.g., Braff et al., 1978; Grillon et al., 1992; Swerdlow & Geyer, 1998): it is thought to reflect a fundamental early stage of information processing.

In order to measure PPI, two types of trials are presented: (a) pulse-alone trial (e.g., a 100 dB noise); and (b) prepulse (85 dB noise) + pulse (100 dB noise) trial, separated by the lead interval (120 ms). If the magnitude of the EMG response for the pulse-alone trial is 100 units, and for the prepulse plus pulse trial, 50 units, then PPI would be 50 per cent (i.e., a 50 per cent reduction in EMG activity when the prepulse is presented). An average for the two trial types is taken (10 presentations for each trial type are enough is obtain a reliable response). As with affective modulation, the acoustic stimulus is presented over headphones and the startle reflex is measured from the orbicularis oculi eye-blink muscle.

The same equipment can be used for affective modulation and PPI, and it is even possible to combine the two procedures into a single experimental session to test whether the induction of emotion influences the extent of PPI (Hawk & Cook, 2000).

As presented in Part III ('Applications'), PPI is a widely used measure of a fundamental neuropsychological process implicated in clinical psychosis and in vulnerability to psychotic breakdown in the normal population. It is also easily measured in lower animals, allowing pharmacological, genetic and neurophysiological studies to be performed, the results of which are of direct relevance to human beings. One of its chief attractions is that it can be easily measured with the appropriate equipment, and it is a very robust phenomenon.

The financial cost of EMG equipment is relatively modest, although a high degree of technical competence is required to record, analyse and interpret the raw signals. Many laboratories use purpose-built EMG systems, which reduce demands in technical competence and standardize procedures across different laboratories.

> **ASK YOURSELF**
> Why has the human eye-blink reflex been the topic of so much research interest?

The ocular system: eye movements

The eyes are part of the brain, therefore eye movements (controlled by the oculomotor system) provide a unique way to examine brain functioning. Dysfunction in eye movements may indicate pathology in the circuits controlling them; but also it may reflect psychological processes, such as inattentiveness. Thus, eye movements are widely used in neurology and in psychology/psychiatry – they have been extensively used to study the neuropsychology of schizophrenia (see chapter 16).

Anatomy of the eye

The eye is made up of a number of structures. The *iris* is disc-shaped and pigmented with a central aperture (i.e., the pupil). The function of the iris is to control the amount of light reaching the retina, which is achieved by changing the size of the pupil: the amount of stimulation of the retina is thus proportional to the size of the pupil. The iris is controlled by two muscles: (a) the *sphincter pupillae* serves to close the pupil by expanding the iris (it is controlled by the parasympathetic nervous system; see chapter 3); and (b) the *dilator pupillae* controls the size of the pupil by contraction, resulting in the retraction of the iris and the enlargement of the pupil (it is controlled by the sympathetic nervous system) (Stern & Dunham, 1990).

Eyelid closure

The seventh cranial nerve innervates the *orbicularis oculi* muscle (this muscle controls eyelid closure and it is routinely measured in eye-blink modulation studies; see above). Three types of eye blink can be measured: (a) the startle reflex (see above); (b) voluntary blinks (e.g., by instructions); and (3) periodic blinks (partly sensitive to environmental factors, such as humidity). These different types of blinks can be differentiated in terms of the waveform produced. For example, voluntary blinks tend to have larger amplitudes than other blinks, with the eyelid closing further and taking longer. There are several ways to measure eye blinks. Early studies used still-frame motion film for recording the image of the eye; video replaced this ingenious if cumbersome technology. Video technology allows the electronic identification of the sclera, iris and pupil: when the pupil is illuminated with light, reflection from the light is brighter from the iris. Other methods include *electro-oculographic* (EOG) procedures consisting of electrodes recording the position of the eye (this does not record muscle potential, as in the case of EMG, but rather the changes in the difference in electrical potential between the cornea and retina as the eye rotates); and special contact lenses. This discussion focuses on infrared technology, which tracks the position of the eye and eyelid closure by the reflection of infrared light.

Types of eye movements

There are a number of different eye movements, and a number of corresponding eye movement experimental paradigms. *Saccadic* movements involve rapid jumps of the eyes from one point to another; they serve the purpose of placing the image of objects on the fovea (see chapter 3). During the saccade the ability to take in information is markedly attenuated (i.e., *saccadic suppression*). The refractory period (i.e., minimum delay between the end of one saccade and the start of another is about 50 ms). A second type of movement is *smooth pursuit* (or slow tracking) where the eyes follow a moving target. Pursuit allows for stabilization of a moving image on the retina.

There are a variety of ways to measure eye movements. For example, infrared oculography exploits the reflection characteristics of infrared light when projected onto the eye (see figure 9.10). A head apparatus is worn which contains sensors that detect reflected infrared rays from the eye, hence providing an accurate measurement of eye position.

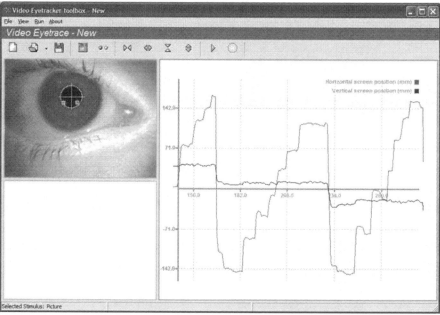

Figure 9.10 Eye movement equipment. Accurate measurement of eye position may be obtained with infrared oculography, which measures the reflection characteristics of infrared light when projected onto the eye. A comfortable head apparatus, as shown, is worn, which contains sensors that detect reflected infrared rays from the eye, and the delivery and recording of infrared information is controlled by a portable eye-tracker (which is linked to a PC for data storage and statistical analysis). (Courtesy of Cambridge Research Systems.)

| Fixation trial | Saccadic trial | Correct response |

Figure 9.11 Saccadic fixation/movement. A saccadic fixation trial begins with the presentation of a central stimulus, which then moves to a peripheral location. The task of the participant is to follow the target as accurately as possible.

Performance is averaged over a series of trials to increase reliability of measurement. Eye movement performance may be scored purely qualitatively or quantitatively. For example, raters can indicate on a scale how well the participant managed to follow the target, providing a qualitative assessment of performance; however, it is now more common to use quantitative measures involving specially designed computer programs that score the main parameters (e.g., accuracy and latency of response).

Eye movements provide information about perceptual, cognitive and affective processes, and they are being widely used in biomedical research, to study psychological processes (e.g., visual perception) and in applied areas of psychology (e.g., car driving). In addition to neuropsychology of psychiatric conditions (e.g., schizophrenia), eye movements are being used to test the effectiveness of different drugs (i.e., the effectiveness of drugs to normalize dysfunctional eye movements and thus normalize the underlying neurological and psychological deficits that gave rise to dysfunctional eye movements in the first place).

The following section focuses on three types of eye movement that have been widely used in experimental and clinical research: (a) *saccadic fixation*, (b) *smooth pursuit* and (c) *antisaccade*.

Saccadic fixation/movement

Visual fixation serves the function of focusing gaze on a stationary object. A saccadic fixation trial begins with the presentation of a central stimulus on which the experimental participant fixates, and then the stimulus moves abruptly to a peripheral location (figure 9.11). The participant's task is to shift gaze from current position to the new position. This is an easy task, and is often used as the control condition in the assessment of other types of eye movements.

Smooth-pursuit eye movement (SPEM)

Smooth-pursuit eye movements (SPEM) serve the function of maintaining an image of a slowly moving object on the fovea (figure 9.12). A pendulum set in motion was originally used to measure SPEM; now it is usual to use computer presentation of a stimulus that mimics the path of a moving pendulum (this permits tighter control over frequency of oscillation and waveform generated).

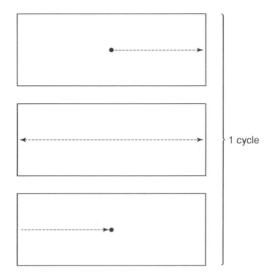

1 cycle

Figure 9.12 SPEM stimuli. Smooth pursuit eye movements (SPEM) consists of a target, moving back and forth at a regular rate, which the participant is required to track as accurately as possible.

Antisaccade eye movement

An antisaccade trial begins with the presentation of a central stimulus, and then the stimulus moves abruptly to a peripheral location. But, unlike the fixation (or saccade) task, the participant's task is to move the eye in the mirror in the *opposite* direction to the target movement (i.e., if the target moves left by x visual angle, then participants should move their eyes right by the same visual angle). The task is theoretically interesting because it requires at least two psychological processes: (a) the inhibition of the prepotent saccadic response (human beings have a natural tendency to follow any moving stimulus); and (b) redirection of gaze to the mirror position of the target stimulus (figure 9.13).

Performance on the antisaccade task is measured in terms of (a) *error rate* (i.e., failing to initiate prepotent response); and (b) *accuracy* of correct response (i.e., the degree to which the eyes mirrored the target movement in the opposite direction).

Both SPEM and antisaccade tasks have been extensively used to study the neuropsychological basis of schizophrenia; for example, schizophrenia patients show a high error rate on the antisaccade task, suggesting that they have particular problems in inhibiting stimuli. These tasks are also being used to measure the integrity of neural circuits as well as serving as a measure of psychological functions, such as attention, working memory and response inhibition.

The technical requirements of presenting stimuli, recording eye movement position and analysing data are much greater than those of skin conductance activity and cardiac activity, and considerable training and skill are required in interpreting raw data (however, the cost of the equipment is relatively

ASK YOURSELF
Why do eye movements contain so much information of psychological interest?

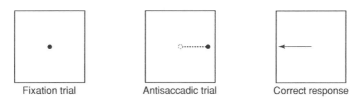

Fixation trial   Antisaccadic trial   Correct response

Figure 9.13 Antisaccade eye movement. An antisaccade trial begins with the presentation of a central stimulus, and then the stimulus moves abruptly to a peripheral location. The task of the participant is to move the eyes in the *opposite* direction to the target movement. This task measures: (1) the inhibition of the prepotent saccadic response; and (2) redirection of gaze to the mirror position of the target stimulus.

modest). For these reasons, eye movement research is typically found in dedicated psychophysiology laboratories.

Eye-blink classical conditioning

This final section focuses on a widely used experimental paradigm in psychophysiology, namely, classical conditioning of the eye-blink reflex. This paradigm relies upon the theoretical principles of classical conditioning developed by Pavlov (see chapter 7). Eyeblink conditioning is widely used for five main reasons: (a) it is theoretically simple and well understood; (b) it is easy to measure; (c) its neural basis is well delineated; (d) it can be used to test hypotheses in many clinical conditions; and (e) it lends itself to research in non-human animals, which can be used experimentally to test hypotheses concerning its neural basis.

There is a large literature pertaining to the rabbit *nictitating membrane response* (NMR); this may be conditioned to an initially neutral stimulus (e.g., tone or light) by repeated pairings of the conditioned stimulus (CS) with a corneal air puff, or mild shock (i.e., unconditioned stimulus; UCS). After repeated pairings, a conditioned response (CR) develops, consisting of an anticipatory response (eyelid closure) to the UCS: the eyelid closes upon presentation of the CS, but before the delivery of the UCS. As in other forms of classical conditioning, repeated presentation of CS without the UCS leads to extinction of the CR (see chapter 7).

Several CS–UCS temporal associations may be manipulated. In *delayed conditioning*, the CS remains on at least until the onset of the UCS and may terminate with the UCS offset. In *trace conditioning* there is a temporal separation between the offset of the CS and onset of the UCS. The duration between the onset of the CS and the onset of the US is the *interstimulus interval* (ISI). Different CR profiles (topographies) are found with these different ISIs; and, importantly, these CR profiles have been mapped onto the activity profiles of neurons in brain areas (specifically, the hippocampus and cerebellum). It has been found that hippocampal lesions do not affect the timing of NMRs using delayed conditioning, but they can be shown to disrupt NMRs using trace conditioning. In contrast, lesions of the cerebellum abolish NMRs. Therefore, the cerebellum may be necessary for classical conditioning, while the hippocampus serves to modulate the conditioned response.

Eye-blink conditioning can be used to test hippocampal and cerebellum integrity in human beings; it is also being used to test hypotheses concerning the involvement of these structures in a variety of clinical conditions (such as autism). Eye-blink conditioning is one of the most widely used experimental paradigms in basic learning studies, psychopharmacology and neurodegenerative diseases (e.g., Alzheimer's disease).

Human eye-blink conditioning

Eye-blink conditioning has been extensively used in human studies (e.g., to test visual processing in blindsight patients; see chapter 8). How are eye blinks measured in human beings? Systems are now available that are reasonably inexpensive and non-intrusive. For example, a headset may be used which employs a low-power infrared photobeam (to measure the amount of light reflected as the eyelid closes; the UCR/CR) and a small-diameter air-puff tube mounted in one lens of an ordinary pair of sunglasses. This set-up is lightweight and comfortable for the participant, delivering low-pressure air puffs (this is the UCS). The CS comprises white noise presented over headphones.

Human eye-blink conditioning has long been used to study anxiety, motivation and personality. Now it is being applied to the study of clinical conditions such as Alzheimer's disease, autism and obsessive-compulsive disorder. Such research is made possible by similarities in this form of conditioning across the animal world. Conditioning experiments can help us understand brain structure and processes and, in return, the study of brain structure and processes helps further our understanding of classical conditioning. To take one example, it is known that classical conditioning becomes sluggish with age, and it is significantly impaired in Alzheimer's disease. This impairment is due to depletion of the neurotransmitter acetylcholine. Now, in rabbits and human beings, acetylcholine impairment may be experimentally caused by the drug scopolamine (which blocks acetylcholine), and it is found that this drug leads to impaired eye-blink conditioning. Pharmaceutical companies are now testing cognition-enhancing drugs in non-human animals using classical conditioning; and once these are developed in the laboratory they can then be tested on human beings using eye-blink conditioning. By this route new insights into brain functioning are possible; and pharmacological treatments are being developed which have direct benefits to the large number of brain diseases that afflict human beings.

ASK YOURSELF
What psychological insights can be gained in the blink of an eye?

Psychoneuroimmunological Assays

Psychoneuroimmunology is concerned with the interaction of psychological, neurological and immunological processes. Although this is a separate specialized research field, *psychoneuroimmunology* assays (i.e., chemical analysis) are used in psychophysiology. As shown in chapter 6, a number of psychological factors are associated with the functioning of the immune system. This section discusses how such assays can be used to examine the effects of various types of experimental manipulation on one important component of the immune system, namely, secretory immunoglobulin A (sIgA; Phalipon et al., 2002; Robert-Guroff, 2000). sIgA is the dominant immunoglobulin that coats mucosal surfaces (e.g., respiratory system, intestines, mouth). It is the first line of defence against pathogenic microorganisms, viruses and bacteria. A lower than normal level of sIgA is a risk factor for upper respiratory infections.

Assay procedures

sIgA can be easily measured from a sample of saliva. The procedure entails the collection of saliva samples over a period of time (e.g., every 15 minutes for 2 hours). Samples are taken with the use of *salivettes*, which contain a cotton dental swab. Participants are required first to empty their mouths of saliva and then to place a salivette roll under their tongue; then they allow the saliva to collect under their tongue without swallowing. After several minutes the swab is removed, placed in the salivette, and then stored at low temperature ($-20\,^{\circ}$C) until analysis. Before analysis the sample is thawed and the saliva recovered by centrifugation (spinning) at 10,000 rpm for 10 minutes. The concentration of sIgA is then calculated (Clow et al., 2003). (The precise procedure for calculating sIgA is described by Carroll et al., 1996. The *secretion rate* of sIgA is calculated: (*concentration* $\times$ *volume*)/*n* (where *n* is the number of minutes over which the sample has been collected – this calculation produces micrograms per minute; μm/minute.)

As seen in chapter 6, stress (e.g., examinations) and high emotionality (induced or personality-based) reduce levels of sIgA. Now, it has been shown that the experimental stimulation of the cortex can also modulate sIgA levels. Stimulating the left and right temporo-parieto-occipital cortex, using transcranial magnetic stimulation (TMS; see chapter 8), leads to different effects on immune system functioning, suggesting some degree of lateralized cortical regulatory influence. Specifically, stimulation of the left hemisphere increases immune system functioning; stimulation of the right hemisphere suppresses functioning – these findings are consistent with lesion studies in rats, where left hemisphere ablation impairs functioning, whole right hemisphere lesions improve functioning (Clow et al., 2003). In human beings, extreme right hemisphere activation (as measured by EEG; see chapter 10) has occurred with significantly lower levels of natural killer cell activity than in those with extreme left hemisphere activation (Kang et al., 1991).

Clow et al. (2003) used TMS to stimulate the right and left hemispheres on different days to examine the influence of hemispheric activation and sIgA functioning: a short period of TMS led to immediate and short-lived effects on the secretion of sIgA; and, in addition, TMS to the left cortex led to up-regulation of the secretion of sIgA. This study shows that sometimes in psychophysiology the dependent (immune system reaction) and independent (TMS) can be physiological variables.

> **ASK YOURSELF**
> What does salivary analysis reveal about psychological reactions?

▢ Conclusion

Psychophysiology is a large part of biological psychology and psychiatry, and encompasses electrophysiology (EEG/ERP) and neuroimaging techniques – as these topics are detailed, they are considered separately in the next chapter. Traditionally, psychophysiology has been associated with measurement of peripheral functions (save EEG) to index physiological processes and events, but this focus was forced more by available technology than theoretical rationale. As seen in this chapter, psychophysiological measures of peripheral systems remain an important technique in psychology, and are especially useful in the study of psychiatric patients, where central processes can be indexed by convenient, inexpensive and well-tolerated procedures. For example, modulation of the eye-blink startle response is known to be sensitive to: emotional state, attentional processes, novelty, distracting stimuli, the central neurotransmitter systems (e.g., dopamine) and clinical symptoms – importantly, this modulation can also be used to assess responses to therapeutic interventions. One major problem, however, with many peripheral measures (especially EDA and HR) is their relative non-specificity; and often it is not clear exactly what is being measured. The application of rigorous theory and appropriate experimental design can reduce these uncertainties, and provide the biological researcher with a toolkit of sensitive procedures powerful enough to address a range of important research problems.

Learning Questions

1. In what ways is the usefulness of psychophysiological tests dependent on basic measurement issues?
2. Why are electrodermal and cardiac measures so commonly used in classical conditioning studies?
3. How are psychophysiological procedures used to differentiate between truth and lies?
4. How has modulation of the eye-blink reflex been used to study emotional and cognitive processes?
5. If you wanted to measure the effects of acute stress on immune functioning, what measures might you use?

NOTES

1 In all science there is the problem of differentiating between *theoretical* constructs and *operational* (measurement) constructs. For a theory to be translated into a form that lends itself to empirical study, theoretical constructs need to be translated into operational constructs. This theoretical-to-operational construct process is problematic, and it is usually the case that the operational constructs have a number of hypotheses attached to them. If these operational hypotheses are not justified, then the construct may not be adequate for testing, fairly and adequately, the theoretical construct of interest. A good example in psychophysiology is the theoretical construct of arousal: this has been measured by a large number of physiological processes (e.g., skin conductance and heart rate), many of which are not highly interrelated. For this reason Thayer (1989) produced a self-report instrument for the measurement of different states of arousal.

2 There is a difference between amplitude and magnitude. Both terms refer to the maximum (peak) EDA reached, but magnitude is computed from *all* trials (including those with a zero

response), and amplitude is measured only from trials with a non-zero response (i.e., a 'response' to the stimulus, as defined by the experimenter). Sometimes probability of response is calculated to measure the extent of non-zero responses. (Formally, magnitude = amplitude × response probability.)

FURTHER READING

Cacioppo, J. T., Tassinary, L. G. & Berntson, G. (eds) (2000). *Handbook of Psychophysiology.* Cambridge: Cambridge University Press.

Ekman, P. (2001). *Telling Lies: Clues to Deceit in the Marketplace, Politics and Marriage.* London: Norton.

Hugdahl, K. (2001). *Psychophysiology: The Mind–Body Perspective.* Cambridge, MA: Harvard University Press.

chapter 10
Neuroimaging

Learning Objectives

To be able to:

1. Outline the rationale and techniques used in electrophysiology (e.g., EEG/ERPs).
2. Describe the different types of neuroimaging methods and explain their applications.
3. Differentiate between structural and functional neuroimaging.
3. Contrast the temporal and spatial resolutions of electrophysiological and neuroimaging methods.
5. Outline the limitations of neuroimaging as a means of relating function to structure.

Chapter 9 discussed how the field of psychophysiology offers a number of valuable tools with which to answer some important questions in psychology; but there are some questions that can only be answered by direct measurement of the brain.[1] This chapter turns our attention to techniques designed to measure brain activity, either from surface (scalp) recording (electrophysiology) or from signals emitted deep within the brain. Electrophysiological techniques are discussed first as these may be seen as a precursor to the more sophisticated neuroimaging techniques developed over the past 20 years, which have revolutionized the physiological study of the living brain. This discussion focuses on the description of these techniques; Part III ('Applications') provides examples of their use in studying normal and abnormal behaviour.

Electrophysiology

Electrophysiology is concerned with measuring and analysing electrical signals from the brain. As discussed in chapter 3, the brain is an electrochemical system; brain processing is associated with the generation of electricity and thus magnetic fields. Electrophysiology provides unique insights into the functioning of the brain, as it is able to record neural activity in the range of milliseconds. In comparison, neuroimaging techniques have relatively poor temporal resolution; they are only sensitive to signals spanning seconds, not milliseconds: much of psychological interest takes place in terms of milliseconds, not seconds.

Electroencephalogram (EEG)

Electrical activity in the brain can be recorded by electrodes placed on the scalp, which collectively comprise the *electroencephalogram* (EEG) – this was first demonstrated by Berger in the 1920s. EEG is now widely used in experimental psychology, neurophysiology and neurology, and is a standard diagnostic tool for such neurological conditions as epilepsy.

The EEG is sensitive to ion currents through nerve-cell membranes (see chapter 4); more specifically, the source of the EEG is the summation of dendritic inputs within the cell, which integrates over time as well as over inputs. The electrical charge outside the dendrite causes current to flow through the surrounding media (brain tissue, cerebrospinal fluid, skull and skin). When it reaches the scalp, the current alters the electrical potentials on the scalp due to the electrical resistance of the tissue: this change in resistance is recorded as the EEG. It is now possible to process EEG signals in terms of *source location*: although the EEG signal is recorded from the scalp, analytical programmes have been developed which allow the experimenter to infer the *source generator* – that is, where in the brain the signals were generated. Such source location programmes allow an activation map of the brain to be produced, which indirectly images cortical and subcortical activity.

International 10–20 System

The EEG is measured by the placement of electrodes on the scalp. The standard method for electrode placement is the International 10–20 System (Jasper, 1958). The electrode locations are denoted with reference to the lobes: F = frontal, P = parietal, C = central, T = temporal, and O = occipital. As shown in figure 10.1, odd numbers refer to the left hemisphere, even numbers to the right hemisphere (Z refers to the midline).

EEG frequencies

The EEG is composed of a mix of electrical frequencies. These frequency ranges are consistent with the popular view of EEG activity as related to cortical arousal, varying from sleep to high activity (figure 10.2).

Alpha

Alpha activity (8–12 Hz) is seen in most people when they are awake and relaxed. Closing the eyes and relaxing produce an increase in this frequency range. The reduction in alpha activity (alpha blocking) has been associated with sensory stimulation and mental activity.

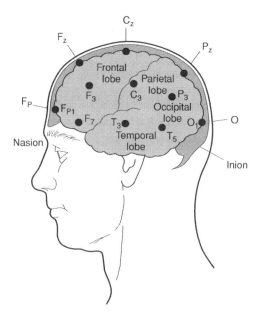

Figure 10.1 International 10–20 electrode system. The '10–20 system', used in the placement of EEG electrodes, derives its name from the relationship between the location of electrodes and area of cortex. Each electrode site has a letter, which denotes the lobe, and a number or another letter, which denotes the hemisphere. The letters F, T, C, P and O stand for frontal, temporal, central, parietal and occipital, respectively – there is no 'central lobe' in the brain, but this is included for identification. Even numbers refer to the right hemisphere; odd numbers to the left hemisphere; and Z refers to an electrode placed on the midline. The '10–20' refers to interelectrode distances (some 10%, some 20%).

Name	Frequency (Hz)
Delta	0.5–3.5
Theta	4–7.5
Alpha	8–12
Slow beta	13–19
Fast beta	20–30
Gamma	30–50
Sleep spindles	12–14

(a)

Delta less than 4 cps	Theta 4–8 cps	Alpha 8–13 cps	Beta more than 13 cps
Asleep	Drowsy	Relaxed	Alert

(b)

Figure 10.2 Table of different EEG frequencies. The EEG is composed of a number of different frequencies, defined (a) and shown (b).

Beta

Beta activity (13–50 Hz), which is also divided into slow (13–19 Hz) and fast (20–30 Hz) beta and gamma (30–50 Hz) waves. Beta is generally used to refer to the 20–30 Hz range, which is associated with tactile, auditory and emotional activation.

Theta

Theta activity (4–8 Hz) is associated with the absence of pleasure, and it is also associated with a variety of processes such as REM (rapid eye movement), sleep, problem-solving, hypnosis. However, it is fair to say that the precise nature of theta is not well understood.

Delta

Delta activity (0.5–4 Hz), consisting of large, slow waves, is associated with sleep and is the predominant frequency of the human newborn during the first two years of life. However, it is also evident in adult human beings.

EEG is prone to a number of *artefacts*, which can corrupt the signal from the electrode channels. There are both biological and technical sources of artefacts. Biological artefacts can result from: (a) the electrocardiogram (ECG; i.e., the heartbeat); (b) the electromyogram (EMG), generated by muscles in the vicinity of the electrodes; and (c) the electrooculogram (EOG), resulting from the movement of the eyes. Technical artefacts have a variety of causes (e.g., 50 Hz mains frequency; equipment is usually shielded from these extraneous sources); movement of the electrodes; and various forms of equipment imperfections (e.g., loose connections to amplifiers). Filtering of low and high frequencies is often used to eliminate irrelevant and extraneous influences. Guidelines for the design and execution of EEG experiments have been developed to standardize research across laboratories (e.g., Picton et al., 2000).

Before turning to EEG responses that are tied to specific psychological events (i.e., evoked potentials), one exciting clinical development of EEG technology is presented.

'Locked-in' patients

Imagine you awoke one morning and once fully conscious became aware that you were totally paralysed: you could not move your hands, legs, mouth, or even your eyes. This rather terrifying prospect is the reality of 'locked-in' patients: the mind is locked into the body and has lost all control. This condition is sometimes a result of a stroke or sclerosis of the motor neurons of the somatic motor system. Worse still, it is not obvious to clinicians whether the patient is conscious or is in a vegetative state; but the patient can hear them talking (the subjective experience of this state is described by Bauby, 1997). Well, how might it be possible to communicate with these patients? Remember, they cannot talk, move their hands or fingers to write, or even blink to develop some communication code; indeed, how is it possible to know that they are even conscious?

In a remarkable study, neural self-regulation of electrophysiological potentials was developed as a means of communication (Birbaumer et al., 1999). Slow cortical potentials (SCPs) were used, and operant training brought these waves under conscious control; this control allows patients to operate a spelling device that drives a cursor on a video screen, allowing patients to select letters of the alphabet. Self-regulation of neural responses is learned by telling patients to keep a ball on the computer screen in one of two boxes. At first this is a difficult task, but people develop strategies (e.g., by relaxing, or focusing) to influence their brainwaves. Once certain aspects of their brainwaves are under conscious control, then these waves can be linked to a cursor that allows the patient to write.

Neural self-regulation is easily achieved in most people, and has been used for a variety of purposes: stress reduction, control of hyperactivity in children, control of cortical states in schizophrenia patients, and control of states to achieve optimal performance in highly accomplished musicians. In clinical conditions this form of brain control is an important, although still relatively new, area of behavioural medicine – significantly it circumvents the side-effects of drug treatment. (A related field is 'biofeedback', which is typically concerned with relaxation techniques to regulate autonomonic nervous system functions, such as heart rate.)

> **ASK YOURSELF**
> How might EEG waves be used in 'mind control' technology?

Event-related potentials (ERPs)

Ever since Berger's observation of scalp recording of EEG, there has been interest in the relationship between EEG recordings and psychological processes. Event-related potentials (ERPs) are EEG responses that are triggered by events: these responses provide valuable data concerning the temporal processing of psychological events. Because the ERP signal is weak compared with the raw EEG signal, it is necessary to increase the signal-to-noise ratio by averaging over a large number of trials.

An ERP contains a number of positive and negative peaks, which are described in terms of their polarity and latency (these are often called *components* of the ERP). For example, a P300 refers to a positive peak with a modal latency of 300 ms.[2] Early responses are assumed to be mediated by sensory analysis, while later peaks are assumed to have more psychological content (e.g., attention and analysis). It is commonly assumed that most scalp ERPs are the summation of the postsynaptic potentials of a large number of neurons that are activated or inhibited synchronously. Different experimental conditions produce different types of responses, emphasizing different parameters. Differences can then be shown between responses taken during a control task and those taken during an experimental task. Figure 10.3 shows the components of a typical waveform elicited by an auditory, infrequent stimulus.

The ERP wave is composed of a number of different 'components', each of which is thought to reflect a different physiological and psychological process.

Sensory potentials

Presentation of a stimulus elicits a very early component (less than 100 ms), and this component is said to be obligatory, resulting from stimulation of the sensory nerves. This

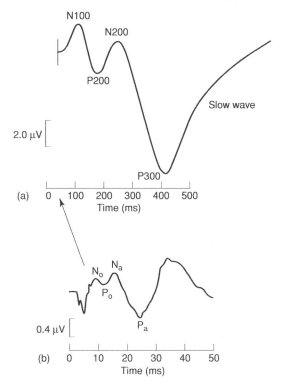

Figure 10.3   ERP wave components.

component is influenced by such stimulus parameters as intensity and frequency, but it seems insensitive to psychological factors, and for this reason is not typically analysed in psychological studies. Obligatory (also called *exogenous*) responses may be contrasted with cognitive (also called *endogenous*) responses.

The early negatives

N100

When a comparison is made of attended and non-attended stimuli, attended stimuli are associated with more negative ERP between 100 and 200 ms. This is sometimes called the *processing negativity*, thought to reflect the selection of information from a particular perceptual channel.

N200

This component is sensitive to deviant (rare) stimuli, thought to reflect a mismatch detector, hence this component is sometimes called *mismatch negativity*. It is also associated with the orienting reflex because it is involved in the automatic processing of surprising (rare) events.

The late cognitive components

P300. Unexpected events that are relevant to the task being performed elicit a large P300. This component may reflect the updating of information in working memory: unexpected and relevant events should lead to an updating of current memory schemas in order to construct an accurate representation of the external world. Thus, it is involved in stimulus encoding.

N400

This component is involved in semantic processing. Its magnitude increases with the incongruous nature of a sentence (e.g., 'he took a sip from the cup'; 'he took a sip from the river', 'he took a sip from the bus'). A large component is also observed in sentence verification paradigms, when either a false affirmative (e.g., a cat is a plant) or true negative (e.g., a cat is not a plant) is given.

As an example of the use of ERP, consider the study by Schott et al. (2003). They addressed the hypothesis that perceptual priming and explicit memory have distinct neural correlates at *encoding*. ERPs were recorded while participants studied words, and then these ERPs were sorted according to (a) whether these words were later used as completions to three-letter word stems in an intentional memory test, and (b) whether the words used for completions were remembered from the study list. Study trials from which words were later used and not remembered (i.e., 'primed trials') and study trials from which words were later used and remembered (i.e., 'remembered trials') were compared with study trials from which words were later not used (i.e., 'forgotten trials'). Primed trials involved an early (200–450 ms) negativity over the parietal cortex; remembered trials involved a late (900–1200 ms) positivity over the right frontal cortex. Such ERP data suggest that processing at *encoding* has an important effect on later retrieval performance. It would be difficult to collect such data in any other way than ERP (save MEG; see below).

Lie detection

As an example of the use of ERPs consider the detection of lies. It is widely known that the conventional polygraph (lie-detector) test, which relies upon increased peripheral nervous system arousal, can be cheated by a variety of means; also it is prone to false positives: that is, identifying innocent people as liars. Could ERPs be used to detect the cognitive processing of guilty (crime-related) knowledge?

In late components (P300, P400), classification of stimuli may be used to detect lies in a way that is not easy to manipulate. In the *guilty knowledge* form of the lie detector test, it is assumed that knowledge of the crime scene (e.g., colour of wallpaper) is classified as relevant (i.e., known) rather than irrelevant (i.e., unknown). Suspects could be presented with three types of stimuli: (a) words related to the crime (*probe stimuli*); (b) words unrelated to the crime and unknown to the suspect (*irrelevant stimuli*); and (c) words unrelated to the crime but known to the suspect (*target stimuli*). The suspect's task is simply to count the target stimuli. The crucial question is whether the suspect categorizes the probe stimuli (guilty knowledge items) as irrelevant (indicating no knowledge) or as target stimuli (indicating knowledge). ERP patterns for these three types of stimuli are then compared in order to make an inference of innocence or guilt. Even if the suspect could distort the patterns of these ERPs, it is difficult to see how guilty knowledge could be deliberately classified as 'irrelevant' because ERPs occur before conscious awareness and cognitive reactions are possible – at best, the suspect could attempt to distort all ERP responses (e.g., by covertly repeating a word) to confuse the picture: but why would an innocent person attempt this deceit?

P300 has been found to provide a good (indirect) measure of recognition memory (i.e., recognizing a stimulus as one that has been previously presented in an experiment, or, by extension, seen at a crime scene), providing a way of differentiating learned (known) from unlearned (unknown) stimuli (van Hooff, Brunia & Allen, 1996). It is also useful in detecting simulated amnesia in low and high psychopathy participants (Miller & Rosenfeld, 2004).

The N400 component is elicited by words that complete sentences falsely. Boaz et al. (1991) examined the utility of the P400 in differentiating those who had knowledge of a crime from those who did not. Experimental participants viewed a videotape of either an enacted burglary ('guilty' condition) or scenes from the city of New York ('innocent' condition). Then they read crime-relevant phrases that had true or false completions, but they did not have to make any response. The results showed that 78 per cent of participants were correctly classified as guilty or innocent. The authors noted that ERPs may be useful in real-life lie-detection procedures (also see Neshige et al., 1991).

EEG and ERP research requires a high level of technical competence as well as a considerable financial outlay in terms of purchase and running costs. Despite the fact the EEG was developed many years ago it is very widely used in the study of the brain, having vital roles to play in experimental research and clinical diagnosis. Increasingly it is being used alongside more recent neuroimaging techniques to provide the high temporal resolution to complement the high spatial resolution of neuroimaging techniques.

> **ASK YOURSELF**
> Are some ERP components impossible to control consciously?

⬚ Magnetoencephalogram (MEG)

Magnetoencephalogram (MEG) is a recent technological innovation that measures the magnetic fields produced by electrical brain activity. By measuring the magnetic field evoked when a specific sensory stimulus is presented, a map of the functional organization of the brain can be deduced. For example, a word might be presented, and this would go first to the visual cortex, then to the frontal cortex for analysis, and then to the motor cortex. These temporal processing stages would be picked up by an MEG. Therefore, the main advantage of the MEG over the EEG is its ability to produce a functional map of brain activation; like EEG, but unlike other neuroimaging techniques, MEG has impressive temporal resolution (in terms of milliseconds). Thus, the spread of activation over the brain's surface can be mapped from initial stimulus onset to final response.

The sources of MEG are, for the most part, the intracellular (intradendritic) currents resulting from postsynaptic potentials (see chapter 4). The main difference is that, while

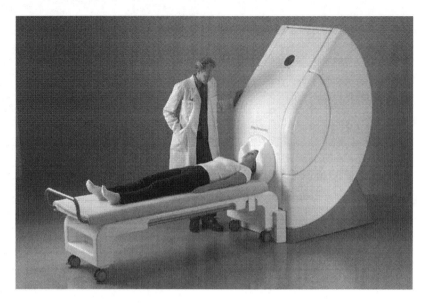

Figure 10.4 A typical magnetoencephalogram (MEG) suite. (Courtesy Neuromag Ltd.)

the head is nearly transparent for magnetic fields, EEG measurements are influenced by such factor as variations in skull resistances. For this reason, MEG is a very sensitive technique.

The technology underlying MEG is complex and the equipment is very expensive. A MEG suite is shown in figure 10.4. The head coils positioned over the participant's head must be housed in a purpose-built shielded room; the coils are bathed in liquid helium to superconducting temperatures of $-269°C$ (this allows the cerebral magnetic field to induce a current in the coils, which in turn induces a magnetic field in a special device called a superconducting quantum interference device, or SQUID; Cohen, 1972). Even a single quantum of magnetic energy is sufficient to induce a measurable current in the coils, thereby making this instrument the most sensitive device known to man. The system contains 37 QUIDSs, or recording channels, which allow for the determination of the spatial distribution of the magnetic field. The raw data are analysed to determine the source of the magnetic field. MEG's time resolution is an impressive 1 ms, and its spatial resolution is 1 mm.

MEG is especially useful for the functional imaging of the brain where a neurological disorder is suspected but there is no evidence of anatomical abnormality. For the purposes of neurosurgery, MEG is used to map the somatosensory and motor cortices (this is necessary in order to minimize damage to sensory and motor systems). It can also be used to detect activation in subcortical structures, although the resolution of MEG decreases as the source of the MEG signal is deeper in the brain.

ASK YOURSELF
Why has there been so much interest in MEG technology?

Neuroimaging

The application of brain imaging to the study of normal and abnormal processes has revolutionized research in biological psychology. Neuroimaging techniques allow researchers to identify structure and function and to examine how structure and function co-vary with variations in genetics, personality, emotion, cognition and psychiatric state. Importantly, they also provide a powerful technique with which to study the effects of experimental manipulations.

Neuroimaging divides into two main areas: (a) *anatomical imaging* and (b) *functional imaging*. Anatomical imaging (also called *structural* or *volumetric analysis*) is concerned with measuring: (1) the total brain size; and (2) specific regions/sites in the brain. These structures can then be correlated with psychological performance (e.g., general intelligence and whole brain volume). In clinical settings, anatomical imaging is used to detect abnormalities (e.g., tumours). In contrast, functional imaging is concerning with measuring brain activation *during* the performance of a psychological task – this type of neuroimaging is of most interest to biological psychologists. A good general summary of neuroimaging is given by Sharma and Chitnis (2000; the book discusses neuroimaging in the context of the neuropsychological study of schizophrenia).

Three main types of neuroimaging are presented in the order of their development: (a) *computerized tomography* (CT), (b) *positron emission tomography* (PET) and (c) *magnetic resonance imaging* (MRI).

Neuroimaging pictures are composed of *pixels* and *voxels*. Images are made up of little squares called 'pixels' (picture elements), each of which takes a grey scale from 1 (black) to 256 (white). Each pixel represents brain tissue about 1 mm on each of the sides. The thickness of the slice is often 3 to 5 mm, thus creating a three-dimensional volume element or 'voxel', which is shoebox shaped.

Computerized Tomography (CT)

Computerized tomography (CT; *tome* is Greek for slice) is based on the well-known X-ray. A CT scanner is shown in figure10.5. Once the head is placed in the scanner, a beam of X-rays is shot through the brain. As these beams exit the brain they are blunted because the brain has dense living tissue. Very dense tissue like bone blocks X-rays; grey matter and fluid block far fewer X-rays. Blunting or attenuation of the passage of X-rays provides the final image. X-rays lose some of their energy by interactions with electrons; and the degree of attenuation of energy is dependent on both the density of the electrons in the tissue and the actual density of the tissue itself. CT provides relatively poor contrast of white (nerve fibres) and grey (cell nuclei) matter; to improve contrast, iodine is injected in the bloodstream (this absorbs more X-rays) and this is especially useful for contrasting blood vessels and surrounding cerebral tissue (e.g., in CT angiography, which is used to measure blood vessel breakage).

Computer programs (algorithms) measure the signal density recorded by the detectors and calculate the degree of attenuation at each voxel (i.e., volume pixel) to form the tomographic images of the brain. CT is widely available and useful for distinguishing the degree of cerebrospinal fluid and brain tissue, demonstrating the size of ventricles

Figure 10.5 A CT scanner and images of brain scans. (Photo © Chris Priest / Science Photo Library.)

and central sulci. However, its disadvantages include the use of X-rays and hence radiation exposure; often an intravenous contrast medium must be used (e.g., iodine); and temporal lobe and subcortical grey matter are difficult to image.

CT scanning came into widespread clinical use in the 1970s. It is used to exclude structural disease in patients who present with a possible psychiatric disorder (e.g., confusion, psychosis and dementia). However, in research settings, CT has yielded to other forms of neuroimaging (such as MRI; see below), which provide far greater detail and spatial resolution.

Positron Emission Tomography (PET)

Positron emission tomography (PET) does not measure the volume of brain structures; it measures cerebral metabolic activity and blood flow, and also neurotransmitter receptor quantity and function. PET cerebral metabolic activity is measured by glucose metabolism (glucose is the energy of the brain that is required during processing) contained in the regional cerebral blood flow (rCBF).

PET uses a radioactive substance that is attached to either a normal body substance (e.g., glucose) or a drug (in the case of receptor binding studies). When labelled with the positron-emitting chemical, it becomes known as a radioactive tracer. The tracer is injected into the bloodstream, where it crosses the blood–brain barrier and circulates with the cerebrovasculature (blood system in the brain). As it decays, the tracer emits positrons, which interact with the surrounding electrons to produce two gamma-ray photons. The

PET scanner has an array of receptors surrounding the head that detect these emissions. It is only the simultaneous arrival of two photons at opposite detectors that is recorded as a signal, and these permit the localization of emissions, since the reaction must have occurred on a line between the two detectors. Computer reconstruction provides a tomographic image of the distribution of the tracer. The scanner itself looks little different from an MRI scanner (see below), but it works on a completely different basis.

Neurochemistry

PET's advantage is its ability to quantify neurotransmitter receptors and to visualize the sites of action of drugs; and measurement of cerebral glucose metabolism and regional cerebral blood flow can be used to study resting brain activity or to map cerebral activation during cognitive and motor tasks. On the side of disadvantages, it uses radioactive substances, thus exposure to radiation is an important factor in its long-term use.

PET has proved extremely useful in understanding brain chemistry and in the investigation of the effects of different drugs on brain chemistry. In the case of drugs, PET involves injecting a radio-labelled tracer that has a high affinity and specificity for the (e.g., dopamine) receptor under study. As the tracer travels around the brain it binds to its affinity receptors. The emissions from the radioactive substance (ligand) over time can be measured and localized to give an indication of where the substance is binding and how strongly. Alternatively this technique can be used to study the site of action of drugs. If an individual is given a drug that selectively blocks dopamine D_2 receptors and is then given a PET scan with raclorpide (a D_2 receptor ligand), then the individual shows reduced binding of the ligand as some of the D_2 receptors have already been occupied by the drug. PET has a spatial resolution of 3.5 mm.

Glucose is the main source of energy for neurons. Abnormal glucose metabolism is an indication of underlying pathology and can be detected. Regional glucose metabolism can be assessed with PET during the resting state, or during the performance of a cognitive task, by monitoring emissions from the tracer as it is metabolized. Computer-processed images are generated that use colour as the code for the degree of glucose metabolism.

PET is appropriate for the assessment of receptor distribution in the brain and the measurement of cerebral blood flow during neuropsychological testing. Also, improved anatomical localization of activity is possible by overlaying PET scan information onto MRI images. Disadvantages include low spatial and temporal resolution when compared with MRI, and the use of radioactive substances, which limits repeated scanning.

Magnetic Resonance Imaging (MRI)

Magnetic resonance imaging (MRI) is the state-of-the-art neuroimaging technique for anatomical and functional scans. It has opened up a whole new way of exploring brain structure and function, and in particular it allows us to see brain activation during the performance of a mental task, including thinking, feeling, judging, deciding, etc. Anatomical MRI is discussed first before moving on to its functional capabilities.

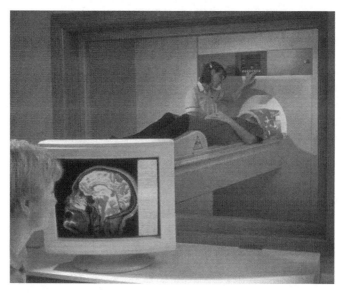

Figure 10.6 An MRI scanner and an image of a brain scan. (Photo © Geoff Tompkinson / Science Photo Library.)

MRI was introduced in the mid-1980s. Its popularity is due to its power of imaging and non-invasive nature – no radioactive tracer needs to be injected into the bloodstream (there are no known risks from magnetic fields). In the early 1990s, its full potential for assessing the relationship between structure and function was fully realized. MRI is very expensive to purchase and run, but is now widely available in clinical practice and for leading-edge neuroscience research. An MRI suite is shown in figure 10.6.

Basics of MRI

In simple terms, the body contains hydrogen atoms (protons), which act like tiny magnets, each with a small dipolar magnetic field (north and south poles). The MRI scanner consists of a powerful magnet. When the head is placed inside this magnet, these protons become aligned to the axis of the magnet, all facing in the same direction. MRI works by blasting these atoms with a radio-frequency (RF) wave; this has the result that the atoms start to rotate and, as they return to their north–south orientation in the magnet field, the atoms emit radio waves that can be detected. The trick is that in every different tissue of the body the atoms rotate at different speeds, so each tissue can be singled out in the scanner and added to the overall picture to build up the final image.

The MR signal can be localized to produce images of slices of the brain by applying the RF pulse at a frequency that only excites protons in a single slice. Currently it is possible to acquire 1 mm thick slices of the entire brain.

The advantages of MRI are its excellent spatial resolution, allowing visualization of structures deep in the brain that are not visible with other techniques. Limitations include the enclosed nature of the scanner and the scanner noise, which induce claustrophobic feelings in some individuals. The purchase cost is high, as are the running costs. It is superior to PET in offering the opportunity of mapping cognitive functions to a very precise neuroanatomical degree, helping to identify structures and functional networks in normal processes and pathological conditions.

MRI-based volumetrics is a well-established technology with a broad range of potential applications in medicine and human neurosciences (the rationale and applications of this technology are described by Caviness et al., 1999). As an example of anatomical MRI, consider a study performed to locate the neural basis of saccadic eye movement performance (see chapter 9). Seventeen participants were scanned using MRI, and their scans were then assessed for certain *regions of interest* (ROI).[3] Prefrontal, premotor, thalamus and cerebellum vermis were assessed, and the volume of the whole brain was also measured. Eye movement performance was assessed at a different time point. Performances on the saccadic task and the volumes of these regions were then correlated (in the regression model, the volume of the whole brain was controlled because the size of a specific region is partially correlated with the overall size of the brain). Only one significant association was found with saccadic performance: cerebellum vermis (Ettinger et al., 2002). Although this result is consistent with the role of the cerebellum in fine-grained motor movement (see chapter 5), there are various explanations for this finding: size differences could be related to glial cells, neurons or neural connections. Size–function correlations do not necessarily imply that the region identified is the main locus of performance effects. For this reason, functional MRI is required to show which regions show activation *during* the performance of the psychological task.

Functional MRI (fMRI)

Biological psychology has undergone a revolution in the past 10 years in the use of MRI to image *ongoing* psychological processes in the brain. Let us now turn to functional MRI (fMRI).

Without doubt, fMRI is one of the most important advances in psychological and psychiatric neuroscience. With spatial resolution as good as 1 mm and temporal resolution of 1 second or less, it is far superior to PET in functional neuroimaging. It can map cognitive functions to very precise neuroanatomical structures, helping to identify normal structure–function relations as well as identifying abnormal structure–function relations in psychopathology. A good introduction is provided by Buxton (2002).

Neurophysiological processes of MRI

What neurophysiological processes give rise to the MRI signal – in other words, what does MRI measure?

fMRI detects regions of neuronal activity by monitoring changes in levels of blood oxygenation: *blood oxygenation level dependent* (BOLD) imaging is the most common form of MRI. This technique rests on the assumption that as neural activity increases so does the flow of oxygenated blood to that particular region. Because the supply of oxygenated blood flow outstrips demand for oxygen, it is possible to detect excess in the amount of oxygenated blood compared with deoxygenated blood. The resulting change in the ratio of deoxyhaemoglobin to oxyhaemoglobin causes the increase seen in the magnetic resonance signal: this serves as an indirect marker of activation and thus of function. The signal is mapped onto the subject's own anatomical scan. Data can be combined across subjects to provide group-averaged images mapped onto standard neurological coordinates.

As noted above, when placed in a strong magnetic field, the hydrogen atoms align to the magnetic field, and when the radio-frequency (RF) pulse is applied this alignment is disturbed. After removal of the pulse, the atoms return to their original position. The time for the atoms to return to their original position is affected by the surrounding tissue type and the local magnetic properties of the tissue: it is this time difference (called relaxation time) that allows the differential properties of tissue to be imaged. This effect can be related to blood oxygenation in fMRI.

Activation in a specific brain region is accompanied by increased blood flow. Oxygenated and non-oxygenated blood have different magnetic properties, so the oxygenated blood in active areas leads to longer relaxation times, which produces a stronger signal from active regions. The signal is dependent on changes in blood oxygenation levels: this is the BOLD effect.[4]

Research designs

Most fMRI studies use a block research design, comprising altering blocks (e.g., a series of the same trials) of experimental conditions. For example, the researcher might be interested in locating those brain areas involved in emotional processing. They could present blocks of three types of faces: (a) faces expressing fear; (b) faces expressing disgust; and (c) neutral faces. If they observed brain activation patterns *separately* for each type of stimulus, they would simply be observing the whole activation of the brain, relevant to the specific facial expression and everything else ongoing in the brain: this would not be too informative. fMRI uses a *subtractive method*: it is assumed that activation during all scans is identical *apart* from those areas involved in the specific emotional experience. According to this subtractive logic, if they subtract (a) fear-face activation from neutral-face activation, and (b) disgust-face activation from neutral-face activation, then they are left with the activation specific to fear and disgust, respectively.

Using a block-design, subtractive technique, the conscious perception of fearful faces (vs. neutral expressions), presented at the level of conscious awareness, activated the *amygdala* (which is known to be implicated in fear processing; LeDoux, 2000); the conscious perception of facial expressions of disgust (vs. control) activated a different brain region, known as the *insula* (Phillips et al., 1997, 1998a,b). This pattern of effects is known as a *double dissociation*.

As discussed in chapter 8, a *double dissociation* is observed when it can be demonstrated that activation in brain region X_1 is related only to function Y_1; and activation in brain area X_2 is related only to function Y_2 (X_1 is not associated with Y_2, and X_2 is not associated with Y_1). Given this pattern of effects, confidence could be placed on the statement that this does not reflect a generalized effect with X_1 and X_2 activating Y_1 to Y_n, or some other artefact (e.g., task difficulty) – these possibilities could not be discounted with a *single dissociation*, where area X is related to function A, but not B (it would not be possible to conclude that function B is mediated by another brain area).

One development in fMRI is *event-related* fMRI, which involves measuring the signal change (activation) resulting from a *single* trial or stimulus presentation (rather than averaging over a block of trials); this allows for much more sensitive experimental designs. With further technical developments, it is expected that fMRI will achieve greater temporal resolutions, measuring in milliseconds rather than seconds. Once this has been achieved, neuroimaging and electrophysiology (EEG and MEG) can be combined into a single investigative tool – although, for convenience and cost, these separate techniques may still be used.

Advantages and disadvantages of fMRI

fMRI is non-invasive and safe; it does not usually need to use radioactivity (although sometimes it does to enhance spatial resolution), and uses the brain's own haemodynamic response to neural activity as an endogenous tracer. As such, repeated scanning does not pose a problem. Description of the functional neuroanatomy of psychological processes provides a framework for investigating the effects of pharmacological treatments: change in functions can be measured before and after drug treatment – this proves especially important in psychiatry, where brain activation in such conditions as schizophrenia may be measured in individual patients to ensure that they are requiring the optimal drug therapy for their specific condition. Another clinical implication is that longitudinal scanning enables changes in brain function to be measured over time: this provides vital information on the progression of brain diseases and points to new therapeutic interventions.

In clinical practice, fMRI is used to localize brain function in patients with tumours or epilepsy who are candidates for surgery. It is important to ensure that tumour removal does not result in postoperative deficits – fMRI allows mapping of cognitive and motor functions in order to identify what regions must be avoided and what functions may be at risk from surgery.[5] Prior to surgery for epilepsy, patients are usually tested to identify which hemisphere is dominant for language; previously, this was done by anaesthetizing each hemisphere in turn and then conducting neuropsychological tests (as discussed in chapter 3, Wilder Penfield performed open-brain procedures to stimulate regions of the cortex to stimulate sensorimotor and cognitive functions).

Magnetic resonance spectroscopy (MRS)

Magnetic resonance spectroscopy (MRS) is used to study neurochemistry. Whereas PET provides information on neurotransmitter receptors, MRS provides information on the metabolites of a range of substances involved in basic biochemical processes (it can be used to study amino acids, neurotransmitters and their metabolites, and compounds involved in brain energy processes; it is also used in the study of neuronal membrane metabolism, and is especially useful in the pharmacokinetics and pharmacodynamics of drugs).

Neurochemistry can be studied because the signal emitted during relaxation yields a spectrum displaying the intensity of different chemical entities and the shift in resonant frequency – in parts per million (ppm). The chemical environment affects the emitted signals, thus allowing the construction of an MRS spectrum (i.e., a *chemical shift*).

ASK YOURSELF
In what ways have MRI techniques opened up whole new fields of investigation?

Summary of Electrophysiological and Neuroimaging Techniques

Each electrophysiological and neuroimaging technique offers a unique insight into the brain; and each has a number of strengths and weaknesses. The main strength of electrophysiology (ERPs) is the impressive temporal resolution of responses, tracking reactions to stimuli in the range of milliseconds; the major disadvantage is the poor spatial resolution and the doubt concerning the source of the generation of the electrical signals (e.g., some signals may be generated some distance from the electrode recording site; these are called *far-field potentials*) – EEG takes a convoluted path between the activated cortex and the electrode on the scalp. MEG, too, has impressive temporal resolution and good spatial resolution. However, neither electrophysiological method comes close to matching MRI in terms of spatial resolution and clarity, but the disadvantage here is the poor temporal resolution (table 10.1).

Table 10.1 Main advantages and disadvantages of EEG/ERP and neuroimaging techniques

Technique	Advantages	Disadvantages
EEG/ERP	Excellent temporal resolution; Relatively inexpensive; Sensitive to sophisticated experimental manipulations; Widespread practical applications (e.g., lie detection).	Poor spatial resolution; Poor source localization; Uncertainty about the precise meaning of components.
MEG	Excellent temporal resolution; Excellent cortical localization.	Poor subcortical localization; Expensive.
CT	Widely available; Comparatively cheap.	Coarse-grained images.
PET	Sensitive to (functional) biochemical activity.	Poor temporal and spatial resolution; Requires injection of radioactive tracer.
MRI	Fine spatial detail; Functional imaging.	Poor temporal resolution; Noisy and claustrophobic environment.

It is now becoming evident that progress in the human neurosciences will be aided by the combination of ERP, MEG and MRI approaches, each offering advantages which help to cancel out the disadvantages of the other techniques.

Functional MRI has been especially influential in brain research, supplementing previous approaches to establishing structure–function relations, namely, (a) post-mortem studies of the interconnection of various neural areas; (b) extrapolation from the known functional anatomy of primates (lesion studies); (c) experiments on the exposed cortical surface during neurosurgery; and (d) evidence of specific functional deficits in brain-damaged patients. None of these approaches yield unambiguous functional data.

However, both fMRI and PET suffer from problems: neither technique provides a measure of primary cortical activity (they are associated with metabolic processes assumed to correlate highly with the functional area); and they rely on subtraction techniques (if the control condition is not precisely specified, then what residual brain activity is left after the subtraction process is unclear). In PET the signal-to-noise ratio is so poor that averages over many individuals must be taken (ignoring the significant structural variation between people). However, given the relative youth of these techniques, it is probable that these limitations will be rapidly overcome by advancing in our knowledge of brain science and neuroimaging technology.

> **ASK YOURSELF**
> Has the power of MRI superseded all other neuroimaging techniques?

Other Brain Imaging Techniques

Finally, there are other brain imaging technologies being developed and used for research purposes, outlined below.

Functional near-infrared optical imaging (fNIR)

Optical imaging of the brain uses infrared technique in a non-invasive way to measure haemodynamic changes (i.e., blood oxygenation and volume) that occur during cognitive tasks (Villringer & Dirnagl, 1997). It is restricted to measuring activity in the cortex – usually the prefrontal cortex – and cannot functionally image activity in deeper areas of the brain. During increased brain activity local cerebral blood flow (CBF) increases, and this blood flow, which exceeds the elevation in oxygen consumption, leads to increased haemoglobin oxygenation. Oxygenated and deoxygenated haemoglobin have characteristic optical properties in the visible and near-infrared light bands. In fact, brain tissue is relatively transparent to light in the near-infrared range (this is the *optical window* – 700 to 900 nm). The equipment consists of light sources and light detectors, and unlike other neuroimaging techniques is portable. It can therefore be used in space-limited environments (e.g., gravity-altered environments, centrifuges, spacecraft and space stations) and military applications where assessment of cognitive performance may be assessed under extreme environmental conditions (e.g., fighter pilot action).

Functional transcranial Doppler ultrasonography (fTCD)

Functional transcranial Doppler ultrasonography uses sound rather than light to assess functional activity in the cortex. Although non-invasive and inexpensive, this technique suffers from low spatial resolution. A strip of sensors are placed over the frontal cortex, and the sound properties of cortical activation (blood flow velocity) are measured. In one study (Vingerhoets, Berckmoes & Stroobant, 2003), blood flow velocity (BFV) in the cerebral arteries was measured in 36 right-handed participants who listened to recordings of actors pronouncing sentences with happy, sad, angry, fearful and neutral meaning, using tones of voice that were either neutral or emotional (the emotional tones were either congruent or incongruent with the meaning of the sentence). Participants were asked to report either the meaning of the sentence or the tone of voice. Using fTCD, it was found that the left hemisphere was equally active when the participants listened for meaning or tone (the 'what' of emotion); however, the right hemisphere was more active when they paid attention to the tone of voice (the 'how' of emotion). This study suggests that the right hemisphere is more important in the processing of emotional tone, while the left hemisphere is more important in assessing emotional meaning (semantics).

> **ASK YOURSELF**
> What other neuroimaging techniques could, in principle, be developed?

▢▢ Conclusion

Each of the neuroimaging techniques surveyed has its own advantages and disadvantages. The old workhorse of neuroimaging, electrophysiology, is still widely used today, and provides a temporal resolution that is still not matched by newer techniques (e.g., MRI) – the development of more sophisticated analysis programmes has helped interpretation of EEG/ERP data (e.g., 'source analysis' of the areas of the brain generating the signals). Increasingly, techniques are being used together to benefit from their combined strengths (e.g., EEG/ERP and MRI). However, one sobering observation of all neuroimaging techniques is their essentially correlational nature: they rely on the association of a change in brain functioning (e.g., BOLD signal) with some psychological event (e.g., processing emotive faces). Although the research designs are experimental – for instance, different types of emotive faces can be presented, either in blocks or individually – what is being observed is *associated* changes in brain activity. In contrast, techniques used in neurophysiology and psychopharmacology allow direct manipulation of the brain, where the *effects* of brain processing can then be measured. In addition, temporal and spatial resolution problems – and some remaining questions concerning exactly which neuronal process are being measured, and from which source – must temper our enthusiasm for these techniques. When first introduced, there were high expectations of what functional neuroimaging would achieve; however, there is now some disappointment that it has not been possible to provide intricate and unambiguous region-to-function mapping (Fletcher, 2004). However, research is progressing apace to refine these techniques, several of which (especially fMRI) have already transformed biological psychology since the 1980s. Further technological innovations will surely expand research opportunities and extend our knowledge of the neural basis of psychological processes.

Learning Questions

1. Why have EEG and ERPs proved so useful in the study of psychological processes?
2. Why is there not one single neuroimaging method preferred by all researchers?
3. What are the aims of functional imaging and how does the information it provides differ from structural imaging?
3. What would be the benefits of combining electrophysiological and neuroimaging methods?
5. Can neuroimaging techniques ever reveal the true nature of structure–function relations?

NOTES

1   According to the definition of psychophysiology provided in chapter 9, electrophysiology and neuroimaging are also psychophysiological techniques; however, they are sufficiently different in procedure and purpose to be considered as a relatively separate class of investigative tool.

2   Often the P300 is termed P3, P400 is termed P4, etc., because these peaks do not always correspond to the precise milliseconds after stimulus onset, but are none the less thought to represent the psychological process associated with the modal times.

3   A regions-of-interest approach is taken when there are predicted or known associations between the psychological measure of interest and brain structures. Measuring all possible regions inflates the probability of finding a statistically significant structure–function association by chance (i.e., a type I error).

4   Many fMRI studies do not analyse or report BOLD changes directly; rather they analyse BOLD signals and process these signals through mathematical models that impose certain assumptions upon the data. Depending on the specific analysis programme used, different results may be obtained – for example, it has been known for one programme to show *activation* in one region, while another programme shows *deactivation*. As in other areas of research design and statistics, the interpretation of results crucially depends upon the assumptions of the underlying mathematical model that is being tested. A second statistical feature of fMRI is the criterion used to identify an area of activation–deactivation: a stringent criterion leads to a relatively small numbers of areas being identified; a more liberal criterion, to a relatively larger number of areas.

5   Prior to the widespread availability of fMRI, location of language functions prior to surgery was performed using a procedure known as *carotid sodium amytal testing*: sodium amytal (a sedating barbiturate) was injected into the carotid artery and this would temporarily anaesthetize the ipsilateral (same-side) hemisphere. Various cognitive functions could then be assessed before surgery was attempted.

FURTHER READING

Andreassi, J. L. (2000). *Psychophysiology of Human Behaviour and Physiological Response*. New York: Lawrence Erlbaum.

Cabeza, R. & Kingstone, A. (eds) (2001). *Handbook of Functional Neuroimaging of Cognition*. Cambridge, MA: MIT Press.

Sharma, T. & Chitnis, X. (2000). *Brain Imaging in Schizophrenia: Insights and Applications*. London: Remedica.

11 Neurophysiology

Learning Objectives

To be able to:

1. Describe recording and stimulation techniques, using specific examples.
2. Outline the methods and strengths/weaknesses of lesion research.
3. Explain how tracing techniques are used to locate neural circuits.
4. Discuss the potential of stem-cell technology for the treatment of neurodegenerative diseases.
5. Consider the ethical implications of invasive research in terms of the cost–benefit consideration.

This chapter describes the major *direct* tools of investigation of the brain by means of such experimental procedures as lesions and implants that stimulate the brain. Of necessity most of these studies are performed on non-human animals, although sometimes these invasive techniques are used for therapeutic purposes in human beings (e.g., electrical implants used to localize the foci of epileptic seizures; or lesion of specific sites to reduce pain). Chapter 3 discussed another form of invasive investigation in the form of Penfield's electrical stimulation of the exposed cortex in neurosurgical patients.

Until comparatively recently, such direct experimental techniques were the main source of experimental data on brain functioning; this was complemented by *clinical neuropsychology*, consisting of correlating brain function with structure (e.g., the cognitive and emotional consequences of accidental damage to the frontal lobes; see chapter 8). Now there are a wide range of brain imaging techniques that allow experimental investigation of the intact human brain (e.g., fMRI; see chapter 10). However, despite the impressive advances in brain neuroimaging techniques, there still remains an important role for traditional experimental procedures that allow a far greater degree of control over key variables and provide a unique source of data that are simply not currently available with the use of other techniques. For example, neuroimaging techniques are basically correlational – although it is now possible to manipulate the psychological variables (e.g., type of emotive faces shown), it is not possible to manipulate the causal basis of emotion reactions, namely the brain. Also, whereas in neurophysiology it is possible to record electrical activity from a single cell (see below), with neuroimaging it is possible only to measure the combined activity of thousands, often millions, of activated cells. Even where it is possible to manipulate the brain directly (e.g., using pharmacological preparations), it is still not possible to target small populations of cells – the researcher must make do with the 'preferential sensitivity' of some cells over others (or neural circuits) and hope that the widespread (albeit weak) effects of the drug on the brain do not confuse the effects of those populations of cells of theoretical interest.

The term *neurophysiology* is used to refer to the experimental (direct) study of physiological processes in the brain, as opposed to merely correlating activity in the brain with function. Neurophysiology is distinct from neuropsychology, psychophysiology and neuroimaging in that it entails the *experimental* manipulation of brain processes, which is necessarily invasive and often destructive.

A number of techniques in neurophysiology are summarized: (a) recording and stimulation studies; (b) lesion studies; and (c) tracing studies. Also covered are the basic details of brain surgery (*stereotaxic procedures*) and the analysis of brain tissue (*histology*). A more detailed treatment of these topics is given by Carlson (2000). Last, exciting developments in neurophysiology, which have important implications for therapeutic brain technology, are outlined.

Recording Techniques

Neuronal activity in the brain is associated with characteristic changes in electrical, metabolic and chemical activity. Neuroimaging allows measurement of electrical (and magnetic), metabolic and chemical activity, but problems of temporal and spatial resolution limit these techniques (see chapter 10). In addition, these neuroimaging techniques measure the complex interaction of processes; they do not *directly* measure activity in specific populations of neurons. In contrast, neurophysiology does directly measure (or, at least, much more directly[1]) neuronal processes and functioning.

One way to investigate the function of a population of neurons is to use electrical or chemical stimulation; another way is to record passively (by electrical or chemical means) while the animal engages in some psychological processing (e.g., responding to a conditioned aversive stimulus). These two approaches are known as *electrical stimulation* and *recording*, respectively.

Two types of stimulation/recording are possible. First, *acute* preparations may be used for a brief period of time during which the animal is anaesthetized – such studies are usually restricted to the investigation of sensory pathways and do not typically entail behavioural observations. Second, *chronic* preparations may be used over an extended period of time after the animal recovers from surgery – in these studies the chronically implanted electrodes can be 'plugged in' to stimulating/recording equipment when required.

Recording electrical activity

Electrical activity is generated by electrical signals in the neuron (e.g., action potentials). This activity can be recorded while the animal is engaged in a variety of behaviours.

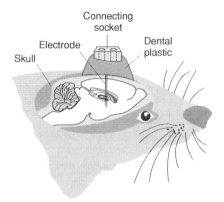

Figure 11.1 An implanted microelectrode. Placement of a chronic electrode showing electrode, dental plastic and plug.

Electrical activity in neurons is recorded with *microelectrodes*: these electrodes have a very fine tip and are able to record electrical activity in individual neurons (known as *single-cell recording*).

Electrodes

Microelectrodes are made of fine glass tubes – glass has the interesting property that, when heated and the ends are pulled apart, the softened glass can be stretched into very fine filaments (no matter how fine it is stretched, a hole runs through its centre). Glass does not conduct electricity, therefore the hole must be filled with a substance that is electroconductive (e.g., a solution of potassium chloride). This type of electrode is suitable for acute preparations.

With chronic recording, a more durable type of microelectrode is needed. Such microelectrodes can be made from fine tungsten wires (the wire is insulated with a varnish). These microelectrodes are attached to miniature electrical sockets; and these sockets are attached to the animal's skull using plastics developed for the dental profession. After recovery from surgery, the animal can be 'plugged in' for recording or stimulation experiments (figure 11.1). In a similar manner to the human EEG, electrical signals from the brain are weak, so these must be amplified and stored for later analysis.

Sometimes the researcher wants to record electrical activity not from a single neuron but from a population of neurons (a region of the brain). These electrodes record the postsynaptic potentials of many thousands, or millions, of neurons. *Macroelectrodes* are used for this specific purpose.

As an example of the application of recording techniques, let us look at the work of Luo, Fee and Katz (2003), who recorded from single neurons in the accessory olfactory bulb of mice – a nucleus that processes pheromonal signals of males engaged in natural behaviours. As shown in chapter 5, many mammalian species use pheromones to communicate social status and reproductive readiness. Pheromones are initially sensed via a specialized sense organ, called the vomeronasal organ, in the nasal cavity. The vomeronasal organ actively pumps samples of pheromones into a sensory cavity, where they are detected by chemical receptors similar to those used in taste and smell. These sensory neurons send connections to a neural structure called the accessory olfactory bulb. Neuronal firing in the area of the brain was modulated by physical contact with male and female conspecifics, with individual neurons activated selectively by specific combinations of the sex and strain of the conspecific, encoding social and reproductive information. This information produces, in essence, a specific 'pheromonal image' of another animal – obviously important information in terms of reproductive fitness.

Such experiments can reveal important information on the selectivity of responses. For example, Luo, Fee and Katz (2003) exposed the mice to different (genetic) strains of male and female mice. Neurons were found that were highly selective for another strain; also other neurons responded selectively to a combination of the strain and gender. In addition, pheromonal neurons reacted about 10 times more slowly than olfactory neurons. This difference in speed might reflect their evolutionary function: the olfactory system needs to react rapidly to the smell of a predator; but the pheromonal system may analyse more complex information relating to reproductive behaviour. Such neurophysiological studies reveal the functions of the chemical senses.

Neurosurgeons sometimes implant electrodes into the human brain. For example, they may want to detect the source of abnormal electrical activity that gives rise to seizures; and then they can remove this abnormal tissue (more commonly an EEG is used to detect the source of epileptic seizures). Also, implants are sometimes used to electrically stimulate brain regions in order to reduce chronic pain (see below).

Some experiments in non-human animals are designed to develop procedures for 'mind control' of robotic devices (*neurobotics*). Consider the experiment by Chapin et al. (1999). They chronically implanted an array of (between 21 and 46) electrodes in the primary motor cortex (M1; see chapter 5) and ventrolateral thalamus, and trained rats to perform a forelimb motor task. Training entailed pressing a spring-loaded lever, which moved a robot arm to a water dropper; once the lever was released, water was transferred to the rat's mouth. Neuron recording during this behaviour was used to derive mathematical functions that predicted forelimb movement: these functions could then be used to stimulate the brain to perform the behaviours. The mathematical functions were derived using neural networks (see chapter 7) to store the temporal information for each lever movement. With peripheral damage (e.g., loss of arms), these results suggest that it may be possible to use training techniques to develop control of a robotic arm: paralysed patients could use electrical recordings to control external devices or their own muscles through functional electrical stimulation. As shown in chapter 10, *neural self-regulation* techniques have already been developed to allow communication with 'locked-in' patients (Birbaumer et al., 1999) – such 'mind control' of external devices, which mimics the usual mind control over output devices (e.g., muscles), is an exciting area of application of biological psychology (for a brief overview, see Kubler, 2004).

Recording chemical changes: microdialysis

Sometimes the researcher is interested in recording the secretion of specific neurotransmitters. *Microdialysis* is the method used to achieve this end. This procedure allows analysis of the chemical environment of the brain while the intact animal is behaving, and is thus a powerful tool in psychopharmacology.

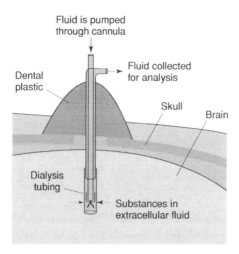

Figure 11.2 Microdialysis apparatus and process. A salt solution (i.e., the *perfusion medium*) is infused through the inner cannula, where it travels to the dialysis site, where it picks up molecules from the extracellular fluid (i.e., the *dialysate concentrations*).

Dialysis refers to the process by which chemical substances are separated by means of an artificial membrane that is permeable to some molecules, but not others. Molecules smaller than the semipermeable membrane pore size pass through the membrane and can be measured; larger molecules do not. This technique is more familiar in the instance of patients waiting for a liver transplant operation (their blood is 'cleaned' several times a week to extract toxic substances).

A microdialysis procedure consists of a probe being inserted into the brain and fixed to the skull (using *stereotaxic surgery*). This procedure capitalizes on the fact that neurochemicals released by the activity of neurons spill into the extracellular fluid surrounding their terminal. The microdialysis equipment consists of a small metal tube that introduces a solution (the *perfusion medium*) into a section of dialysis tubing (i.e., a piece of artificial membrane shaped into the form of a cylinder); the semipermeable membrane is continuously flushed by the perfusion ('pouring through') fluid; another small metal tube leads the solution away after it has been circulated through the pouch, for analysis of specific chemicals (the *dialysate concentrations*) (figure 11.2).

Now let us use the method of microdialysis to answer an important research question.

Microdialysis in the nucleus accumbens

Various drugs that increase dopamine functioning (e.g., amphetamine) influence reactions to conditioned rewarding stimuli. We may ask, where in the brain do these drugs work to facilitate reward-mediated behaviour? One site that has been identified is the *nucleus accumbens* (e.g., Fibiger & Phillips, 1988) – this region is part of the *basal ganglia* in the forebrain (see chapters 3 and 4 above). However, there is debate over the precise role of this structure. Some evidence suggests that dopamine is released also during aversive conditioning; and unconditioned stimuli also lead to an increase in dopamine in this brain site (e.g., Besson & Louilot, 1995; Young, Joseph & Gray, 1993). However, these *conditioning* studies leave unanswered the question of whether the dopamine release to the CS is contingent on the specific reinforcing properties of the UCS (reward or punishment), or whether it is the association per se (irrespective of reinforcement) that is responsible for the release of dopamine. Young et al. (1998) set out to answer this question.

Young et al. (1998) used microdialysis to examine changes in dopamine levels in the nucleus accumbens during the formation of an association between two *neutral* stimuli (i.e., tone and flashing light), which do not themselves evoke changes in dopamine levels as measured in the extracellular fluid. A sensory preconditioning paradigm was used (see chapter 7). Since the neutral stimuli (CS1 and CS2) have no inherent motivation value, they do not elicit a behavioural response, therefore their associative formation is behaviourally silent (i.e., it cannot be measured behaviourally during its formation); therefore, there is a need for a second stage of the experimental procedure to reveal the effect of this association. CS1 is now paired with a UCS, and the CR is established; let us now assess the CS1–CS2 associative strength by presenting the CS2 alone: this now has the power to elicit the CR formed by CS1–UCS conditioning, even though CS2 has never been associated with the UCS. (The UCS here was a mild foot shock, and the CR was a suppression of ongoing licking performance.[2])

Young et al.'s results showed that dopamine was released to the presentation of the paired stimuli; the authors concluded that 'dopamine release in the nucleus accumbens is sensitive to the associative contingencies of the stimuli presented and increases during the formation of a conditioned association, even when neither of the stimuli entering into the association has biological significance, nor inherently releases dopamine' (Young et al., 1998, p. 1181). Thus, using a microdialysis probe, it is possible to say that dopamine release in this region of the brain is not conditional upon reinforcement (reward or punishment); but it occurs with simple associative learning. It would be difficult to answer the above questions by means other than microdialysis.

As is shown by this example, microdialysis is a powerful way to assess the chemical activity associated with the performance of a psychological *function* – in the case of sensory preconditioning, where there was no behaviour to measure during the associative phase of learning. Young et al.'s experiment showed that it is possible to measure chemical processes associated with *inferred* central psychological states; and as sensory preconditioning demonstrates, it is sometimes necessary to infer central states to make sense of subsequent behavioural reactions (in this instance, conditioned suppression by CS2).

Other applications of microdialysis include the chemicals released by electrical self-stimulation (see below), and thus offer a unique experimental perspective on the brain basis of addiction.

> **ASK YOURSELF**
> What different sources of information do electrical and chemical recording techniques yield?

▢ Stimulating Neural Activity

A complementary approach to recording brain activity is stimulation. Either electrical or chemical stimulation may be used to investigate the effects of brain activation on various classes of behaviour (e.g., when feeding, copulating, avoiding). For example, if the hypothalamus is stimulated, then, depending on the specific site of action, behaviours such as feeding, drinking, grooming, attack and escape are elicited. Another form of stimulation is intracranial self-administered (ICSS): here the stimulation is contingent on operant behaviour – in this form of instrumental conditioning, pressing a bar initiates the electrical current (this approach has proved useful in studying the neural basis of reward; see below).

The logic of stimulation studies is closely related to lesion studies of the brain (see below); if area x is lesioned and function y is lost, then it should be found that *stimulation* of area x elicits function y (for a discussion of single and double dissociation, see chapter 8). However, if such stimulation does not have the opposite effect of a lesion, then this would caution interpretation that area x is really responsible for controlling function y. Let us take the example of lesion of an area of the brain that leads to loss of sexual interest in opposite-sex mates. It may be inferred that this area is involved in sexual motivation (but there are many other interpretations of this association – e.g., the lesion might have impaired sensory or motor processing). But when electrical stimulation does not arouse interest in non-lesioned animals, then it would make sense to pay closer attention to these alternative explanations for this apparent loss of sexual interest.

However, there are problems with interpreting both stimulation and lesion studies. Even if a lesion to area x impairs function y, and electrical stimulation of area x elicits function y, then it is still not certain that area x is the neural centre for that function. In the case of sexual motivation, there are many other interpretations (e.g., area x might be involved in the processing of sensory qualities that increase the incentive value of all stimuli, not just sexual partners). However, these problems are in the nature of scientific research, which requires a continuous process of testing and refinement of theory.

Electrical vs. chemical stimulation

Electrical stimulation involves passing an electrical current through a wire inserted in the brain (positioned by *stereotaxic surgery*). Chemical stimulation involves injecting a small amount of an excitatory amino acid (e.g., glutamic acid; this is the principal excitatory amino acid in the brain). Injection of the chemical is achieved with the use of an apparatus permanently attached to the skull: a metal cannula is used for this purpose.

The principal disadvantage of chemical stimulation is that it is slightly more complicated than electrical stimulation, but its main advantage over electrical stimulation is that it activates cell bodies but not axons, because only cell bodies (and their dendrites) contain neurotransmitter receptors. It is known that the injection of an excitatory amino acid into a particular brain region excites cells there and does not excite the axons of other neurons that pass through this area. Thus chemical stimulation is more localized and specific than electrical stimulation.

Stimulation of a single cell by chemical means is achieved with a technique known as *micro-iontophoresis* (this refers to the injection of a very small quantity of chemicals that are ion carrying): when transmitter substances bind with postsynaptic receptors, ion channels open, producing excitatory or inhibitory postsynaptic potentials (chapter 4), which can be measured. To determine the effects of specific neurotransmitter substances (or drugs that stimulate or block particular receptors) on the activity of an individual neuron, a *multi-barrelled micropipette* is used: this device consists of two or more glass microelectrodes

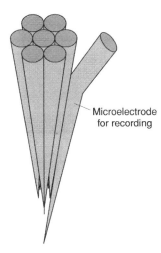

Microelectrode
for recording

Figure 11.3 Micro-iontophoresis procedure showing a seven-barrelled micropipette and a recording microelectrode. Each of the seven micropipettes is filled with transmitter substance, neuromodulators, drugs, or hormone; and an electrical current is passed through one of the micropipettes and molecules discharged; and then the neural activity of the cell exposed to the molecules is measured.

(micropipettes) bundled together so that their tips are close to one another. A recording electrode is also attached to measure the activity of the neuron.

As shown in figure 11.3, a seven-barrelled micropipette glued to a recording microelectrode can be used. Each of the seven micropipettes can be filled with transmitter substance, neuromodulators, drugs or hormones. An electrical current is passed through one of the micropipettes, and molecules discharged. The recording electrode detects the neural activity of the cell exposed to the molecules. If the neuron changes its firing rate when some of the substance is injected from the micropipette, it can be inferred that the neuron contains receptors for that substance.

As an example of chemical stimulation, Woodnorth et al. (2003) examined the sites of activation that lead to theta rhythm in the hippocampus (theta is observed during voluntary behaviours and information seeking, and is thought to play a role in memory, arousal, orienting and attention, as well as in anxiety; see Gray & McNaughton, 2000; Woodnorth & McNaughton, 2002). Woodnorth et al. (2003) tested whether chemical stimulation of the hypothalamus affects the theta rhythm: they used a drug that increases inhibition by GABA (chlordiazepoxide, which is an anxiolytic benzodiazepine). A total of between 5 and 7 cannulae were employed, which recorded electrical activity, as well as injecting the chemicals, across different regions of the hypothalamus. Both forms of chemical stimulation were found to reduce or increase the frequency of theta, depending on the precise region of the injection. They were thus able to determine which regions of the hypothalamus played a role in the electrophysiological activity of another brain structure, the hippocampus. These data allowed the authors to conclude that 'theta frequency may be determined by a complex interplay between distinct but interacting modulatory regions in the medial hypothalamus' (p. 319).

Intracranial self-stimulation (ICSS) studies

Intracranial self-stimulation (ICSS) and intracranial place conditioning (ICPC) studies have been used to study the reinforcing effects of electrical stimulation and drug effects. In rodents, ICSS has identified the ventral tegmental area (VTA) as the site of the reinforcing effects of some drugs (e.g., morphine and ethanol); in addition, injection of these drugs directly into the VTA produces ICPC (i.e., the animal chooses to move to the position associated with the administration of these reinforcing, rewarding drugs; McBride, Murphy & Ikemoto, 1999). The VTA projects to several forebrain regions, including the septum, amygdala, medial prefrontal cortex and entorhinal cortex.

Olds and Milner (1954) performed one of the best-known studies in psychology. They noted that stimuli have two effects: (a) they elicit responses; and (b) they reinforce responses. In studying the elicitation of responses, the focus is on the stimulus; in studying reinforcement, the focus is on the responses that *precede* the stimulus. Reinforcement consists of a stimulus increasing responses (reward), decreasing responses (punishment) or leaving them unchanged (neutral). Olds and Milner (1954) focused on the reinforcing properties of electrical stimuli, not merely their eliciting properties. (It may be noted in passing that these experiments were performed under the guidance and encouragement of Donald Hebb, who did so much to advance neuropsychology; see chapter 1.)

Olds and Milner (1954) used 15 male rats; electrical current to the brain was contingent on lever pressing in a Skinner box (see chapter 7) – a form of ICSS. The performance measure was the proportion of total time given to responding – this score was compared with responses taken during extinction (where no electrical stimulation was given for lever pressing). After recording behaviour, the animals were sacrificed, and their brains fixed with formalin, frozen, sectioned, stained and examined to determine which structure of the brain had been stimulated by the electrode (see the *histology* section below). The results showed that reward seemed to be located in the septal area of the brain.

Brain stimulation reinforcement has confirmed in all animals studied, including human beings, the reinforcing (pleasurable) nature of electrical stimulation of certain brain circuits. However, the optimal sites for 'pleasurable' responses differ from those reported initially by Olds and Milner (1954). Subsequent experiments show that stimulation of the *medial forebrain bundle* (MFB) is the most effective site for continuous self-stimulation (Olds, 1962) – the MFB passes through the hypothalamus, connecting forebrain and midbrain structures (because of its interconnections, stimulation of the MFB has the capacity to stimulate a number of axons in different forebrain systems).

These data tie in well with what is known about the evolution of adaptive systems (see chapter 2). Animals could not have evolved if they had not developed the ability to learn from experience – as discussed in chapter 7, learning in this context means repeating behaviours that lead to reward (obtaining food, water and a mate; associated with an increment in genetic fitness) and avoiding behaviours that lead to punishment (avoiding predators and noxious substances; associated with a decrement in genetic fitness). Learning entails a reorganization of neuronal processes so that behaviours better fit the environmental demands (an example of *neural plasticity*; see chapter 7). Olds and

Milner's seminal work gave the first insights into the neural basis of this fundamental biological function.

Hypothetical intervening variables hold no appeal for radical behaviourists, who argue that there is no need to infer intervening (unseen) variables when behaviour can be predicted from knowledge of the environment, reinforcement history and stimuli (see chapter 7). To them, talk of 'pleasurable stimulation' is misleading. Intervening variables are hypothesized because stimulation leads to responses which increase the probability of stimulation – by definition animals work for 'rewarding' stimuli and avoid 'punishing' stimuli. This is a rather circular argument, but it is meaningful when it is linked to the evolution of motivational systems that serve an adaptive purpose: to increase genetic fitness. In any case, to understand certain behavioural phenomena it is necessary to formulate theories of central states. Such central states have already been discussed in terms of sensory preconditioning, which is behaviourally silent during associative formation of two neutral stimuli (see chapter 7). Another form of an inferred central state is seen with the termination or omission of an expected rewarding stimulus: this is not treated as a non-event (as must be assumed by strict behaviourists); rather, it acts as a form of punishment (in this case, *frustrative non-reward*).

Interpretation of stimulation studies

The interpretation of brain stimulation studies is not without its problems. For a start, a pulse of electrical current does not parallel the precise electrical activity of the brain. Carlson (1998) likens electrical stimulation to 'attaching ropes to the arms of the members of an orchestra and then shaking all the ropes simultaneously to see what they can play'. In particular the complex interplay of spatial and temporal patterns of neural firing is lost. It has already been said that the VTA seems to be the site of action of several drugs that have reinforcing properties; but this effect may be due to increased release of dopamine somewhere else in the 'reward' circuit that begins in the VTA (e.g., the nucleus accumbens, where all drugs of addiction seem to exert an effect). It is known that rats will self-infuse a variety of drugs of abuse – such as amphetamine, morphine, cocaine – when release of these drugs in the nucleus accumbens is made conditional upon some instrumental response.

Do ICSS studies provide information on the neural response to natural reward (e.g., food and water)? In some respects, ICSS data are not consistent with natural rewards. For example, electrical brain stimulation can be remarkably powerful: rats may press almost continuously for many days to receive brain stimulation – in fact, much more than they would respond to obtain natural reward. (In a similar manner, the craving and thus the rewarding properties of cocaine are greater than those of natural rewards, such as sugar.)

Animals prefer electrical brain stimulation over natural rewards; and there have been claims that, if allowed, they would starve themselves to death in order to get this artificial, but highly pleasurable, source of stimulation. The similarity of this behaviour with that of the human drug addict is obvious. Addictive drugs seem to work by subverting normal responses to natural reinforcers in favour of a more direct chemical action on the 'pleasure' circuits in the brain.

> **ASK YOURSELF**
> What cautions must be borne in mind when interpreting stimulation studies?

Lesion Research

Lesion research is one of the most widely used procedures in neurophysiology. This type of research involves destruction of part of the brain in order to determine the functions subserved by that part. This approach is also known as experimental ablation (from the Latin word *ablatus*, 'to carry away'). Experimental ablation entails the anaesthetized animal's head being immobilized in a fixed position by the *stereotaxic apparatus*. A *stereotaxic atlas*, which is a three-dimensional map of the brain, is used to locate the exact coordinates for the placement of an electrode. Following behavioural testing (e.g., avoidance behaviour), the animal is sacrificed and a histological analysis of the brain is performed in order to ensure that the lesion was at the intended location. A group of control animals (also called the *vehicle*, or *sham lesion*, group) undergo the same procedure, with the exception of the electrical lesion (this group ensures that the behavioural effects observed are not the result of the surgical procedure, the anaesthetic or damage of the tissue through which the electrode travelled before it reached its intended target).

Cortical and subcortical ablations

It is relatively easy to destroy tissue located immediately under the skull. The animal is anaesthetized, part of the skull is removed, and then a section device can be used to 'aspirate' brain tissue: a glass pipette is placed on the surface of the brain and this sucks away tissue with the aid of a vacuum pump. Lesions deeper in the brain require different methods.

Subcortical lesions are usually produced by passing an electrical current through a stainless steel wire that is coated with an insulating varnish except at the tip. The wire is guided stereotaxically to the desired location. The electrical current comprises a radio frequency (RF) current (alternating current of a very high frequency). The passage of the current through brain tissue produces heat, which kills cells in the region surrounding the tip. This method kills all tissue in the region of the electrode tip.

A more selective method of producing brain lesions employs an excitatory amino acid (which stimulates chemicals within the neuron), which kills neurons by stimulating them to death: these are *excitotoxic lesions*. When an excitatory amino acid is injected through a cannula into a region of the brain, the chemical destroys neural cell bodies in the vicinity but spares axons that belong to different neurons that happen to pass through this region. This selectivity allows the researcher to determine whether the behavioural effects of destroying a particular brain structure are caused by the death of neurons located there or by the destruction of axons that pass through the region.

Procedures are also available that allow the destruction of a certain class of neuron, characterized by its neurotransmitter. For example, *6-hydroxydopamine* (6-HD) resembles the catecholamines norepinephrine and dopamine; and, because of this resemblance, 6-HD is taken up by transporter molecules in axons and terminal buttons of dopaminergic and noradrenergic neurons. Once inside the cell, the chemical poisons and kills neurons.

Let us take an example. Both dopaminergic and noradrenergic circuits seem to be associated with reward systems that play a role in maternal behaviour. Rats injected with

6-HD in the ventral tegmental area (VTA) during lactation show a deficit in pup retrieval (a vital component of maternal behaviour) (Hansen et al., 1991). As this neurotoxin does not affect nursing, nest-building or maternal aggression, it was assumed that the VTA is involved specifically in the initiation of maternal behaviour – other evidence shows that the VTA is involved in sex, feeding and a range of other appetitive behaviours.

By their very nature, most lesions are permanent and irreversible. However, it is possible to produce temporary lesions. The easiest way to achieve this is to inject a local anaesthetic into the appropriate part of the brain: this blocks action potentials in axons entering or leaving that region, thus producing a temporary lesion (called a *reversible lesion*). Such an effect is produced by cooling brain tissue enough to suppress neural activity. A device called a *cryode*, which consists of a series of stainless steel tubes through which a chilled liquid can be circulated, is implanted between the skull and the surface of the brain. This device is used in studying brain functions in monkeys. Chapter 8 revealed that transcranial magnetic stimulation (TMS) can be used to disrupt the normal electrical activity of the cortex in awake human beings, and by this means achieve something very close to experimental cortical ablation.

Stimulation and lesion studies at work: latent inhibition and the nucleus accumbens

As an example of the theoretical value of stimulation and lesion research let us consider the role of the nucleus accumbens in latent inhibition (LI). Chapters 7 and 8 noted that LI refers to a general learning process consisting of the retardation in learning a CS–UCS association when the CS has previously been 'pre-exposed' without consequence (i.e., it is not reinforced by a UCS). LI is of particular interest to psychologists because it involves a learning process (in this case, learning that the CS has no predictive, reinforcement, value); but, in addition, disrupted LI (i.e., lack of an effect of pre-exposure of the CS on subsequent CS–UCS associability) has been proposed as a model of the attentional deficits in schizophrenia, whereby familiar stimuli are processed as if they are new and novel (Gray et al., 1991; for further discussion of this association, see chapter 16).

Now, it is known that drugs that increase levels of dopamine worsen schizophrenia symptoms, while drugs that reduce levels of dopamine improve symptoms. In this respect, LI is a simple but interesting behavioural paradigm because: (a) it is disrupted in rats by repeated amphetamine administration (a dopamine agonist); and (b) the effects of amphetamine are reversed by administration of neuroleptic drugs (dopamine antagonists). In addition, LI is disrupted in acute schizophrenia patients, as well as by acute administration of amphetamine in normal human beings.

If it were possible to localize the effects of dopamine-altering drugs on LI, then the goal of describing the neural pathways in schizophrenia would be closer. On the basis of several experimental studies showing that drug effects on LI are mediated by the nucleus accumbens, these authors conducted a series of lesion studies. These studies were performed because drugs such as amphetamine influence a number of neurochemical circuits, not just dopaminergic ones. Thus, experimental investigation of the actual brain site of interest provides a unique insight not afforded by psychopharmacology alone.

There is an important caveat in interpreting the results of stimulation and lesion studies. The behaviour of reading the words on this page involves the coordinated action of many different functional circuits: eye movements, focusing of lens, perceiving and recognizing words and letters, comprehending the meaning of words, and the active processing of the context of the sentences being read. Behaviour recruits many different functions. The interpretation of lesion studies is thus complicated by the fact that all regions of the brain are interconnected: lesion or stimulation of one area may, and often

ASK YOURSELF
Is destruction of neural tissue a good way to understand its normal functions?

does, cause effects in other areas. Such studies can show that the region is *somehow* involved; and, with the integration of many such studies, it is often possible to develop empirically grounded models of the neural functions underlying a specific behavioural expression.

Therapeutic Interventions in Human Beings

The stimulation and lesion studies already considered have all been conducted on non-human animals, aimed at advancing knowledge on the relationship between neuronal processes and behaviour. However, similar procedures – albeit for very different purposes – are also conducted in human beings. Let us now turn to these applications.

Therapeutic lesions

There is a long history of using lesions to ameliorate a number of neurological conditions in human beings. Human stereotaxic surgery was born in the 1940s (Spiegel, Wycis & Marks, 1947) and neurological diseases, such as Parkinson's disease (PD), have been treated by a variety of invasive techniques, such as thermal lesioning or injection of alcohol into the thalamus and pallidum: lesions to the thalamus reliably abolish tremor. However, in the case of PD, stereotaxic surgery was largely replaced by drug therapy (i.e., levodopa, L-dopa, which is a dopamine agonist). However, L-dopa therapy often causes undesirable side-effects (notably, motor problems). As a result, in the 1980s there was a renewed interest in the therapeutic benefits of lesioning the pallidum (i.e., *pallidotomy*) – the pallidum is part of the basal ganglia, which is involved in motor planning and movements (see chapter 5). By the 1990s, such surgery was shown, at least in some patients, to be effective in reducing the side-effects of long-term use of L-dopa.

Therapeutic electrical stimulation

Electrical stimulation is also used in human beings for a number of medical reasons. It is sometimes used to detect the focus of epileptic discharge before ablative surgery to remove the diseased brain tissue that is generating the pathological discharge of electricity. It is also used in PD, initially to localize the thalamic site of tremor: high-frequency electrical stimulation was found to suppress tremor – this electrical stimulation is thought to provide an inhibitory input, thus cancelling the excitatory processes that cause the tremor. (Chronic electrodes in the thalamus have also been used for the treatment of chronic pain; and electrical stimulation has been used for a wide range of pain conditions.) Electrodes are also sometimes chronically implanted in the pallidum to alleviate motor disturbances seen in PD patients. Stimulation has the obvious advantage over lesions in that it is reversible.

Stereotaxic Surgery and Histological Analysis

This section describes how electrodes are implanted and areas of the brain lesioned; and how neural tissue is analysed (histology).

Stereotaxic surgery

Stereotaxic surgery is the procedure used to locate the position of the tip of the electrode or cannula in the brain. This stereotaxic apparatus immobilizes the animal's head in a standard position, and the electrode or cannula is moved through the three axes of space. A *stereotaxic atlas* is consulted to find the location of specific brain regions – there is enough similarity among individuals to predict the location of particular brain structures from external features of the head (however, the precision of the electrode/cannula placement needs later to be confirmed by histological analysis).

Once the stereotaxic location of a target region has been identified from the atlas, the animal is anaesthetized, placed in the apparatus and the scalp is cut open. The appropriate numbers on the stereotaxic apparatus are set, and a hole is drilled though the skull and brain; the electrode or cannula is then lowered into the target area of the brain (figure 11.4). When surgery has been completed, the wound is sewn up and the animal is allowed to recover from surgery. (A similar procedure is used with human beings, who may have part of their brain lesioned to prevent, for example, severe tremors caused by such disorders as Parkinson's disease – in this instance, MRI is used to locate the precise spatial position of the target area.)

Histology

After lesion and behavioural observations have been taken, the experimental animal is *sacrificed* (i.e., killed, usually by an overdose of general anaesthetic). Histology involves the preparation of brain tissue in a form that permits analysis under the microscope.

Perfusing, fixing and slicing

Upon death, brain tissue rapidly degrades; therefore, to prevent this, *autolytic enzymes* (autolytic means 'self-dissolving') must be destroyed, and the tissue must also be protected against bacteria and moulds. First, blood is removed and the brain is perfused with a dilute salt solution; then the brain is placed in a *fixative*, the most common form of which is formalin (it also hardens brain tissue, which is convenient for the purpose of slicing). Often the brain is also frozen.

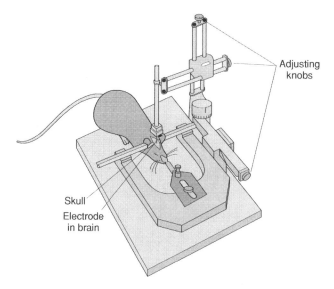

Adjusting
knobs

Skull
Electrode
in brain

Figure 11.4 Stereotaxic apparatus used to locate precisely the tip of the electrode or cannula in the brain. The coordinates of the brain are obtained from a *stereotaxic atlas* unique to each species (a similar procedure is used in human brain surgery).

Once fixed, the brain may be sliced by a *microtome*, which produces very thin slices (or *sections*). After the tissue is cut, slices are attached to glass microscopic slides. Tissue can then be stained by putting the entire slide into various chemical solutions.

Staining

Looking at the slice under a light microscope it is possible to see the outlines of some large cellular masses and the more prominent fibre bundles, but no fine detail is evident. Further histological techniques are applied to highlight the structure of the neuron. To observe fine anatomical details (e.g., synapses), an electron microscope is used: a beam of electrons is passed through the tissue, and a shadow is cast on a sheet of photographic film, which is exposed by the electrons – as electrons tend to pass through the tissue, the degree to which they appear at the film and expose it depends on the physical properties of the tissue.

Staining techniques highlight specific neuronal processes, so are especially useful in revealing fine detail. The *Golgi stain* reveals the whole cell (its structure, *morphology*); the *Nissl stain* reveals the cell body. Other stains highlight neurons that are sensitive to a certain neurotransmitter: a pathway made up of such neurons would stand out against a background of neurons that remain unstained (e.g., the Weigert's myelin stain colours the nerve fibres to see pathways). For example, the Nissl stain is a dye known as *methylene blue*; it selectively stains cell bodies because it is taken up by RNA, DNA and associated proteins located in the cell nucleus. (Golgi shared the 1906 Nobel Prize in medicine with Santiago Ramon y Cajal for their work on understanding the nervous system – Cajal specifically for his work on the structure and connections of neurons.)

The importance of Golgi's work was in revealing neuronal processes in such fine detail; his method is still used today, and has spawned a whole array of staining techniques that allow microscopic analysis of neuronal processes and connections throughout the brain.

ASK YOURSELF
What role has histological analysis played in revealing the structure of neuronal tissue?

Now let us move on to other techniques used to identify which brain areas are involved in which behaviours.

Tracing Techniques

Tracing neurochemical pathways is achieved by injecting a quantity of a chemical in the target brain areas – once again using stereotaxic surgery to implant a cannula (e.g., horseradish peroxidase, HRP, is often used to trace pathways). The molecules of the chemical are then taken up by the dendrites of the neuron and transported through the soma to the axon, where they then travel to terminal buttons. Several days later neurons in this circuit are filled with molecules of the chemical. By this means it is possible to determine where neurons in one brain area travel.

Tracing comes in two forms: (a) *anterograde labelling* (anterograde is used to refer to the direction of flow in the same direction as the action potential – anterograde means 'moving forward'); and (b) *retrograde labelling* (which refers to the direction opposite to the flow of the action potential) (figure 11.5). Once again, using stereotaxic techniques, chemicals are injected in the cell body of the neuron; these chemicals are taken up by the cell body and its dendrites. They are then slowly transported along the axon towards the terminal buttons. In order to establish which neurons send information *to* the nucleus,

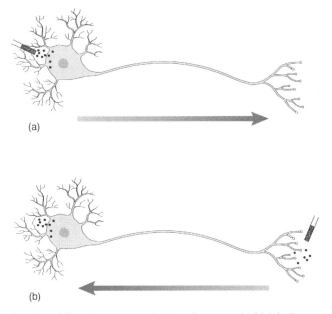

(a)

(b)

Figure 11.5 Direction of flow in anterograde (a) and retrograde (b) labelling

retrograde labelling is used. Here the chemical is transported, against the direction of the action potential, from the terminal buttons to the cell body. These methods allow neural circuits to be identified. *Immunocytochemical* procedures are then used to trace the neuronal paths (see below).

Double labelling

It is possible to combine anterograde or retrograde tracers with the chemical analysis techniques described above. This method of *double labelling* allows us (a) to determine what chemicals a particular neuron contains, and (b) to determine the connections of neurons throughout the brain.

Localizing Neuronal Activity

Another set of commonly used techniques consists of localizing neurochemical activity in the brain: (a) *neuronal metabolic activity*; (b) *proteins* synthesized by the cell's activity; and (c) *messenger RNA* (mRNA) involved in protein synthesis. Procedures are used to localize which brain areas were most active during the performance of a task: this analysis takes place after the animal has been sacrificed.

Recording metabolic activity: autoradiography

Electrical activity is only one of the events that accompany neuronal activity. As seen in the case of PET (chapter 10), metabolic processes may also be used to index brain activity. To measure metabolic activity, a radioactive *ligand* for a particular receptor is injected into the animal (a ligand is a chemical that binds to a particular receptor type), for example, 2-deoxyglucose (2-DG) – this chemical is similar to glucose, so it is taken up by neurons. The more active the neuron, the more 2-DG is taken up: this take-up can be measured. Unlike glucose, 2-DG stays in the neurons; therefore, once the animal has been sacrificed, its brain removed, fixed and sliced, it can be analysed to discover which brain areas were most active during a particular behaviour.

Autoradiology entails brain slices being coated with photographic emulsion (the substance found on normal photographic film), and after several weeks the slides are developed just like a photographic film. The molecules of radioactive 2-DG show themselves as spots or silver grains in the developed emulsion because the radioactivity exposes the emulsion (in the same way that X-rays or light would). The most active regions of the brain contain the most radioactivity, showing this radioactivity in the form of dark spots in the developed emulsion.

Recording protein changes: immunocytochemistry

When cells are active, DNA in the nucleus leads to the production of peptides and proteins. These proteins maintain the cell as well as producing neurotransmitters; also they produce the receptors which need to be identified. These proteins can be identified and measured using a procedure known as *immunocytochemistry*. One of these proteins produced is *fos*. One gene that is expressed is called *c-fos*: this gene is involved in regulating the transcription of other genes, cell proliferation and differentiation, and is a good indicator of neuronal responses to behavioural tasks. The proteins produced by the gene are easily measured and offer a sensitive way to assess gene transcription during performance of a behavioural task. Obviously, this is a time-sensitive procedure: the animal has to be sacrificed and the brain preserved before the protein synthesis associated with a specific behaviour dissipates. For example, the researcher might condition a group of rats to a CS (e.g., light, associated with foot shock); and then expose the rats to a period of CS presentations. They could then compare fos expression in their amygdala to determine whether this structure is involved in anxiety – they could compare this *experimental* group's fos expression with a *control* group who have been exposed to the light that, for them, has not been conditioned to a foot shock. They might also want to correlate the degree of fos expression with the degree of behavioural anxiety shown (e.g., as measured by conditioned suppression of licking).

The way in which *immunocytochemical* analysis works is by exposing the brain slices to an antibody, labelled with a fluorescent dye, for the peptide; the slices are then inspected under a light microscope using light of a particular wavelength. The presence of transmitters shows up in different colours on a *photomicrograph*.

Recording messenger RNA (mRNA)

Another way to localize a substance is to use *in situ hybridization*: all peptides and proteins (including their enzymes) are synthesized according to the information contained on the chromosome. As discussed in chapter 2, when a particular protein is produced, the necessary information is copied from the chromosome onto a piece of mRNA, which leaves the nucleus and travels to the ribosome, where protein synthesis occurs. The recipe for the protein is coded on a particular sequence of nucleotides that make up the mRNA. It is possible to synthesize a piece of radioactive RNA that contains a sequence of nucleotides complementary to the sequence on the mRNA. The researcher would expose slices of brain tissue to the radioactive RNA, which sticks to molecules of the appropriate mRNA. Then they use autoradiographic methods to reveal the location of the mRNA and thus the location of the protein synthesis the RNA initiates.

> **ASK YOURSELF**
> What are the limitations of using gene expression products in localizing neuronal activity?

▢▢ Ethics in Animal Experimentation

There is heated debate over the morality and scientific value of animal experiments. As discussed in this chapter, (non-human) animal research provides a rich source of knowledge that simply cannot be obtained by any other means; we see in chapter 13 that (non-human) animals are also widely used in genetics research, partly because there is considerable overlap between the genomes of the mouse (and other species) and those of human beings. This is a highly complex, not to mention emotive, debate, and full justice cannot be done to it here. But let us sketch out some of the positions, and survey the ethical and legal constraints that pertain to animal experimentation. The basic issue that must be decided is: in order to eliminate any animal suffering, are we – as individuals and as a society – willing to forgo scientific knowledge and technological innovation in the brain sciences (including treatments for a range of neuropathologies)? If we are willing to forgo such innovation, then perhaps we should also be willing to stop the use of animals for all purposes (e.g., food, clothes, etc.).

Those who object to animal experimentation do so on a number of grounds. First is the morality argument: non-human animals have equal moral status to human beings; therefore, if we are not willing to experiment (using invasive and harmful procedures) on human beings, then we should not experiment on other animals. This is the position of the 'animal rights' movement, who oppose all forms of animal experimentation. This is ultimately a philosophical position, and one either believes it or not (there are philosophical arguments *against* the animal rights viewpoint: for rights to be awarded, there must be duties, but animals do not have duties in any moral sense – remember we take away the rights of human beings if they do not fulfil their duties, for example, as in the case of incarcerated criminals). Second is the viewpoint that animals are so different from human beings that making comparisons is dangerous. It is true that all species are not the same – for that matter, all human beings are different; but most scientists working in this area believe that there are considerable similarities between the species, and sensible comparisons can be made. For this reason all drug and medical treatments are first developed on non-human animals.

René Descartes believed that non-human animals were merely machines, devoid of a soul (mind; see chapter 1). Therefore, according to his philosophical position, experimentation on animals was tenable, as it did not cause pain or any form of insult to the mind. This view is now defunct. (I doubt whether any professional scientist still holds this viewpoint – even if there are philosophical arguments to support this position, it should be assumed that animals do feel pain.) Indeed, there is every reason to think that animals experience pain in much the same way as you and I: they have the nociceptive receptors and the nervous systems that mediate pain; and they respond to analgesia in much the same way as humans do; also they behave much the same way as we do when exposed to noxious stimuli. Scientists working on animal models contend that the nervous systems of animals are so similar to that of human beings that comparative work is not only possible but necessary to advance scientific knowledge. As shown above – and more examples are given below – for ethical reasons, it is not possible to perform many of the scientifically interesting procedures on human beings.

It is difficult to avoid the conclusion that, if animal experimentation were stopped, then fundamental work in the brain sciences, especially those related to therapies for neural degeneration (e.g., Parkinson's disease) and damage (e.g., stroke), would come to a sudden halt; and there would be no alternative ways to pursue these fundamental lines of research. Of course, to many people who oppose animal experimentation, this is worth the price for saving animal suffering.

In order to conduct animal research in the UK, it is necessary to be licensed by the Home Office of the British government. Both the individual experimenter and the research project must be approved; and the research team is under a *legal* responsibility to adhere to procedures for working with animals. This responsibility relates to: (a) using the smallest number of animals possible; (b) the use of reward, deprivation and aversive stimuli; (c) housing and care; and (d) anaesthesia, analgesia and euthanasia.[3] There is a trade-off between the importance of the results and the potential suffering of the animal (however, suffering is minimized). Laboratories are regularly inspected by Home Office inspectors to ensure standards are being maintained.

Stopping animal research would prevent – or at the very least, significantly delay – the development of effective treatment for, among other things, the cancers, dementia, stroke, Parkinson's disease, brain injury – and this could be a rather long list. Set against this benefit is the saving in terms of animal suffering, which, although it is kept to a minimum, is not totally eliminated. The cosy idea that it is possible to stop animal research – a desire that most people hold – and replace it with an equally effective *alternative* is, alas, wishful thinking. If it were this easy, well-intentioned scientists would already have stopped working with animals. Unfortunately, tissue cultures and computer models do not have heart attacks, strokes, Alzheimer's disease, schizophrenia or anxiety. Whatever one's position on this debate, there remain many thorny issues to confront.

> **ASK YOURSELF**
> What are the important factors that we should consider when evaluating the ethical basis of animal experiments?

Stem-cell Technology

Recent years have seen great interest in stem-cell technology and the promise it holds for the renewal of cells in the body (including the brain, via neural transplantation procedures). The development of this exciting medical advance has come from experimental brain research in non-human animals, and it is currently being tested on these animals. Before the conclusion of this chapter, let us cast our eye over the outlines of this technology and what it promises for clinical neuroscience.

Intensive research work in the 1990s focused on the development of the science and technology of stem-cell research; the dawn of the new century saw the early stages of the realization of the promise of cell renewal. During the early years of the twenty-first century, stem cells were implanted in various organs in the body (e.g., stem cells taken from patients' own bone marrow and injected into damaged areas of their hearts: these stems developed into muscles and blood vessel cells, and led to significant improvement in their medical condition). There are many physical conditions that will benefit from this technology.

There is particular interest in stem-cell technology for neurodegenerative conditions (Weiss, 1999). First, there are a large number of degenerative brain diseases for which current medical practice offers only partial solutions (e.g., Parkinson's disease), or no viable solutions at all (the variety of dementias, e.g., Alzhiemer's disease); and many thousands of people a year suffer cerebral accidents (such as stroke), which lead to cell death in the brain. The hope of stem-cell technology is to replace this diseased tissue with new tissue. Today many biotechnology firms are in the race to develop and patent viable stem-cell technologies for these brain disorders (e.g., www.ReNeuron.com). To date, there have been promising results in non-human animals: for example, implanted stem cells can restore cognitive functions following experimental brain damage (e.g., Grigoryan et al., 2000).

What are stem cells?

Stem-cell technology is helping us understand how an organism develops from a single cell and how healthy cells can replace damaged cells in adult organisms (see also chapter 4). Stem cells are special types of cells that have three important properties: (a) they are unspecialized; (b) they are capable of dividing and renewing themselves for long periods of time; and (c) under certain conditions, they can be induced to become specialized cells (e.g., neurons) – they can become almost any cell in the body (Temple, 2001).

Two types of stem cells are studied: (a) embryonic stem cells and (b) adult stem cells. These two types have different functions and characteristics. In the 3- to 5-day-old embryo, called a *blastocyst*, a small group of about 30 cells, called the inner cell mass, gives rise to around 300 different or highly specialized cells needed to make up adult organisms (heart, lung, skin, brain), totalling some 100 trillion cells. In some adult tissues, such as bone marrow, muscle and brain, discrete populations of adult stem cells generate replacements for cells that are lost through normal wear and tear, injury or disease (adult stem cells are found in many more forms of tissue than previously thought).

One of the fundamental properties of a stem cell is that it does not have any tissue-specific structures that allow it to perform specialized functions. In their original form, stem cells do not carry out physiological functions; however, these unspecialized cells can give rise to specialized (functional) cells (a process called *differentiation*). Unlike nerve cells – which do not normally replicate themselves – stem cells may replicate many times (a process called *proliferation*).

The technological trick is to develop stem cells that can be cultivated outside the laboratory and implanted into circumscribed areas of the brain in order to replace diseased tissue without interfering with the functioning of healthy tissue. For example, some stem-cell cultures are available that proliferate in low temperatures (ideal for their development), but which in the higher temperature of the brain have a much lower rate of proliferation and therefore less chance of becoming cancerous.

Stem cells in Parkinson's disease

Parkinson's disease (PD) affects more than 2 per cent of the population over 65 years of age; it is caused by a progressive degeneration and loss of dopamine (DA)-producing neurons, which leads to tremor, rigidity and hypokinesia (abnormally decreased mobility). It is thought that PD may be the first disease to be amenable to treatment using stem-cell transplantation. Factors that support this notion include the knowledge of the specific cell type (DA neurons) needed to relieve the symptoms of the disease. In addition, several laboratories have been successful in developing methods to induce embryonic stem cells to differentiate into cells with many of the functions of DA neurons. However, much more research and technological development will be required before stem-cell implantation becomes a standard form of therapy.

ASK YOURSELF
How likely is it that the great promise of stem-cell technology will become a common medical reality?

For many of us in the future, stem-cell technology will not be merely an interesting section in a textbook but our best hope for a longer and better quality of life: this is a serious and important topic.

Brain Prostheses

Other chapters in this book have discussed the development of various prostheses, such as the artificial retina (chapter 5). Now, neurophysiological research is leading to the development of artificial brain parts. The first brain prosthesis is the artificial hippocampus (Graham-Rowe, 2003). Unlike previous prostheses, such as the artificial retina and cochlear implants, which stimulate brain activity, the artificial hippocampus, in the form of a silicon-chip implant, will perform the same processes as the real hippocampus. Ultimately it may be used to replace lost cognitive functions, for instance in patients who have suffered brain damage due to stroke, epilepsy or Alzheimer's disease.

How does the artificial hippocampus work? First, it is necessary to build a mathematical model of how the hippocampus performs under all possible conditions; second, this mathematical model must be replicated on a silicon chip; and third, the chip will have to interface with the brain in some way. To achieve the first aim, researchers took slices of rat hippocampus and electrically stimulated them until they determined which electrical input produced which output. Putting the information from various slices together gave the team a mathematical model of the entire hippocampus. The actual chip would not need to be implanted in the brain; it can rest on the skull, communicating through arrays of electrodes (one set of electrodes records the electrical activity coming in from the rest of the brain; the other set of electrodes sends appropriate electrical instructions back out to the brain).

It is possible to develop neural network functions of the actions of populations of neurons involved in a motor task, which in a real sense is downloading into an artificial medium (the neural network system) the pattern of neural activity controlling behaviour. This artificial hippocampus moves us closer to the day when the downloading of the mind onto a computer is less a figment of the imagination than a realistic neuroscience technology!

> **ASK YOURSELF**
> Will there be a time in the foreseeable future when psychological functions are augmented by brain–computer interfaces?

Conclusion

The direct neurophysiological techniques surveyed in this chapter open up a perspective on brain functioning that simply is not available from other approaches. In particular, these techniques allow an experimental approach to be adopted; this stands in contrast to the essentially correlational approaches of many other techniques (e.g., neuroimaging; see chapter 10). Not only does basic neurophysiology in non-humans provide information on brain structure and function – going down to single neurons and gene expression; it also opens up the opportunity of developing neuroscience interventions for human neurodegenerative diseases (e.g., the dementias). But, as discussed above, the ethical issues entailed by such research are important. The development of neuroprostheses is another exciting new area that should come to play an important role in the treatment of brain disease – these developments should also contribute to the development of more realistic computer simulations of brain processes (see chapter 7), adding to our knowledge of the computational processes of the brain.

Learning Questions

1. What is unique about neurophysiological procedures?
2. What are the respective strengths and weaknesses of recording, stimulation and lesion procedures?
3. What techniques are used to measure the expression of genes in neurons?
4. How might stem-cell technology be used for the treatment of human neurodegenerative diseases?
5. How can we evaluate the benefits of neurophysiological research in relation to its ethical and moral costs?

NOTES

1   Experimental observations are theoretical, and filtered through the lens of underlying theory, hypothesis and operational procedures. However, many neurophysiological observations are partially indirect in other ways: for example, the measurement and analysis of chemicals in the extracellular space during the performance of some behavioural task is not a totally *direct* measure of the chemicals in the synaptic cleft (see the *microdialysis* section in the present chapter); however, within the limitations of currently available experimental procedures, they are as close as research can get. In any case, they are certainly much more direct than that obtained with neuroimaging techniques.

2   Conditioned emotional suppression of ongoing behaviour is a standard way in rat experiments to assess CS–UCS strength. This response reflects one of the main behavioural effects of the presentation of an aversive CS, which is to inhibit ongoing behaviour (i.e., suppressive behaviour): the degree of behavioural suppression is taken as the strength of the CS–UCS formation. In passing, it is interesting to note that this *behavioural inhibition* CR is very unlike the UCR elicited by the UCS (i.e., the foot shock), which is characterized by flinching, jumping, vocalization, etc. (This is yet another example of the fact that the CR is not simply a substitute for the UCR; see chapter 7.) Chapter 14 returns to these phenomena when it discusses the neurobiology of fear and anxiety.

3   The British Psychological Society's ethical guidelines may be found at www.bps.org.uk.

FURTHER READING

Carlson, N. R. (2000). *Physiology of Behavior.* London: Allyn & Bacon.

Kalat, J. W. (1998). *Biological Psychology.* London: Brooks/Cole.

Kiessling, A. A. & Anderson, S. C. (2003). *Human Embryonic Stem Cells: An Introduction to the Science and Therapeutic Potential.* London: Jones & Bartlett.

chapter 12 Psychopharmacology

Learning Objectives

To be able to:

1. Outline the various forms of psychopharmacological research and the types of experimental designs employed.
2. Describe the drug discovery process and how drugs are tested in clinical trials.
3. Distinguish between clinical efficacy and toxicity.
4. Consider the technical aspects of drug action in the body and how this relates to clinical effects.
5. Discuss the scientific and ethical/moral implications of DNA-based differences in efficacy and safety profiles.

This chapter builds upon the theoretical foundations of neurons and neurotransmission (chapter 4) in its focus on the research techniques used in psychopharmacology, which is defined as the mode of action and effects of chemicals on psychological processes. Included in our discussion are the common types of psychopharmacological research; the various research designs used in this research; drug discovery and development (including clinical trials); some of the technical aspects of how drugs move through and affect the body; and the interplay of neurotransmitters and genetic factors (*psychopharmacogenetics*), which is one of the exciting new developments that is shaping the future of psychopharmacology.

Most of us have first-hand experience of the effects of changes in neurotransmitters on psychological functions. The majority of us take everyday drugs: coffee, tea, nicotine and alcohol; and a smaller number of us take either physician-prescribed medication to change psychological state (e.g., antidepressant medication) or 'self-medication' (e.g., marijuana, amphetamine and cocaine). These drugs have psychological effects because there are receptors in the brain that are sensitive to these chemicals. Without these binding sites (i.e., postsynaptic receptors), drugs would have no effect.

Often drugs are viewed as having a direct effect on neurotransmission, often couched in terms of remedying some chemical deficiency or imbalance. However, drugs and endogenous neurotransmitters (know as *ligands*) not only influence neurotransmission by binding to postsynaptic receptor molecules; they also have effects upon the expression of genes in the nucleus of the cell (see chapter 4). As shown in this chapter, the topic of psychopharmacology is becoming increasingly tied to that of genetics; and much research effort is now being devoted to understanding the interplay of pharmacological and genetic processes (an area known as *pharmacogenetics*; see below). In addition, psychopharmacology and molecular genetic strategies are now being used in neuro-imaging studies of brain activation, where it is becoming increasingly common to see studies that examine functional brain activation patterns in relation to specific genes and pharmacological functions (e.g., do schizophrenia patients show an abnormal pattern of functional responses on a relevant task, and do specific genes predict the ability of certain drugs to restore normal functioning?). The promise of an integrated brain science is rapidly becoming not only a reality, but also standard practice in neuroscience research (Callicott, 2003).

▮▯ Types of Psychopharmacological Research

There are three main types of research in *psychopharmacology*, each with a different set of research questions and tools – although relatively separate domains of study, these different types of research are mutually reinforcing (figure 12.1).

1. *Basic research* aims to understand the nature of neurotransmission at the molecular and cellular levels of analysis. Such research is needed for all other types of psychopharmacological research, and contributes to our knowledge on all aspects of neurotransmission,

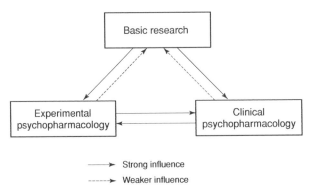

Figure 12.1 Interaction of types of research. The three main types of psychopharmacological research are mutually beneficial. *Basic research* strongly influences *experimental psychopharmacology* and *clinical psychopharmacology* (e.g., basic genetic effects on drug action); there are strong influences between *experimental psychopharmacology* and *clinical psychopharmacology*; and both types of research inform (albeit less strongly, but no less importantly) basic research (e.g., highlighting practical issues in need of a fundamental theoretical development). Although useful for exposition, these types of research tend to get blurred in actual practice.

from neurotransmitter synthesis and release, receptor molecule binding and action potentials, to secondary messenger effects on DNA expression.

2. *Experimental psychopharmacology* uses drugs as a methodological tool to probe brain systems. For example, the researchers may want to understand the neural basis of memory or schizophrenia. To achieve these ends, they may manipulate known pharmacological systems in the brain in order to understand their neurochemical bases. The researcher might also combine this approach with: (a) behavioural tests of psychological functions; (b) neuroimaging to localize neurochemical processes; and (c) genetic analysis (e.g., examining the role of candidate genes). In regard to schizophrenia, the drug amphetamine has been widely used to influence dopaminergic circuits that are putatively related to schizophrenia symptoms; these neurochemical effects can then be related to performance on cognitive tasks that are thought to model the cognitive disruptions seen in the schizophrenia patient (e.g., latent inhibition; see chapter 17).

3. *Clinical psychopharmacology* is interested in identifying and developing drug treatments for specific clinical conditions. Here the concern is less with the neural basis of the effects of these drugs – although, for sure, these are important – but with clinical efficacy and safety: does the drug alleviate symptoms without causing adverse side effects? Unlike basic and experimental research, clinical research must deal with the full range of practical and ethical issues that pertain to testing new drugs on human beings. In addition, human beings have psychiatric diseases that are not so evident in other animals (or, indeed, evident at all) – behaviours in non-human animals that seem to resemble anxiety in human beings may be studied, but where in non-human animals are thought disorders, such as magical ideation (e.g., believing that one's thoughts can directly influence the material world)?[1]

> **ASK YOURSELF**
> How do the various types of psychopharmacological research complement each other?

Experimental design

The preferred form of experimental design is the double-blind randomized design in which participants are randomly assigned to experimental groups (e.g., drug vs. placebo); sometimes the design is 'crossed over', meaning that on one occasion the participant received either placebo or drug, and on the second occasion the alternate placebo/drug – this type of design controls for (between-participant) individual differences, which add error variance to data. The 'double-blind' feature of this design refers to the fact that neither the participant nor the experimenter is aware of who has been given the drug or the placebo – such knowledge can have a subtle effect on expectations and ratings. After the experiment is completed and the data analysed, then the code is broken to reveal which group received the drug and which the placebo.

The placebo effect

A few words need to be said about placebos and the 'placebo effect'. A placebo is an inert substance with no pharmacological mode of action; however, it often has an effect. A placebo is used to control for expectancy effects: often if the patient *believes* they have been given a drug, then their symptoms will improve (for an evolutionary account of this effect, see Evans, D., 2003). Chapter 6 showed that stress can impair the immune system, and it is likely that at least some of the placebo effect is mediated by enhanced immune system functioning. In animal studies, too, a placebo is used: this usually consists of a 'vehicle' or 'sham' group: this group is treated in an identical manner to the experimental group but without the drug (i.e., they are handled in the same way, etc.). It is possible that the treatment of the animals, and not the drug itself, may have real physiological effects (e.g., being injected may produce unexpected behavioural effects).

Issues of validity

In all research there are issues of validity to consider when interpreting experimental data. Two types of validity are important: (a) *internal validity*; and (b) *external validity*.

Internal validity

Internal validity refers to the extent to which the interpretation of an experiment is logically consistent with the internal features of the experiment. For example, if a test of the effects of caffeine on some measure of cognitive performance were conducted, it would be important to look closely at the design details of the study to ensure that interpretations are valid. Were participants randomly assigned to the caffeine and placebo conditions? Were participants and experimenter blind to the drug/placebo groups? It might also be desirable to conduct tests to ensure that the two groups were not markedly different in terms of age or weight (age might be independently related to cognitive performance; weight to the psychological effects of caffeine due to metabolism differences).

External validity

External validity refers to the extent to which our interpretations generalize beyond the experimental sample to the wider population – that is, the target population. After careful scrutiny, the internal validity of the caffeine experiment might be supported. If caffeine were found to retard the performance decline seen in the placebo group over the course of the experiment, then it might be concluded that these effects generalize to the wider world. But does our experiment have external validity? On closer inspection, it might be realized that the experiment was conducted in the morning and contained mainly people of an introverted character who were willing to turn up so early for a psychology study. For these reasons, the experiment may not have good external validity, because it is known that cognitive performance is not affected by caffeine in a simple manner, but is influenced by time of day of testing and introversion–extroversion (Corr, Pickering & Gray, 1995). In order to provide support for its external validity it would prove necessary to rerun the experiment at different times of the day and with introverts and extroverts.

In the case of clinical trials (see below), issues of internal and external validity are crucial. For example, it would be little use developing a drug to treat depression in elderly females by conducting the clinical trials on young men. There are a number of crucial issues that need to be taken into account when designing a study with good internal and external validity.

Types of design

A randomized *between-groups* design has good internal validity, but it may conceal true drug effects because of the variability (i.e., statistical error) between the groups. Pharmacogenetics (see below) warns us that different people have different reactions to the same drug, and this too may obscure the main effect of the drug. One solution is to match the groups on key characteristics (e.g., age and sex), while still maintaining randomization (i.e., every individual has an equal chance of being assigned to the experimental conditions). Matching will increase the statistical *power* of the test by reducing, if not eliminating, differences between the groups (*power* refers to the ability of the statistical test to detect a difference when one actually exists between the groups – increasing the sample size is a common way to increase statistical power).[2]

Often a *repeated-measures* (also known as *within-participants*) design is preferred because all participants receive all drugs and the placebo (the order of these conditions is 'counterbalanced' to eliminate order effects). As with the between-participants design, administering the drugs/placebo double-blind is crucial. This has the desirable effects of controlling individual differences and thus increasing statistical power. However, the disadvantages include practice effects on performance, and general familiarization with the experimental environment. On some measures of performance, learning occurs, so performance on the second occasion of testing will be better than on the first occasion (this learning effect even occurs on tasks which are not explicitly measuring learning, e.g., eye movements; see chapter 9).

External validity may be threatened for a variety of reasons. For example, the experimental results may only generalize to individuals who get multiple treatments; experimental participants may be sensitized to the purpose of the study, and this expectation may influence their response to the drug; being part of a trial and continuously monitored may interact with the drug effects (especially with psychoactive drugs). In fact, a very long list of factors that may compromise the external validity of drug trials could be compiled. For this reason, it is important that the effectiveness and safety of drugs are monitored in ways that mimic the conditions prevailing in the final target environments in which the drug is to be administered (e.g., primary health-care clinic) (figure 12.2).

> **ASK YOURSELF**
> What are the advantages and disadvantages of the different research designs used in psychopharmacology?

Drug Discovery and Development

Before trials are conducted to assess clinical efficacy and safety, the drug must be first discovered and developed. Basic research informs the process of drug discovery; clinical studies show which chemical compounds affect psychological states; and experimental approaches help to build sophisticated models of the complex interplay of genetic,

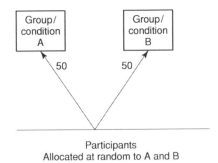

(a) **Randomized Between-groups Design**

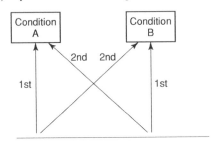

(b) **Repeated-measures Design**

Figure 12.2 The two basic research designs used in psychopharmacological research. (a) In the *between-groups design* participants are randomly assigned to one of the experimental conditions (e.g., drug or placebo); and (b) in the *repeated-measures design* participants are tested in all experimental conditions, usually in a counterbalanced way (e.g., half of the sample have an AB combination; the other half, a BA condition – this controls for order effects). There are several variations on these two basic designs.

neurochemical and cellular processes – including the construction of neural network models of brain–mind relations (Park, 1998).

Drug discovery

Traditionally, the identification of a chemical compound that serves as a useful drug has relied more on serendipity than a rational process of deduction, hypothesis and empirical test. Each drug on the market has its own discovery history: the history of drug discovery is the development of a drug for one purpose only to find that it has a quite different effect. Typically, drug development uses as many approaches as are available. However, increasingly, basic neuroscience and genetics are leading to the development of specific drugs for specific diseases: once the disease process is known, then it is possible to target the process with a drug intervention. For example, it might be discovered that the cause of a specific disease is the under- or overproduction of an enzyme, and this knowledge would allow the development of drugs that either stimulate or inhibit the production of this enzyme.

Knowledge of how the body works is essential, and then compounds are isolated that impact upon the processes of the disease system. Most disease processes are complex, involving a cascade of biochemical events. This complex process must be broken down into its separate parts, and each part is then analysed. Then the decision must be made as to the most appropriate stage to intervene with the new drug. At the end of the discovery and development process, only one question needs to be answered: 'Does the drug change the disease process in a positive direction without having significant adverse side effects?'

Once the disease process is known (*pathogenesis*), it is possible to test in a series of test-tube experiments, known as *assays*, the effects of compounds as they are added to enzymes, cell cultures or cellular substances grown in a laboratory. Hundreds, perhaps thousands, of assays will be performed before any effect is observed. Once a chemical compound is identified, then testing in non-human animals can commence.

Typically, two or more species are used to test the biological effects of new drugs – drugs can have different effects in different species. Animal testing is primarily concerned with assessing toxicity and safety. Animal research is essential because it is simply not possible to know in advance how a new drug compound will affect the intact animal. Such testing facilities are required to adhere to stringent legislation concerning the care and treatment of animals, and it is a requirement that as few animals as possible are used. Animal testing reveals vital information concerning how much of a drug is absorbed into the blood; how it is broken down chemically in the body; the toxicity of its metabolites; and how quickly the drug and its metabolites are excreted from the body.

However, as knowledge accumulates, computer models of biological processes may be used to simulate enzyme functions and to design drugs that influence the action of these functions. Computer models can show what the receptor site looks like and how the chemical compound might either stimulate or inhibit the enzyme. Knowledge of the disease process enables *rational* development of drugs. (*Rational* in the context refers to development according to existing knowledge. In contrast, *empirical* refers to the trial-and-error approach of seeing what works. Although it is a hit-and-miss approach, the empirical strategy has proved very successful in leading to the identification of the vast majority of drugs used today: necessity may be the mother of invention, but serendipity has been the father of drug discovery.)

> **ASK YOURSELF**
> Will the trial-and-error approach to drug discovery ever be replaced by a more 'rational' approach based on theoretical models?

Clinical Research Trials

Once animal experiments have been completed, then the next stage of the drug development process is to move on to clinical trials. A clinical trial is an *experiment* conducted with either healthy volunteers or patients. The principles of good experimental design and appropriate statistics are important: research questions can only be adequately answered by an appropriate research design.

New drugs are tested in human beings through a series of clinical trials (phase I–IV trials). These trials must be undertaken in order for a new drug to receive regulatory approval (i.e., a licence to market). Each country has its own regulatory framework, but most adopt the standard protocols of the USA and the UK. Psychologists are often involved in clinical trials, providing necessary expertise in a variety of areas: mood ratings, psychomotor tests (e.g., reaction time), advice on drug protocol (especially the optimal times points for psychological testing) and training of experimenters.

Phase I trials

Phase I trials comprise the first test of the drug in human beings. Typically small groups of healthy young (usually male) individuals are recruited; but sometimes, where the drug is designed for use in patients with a particular disease, patients may be used. All participants are fully briefed on the nature of the clinical trials, and they must give informed consent before the trial commences. Often a dose-escalation design is employed: the first small group of volunteers (approximately 10 people) will be given a low dose of the drug; if no adverse effects are found then the next group of volunteers will be given a higher dose; and this dose escalation continues for a predetermined number of doses (unless adverse effects are reported, which would halt the clinical trial). Volunteers are tested in a purpose-built clinical setting with continuous monitoring of vital signs and an emergency team available to cope with life-threatening adverse effects.

The main purpose of phase I research is to assess the metabolic and pharmacological actions of the drug in the body, and to determine whether adverse effects occur. Often psychological measurements are also taken to assess any subtle changes in mood and behaviour (e.g., sleep disturbance) – these effects may suggest other applications for the drug. The aim of a phase I trial is to gather information on how the drug is handled by the body (*pharmacokinetics*) and how it affects the body (*pharmacodynamics*) (see below), as well as to determine the maximum tolerated dose. About one-third of drugs tested at this stage fail.

Phase II trials

Phase II trials include a controlled clinical study aimed at determining the clinical efficacy of the drug (to cure, relieve or prevent disease) and assessing its short-term side effects. These studies typically use a double-blind, placebo-controlled, randomized study with upwards of 200 patients with the disease. Such trials are commonly conducted in hospital units specializing in clinical research. Monitoring of patients is typically less intensive than in phase I, but patients are still very closely monitored. Pharmacokinetics – how the body handles the drug – are re-evaluated because patients may have different kinetic profiles from the healthy young men typically used in phase I trials. The main aim of phase II research is to determine the optimum dose in terms of clinical efficacy, safety and tolerability. At this stage approximately one-half of drugs fail.

Phase III trials

Phase III trials are an extension of phase II trials: they entail the administration of the new drug, at the optimum dose, to a much larger clinical sample of patients. Information gathered at this phase is used for evaluating the overall benefit–risk relationship of the drug, and to provide a basis for physician labelling. In this phase, the drug is used in the same way that it will be marketed and used in the general population. Phase III trials typically use several hundred to several thousand patients. Once safety is assessed and clinical efficacy demonstrated, then the pharmaceutical company may apply to a government regulatory authority to gain a licence to market the product.

Depending on the nature of the disease and the availability of alternative drugs, the new drug may be compared against the currently available treatment rather than a placebo. This procedure is often demanded by ethical consideration: it would be wrong to withhold a currently effective drug from a patient in order to test the efficacy of a new drug. Only about half of all drugs tested at phase III find their way onto the market.

Phase IV trials

After the licence to market has been granted, further trials examine particular aspects of the drug in specific populations, often comparing its efficacy, side effects and tolerability with competitors' drugs. Also, the drug can be tested for its effectiveness in treating other disorders, or its interactions with other drugs. Physicians will be recruited to report back to the company any adverse or peculiar effects patients report after taking the new drug.

All four clinical phases require approval by an appropriate ethics committee, composed of experts in the field and related fields and laypeople, who examine the details of the protocols carefully.

There are several problems with extrapolating from clinical trials to real-world practice. For example, let us take the case of antidepressants. Clinical trials conducted under ideal conditions for up to 1 year usually have high compliance (e.g., patients take the drug at the correct time and in the correct dose) and low dropout rates because patients feel that they are being routinely monitored. However, under everyday conditions, compliance is likely to be much poorer; therefore the drug efficacy estimated from clinical trials may overestimate the efficacy seen under more usual medication conditions – this is a particular problem for drugs that may have undesirable side effects (e.g., impotence). In addition, clinical trials are usually conducted for a relatively brief period of time, and the long-term effects of antidepressant medication – a crucial variable in preventing relapse – is often not thoroughly investigated.

> **ASK YOURSELF**
> Why are not all adverse side effects of drugs identified during clinical trials?

▩ Technical Aspects of Drug Effects

This section summarizes some of the technical aspects of psychopharmacological research: (a) the route of administration; (b) how drug molecules move around the body (i.e., *pharmacokinetics*); and (c) clinical efficacy (i.e., *pharmacodynamics*).

Drug delivery routes

There are a number of different routes by which drugs are administered, and each has its own set of advantages and disadvantages, influencing absorption, toxicity and clinical effectiveness (Carlson, 2000). In the case of human beings, it can be shown how some routes are more likely to lead to addiction.

1. *Intravenous (IV) injection*: Drug molecules are dissolved/suspended in a liquid and then injected into the bloodstream (this route of administration is commonly used in animal research). The time between injection and action of the drug in the brain is a matter of seconds. Disadvantages include: (a) the full dose (i.e., the dose required for optimal effects) is administered (this may not be desirable all at once, and to avoid adverse physiological reaction it needs to be gradually introduced); (b) some skill is required to inject the vein properly; and (c) in the case of human beings, some people are fearful of injections (leading to participant dropout and a possible effect of anxiety on the drug response). This route is often preferred by advanced drug abusers because of its speed and power of action.

2. *Intraperitoneal (IP) injection*: The drug is injected through the abdominal wall into the *peritoneal cavity* (i.e., space that surrounds stomach, intestines and liver). This route of administration is not as rapid as IV injection. It is typically used with small laboratory animals.

3. *Oral administration*: In human beings a convenient route of administration, but IV or IP routes are better for getting the drug, in the required dose, directly into the bloodstream. In addition, some drugs are destroyed or degraded by stomach products (i.e., digestive acids and enzymes), rendering this route of limited use.

4. *Intramuscular (IM) injection*: The drug is injected into a large muscle (e.g., buttocks), where it is absorbed into the bloodstream via the capillaries that supply the muscle. The speed of travel to the central nervous system is slower and less concentrated than either the IV or IP routes (its speed of travel to the brain can be slowed by a second drug that constricts blood vessels). This route is sometimes used with psychiatric patients in the form of *depot* medication, which works over a long time period (the rate of release of the drug can be further slowed by placing it in various substances).

5. *Subcutaneous (SC) injection*: the drug is injected into the space beneath the skin (sometimes used in human studies where only a small amount of the drug is needed – a convenient route for the slow release of a drug). For example, this route is used when administering nicotine to human non-smokers in experimental studies of nicotine action in the brain.

6. *Intrarectal administration*: Drugs can be placed in the rectum (in the form of suppositories) – this method is not often used in animal studies (they defecate when fearful). This route of administration is very useful, though, for drugs that may upset the digestive tract.

7. *Inhalation*: Drugs can be infused through the lungs, and this is the usual route for many drugs of abuse: nicotine, marijuana, 'free-base' cocaine, etc. The benefit, and danger, of this route of administration is the short distance between the lungs and

the brain: this increases the addictive power of inhaled drugs (i.e., there is a short interval between the CS/environment and UCS/drug; see chapter 7).

8. *Topical administration*: Drugs can be absorbed directly through the skin (e.g., nicotine-replacement patches). This is a relatively slow process allowing small amounts of the drugs to enter the body over a long time period.

9. *Mucous membrane administration (insufflation)*: The mucous membrane lining the nasal passage offers another convenient route of administration. Some drugs of abuse are sniffed for this very reason (e.g., cocaine). The major advantage – and disadvantage in terms of addiction potential – is that the drug reaches the brain in a very short time.

10. *Intracerebral administration*: In experimental animals, drugs can be injected directly into the brain. Also, drugs can be administered into the cerebrospinal fluid in the ventricles: this route of administration achieves rapid and widespread effects in the brain – it is sometimes used in human beings to administer antibiotics in severe forms of brain infection.

These are important consideration when developing a new drug for widespread use in human beings. For example, it is doubtful whether IV, IM or IP routes would be popular for a cold-preparation remedy!

Dose-response curve

Once the drug has entered the bloodstream it must then reach its site of action to exert its biological effect. The effectiveness of a drug is described by the *dose-response curve*: this is calculated by administering various doses of the drug (defined in terms of milligrams of drug per kilogram of body weight), and the effects of the drug are plotted. This is one of the most important concepts in *pharmacodynamics*, which is the study and understanding of the biochemical and physiological effects of drugs and their mechanisms of action.

In this dose-response curve, two responses must be plotted: (a) the therapeutic response; and (b) side effects (see figure 12.3): the difference between these two curves provides an estimate of the drug's margin of safety (but as discussed below, responses to drugs can vary widely between individuals). Different drugs have different dose-response curves because: (a) they have different routes of administration; (b) they have different sites of action; and (c) they have differing levels of *affinity* for receptors (i.e., some drugs have high affinity and bind easily with receptors, thus they exert good effects even at low doses; other drugs have low affinity and therefore require a higher dose for an adequate response to be observed).

Therapeutic index

The *therapeutic index* of a drug is the ratio of: (a) the dose that produces the desired effect in 50 per cent of participants, and (b) the dose that produces toxic effects in 50 per cent of participants. For example, if it were found that, for a new drug, the dose that produced

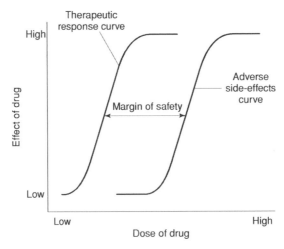

Figure 12.3 Dose-response curve for a hypothetical drug. The left-hand curve is the therapeutic response; the right-hand curve the adverse side effects; and the difference between these curves the margin of safety (the larger the margin, the safer the drug).

toxic effects in 50 per cent of participants was 10 times higher than that which produced the desired effect in 50 per cent of participants, the therapeutic index would be 10. Obviously, drugs with a large therapeutic index are safest.

The therapeutic index is an important consideration in the development of psychiatric drugs, where accidental or deliberate overdoses are a real concern. In contrast to the older classes of anti-anxiety drug, such as the barbiturates and tricyclics, with a therapeutic index of 2–3, modern tranquillizers have a therapeutic index of over 100 (see chapter 15). This therapeutic index means that the drug has a high affinity for sites of action relating to clinical efficacy, and low affinity for sites of action relating to toxic effects. Drug development must balance these two effects in the attempt to design drugs that are clinically powerful but low in terms of adverse reactions.

Drugs are rarely administered on only one occasion; therefore, in evaluating their effects it is important to consider the effects of repeated administration. Over time, drug effects are likely to change: (a) *tolerance* refers to diminishing drug effects; and (b) *sensitization* refers to enhanced drug effects. Tolerance is seen in the case of many drugs of abuse, with increasingly large doses of the drug required to achieve the same effect – physiological adaptation to the drug (probably resulting in fewer postsynaptic receptors) leads to *withdrawal symptoms* when the drug is no longer taken. These symptoms result from the drug replacing the action of naturally occurring (endogenous) ligands (neurotransmitters): if the drug is not taken then the system is in a depleted state. Drugs may lead to tolerance by: (a) making the receptors less sensitive (reduced affinity), or (b) reducing receptor numbers. *Recovery* consists of returning the system to a normal state of functioning with the natural ligands. Such effects must be assessed when developing a new drug. A drug that only achieves clinical efficacy for the first few doses or leads to long-term dependency, is not desirable.

Pharmacokinetics

Pharmacokinetics is concerned with the time course of a drug and its metabolites in the body after administration by any route – loosely speaking, how the body handles drugs. This is an important topic because, for the drug to be effective, it must reach its site of action in a sufficient amount. First, the drug must enter the body (unless it is delivered directly into the brain); second, it must enter the bloodstream and travel to the site of action; third, once at the site of action, the drug must leave the bloodstream and interact with molecules at the site of action; and fourth, the drug must be removed from the body. An effective response to a drug requires the appropriate concentration of drug at the site of action; the dose required to attain and maintain the appropriate concentration depends on pharmacokinetics, which is defined as the movement of drugs around the body. Pharmacokinetic analysis entails the estimation of the following biological parameters (the parameters differ for the various routes of administration summarized above).

Volume of distribution

The *volume of distribution* (Vd) is the amount of drug in the body divided by the concentration in the blood. Some drugs that are lipid (fat)-soluble have a very high volume of distribution; whereas drugs that are lipid-insoluble remain in the blood and have a low Vd. This parameter is important because the amount of drug in the blood is a crucial variable for how much of the drug reaches the target organ; in addition, a high Vd means that the drug is building up in the fatty tissue of the body, which could produce toxic effects. A closely related parameter is *bioavailability*, which is the amount of the drug dose that reaches the blood circulation (with intravenous injection, bioavailability is 100 per cent; but it varies for other routes).

Absorption rate constant

The *absorption rate constant* expresses the speed of absorption. This parameter influences the maximum (peak) concentration, the time at which the maximum concentration occurs (peak time) after a single oral dose. During long-term drug therapy, the extent of absorption is the more important measurement because average concentration depends on it.

Clearance

The *clearance* (Cl) is the volume of plasma from which the drug is completely removed per unit time. The amount eliminated is proportional to the concentration of the drug in the blood. The *elimination constant* relates to the amount of the drug in the body eliminated per unit of time. These parameters are important for working out the dose and frequency of administration. The *elimination half-life* (t1/2) is the time taken for plasma concentration to reduce by 50 per cent. This information is important for considerations of clinical efficacy as well as for toxicity.

> **ASK YOURSELF**
> Is there is a lot more to know about the action of drugs than merely their effects at target receptors?

▉▉▢ Psychopharmacogenetics: DNA Meets Drugs

One of the most exciting outcomes of the genomic revolution is the prospect of drug development based upon knowledge of genetic differences and their effects. *Pharmacogenetics* is the study of genetically related individual differences in responses to drugs; *psycho*pharmacogenetics focuses on the role of genes in reaction to drugs that affect the central nervous system (figure 12.4). The importance of this approach is underscored by the fact that adverse drug reactions (ADRs) comprise the fourth largest cause of premature deaths in the Western world: a clinically efficacious drug may be harmless to one person, but lethal to another.

ADRs are more of a problem than previously thought. A meta-analysis revealed that serious adverse drug reactions occur among 6.7 per cent of all hospitalized patients and that 0.32 per cent of all hospitalized patients develop fatal adverse reactions, causing more than 100,000 deaths annually in the US (Lazarou, Pomeranz & Corey, 1998).

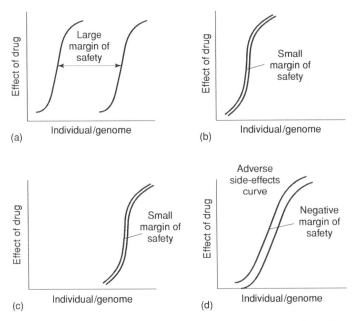

Figure 12.4 Psychopharmacogenetics. Hypothetical dose-response curves for different individuals/genomes administered the same drug, illustrating the role played by individual differences in genetics in therapeutic responses and adverse side effects. (a) Large margin of safety, producing significant therapeutic benefit, with adverse side effects occurring only at a much higher dose; (b) small margin of safety, with the normal dose or therapeutic benefits very close to the dose for adverse side effects; (c) a high dose is required for therapeutic benefit, but this dose coincides with the dose for adverse side effects; and (d) a dangerous profile showing that adverse side effects occur at a lower dose than required for therapeutic benefits.

Pirmohamed et al. (2004) estimated that 6.5 per cent of hospital admissions are due to ADRs, and in the UK approximately 10,000 people a year die as a result of ADRs.

Inter-individual variability in drug metabolism and response is extensive; and drug level in plasma can vary more than 1,000-fold between two individuals having the same weight and with the same drug dosage. Genetic variability is also known for drug absorption, drug metabolism and drug interactions with the receptors. Ageing is known to result in less capacity for drug metabolism as well as less capacity to induce drug-metabolizing enzymes. Genetic factors may account for about 20–40 per cent of the inter-individual differences in drug metabolism and response, but for certain drugs or classes of drugs the genetic factors will be of utmost importance for the outcome of the drug therapy.

Developments in pharmacogenetics promise to produce a number of important benefits: (a) the prediction of drug effectiveness; (b) prior knowledge on drug safety; and (c) the tailoring of drug therapies to the specific genomic make-up of the individual. More precisely, psychopharmacogenetics is defined as the study of variations in the coding or regulatory regions of genes that lead to inter-individual variability in drug effect (efficacy) or in adverse effect profile (toxicity) (for a review of pharmacogenetics, see Aitchison & Gill, 2003).

At present, drugs are prescribed on the basis of what works 'in general', not what is likely to work for the individual patient in question: you and me. In psychiatry this is a big problem, because drugs often simply do not work, or work ineffectively, or produce unpleasant side effects (which sometimes lead to patients not taking their medication). This situation is costly in terms of the chronicity of the illness, the adverse side effects, the increased risk of suicide, and occupational, domestic and social impairment, as well as the financial costs of prescribing expensive but useless drugs. A more rational basis on which to prescribe drugs is needed.[3]

Pharmacogenetics includes the study of two sets of factors: (a) *pharmacodynamic* genetic factors, affecting the drug response at the level of the target organ; and (b) *pharmacokinetic* genetic factors, affecting drug absorption, metabolism and excretion. The effect of drugs at the target organ is indexed by such measures as severity of clinical symptoms, as well as changes in physiological and psychological gating (or changes in standardized behavioural paradigms, in the case of animal studies). Pharmacokinetic responses are assessed by physiological study of the metabolism of the drug in the body.

Ethical issues

Pharmacogenetics is indeed an exciting new approach to the development of drugs, and it promises many benefits; but it brings into clear view some of the ethical issues that echo throughout psychopharmacology.

The first concern is that some people will have to be told that current drug therapies that are *generally* effective for a specific disease are not effective for *them*: when no alternative treatment is available, this information will be unwelcome and may result in an adverse psychological reaction. One psychological consequence might be a reduction in optimism and hope: such reactions are likely to impair the efficiency of immune system functioning (see chapter 6) and thereby contribute to the disease process. Careful thought will need to be given to how such information should be communicated to the patient, and how to deal with adverse psychological reactions, if they occur.

The next issue concerns drug discovery and development. The vast majority of drugs are developed by commercial pharmaceutical companies, who invest enormous amounts of money to develop the everyday drugs that are taken for granted. The research and development programmes that lead to the production of a successful drug can run into hundreds of millions of pounds/dollars and take between 6 and 10 years. Now, pharmacogenetic research – at least, to the extent that it is successful – will identify different groups of people who have differential reactions to drugs. Some of these groups – perhaps those who show particularly strong adverse reactions – may be relatively small in number. Here is the concern: will pharmaceutical companies have the financial incentive to develop effective drug treatments for this small group of people? If they are likely to make a financial loss in such a development programme then why should they? The solution to this dilemma will need to involve a contract between the pharmaceutical industry, government and society as a whole (are you be willing to pay higher taxation to pay for the development of drug therapies for a minority of the population?). As currently seen by the paucity of investment in rare genetic conditions, it would be unduly optimistic to assume that society will willingly underwrite the development costs of drug treatments for the (perhaps very small) minority.

Pharmacogenetic research, in all probability, will produce results in terms of the *likelihood* of adverse reactions and clinical efficacy – few things in genetics are totally certain. Therefore, the next ethical concern relates to the extent to which patients should be allowed to 'take a chance' with potentially dangerous drugs. Patients will need considerable information to make an informed and sensible choice; and society as a whole will need to be educated in the basic science and implications of psychopharmacogenetics.

A particularly difficult ethical issue concerns psychiatric patients. Many countries are now either considering or passing laws to ban the theft of DNA material (e.g., covertly acquiring a strand of hair to test for paternity or disease-proneness): it will be a criminal offence not to obtain informed consent before taking and analysing someone else's DNA sample. There will need to be exceptions to this general requirement: for example, suspected criminals may not have a choice; and accident patients, who cannot give informed consent, may be genotyped for sound medical reasons. But what about the seriously ill schizophrenia patient who believes that the hospital staff are really MI6/CIA agents who want to manipulate his DNA? Under these conditions should this patient's DNA be taken without consent? One consequence of not taking DNA might be the prescription of ineffective and potentially harmful medication; or, at the very least, a continuation of psychotic symptoms, with all that entails. Or should parents be allowed, on religious grounds, to withhold (genetically identified) life-saving drugs from their young children because they do not believe in scientists and physicians 'playing God'? In the nature of ethical concerns, simple solutions are elusive. (Other ethical issues are discussed by Issa, 2000.)

ASK YOURSELF
Should advances in pharmacogenetics make us excited, frightened, or both?

The development of other medical technologies has already thrown up ethical and legal dilemmas. For example, does a man have the right to refuse his (otherwise infertile) ex-partner's use of a frozen embryo created with his sperm? With the development of new medical technologies, such dilemmas are bound to increase in number and complexity. As seen in chapter 13, a proportion of the funding for the Human Genome Project is devoted to addressing these ethical problems. There will undoubtedly be increased public debate over the ethics of pharmacogenetics.

Conclusion

This chapter has discussed how drugs are discovered and developed to provide effective and safe treatments for medical and psychiatric conditions, and the types of basic and experimental research that help build up models of normal and abnormal chemical processes in the brain. This approach in biological psychology is very important in the case of the clinical conditions of depression, anxiety and schizophrenia (see chapters 14–16): not only does psychopharmacology produce treatment for these disorders but it also provides an analytical tool with which to probe and understand neural mechanisms. The close interaction of neurotransmitters and genetic processes, in terms of receptor actions on DNA synthesis (see chapter 4), and the role that genetics plays in influencing the effectiveness and safety of drugs (i.e., psychopharmacogenetics) have also been presented: seen in this light, neurotransmission and molecular genetics are, in some crucial respects, opposite sides of the same neuronal coin.

Learning Questions

1. Why are issues of internal and external validity important in psychopharmacological research designs?
2. What is the 'generalizability problem' in the context of clinical trials?
3. What is the 'therapeutic dose' and why is it important?
4. What is 'pharmacokinetics' and what roles does it play in the design of new drugs?
5. What are the main ethical dilemmas presented by pharmacogenetics, and how might they be handled?

NOTES

1   The Merck *Manual of Diagnosis and Therapy* offers an excellent introduction to the basic, technical and applied aspects of clinical psychopharmacology from the standpoint of a leading international pharmaceutical company (www.merck.com/pubs/mmanual/).

2   More formally, *power* is inversely related to type II error, which is failing to detect a real difference between groups due to such features as statistical noise (error) and inadequate sample sizes. Type I error is the identification of a difference between groups where none really exists (that is, the null hypothesis of no difference is true) – this is indexed by the *significance level* or statistical *probability* of making a type I error.

3   Psychopharmacogenetics is also important in adverse drug reactions seen in those who abuse illegal drugs: often we are told that this or that drug is 'safe' if taken sensibly (and much public

money is spent in disseminating 'information'); but the truth is that, for some people with a certain genetic make-up, even so-called 'harmless' drugs may be quite lethal. For a larger number of people, adverse reactions comprise subtler short-term and long-term psychological effects. Taking any form of psychoactive drug is a gamble, and the dice are loaded by our genetic constitution: if we are lucky, we may just enjoy a few nights of fun; but, if we are less fortunate, we may go on to develop depression, anxiety, psychosis and even perhaps longer-term neurodegeneration (e.g., dementia).

FURTHER READING

Leonard, B. E. (2003). *Fundamentals of Psychopharmacology.* London: Wiley.

Stahl, S. M. (2000). *Essential Psychopharmacology: Neuroscientific Basis and Practical Applications.* Cambridge: Cambridge University Press.

Wendell, W. (1997). *Pharmacogenetics.* Oxford: Oxford University Press.

chapter 13

Psychogenomics

Learning Objectives

To be able to:

1. Explain what is, and is not, meant by 'heritability'.
2. Outline how genetic influences are assessed and the types of genetic study designs used.
3. Evaluate the importance of environmental effects in genetic designs.
4. Discuss what is known about the human genome and how DNA coding regions (i.e., genes) are discovered.
5. Describe methods of studying individual (genetic) differences in normal and abnormal behaviour.

The Human Genome Project has opened up a whole new vista on the role of genetics in psychology. In particular, powerful new methodologies allow a search of the entire human genome for coding sequences (genes) that contribute to complex psychological phenotypes (including behaviours, traits, etc.); and it is now possible to integrate two hitherto separate approaches: *quantitative* (statistical) *genetics* and *qualitative* (molecular) *genetics*. This chapter summarizes these two approaches, and illustrates how they are being simultaneously employed in biological psychology (for a thorough survey of this topic, see Plomin et al., 2001). Part III of the present book (*Applications*) demonstrates how these concepts and methods are being put to use in the study of psychological traits and psychiatric disorders.

The *genome* refers to the totality of genes on all chromosomes – the blueprint for life. Hidden in this 3-billion-letter sequence are some of the major influences on our physical and psychological development; hidden too are the silent genes that play a role in our physical and psychological decline. This search of the genome for the genes involved in psychological processes I have chosen to call *psychogenomics*. The term *behavioural genomics* (Plomin & Crabbe, 2000)[1] is often preferred; but this chapter is concerned not just with overt behaviour, but with all central psychological states (e.g., behaviourally silent learning, as in sensory preconditioning; see chapter 6). Many of the important influences on behaviour are intermediate between neurology and behaviour (i.e., truly *psychological*) – examples are given in chapter 15, when the concept of the *endophenotype* in psychiatric research is discussed.

This chapter starts with a description of quantitative genetic methodologies, designed to estimate by statistical means the influence of genes on psychological phenotypes; then it moves on to qualitative methodologies, designed to identify specific genes at the molecular (genomic) level; and, finally, it integrates these levels of description in our search for the molecular genes that can be related directly to psychological phenomena.

Anyone with even the faintest knowledge of psychology – and the majority of the general public – know something about genetics: popular television programmes, books, newspapers, etc., regularly feature articles on medical 'breakthroughs' in genetics. Much of this public debate is based on biased reporting of scientific data, as well as fundamental misunderstandings of genetic methodologies and the correct interpretation of data. One major aim of this chapter is to clarify some of these misunderstanding so that genetics research is put into proper perspective.

Quantitative (Statistical) Genetics

Until the recent past, genetics in the behavioural sciences comprised quantitative methodologies, a branch of science first introduced by Fisher (1918) and Wright (1921). This set of statistical analytical tools is concerned with the partitioning of variance (individual differences) of a phenotype (trait) into two main components: genetic and non-genetic (environmental) components.[2] Quantitative genetics has comprised two main approaches: twin and adoption studies. Quantitative genetics says nothing about the molecular level of analysis – about the number of genes or the complexity of their interaction – but it can show that genetics makes a contribution to explaining differences observed in a phenotype (e.g., extroversion). Plomin (1994) summarizes the role that genetics has played in developmental psychology.

A less appreciated aspect of this approach is that it permits inferences concerning the contribution of *non-genetic* (environmental) influences. It is thus a mistake to think that quantitative genetics is interested only in genetic influences: in fact, the use of sophisticated genetic methodologies confirms the indispensable role of environmental factors in psychology. To give one example: the probability of a monozygotic (MZ; identical) twin being *concordant* for schizophrenia (i.e., having the condition), if their twin has been diagnosed as having schizophrenia, is slightly less than 50 per cent – despite the fact that they have the same genome, they may have different phenotypes. In this example, quantitative genetics removes any doubt about the non-genetic (environmental) influence on this severe form of psychosis (however, knowing that there *is* an environmental effect does not tell us anything about this effect).

It thus seems that the possession of a gene that predisposes to a particular phenotype may be a *necessary* but not a *sufficient* condition for the expression of that phenotype: environmental influences seem to set the *sufficient* conditions (or, more exactly, the gene–environment interactions; see below). The search for these environmental conditions thus becomes an important part of understanding the genetics of behaviour, especially as the environment may lay the conditions in which genetic influences are expressed (recall the case of PKU; see chapter 2).

As noted by the American Society of Human Genetics (Sherman et al., 1997), until a few decades ago it was believed that human psychological characteristics were almost entirely the result of environmental influences. But now it is known that this belief is untrue: the vast majority of psychological characteristics have a genetic contribution, sometimes to a high degree: intelligence, memory, novelty-seeking and activity level, most forms of psychiatric illness, and introversion–extroversion, all show some degree of genetic influence. In another development, quantitative genetic studies have required developmental psychologists to revise their theories. For example, traditional theories contended that genetic influences were important in infancy and early childhood, but much less so as the child matured – research now shows that, for many traits, genetic effects *increase* throughout early childhood and adolescence. Also, it was asserted that environmental influences on behaviour were shared by family members, rather than experienced uniquely by individuals: it is now known that, in contrast to this view, for many traits, environmental influences make family members different, rather than similar.

The measurement of genetic influence

Quantitative genetic methodologies estimate the percentage of variance in a phenotype attributed to genetic influence and the percentage of variance attributed to non-genetic (environmental) factors. But what does this mean? What does it mean to say that 'height is 80 per cent genetic'? Does it mean that 80 per cent of our height is due to our genetics, with the remaining 20 per cent due to other factors (e.g., nutrition)? Before this question can be answered, it is necessary first to understand the concept of *variance*: genetic methodologies analyse variance, not absolute measures of the phenotype. What this statement means is that a quantitative genetic study of height is concerned with estimating the genetic contribution to *differences* (variations) between the mean height of the population and variation of heights around this mean height. If there is no variance in the phenotype, then the genetic contribution must be zero.[3]

Before discussing variability, it should be noted that all human beings, irrespective of, so-called, 'race', are virtually identical in genetic terms. Only about 1 in every 1,000 base pairs differs (some 2 million in the entire genome). But it is these differences that are important in influencing individual differences. It is, therefore, important to understand the concept of *variance*, because this is at the very heart of quantitative genetic methodologies (Ridley, 2003, provides a good overview of quantitative genetics in the context of evolutionary theory).

The concept of deviation (variance)

Look around you; objects that belong to a single class (e.g., books) vary in width, height, depth, weight, etc. For each of these attributes, you could calculate a mean; then you could work out the extent to which each book differs from this mean value. Then you could take the mean of these deviations, which would leave you with a measure of the mean *dispersion* of your books. This is essentially what is meant by variance, but the calculation is slightly different from the one given here (i.e., the difference being that individual score from the mean is squared before summing the deviations and dividing by the number of deviations[4]).

Let us take a psychological example. If it is assumed that the mean IQ of a population is 100, then individuals in the population should have scores distributed around this mean value. An IQ score of 120 would represent a deviation of +20 (i.e., 120 minus 100); someone with an IQ of 70, would have a deviation score of −30 (i.e., 70 minus 100); and so on for all data points. The basic point is that quantitative genetics assesses the genetic contribution to *these* deviations: it does not refer to absolute scores.

Discrete and continuous distributions

Another important aspect of quantitative genetics is the relationship between genes and distribution of scores.

What is the rationale for expecting *continuous variation* in psychological phenotypes (there is very little variance in morphological features)? Such variation results when the phenotype is influenced by a large number of genes (*polygenic* influences), each contributing a small effect.

In contrast to complex traits, simple Mendelian characteristics (e.g., one's blood group) have discrete variation. This can be illustrated by the relationship between the number of genes and the distribution of the phenotype in a population (figure 13.1). The idea that multiple-gene effects lead to continuously distributed traits is the basis of quantitative genetics.

With a single pair of Mendelian alleles at one locus, with one allele dominant and the other recessive, the distribution of the phenotype in the population would contain two categories of the phenotype (AA, Aa, aa; a 2:1 ratio). Now imagine that there were two loci, with two alleles each – this leads to the following combinations: aabb, AaBB, AaBb, AABB, AABb. Now the distribution is starting to look like a normal distribution. With six loci, each with two alleles, the distribution of phenotypes approaches the normal distribution; and, with many loci, the normal distribution is achieved. The latter part of this chapter looks at some of the strategies being used to identify the genetic basis of these polygenic traits, a method called *quantitative trait loci* (QTLs; Plomin et al., 2003).

Quantitative genetics is usually concerned with psychological phenotypes that are *polygenic* (involving many genes) in nature. For such traits it is not possible to track the flow of genetic transmission through the generations (this *pedigree* approach is used for simple Mendelian traits – indeed, this approach is used to determine if the flow of transmission accords with Mendelian principles of the *law of segregation* and the *law of independent assortment*; see chapter 2).

The concept of heritability (h^2)

Figure 13.2 shows a single-point deviation from the population. This could be made up of genetic variance, environment variance, or, more probably, a combination of the two influences.

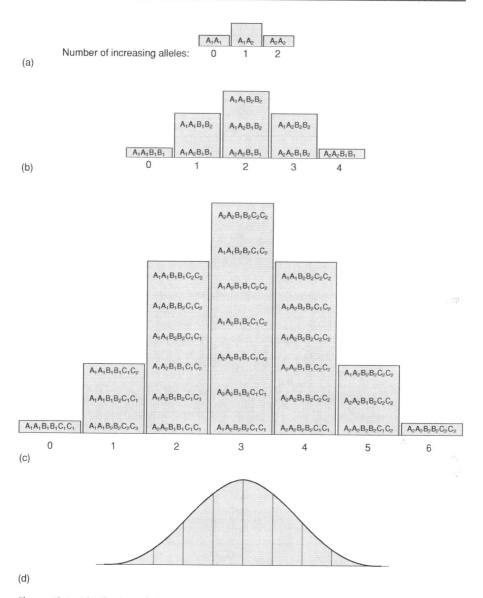

Figure 13.1 Distribution of phenotype for one-to-multiple gene loci. Increasing the number of genes and alleles leads to a distribution that approximates a normal distribution. Assuming additive effects and pure genetic influence, (a) one gene with two alleles yields three genotypes/phenotypes; (b) two genes with two alleles, nine genotypes/phenotypes; and (c) three genes with two alleles 27 genotypes/phenotypes, at which point there is an approximation to a normal distribution of phenotypes. Most psychological phenotypes are affected by multiple genes with more than two alleles, which have their own interaction with the environment. (*Source*: Plomin et al., 2001; used with permission.)

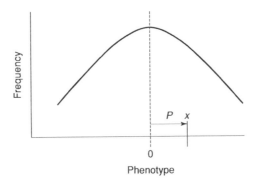

Figure 13.2 Phenotype deviation from population mean. Individual (*x*) deviation from population mean (standardized to have a mean of 0).

Deviation (as assessed by variance) is the central concept in heritability (h^2). Thus, heritability (h^2) = V_A/V_P. V_A is variance in (additive) genetic effect, and V_P is variance in phenotype.

In order to estimate heritability, V_A needs to be estimated. In the case of human beings this is where twin studies and adoption studies come in to place – in non-human animal studies, it is more useful to use more powerful inbreeding studies, where environmental effect can be tightly controlled, to estimate heritability.

If it were found that heritability was 1, then all the variance in the phenotype would be genetic in nature: in other words, all differences between people on the phenotype could be explained by genetic differences. In contrast, if heritability were 0, then there would be no genetic influence: in other words, all differences between people in the phenotype are unrelated to genetic differences.

In calculating heritability, the assumption is made that the environments for this population are identical. If members of the population experience different environments, then the estimate of heritability loses much of its meaning – for example, if some parents and offspring experienced advantageous environments (e.g., superior nutrition), but other families less advantageous environments, then comparisons between families, and thus heritability, would no longer be meaningful: this would be measuring environmental effects. As shown below, certain genetic effects and features of twin/adoption designs can bias this heritability estimate (over- and underestimating genetic influence).

Effect size

Heritability estimates are concerned not only with whether genetics influences behaviour but also by how much: that is, with the *effect size* of the genetic contribution. It is important for us to remember that effect sizes refer to individual differences in the *population*, not to *individuals*. A simple example should suffice to prove this point. If PKU were left untreated, it would have a severe effect on the cognitive development of individuals homozygous for the recessive allele – as close to 100 per cent genetic influence as perhaps can be achieved. But, if a genetics study of a random population were conducted, then the effects size of PKU would be very small, simply because very few individuals (approx. 1 in 10,000) are homozygous for the PKU gene. When treated, there is an even smaller (approaching zero) effect of PKU in the population. This example shows the care that is needed in making inferences from heritability coefficients (it is rather like inferring the size of someone from knowing only their weight but not their height – without the height information, the weight information, though useful, is not terribly helpful). Heritability is a statistic that describes the contribution of genetic differences to observed differences between individuals in a particular population at a particular time, using certain methods. It is *not* some abstract true value.

Where there are both genetic and environmental influences, the phenotype (P; expressed as the deviation from the population mean) is expressed as the sum of genotype (G) and environmental (E) influences. This is what is meant by *partitioning of variance*. Thus, P = G + E. This is the fundamental mathematical model of quantitative genetics.

What heritability *does not* mean

Much of the controversy surrounding the genetics of psychology has been the result of a misunderstanding of the heritability estimate (h^2). An important aspect of interpreting genetic influences is the difference between *population* estimates and the expression of genetic influences in *individuals*. If it is accepted, for the sake of argument, that general intelligence has a heritability of 50 per cent, then what does this heritability estimate mean? It may be inferred that, at the population level (in the population studied), on average, 50 per cent of variance for this trait is attributed to genetic (non-environmental) factors; and, on average, 50 per cent is attributable to environmental (non-genetic) factors. However, what do these data mean for an *individual's* genetic and environmental influence: in principle, the individual's genetic influences can range from 0 to 100 per cent. Population statistics refer to populations, not to specific individuals within the population.

Thus, heritability estimates refer to genetic and environmental influences on a *specific trait* in a *given population* at a *specific time* of testing: it is not the discovery of the genetic contribution to a specific trait. Parameter values for genetic and environmental factors operating with the given population at a given point in time can have a great influence on heritability estimates (e.g., as in the case of PKU): heritability does not imply inevitability. The more effective the environmental interventions, the less important genetic factors may appear to be, despite the fact the actual DNA has not changed.

Now, if a genetic contribution to trait variations *within* a population is found, then it may seem legitimate to infer that any differences *between* populations must also have a genetic basis: such an inference from quantitative genetics is wrong – that the population difference *may* be genetic is not answered by quantitative genetics. Within-population estimates of heritability say absolutely nothing about the genetic differences *between* populations – and this is true *even if* heritability is estimated to be identical in the two groups. The investigation of the genetic basis of between-population differences must ultimately rely upon a molecular genetics approach and an understanding of the interaction of genes and environments (Plomin, 1994).

ASK YOURSELF
Why are there so many misunderstandings concerning the meaning of heritability?

Gene effects

Before discussing the workhorses of quantitative genetics (i.e., family, twin and adoption studies), it is necessary to consider some of the different forms genetic effects can take. These different forms have an impact on how heritability estimates are interpreted; also they show the complex nature of genetic effects.

First, specific genes have different effects, with some effects being small, others much larger: this is the gene's *effect size*. Second, gene effects may be either independent of or dependent on other genes. The heritability formula given above refers to *additive* genetic effects: such gene effects are independent of each other, and each additive gene adds its contribution in a straightforward fashion. In contrast, *non-additive* effects refer to gene effects that are dependent on other genes, either at the same locus (i.e., *dominance*) or at other loci (i.e., *epistasis*, referring to the interaction, or configuration, of genes that go together to produce a unique phenotype – such effects may not run in families; see below) (Sherman et al., 1997; again, see below). Alleles can have both additive and non-additive effects. As discussed below, non-additive effects complicate the estimation of heritability. There is also evidence that the effect of a gene may depend on whether it is passed from the mother or father, a phenomenon known as *imprinting* (see chapter 2).

Study designs

Let us now put to work the concepts of variance, continuous distributions and heritability in the three main methodologies employed in quantitative genetics: family, twin and adoption studies. Family studies are based on observation; twin studies may be thought of as experiments of nature, adoption studies, experiments of nurture – the latter two types of studies can be used to explore the subtle interplay of both genetic and environmental influences.

Family studies

Offspring share 50 per cent of their genes with each parent. Heritable genetic influences must run in families – of course, not all genetic influences (e.g., mutations) run in families. Therefore, the first obvious research design is to trace the transmission of the phenotype (e.g., schizophrenia) across several generations of a single family – these families are sometimes known as 'pedigrees'. The precise pattern of inheritance provides important clues to the nature of the genetic transmission. For some disease (e.g., Huntington's disease) there is a simple Mendelian pattern of dominance, with on average 50 per cent of offspring being affected (see chapter 2). With a sufficient number of generations, this pattern should become clear. However, with more complex disorders which contain many contributing genes (polygenic diseases), which may not have complete penetrance or may show complex gene–gene and gene–environment interactions, family studies may not reveal clearly the precise pattern of inheritance – but, at the very least, they can show the pattern is not Mendelian.

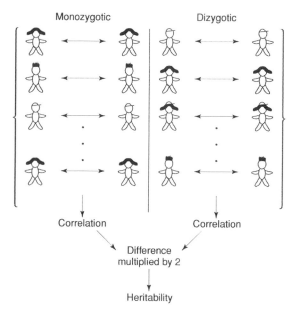

Figure 13.3 The twin study method compares monozygotic (MZ; identical) and dizygotic (DZ; fraternal) same-sex twins on variables of interest, by computing correlations separately for the MZ and DZ groups and then multiplying the difference in correlations to provide a simple measure of heritability.

Twin studies

Twin studies compare the similarities in the variance in phenotypes within pairs of MZ twins (identical genomes) and DZ twins (who share, on average, 50 per cent of the variations in their genomes). The basic logic of twin studies runs that, if genetic differences are important for a trait, then genetically identical individuals (MZ) must be more similar on the trait than less genetically related individuals (DZ). Twin studies typically use same-sex DZ twins (who need not be the same sex) because they are a better comparison for MZ pairs (who are always the same sex).

Twin studies are based on two assumptions: (a) if DZ twins are different genetically but experience the same environment, then any differences between the two twins can be attributed to genetic factors; and (b) if MZ twins have identical genes, then any difference between them must be due to environmental factors (figure 13.3). Using MZ and DZ differences (variance), quantitative genetics research designs partition variance into genetic and environment sources of influence. The difference in MZ and DZ correlations are multiplied by 2 to yield the estimate of heritability: i.e., $(r_{MZ} - r_{DZ}) \times 2 = h^2$. (For first-degree genetic relatives, their correlation reflects half of the effect of genes because they are 50 per cent similar genetically, therefore if heritability is 100 per cent, the correlation is 0.50: this is the reason why the MZ–DZ difference is multiplied by 2.) Weight is a good example of the calculation of heritability: $(r_{MZ} = 0.80, r_{DZ} = 0.43) \times 2 = 84$ per cent.

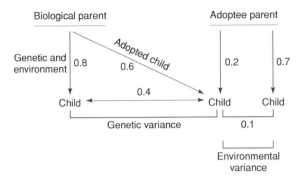

Figure 13.4 Adoption studies rationale. Adoption studies, which come in a variety of designs, provide the opportunity to disentangle genetic and environmental influences by comparing correlation coefficients from children and biological/adoptee parents. Adoption creates family members who share the same environment but are genetically unrelated: their similarity in phenotype variance provides an estimate of family environment influence. Multivariate statistical analysis decomposes the variance into genetic and non-genetic (environmental) sources of influences, and environmental variance into shared (common) and non-shared (unique) variance.

It should be noted at this point that correlations between MZ twins reflect all of the genetic variance, irrespective of the form the genetic effects take (i.e., additive and non-additive); but correlations between DZ twins reflect only one-half of the *additive* genetic variance, plus a smaller fraction of non-additive components. When non-additive effects are minimal, simply doubling the difference between MZ and DZ twin correlations provides an approximate estimate of heritability. However, if non-additive effects are substantial, this comparison overestimates genetic influence (Sherman et al., 1997).

Adoption studies

Similarity in phenotype variation may be due to genes or environment. The most direct way to disentangle these sources of influence is adoption, which creates pairs of genetically related individuals who do not share the same family environment. Adoption also creates family members who share family environment but are not genetically related: their similarity in phenotype variance provides an estimate of family environment to family resemblance. The adoption method also allows the study of 'genetic' siblings and 'environmental' siblings (figure 13.4).

The adoption method separates genetic and environmental influences: when biological parents give up their children for adoption at birth, any similarities in phenotype variance between the parents and their adopted-away offspring can be attributed to shared heredity, not shared environment (assuming no selective placement; see below). In addition, any similarities in phenotype variance between the adoptive parents and their adopted children can be attributed to shared environment, not shared heredity.

Adoption designs come in a number of varieties, but all consist of an assessment of genetic influences in adopted-apart relatives, including: (a) biological parents and their adopted-away offspring; (b) adoptee parents and adoptive children; and (c) twins separated early in life. Environmental influences are assessed by estimating the similarity of phenotype variance of unrelated individuals living together (e.g., genetically unrelated children reared in the same family). It is possible to conduct a simultaneous analysis of genetic and non-genetic family relations using structural equation modelling, which allows various models of genetic and environmental transmission to be tested. Adoption designs can also yield information concerning the influence of specific environmental influences (e.g., early trauma), which are not confounded by heredity.

Put another way, adoption studies examine the similarities and differences in phenotype variance between MZ twins raised in the same and different environments – however, the logic of this method is not restricted to MZ twins (DZ twins, and siblings with various degrees of relatedness, e.g. half-sibs, can also be used). Phenotype similarities, despite rearing in different environments, suggest the action of genetic factors; in contrast, phenotype differences, despite identical genes, suggest the action of environmental factors. Phenotypic similarity between non-genetically related individuals reared together must be environmental.

Most psychological traits considered in adoption studies show a significant genetic contribution. For example, in the case of cognitive ability, there is a contribution of genetic and environmental variance. Genetic parents and offspring and genetic siblings significantly resemble each other even when they are adopted apart and do not share the family environment – this is as true for psychological traits, such as cognitive ability, as it is for physical traits, such as weight. For example, the risk of schizophrenia is just as great for offspring of schizophrenic parents whether they are reared by their biological parents or adopted away at birth (see chapter 16).

Other types of family study

Changing social trends have allowed new types of family studies to be conducted (e.g., step-families created as a result of divorce and remarriage). Half-siblings typically occur in step-families because, typically, the woman brings a child from the former marriage to her new marriage and than has another child with her new husband. These children have only one parent in common and share only 25 per cent of genetic variation. These half-siblings can be compared with full siblings in step-families to assess genetic influence. A useful test of whether step-families differ from never-divorced families is the comparison between full siblings in the two types of families. As is immediately evident, there are many problems with these types of study, but large sample sizes and sophisticated research design can reveal important information about the genetic and environmental contributions to child development.

Problems of interpretation

Doubt is often voiced concerning the adequacy of twin and adoption studies to estimate correctly the influence of genetic factors on psychological phenotypes. Assumptions of the twin method are: (a) equal shared-environmental influences for both types of twins; and (b) little or no assortative mating (i.e., mating on the basis of greater than chance similarity in genetic differences). However, the assortative mating 'assumption' is more an empirical issue that can be taken into account in twin analysis and, if anything, it serves only to underestimate heritability.

Do MZ and DZ children have the same family environments? Specifically, are MZ siblings treated more similarly than DZ children? If they are, then genetic effects tend to be *overestimated*. Often MZ twins are dressed in identical clothes and exposed to the same environments; also people's reactions to MZ twins is likely to be more similar than to DZ twins, who look more different than MZ twins. MZ twins sometimes report having a 'special bond' in being able to predict the actions of their twin: genes apart, this is understandable if they have been exposed to similar learning experiences. These effects are a form of *gene–environment correlation*: that genes lead to exposure to similar environmental factors (Rowe, 2003). Once again this is an empirical issue, which can be taken into account in genetic analyses.

For some psychological phenotypes (e.g., intelligence and social attitudes) assortative mating may be substantial (Sherman et al., 1997). Therefore, doubling the difference between MZ and DZ twin correlations (see above) would *underestimate* genetic influence. Other effects might reduce the influence of genes and inflate the estimate of the environment. For example, MZ twins show greater birth weight differences than fraternal twins, and thus may have different prenatal environments (these differences may be due to prenatal competition).

In the case of adoption studies, do adoptee families have similar environments to non-adoptee families? This is the problem of *selective placement*. Clearly, it is difficult for childless couples to adopt, and usually adoptive children (at least babies) go to rather well-to-do homes, with highly motivated adoptive parents who want to do their best for their new baby. Also, if bright babies are adopted by bright families (i.e., selective placement matches biological and adoptive parents), then genetic influences could inflate the correlation between adoptive parents and their adopted children. Today there are far fewer traditional adoptions of very young babies than in the past (due to contraception, abortion and more liberal social attitudes towards childbirth outside wedlock). As a result, there are fewer opportunities for adoption studies; therefore, it is more difficult to replicate and extend previous findings.

Proponents of the genetics approach (e.g., Plomin et al., 2003) would agree with some of these criticisms of twin and adoption studies, but would also add that the answer is not to abandon one of the most powerful analytical procedures in the behavioural sciences but rather to improve and refine existing methodologies (as discussed below, qualitative genetics allows the answer to these criticisms from the viewpoint of differences in DNA sequences).

Application to psychiatry

Quantitative genetics continues to play an import role in psychiatry. High levels of co-morbidity are consistently seen for psychiatry disorders, which suggests that the many risk factors for psychopathology are not disorder-specific. Indeed, it is thought that the broad array of common psychiatric disorders may be explained by a smaller number of underlying factors (we see a specific example of this process when we consider the anxiety disorders in chapter 15, and their underlying factors in chapter 17). Kendler et al. (2003) tested the hypothesis that this pattern of co-mordibity can be explained by two broad groups of 'internalizing' and 'externalizing' disorders. 5,600 twin pairs were assessed for lifetime diagnosis on a number of psychiatric syndromes, and multivariate statistical analysis – which allows many variables to be simultaneously analysed – was used to test different statistical models of the data.

The first stage of the analysis fitted models to seven syndromes: major depression, generalized anxiety disorder (GAD), phobia, alcohol dependence, drug abuse/dependence, adult antisocial behaviour, and conduct disorder (for a description of the depression and anxiety/phobia disorders, see chapters 14 and 15). Two underlying factors were identified: the first ('externalizing') factor contained alcohol dependence, drug abuse/dependence, adult antisocial behaviour and conduct disorder; the second ('internalizing') factor contained major depression, GAD and phobia. Within the second internalizing factor, depression and GAD loaded onto a separate factor from animal and situation phobia (for the neuropsychological basis of this distinction, see chapter 17).

The authors reported that the underlying structure of the genetic and environmental risk factors for the common psychiatric and drug abuse disorders are very similar in males and females; and genetic risk predisposes to two broad groups of internalizing and externalizing disorders; and two genetic factors predispose to anxiety and phobia (fear). Substance-use disorders have disorder-specific genetic risks. For at least a subgroup of externalizing disorders, shared environment (e.g., family disruption and poor parental monitoring) is also important. Within syndromal groups, unique (non-shared) environmental experience helps to explain the development of the specific disorders in vulnerable individuals. Thus, there is an underlying genetic predisposition that can be classified along two major factors (internalizing and externalizing), and this genetic predisposition leads to specific disorder depending on unique environmental exposure.

Kendler et al. (2003) is invaluable in revealing the similarities and differences between psychiatric disorders, as well as in identifying the genetic and environmental risk factors. It would be difficult to obtain such knowledge in any other way than by quantitative genetic analysis. This type of approach is also important in showing that many apparently disparate phenotypes may show a common causal basis, and that classification of psychiatric disorder may be based on a rational system of knowledge rather than on the presentation of signs and symptoms.

> **ASK YOURSELF**
> Can *all* questions concerning heritability be answered by an appropriately powerful quantitative design?

Theoretical Issues in Genetic Effects

When considering genetic effects, several issues are of importance.

Genetic influences on 'downstream' behavioural phenotypes

Plomin, Owen and McGuffin (1994) presented the heritabilities for a number of behavioural disorders and compared these with those for some major medical disorders.

It is interesting that behavioural disorders are more consistently heritable, which challenges the assumption that medical disorders are predominantly genetic in origin while behavioural disorders are largely environmental in origin. If some thought is given to this matter for a moment, then the high heritability seen in complex psychological traits is not surprising. Many behavioural traits that are 'downsteam' (i.e., those that are a long way down the causal chain) pick up a large number of influences (both genetic and environmental) before the final trait is expressed.

Epistasis: gene–gene interactions

The first complication relates to the interdependence of gene effects; that is, *epistatic interactions* (Grigorenko, 2003; see Lykken, 1982). These effects are not additive but interactive: the expression of one gene depends upon the expression of another gene (figure 13.5). These effects result from the interplay of genes at different loci: that is, the particular combination (configuration) of genes. These effects are not passed from parent to offspring. They serve to complicate the discovery of genetic influences and obscure the pattern of transmission. With reproduction, entailing the selection and recombination of genes, these effects may disappear.

Epistasis may explain why genetic-influenced traits do not always seem to run in families: the separate alleles that combine to produce this effect run in families, but their interactive effects (phenotypes) do not. Still so much is unknown about the genetics of complex psychological traits that this *interplay* of genes poses a serious problem for unravelling the genomic basis of psychological traits: genetic studies are only beginning to address this effect.

Let us take a hypothetical example of epistasis and consider its effect on some phenotype. If individuals with A_1B_2 alleles show a higher deviation from the population mean than the combined (additive) average deviations of A_1 and B_2, then this extra deviation

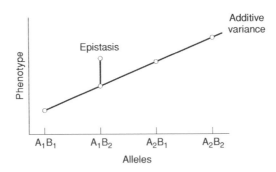

Figure 13.5 Epistasis is evident when the combination of two or more alleles (A_1B_2) contributes more to the phenotype than the addition of the alleles considered separately. In other words, the effects of the alleles are multiple in this specific combination (or configuration).

is *epistatic*. If A and B loci are not linked, then the extra epistatic effect is not be passed on to future generations; but, if the two loci are linked, then the epistatic effect is passed on with a probability equal to 1 minus the recombination rate between the loci. Usually in genetics it is convenient (and tenable) to assume *additive* effects.

However, it must be said that the evidence for epistasis is weak, and it is more a theoretical possibility than a proven fact. For example, it should be expected that MZ correlations should be more than double DZ correlations because of added gene–gene effects, but this is not often found. Additive effects models do well in accounting for the pattern of MZ and DZ correlations found.[5]

Gene–environment correlations

Other effects can arise because of gene–environment interaction: that is, when the same gene produces a different phenotype in different environments (Rowe, 2003). Another type of effect is gene–environment correlation: that is, when particular genes are found more often than random in particular environments.[6] Using statistical methodologies, a finding of $rMZ > 2rDZ$ would suggest that the sources of influence on the phenotype are more than additive genetic effects.

Gene–environment interactions remind us once again that thinking in terms of nature *versus* nurture, rather than nature *and* nature, is unhelpful in understanding the interplay of both sets of factors in all complex psychological traits: there can be no genetic influences without the environment; and there can be no environment without genes. Working out how genes and environment interact in producing the human brain, as well as its outputs (collectively termed the mind), is the scientifically viable way to advance psychological science.

Phenotypes: genes and environment

Animal ethology drew a distinction between instinctive and learned behaviour: lower animals' behaviour was thought to be more instinctive, and thus more under genetic control; human beings' behaviour more learned, and thus more under environmental control (the overzealous adoption of this latter assumption led to J. B. Watson's behaviourism). This distinction now seems both artificial and misleading. For example, songbirds are genetically wired for particular birdsongs, but these songs either do not appear or are retarded in the absence of environmental exposure to conspecifics' singing. Human beings' language seems to offer a good parallel with birdsong: the verbal environment to which the individual is exposed during childhood determines verbal behaviour (i.e., language, dialect, accent, etc.). It would be extraordinary to think that there are specific genes for English, Russian, etc., as it would be extraordinary to think that human beings could learn a language without the brain hardware of genetic origin (the *extent* of the influence of genes on language competence and performance is still debated). Thus, genetics and environmental factors go hand in hand in building psychological phenotypes.

Environmental variables are usually vital in the expression of genetic liability. For example, unpleasant life events may potentiate the (genetic) liability to depression. In this case, it may be expected that the expression of depression in those with a genetic liability would be greater in those who have actually experienced a recent unpleasant life event (e.g., serious illness, death of close relative, unemployment, etc.). This is an example of gene–environment interaction. The form of this interaction modifies our early definition of the contributory factors to the phenotype (P):

$$P = G + E + (G \times E) + e$$

ASK YOURSELF
Does the complexity of gene and environment effects limit the value of the reductionist approach to psychology?

As before, G is the genetic variance, E the environmental variance, and (G × E) is the interaction of genetic and environmental influences that are independent of the main effects of G (e is the error associated with measurement – that is, all other sources of influences on the phenotypes that have not been measured).

Measuring the Environment

This discussion so far has focused on describing and estimating genetic effects on variance in the phenotype. Let us now turn our attention to describing the environment. If a genetic influence on a phenotype is detected, then it is obvious that this effect must result from at least one gene; but, if an environmental effect is detected, then nothing can be assumed about the underlying mechanism. Quantitative genetics is able to investigate environmental influences in two ways. Twin and adoption studies allow environmental influences to be partitioned into those *shared* between relatives (e.g., those that make relatives resemble each other) and those that are *non-shared* (i.e., those that make relatives different from each other). Plomin (1994) and Plomin, Asbury and Dunn (2001) review the literature on shared and non-shared environments.

Quantitative genetics provides the methodology to examine the influence of shared and non-shared environments (family relations, peer relation, socio-economic status). *Shared environment* consists of those environments shared by siblings within the family (e.g., family values, child-rearing practices); *non-shared environment* consists of those environments not shared by siblings within the same family (e.g., siblings being treated differently because of birth order, sex, life events, extra-family influences). One of the most striking findings from quantitative genetics research is that shared environment effects are not nearly as important as non-shared environment effects: that is, experiences unique to the sibling within and outside the family appear to be much more important than shared environmental experiences. This finding explains why children from the same family are so very different.

Two of the most important findings are: (a) contrary to most early socialization theories of development, non-shared environmental influences serve to make children growing up in the same family as different as children growing up in different families; and (b) the *nature of nurture* is relevant in that genetic factors influence the way environments are experienced (Plomin, 1994).

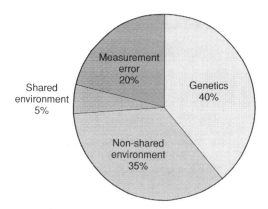

Figure 13.6 Shared and non-shared environments. As a broad estimate of genetic and environmental influences on measures of individual differences, quantitative research reveals the following: (a) genetics (approx. 40%), (b) non-shared, unique, environments (approx. 35%), (c) shared environments (approx. 5%), and measurement error (approx. 20%).

In environmental research designs the phenotype ('behaviour') is a measure of the environment (e.g., perception of peer relations): if environments are independent of individuals' genes then this research strategy is flawed. Quantitative genetic research shows that the variance (i.e., individual differences) may be attributed to several sources of influence: (a) genetics (approx. 40%), (b) non-shared, unique, environments (approx. 35%), (c) shared environments (approx. 5%); and measurement error (approx. 20%). Furthermore, non-shared environmental variance is itself partly genetic in origin (Plomin, 1994): our choice, modification and interpretation of our environments are partly under genetic influence (figure 13.6).

In summary of this section, quantitative genetics is important in showing the genetic contribution to a psychological phenotype; and it can also be used to estimate the influence of different types of environment (e.g., shared and non-shared environments). As already noted, estimating genetic effects is not without its problems, and in interpreting twin and adoption studies, as well as other types of family studies, it is important to take into account a number of caveats. However, quantitative genetic studies provide information on the causal influences of psychological phenotypes that is simply not available in other areas of psychology. In addition, this approach has revealed surprising findings, notably the influence of non-shared environment on development, and the relative importance of genetic influences throughout the lifespan. Theories of human development have been forced to change as a direct result of these quantitative genetic data.

> **ASK YOURSELF**
> Can genetic designs detect all important sources of variance in the environment?

▦ Qualitative (Molecular) Genetics

Quantitative genetics can estimate the genetic contribution to a psychological phenotype, but it does not tell us anything about the *biological* nature of the genes involved.
For this information it is necessary to turn to qualitative genetics and to the human genome.
Modern genetic research in the behavioural sciences comprises a mix of quantitative
and qualitative strategies. These joint strategies are surveyed in the next section of
this chapter, but first it is important to understand the basic logic and procedures of
qualitative, or molecular, genetics. For an excellent introduction to the applications
of genomics to human biology, including the molecular gene technologies, see Primrose
and Twyman (2004). This section starts with background information about the human
genome.

Genomes: does size matter?

Before publication of the draft of the human genome sequence, it was thought that the
human genome contained as many as 100,000 genes. The draft publication came as a
shock, with an estimate of only some 35,000 genes.[7] This is a surprising figure when
seen in the light of the number of genes in more humble animals and plants: the mustard
plant has 27,000; the nematode worm, 20,000; and the fruit fly, 14,000! Indeed, even the
estimate of 35,000 genes may be an exaggeration because, over evolution, certain genes
have spun off sets of related genes, resulting in groups of similar genes with subtly
different functions (these *gene families* result during the production of gametes, where a
chunk within the chromosome is duplicated, leading to two copies of a gene). These
data indicate that there is not a good correlation between the number of genes a species
possesses and its complexity.

There is, however, a correlation between size of genome (including non-coding and
regulator genes; see below) and phenotype complexity. The human genome is over
30 times larger than the worm's, but its genes are not even double that of the worm's.
This accumulation of 'junk' DNA during evolution results from natural selection not operating on these non-coding DNA sequences – this DNA may be selfish in the sense described
in chapter 2, freeloading on the functional genes that make a viable life form (gene
replication machine). As with domestic junk, DNA junk tends to increase, not decrease
(Watson, 2003). But as noted above, this so-called junk DNA may have a role to play in
human beings, especially in individual differences.

Regulator genes: functional complexity

It has already been noted that gene number seems not to be vital to phenotype complexity. Well, what does account for this complexity: how do mice and men (and
women) differ? Phenotype complexity is the result of the *functional complexity* of genes,
which is greater in human beings than in other animals: *regulator* genes are responsible
for turning on and off other genes. Regulator genes flank protein and polypeptide coding
sequences of DNA (genes), acting to coordinate the activity of the production of proteins.

In addition, a given gene may produce different proteins, either because different exons (coding sequences) are coupled together to create slightly different proteins, or because biochemical changes are made to the proteins after they have been produced.

DNA molecule

In chapter 2, the basic structure and units of the DNA molecule were outlined. To summarize, it consists of a sequence of units called *nucleotides*, which consist of a phosphate and sugar group with a *base* attached. The alternating sugar and phosphate groups of successive nucleotides form the backbone of the DNA molecule – it was the structure of this backbone that was revealed by Rosalind Franklin's X-ray diffraction pictures, and which provided Watson and Crick (1953) with the clue to the helical nature of the backbone. The full DNA molecule consists of two paired complementary strands (the double helix), each made up of sequences of nucleotides; the nucleotides of opposite strands are chemically bonded together: it is these bonds that carry the letters GACT that comprise the blueprint for life.[8]

DNA is some 3 billion bases long, but most of these bases are 'junk' in that they do not seem to serve any purpose.[9] The total length of DNA is divided into regions called genes (*exons*; sequences of DNA that code for proteins), and non-coding stretches of sequences between them (*introns*); and proteins are composed of only 20 amino acids. The mapping of DNA onto these amino acids is what is meant by the *genetic code* (it is often incorrectly assumed to be the sequences of bases themselves). It is the *shape* (i.e., three-dimensional configuration) of the final protein that gives it its functional properties. Differences in the base sequences that go to make up the gene are *alleles*. These different sequences result in different amino acids being produced, and thus different proteins: such differences are sometimes called *protein polymorphisms*.

Some degree of complexity now needs to be added. A gene does not code necessarily for only one protein. It is more accurate to say that a gene encodes for a *polypeptide* (i.e., a chain of amino acids). This description is more accurate because some proteins, such as haemoglobin, are assembled from more than one polypeptide, and the different polypeptides are encoded in separate regions of the genome (e.g., haemoglobin is made from four polypeptides).

Individual differences

The human genome is a misnomer: your genome is different from mine. All of us have different genomes (only monozygotic, MZ, twins have an identical genome); in fact, each of us has *two* genomes, contained on the two pairs of chromosomes (only gamete sex cells have one genome). However, you and I, and all other members of the human species, have genomes that are virtually identical: it is necessary to look long and hard to spot differences in our base sequences (about 1 out of every 1,000 bases, totalling a few million base-pair differences). Indeed, much of our genome is shared with animals and plants. But these differences, small as they are, have important effects: they make mice or men (and women), and you and me.

When considering individual differences between conspecifics (members of the same species), it is important to think not about the absolute number of base-pair differences but the functional effects on protein production of these differences. As noted in chapter 2, relatively small changes in base-pair sequences (mutations) can have dramatic effects on the expression of the final phenotype. In fact, a *single* base substitution can have the largest effect because it produces a *frameshift*, that is, changing all polypeptides and proteins in the gene sequence. In fact, most of these DNA differences involve a substitution of a single base pair, called *single nucleotide polymorphisms* (SNPs; see below). Identification of base sequence differences (polymorphisms) is the most important task for individual differences research. Plomin (2002) argued that, if subtle

DNA differences are responsible for differences between the worm and you and me, then even more subtle differences are responsible for differences between you and me. This is the argument underlying the research strategy for looking to molecular genetics to explain individual differences in human beings.

> **ASK YOURSELF**
> Are individual variations in the genome too small to make much of a difference in behavioural phenotypes?

Techniques in molecular genetics

To understand how qualitative genetics is used to study human phenotypes and individual differences in these phenotypes, it is necessary to know something about molecular genetic techniques. The basic principles are relatively easy to grasp; the complexities need not distract us from the important issues.

Molecular genetics began humbly enough in the notoriously filthy laboratory of Morgan at Columbia University (USA) in the early 1900s. He studied the chromosomes of the fruit fly (*Drosophila* – this species is now much beloved by geneticists because of its short lifespan and cheapness), which was readily available in large quantities in the university at that time. Starting in 1907, Morgan discovered that chromosomes (which had been first seen in the late 1890s, and later suspected of carrying genetic information due to the fact that they come in two varieties, which mirrored Mendel's breeding experiments) break apart and re-form during the production of sperm and egg cells (gametes). Recombination (crossing over) during gamete production (see chapter 2) allowed Morgan to map out the positions of particular genes along the chromosome. This has been the basic approach used ever since in linkage and association studies (see below).

The logic of this strategy is that the chromosome break (during crossing over) is statistically more likely to occur between two genes that are far apart (simply because there are more potential break points in the intervening DNA). Therefore, if there is a lot of reshuffling for any two genes on a chromosome, it can be concluded that they are a long way apart; the rarer the reshuffling, the closer genes are together. This is the basic principle that underlies all genetic mapping, and was the start of what culminated in the form of the Human Genome Project. Morgan had to rely upon naturally occurring mutations in the fruit fly: collecting, inspecting, reproducing and analysing.[10] Nowadays it is common to help Nature along with experimentally caused mutations (see below).

Overview of techniques

In order to sequence DNA and to identify genes associated with phenotypes, it would be helpful to outline a number of important procedures. First, a segment of DNA must be amplified in order to have enough of the segment of the molecule to analyse (currently a cheek swab of saliva allows hundreds of markers to be analysed). Second, the order of the base pairs must be sequenced. Once there is enough DNA for analysis and the sequence of the molecule has been determined, then it is possible to look for interesting coding sequences (genes).[11]

DNA amplification: polymerase chain reaction (PCR)

PCR has made possible large-scale genomic analysis. It is a way to clone DNA segments (the term 'genetic cloning' usually refers to copying DNA segments, not producing genetically identical animals or plants). PCR amplifies a single piece of DNA in a couple of hours – previous cloning methods required DNA to be inserted into bacteria for the purpose of replication. (PCR was invented by a surfing Californian, Kary Mullis, who won a Nobel Prize in 1993 for his invention.)

Genomic sequencing: the Sanger method

PCR became the major workhorse in the Human Genome Project, and produced enough DNA for high-throughput machines to sequence half a million base pairs per day. The other workhorse in the Human Genome Project was the sequencing method itself, using a method developed by Sanger in the 1970s (Sanger was to receive his second Nobel Prize in 1980 for developing this method – his first Nobel Prize was in 1958 for his work on the structure of proteins, especially insulin).

How are the 3 billion bases of the DNA molecule sequenced? At the beginning of the Human Genome Project, technology was still slow, laborious and expensive; and many scientists questioned the wisdom of sequencing the whole genome when it is suspected that most of it is composed of junk DNA. However, as so often the case, necessity proved to be the mother of invention, and technology rapidly advanced to make genomic sequencing fast and cost-effective. The Sanger method is shown in figure 13.7.

The Sanger method cuts up strands of DNA at specific points in the molecule chain that correspond with the four base pairs. For each segment of DNA this yields strands of different lengths, and where the strand ends (the 'stop' points), the base pair at that position can be 'read-off'. (Sanger is rightly famous for inventing a method to produce these stop points.) These lengths are set in a special gel and electricity applied. There is then a timed race, and the final position of strands indicates base pairs. By this method, the sequence of base pairs is known, and the entire sequence of the DNA molecule can be determined. This is an elegant way to sequence DNA; but it is costly in terms of hours required to sequence each base.

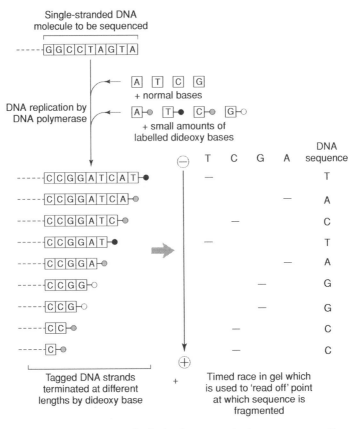

Figure 13.7 Sanger's sequencing method. The Sanger method uses an enzymatic procedure to synthesize chains of DNA of varying length and read off the base pair at the 'stop' point. First, a single strand of DNA is selected and a different dideoxy base is added to each of the four base pairs (this labels each base pair). Now it is possible to 'cut' the DNA strand at each dideoxy base, as shown. These strands are then separated by a process of electrophoresis, which consists of a timed race through gel, their position corresponding to the base pair. Then it is simple for a machine to read these positions and thus identify the base pair at the 'stop' point in the chain. By this repetitive procedure, all the bases of a DNA molecule can be identified.

To save time, each fragment can be tagged with a fluorescent dye corresponding to its chain-terminating base: the colour emitted by the fragment provides the identity of the base. A laser scanned across the bottom of the gel, activating the fluorescence, and a photosensitive electronic eye detect the colour being emitted by each piece of DNA.

Gene identification

The sequence of the DNA molecule does not tell us anything directly about genes: a coding DNA segment (gene) looks very much like junk DNA: the genome is just a string of As, Ts, Gs and Cs. So how are genes found in the relatively barren landscape of the whole genome? Our search is made more difficult by the fact that introns are found in coding regions. For example, the human gene *dystrophin* (the gene responsible for muscular dystrophy) spreads over 2.4 million base pairs, but only 0.5 per cent of these bases actually code for proteins; the rest consist of 79 introns (a typical human gene has 8 introns). Plomin and McGuffin (2003) outline the various gene identification strategies used in human psychopathology (see below).

Cross-species comparisons

One way to differentiate genes (exons) from introns and junk DNA is to compare the genomes of different species. The mouse genome has proved especially popular for this purpose, and its genome has been specifically sequenced to facilitate the search for human genes (Crabbe, 2003). The rationale for this approach is based on evolution: in their protein-coding (exon) segments (genes), human and mouse genomes are highly similar. In contrast, junk DNA has mutated over the millions of years of evolution, and, as it has escaped control by natural selection, it has diverged. There are thus similarities in exon protein-coding sequences (genes) across species, but much less similarity in intron (junk) sequences.[12]

As already noted, non-human animals have much less junk DNA (e.g., the puffer fish, *fugu*; Brenner, 2001), so these animals are a good place to start the search for genes: less time is wasted searching the vast, barren wastelands of junk DNA.

From RNA to DNA: reverse transcriptase technology

A very different way to identify genes is *reverse transcriptase technology* (figure 13.8). The rationale for this approach is very simple: DNA codes for RNA, and then polypeptides and proteins. Therefore, if the sequence of DNA is known, then the sequence of RNA is also known. Turning this logic around: if the sequence of RNA is known, then so too is the sequence of DNA: the gene-coding sequence.

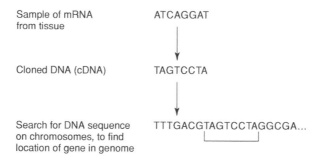

Sample of mRNA from tissue	ATCAGGAT
Cloned DNA (cDNA)	TAGTCCTA
Search for DNA sequence on chromosomes, to find location of gene in genome	TTTGACGTAGTCCTAGGCGA...

Figure 13.8 Reverse transcriptase technology is a way of identifying gene sequences from messenger RNA (mRNA) expressed in tissue. Once the mRNA sequence is known, the DNA sequence is known, and the human genome can then be searched for a segment that corresponds to the sequence of DNA expressed in the analysed tissue.

This procedure involves first purifying a sample of messenger RNA (mRNA) from tissue (e.g., the brain). This sample provides the RNA for all the genes that have been expressed in this tissue – more precisely, those genes that are sufficiently active to produce detectable amounts of RNA. Now, using reverse transcriptase, DNA can be re-created (known as cDNA – 'c' standing for cloned), and thus reproduce the sequence of exons that led to the production of RNA in the first place: the gene sequence is now known. This is where the power of the Human Genome Project comes into its own. It makes the localization of genes a relatively trivial activity. (This approach, of course, can be used in any tissue in the body, and holds out great hope for the identification of genes that are active during the growth of cancerous tissue: in the future drugs will regulate the activity of these genes and thus regulate their effects.)

Reverse transcriptase technology is a 'quick and dirty' way to identify genes – more precisely, polypeptide/protein-producing genes. As already discussed, some of the interesting parts of the genome lie outside polypeptide/protein-producing genes, and thus do not produce RNA; they are the control mechanisms (regulatory) that switch genes on and off. If the cloned DNA (cDNA) approach is pursued, then a good overview of which genes are expressed is achieved, but not how they are turned on. In the latter part of this chapter, the methods employed to find genes related to specific psychological and psychiatric behaviours (i.e., quantitative trait loci, QTL, studies) are discussed.

Two new fields have emerged following the Human Genome Project: *proteomics*, which is the study of proteins encoded by genes; and *transcriptomics*, which is the study of where and when genes are expressed (transcribed). *Once* genes (i.e., coding exons) have been identified, then mRNA can be taken from body tissue and used to identify which genes were active in the tissue sample: *DNA microarrays*.

DNA microarray

Microarray, or 'DNA chip' technology (also known as *expression array profiling*), first introduced commercially in 1996, is an exciting new tool of widespread importance in medicine and pharmacology. Microarrays permit patterns of gene expression to be identified in different tissue (or individuals), and thus can point to important genetic differences in the expression of disease. For example, to take an application from medicine, microarrays are being used to differentiate the molecular genetics of different versions of the same class of cancer, leading: (a) to the identification of the molecular processes involved in the dysfunction of the cell (i.e., which genes are turned on/off and which proteins are produced); and (b) a diagnostic test to differentiate between different versions of cancer (often this information is available only after the cancer has returned). Introductions to this technology can be found in Shoemaker et al. (2001), and Friend & Stoughton (2002), where links to further information are provided.

DNA microarrays work by depositing DNA sequences in a matrix of tiny wells – the matrix could contain all genes in the genome. The mRNA (extracted from tissue in the body; e.g., the brain) is biochemically tagged with a chemical marker that fluoresces under ultraviolet (UV) light. The mRNA sample is then washed across the DNA microarray, filling all the tiny wells that contain different gene sequences. The base-pairing bonds that hold together the two strands of the double helix compel each mRNA molecule to

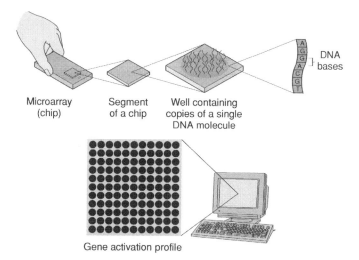

Microarray
(chip)

Segment
of a chip

Well containing
copies of a single
DNA molecule

DNA
bases

Gene activation profile

Figure 13.9 The DNA chip process. Microarray technology works by depositing DNA sequences in a matrix of tiny wells over which messenger RNA (mRNA) is washed, which is biochemically tagged with a chemical marker that fluoresces under ultraviolet (UV) light when it binds to a complementary DNA sequence. By this process, the genes expressed in tissue, as measured by mRNA, can be identified.

pair off with the gene from which it was derived. Then it is a relatively simple procedure to observe which spots have picked up the fluorescent mRNA. Some cells fluoresce strongly, indicating that the cell is very active in the tissue from which the mRNA was taken (figure 13.9).

As most genetic differences, including those in disease, consist of *single nucleotide polymorphisms* (SNPs; see above), a chip containing illness-linked gene variants could be used to uncover an individual's SNPs and thus their likelihood of acquiring the disease. The promise is that one day microarrays could be used to detect an individual's genetic propensity to a host of disorders. These 'at risk' people – most of us are 'at risk' from some disease process – could then be monitored and appropriate (early) treatment provided. Another important application is tailoring drugs to specific genotypes in order to increase clinical efficacy and minimize adverse side effects (that is, pharmacogenetics; see chapter 12). This technology is now mainstream in drug research aimed at targeting specific molecular processes (see Friend & Stoughton, 2002).

Microarrays can also be used to reveal gene expression during psychological processes. For example, one group of experimental animals could be placed in an enriched environment and the other group in an impoverished environment, and then tissue from different regions of their brains could be submitted to microarray analysis to identify the type and degree of genetic expression. For instance, in one study, a specific pattern of gene expression changes (e.g., in protein kinases) was observed in the nucleus accumbens from primates exposed to cocaine for over a year (Freeman et al., 2001). Such studies can show that genes are involved in addictive processes. In another study, gene expression in frontal cortical tissue was assessed in alcoholic vs. control patients; these data showed a pattern of gene expression related to the cell cycle (Lewohl et al., 2000). (For a discussion of microarrays in complex traits research, see Crabbe, 2003.) This type of analysis can also be used to study psychological phenotypes in human beings (e.g., depressed patients vs. controls), but this analysis can only occur at post-mortem.

Microarrays are also used to compare the genetic expression of different species. In the case of human beings and chimpanzees, it has been found that similar genes are expressed in liver and blood cells, but not in brain tissue, suggesting that the pattern of gene expression in the brain underlies psychological differences between these two animal species.

Microarray technology provides yet another example of the importance of such innovative methods in advancing knowledge. Today microarray technology may seem a rather obscure method used only by white-coated boffins in biotechnology laboratories, but in the not too distant future it might be the case that a routine blood test will result in a personalized microarray profile that will inform medical treatment.

Experimental mutations, knock-out, knock-in and over-expression

We are all the consequence of chance mutations – the results of the accumulation of errors and mistakes! In non-human animal research, identification of genes and the role of these genes is achieved in a number of different ways.

Mutations

Mutations in DNA can be induced either chemically or through X-irradiation. These mutations in DNA result in the phenotype for which it codes (if any) being altered: once the researcher observes an altered phenotype (e.g., colour or limb size), then the position on the genome of the altered DNA can be identified (Crabbe, 2003). These strategies are valuable for genes that have little natural variation – for example, genes that code for limb number. This technique produces variation in the gene (polymorphisms), thus allowing statistical association with phenotype expressions.

Knock-outs

Another way to study the action of genes is to selectively knock out genes (i.e., selectively turn off specific genes, and thus they are not transcribed and expressed in protein synthesis) and observe the resulting change in phenotype. This technique is widely used to produce experimental animals who are bred for specific behavioural features (Capecchi, 1994). Genes can also be inserted ('knocked in'), that is, inserted to observe their effects.

> **ASK YOURSELF**
> In what ways is molecular genetics starting to revolutionize psychology?

Over-expression

Stimulating the over-expression of a gene may also give important clues to its functions.

Quantitative *and* Qualitative Genetics

How can quantitative (statistical) and qualitative (molecular) genetics research strategies be combined in the search for the genetic basis of individual differences? This section surveys research strategies designed to reveal the genetic basis of complex psychological traits.

There have been two separate trends in genetics research: (a) the *Mendelian disease model*; and (b) the *biometric trait approach*. The Mendelian approach focused on the effects of mutations, and followed the strategy of looking at the effects of single genes; in contrast, the biometric approach, following in the statistical footsteps of Sir Francis Galton, focused on quantitative variations in complex traits (Plomin et al., 2003). The Human Genomics Project has now made the integration of these two approaches feasible.

Before searching for the genetic basis of complex psychological traits, it should first be acknowledged that there are a large number of disorders (e.g., Huntington's disease) that do follow a relatively simple form of Mendelian inheritance (some 2,000 diseases[13]). For these traits, a traditional Mendelian analysis is sufficient to infer the form of transmission, and thus provide clues to their chromosomal loci. However, a Mendelian analysis is not appropriate for the genetic analysis of most traits of interest in psychology (e.g., cognitive ability and extroversion) and psychiatry (e.g., schizophrenia): these phenotypes simply do not follow a Mendelian route of transmission; instead, they suggest the action of many genes (polygenes), perhaps many acting in union (*epistasis*).[14]

Complex traits: quantitative trait loci

Complex traits are either *oligogenic* (a few genes, each with a moderately large effect) or *polygenic* (many genes, each with a small effect). A gene in a multiple gene system responsible for a complex trait is called a *quantitative trait locus* (QTL; plural, *loci*). Unlike single-gene effects, QTLs are neither necessary nor sufficient for the development and expression of the disorder or phenotype.[15] QTLs serve as probabilistic risk factors and are incremental in nature. The resulting trait is distributed quantitatively as a dimension rather than qualitatively as a disorder (see above), as first described by Fisher (1918).

An example of a genetic risk factor is the apolipoprotein E (*ApoE*) gene associated with Alzheimer's disease (a form of dementia). An allele of this gene, *ApoE4*, is found at a higher frequency in sufferers. However, not all people with this allele develop the disease. The gene is thus a *liability* to Alzheimer's disease: it is a *probability*, not a *certainty*. Another issue to be considered in genetics research, including QTLs, is gene *penetrance*: this is the degree to which the gene is expressed in the phenotype. Some genes (e.g., that for Huntington's disease) are highly penetrant; but many genes are less penetrant. However, some researchers argue that 'penetrance' is used to refer to cases in which there is not a perfect correlation between genotype and phenotype – in other words, a 'weakly penetrant gene effect' refers to a phenotype that is not caused by a simple single-gene Mendelian process (that is, there are important non-genetic, i.e., environmental, sources of influence on the phenotype).

Detection of QTLs

Large-scale studies are under way to identify QTLs involved in a variety of psychological and psychiatric phenotypes. The methods for gene identification reviewed above are not powerful enough to detect multiple genetic influences of small effects. Another approach is required (Sham, 2003, provides a thorough discussion of research strategies used in QTL research). However, QTL research is not without its methodological problems (Cardon, 2003); and some scientists question the theoretical basis of the whole approach (e.g., Balaban, 2002).

Two main research strategies are used to identify QTLs: (a) *linkage*, and (b) *association* (Sham, 2003). These two approaches are complementary: linkage is good at detecting large effects over a great genetic distance; association is good at detecting small effects over a small distance (Craig & McClay, 2003; Rao & Gu, 2002).

Linkage studies

For single-gene disorders, linkage can be identified from the pattern of family inheritance (so-called family pedigree studies, in which the co-transmission of a marker allele and phenotype can be traced – this is easy to achieve in the type of disorders presented in chapter 2). Linkage is based on the observation that certain characteristics seem to run in families; but this observation says very little about the respective genetic and environmental contribution to the characteristic. Linkage studies attempt to estimate this genetic contribution.

This classic approach focuses on multi-generational or extended pedigrees that contain multiple affected members. The aim is to detect one or more genetic markers that do not assort independently of the disease: that is, the disease expression is linked to a 'genetic marker' (see below). This finding would indicate that the marker and the disease susceptibility locus are in close proximity on the same chromosome; the next step after this region of interest has been identified is to narrow down this region in order to identify the gene(s).

The rationale underlying linkage studies is that recombination (crossing over; see chapter 2) occurs, on average, once per chromosome in the formation of gametes; and the marker DNA and an allele for the characteristic on the same chromosome are inherited together within a family. The probability that two genes are found on the same chromosome after crossing over is related to their proximity on the chromosome: if they are close, then they are more likely to be passed on together; genes more distant are more likely to separate during crossing over. This is the basic rationale used by Morgan in the early 1900s.

Association studies

When the search for a gene involved in some complex trait is started, little or nothing may be known about its location. To narrow down the location of the gene – that is, to identify a 'hot spot' of gene activity – genetic markers are used (DNA sequences the location of which is known) – markers are not functionally related to the phenotype (see below). If a marker is consistently found in an individual with the trait in question, then this may represent a 'marker for the gene': not the gene itself, but the chromosome and location on the chromosome. In other words, the marker is 'linked' to the gene. Sometimes a gene has already been identified, but not linked to the characteristic under investigation. Here, instead of using a genetic marker, it is possible to use the gene itself to determine whether it is related to the characteristic: this is the 'candidate gene' approach. Candidate genes may be suggested by non-human animal studies (e.g., mouse genome).

With QTLs, a linkage approach is limited: it is good at locating genes with large effects on phenotypes, but much less powerful when it comes to identifying the numerous genes of small effects involved in complex traits that have a normal distribution in the population – most psychological traits are of this type. Most QTL studies use *allelic association*, which is more powerful for detecting these small effect sizes.

QTLs can be found for human behaviour by comparing allelic frequencies for individuals with high scores on a trait (e.g., fearfulness; or those who met some diagnostic criteria) with those who score low on the trait (or controls who do not meet diagnostic criteria). The major strength of linkage is that it is systematic in the sense that a few hundred DNA markers can be used to scan the genome. In contrast, because allelic association with a quantitative trait can only be detected if a DNA marker is itself the QTL, or very close to it, tens of thousands of DNA markers would need to be required to scan the genome thoroughly. For this reason, allelic association has been used primarily to study associations with candidate genes, or locations narrowed down by linkage studies.

In the case of fearfulness in rats (defined by behaviour characteristics such as defecation and activity), regions of chromosomes 1, 12 and 15 contain QTLs (Flint et al., 1995). The statistical index of allelic association is the LOD score: this is the logarithm to the base 10 of the odds. Simply put, LOD relates to the 'odds' that a specific allelic association belongs to one group and not the other (e.g., low vs. high fearful individuals). A LOD score of 3 or greater is generally accepted to be statistically significant.

Coda: genetic markers

The above discussion has referred to *genetic markers* in a number of places, without describing them in detail (for a detailed discussion, see Craig & McClay, 2003). These markers cut DNA into segments, and it is through the study of these segments that genes are located on specific chromosomes. Usually, when the news is announced that a gene has been 'found' it means that it has been localized to a part of one of the chromosomes by the use of these markers.

Markers are thus landmarks in the genome. There now exist millions of markers. But what are markers? Markers are DNA polymorphisms (stretches of DNA that come in different forms) that can be used to localize variations in some phenotype to polymorphisms in some location in the genome. It is a way of homing in on the region of genetic interest. As with all landmarks, aiming for it does not mean you have arrived at your precise location (in this case, the gene sequence). However, a systematic search (e.g., by allelic association) is much easier when it is known where roughly to look.

DNA markers can be identified by using *restriction fragment length polymorphism* (RFLP). Using this method, DNA is chopped up by an enzyme called a *restriction enzyme* – there are hundreds of different types of these enzymes, each of which cuts DNA at a particular location (i.e., where a polymorphism is known to occur) – these enzymes are like chemical scissors. For example, *ecru* recognizes the sequence GAATTC and severs the DNA molecule between G and A bases on each strand (this sequence occurs thousands of times throughout the genome).

If, when searching for a particular gene, its DNA spans the cutting site of the enzyme, then it will be cut by the enzyme; a different allele, in the same location but not containing the cutting sequence, does not cut. If an association between variation in the phenotype and variation in the DNA, cut by the enzyme, is found, then there is good reason to believe that the search is homing in on the gene sequence responsible for the phenotype. Examples of genetic markers (i.e., polymorphisms) are *simple sequence repeats* (SSRs) and *single nucleotide polymorphisms* (SNPs, i.e., substitution of one base pair). The ultimate way to detect all polymorphisms is to sequence the DNA of many people. SNPs constitute 85 per cent of all DNA differences that are likely to be the genetic cause of most disorders.

In interpreting gene–behaviour associations, it is important to know the cautionary tale of the 'chopstick gene'. A correlation between a gene and a phenotype does not necessarily imply that the gene codes for that phenotype. Is there a specific gene for the use of chopsticks? Obviously not, but it would be easy to associate a genetic locus with this skill proficiency. How is this possible? This association (correlation) is a result of, on average, blue-eyed people being less proficient than brown-eyed people (from certain parts of the world) – that is, brown-eyed people tend to be proficient with chopsticks, whereas blue-eyes do not to the same extent. Therefore, care must be exercised so as not to associate purely cultural (learned) behaviours with genetic causation.

This tale reminds us that linkage and association studies are dealing with correlations; and, as is well known, 'correlation does not imply causation'. However, if the gene responsible for the phenotype is determined – and this would take considerable experimental evidence – then it is sensible to infer, from this correlational data, that the alleles of the gene *cause* differences in the phenotype because behaviour cannot cause differences in DNA (only DNA can cause behaviour). In all other areas of psychology, such an inference from correlational data would not be correct. For example, if it is found that socially dominant males have higher levels of testosterone, then this finding is compatible with a number of conclusions: high levels of this hormone lead to dominance behaviour; achieving a dominant position in a social hierarchy leads to elevated levels of testosterone; or both effects take place. Without experimental manipulations of (a) the hormone or (b) social status, these alternative conclusions could not be checked. Genetics does allow legitimate reduction of behaviour to DNA sequences (bearing in mind caveats concerning necessary–sufficient conditions, gene–environment effects, etc.).

ASK YOURSELF
How does the QTL approach differ from classical Mendelian genetics?

Genetics and General Intelligence

Knowledge concerning the genetics of intelligence has benefited from advances in molecular techniques, which complement quantitative genetic methods, which have consistently shown a high heritability in this factor. Indeed, there is an important interplay of all three approaches to understanding intelligence, which illustrates the broader relevance of adopting a multi-track research strategy: (a) estimating genetic and environmental influence (*quantitative genetics*); (b) identifying genes associated with intelligence (*molecular genetics*); and (c) understanding the function of genes (*functional genomics*).

General intelligence – denoted by g – may be defined as the variance common to all tests of cognitive ability; that is, the common thread that links tests of seemingly different abilities. The notion of g is supported by the somewhat remarkable fact that all tests of cognitive ability are positively correlated – this is known as the 'positive manifold' – in correlational matrices. What this means is that, although there is unique variance in all tests of ability (e.g., spatial, verbal, performance, perceptual and mathematical), there is also shared (or common) variance as revealed by positive correlations. Statistical techniques (e.g., factor analysis; see chapter 17) may be used to measure these common and unique sources of variance. The common factor of intelligence (i.e., g) accounts for a substantial proportion of the variance among tests (approx. 40%).

As noted by Plomin (2003), multivariate genetic analysis – which allows variables to be simultaneously analysed – shows that the genetic overlap among tests of cognitive ability is twice as great as the phenotype overlap, an observation suggesting that 'g is where the genetic action is' (p. 1). Plomin goes on to state that 'Although g is not the whole story, trying to tell the story of cognitive abilities without g loses the plot entirely' (p. 1).

This literature is important for a number of reasons. First, quantitative genetic studies show that intelligence is strongly influenced by (additive) genetics (approx. 60%) – this genetic influence stabilizes from infancy (approx. 20%), childhood (approx. 40%) to adulthood (approx. 60%). Second, it is interesting to note that as g is molar (i.e., at a high level of integration), the strong genetic factor running through the diverse tests of cognitive ability flies in the face of the assumption in neuroscience that brain functions are essentially modular, consisting of relatively independent processing units with their own genetic basis (for a discussion of modularity, see chapter 18). Third, mental retardation also appears to be g-related – there are some 200 single-gene disorders that include mental retardation among their symptoms. Fourth, g is surprisingly stable throughout adulthood, and it does not greatly change as a result of life experience – if any psychological phenotype should change, then it might be expected to be g. Fourth, the practical implications of cognitive ability are vast, and g widely predicts educational and occupational success more than any other trait, and it is routinely used in employment selection and placement. Surprisingly for a trait that is often not considered seriously in psychology – indeed, it is hardly taught at undergraduate level – it is one of the most obvious and practical applications of psychology. Therefore, understanding its genetic and environmental foundations is of no small importance.

The genetic contribution to intelligence is better documented than for any other biological or behavioural dimension or disorder and this has meant that it is possible to refine the research questions to ask about the interplay of nature and nurture and the molecular genetics of these statistical findings. Of particular importance in this regard is the finding that, although the phenotypic correlation among cognitive tests is about 0.30, multivariate genetic analysis shows that the genetic correlations among these tests are around 0.80 – a genetic correlation measures the degree to which genetic effects on one trait are associated with genetic effects on another trait (i.e., knowing the genetic contribution on one measure accounts for that of another measure). Such analysis would

> **ASK YOURSELF**
> What does the genetics of intelligence tell us about the structure of different cognitive abilities?

assess not the genetic contribution to phenotype intelligence but genetic contribution to the covariation observed among such tests – it is also possible to extend this type of analysis to the covariation observed between g tests and behaviour, or between normal variation in the population and clinical disorders. It is interesting to note that genetically related to g are grey and white matter densities in diverse brain regions, which are themselves highly genetically influenced. High genetic correlation implies that genes associated with one cognitive ability factor are highly likely to be associated with all other cognitive abilities (or brain processes). However, not all intelligence-related phenotypes show a high genetic correlation. For example, severe retardation does not seem to share a common genetic effect with the g of siblings: severe disorders are often the result of rare single-gene or chromosome disorders and often occur spontaneously. In contrast, less severe retardation is associated with the genetic g of siblings (see Plomin, 2003), suggesting a common QTL contribution to both phenotypes. For a discussion of this literature and for further reading, see Plomin (2003) and Plomin and Spinath (2004); for a review of the neuroscience of intelligence, see Gray and Thompson (2004).

Ethical and Moral Issues in Genetics

A number of scientists take issue with behavioural genetics (e.g., Kamin, 1974; Lewontin, Rose & Kamin, 1984; Rose, 1997; Rose & Rose, 2001).[16] These authors highlight the necessity of taking adequate account of the social, political and ethical aspects of genetics research: history has already proved that these issues are ignored at our peril. (History also shows that the social, political and ethical aspects of environmental research are ignored at our peril.) Their specific criticisms of psychological genetics revolve around: (a) the complexity of psychological characteristics; (b) the validity of estimating influences from genetic and non-genetic (environmental) factors (they argue that these influences are complex and bound together in a way that is not easily divisible); and (c) the suspicion that genetics research has a sociopolitical hidden agenda, to reduce human beings to purely biological entities, robbed of historical, social and political context.[17]

One of the important names in the Human Genome Project (Sir John Sulston) has also discussed the social, commercial and ethical issues coming out of molecular genetics (Sulston & Ferry, 2002) – he is especially concerned about the privatization of genetic knowledge and technology to the detriment of public accessibility. (Watson, 2003, provides a succinct account of the difficult issues surrounding the use of genetics for social and commercial purposes.) This is not the place to go into these complex issues, but, to other scientists, current knowledge of psychological genetics constitutes an advanced base camp in the assault on Mt. Ignorance, a camp so far up the slope that it permits glimpses, through the fog, of the summit where enlightenment about the nature of individual differences and the factors that impact on their plasticity will prevail. (Gottesman, 2003, p. xiii)

> **ASK YOURSELF**
> Does genetic research *always* have a sociopolitical dimension?

The Future: Applications and Angst

The future is here: DNA tests are available for a range of physical and psychological disorders. For example, it is now possible to know whether you and I carry the Huntington gene, and thus it is possible to know if we are destined to go on to early psychological decline: knowledge often comes with a heavy price! In the future, with advances in *proteomics* (i.e., the study of protein expression and function), coupled with strategies to modify gene expression (*transcriptomics*; the study of messenger RNA to determine when, where and under which conditions genes are expressed), it will be possible to take remedial action to reduce or eliminate the pathological effects of gene expression.

In our consideration of the techniques used in genetics applied to human beings, it is important to consider ethical, legal, psychological and social issues – such issues do not belong in a different book or chapter: they need to be at the forefront of our thinking about the technological applications of scientific techniques.

Few of us worry about the positive benefits of genetics research in human disease: in fact, most of us look forward to the day when medical practice has caught up with the opportunities opened by the Human Genome Project; and I doubt whether many of us would refuse life-saving treatment based on molecular genetic technology. However, it would be naive to assume that there will not be a price to be paid for this technological progress.

There is the concern that information regarding individuals' genomes will be used to classify people into low and high risks for insurance, employment and other purposes, creating a genetic underclass. Also, if molecular genetics can reduce the influence of genes that code for pathological phenotypes, then it is highly probable that it will also be possible to use this technology to *enhance* characteristics that are in the normal range of scores (e.g., the trait of general intelligence). Often it is said that this prospect is unlikely, and reflects a misunderstanding of the relationship between genes and complex phenotypes. However, it is possible that (a) genes have relatively large psychological effects that will be identified; and (b) even if all psychological phenotypes are highly polygenetic, there will come a day (maybe in the distant future) when scientific knowledge and technological advance allow for genetic manipulation of genes for enhancement. There is a thin and shifting line between modifying a gene that codes for a clearly defined categorical pathology (e.g., PKU) and modifying a gene that codes for a quantitative trait in order to boost psychological processing.

When technology is available – and surely it will be – who is to tell the parent that they are not allowed to give their child the best possible start in the world? Will parents be content to continue to allow the blind chance involved in genetic transmission to decide the fate of their children? Will there be a pressure to modify genes so that each and every person born has equal psychological potential? If not, then why not? Such issues will raise personal dilemma and hard problems for society.

Since its inception, the Human Genome Project has provided funds to study the ethical, legal and social issues surrounding the availability of genetic knowledge and technology. Issues that have been addressed include: (a) privacy and confidentiality of genetic information (who owns DNA information and who has rights of access to it?); (b) fairness in the use of genetic information by insurers, employers, courts, schools, adoption agencies; (c) psychological impact, stigmatization and discrimination due to individual differences; (d) reproductive issues, including adequate and informed consent in reproductive decisions; (e) fairness in access to advanced genomic techniques (who is to pay, and for what?); (f) desirability of testing for genetic vulnerability for which there is no remedial therapy; (g) conceptual and philosophical issues concerning personal responsibility, and free will vs. genetic determination (will it be possible to plead as mitigation one's genome in the case of a crime?); and (h) commercialization of gene products.[18] Ethical and social issues, including genetic counselling, studies of group differences and the responsibilities of the scientist, are discussed by Sherman et al. (1997).

> **ASK YOURSELF**
> In psychogenomics, to what extent have science (i.e., knowledge) and the use of science (i.e., technology) become confused?

Conclusion

In summary, the Human Genome Project has ushered in a new age of discovery and innovation in the biological sciences. Until recently, genetic studies of psychological phenomena relied on statistical studies of phenotypes, using either twin or adoption studies. These statistical studies have shown the importance of genetics (and environments) for virtually all psychological characteristics; however, they do not tell us *how* genes work at the biological level. The ultimate scientific goal is not just finding genes associated with behaviour but also understanding how these genes function (*functional genomics*): science is rapidly entering this new era of discovery (*neurogenetics* will be especially important in showing how genes control brain processes). Within our sights is the emergence of a true molecular science of the mind: *psychogenomics*.

> ## Learning Questions
>
> 1. How should 'heritability' be properly interpreted?
> 2. Have molecular genetic technologies superseded traditional quantitative genetic designs?
> 3. Why are gene–gene and gene–environment effects important in explaining complex behaviour?
> 4. What is the 'quantitative trait loci' (QTL) approach and how does it differ from the classical Mendelian approach?
> 5. Is it true that the more we know about genetic influences the more we know about environmental influences?

NOTES

1 *Functional genomics* is also sometimes used instead of the term *behavioural genomics*, but this term is more often used for the molecular processes of genomics. Therefore, to avoid confusion, behavioural genomics (or psychogenomics) is preferred.

2 The Behavioral Genetic Interactive Modules are a series of freely available interactive computer programs designed to convey a sense of modern behavioural genetic analysis; these cover basic statistical concepts and some of the applied analytical approaches used in genetics: http://statgen.iop.kcl.ac.uk/bgim.

3 Such a finding would not mean that genetics is not important in determining height of the sample. For example, you and I have two arms and two legs; and these are genetically controlled. But, if a quantitative genetic study of this phenotype were conducted, then it would come to the conclusion that there is no genetic influence because there is no *variance* (save rare genetic mutations, and environmental injury, which would not be detected by the statistical procedures used).

4 The statistical concept of *variance* is defined as the sum of squared deviations from the mean divided by the sample size. In standard notation, this reads:

$$Vx = 1/n \sqrt{(x_i - x)^2}$$

where: Vx is the variance of variable x
Σ is the sum
x_i is the set of numbers
x is the sample, or population, mean
$(x_i - x)^2$ means to square each number after the subtraction of $x_i - x$.

The procedure: (a) work out the mean of a set of number (e.g., $(4 + 5 + 2 + 9 + 6 + 7)/6 = 5.5$); (b) take the deviation of each number from this mean (e.g., $9 - 5.5 = 3.5$) and then square it (e.g., $3.5^2 = 12.25$); (c) sum/add these squared deviations; and (d) divide this sum by the sample size. Usually in psychology the square root ($\sqrt{\ }$) of variance is taken to yield the standard deviation, which produces a measure of deviation in the original units. (Squaring eliminates minus numbers, which otherwise would get used in a simple mean-difference procedure.) (Deviation also underlies the statistical concept of correlations: if two variables are correlated then this means that the deviation from the mean for the two variables goes in the same direction (the extent of this concordance is known as the *correlation coefficient*: a coefficient of 0 means no concordance, a coefficient of 1 means perfect concordance).

5 I am grateful to Professor Robert Plomin (June 2004; personal communication) for bringing this fact to my attention.

6 The proportion of variance due to different effects is important when we wish to understand how a population responds to selection (i.e., breeding experiments): if all the variation exists because different individuals experience different environments, then there is no genetically influenced phenotype to favour; but if the variation is mainly genetic, then the phenotype to favour is large. Using a breeding methodology in non-human animals, it is possible to work out how much differences in the phenotype are due to environmental factors and how much are due to genetic factors; it is also possible to work out whether the genetic effects are additive or epistatic. Obviously, with human beings this strategy is not possible.

7 It was thought by some people that the relatively small number of genes in the human genome entailed the conclusion that much of human behaviour *must* be learned; whether or not this conclusion is warranted – and there is still considerable debate surrounding this problem – it cannot depend on this number-of-genes argument.

8   This blueprint *for* life is no more life itself than a blueprint for a factory is a factory capable of manufacture: it is only a first step – albeit a fundamental one – for the further manufacture of the building blocks of life: proteins, etc. During the building process, the final shape of the building can be altered; so too in the human body, where the DNA blueprint contains only the rudiments of the final form of the phenotype. Even in the case of major gene effects, this blueprint can effectively be nullified by changes during the building process (e.g., PKU). Seen in this light, 'genetic determinism' loses its meaning.

9   Junk DNA, however, does have it uses, one of the most important being 'genetic fingerprints' for identifying criminals. Jeffreys, Wilson & Thein (1985) noted that a short piece of DNA is repeated many times over, and the number of repeats varied between individuals. A number of repeating regions are used (the FBI uses 12), and then statistical probability theory is applied to calculate the probability that there is a match between DNA left at the scene of the crime and the suspect's DNA.

10   Morgan and his students – affectionately known as 'Morgan's Boys' – would trap the flies with the allure of rotting bananas. Reputedly, the laboratory was infested with cockroaches, attracted by the terrible smell. Morgan and his students did not mind working night and day: theirs was an interest in a fascinating topic of study. Today, high-throughput DNA laboratories are highly technical and spotlessly clean: yet they could not have existed without inspired scientists like Morgan and his dedicated students (see Watson, 2003).

11   It has been possible since the 1970s to 'cut-and-paste' stretches of DNA: a pair of molecular scissors is required to cut DNA into sections; then a molecular glue is needed to manipulate the pieces; and lastly a molecular duplicating machine is required to amplify DNA (PCR). These tools comprise what is known as 'recombinant DNA' technology. This technology allows the manufacture of new DNA sequences: new genes. (Watson, 2003, provides a good introduction to the uses and methods underlying this technology.)

12   The similarity of protein-coding sequences (exons) and the divergence of junk sequences shows that natural selection has been very effective in eliminating mutations: these are rare in exons, but common in introns and junk DNA.

13   An online research of Mendelian disorders may be found at: http://www.ncbi.nlm.nih.gov/

14   Although complex traits may not follow a Mendelian form of inheritance, the many individual genes that go together to comprise the genetic basis of the trait are fundamentally Mendelian in nature: that is, they comprise separate alleles (which come in a variety of forms), and may be dominant or recessive (or some intermediate of these two extreme positions).

15   QTLs are, of course, nothing more than separate genes that contribute to a phenotype. However, the QTL *approach* is different from the Mendelian and candidate gene approaches in that QTLs are seen within a gene *complex*: in order to understand the genetic basis of complex quantitative phenotypes it is necessary to identify the interplay of a large number of genes, each of which has a small effect.

16   These authors are outspoken critics of the scientific and sociopolitical bases of genetics research in psychology and psychiatry. They are in a 'minority' among those working in genetics, but this partly reflects the fact that other scientists who do not endorse the scientific power of human genetics simply do not work in this area, and thus do not write here either: they are off working in other areas of science that they find more conducive to their beliefs.

17   Another form of opposition to quantitative genetics comes from the unlikely quarter of evolutionary psychology (EP). EP focuses on species-typical phenotypes, and compares differences *across* species in an attempt to understand the evolutionary basis of psychology: its focus is on mean differences. In contrast, quantitative genetics (QG) is not interested in mean differences between species, but in differences in variance *within* species (especially human beings). This difference alone does not explain the opposition of EP to QG: it is likely that this opposition emanates from a desire of EP to distance itself from the misuse of evolution

(social Darwinism) and classical (Mendelian) genetics in the earlier part of the twentieth century in the corruption of genetics for political purposes (i.e., eugenics). After all, EP and its predecessor, sociobiology, have a hard enough time arguing for a Darwinian basis to the mind without getting bogged down in arguments concerning differences between human beings. (See chapter 2 for a discussion of sociobiology and EP.)

18   For a discussion of the Human Genome Project, including ethical, legal and social issues, go to: www.ornl.gov/hgmis/.

FURTHER READING

Plomin, R., DeFries, J. C., Craig, I. W. & McGuffin, P. (2003). *Behavioral Genetics in the Postgenomic Era*. Washington: American Psychological Association.

Plomin, R., DeFries, J. C., McClearn, G. E. & McGuffin, P. (2001). *Behavioral Genetics*. New York: Worth.

Primrose, S. B. & Twyman, R. M. (2004). *Genomics: Applications in Human Biology*. Oxford: Blackwell.

Part III applies our understanding of the 'Foundations' (Part I) and 'Approaches' (Part II) of biological psychology to a number of key areas of importance in normal and abnormal behaviour. It would be impossible to review every possible topic in detail – such an ambition would be futile given the vastness of the literature and our limited space. Instead, this part has the more modest goal of focusing on five topics, three of which relate to psychopathology and two of which relate to normal, everyday processes and behaviours. Throughout these chapters, illustrative examples are taken from theoretical and methodological perspectives, both to demonstrate the utility of these theories/approaches and as a way to understand the specific topics. The five topics are covered in some detail in order to provide a depth of analysis and reveal the actual scientific state of our knowledge – where appropriate, our *lack* of knowledge is highlighted: knowing what is *not* known is sometimes just as important as knowing what is known!

Chapter 14 ('Clinical Disorder I: Depression') describes the major signs and symptoms of depression, and the psychiatric classification of depressive disorders (principally major depressive disorder and bipolar disorder). Cognitive explanations are considered alongside physiological explanation, as revealed by psychopharmacology, genetics and neuroimaging. Also considered is a novel treatment of depression, transcranial magnetic stimulation (TMS), used principally in experimental studies of brain function (see chapter 8). Possible evolutionary functions of depression are also surveyed. A personal account of the experience of bipolar depression by a professor of experimental psychology, Stuart Sutherland, is given in an attempt to convey the qualitative nature of this disorder.

Chapter 15 ('Clinical Disorder II: Anxiety') describes the major classification of the anxiety disorders, in the context of psychopharmacology, psychophysiology, neuroimaging and genetics studies. Cognitive models are also discussed to show how they relate to purely biological explanations. Once again, evolutionary explanations are presented, and a personal account of anxiety (obsessive–compulsive disorder; OCD) is provided by the experiences of the biological psychologist Dr Frederick Toates.

Chapter 16 ('Clinical Disorders III: Schizophrenia') discusses the nature of psychosis and schizophrenia, serving to dispel some of the myths and misunderstandings surrounding these conditions. The diagnostic symptoms of schizophrenia are presented and contrasted with other forms of psychosis. Cognitive processes and biases, especially in relation to delusions, are discussed, as are the meanings attached to delusions and hallucinations. Approaches surveyed include neuropsychological assessment, behavioural tasks, psychophysiology, psychopharmacology, neuroimaging and genetics. Also summarized is the 'high-risk approach' to identifying those individuals who may be prone to developing schizophrenia, before considering some of the possible evolutionary reasons for the existence of this highly deleterious disorder. An account of the subjective experience of psychosis is provided in a detailed account by the person-centred (humanistic) psychologist Dr Peter Chadwick, who received his (second) doctoral degree for his study of cognitive processes in schizophrenia.

Chapter 17 ('Personality: Emotion and Motivation') presents a review of normal variation in personality related to neurotic disorders. First, the meaning of individual differences and uniqueness is clarified; then Darwin's account of the expression of emotion in animals is presented as an introduction to the emotional basis of personality. The main structural models of personality are described, and then a detailed account is given of the neuropsychology of approach and avoidance motivational tendencies, which are thought to underlie the major dimensions of personality (namely, extroversion and neuroticism). The genetics of personality, including recent molecular studies and the relevance of selection studies, is also discussed. One of the leading neuropsychological models of individual differences in approach and avoidance motivation is described in some detail, namely Jeffrey Gray's Reinforcement Sensitivity Theory (RST). Neuroimaging studies of reactions to emotive stimuli and the role of personality in these reactions are summarized. Lastly, the evolution of individual differences is discussed.

Chapter 18 ('Cognition: Computation and Consciousness') turns to the biological basis of cognition, specifically to the problems of brain computations and the mysteries of consciousness. Here some of the thorny theoretical problems in the brain–mind debate are discussed, including how to close the gap between the physical stuff of the 'brain' and the objective stuff of the 'mind'. The brain as a general-purpose computer is described and critiqued, and the role of computation in evolutionary psychology summarized, including discussion of the existence of innate content in computational processes as seen in processing biases (e.g., logical reason and cheating detection). How ideas jump from brain to brain to form culture is discussed in terms of the speculation of a 'meme' system of selection and inheritance. The problems of consciousness are then delineated and discussed within a biological framework; followed by experimental evidence (from neuropsychology, for instance) that bears upon the form and function of conscious awareness. The chapter closes with a description of a biologically viable account of the evolution and function of consciousness, produced by Jeffrey Gray, before ending on a speculative note concerning one of the remaining problems: why are we conscious at all?

Much of the discussion in these chapters is intended to demonstrate that an integrated view should be taken of the brain–mind, and, although clearly defined headings are a convenience for textbook writers (and readers), they do not reflect the coordinated functioning of the brain. In this respect, the work of Jeffrey Gray, who made a significant contribution to all five areas covered in Part III, attests to the viability of applying a common theoretical neuropsychological approach to what may seem separate problems – this is the approach advocated by Donald Hebb, in whose footsteps Gray followed.

What such work, by Gray and others, demonstrates is that even apparent mysteries of the brain–mind *are* problems for biological psychology, and that the application of theoretically cogent approaches, along with the use of sophisticated empirical tools, produces real (but, as yet, not total) understanding, as opposed to the data-retardant speculation common in other areas of philosophy and psychology.

Clinical Disorder I: Depression

14

Learning Objectives

To be able to:

1. Describe the diagnostic features of major depressive disorder and bipolar disorder.
2. Outline what is known about the structural abnormalities observed in depression.
3. Discuss the major psychopharmacological hypotheses and treatments of depression.
4. Evaluate the genetic bases of depression and the role of environmental factors.
5. Describe and critique evolutionary explanations of the possible functions of depression.

Biological psychology makes an important contribution to the understanding and treatment of abnormal states of mind, collectively termed *psychopathology* (disease of the mind). In this and the next chapter some of the major conditions falling under the general heading of *neurosis* are presented; then in the following chapter the discussion turns to *psychosis*, focusing on schizophrenia. These conditions are of considerable theoretical interest; but more importantly they are of great clinical importance: a significant number of people suffer from one or more of these conditions, leading to costs in terms of impoverished quality of life (to the afflicted and their family/friends), health care and lost educational/occupational opportunities. There are few families that have not been directly or indirectly affected by these conditions. Useful information and advice on clinically relevant aspects of mental illness is available, in the UK, from the Royal College of Psychiatrists (www.rcpsych.ac.uk) and, in the USA, the American Psychiatric Association (www.psych.org).

The two major clusters of neurotic disorder are depression and anxiety. There are many symptoms associated with these disorders, including voluntary action, motoric behaviour, motivation, and disrupted cognitive processing; but at their core is a disorder of emotion. Treatment for these conditions is predominantly pharmacological, and much is known about their psychopharmacological bases. The fundamentals of neurons and neurotransmission were covered in chapter 4, and the techniques of psychopharmacology in chapter 12: these chapters form the foundations of much of the material surveyed in the next three chapters. Other technical approaches (e.g., psychophysiological) are sampled in order to throw further light on the biological bases of these disorders.

What are Emotion and Mood?

Most of the disorders falling under the rubric *neurosis* entail a disorder of emotion and mood; and these pathological expressions of emotion/mood are often seen to reflect the extreme end of a continuum of normal functioning. As we will see in chapter 17, there is a very close connection between the everyday emotion/mood and their clinical expression.

We all know the nature of emotion first-hand: the anxiety before a dentist's appointment; the sense of anticipation before going on a first date; the rush of fear when seeing a snake; the feeling of anger when annoyed; the frustration of not achieving some desired goal; the sadness of death; the happiness of a close relationship; and the excitement of success. Some of us have also experienced extremes of emotion: these can be *normal*, in the sense that the level of emotion experienced is appropriate to the objective situation (e.g., knowing a relative is just about to die), or *abnormal* (pathological), in the sense that the level of emotion experienced is out of proportion to the objective situation (e.g., fear of a household spider). Emotions are psychological states that make us feel most alive – they take us to the elated highs of joy and to the depressed lows of despair. They are important personally and scientifically. But, while we may know what emotions *feel* like, it is very difficult to verbalize and conceptualize their nature in psychological terms – among other reasons, this is why the behaviourists elected to treat emotional experience as invalid scientific data. Like it or not, emotions are real, or, at the very least, *seem* real; therefore, they are the object of valid psychological enquiry. However, our first-hand experience of *our own* emotions does not necessarily equip us to understand the emotions of other people, especially when their emotions are extreme. Accordingly, caution needs exercising when interpreting the emotions of other people on the basis of our own experience – the problem of knowing the experience of other people is discussed further in chapter 18.

An emotion may be defined as a feeling (or affection) experienced consciously (or at least accessible to consciousness) that pervades thoughts and which is neither essentially cognitive in nature (although it has a cognitive component) nor voluntary. It is usually outside our immediate conscious control and it is rather like a flood wave of pure psychological sensation. At pathologically high levels, it dominates our consciousness, preventing the normal working of our cognitive processes and interrupting our usual behaviour. Pathological emotion may thus be defined as an affective state (out of proportion to the objective reality) that pervades consciousness, impairing adaptive reactions to everyday stimuli. Strong emotion that is proportional to objective reality (e.g., facing a real threat) should not be seen as pathological, although it may require similar therapeutic interventions (e.g., anti-anxiety medication for someone who is facing death).

The term *emotion* is usually reserved for affective feeling towards some distinct object or situation. More formally, emotion is related to a reinforcing stimulus: it is usually about something (this 'something' can be specific or general) and tends to be short-lived. In contrast, the term *mood* is usually reserved for longer-lasting feelings that are not necessarily tied to some event (e.g., we have all woken up in a 'bad mood' that persisted throughout the day for no apparent reason). Although this emotion–mood distinction is somewhat arbitrary – for example, mood may often be traced to a specific reinforcing stimulus (although its effect may be as evident as for a short-lived, distinct emotion) – it is a usual starting point for understanding affective states (see Matthews, Deary & Whiteman, 2003).

Emotion and mood are often classified along two fundamental dimensions: *positive* (appetitive) and *negative* (aversive) – animals subjectively favour the former and shun the latter. In terms of effects, it is possible to describe emotion along four dimensions: (a) behavioural; (b) physiological; (c) cognitive; and (d) subjective. For example, when we are fearful (e.g., hearing a noise in the house when alone late at night), (a) ongoing behaviour is initially inhibited, and we listen carefully (*behaviour*); (b) hormones and neurotransmitters are released to prepare us for rapid action (*physiology*); (c) cognitive resources are directed to the potential source of threat (e.g., attention and reasoning; *cognition*); and (d) a sense of tension and apprehension overwhelms us (*subjective*). These four aspects are important for understanding the physiology and psychological significance of emotion. Mood also involves these four elements, but their activation is less marked and longer-term – there is no doubt that, when in a 'bad mood', our behaviour, physiology, cognition and subjective states are all altered.

When these emotion/mood states become semi-permanent, habitual responses, they form personality traits, as assessed by psychometric measures. Thus, it is possible to talk of the 'anxious person', as someone who is quick to show the characteristics signs of anxiety at the slightest provocation. Chapter 17 discusses how these habitual normal emotional processes are related to a variety of neurotic psychopathological disorders, and how the nature of pathological emotions may be understood from the perspective of normal expressions of emotion.

Before discussing the symptoms (expressions), aetiology (causes), treatment (therapy) and prognosis (expected outcome), I first outline the classification of mental disorder by psychiatrists in their clinical practice. For each condition the main symptoms are summarized based upon the fourth (revised) edition of the *Diagnostic and Statistical Manual of Mental Disorders* (DSM-IV-R; American Psychiatric Association, 2000).

ASK YOURSELF
To what extent can we use our own experience of emotional states to understand other people's emotional experiences?

Psychiatric Classification: DSM-IV-R

DSM-IV-R is one of the major classification (*nosological*) systems used in psychiatry; the alternate classification system is the World Health Organization's (WHO) *International Statistical Classification of Diseases and Related Health Problems* (ICD-10; WHO, 1992). DSM-IV-R provides descriptive criteria and statistical information for the diagnosis of the whole range of psychiatric conditions.

DSM is deliberately *atheoretical*, avoiding aetiological and treatment recommendations – a decision largely based on: (a) the considerable debate still surrounding the cause of mental disorder; and (b) the desire to achieve diagnostic standardization and reliability. Disorders are classified according to five axes: (a) Axis I comprises *Clinical Disorders* (e.g., Mood Disorders, Eating Disorders, Anxiety Disorders); (b) Axis II comprises *Personality Disorders* and *Mental Retardation* (e.g., schizotypal personality disorder), which can often confuse a primary diagnosis of a clinical disorder; (c) Axis III refers to *General Medical Conditions* (e.g., infectious and parasitic diseases), which are potentially relevant to the understanding or management of clinical disorder; (d) Axis IV assesses *Psychosocial and Environmental Problems* (e.g., housing problems), which are factors that may affect the diagnosis, treatment and prognosis of mental disorders; and (e) *Global Assessment of Functioning* (psychological, social and occupational functions) provides information necessary for the planning of treatment and measurement of outcome.

The purpose of the DSM system is to impose diagnostic rigour in psychiatry, leading to reliability of diagnosis. Reliability is especially important in the context of evaluating treatment interventions: it needs to be known that what is being classified as a major depression in Detroit, USA, is the same as that in London, UK (of course, it is important not to confuse reliability with validity: a consistency of diagnostic practice does not necessarily mean that the diagnosis is correct[1]). The DSM system forces consideration of a number of different aspects of the patient's life: the presenting symptoms are only *one* source of information. For example, an acute episode of paranoia does not necessarily imply a psychotic condition (it could be caused by a temporary infection), or it may represent a long-lasting personality trait, representing a personality disorder. A 'depressed' patient may well have much to be depressed about in their social or occupational life, and their condition may be an entirely understandable reaction to a real loss of control; a highly anxious patient may well be confronting highly aversive events in their everyday life. Symptoms are only a guide: they are not the diagnosis. The DSM system defines the necessary and sufficient signs and symptoms for the diagnosis of a mental condition.

ASK YOURSELF
What factors need to be taken into account when diagnosing a psychiatric condition?

Definition of Depression

Depression is one of the major *affective disorders*. It represents a cluster of symptoms (syndrome), relating to emotion/mood, motoric, motivation and cognitive disturbances – only one symptom, although it is an important one, is an abnormality of (low) mood. There are abnormalities in *vegetative functions* (e.g., sleep, appetite, weight and sex drive), *cognitive features* (e.g., attention span, memory, impulse control), *behavioural features* (e.g., motivation, pleasure and interests) and *physical features* (e.g., headaches and muscle tension – these physical complaints, themselves, can be very debilitating).

It has been estimated that more years of healthy functioning are lost through depression than any other disorder (except for perinatal and communicable diseases of childhood), and, by 2020, the economic burden imposed by affective disorders will be exceeded only by ischaemic heart disease (Murray & Lopez, 1997). Economic costs are one thing; the terrible personal costs to sufferers are quite another. Lifelong prevalence stands around

Figure 14.1   Sir Winston Churchill, with his characteristic 'V for victory' sign of defiance during the Second World War. (Photo © Underwood & Underwood / CORBIS.)

10 per cent, and many cases go unreported and untreated, sometimes leading to suicide. However, despite the daily challenges of depression, some people struggle through and achieve great things.

For example, Sir Winston Churchill was a highly emotional person, suffering from periodic bouts of depression for much of his adult life – his daily struggles with depression were documented by his personal physician Lord Moran (Moran, 1966), something that Churchill called his *black dog* (for a psychiatric analysis, see Storr, 1989).[2] But, despite his considerable psychological problems, Churchill maintained a formidable work rate for most of his 60-year career and excelled during the Second World War – indeed, it may be speculated that, during the dark days of the early part of the war, when Britain was on the verge of defeat, Churchill's inability to distinguish his own personal depression and the sense of doom from that warranted by objective circumstances enabled him to soldier on defiantly (in a real sense, he was as defiant of his own depression as he was of Hitler; figure 14.1). Churchill's life shows several important aspects of depression, and suggests that, under *certain circumstances*, it may be useful.

Attributional (explanatory) style

Before embarking on our journey of biological theories of depression, the important role of cognition should be acknowledged – in particular the interaction of 'biological' and 'cognitive' factors is important. 'Biological' factors do not operate in a different realm from 'cognitive' factors: both are part of the same psychophysiological system.

We all experience disappointments and setbacks that may be defined as 'depressing' – we are even often heard to say that the 'weather is depressing' (which in the case of seasonal affective disorder, SAD, it may well be; Mersch et al., 1999). Clinical depression, however, is more than everyday disappointment or sadness; it is, to varying degrees, a profound sense of loss, worthlessness, low self-esteem, and a feeling of helplessness that life is beyond control – crucially, a feeling that one is to blame for the bad things that happen. There is a *cognitive triad*, concerning negative beliefs and attributions about: (a) the world, (b) oneself, and (c) the future. A typical depressed person's attributions (e.g., assumed causes) for bad events (e.g., failing an exam, losing a boy/girlfriend) is: (a) 'it's my fault' (*internal* attribution); (b) 'it will always be my fault' (*stable* attribution); and (c) 'I'm useless at everything' (*global* attribution). These attributions – that is, the habitual reasons given for good and bad events in the world – are known as *attributional* or explanatory *style* (Abramson, Seligman & Teasdale, 1978); these can be measured by such questionnaires as the Attributional Style Questionnaire (ASQ; Peterson et al., 1982).[3] Cognitive-behavioural therapy (CBT) aims to restructure these biased cognitions, to develop a more rational (i.e., positive) outlook on life. There is now a vast literature on the cognitive biases seen in depression, reflecting a range of memory and decision-making processes (e.g., Fossati et al., 2004; van Vreeswijk & de Wilde, 2004).

In one study, a modified Stroop task was used with self-descriptive emotional information, consisting of naming the colour in which positive and negative adjectives differed in the degree to which they described the person; these target adjectives were primed by emotional phrases that varied according to the degree of self-reference. The results showed that depressed patients, compared with healthy controls, were slowed by self-descriptive targets primed by self-descriptive negative phrases more than any other prime–target combination (e.g., target negative adjectives primed by non-self-descriptive phrases) (Segal et al., 1995) – this finding suggests that negative information about the self is highly interconnected in the cognitive system of depressed patients. Elliot (1998) provides a review of the complex neuropsychological literature and discusses some of the related methodological and theoretical issues.

Understanding the behavioural and cognitive bases of depression is just as important as understanding the purely biological bases (e.g., action of drugs at specific receptors). For example, drugs do not exert a magic effect on psychological state; rather, they influence the neuropsychological systems that subserve these states. Behavioural and cognitive processes also have the power to influence these states. Let us return to the case of Sir Winston Churchill. He was one of history's great orators, and seemed a naturally gifted performer, but this appearance is deceptive. Churchill achieved his public speaking success not by gift of nature but by a number of cognitive-behavioural strategies. In fact, he had a chronic fear of public speaking, which he overcame by meticulous preparation. Also, he fought his recurrent depression with physically creative pastimes, such as bricklaying; and he reduced his worrying with an improvised form of cognitive-behaviour therapy (CBT): 'It helps to write down half a dozen things which are worrying me. Two of them, say, disappear; about two nothing can be done, so it's no use worrying, and two perhaps can be

ASK YOURSELF
Does the theory of attributional style help to explain Sir Winston Churchill's 'black dog' depression?

settled' (Moran, 1966, p. 167). What such forms of 'self-therapy' allow is the gaining of instrumental control over otherwise unpredictable and threatening events; and the most direct way to achieve this instrumental control is via behaviour (including cognitive behaviour). For this reason, learning-theory approaches (see chapter 7) are important in all forms of psychopathology.

▨▢ Diagnostic Categories

DSM-IV-R divides the mood disorders into a number of broad categories: *Depressive Disorders* (unipolar depression) and the *Bipolar Disorders* (comprising varieties of manic-depressive psychosis). The depressive disorders comprise two major disorders: *Major Depressive Disorder* and *Dysthymic Disorder*. Depressive disorders are distinguished from the *Bipolar Disorders* by the absence of any history of manic or hypomanic episodes (mixed episodes, containing both depression and mania). The aim of treatment is to tailor intervention to suit the specific condition of the individual patients. There are thus many different types of depression. Patients present with different symptoms and their symptoms are unique to their life experiences.

Major depressive disorder

Major depressive disorder is characterized by one or more depressive episodes (i.e., at least two weeks of depressed mood or the loss of interest or pleasure in nearly all activities). A diagnosis requires the patient to have at least four other symptoms relating to: changes in appetite or weight, sleep and psychomotor activity; decreased energy; feelings of worthlessness or guilt; difficulty thinking, concentrating or making decisions; or recurrent thoughts of death or suicidal ideation, plans or attempts. Sadness may be denied at first, but revealed during interview; some patients have somatic complaints rather than feelings of sadness; and many individuals report increased irritability, anger and frustration.

Depression can develop over days or weeks; and a *prodromal* period, prior to the depressive episode, may include anxiety symptoms and mild depressive symptoms that have persisted for weeks or months. An untreated depressive episode may last 4 months or longer.

Dysthymic disorder

Dysthymic disorder is characterized by at least two years of depressed mood for more days than not, accompanied by additional depressive symptoms that do not meet the criteria for major depressive disorder. Dysthymia is a low-grade but very chronic form of depression; it may represent a relatively stable and unremitting illness, or it may occur between episodes of major depressive disorder. When major depressive episodes are superimposed on dysthymia, the resulting condition is sometimes called *double depression*.

Bipolar disorder

A manic episode is defined as a distinct period during which there is an abnormality and persistently elevated, expansive or irritable period, lasting for at least 1 week. This mood disturbance must be accompanied by at least three additional symptoms from a list including: inflated self-esteem or grandiosity, decreased need for sleep, pressure of speech, flight of ideas, distractibility, increased involvement in goal-oriented activities or psychomotor agitation, and excessive involvement in pleasurable activities with a high potential for harmful consequences. The disturbance must be sufficient to cause a marked impairment in social and occupational functioning or to require hospitalization, or it is accompanied by psychotic features, such as having a special relationship with God or some public figure, such as a famous politician or entertainment figure. Patients in the manic phase often do not recognize that they are ill and resist attempts to be treated, often becoming irritated that people cannot understand or accept their ideas and behaviour, which to them may appear perfectly normal. There are various subtypes of bipolar disorder: (a) bipolar I disorders, (b) bipolar II disorder, and (c) cyclothymic disorder.

Bipolar I disorder is characterized by one or more manic or mixed episodes, usually accompanied by major depressive disorder; *bipolar II disorder* is characterized by one or more major depressive episodes accompanied by at least one hypomanic episode; *cyclothymic disorder* is characterized by at least 2 years of numerous periods of hypomanic symptoms that do not meet criteria for a manic episode and numerous periods of depressive symptoms that do not meet criteria for a major depressive episode – yet the presence of hypomania and depression are evident to the skilled clinician. (For an authoritative resource site, go to: www.mentalhealthcare.org.uk/.)

The longitudinal course of bipolar illness is characterized by many recurrent episodes, some depressive, some manic or hypomanic, and some mixed with simultaneous features of mania and depression. These alternating episodes can become rapid cycling, with at least four ups/downs in 12 months. Although statistics differ, many bipolar patients are hospitalized on several occasions throughout their lives; as many as one-half attempt suicide; and many are unmarried, unemployed and receiving welfare benefits. These personal and social consequences are partly a result of inadequate diagnosis, treatment and outcome – and the social stigma attached to mental illness is an additional source of strain – all of which have markedly improved in recent years, leading to a more positive outcome for many patients. Many bipolar patients can and do lead successful and fulfilling lives.

In a mixed episode, over a period of at least 1 week, the patient experiences rapidly alternating moods, and meets the criteria for both a manic episode and a major depressive episode. In the hypomanic episode, there is a distinct period during which there is an abnormality and persistently elevated, expansive, irritable mood that lasts at least 4 days. As with a manic episode, this period of abnormality must be accompanied by at least three additional symptoms.

> **ASK YOURSELF**
> Does DSM-IV classification account for all aspects of depression?

☐☐ Professor Stuart Sutherland: Psychologist and Bipolar Patient

Stuart Sutherland, a professor of experimental psychology, wrote a poignant account of his experience of his depression and mania, as well as his reaction to the various psychological therapies he received (Sutherland, 1976; *Breakdown: A Personal Crisis and Medical Dilemma*). This book is well worth reading for its insight into the subjective nature of bipolar depression (the *personal crisis*), as well as its discussion of the role of psychiatry and psychotherapy (the *medical dilemma*). His book goes some way to conveying the real misery and great distress of mental illness; as Sutherland (1976, p. 8) noted,

> Until I collapsed myself, I found it difficult to sympathize properly with friends who were to a greater or lesser degree neurotic. For forty-five years I had never known what it was like to be depressed or anxious, and although, being slightly hypochondriacal myself, I could sympathize with friends who were physically ill, I was unable to understand at an emotional level the feelings of someone suffering purely mental torment – and this despite the fact that I am myself a psychologist, and had therefore read a great deal on the subject of mental illness.

This passage shows how difficult it is to truly understand the psychological experiences of other people, despite our sincere wish to – often expressed in the banal phrase, 'I understand'.

Sutherland goes on to describe the experience of anxiety:

> The onset of my neurosis was marked by levels of physical anxiety that I would not have believed possible. If one is almost involved in a road accident, there is a delay of a second or two and then the pit of the stomach seems to fall out and one's legs go like jelly. It was this feeling multiplied a *hundredfold* that seized me at all hours of the day and night. (p. 2; italics added)

When the depression lifted, positive mood drastically returned, and within 24 hours Sutherland went from a state of hopeless gloom to a mood state of optimism and fascination with the world around him. However, all was not well in this 'aftermath'. During the next 3 months Sutherland, by his own admission, behaved in a way that was 'almost as mad as my behaviour during the depression' (p. 63). He was hypermanic ('high'), and behaved without shame or reserve, combining wild optimism with reckless spending of money, an inability to stop talking and a tendency to engage in pranks (including an embarrassing incident involving his wife in a sex shop in London and an amusing encounter with a prostitute on the midnight train from London to Brighton). He was also convinced that he would make a fortune by writing a highly successful introductory textbook on psychology – truly the ramblings of a disturbed mind! His hypermanic state was experienced as enjoyable and lasted for 3 to 4 months, when the depression returned.

Another famous scientist and bipolar patient is Professor Kay Jamison, who surprised her psychiatry colleagues in 1995 by declaring that she was a long-time sufferer of bipolar depression. She has written a number of books on this disorder: *An Unquiet Mind* (1995), which describes her experiences; *Touched with Fire* (1993), which explores the links between bipolar disorder and creativity; and *Manic-Depressive Illness* (2002), which provides a summary of the science of bipolar disorder.

These accounts give an insight, albeit a second-hand one, into the subjective state of bipolar depression. Such accounts can also give important clues to the nature of the disorder, and can take us beyond the checklist of symptoms found in a psychiatric classification system: these clues might suggest psychological processes inherent in the disorder and thereby serve a function in advancing research (examples of this process are seen in relation to schizophrenia; see chapter 16).

Attempts to understand the biological basis of depression encompass a large and diverse field. This chapter can only scratch the surface of this literature. The following sections survey what is known in four areas: (a) brain abnormalities as revealed by neuroimaging studies of the volume (size) of regions/structures; (b) psycho-pharmacological approaches; (c) transcranial magnetic stimulation (TMS) as a potential treatment; and (d) quantitative genetic studies (relevant molecular genetic studies are covered in the next chapter). The fundamentals of these techniques have already been covered in Part III ('Techniques').

> **ASK YOURSELF**
> What does Stuart Suther-land's personal account bring to our understanding of bipolar disorder?

Neuroimaging: Structural Volume

A variety of neuroimaging procedures have been used to study depression. For example, these studies have found decreased blood flow in the left, and sometimes the right, pre-frontal cortex; reduced volume in the orbitofrontal cortex (Bremner et al., 2002); and functional abnormalities in limbic structures, such as the amygdala and the hippocampus, basal ganglia and the cingulate gyrus (George, 1997; Sheline, 2003).

Van Elst et al. (2000), using volumetric MRI, reported that depressed patients displayed significant enlargement of the right and left amygdala; and Kumar et al. (2000) found a reduction in the normal volumetric asymmetry in the frontal regions. In a review of the literature, Oquendo and Mann (2001) concluded that frontal lobe volume is reduced in major depression. However, not all studies have reported reduced prefrontal cortex in depressed patients (e.g., Brambilla et al., 2002) – such inconsistencies have also been reported for other putative abnormal sites, for example, atrophy in the hippocampus (Rusch et al., 2001).

Sheline (2003) provides the following summary of the major findings relating to the brain structural abnormalities found in depression (including bipolar disorder). Brain changes, associated especially with early-onset depression, have been reported in the hippocampus, amygdala, caudate, putamen and frontal cortex. These structures comprise a neuro-anatomical circuit known as the *limbic–cortical–striatal–pallidal–thalamic tract* – this set of interconnected brain structures was first described by Nauta (1972).

> **ASK YOURSELF**
> What might structural neu-roimaging findings tell us about the symptoms ob-served in depression?

The Neural Toxicity Hypothesis

Episodes of depression are associated with elevated cortisol levels; and hypothalamic–pituitary–adrenal (HPA) axis (see chapter 6) dysfunction is implicated. These elevated cortical levels are excitotoxic in several brain regions (e.g., hippocampus, amygdala and prefrontal cortex; all areas with high concentrations of glucocorticoid receptors); gluco-corticoid neurotoxicity is well documented, and this may explain reduced volume and the impairment of function associated with these structures (Sapolsky, 2000). However, neural plasticity (especially in the hippocampus) may to some extent remedy these toxic effects, but only if the stress and depression are reduced – as discussed below, such a reduction is an important function of antidepressant drugs. However, early life stress may produce a permanent hypersensitivity to stress, mediated in part by a dysfunctional HPA axis (Heim et al., 2001). There is evidence that the total amount of time patients have been depressed is associated with the size of reduction in hippocampal volume (for a review, see Sheline, 2003). In one study, a correlation was shown between higher cortisol levels measured longitudinally and more hippocampal volume loss in normal human ageing (Lupien et al., 1998). Thus, depression is as much a physiological disease as it is a psychological disease, significantly increasing risk of a wide variety of associated pathological processes (e.g., dementia).

The links between limbic and cortical structures also raise the possibility that excitotoxic damage to one region may spread to other regions. One mechanism for this process of destruction involves glial cells: they reduce excess (excitotoxic level of) glutamate (the major excitatory neurotransmitter), maintain metabolic functions and produce nerve growth factors and trophic factors (essential for the formation of new connections). Loss of glial cells may increase the probability of neurotoxic damage. In this regard, it is interesting that one of the distinctive features of Albert Einstein's brain was a greater density of glial cells (see chapter 3). Loss of glial cells could thus be responsible for the volume loss in the limbic–cortical–striatal–pallidal–thalamic circuit. Stress-induced inhibition of neurogenesis is another possible mechanism for producing volume loss – in experimental animals, early stress (e.g., isolation rearing) leads to a number of structural, functional and neurochemical changes. Little work has been conducted in human beings, although there is evidence of stress-induced structural changes in post-traumatic stress disorder (PTSD; see next chapter). Possible relations between brain volume changes and depression are shown in figure 14.2.

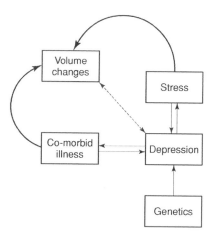

Figure 14.2 Sheline (2003) model of the hypothesized interactions accounting for some of the brain structural changes reported in depression. Many co-morbid illnesses are associated with structural brain changes, and animal models demonstrate stress-induced brain structural changes (solid arrows). Depression is associated with both stress and co-morbid illnesses, but it is not clear if there is an independent contribution of major depression to structural brain changes (dotted arrow).

Interpretation of such findings is, however, problematic, because neuroimaging studies are still, in essence, correlational (see chapter 10). In this regard, it is difficult to know whether abnormal brain volume or activation patterns are the cause or result of depression; and the role of medication in these effects is another confounding variable, even when fairly clear associations are found between structural volume and illness status (e.g. DelBello et al., 1999). There may be effects on structural volume (e.g., hippocampus) as a result of disease severity, gender and treatment response (Vakili et al., 2000), or it may result from depression-associated but independent effects (e.g., illness). However, theories in this area remain largely speculative.

To illustrate the complexity of this literature, Frodl et al. (2003) found that first-episode depressed patients had larger amygdala volumes, but, when amygdala size was compared between recurrent depressive patients and matched controls, no differences were found. One explanation of this finding could be the atrophy effects of disease progression (via excitotoxic processes; see chapter 12), eliminating the enhanced amygdala volume in recurrent patients. However, for this interpretation to be supported, first-episode patients would need to be followed over time, in a prospective study. The majority of neuroimaging studies are cross-sectional, often use relatively small sample sizes and do not report such prospective data: this makes results difficult to interpret with confidence.

To get an answer to this hard causal question would require an (ethnically unacceptable) experimental induction of depression – this is possible only in experimental (non-human) animals. Other research strategies thus need to be pursued; for example, comparing first-episode with chronic patients; conducting longitudinal studies to assess the effects of disease progression on brain volumes and functions; correlating volumetric and functional abnormalities with type and severity of symptom; and investigating the normal range of functional and structural relations in the normal population to assess vulnerability (high risk) factors in the general population.

The sophistication of neuroimaging studies is developing fast; and volumetric findings in depression are being investigated in terms of neurotoxicity (e.g., by gluco-corticoids), decreased brain-derived growth factor, decreased neurogenesis and loss of plasticity (Sheline, 2003). As seen in chapter 12, neurochemicals are only one part of the complex chain of neuronal events that cascade from the molecular expression of genes to neural reorganization (plasticity) in response to environmental stimuli. In the case of brain volume, the important role of psychopharmacological factors is evident.

This brief summary of anatomical neuroimaging studies in depression reveals the complexity of interpreting data, even when consistent patterns of results are available. Although it is tempting to make sweeping statements when summarizing such data, this is inappropriate because, in common with other areas of psychology, this literature *is* complex. In this regard, it is also worth noting that scientists often disagree with each other over the relevance, importance and interpretation of data; and in fast-moving research areas a consensus of opinion is not easily found – nor indeed should such a consensus be expected, because science is a highly competitive activity. If much of biological psychology seems fragmented, with many differences of scientific opinion and more questions than answers, then even this is an important advance in understanding the nature of psychological science, as well as science in general.

In addition to neuroimaging studies – including the many functional studies not included here – there have also been a large number of psychophysiological studies of depression, including all of the techniques surveyed in chapter 9. In place of attempting to summarize this entire literature, this section examines one tool that has attracted considerable research attention as a novel form of therapy.

> **ASK YOURSELF**
> What are the problems with the hypothesis that disrupted neurotransmission is the cause of depression?

Psychopharmacology: Introduction

Although there exist various treatment approaches to depression, including the various psychological therapies (especially cognitive-behavioural therapy), drug treatment is by far the most common and convenient. Many patients receiving medication for depression never get to see a psychiatrist; often they are treated in primary-care settings (e.g., by a general practitioner). Less frequently, some form of psychological treatment is offered: this can range from individual, intensive psychodynamic therapy, to cognitive-behavioural therapy, to family-based therapy. Of course, these psychological treatments are no less 'biological' than drug treatments: all treatments work by changing neuronal activity in the brain. However, pharmacological treatments, and their modes of action, have been most thoroughly investigated.

In one sense (but only one), it is not important to know *how* psychological therapies work; what is important is *whether* they work, as assessed by a properly conducted controlled clinical trial. However, this atheoretical, empirical position is inadequate: practical therapies develop from theories. There is now an increasing realization that research is needed to understand the neurological and psychological aspects of all forms of therapy (i.e., a neuropsychology) – this includes the interaction of drug-based and psychological-based therapies. As has been stressed throughout this book, a truly integrated neuropsychology is needed, combining the *neuro* and the *psychological* in equal measure (see chapter 12).

Neurotransmission

There is now compelling evidence that depression is, at least in major part, a disorder of neurotransmission, which itself may be part of an underlying pathophysiological process. For this reason, considerable effort has been devoted to: (a) understanding its basic neurochemistry and neurotransmission; and (b) developing effective drug treatments. *Why* there is a problem of neurotransmission is less clear. Is it an overreaction to aversive environmental events? Is it a genetic liability, possibly of inadequate protein expression? Are neuronal processes compromised somehow? The fact that drugs improve the symptoms of depression does not logically imply that the symptoms are *caused* primarily by a dysfunction in the neurotransmitter systems – although the causation would be *mediated* by neurotransmitter systems – with a sufficient level of aversive life events, most of us would get depressed. What can be said, without too much fear of contradiction, is that neurotransmitters play an important role *somehow* in the causal chain of events that result in depression.

Treatment responses

Drugs that alleviate symptoms of depression are collectively known as *antidepressants*. For many people they are, quite literally, a lifesaver – there is a greatly increased risk of suicide in depressed patients. Before discussing the success rate of antidepressants, first it is necessary to summarize some terms commonly used to describe treatment responses to drugs.

Three terms describe the improvement of a patient after treatment: *response*, *remission* and *recovery* (the three Rs). *Response* is used to refer to a patient who has experienced at least a 50 per cent reduction in symptoms (these patients are called 'responders'); *remission* is used to refer to a patient who has experienced a disappearance of symptoms; and *recovery* is used to refer to a patient who has been in remission for 6 to 12 months. Two terms describe a worsening in a patient following treatment: *relapse* and *recurrence* (the two Rs). A *relapse* is used to describe a patient whose condition worsened before there was *remission*, or before the remission turned into *recovery*; *recurrence* is reserved to describe a patient whose symptoms worsen after complete recovery (Stahl, 2000).

Some statistics

At first treatment, antidepressants are effective in only two out of three people, with one-third showing little benefit. After 1 year of drug treatment, approximately 40 per cent still have the same diagnosis; approximately 40 per cent have no diagnosis; and approximately 20 per cent are either partially recovered or develop dysthymia (see above). Fortunately, most people (more than 90 per cent) respond eventually, although for some patients this happens only after trying different antidepressants or combinations of antidepressants. Approximately a third of patients respond to a placebo (i.e., chemically inert substance) – for this reason it is vital to compare pharmacological and psychological treatments against a placebo or control group: some people just recover on their own.

Approximately half of responders to antidepressants experience a complete remission within 6 months of treatment; and some two-thirds of the responders remit within 2 years. Antidepressants are also known to reduce relapse during the first 6 to 12 months following initial response to medication. About half of patients relapse within 6 months of response if they are switched to placebo, but only about 10 to 25 per cent relapse if they are maintained on the drug. For this reason drug treatment is thus often continued after response: this therapy is known as *relapse prevention*.

> **ASK YOURSELF**
> What does the heterogeneity of response to antidepressants imply about the neurochemical nature of depression?

▢▢ Psychopharmacology: Pathophysiology

There is another important reason why psychopharmacological understanding of the neural basis of depression is important. As already discussed in chapters 4 and 12, depression may be part of a *pathophysiological mechanism*. There is accumulating evidence that the pathological mechanisms that are expressed as depressive symptoms are neurologically toxic. There is evidence from related conditions; for example, it appears that post-traumatic stress disorder (PTSD) results in major physical changes in the brain, including loss of neurons in areas like the hippocampus (e.g., Bremner et al., 1995).

As discussed in chapter 12, the rate and quantity of neurotransmitters have effects on cellular processes above and beyond merely causing an action potential. For example, too much calcium triggers the production of intracellular enzymes and this can lead to the production of toxic *free radicals*: these radicals roam around the cell destroying its components (especially dendrites). Given enough time, this riot of free radicals triggers the excitotoxic process of apoptosis (cell death). Depression may have long-lasting neuropathological effects on the brain – this would be revealed in a gradually worsening clinical profile with age (i.e., more frequent and severe episodes), making treatment less effective.

In addition to these pathophysiological effects, long-term changes to stable traits of personality may occur following environmentally induced depressive episodes: a depressiogenic personality style may develop, which increases the chances of future episodes of depression in reaction to environmental events that previously would not have been sufficient to provoke such a reaction (Gray & McNaughton, 2000). This possibility takes us back to the issue of *causation* (clinical aetiology in depression and in other psychiatric conditions): whatever the primary cause for the development of a psychiatric disorder, the involvement of neurotransmitter systems may have subsequent (causal) effects that are unconnected with the original cause. What exists is not a simple causal link from cause ⇒ symptoms, but a two-way pathological processes of cause ⇔ symptoms (of course, it is not the symptoms themselves that are pathophysiological – although sometimes they may lead to a worsening of the condition via instrumental behaviour (e.g., impulsive, reckless actions) – but the underlying physiology). Whatever one's theoretical perspective on the cause of depression – environmental, genetic, family, psychodynamic, even political or humanistic – the role of neurotransmission, and how it can lead to permanent changes in neuropsychological processes, must also be taken into account. In this real sense, there is no sensible dividing line between 'biological' and 'non-biological' theories of psychopathology: non-biological causes may have important biological effects.

The next section surveys two major psychopharmacological theories of depression: the *monoamine hypothesis*, and the *neurotransmitter receptor hypothesis* (for a review of this literature, see Stahl, 2000).

> **ASK YOURSELF**
> How might depression result from long-term exposure to stressors?

▮▯ Psychopharmacology: Monoamine Hypothesis

The monoamine hypothesis was the first major theory of the neurochemical nature of depression. The theory states that depression is related to a dysfunction in one or more monoamine systems; more precisely, depression is *caused* by (strong version of the theory), or *associated* with (weak version of the theory), a deficiency in monoamine neurotransmission. The principal monoamine neurotransmitters in the brain are the catecholamines, norepinephrine (NE) and dopamine (DA), and the indoleamine, serotonin (5-HT). Monoamine neurotransmitters are synthesized by means of enzymes, which assemble neurotransmitters in the cell body or the terminal of the neuron. This theory was built upon experimental findings that showed: (a) drugs that deplete the synthesis or release of these neurotransmitters induced depression; and (b) drugs that increased the synthesis or release of these neurotransmitters (antidepressants) improved the symptoms of depression (Carlson, 2000). Let us now look at these three monoamines in turn.

Norepinephrine (NE)

Norepinephrine (NE) is released from the noradrenergic neuron. The synthesis (i.e., production) of norepinephrine begins with *tyrosine* (an amino acid precursor), which comes into the nervous system from the blood; once inside the neuron, tyrosine is acted on by three enzymes: *tyrosine hydroxylase* (TOH), *dihydroxyphenylalanine* (DOPA) and *decarboxylase* (DCC), which finally converts DOPA into dopamine (DA, one of the major neurotransmitters). In the case of norepinephrine in noradrenergic (NE) neurons, DA is merely a precursor. The final enzyme, *dopamine beta-hydroxylase* (DBH), converts DA into norepinephrine.

As discussed earlier, NE is produced by enzymes; so too is it destroyed by enzymes after release at the synapse: two main destructive enzymes act on NE to turn it into inactive metabolites: first is *monoamine oxidase* (MAO); the second is *catechol-O-methyl transferase* (COMT). These enzymes destroy NE and thereby terminate its action – as discussed below, MAO inhibitors were commonly used antidepressants. There is also a transporter (reuptake) pump that removes NE from the synapse without destroying it. Thus drugs that either (a) inhibit MAO, or (b) slow down the reuptake pump have the effect of increasing the availability of NE in the synapse. The NE neuron is rather complex, but it is necessary to know some of its detail in order to understand how antidepressants work.

NE postsynaptic receptors come in two main forms: *alpha* and *beta* (with various subtypes of each). Different receptors may mediate differential effects of NE in the frontal cortex (e.g., postsynaptic $beta_1$ receptors for mood, and postsynaptic $alpha_2$ receptors for attention and cognition). The $alpha_2$ receptor is the only presynaptic NE receptor on NE neurons: this receptor type regulates NE release from the presynaptic terminal and is called an *autoreceptor*. Presynaptic $alpha_2$ autoreceptors are found on the axon terminal, as well as at the cell body and dendrites (*somatodendritic $alpha_2$ receptors*).

NE presynaptic receptors are important because when they recognize NE they turn off further release – this is an example of a negative feedback mechanism. The job of the $alpha_2$ autoreceptor is to ensure that there is not an excess of NE in the synapse.

Drugs that antagonize this receptor lead to enhanced release of NE. Overactivity of NE can be reduced by alpha$_2$ agonists – that is, increasing the mopping-up action of the reuptake pump.

Most of the cell bodies for NE neurons are located in the brainstem, in the locus ceruleus, which has been implicated in focusing attention. NE deficiency is hypothesized to underlie impaired attention, problems in concentrating, difficulties with working memory and speed of information processing, as well as psychomotor retardation, fatigue and apathy – these are all symptoms commonly seen in depression, as well as a range of other psychopathological disorders. However, there are many specific NE pathways in the brain, each mediating a different physiological function.

Dopamine (DA)

Dopamine is synthesized by two out of the three enzymes involved in the synthesis of NE – the dopamine neuron lacks the third enzyme (*dopamine betahydroxylase*), thus it cannot convert DA into NE. Like the NE neuron, the DA neuron has autoreceptors and a presynaptic transporter (reuptake pump). The same enzymes that destroy NE also destroy DA (i.e., MAO and COMT). Many dopamine receptors exist, including at least five subtypes. The most studied receptor type is D$_2$: it is stimulated by DA agonists for the treatment of Parkinson's disease and blocked by DA antagonists (*antipsychotics*) for the treatment of schizophrenia (which also affect D$_1$ and D$_4$ receptors).

Serotonin (5-HT)

In a similar manner to NE and DA neurons, presynaptic receptors exist for 5-HT neurons. 5-HT is synthesized from the amino acid *trytophan*, which is transported to the brain from blood plasma. Two synthetic enzymes convert tryptophan into serotonin: *tryptophan hydroxylase* converts tryptophan into *5-hydroxytryptophan*, which is then converted by the amino acid *decarboxylase* into 5-HT. Like NE and DA, 5-HT is destroyed by MAO. Also, the 5-HT neuron has a presynaptic transport pump, called the serotonin transporter – this serves the same role as the NE neuron transporter and the DA transporter: to regulate, by recycling, excess neurotransmitter from the synapse back to the terminal buttons.

When precursor tryptophan is depleted in depressed patients and 5-HT synthesis is suddenly diminished, patients who have responded to SSRIs transiently deteriorate until 5-HT synthesis is restored. This is one piece of evidence that points to the important role of 5-HT in depression. Interestingly, acute tryptophan depletion in volunteers leads to a lowering of mood only in those individuals with a family history of unipolar depression (Riedel, Klaassen & Schmitt, 2002).

There are two main presynaptic receptors (5-HT1A and 5-HT1D; autoreceptors) and several postsynaptic receptors (5-HT1A, 5-HT1D, 5-HT2A, 5-HT2C, 5-HT3 and 5-HT4). Autoreceptors allow 5-HT to be detected at the dendrites and cell body; this occurs via the 5-HT1A receptor, which is also called a *somatodendritic autoreceptor*: this causes a slowing of neuronal impulse flow though the neuron. The 5-HT1D receptor is a *terminal autoreceptor*, responsible for detecting 5-HT in the synapse: 5-HT occupancy of 5-HT1D receptors inhibited further release of 5-HT release. Drugs that block the 5-HT1D auto-receptor promote 5-HT release.

The 5-HT neuron is complex because it also contains NE receptors: there are both 5-HT and NE autoreceptors on the 5-HT neuron. NE presynaptic receptors thus regulate 5-HT release. In fact, on the axon terminal of 5-HT receptors are located presynaptic (NE) alpha$_2$ receptors. When NE is released from nearby NE neurons it can diffuse to alpha$_2$ receptors on 5-HT neurons: this serves to turn off 5-HT release. (The alpha$_2$ receptor on the NE neuron is called an *autoreceptor*; but the alpha$_2$ receptor on 5-HT neurons is called a *heteroreceptor*.) There is also an alpha$_1$ autoreceptor on 5-HT cell bodies, but, unlike the alpha$_2$ autoreceptor, its activation causes 5-HT release. This arrangement shows how different neurochemicals interact in important ways.

5-HT cell bodies are concentrated in the brainstem, in the raphe nucleus. Projection from this nucleus to the frontal cortex is important in mood; projection to the basal ganglia is involved in the control of movement, and possibly obsessions and compulsions; projection to the limbic area is involved in anxiety and panic; and projection to the hypothalamus regulates appetite and eating behaviour. Brainstem sleep centres regulate sleep, especially slow-wave sleep. It is thus easy to see how a dysregulation in the 5-HT neuron can exert a range of seemingly unrelated symptoms: mood, movement, anxiety, appetite and sleep disorder.

With an understanding of the action of the monoamine neurons, it is very easy to identify targets for drug development. In order to develop a drug to boost monoamine activity, the following actions could be targeted: (a) inhibition of the action of enzymes involved in the breakdown of neurotransmitters; (b) excitation of the action of precursor enzymes involved in the synthesis of neurotransmitters; (c) blockade of the action of autoreceptors involved in reuptake pumps; and (d) activation of the action of autoreceptors involved in stimulating neurotransmitter release (figure 14.3). In developing therapeutic drugs, the fact that there are several receptor subtypes for each type of neurons needs to be taken into account – some of these receptors would have a therapeutic effect, but others would have unpleasant side effects. The trick is to develop compounds that operate only on those neurons in specific neurochemical pathways in the brain, and only on those receptors involved in the desired therapeutic response.

Problems of monoamine hypothesis

There are a number of problems with the monoamine hypothesis (Stahl, 2000). The first is the lack of precision concerning the pharmacological mechanisms involved. Second, the monoamine hypothesis cannot account for the fact that there is a substantial time delay between: (a) administration of the drug effect and its effects on neurotransmitter systems (minutes to hours), and (b) therapeutic effectiveness (weeks to months). Put simply, if symptoms are caused by an imbalance in neurotransmission, then correcting the imbalance should lead to an immediate improvement in mood. This relationship is not observed, which suggests that there are other neuronal processes involved in the therapeutic response to antidepressants (e.g., slower effects within neurons, or psychological effects facilitated by increased monoamine activity, which takes time to develop and to be made permanent by neural plasticity processes). However,

ASK YOURSELF
Is the time delay of therapeutic action of antidepressant drugs conclusive evidence against the 'monoamine hypothesis'?

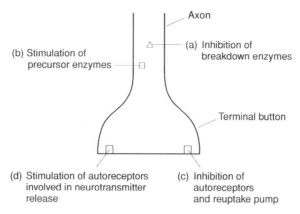

Figure 14.3 Possible actions of antidepressant drugs. There are a number of possible targets of antidepressant drugs, all aimed at producing a net increase in the availability of monoamine at postsynaptic receptors: (a) inhibition of the action of enzymes (e.g. by disrupting their production) involved in the breakdown of neurotransmitters; (b) excitation of the action of precursor enzymes involved in the synthesis of neurotransmitters; (c) blockade of the action of autoreceptors involved in reuptake pumps; and (d) activation of the autoreceptors involved in stimulating neurotransmitter release.

the monoamine hypothesis focused attention on the availability of neurotransmitters in the synapse; more recent research attention has shifted attention towards the role of receptors and the plasticity in receptor activity.

Psychopharmacology: Receptor Hypothesis

The theory behind the shift away from neurotransmitter availability to receptor action proposes that the key to neurotransmission (as opposed to neurotransmitter) abnormalities in depression lies in the regulatory processes of receptors. Specifically, it states that the depletion of neurotransmitters causes a compensatory process of up-regulation of post-synaptic receptors – that is, greater receptor activity. Evidence for this hypothesis is still sparse, but there are some data showing, from post-mortem studies, that there are increased numbers of 5-HT$_2$ receptors in the frontal cortex of patients who committed suicide. It may be that there are abnormalities in gene expression of neurotransmitter receptors and enzymes in families with depression. This theory has the benefit of being able to account for the delay between the effect of antidepressants on neurotransmitter levels and effect on symptoms.

The neurotransmitter receptor hypothesis proposes that antidepressants eventually cause a desensitization, or down-regulation, of key neurotransmitter receptors in a time course consistent with the delayed onset of antidepressant action. A simple version of the neu-rotransmitter receptor hypothesis is that the normal state becomes one of depression as a result of the up-regulation of postsynaptic receptors due to the natural depletion of neurotransmitter. Boosting neurotransmitters by MAO inhibition, or by blocking reup-take pumps for monoamine neurotransmitters, eventually results in the down-regulation

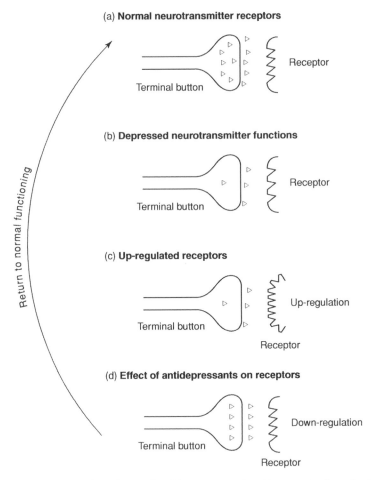

(a) **Normal neurotransmitter receptors**

Terminal button

Receptor

(b) **Depressed neurotransmitter functions**

Terminal button

Receptor

(c) **Up-regulated receptors**

Terminal button

Up-regulation

Receptor

(d) **Effect of antidepressants on receptors**

Terminal button

Down-regulation

Receptor

Return to normal functioning

Figure 14.4 The receptor hypothesis of antidepressant action. The receptor hypothesis was proposed to account for the significant time lag between drug administration and clinical effect. According to this hypothesis, monoamine may be depleted (e.g., as a result of stress), which leads to a compensatory increase in receptor numbers and sensitivity (i.e., up-regulation). Antidepressant medication serves to increase the availability of neurotransmitters, which then down-regulates receptors, leading to clinical improvement.

of neurotransmitter receptors in a delayed time course more closely related to the timing of recovery from depression (figure 14.4).

Although firm evidence is lacking concerning the monoamine hypothesis and the receptor hypothesis, there is a large amount of evidence that, even despite apparently normal levels of monoamines and their receptors, monoamine systems in depressed patients do not respond normally. This dysregulation can be shown by probing monoamine receptors with drugs that stimulate, which in depressed patients leads to deficit output of certain neuroendocrine hormones, which can be used to index the activity of these systems (e.g., Cleare, Murray & O'Keane, 1998; Kapitany et al., 1999; Riedel, Klaassen & Schmitt, 2002). It is also possible to use PET to observe the deficient changes in neuronal firing rates after the administration of monoamine-stimulating drugs (e.g., Mann et al., 1997).

Related to this alternative hypothesis is the view that depression may be a *pseudomonoamine* deficiency: that is, there may be a problem in signal transduction resulting from a deficiency in the molecular events that cascade from receptor occupancy. Thus, the problem could be a deficient cellular response. As noted in chapter 4, neurotransmitters serve a variety of roles, only one of which is fast-onset nerve conduction; an equally important role is in gene expression. Thus, secondary messenger systems that lead to intracellular transcription factors that control gene regulation could be the site of deficient functioning of monoamine systems (Stahl, 2000).

Attention has focused on one candidate mechanism in this process: the brain-derived neurotrophic factor (BDNF). BDNF sustains the viability of brain neurons, but under stress the gene for BDNF is repressed, leading to atrophy and possible apoptosis of vulnerable neurons in the hippocampus, where BDNF is switched off – this might be the mechanism underlying hippocampal atrophy seen in PTSD (see below). If true, this deficiency may lead to depression, with increasingly frequent and severe episodes, and a weaker response to treatment. Antidepressants could work by stimulating the gene expression of neurotrophic factors.

Although much is known about neurotransmitters and how neurons work, the precise mechanism underlying the mode of action of antidepressant drugs is still poorly understood. It is known that all effective antidepressants have immediate interactions with one or more monoamine neurotransmitter receptors or enzymes. In fact, there are at least eight separate pharmacological mechanism of action: most block monoamine reuptake, but some block NE alpha$_2$ receptors and others MAO. Some antidepressants preferentially affect only one monoamine system; others affect several systems. Whatever the mode of action, all antidepressants have the end effect of boosting levels of monoamine neurotransmission.

The classical antidepressants are no longer the first-line treatment for depression; these have been superseded by a new class of antidepressant with a more attractive therapeutic response (i.e., the ratio of benefits to side effects).

> **ASK YOURSELF**
> How does the 'receptor hypothesis' account for the problems with the 'monoamine hypothesis'?

▧▢ Psychopharmacology: Types of Drugs

With knowledge of the workings of monoamine neurons and receptors, it should be possible to suggest designs of drugs to alleviate depression. This class of drugs may be conveniently divided into *classical antidepressants* and newer *selective reuptake inhibitors*.

Classical antidepressants

There are two major classes of antidepressant widely used since the 1960s: *monoamine oxidase* (MAO) *inhibitors* and *tricyclics* (named after their three-ringed chemical structure).

MAO inhibitors increase the availability of monoamines by inhibiting the action of MAO – this enzyme breaks down monoamines, so its inhibition increases the availability of the neurotransmitter. These are the desirable pharmacological effects; less desirable are effects on other neurotransmitter systems, thought to be involved in adverse side effects (e.g., they block sodium channels in the heart and brain, and can cause cardiac arrest in overdose; blockade of alpha$_1$ adrenergic receptors causes hypotension and dizziness).

The tricyclic antidepressants increase the availability of monoamines by blocking monoamine transport (reuptake) pumps (see chapters 4 and 12 above) – there are a variety of such pumps, for each of the different neurotransmitter systems. Tricyclics block NE and 5-HT, and to a lesser extent DA reuptake pumps; some have more potency for inhibition of the 5-HT pumps (e.g., clomipramine); others are more selective for NE (e.g., desipramine). More technically, tricyclics function as negative allosteric modulators of the neurotransmitter reuptake (allosteric interactions are described in chapter 4). This process works as follows: once NE or 5-HT binds to its own presynaptic autoreceptor it is normally transported back to its presynaptic membrane for repackaging and reuse. This process is interrupted because tricyclics bind to an allosteric site close to the neurotransmitter transporter receptor, which has the effect that the neurotransmitter no longer binds there. The net effect is a blocking of the reuptake pump.

Although consistent with much of the available evidence, the monoamine deficiency hypothesis was too simple to explain the full range of effects; in particular, it could not explain the significant delay of onset of action: if drugs replenish neurotransmitter supply within a few hours then why does it take weeks for a clinical benefit to be found? However, this hypothesis did serve to focus research attention on the role played by monoamines; and subsequent research has confirmed the importance of these chemicals, although the complexity of their actions has also been revealed. It is known that all antidepressants boost the action of one or more of these monoamines (Stahl, 2000). The adverse side effects of these drugs are very serious, especially when seen in the light of the elevated risk of suicide in depressed patients.

Selective serotonin reuptake inhibitors (SSRIs)

Selective serotonin reuptake inhibitors (SSRIs) are a newer class of drugs comprising five main members (fluoxetine, sertraline, paroxetine, fluvoxamine and citalopram; for a review of these drugs in the major psychiatric disorders, see Vaswani, Linda & Ramesh, 2003). Although these drugs are chemically different, they all share the same major pharmacological effect: selective and potent inhibition of serotonin reuptake. (Unlike the tricyclics, they do not block sodium channels, even in overdose, and are therefore much preferable in suicide-prone depressed patients.) SSRIs are similar in many respects to the classical antidepressants, but they have the benefit of being a more effective blocker of serotonin reuptake at doses with fewer and weaker adverse side effects (they are thus much better tolerated and patients are more likely to take them as prescribed).

Newer antidepressants

In addition to SSRIs, there are also selective noradrenergic reuptake inhibitors (NRIs), and some drugs are combining these pharmacological actions. These dual reuptake inhibitors (SNRIs) are, in some ways, similar to the tricyclic antidepressants, which are also dual reuptake inhibitors of NE and 5-HT. However, the newer class (e.g., venlafaxine, the prototypal SNRI) affect reuptake of NE and 5-HT (and to some extent dopamine) but without the side effects associated with the older class of drugs (i.e., they are selective for therapeutic receptor targets). Venlafaxine has different degrees of inhibition of 5-HT reuptake (most potent and therefore present at low dose), NE reuptake (moderate potency and therefore present at higher dose), and DA reuptake (least potent and therefore present only at highest dose).

The original tricyclics were 'dirty drugs', affecting many receptors at once; SSRIs cleaned up this scattergun approach to monoamines, aiming instead for selectivity. However, in some circumstances it is desirable to use drugs that have non-selective, multiple pharmacological actions, especially in treatment-resistant patients. Such complex drugs work via the synergies that exist when two or more monoamines are simultaneously targeted (as noted above, there are NE receptors on 5-HT neurons). In contrast to the tricyclics, dual-action SNRIs are selective in targeting receptors involved in the therapeutic response, sparing receptors involved in mediating adverse side effects, hence their safety profile is much better (see chapter 12).

Mood stabilizers

Bipolar disorder is classified as a form of depression, but it shows many of the features of psychosis, and often involves anxiety (see Stuart Sutherland's account above). Lithium was the first mood stabilizer to be used to treat bipolar disorder, and it continues to be widely used today. It is effective in treating the acute episodes of mania, and is especially effective in providing a prophylactic (i.e., preventive) effect. Interestingly, lithium even treats depression in bipolar patients, although it is not so clear that it is a powerful antidepressant for unipolar depression. It is sometimes used to augment antidepressants for treating resistant cases of unipolar depression. Antipsychotics (i.e., drugs used in the treatment of psychotic conditions; see chapter 16) are also used in bipolar disorder, particularly in the form of short-term management of the acute phases of mania or hypomania.

Antidepressants also modify the long-term course of bipolar disorder: when given with mood stabilizers, they may reduce depressive episodes. But antidepressants can flip a depressed bipolar patient into mania, or mixed mania and depression, or rapid cycling every few days, or even hours, especially in the absence of mood stabilizers. Thus many bipolar patients require a clever mix of mood stabilizers and antidepressants.

The long-term course of bipolar disorder is chaotic, with psychotic episodes and relapses; and medication is seen to be essential in preventing recurrent episodes. The concern is that the intermittent use of mood stabilizers, poor compliance and increasing numbers of episodes lead to even more episodes of bipolar disorder, with less responsiveness to lithium. Thus the continued use of mood stabilizers, atypical antipsychotics and antidepressants is important: (a) to reduce symptoms and aim for remission; and (b) to prevent unfavourable long-term outcomes.

Kindling

Relapse prevention is important in depression in order to avoid further deterioration. Consider the case of mania in bipolar disorder. One theory of mania is that recurrent episodes may 'kindle' further episodes, a hypothesis first put forward by Post and colleagues (Post et al., 1984; Post, Rubinow & Ballenger, 1986; see also Ehnvall & Ågren, 2002). This is based on the observation that seizures kindle more seizures. It is, therefore, of interest that trials with anticonvulsants (e.g., carbamazepine) have demonstrated efficacy for improving the manic phase of the disorder (the anticonvulsant, valproic acid, is approved for this condition). Carbamazepine was the first anticonvulsant to be shown to be effective in the manic phase of this disorder (this drug is routinely prescribed for many forms of epilepsy). Its mode of action may be to enhance GABA (inhibitory) function, perhaps by actions on sodium and/or potassium channels. Although the mode of action of anticonvulsants is not well understood, they are thought to work at the cell membrane, affecting ion channels, including sodium, potassium and calcium channels.

> **ASK YOURSELF**
> What does the heterogeneity of response to antidepressants imply about the neurochemical nature of depression?

Transcranial Magnetic Stimulation (TMS): A Novel Therapy

Chapter 8 summarized transcranial magnetic stimulation (TMS), which uses a strong magnetic field to induce electrical changes in the brain. Depending on the precise method used, this technique can be used to stimulate the cortex (to map the cortex) or to inhibit its effective functioning (enabling temporary, and reversible, 'lesions'). In addition to TMS being used as an experimental tool in basic neuroscience, it has also been tested as a potential therapeutic tool.

TMS has been suggested as a therapeutic tool in a number of neuropsychiatric conditions (George, 1996; Zyss, 1996). The idea that TMS may be effective, in part, may be traced to the effectiveness of electroconvulsive therapy (ECT) for treatment-resistant (refractory) depression.[4] In contrast to ECT, TMS is selective and affects only small portions of the cortex (it does not induce seizures, nor does it seem to have any detrimental effects). Several studies have assessed the efficacy of TMS in depression.

One study assessed the effectiveness of TMS in depressed patients receiving antidepressant drugs: one group received antidepressants plus TMS, the other group just antidepressants (Conca et al., 1996). TMS was given daily for 10 days. By the third day, a significant remission of depressive symptoms was observed; and, on the last day, a larger difference between the groups was found.

A controlled, randomized comparison of ECT and TMS on non-psychotic major depressive disorder showed that TMS achieved similar remission rates to ECT in non-psychotic depression (Grunhaus et al., 2003); however, ECT may still be better in psychotic depression. A similar antidepressant effect in depression was reported by Padberg et al. (2002). The fact that TMS seems as good as ECT is an important result, as TMS is preferable to ECT for a host of reasons (e.g., its localized effect and lack of side effects).

Michael and Erfurth (2004) compared patients with bipolar disorder with mania and found TMS (as an add-on to partially effective medication), applied over 4 weeks, to be effective in reducing mania, but this was not a controlled study. (As TMS was added to existing drug therapy, it is not possible to say conclusively that the improvement was due to TMS alone.)

Dannon et al. (2002) compared 3- and 6-month outcomes of depressed patients treated with either ECT or TMS (all patients had been initially referred for ECT treatment). Twenty per cent of the patients relapsed (the same percentage for both treatment groups); and there was not a significant difference between the groups at 6-month follow-up, indicating that TMS is just as effective as ECT in treating treatment-resistant patients who were initially referred for ECT.

In a sham-control (they went through the TMS procedure but did not receive the train of pulses) or daily treatment for 2 weeks, there was a significant improvement in depressive symptoms in the TMS group: 9 out of 20 responders in the TMS group, none out of 10 in the sham-control (George et al., 2000).

The biological mechanism for therapeutic effects of TMS is complex; it seems to affect specific and selective alterations which are distinct from those induced by antidepressants, pointing to a unique mechanism of action: this line of research holds the potential to lead to research to identify novel pharmacological targets in depression.

In a neurophysiological investigation of the underlying neurobiological mechanism of TMS, microdialysis techniques (see chapter 11) were used to measure the patterns of release of dopamine in various areas of the rat brain (Keck et al., 2002). Rapid TMS led to a significant increase in dopamine in the dorsal hippocampus, the nucleus accumbens and the wider striatum. Thus TMS affects mesolimbic and mesostriatal dopaminergic systems, and these effects may be related to the effectiveness of TMS across a wide range of neuropsychiatric conditions, including depression.

TMS represents a promising tool to probe psychological functions in patients and controls; and it offers the promise of a safe and simple means to improve symptoms (it would be more acceptable than ECT). However, more rigorously controlled clinical studies are required before TMS can be used as a frontline treatment for depression (Wassermann & Lisanby, 2001).

> **ASK YOURSELF**
> In what ways does transcranial magnetic stimulation (TMS) differ from electroconvulsive therapy (ECT)?

Quantitative Genetics

Chapters 4 and 12 summarized the literature showing that neurotransmission is often the first step in the complex cascade of cellular events that lead eventually to gene expression in neurons in the central nervous system. Psychopharmacological research provides clues to the type of genes that might be implicated in psychopathology, including depression. The rationale of this approach runs as follow: if drugs that are effective in treating depression work by affecting the action of transporter (reuptake) receptors, then maybe the genes responsible for the synthesis and regulation of these receptors are involved in the vulnerability to depression. This research approach can only ever point to the possibility of such an action – it could be that autoreceptors are dysregulated by some other process in the neuron, and it is the genes responsible for these (unknown) processes that are ultimately responsible for the vulnerability to depression. In any event, research must start somewhere, and the only place it can ever start from is current knowledge.

Before searching for the actual genes that predispose to depression, it is necessary to ask the important question: is there evidence that depression has a genetic influence? The genetic analysis of depression started with family studies (Sullivan, Neale & Kendler, 2000):

biological relatives of unipolar patients show an excess of unipolar disorder (but not bipolar depression); however, family studies of bipolar depression reveal an excess of *both* unipolar and bipolar disorder among relatives (Kalodindi & McGuffin, 2002). Twin studies too show a substantial genetic contribution to unipolar depression. In a survey of the literature, Sullivan, Neale and Kendler (2000) reported that the variance in liability to depression could be explained by unique environmental effects (58 to 67 per cent) and additive genetic effects (31 to 42 per cent), with little contribution from shared environment (0 to 5 per cent). Depending on the specific study – they have different samples, diagnostic criteria, etc. – estimates of genetic contribution range from 40 to 70 per cent (McGuffin et al., 1996), and are therefore substantial.

A genetic influence on depression does not, of course, tell us anything about the causal factors involved; nor does it inform us that there are specific genes 'for' depression. For example, there could be a general vulnerability to neurosis, with depression being only one possible expression of this vulnerability. There is still a long way to go before specific genes *for* depression are identified.

In an interesting study, Gottesman and Bertelsen (1989) tested the *offspring* of discordant bipolar twins: the offspring of the unaffected MZ twins were just as likely to develop unipolar depression as the offspring of the affected twins, a finding that suggested a genetic mode of action and transmission. This study indicated that the unaffected twins had the same *genotypic* susceptibility to bipolar depression as the affected twins, yet their *phenotypes* were different.

In the case of bipolar depression, there is evidence of an overlapping genetic susceptibility with the spectrum of schizophrenia disorder. In particular, schizoaffective disorder, and less commonly schizophrenia, has been reported in the MZ co-twin of bipolar pairs. One study that relaxed the conventional diagnostic hierarchies (i.e., when a diagnosis of schizophrenia excludes a diagnosis of bipolar disorder) and allowed patients to have more than one diagnosis supported the existence of an overlap between genes causing liability to bipolar disorder and schizophrenia (Cardno et al., 2002).

Evidence from adoption studies too shows a strong genetic effect in bipolar depression. Probands who were adopted were found to have a significantly higher rate of affective disorder, consistent with their biological twin's status rather than with their adoptive parents' psychiatric status. However, there have been very few adoption studies, and not all have found a strong genetic effect (Sullivan, Neale & Kendler, 2000; see Kalidindi & McGuffin, 2002).

Genetic studies suffer from a number of problems. As is common in many other areas of psychopathology, there is a significant *co-mordibity* between affective disorders and other psychiatric disorders. The same genes appear to contribute to susceptibility to both major depression and generalized anxiety disorder (Kendler et al., 2003; see chapters 13 and 17). An overlap in genes contributing to depressive and anxiety symptoms has been found in other studies, but there is also evidence of a separate and specific genetic contribution to anxiety (e.g., Thapar & McGuffin, 1997). In many psychopathological studies, it is difficult to find clear-cut cases of any disorders, and combinations of different symptoms are more common than well-defined cases. Psychiatric diagnosis and treatment work by considering the more serious symptoms. For example, a patient diagnosed as having schizophrenia may also be depressed, which in the absence of schizophrenia symptoms may well lead to a diagnosis of a major depression. Co-morbidity is major problem in research studies: on the one hand, it is desirable to have well-defined cases of the disorder under investigation, but on the other hand these well-defined cases may not be representative of the full range of symptoms seen in the typical case presenting with the disorder.

A Mendelian, single-gene model can be discounted in depression – if such a model were correct then the mode of transmission would show a classical pattern of recessive–dominant effects (see chapter 2) across the generations. This fact makes the search for specific genes very difficult. A further complication is that there may be different genes predisposing to the disorder in different families. Another problem is one of classi-fication: how are 'affected' and 'unaffected' family members defined? As discussed in chapter 13, traits are normally distributed, and there rarely exists a clear dividing line between the 'normal' and 'abnormal'. To date, the picture from linkage studies is con-fused, although a number of 'hot spots' have been identified. The next chapter surveys the molecular genetics of affective disorders.

Depression and the environment

In addition to the involvement of genetic factors in depression, heritability estimates high-light the importance of the environmental (non-genetic) effects. Environmental influ-ence is clearly shown by the imperfect concordance seen in monozygotic (MZ) twins (i.e., there is about a 70 per cent chance of an MZ twin pair being depressed if their twin is affected; this compares with around 20 per cent for dizygotic (DZ) twins). Attention is increasingly turning to the role played by the environment, especially in the context of gene–environment interactions (see chapter 12): genes may be a *necessary* condition in vulnerability to disorder, but the environment seems to set the *sufficient* conditions for the expression of the disorder – this argument holds for environments in which there is variability in the expression of depression and a quantifiable genetic contribution.[5] There are obvious and confirmed links between recent life adversity and the onset of depres-sion (Brown & Harris, 1978), but, as should now be expected, the relationship between genetic vulnerability to depression and reactions to adverse life events is complicated.

The first problem is separating and defining 'genetic' and 'environmental' effects (Plomin & Bergeman, 1991). There is evidence that the perception of adverse life events is itself partly explained by genetic differences: relatives of depressed patients not only show increased rates of depression but also increased rates of experiencing or reporting threatening life events (McGuffin, Katz & Bebbington, 1988). Evidence is pointing to the possibility that the environment is not simply 'out there', but is, to some extent, selected, shaped and perceived by us – such perceptions may form an important part of personality differ-ences that predispose people to suffer from a variety of neurotic and psychotic condi-tions (see chapter 17).

This line of research has led to the hypothesis that genetic factors may influence the liability to depression indirectly (a) by a bias in threat perception, which may predispose both towards symptomatology and reported unpleasant happenings, or (b) by predis-posing individuals to select more aversive environments and a 'hazard-prone' lifestyle – of course, people do not deliberately choose harsh environment, but they nevertheless seem to seek out or create them (e.g., engaging in risky financial transactions that may

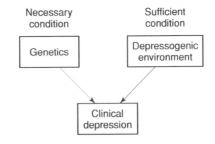

(a) **Additive model of depression**

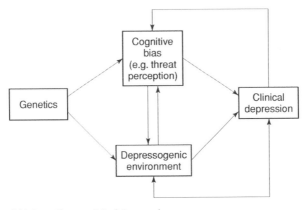

(b) **Interactive model of depression**

Figure 14.5 Genetic and environmental models of depression. Two models of depression: (a) an (over)simplified additive model, with genetic predisposition and depressogenic environment exerting separate influences; and (b) a more realistic model emphasizing the role played by genetic predisposition on perception and choice of environments which lead to depression and which are influenced by depression itself in a vicious circle.

well lead to an objectively defined adverse life event, for example, debt, occupational and family troubles – such long-term counterproductive behaviours may be a sensible short-term strategy to reduce the suffering of symptoms) (figure 14.5).

It has already been noted that attributional style can lead to cognitive distortions in perception and reactions to the world. However, it is important to keep in mind here the difference between blame and understanding: to say that depressed people may select more harsh environments is not to blame them for their depression – no more than it is appro-priate to blame cigarette smokers for their increased likelihood of developing lung cancer (few people make the rational choice to smoke in order to get lung cancer): the aim of science is to *understand* such complex and counterproductive behaviours, not throw the veil of blame over psychological phenomena and thereby ignore them.

ASK YOURSELF
What has quantitative genetics told us about the importance of the environment in depression?

▊▢ Evolutionary Perspectives

As detailed in chapter 2, evolution by natural selection is a random process, and the 'gene's-eye view' of evolution implies, according to Dawkins (1976), that animals – including *you* and *me* – are merely gene replication machines. There is another aspect of this gene's-eye view that is especially important for psychopathology: genes are selfish in that the 'successful' ones (i.e., those that have survived and replicated) code for phenotypes that, at the individual level, may not appear to be advantageous or even adaptive. One result of this selfish gene strategy – but see chapter 2 for what is meant by 'selfish' – may be disorders which cause considerable suffering to the individual but serve to propagate the gene's frequency in the gene pool. In recent years, an evolutionary perspective has been applied to anxiety and depression; and the attempt has been made to explain why such seemingly maladaptive phenotypes have evolved, or, at the very least, survived – the *maladaptive mind* (Baron-Cohen, 1997) parallels the evolutionary factors in the *adaptive mind* (Barkow, Cosmides & Tooby, 1992).

The basic argument for the importance of evolutionary explanations in psychopathology is that mental illness is a product of the brain functioning, and the brain is a biological organ that has evolved by the same processes of natural and sexual selection as all other living things. The fact that the mind *appears* to be so different from brain processes, and thus to evolutionary factors, does not mean that the mind is not subject to these evolutionary forces: to *some extent*, it must be. However, the power of any scientific theory is its ability to explain and predict. In this regard, evolutionary theories offer a perspective that is novel. Although still in its infancy, already some intriguing insights have been gained.

In terms of depression, the evolutionary explanation is less easy to grasp than that of anxiety: what, if any, could be the function of low mood, withdrawal, agitation, lack of pleasure (anhedonia) and increased risk of suicide? What is the point of crying for much of the day; waking early or sleeping too long; having delusions of physical illness; and losing contact with social support? The evolutionary approach argues that it may not be as preposterous as it at first may seem to consider these symptoms to have an adaptive function. They go on to argue that because depression is so common and so closely associated with *normal* everyday sadness, then it should be asked: (a) is it a true abnormality?; (b) is it a dysregulation of a normal capacity of sadness?; or even (c) is it an adaptive mechanism? The evolutionary approach asks the type of questions not usually asked in the context of psycho*pathology*.

Acute vs. chronic stress

Before considering positive functions for depression, it would be useful to consider one explanation that views depression as a pathology. Cannon (1929) proposed that stress is part of a 'fight–flight' system of defensive reactions, which can become chronic in operation and thereby represent a problem. Hans Selye (1976) emphasized the 'general adaptation syndrome', in which the physiological reaction to stressors outside the capacity of the body to maintain a *homeostasis* represents stress. In *stage I*, the alarm reaction entails the hypothalamic–pituitary–adrenal (HPA) axis (see chapter 6), which causes the characteristic signs of alarm (sweating, raised blood pressure, etc.): this prepares us physiologically for fight or flight action. In *stage II*, the body attempts to adjust to the stressor (i.e., physiological strain), reducing arousal (but not to normal levels); but this represents a continued strain on the body and may lead to side effects in the form of physical (e.g., impaired immune functioning; see chapter 6) or psychological problems, via either physiological processes (e.g., HPA overactivation, involved in depression) or psychological processes (e.g., the cognitive interpretation of the source of stress). In *stage III*, continued chronic stress may exhaust the body's capacity to cope and it may break down, which, in extreme cases, may result in death. Stage I is a highly adaptive process.

Chapters 15 and 17 show that defensive reactions to potentially dangerous stimuli and events have a powerful evolutionary function. Our brains evolved to deal with immediate, acute reactions: we see the lion and run to safety. However, in the modern world we are confronted by a continual bombardment of aversive stimuli, pumped out by the daily news – which works on the principle that 'good news is no news' – and experienced in everyday life (e.g., crowded cities) – these continual sources of aversive stimulation are what is known as 'stress'. The defensive systems in the brain have not evolved to deal with this type of stress; in many people, these functional capacities are stretched to their maximum and lead to a neurochemical dysfunction resulting in depression.

In this regard it is interesting to note that Brandstatter and Guth (2000) studied saving and consumption consumer decisions as a function of life expectancy (which comprised the source of aversive stimulation). They found considerable individual differences in the perception of this source of aversive stimulation; specifically, individuals with a personality of neurotic introversion (which corresponds to high trait anxiety) were most responsive to this form of aversive stimulation: it was as if, for any given value of life expectancy, these individuals perceived the time to death as being much shorter. So too in everyday life: it is the neurotic-introverted individuals who tend to suffer depressive symptoms. Chapter 17 returns to individual differences in the perception of threat.

There is a suspicion – supported by animal models – that the material rewards and opportunities made available by society itself are another major source of depression. In chapter 17 it is argued that anxiety is induced by conflict of *any* kind, including reward–reward conflict: the resulting frustration, fuelled by the otherwise desirable choices confronting us, is a form of aversive stimulation. Thus, the consistent presentation of aversive stimuli, along with the frustration induced by choice, can and does in many people lead to impairment of the brain's ability to cope effectively, resulting in emotional, behavioural and cognitive 'breakdown'. It is somewhat ironic that the very material benefits of modern society may also be the very cause of our misery. The whole point of commercial advertising is to induce a 'want' state, and competition ensures that several opposing want states exist at any one time: although economically we may be 'better off', psychologically this is a source of stress and will often compromise the very happiness we are trying to maximize: ironic indeed.

Positive functions

Is it possible that depression itself is a result of a positive adaptation – that is, depression is not a pathological outcome of some breakdown in the normal functioning system?

One evolutionary explanation of sadness – and perhaps even clinical depression – relates to the response to events that signal loss: depression is often associated with the withdrawal of some previously positively reinforcing stimulus (e.g., job, reputation, health, relative, spouse). In this context, sadness/depression reflects losses of reproductive resources. Under these circumstances, what would be the most adaptive strategy? Loss is a signal that previous behaviour has been unsuccessful and needs to be changed: it is adaptive to learn from such loss. In order to undertake this process of re-evaluation, it is argued that sadness/depression disengages the person from the immediate (potentially threatening) situation that cannot simply be avoided ('don't just do something, sit there!'), and encourages a form of emotional and cognitive reappraisal (a grief process). That is, following a loss, the first thing to do is to stop whatever you were doing before the loss; sadness motivates this behaviour. Nesse and Williams (1997) provide a discussion of possible evolutionary functions of depression.

Some studies show that most of us consistently overestimate our abilities and effectiveness; depressed people are said to have *depressive realism*, taking off the rose-tinted glasses through which most of us view the world (Taylor & Brown, 1988; Haaga & Beck, 1995). Coupled with this re-evaluation are submissiveness (to avoid punishment from potential danger; e.g., other people) and resource dependency on others, with behavioural strategies of crying, child-like dependency, etc., designed to elicit sympathy and resources, sufficient to tide them over their period of grief and re-evaluation. It must be stressed that none of these 'strategies' are conscious and certainly not deliberately 'manipulative' in the sense that the word is commonly used – in a more formal sense, it is an evolved phenotype with the effect of manipulating others.

The case of the experimental psychologist Stuart Sutherland, who suffered a midlife bipolar disorder provoked by sexual jealousy (after finding out that his wife was having an affair with a close friend, who was also seen as a professional rival, reported that, during his illness, 'My mind was occupied solely with my jealous thoughts: cruelly detailed and painful visual images succeeded one another on never-ending succession', p. 33). Many of the symptoms reported by Sutherland fit well the pattern of a submissive, child-like strategy:

> I could not bear to be separated from my wife, and most of the time was spent in her company. I followed her around the house and on shopping expeditions: if I lost sight of her in the supermarket I would panic and think I would never see her again. (p. 5)

This type of analysis also separates ultimate (evolutionary) functional causes from the proximal (local) mechanisms that tend to dominate psychological and psychiatric approaches. Whereas the social psychiatrist may ask questions about the role of social support in the aetiology of depression, the evolutionary psychiatrist is interested in *why* such support is so important.

ASK YOURSELF

Are the evolutionary theories of depression merely 'just-so' stories with little, if any, explanatory and predictive power?

Conclusion

Depression is a complex set of disorders, with multiple causal influences and a complex course. Its prevalence seems to be rising in modern society, but whether this is a result of more precise diagnosis or a reflection of the effects of the stress of modern society is not known – it is also possible that more people seek medical advice now that there is less social stigma attached to the disorder. Many people seek their own remedy in the form of alcohol, which temporarily suppresses the neural systems that mediate stress. Whatever the true state of affairs, depression is one of the major disorders afflicting many people in society – there are probably few families that have not been touched by it. In order to understand this class of disorder, it is important to appreciate the dynamic interplay of many factors, including social influences, cognitive biases, neurotransmitter systems and structural and functional brain processes.

> ## Learning Questions
>
> 1. At what point do everyday disappointment and sadness become clinical depression?
> 2. What is bipolar depression and why is it such a debilitating illness?
> 3. Are the 'monoamine hypothesis' and 'receptor hypothesis' complementary explanations?
> 4. What do genetic studies reveal about the possible role played by environmental factors in depression?
> 5. Are evolutionary accounts of depression purely speculative?

NOTES

1 How a diagnosis is defined as 'correct' is not an easy task, and is one of the main topics of debate in psychopathology (e.g., the separation of depression and anxiety conditions). Conditions are defined as distinct when they have different: (a) aetiological processes; (b) pathophysiologies; (c) therapies; and (d) treatment outcomes. However, many conditions have considerable overlap in all these features, making the boundaries between conditions rather fuzzy.

2 It is suspected that Churchill may have suffered from one of the various forms of bipolar disorder, for example, bipolar II disorder, which is characterized by one or more major depressive episodes accompanied by at least one hypomanic episode. In his younger years and in government, Churchill had a very active mind, and would routinely suggest ideas and schemes that were either reckless or impractical (e.g., he had to be deterred by the King from accompanying the landing party on D-Day, the invasion of Europe); and some of his economic and military actions were later heavily criticized for lacking restraint. There is, however, scant evidence than he had frank manic episodes. Whether his behaviour was the result of a bipolar disorder or the normal behaviour of an individual in exceptional circumstances must remain in the realm of armchair speculation.

3 There has been interest in the opposite attributional style: people who blame bad events on others and take credit for good events: these individual have a positive (optimistic) attributional

style, which is related to occupational and educational success (e.g., Corr & Gray, 1995; Seligman, 1991).

4   Electroconvulsive therapy (ECT), which is the only therapeutic agent for the treatment of depression that is rapid in onset and can start being effective after a single treatment, is used for the treatment of treatment-resistant (refractory) depressed patients, who otherwise have a higher chance of self-harm and attempted suicide. Although the precise mechanism of action is unknown, it is probably related to the activation of neurotransmitters caused by the seizures. There is, of course, a social stigma associated with ECT, and, on the face of it, it seems a very crude, even cruel, form of treatment. However, it is painless and well tolerated, with few documented long-term effects, although there is often temporary memory loss. ECT may be undesirable, but, in extreme cases, less undesirable than the misery of severe depression, which all too often ends in suicide.

5   In some extreme environments, there may not be a necessary genetic component to depression, as it is possible to imagine circumstances in which even the least vulnerable person would eventually develop depressive symptoms – in such environments, the variation explained by genetic differences would be eliminated (such a genetic elimination in phenotype is seen in the case of PKU, where the environment is favourably changed to eradicate the expression of genetic differences into phenotype differences; see chapter 2).

FURTHER READING

American Psychiatric Association (APA) (2000). *Diagnostic and Statistical Manual of Mental Disorders*, fourth edn. Washington: American Psychiatric Association.

Jamison, K. R. (1995). *An Unquiet Mind*. New York: Knopf.

Sutherland, S. (1976). *Breakdown: A Personal Crisis and Medical Dilemma*. London: Weidenfeld and Nicolson.

<table>
<tr><td>chapter
15</td><td># Clinical Disorder II:
Anxiety</td></tr>
</table>

Learning Objectives

To be able to:

1. Describe the psychiatric classification of the anxiety disorders.
2. Evaluate the use of the modulated startle reflex technique to understand the anxiety disorders.
3. Explain the classical conditioning model of the development and maintenance of anxiety.
4. Discuss psychopharmacological and molecular genetic bases of anxiety.
5. Describe and critique evolutionary explanations of the possible functions of anxiety.

Depression and anxiety share many features in common and are often co-morbid; in addition, these conditions respond to similar pharmacological treatments. None the less, however fuzzy the boundary, there are marked differences. DSM-IV-R (see the discussion in chapter 14 above) defines a number of major anxiety disorders: (a) *generalized anxiety disorder* (GAD), (b) *phobia* (specific and social), (c) *panic attack*, (d) *agoraphobia*, (e) *obsessive–compulsive disorder* (OCD), and (f) *post-traumatic stress disorder* (PTSD).

In the sections to follow the main diagnostic features of each of the major anxiety disorders are summarized, followed by discussion of their psychopharmacological profiles. Then psychophysiological approaches are surveyed, along with molecular genetics and the possible evolutionary basis of anxiety.

The term 'anxiety' is used to refer to a range of distinct conditions, with different symptoms, courses and treatments. In chapter 17, scientific reasons for questioning this lumping together will be presented. However, for the present, the standard psychiatric classification of this class of neurotic disorders is followed. Let us start with a clear form of anxiety, *generalized anxiety disorder* (GAD).

Generalized Anxiety Disorder (GAD)

Generalized anxiety disorder (GAD) consists of persistent and excessive anxiety and worry (apprehensive expectation), occurring more days than not, for a period of at least 6 months. For a clinical diagnosis, anxiety and worry must be accompanied by at least three additional symptoms from a list that includes: restlessness, being easily fatigued, difficulty concentrating, irritability, muscle tension and disturbed sleep. GAD impairs everyday functioning as patients have difficulty controlling their worry, and as a result experience disruption of social and occupational functioning. The intensity, duration and frequency of this anxiety and worry are far out of proportion to the feared event – often patients seem to be 'worrying about nothing'.

Various psychopharmacological and psychological approaches are available to treat GAD, and neuropsychological tasks can be used to evaluate the effectiveness of these treatments on cognitive functioning. For example, in one study, the emotional Stroop task (see chapter 8) was used to examine attention to threat stimuli before and after psychological therapy: GAD patients showed interference in colour-naming negative words before treatment, but this difference with the control group disappeared after treatment, indicating that the preconscious bias for threat stimuli alters over time with reductions in anxious thoughts and intrusive worries (Mogg et al., 1995).

An fMRI study that compared brain volumes (superior temporal gyrus, thalamus and prefrontal cortex) in children/adolescents with GAD and healthy matched controls revealed a significantly larger superior temporal gyrus in GAD patients, and also a more pronounced right–left asymmetry in total white matter – this volume of white matter was significantly and positively correlated with anxiety scores (de Bellis et al., 2002).

> **ASK YOURSELF**
> Are the diagnostic features of generalized anxiety disorder (GAD) little more than a description of the disorder?

The amygdala is also an important structure in fear/anxiety responses, and its projections to the superior temporal gyrus, thalamus and prefrontal cortex are thought to comprise the neural basis to interpret social behaviours (for a review of the amygdala and prefrontal cortex in emotion, see Davidson, 2002; also see chapter 17 below).

Phobia

There are three main classes of phobia: (a) specific phobia, (b) social phobia, and (c) agoraphobia. (Agoraphobia is included under the general heading of phobia, but in DSM-IV-R it is listed as a separate disorder.)

Specific phobia

A specific phobia (also known as a *simple phobia*) is characterized by clinically significant (i.e., excessive and unreasonable) fear provoked by exposure to a specific object or situation (e.g., flying, heights, animals, blood, spiders), often leading to avoidance behaviour. Exposure to the feared situation/object causes an immediate and expected fear response and, in extreme cases, a full-blown panic attack.

Studies using fMRI have reported that, unlike in other anxiety conditions, the amygdala does not seem to be hyperactive. In one study, specific animal phobics were compared with matched controls. During fMRI, patients and controls viewed emotionally expressive and neutral faces, and blood oxygenation level dependent (BOLD) responses were compared. Both groups showed enhanced amygdala activation to fearful faces, but there was no differential effect of group. Thus, there may be a restricted role for the amygdala in specific phobias, as compared with other anxiety disorders (e.g., PTSD). There was greater activation in the right insular cortex in the specific phobia group (Wright et al., 2003). Chapter 17 returns to the possible neural substrates of phobia.

Psychological treatment involves exposure therapy for simple phobias and more complex types: the fear/anxiety response wanes with gradual and repeated exposure to the feared stimuli (this is the process of *systematic desensitization*, formerly called *reciprocal inhibition*, which refers to substituting relaxing parasympathetic nervous system activation for arousing sympathetic activity).

Social phobia

A social phobia is characterized by clinically significant fear provoked by exposure to certain types of social situations (especially where a performance is required), often leading to avoidance behaviour. Social phobia is divided into discrete and generalized forms. In the discrete form, the individual fears a very specific situation (e.g., public speaking); in the generalized form, the individual fears almost all social situations in which evaluation and scrutiny may be possible. Whereas panic patients fear being in crowds, etc., because they may lose control and be unable to escape, social phobics fear social evaluation, humiliation, shame and embarrassment – where panic occurs, this is *expected* and in response to a specific situation or stimulus. For obvious reasons, generalized phobia is more disabling than specific phobia.

Social phobia has a prevalence of up to 10 per cent of the population, and twice as many women as men are affected. It usually has an early onset, occurring during adolescence, and has a chronic and unremitting course. Children as young as 2 years old show behavioural inhibition (intense anxiety when faced with new social situations or a stranger), and these children have increased prevalence of developing phobia in adulthood (Merikangas et al., 1998). Unsurprisingly, this disorder is very disabling in social, academic and occupational terms. There are gradations of this condition and it shades into normal behaviour: for example, most of us experience some degree of apprehension and fear when first giving a talk in front of a large group of people.

There are effective drug treatments (see below) as well as effective cognitive-behavioural therapies for this disorder – these may be used in conjunction with drug therapy or alone. These therapies target the major cognitive distortions in social phobics, including: overestimating the scrutiny of others and the consequences of such scrutiny; attributing critical thoughts to people; and underestimating one's own social skills.

Therapy aims to challenge and restructure these unrealistic, emotional and catastrophic thoughts, and to develop a more rational and realistic cognitive understanding of social situations.

Experimental cognitive studies of social phobia reveal a bias towards negative social-evaluative words. In one study using the emotional Stroop task, patients with social phobia showed attentional biases to socially threatening words, such as those describing negative evaluation (e.g., 'criticize') and those describing anxiety symptoms that are noticeable to others (e.g., 'blushing'), but not to anxiety symptoms less noticeable to others (Spector, Pecknold & Libman, 2003; see Mogg et al., 2000).

Agoraphobia

Agoraphobia is fear of being in places or situations from which escape might be difficult or embarrassing, or where help may not be available in the event of a panic attack (which often accompanies agoraphobia) – it is literally translated as 'fear of the marketplace'. The resulting fear and anxiety lead to a pervasive avoidance of situations, including being alone outside the safety of the home, being in a crowd of people, travelling in a car, bus or aeroplane, or being on a bridge or in a lift (elevator). Such phobic patients find it very difficult to leave the home and fear that something terrible will happen to them if they do. These avoidance behaviours are often occupationally and socially crippling. The type of avoidance response seen in this condition and its possible biological bases are analysed in detail in chapter 17, where it is shown that phobia in general may be better thought of as a type of fear rather than anxiety.

As with the other anxiety conditions, numerous studies have been conducted to investigate information processing deficits and biases. For example, in one experiment, the emotional Stroop task was used in patients with panic attacks and agoraphobia, with three different types of words: panic-related, interpersonal threat, and neutral words, presented either above (overt) or below (covert) the threshold of consciousness awareness. The results showed a robust Stroop interference for panic words, whether presented overtly or covertly (Lundh et al., 1999), suggesting that panic patients have fast processing of panic-related material.

> **ASK YOURSELF**
> What distinguishes the clinically phobic patient from the socially shy individual?

▢ Panic Attack

A panic attack is a discrete period in which there is a sudden onset of *unexpected* intense apprehension, fearfulness or terror, often associated with feelings of impending doom; symptoms include: a shortness of breath, palpitations, chest pain/discomfort, choking or smothering sensations, fear of losing control and catastrophic thinking (e.g., 'I am going to die'). There is a strong desire to flee from the situation and get to a place of safety. Panic attacks can last between 5 and 30 minutes – although sometimes they may persist for hours. They may also occur during sleep (nocturnal panic attacks). These attacks can lead to the instrumental learning of avoidance behaviours, reinforced by the reduction of panic and relaxation. This learning can produce a secondary avoidance disorder, such as agoraphobia (approximately a 30 per cent chance).

Panic attacks are often co-morbid with other psychiatric disorders, or they may exist on their own, in which case a panic disorder (PD) is diagnosed. It is common for patients with social phobia, post-traumatic stress disorder and/or specified phobias to experience panic attacks, but these attacks are *expected* and in response to a known, feared specific object or situation; therefore they do not meet the criteria for a diagnosis of panic disorder. Panic disorder proper – as distinct from panic attacks associated with other anxiety disorders – is diagnosed when there are recurrent unexpected attacks followed by at least a 1-month period of persistent anxiety or concern about them.

It is estimated that about 10 per cent of the population experience at least one panic attack some time in their life, although this estimate may represent under-reporting. Panic disorder affects approximately 2 per cent of the population, and it usually starts in adolescence or early childhood (only rarely does it present for the first time in people over the age of 45). It seems to be more prevalent in women, and there is a high concordance rate in MZ twins (Perna et al., 1997). Suicide is more likely, as indeed it is in the case of the whole range of anxiety disorders (Khan et al., 2002).

The suffocation hypothesis

Klein (1993) proposed that panic disorder patients have a false suffocation alarm that may be associated with a lowered threshold for carbon dioxide detection. Support for this theory comes from studies showing that panic disorder patients more readily panic than normal controls after exercising, when breathing carbon dioxide or when given lactate (lactate produces panic because it is a potent respiratory stimulant – panic patients may be more sensitive to agents that promote respiratory drive). This theory proposes that panic disorder patients have a suffocation monitor in the brainstem that misinterprets the respiratory drive signal and misfires, triggering a false suffocation alarm. Serotonergic (5-HT) deficiencies enhance this ventilatory response in PD patients, suggesting that 5-HT normalizes the ventilatory response. Although some studies support this theory (e.g., Beck, Ohtake & Shipherd, 1999; Rassovsky et al., 2000), other studies do not (e.g., Katzman et al., 2002; for a review of the literature, see Griez & Schruers, 1998). There does appear to be a genetic component to panic reactivity to CO_2 inhalation, supporting the idea that CO_2 hypersensitivity might be the expression of an underlying genetic vulnerability to PD (Arancio et al., 1995).

In addition to drug therapy, cognitive and behavioural therapies are commonly combined in the treatment of panic disorder, whether it is presented with or without agoraphobia. Cognitive therapy focuses on identifying the cognitive distortions (e.g., 'I'm going to die', when an attack is starting) and modifying them; behavioural therapy attempts to modify a patient's responses through exposure to situations and stimuli that provoke attacks. Behavioural treatments are especially effective in treating the behavioural (phobic) responses to panic, but not panic itself.

The neurobiology of panic disorder has yet to be clarified. However, there is evidence of EEG abnormalities. Panic disorder patients with and without EEG abnormalities (non-epileptic) were compared with matched healthy controls. Panic patents showed a higher than expected rate of EEG abnormalities (29 per cent); and EEG screening was effective in identifying patients with a high probability of structural brain abnormalities: MRI abnormalities were found in 61 per cent of EEG-abnormal patients and 18 per cent of EEG-normal patients (the controls had a rate of 4 per cent). In addition, a high rate of septo-hippocampal abnormalities has been reported (Dantendorfer et al., 1996). The cause and effect of these *associations* are still largely unknown.

Obsessive–Compulsive Disorder (OCD)

Obsessive–compulsive disorder (OCD) is characterized by obsessions (which cause marked anxiety) and/or compulsions (which serve to neutralize the anxiety) – usually, both obsession and compulsions are present (having a compulsion without some obsession is rare). Obsessions are experienced subjectively as internal thoughts, impulses or images that are intrusive and inappropriate, causing anxiety and distress. Common obsessions comprise contamination, aggression, religion, safety/harm, need for exactness/symmetry, and somatic (body) fears. Compulsions are repetitive behaviours or mental acts, comprising checking, cleaning/washing, counting, repeating, ordering/arranging and hoarding/collecting. Once again, these behaviours may be seen as the extreme end of a largely normal continuum: how many of us have not doubled-checked that the doors are locked, or felt the urge to wash our hands when this was not necessary?

It is not possible directly to observe an obsession, but compulsions can usually be observed: they consist of some behavioural ritual, either in response to an obsession or according to rigid rules aimed at preventing distress or some dreaded event. Compulsive acts are irrational in the sense that they do not prevent the feared event – however, the fact that the dreaded event does not occur leads to a conditioning process of *superstitious* behaviours (i.e., inferring a false causal link between the compulsive act and the avoidance of the dreaded event).

For a diagnosis of OCD, obsessions and/or compulsions must last for at least 1 hour per day and be sufficiently severe to impair normal social and occupational functioning. The prevalence of OCD in the general population is approximately 2 per cent. But some clinicians would broaden the definition of OCD to include a spectrum of disorders, including pathological gambling, eating disorders, paraphilias (i.e. recurrent, intense sexually arousing fantasies and urges directed towards some object), kleptomania (i.e., recurrent failure to resist impulses to steal items, even when not needed) and body dysmorphic disorder (i.e., a preoccupation with a defect in appearance that is either imagined or out of proportion to a slight physical anomaly). A survey of the clinical and non-clinical OCD literature shows that low-level OCD symptoms may be quite common in the general population – one wonders whether the constant urge of some of us continually to check our emails is a modern-day manifestation of this disorder.

Figure 15.1 Dr Frederick Toates, the biological psychologist, who has been a long-time sufferer of obsessive–compulsive disorder (OCD) and who has written widely on the subjective experience, science and treatment of this anxiety disorder, as well as pursuing a highly successful academic career and publishing the highly regarded *Biological Psychology: An Integrative Approach*. Pictured here is also his wife, Dr Olga Coschug-Toates, who co-authored *Obsessive Compulsive Disorder* (2002).

Dr Frederick Toates: a psychologist with obsessive–compulsive disorder

A superb account of the first-hand experience of obsessions and compulsions is provided by the biological psychologist Dr Frederick Toates, who has produced, among many other excellent books, the impressive *Biological Psychology: An Integrative Approach*. The previous chapter presented an account of bipolar depression by another psychologist, Professor Stuart Sutherland, and in the next chapter the 'psychotic consciousness' of Dr Peter Chadwick, who is an expert in schizophrenia research, is presented. This section aims to provide some sense (albeit second-hand) of the misery that anxiety can bring to everyday living.

Toates and Coschug-Toates (2002) describe the subjective nature of OCD and then summarize what is known about the biological and psychological bases of this disorder. This interweaving of first-hand experience and scientific knowledge provides a cogent insight into what still remains one of the unexplained disorders of everyday life. Below are a few examples of some of Dr Toates' obsessions and compulsions; they show how obsessions can lead to compulsive behaviour.

> Sitting on a bus, I would fix on a passenger who had just alighted, and try to hold him in my gaze for as long as possible. If I couldn't hold him until the bus turned the corner, I was worried that this was an omen that tragedy might shortly befall me. Crazy? Irrational? Yes, particularly for a scientist who had hitherto prided himself on the disinterested and objective pursuit of knowledge, but it was compelling. It lasted for some months and then slowly went away. (p. 36)

> I also found myself checking and double-checking that I had switched off electrical equipment, locked doors, etc. I could not resist going back for yet one more 'final' check. This behaviour was about to add to the discomfort of what was to be the worst day of my life

until then, as I slipped deeper into depression. . . . Could all that pleasure in living really be over for good? How long would this hell last and would I get even worse? I couldn't imagine what it would be like to be in a mood even worse than this. I was now in a state of panic, feeling, I guess, something like the proverbial rat trapped in a corner. (p. 37)

Apart from wasting time on checking doors and electric switches, I spent time checking the contents of letters. I would write several letters, seal them and take them to the post, only to feel insecure that I had put the right letter in the right envelope. I would then open them up to read the contents. (p. 38)

Dr Toates is not alone in his obsessions and compulsions. Toates and Coschug-Toates (2002) list a number of famous people who showed evidence of OCD: Samuel (Dr) Johnson (1709–84), writer, poet and philosopher; Hans Christian Andersen (1805–75), writer; Charles Darwin (1809–82), biologist and originator of the theory of evolution by natural selection (see chapter 2); Søren Kierkegaard (1813–55), the philosopher; and Kurt Gödel (1906–79), the mathematician and logician.

Most of us have experienced obsessions and compulsions, if only to a slight degree. How many of us have not gone back to check that something electrical was switched off, or that the taps were closed? For example, on my way to a scientific conference I turned the car around after just leaving the house to check the taps – but this might have been a learned and, indeed, totally rational response: a failure to check the sink taps some years earlier resulted in a flooded flat and very wet and very annoyed neighbours!

The next chapter examines the possibility that conditions such as OCD are on a spectrum from the normal/adaptive (no more wet and annoyed neighbours – a form of negative reinforcement; see chapter 7) to the pathological (e.g., checking the taps 100 times a day). At this point it should be noted that OCD seems to entail the malfunctioning of motor programmes: there is goal (e.g., 'I must check the taps are off'), a motor plan ('I will visit the bathroom and kitchen and feel whether the taps are tightened'), which is then executed, and once this plan has been implemented there is feedback information that 'puts the mind at rest'. Somewhere in this chain of events there is failure, perhaps in the final stage of processing feedback.

Evidence exists to support the claim that there are neurobiological abnormalities in OCD. Structural and functional neuroimaging studies provide evidence for elevated glucose metabolic rates in the orbitofrontal cortex, caudate nuclei and thalamus; and neurological disorders such as Tourette's syndrome, and other disorders with basal ganglia dysfunction, frequently involve OCD symptoms, thereby supporting the idea of a biological basis of this disorder. OCD is associated with increased familial risk in sibling pairs concordant for Tourette syndrome. Furthermore, patients with OCD often exhibit neurological soft signs, which point to neurological compromise (for a review of this literature, see Kuelz, Hohagen & Voderholzer, 2004).

In unravelling the biological bases of OCD, attention has been drawn to the close link between Tourette's syndrome and OCD: this link points to the involvement of dopamine action in the basal ganglia. Tourette's syndrome is a chronic neuropsychiatric condition characterized by multiple motor and vocal tics. Interestingly, between 45 and 90 per cent of these patients also have obsessions and compulsions. Family genetic studies show a link between Tourette's syndrome and OCD, leading to the hypothesis that there exists a common

ASK YOURSELF

Is obsessive–compulsive disorder (OCD) an exaggeration of normal risk-avoidant behaviour?

genetic factor that manifests itself as tics or OCD: tics may be the behavioural manifestation of a genetically based basal ganglia dysfunction, with Tourette's syndrome being manifested as 'tics of the body' and OCD as 'tics of the mind' (Stahl, 2000).

Post-traumatic Stress Disorder (PTSD)

Post-traumatic stress disorder (PTSD) is characterized by the re-experiencing of a traumatic event, accompanied by symptoms of increased arousal, avoidance of stimuli associated with the trauma and, sometimes, panic attack – however, this is different from panic disorder or social phobia in that it is a response to a real threat (e.g., war trauma or rape). Although a minority of people exposed to such life-threatening situations develop a full-blown disorder, its prevalence is much higher then previously thought (indeed, until the early 1990s, some psychiatrists denied it existed at all).

PTSD is a serious disorder, often leading to suicide, even among the apparently tough (e.g., soldiers). Symptoms include intrusive memories and thoughts, and flashbacks of the original trauma, involving activation of the memories relating to the incident, nightmares, high arousal, depression, aggression, irritability and impulsiveness. Co-morbidity with other psychiatric disorders, especially depression and drug and alcohol abuse, are the rule rather than the exception: these make the diagnosis difficult and may explain why PTSD took so long to be recognized as a valid psychiatric disorder.

A number of information-processing deficits are found in PTSD, including: memory dysfunction (perhaps consistent with toxic effects in the hippocampus, resulting from excessive neuroendocrine responses; see chapter 14); and an attentional bias towards trauma-related stimuli, especially at post-recognition stages of processing. Premorbid level of intelligence also seems to have an effect (Buckley, Blanchard & Neill, 2000): there is evidence, from a number of different sources, to suggest that high cognitive ability may act as a buffer to negative events and to the development of psychiatric disorder. PTSD has a substantial genetic component (Radant et al., 2001).

It is estimated that over one-third of US soldiers serving in Vietnam experienced PTSD. It is also suspected that more UK soldiers in the Falklands conflict of the early 1980s subsequently committed suicide than were actually killed (N = 252) in action. In everyday life, road traffic accidents, physical assaults and rapes are among the most common incidents that lead to PTSD.

The amygdala is implicated in the pathophysiology of PTSD, as well as many other anxiety disorders. For example, in one study, fMRI reactions to masked presentations of emotive faces in combat-exposed veterans with and without a diagnosis of PTSD revealed that PTSD patients had an exaggerated amygdala response to fearful faces, even when these were masked (i.e., not consciously perceived) (Rauch et al., 2000). Such results indicate that PTSD patients have a rapid, automatic (preconscious) identification and processing of general covert threat stimuli, which results in hyper-arousal to negative stimuli. Of relevance in this regard is the finding that stimulation of the amygdala in human beings can induce memory flashbacks, pointing to a search for emotionally tagged material that is brought into conscious awareness – the amygdala is involved in emotional arousal so should therefore be expected to amplify any ongoing negative thoughts and feelings. ERP research has shown that attentional and/or concentration deficits are evident in the

P300 component of Vietnam combat veterans, but only in the unmedicated (medication seems to normalize these deficits), indicating that ERP technology can be used to assess effectiveness of treatment (Metzger et al., 1997).

The anterior cingulate cortex has been associated with functional abnormalities in PTSD. Vietnam combat veterans with and without a diagnosis of PTSD underwent fMRI while performing an emotional counting task (the veterans counted the number of different types of words: combat-related, general negative and neutral words). The non-PTSD veterans showed significant difference in fMRI blood oxygenation level dependent (BOLD) responses (indicative of greater activation) between the combat and general negative word processing; but this difference was absent in the PTSD veterans. This result suggests a diminished response in the cingulate cortex in the presence of emotionally relevant stimuli in PTSD; and that this diminished activity may mediate, to some extent, symptoms such as distress and arousal when exposed to trauma stimuli (Shin et al., 2001).

Neural network approaches have also been applied to PTSD (see chapter 7). Connectionist neural networks attempt to model the associative links between cognitive systems, sufficient to account for existing data, as well as being able to generate new predictions based on changing input values or parameters and functions within the network. These predicted outcomes can then be tested in patient groups. For example, one such model (Tryon, 1998) provides a theoretical basis for explaining the clinical symptom constellation of PTSD, with special emphasis on why trauma is re-experienced through memory. It accounts for individual variation in symptom severity, including why some people do not develop PTSD; explains why persons with PTSD are co-morbid with depression, generalized anxiety and substance abuse; and shows how abnormal behaviour derives from normal memory formation processes (neural networks can also be extended to psychopharmacological processes; e.g., Politi et al., 1999). For an excellent overview of neural networks in psychopathology, see Stein and Ludik (1998).

Emotional Stroop studies show an interference effect of Vietnam-related negative words in Vietnam PTSD patients; and in these patients there was superior free-recall and recognition memory for the emotion words, suggesting that the slower colour naming of threat words was related to an attentional bias towards them rather than their avoidance (Vrana, Roodman & Beckham, 1995).

> **ASK YOURSELF**
> What does post-traumatic stress disorder (PTSD) say about the influence of the exposure to threat on brain processes?

▢▢ Psychopharmacology

The fundamentals of psychopharmacology were covered in chapters 12 and 14, and material relevant to anxiety was discussed in the context of depression (chapter 14): this knowledge forms a basis for the present chapter.

General background

In the 1950s, barbiturate drugs were commonly used to relieve anxiety; but the effectiveness of these drugs was proportional to their power to sedate. Although useful drugs, they were far from ideal because of problems of dependency and withdrawal, and their safety profile was poor (especially when used with other drugs or with alcohol – alcohol has long been the drug of choice for those who 'self-medicate' to relieve anxiety). A particularly unpleasant aspect was their toxicity at high doses, and for this reason they were often used by patients to commit suicide.

The 1960s saw the development of new classes of drugs. At this time, a distinction was made between two major classes of drugs: the antidepressants (e.g., tricyclic antidepressants and MAO inhibitors; see chapter 14) and the anxiolytics (anti-anxiety drugs; e.g., benzodiazepines). This distinction reflected diagnostic distinctions that tended to separate major depressive disorder from generalized anxiety disorder. However, this nosological (classificatory) distinction was challenged by empirical findings showing that some tricyclic antidepressants and MAO inhibitors were also effective in treating panic disorder. There began a trend to viewing anxiety and depression as overlapping rather than as distinct disorders. By the 1990s, antidepressants from the selective serotonin reuptake inhibitor (SSRI; see chapter 14) class became recognized as preferred first-line treatment for many anxiety disorders, ranging from OCD to panic disorder, and now to social phobia and PTSD, although not for generalized anxiety disorder (for a review of SSRIs in the major psychiatric disorders, see Vaswani, Linda & Ramesh, 2003).

Noradrenergic anxiolytics

In addition to the role of 5-HT, norepinephrine (released from noradrenergic, NE, neurons) has also been linked to anxiety. The observation that electrical stimulation of the locus ceruleus produces a state analogous to anxiety in experimental animals led to the hypothesis that anxiety is related to NE overactivity (in human beings, NE overactivity is related to anxiety symptoms, such as sweating and tremor). This hypothesis then led to the prediction that, if overactivity of the locus ceruleus NE neurons is associated with anxiety, then administration of an alpha$_2$ (autoreceptor) agonist should act in a manner similar to the action of NE itself on its presynaptic alpha$_2$ autoreceptors – that is, reuptake of norepinephrine should be increased and, therefore, anxiety should be reduced. The NE hypothesis thus predicts that anxiety is reduced because an alpha$_2$ agonist stimulating alpha$_2$ autoreceptors imposes a brake on NE release. In support of this theory, the alpha$_2$ agonist clonidine has some clinically recognized anxiolytic actions (e.g., de Angelis, 1995). It is especially useful in blocking the NE aspects of anxiety (sweating, dilated pupils, etc.); but it is less powerful in blocking the subjective and emotional aspects of anxiety. Clinically, yohimbine, an NE alpha$_2$ antagonist, increases the core symptoms of some anxiety disorders; and idaoxan, another NE alpha$_2$ antagonist, increases anxiety scores in healthy volunteers (Schmidt et al., 1997).

Overactivity of NE neurons creates too much postsynaptic norepinephrine at NE receptors, particularly beta receptors: consistent with the hypothesis of a state of NE excess in anxiety, it is possible to reduce symptoms of anxiety in some cases by blocking beta receptors with beta blocking drugs – this seems especially useful in the case of social phobia (Greist et al., 1996), where there seems to be a vicious circle of anxiety upon exposure to the feared social environment (figure 15.2).

The case of NE neurotransmission shows a number of important features of the psychopharmacology of anxiety: (a) anxiety is related to a number of neurochemical

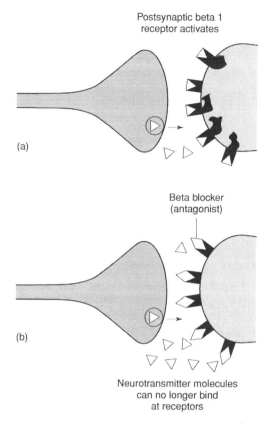

Postsynaptic beta 1
receptor activates

(a)

Beta blocker
(antagonist)

(b)

Neurotransmitter molecules
can no longer bind
at receptors

Figure 15.2   NE neuron and anxiolytic drug action. Evidence points to overactivity of norepinephrine (NE), particularly at beta receptors, being associated with anxiety (a). Anxiety can be reduced by blocking beta receptors (b). NE overactivity is also indexed by: dilated pupils, tremor, fast heartbeat and sweating.

systems (sometimes working synergistically; i.e., allosterically); (b) different anxiety disorders may be caused, or related to, a different profile of activation and inhibition of neurochemical systems; and (c) a subtle combination of activation/inhibition is required to treat effectively any one anxiety disorder.

In panic disorder several lines of evidence support the involvement of NE: (a) panic patients are hypersensitive to alpha$_2$ antagonists and hyposensitive to alpha$_2$ agonists (yohimbine, an alpha$_2$ antagonist, acts as a promoter of NE release by cutting the brake cable of the presynaptic NE autoreceptor: the result is an exaggerated response in panic disorder patients); (b) caffeine is also a panicogenic (i.e., panic-inducing), as it facilitates NE release; and (c) panic patients have a blunted response to postsynaptic NE agonists, perhaps as a consequence of a overactive NE system. Using microdialysis and lesion techniques, norepinephrine levels were assessed in the dorsomedial hypothalamus of the rat (Shekhar et al., 2002): in support of the norepinephrine–panic association, experimentally manipulated levels of extracellular norepinephrine were found to elicit panic-like responses (e.g., increases in heart rate, blood pressure, respiration rate and anxiety).

Benzodiazepines

Before the use of SSRIs in anxiety, benzodiazepines were the first-line treatment. The action of this class of drug demands some familiarization with the pharmacology of (inhibitory) GABAergic neurotransmission.

There are two known GABA subtypes: $GABA_A$ and $GABA_B$. $GABA_A$ receptors are the gatekeepers for a chloride channel: they are allosterically modulated by nearby receptors – benzodiazepine is one such receptor. (A second GABA receptor subtype, $GABA_B$ receptor, is not allosterically modulated by benzodiazepines – this slow-action receptor type seems not to be related to anxiety) (figure 15.3).

Thus benzodiazepines do not work directly on GABA receptors, but rather modulate (i.e., through allosteric interaction) their operation: in other words, activation of the benzodiazepine receptor has the power to change the functioning of nearby GABA receptors. (Allosteric interactions are discussed in chapter 12.)

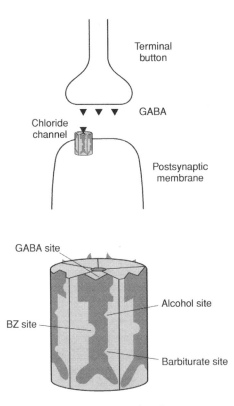

Figure 15.3 Benzodiazepine–$GABA_A$ receptor complex. $GABA_A$ postsynaptic receptors are the gatekeepers for a chloride channel and are allosterically modulated by nearby benzodiazepine (BZ) receptors. Thus, the anxiolytic effects of benzodiazepine are mediated by their action on GABA receptors. Also shown are the allosteric sites of other anxiolytics (e.g., alcohol and barbiturate) commonly used to reduce anxiety.

In addition to the benzodiazepines, other chemicals increase GABAergic neurotransmission (e.g., barbiturates and alcohol, but these chemicals interact with other receptors that allosterically modulate GABA receptors). The benzodiazepine–GABA complex is found widely throughout the brain (e.g., cerebellum and spinal cord). Its anxiolytic effects are thought to operate in the systems in the brain (e.g., septo-hippocampal system) implicated in the generation of anxiety (see chapter 17).

The fact that benzodiazepines act at naturally occurring receptors in the brain suggests the hypothesis that the brain has its own benzodiazepines, or 'endogenous Valium'. However, identification and characterization of the naturally occurring ligand are not yet complete. Accordingly, it has been suggested that reduced actions of GABA, as well as the reduced action of endogenous benzodiazepine ligands at the GABA–benzodiazepine receptor complex, may be associated with normal variations in the emotion of anxiety.

GABA, and its allosteric modulation by benzodiazepine, seems to be involved in panic (indeed, the Shekhar et al. (2002) study used blockade of $GABA_A$ receptors to increase NE release). One theory is that the ability of benzodiazepines to modulate GABA is out of balance. As so little is known about benzodiazepine ligands, most of the research has focused on benzodiazepine receptors. It is possible that the brain makes less than the required amount of the endogenous ligand (naturally occurring neurotransmitter) and thus has less ability to decrease anxiety on its own by failing to activate GABA-inhibiting neurotransmission. It is also possible that the brain produces an excess of anxiogenic inverse agonists (i.e., neurochemicals that bind to the receptor and actively inhibit it), leading to a lack of activation of GABA receptors and thus panic disorder and anxiety.

> **ASK YOURSELF**
> Is there likely to be a single neurochemical disorder common to anxiety conditions?

☐☐☐ Psychophysiology

There have been numerous and many different types of psychophysiological studies of anxiety. In this section two types of studies are summarized: (a) affective modulation of the startle reflex (see chapter 9); and (b) classical conditioning of neurosis, using heart rate and electrodermal responses (see chapters 7 and 9). In the case of the modulated startle reflex there is theoretical interest in its neural processes; however, heart rate and electrodermal measures are used as convenient (indirect) indices of emotional responding.

Affective modulation of the startle reflex

Affective modulation of the startle reflex has been extensively used to study emotional processes in normal and clinical populations. In relation to clinical states of excessive, diminished or distorted emotional responding, this technique provides answers to a number of important research questions, for example: is clinical anxiety related to hypersensitivity to aversive stimuli; and is depression related to hyposensitivity to appetitive stimuli? This technique also permits the investigation of the possible interaction of sensitivities to aversive and appetitive stimuli (see Corr, 2002b), answering such questions as: does reactivity to appetitive stimuli depend upon sensitivity to aversive stimuli? In a clinical context, it may be asked: might a clinically anxious patient's greater sensitivity to aversive stimuli impair their reactions to appetitive stimuli, and thereby lead, in vulnerable individuals, to a depressive condition resulting from heightened levels of anxiety? Affective modulation of the startle reflex is thus a very useful, objective and flexible tool to probe emotional responding. Grillon and Baas (2003) note that:

> The absence of an objective measure of emotion has been an impediment to psychophysiological research on emotion and its application to psychopathology. The startle reflex very well complements verbal reports, which are vulnerable to individual perception, demand characteristics, and intentional distortion. (p. 1558)

Due to the objective nature of the startle reflex procedure – that is, participants do not need to know what it is measuring for the technique to be effective – it has attracted considerable research attention in recent years. Another powerful feature of this procedure is that startle modulation by different types of emotional stimuli is easily observed in both human and non-human animals – in non-human experimental animals, it is possible to conduct more rigorous and controlled neurophysiological experiments involving invasive brain procedures (see chapter 11). There has now been extensive study of the pharmacological, anatomical and electrophysiological basis of the fear–startle circuit in non-human brains (for a review, see Walker, Toufexis & Davis, 2003), and much is known about the brain basis of emotional responses. Affective modulation of startle thus allows important insights into the neural circuitry involved in affective processing in general, as well as specific forms of disordered processing.

Anecdotal evidence for greater startle reactivity in fearful/anxious individuals provided the impetus for the first study of fear-potentiated startle in rats (Brown, Kalish & Farber, 1951); one of the first demonstrations in human beings of exaggerated startle was reported by Spence and Runquist (1958). In recent years there has been a flood of studies in human samples using this promising psychophysiological technique.

As described in chapter 9, affective modulation of the startle reflex is useful because the increase in amplitude observed when the startle probe is presented during the viewing of unpleasant slides, as compared with neutral slides, is known to be related to fear/anxiety[1] – an effect known as *fear-potentiated* startle. When probes are delivered during the viewing of pleasant slides, there is a significant attenuation of the startle reflex – an effect known as *pleasure-attenuated* startle. This technique has a wide applicability to psychopathology and has been used to study emotional responses in different anxiety conditions (for a review of this literature, see Grillon & Baas, 2003).

Phobia

Hamm et al. (1997) compared a specific phobia group (either animal or mutilation/blood fears) with a non-phobic control group. Acoustic startle probes were presented during the presentation of pleasant, unpleasant and neutral slides, as well as during slides of the specific fear objects of the phobia group. Both groups showed the affective modulation pattern: pleasant slides attenuated the startle reflex, unpleasant slides potentiated it, both compared with neutral (control) slides; and, in addition, the phobia groups showed significantly greater startle potentiation to a slide of their own phobic objects.

PTSD

It was noted in the case of PTSD that one of the signs was increased startle (Orr & Roth, 2000), but this sign is based only on clinical observation of patients' behaviour. A number of startle studies have now been conducted on PTSD adults and children to experimentally test this observation. The data are mixed, though: looking at the basic startle reflex (i.e., reaction to the startle probe without any manipulation of emotion), some studies show either no exaggerated startle or even a reduced startle (Lang et al., 1992). However, in a meta-analytic review of this literature,[2] Metzger et al. (1999) concluded that, although not all studies found statistically significant results, across all studies there was support for exaggerated startle.

More consistent findings have been found with affective *modulated* startle. Grillon and Morgan (1996) tested Vietnam veterans with a diagnosis of PTSD, both with (threat condition) and without (safe condition) experimental stressors. Baseline startle did not differ between the groups of PTSD veterans, compared with groups of combat soldiers and normal controls; however, in the threat condition (i.e., the threat of electric shock), startle was potentiated (i.e., fear-potentiated startle), but this fear-potentiated startle did not differ between groups; however, the overall magnitude of startle was greater in the PTSD patients, pointing to a shift from baseline startle. These data suggest that PTSD patients generalize threat perception to even the safe (non-shock) condition, and this might be an important feature of their clinical presentation.

Depression vs. anxiety

In relation to major depressive disorder, Allen, Trinder and Brennan (1999) examined affective modulation of startle in patients matched with a control group. They reported that, although both groups gave similar ratings of the pleasantness/unpleasantness of pleasant, unpleasant and neutral slides, their patterns of startle reactions were quite different: contrary to the standard pleasure–attenuation response, the severely depressed patients showed *potentiated* startle during pleasant slides, pointing to the intriguing suggestion that depressed patients may respond to pleasant slides as if they were aversive, possibly because such stimuli are seen as signals of frustrative non-reward.

Hypoanxious psychopaths

An opposite pattern of effects has been observed in criminals who have been diagnosed as having a psychopathic personality[3] – these individuals are emotionally cold, unempathic, callous, manipulative and have disregard of others (see Cooke & Michie, 2001). Patrick, Bradley and Lang (1993) studied their pattern of affective modulation. Prisoners low in psychopathy had a similar affective pattern to college students; but, in the criminals high in psychopathy, startle reactions to *both* pleasant and unpleasant slides were reduced (compared with neutral slides), indicating that psychopathic criminals processed unpleasant images as if they were pleasant. Although the precise interpretation of these data is problematic – experiencing unpleasant slides as appetitive is only one explanation of the data – they do seem to show that, for whatever reason, psychopathic individuals process emotional stimuli differently from non-psychopathic individuals (be they criminals or students). Of theoretical interest is the fact that, of the two separate factors that comprise the general factor of psychopathy, only *emotional detachment* (not *antisocial behaviour*) was related to dysfunctional emotion processing, confirming that psychopathy is more than antisocial behaviour, and reflects fundamental deficits in information processing (e.g., failures of planning; failure to learn from negative experience; and failure to experience appropriate emotions).

Attributional bias

To illustrate the flexibility and subtlety of affective modulation of startle technique, consider the experiment by Lawson, MacLeod and Hammond (2002). To assess whether depressed patients display a negative attributional bias – that is, give negative attributions to ambiguous stimuli – potentiated startle was first shown to occur to emotional interpretation of ambiguous stimuli (probes were presented during imagery cued by an emotional stimulus); and then it was demonstrated that healthy individuals who scored high on a questionnaire of depression (i.e., the Beck Depression Inventory, BDI) had an elevated tendency to impose negative interpretations on ambiguous information. This type of finding suggests that negative attributional bias may be a trait of depression, and not simply a result (i.e., state) of being depressed (see chapter 14).

Applications of startle reflex

One of the major strengths of the affective modulation of startle procedure is that it permits cross-species comparisons (where self-report ratings are obviously not possible). The type of research possible only with non-human animals is fundamental to building a basic neuroscience of emotion. Testing hypotheses, perhaps derived from the human clinic, in non-human animals and then taking these results back to the clinic are a powerful way to develop effective treatments for clinical disorders. Modulated startle can also be used in non-clinical volunteers, where a range of research questions can be addressed, including the vulnerability factors found in the general populations (e.g., fear-potentiated startle in individuals who score high on personality measures of anxiety, for example, harm avoidance; Corr et al., 1995). In addition, the study of non-clinical (high-risk) samples can overcome some of the problems found in clinical studies: patients often present with a complex mixture of symptoms, and it is not clear whether these symptoms are core to the primary causal basis of the disorder or a product of the ongoing pathophysiology (disease progression) or the effects of medication (or other disease-related effects, e.g., infections). Thus, study of non-clinical healthy samples (where risk factors can be examined) and non-human animals (where some forms of basic neuroscience are only possible; e.g., experimental brain lesions), both conducted alongside clinical studies, provide a powerful means to understand the complex nature of affective disorder. In the next chapter another example of the high-risk strategy, this time in relation to schizophrenia, is seen.

ASK YOURSELF
What has the affective modulated startle technique revealed about the differences between anxiety disorders?

Endophenotypes

The complexity of most disorders presents a challenge to attempts to understand their causal basis. The traits that underlie clinical disorders are called *endophenotypes* (Gottesman & Shields, 1967, 1972),[4] and have been applied to most forms of psychiatric disorder. This idea goes back to Wilhelm Johanssen, who reported, from his work on self-fertilized lines of beans, that the phenotype is an imperfect indicator of the genotype, and the same genotype may give rise to a variety of phenotypes; also, the same phenotype may have arisen from different genotypes (see Gottesman & Gould, 2003). Thus, it cannot simply be assumed that a single phenotype (be it the colour of beans or a psychiatric condition) has a same genotype, or that different phenotypes must have different genotypes. This genetic reality poses a problem for psychiatric diagnosis and aetiology. The endophenotype approach attempts to circumvent this problem, for only in diseases with a classic Mendelian pattern of inheritance is the genotype indicative of the phenotype – however, most psychiatric conditions are polygenic.

The endophenotype approach argues for the search for the basic underlying dispositions and dysfunctional neural systems implicated in the disorder – in the case of schizophrenia, eye movement dysfunctions have been extensively studied – rather than exclusively focusing on the surface features of signs and symptoms (see chapter 17). Gottesman and Shields (1967) described endophenotypes as internal phenotypes (sometimes called 'intermediate phenotypes', 'biological markers' or 'vulnerability traits') discoverable by 'biochemical test or microscopic examination', not observable to the unaided eye. It may be these intermediate phenotypes that are acted on by evolutionary pressures. Psychophysiological procedures play a fundamental role in measuring these endophenotypes, and thus make a fundamental contribution to our understanding of the aetiology and pathophysiology of psychiatric disorder – in fact, endophenotypes may be measured by neurophysiological, biochemical, endocrinological, neuroanatomical, cognitive and neuropsychological measures. For example, in relation to the complex (exo)phenotypic nature of PTSD, the following strategy has been advanced.

> One way to circumvent these problems is to perform genetic analysis of traits *associated* with PTSD, rather than PTSD itself, an approach that has been fruitful for other diseases with complex modes of inheritance. Hypothalamic–pituitary–adrenal axis hypofunction, physiologic markers of increased arousal, and increased acoustic startle response are all potential PTSD-associated traits that might be susceptible to genetic analysis. (Radant et al., 2001, p. 203; italic added)

ASK YOURSELF
what are the advantages of the 'endophenotype approach' over the conventional focus on symptoms?

Classical Conditioning

Conditioning and learning processes have played an important role in understanding the aetiology and treatment of many anxiety conditions. *Cognitive-behavioural therapy*, which is now used for many forms of neurotic disorder (especially depression), traces its theoretical roots to behavioural principles based on conditioning theories, namely classical and instrumental conditioning.

Conditioning studies have been used in high-risk research to identify premorbid risk factors implicated in vulnerability to disorder. For example, children at risk for later anxiety disorder, followed over an 8-year period, were characterized as having: (a) increased startle reflex; (b) heightened autonomic stress reactivity; and (c) deficits in associative learning (Merikangas et al., 1999).

The classical conditioning theory of neurosis states that conditioned stimuli (CSs; initially neutral stimuli) become associated with aversive unconditioned stimuli (UCSs), and that the anxious response is a conditioned (emotional) response (CR; see chapter 7). Where the UCS has not been particularly traumatic, it is usually assumed that individual differences in the ease with which some people develop CRs explains the clinical manifestation. It is also assumed that a generalization process occurs so stimuli that are similar to the original CSs take on the power to elicit the CR; here too individual differences may be observed (Gray, 1975).

However, there is surprisingly little *direct* support for this conditioning theory, and the processes of conditioning involved in anxiety seem to be complex. For example, there may be an important *incubation* process, which serves: (a) to *prevent* extinction of the non-reinforced CS; and (b) to *increment* the strength of the CR (in the context of non-reinforcement, where extinction should be expected). In addition, once an aversive CS has been established, it is assumed that, in many clinical conditions (e.g., agoraphobia), instrumental conditioning occurs: avoidance of the feared stimulus leads to the conditioning of an instrumental (avoidance) response. This is known as the two-process theory of neurosis (see chapter 7).

Social phobia

In a classical conditioning study in social phobia patients, neutral faces were used as the CS and aversive odour as the UCS (Hermann et al., 2002). Both the social phobia and control groups conditioned: that is, they showed a CR (as measured by subjective and physiological reactions) to the face (CS+) associated with the UCS, as compared with the face (CS−) unpaired with the UCS. (It is typical to assess CRs in the extinction part of the experiment, where only the CS is presented – thus, the response cannot be an unconditioned one to the UCS.) Although the social phobics did not show enhanced conditionability, they did show a greater expectancy of the UCS, especially for the CS− faces that were never associated with the UCS; and also they showed a delay in extinction of their CR.

This study demonstrates that, by using a relatively simple classical conditioning procedure, considerable insight may be gained into the factors involved in the development of social phobia: this study also showed that social phobics generalize aversive associations to neutral (non-reinforcement) stimuli (in this case, faces); and once this spurious association is formed, they extinguish this response slowly. These findings make sense when seen in the light of the nature of social phobia. You and I are fearful of some stimuli and events, but most of us do not generalize this fear to all related events; in contrast, social phobics seem to have distorted associative learning that does link these unrelated events and thus sets up considerable fear and anxiety to social stimuli and events that for most of us would produce only the mildest of emotion reaction. The type of knowledge gained with this classical conditioning procedure would not be obtainable using other research approaches.

CS–UCS predictability

As described in chapter 7, conditioning involves the learning of the regularities of the environment, allowing modelling of the environment and therefore prediction and control. In this context, it is interesting that a deficit in associative learning increases the symptoms of anxiety: unpredictability is core to anxiety. Grillon (2002) undertook a differential conditioning procedure, in which one CS(+) predicted the UCS shock, the other CS(−) was not paired with UCS shock. CRs were measured by fear-potentiated startle (greater startle reactions to CS+ than to CS−), skin conductance and behavioural avoidance (i.e., not returning for the second testing session). Individuals who were unaware of the CS–UCS contingency did not show the differential conditioning; this was seen only in the aware individuals. Importantly, individuals who were unaware, and who did not condition, showed greater signs of anxiety and greater avoidance of the second session (however, it is possible to generate other explanations of this *association* other than a lack of control).

Conscious awareness

The role of conscious awareness in conditioning has been debated for many years. Some studies indicate that awareness is necessary (e.g., Grillon, 2002; see above), and this observation is often interpreted as showing the importance of cognitive factors in conditioning. However, other evidence seems to show that awareness is not important in conditioning.

Pavlovian conditioning paradigms, with backward masking of the CS, have been used to examine pre-attentive conditioning in various anxiety groups. In these experiments, the CS is presented, and after (approximately) 30 ms a second image is superimposed on the CS: this second image overwrites the CS image in the short-term memory and prevents further processing. (psychophysical experiments[5] are performed before the conditioning study to ensure that the backward mask has prevented the CS entering into conscious awareness). Some pictures (CS+) are paired with a UCS (electric shock), while other pictures (CS−) are not paired. Fear-relevant (FR; spiders and snakes) and fear-irrelevant (FI; flowers and mushrooms) serve as the CSs (half of each type are reinforced by the UCS) – this type of design is shown in table 15.1.

Table 15.1   Experiment with backward masking of the CS

	UCS paired	UCS unpaired
FR	CS+	CS−
FI	CS+	CS−

Preparedness

Ohman and Soares (1993) conditioned human beings to (unmasked) picture CSs of snakes or spiders and then presented these picture CSs again during (non-reinforced) extinction trials, but this time they were masked (i.e., presented below the threshold of awareness). The data revealed enhanced responding to masked shock-associated picture CSs+ compared with masked non-shocked picture CSs–, but only when they were fear-relevant (snakes or spiders). Such data points to preferential pre-attentive processing of fear-relevant stimuli, even when they are not (apparently[6]) consciously perceived. Similar results have been obtained with angry (fear-relevant) and happy (fear-irrelevant) faces, backward masked by neutral faces: the CRs to fear-relevant angry faces survived backward masking in extinction (e.g., Esteves et al., 1994). Wong, Shevrin and Williams (1994) replicated these findings and also reported EEG data relating to CS+ onset, which produced a slow negative potential, which is thought to be related to expectancy of a second, motivationally relevant stimulus.

Ohman and Soares (1998) found differential Pavlovian conditioning to masked picture CSs of snakes and spiders, but not flowers and mushrooms, during acquisition. The data show that participants do not need to be aware of the CS in order for conditioning to occur – such findings oppose the theory that conditioning occurs *only when* there is conscious awareness of the contingency between CS and UCS. Esteves et al. (1994) used happy or angry faces as CSs and neutral stimuli as masks during acquisition, and, once again, differential conditioning occurred (but only to 'prepared' angry-face CSs) in the absence of conscious awareness.

There is thus some evidence for the preparedness hypothesis of fear (see chapter 7), which argues that certain types of evolutionarily important stimuli (e.g., snakes/spiders) are biologically prepared to elicit strong physiological reactions and thus enter into rapid association with other stimuli. However, traditional conditioning theory, even when refined by the preparedness hypothesis, still does not easily explain the 'neurotic paradox' (see Eysenck, 1979): clinical anxiety does not follow the usual path of extinction that, according to classical Pavlovian theory (see chapter 7), should occur following withdrawal of the aversive UCS. It is often stated that conditioned emotional states are maintained by instrumental avoidance of the feared object; and, by this means, the CS does not receive adequate CS-alone presentation to support the process of extinction. This theory alone is rather inadequate to explain: (a) the continued maintenance of conditioned emotional responses; and (b) their actual increment without further reinforcement. Thus there is a 'neurotic paradox' to solve.

The 'neurotic paradox': incubation

Eysenck (1968, 1979, 1985) proposed an interesting incubation model of neurosis to explain this paradox. In addition to the lack of extinction, Eysenck argued that there are three conditions that promote incubation (i.e., the *increase* in strength of the CR on non-reinforced trials): (a) an intense UCS; (b) prepared stimuli (e.g., spiders/snakes); and (c) short exposure during extinction. In this complex theory, Eysenck argued that the type of classical conditioning that takes place during conditioning of neurosis is different from that in typical classical conditioning experiments, especially of the type used by Pavlov. First, CS–UCS conditioning produces a noxious CR (e.g., fear), and this CS-induced state has physiological properties similar to the original UCS-induced state; therefore, when the CS is presented, and the CR elicited (even in the absence of the aversive UCS), the CR represents a physiological state comparable to the original UCS. By this process, presentation of the CS-alone (in experimental extinction) is not psychologically experienced as CS-alone, but rather as CS plus a physiologically aversive reaction (CR) that has the reinforcing properties of the original aversive UCS. Accordingly, CS-alone has the power to reinforce (i.e., strengthen) the CS. By this process, CS-alone presentation can serve to increment (or incubate) emotional reactions. (For a discussion of incubation theory, see the peer commentaries on Eysenck, 1979.)

The validity of incubation theory has yet to be fully examined. There is evidence that fear-relevant stimuli enhance the acquisition of classical conditioned responses; and there is also good evidence that higher-intensity UCSs (e.g., shock or noise) also enhance acquisition; however, there is little evidence that the length the CS presented alone during extinction either maintains or increments emotional CRs.

In relation to the neurotic paradox and conditioning in general it is very surprising that temporal (time) factors are rarely systematically manipulated. Most classical conditioning studies measure behaviour in a very limited period of time (1 to 2 hours). Conditioned emotional reactions in the real world develop over time, and it would be unsurprising if there were not important temporal features to the development of pathological conditioned emotional responses. There is evidence that temporal delays and sleep have significant effects on memory and learning (e.g., Walker, 2005).

The 'neurotic paradox': cognitive mediation

One major alternative theoretical perspective that attempts to explain the neurotic paradox stresses the cognition mediation of UCS–CS relationships. According to this point of view, it is appraisal and expectations that strengthen emotional reactions to CSs, not an automatic process of stimuli associability. This theory can explain the neurotic paradox: extinction is retarded because of the covert rehearsal of the aversive stimuli, which serves to maintain, even strengthen, their association.

In support of this cognitive perspective, Davey (1995, 1997) proposed that phobic responding is related to a bias towards expecting aversive outcomes following encounters with the phobic stimulus, which in terms of conditioning may be described as a bias towards expecting an aversive unconditioned stimulus (UCS) following a phobic conditioned stimulus (CS). Contemporary conditioning accounts of specific phobias view these selective associations as a UCS expectancy bias, and hypothesize that this kind of overestimation may underlie the development and maintenance of phobias. This cognitive-created expectancy is rather like the difference in the ease of conditioning with prepared and non-prepared CS: individuals with this expectancy bias subjectively experience the UCS as more aversive and of higher intensity (higher-intensity stimuli usually lead to stronger conditioning effects).

The disease-avoidance hypothesis

In addition to the expectancy bias, other processes seem to contribute to fear reactions. Take the case of animal phobias, which are among the most common of all the phobias. It is obviously sensible to fear animals such as snakes, spiders and large predators, as they are potentially dangerous; but it is not so clear why some many people are afraid of invertebrates, such as cockroaches, snails, etc. To account for this observation, Matchett and Davey (1991) proposed the *disease-avoidance model*, which predicts that common animal fears are mediated by two kinds of selective associations: (a) a bias towards expecting physically harmful consequences associated with predatory animals (e.g., tigers, alligators, sharks), consistent with traditional models of specific fears that assume that phobic responding is driven by the fear of physical harm; and (b) a bias towards expecting disgust or disease-relevant consequences (e.g., slugs, cockroaches, rats). In a test of the disease-avoidance model, Davey, Cavanagh and Lamb (2003) compared UCS expectations elicited by: (a) high-predation animals; (b) low-predation animals; and (b) safe animals. Using a 'thought conditioning procedure', experimental participants were asked to estimate the probability of pictures of high-predation animals (e.g., tigers, sharks, alligators), low-predation animals (e.g., spiders, slugs, cockroaches, rats) and safe (fear-irrelevant) animals (e.g., kittens, rabbits) being followed by either (a) an electric-shock UCS (painful consequence), or (b) a nausea-inducing drink UCS (disgust-relevant consequence), in a hypothetical classical conditioning experiment. The results showed that high-predation animals were selectively associated with a pain UCS, while low-predation animals were selectively associated with a disgust-relevant UCS (safe animals were not strongly associated with either class of UCS). The authors concluded that these findings provide evidence for a possible associative mechanism by which changes in non-specific levels of disgust sensitivity may directly affect levels of fear to low-predation animals. The important point about such data is the indication that people have expectations about innate stimuli which serve to enhance their salience and their ease of associability, especially with UCSs.

> **ASK YOURSELF**
> Do psychophysiological techniques offer the best way to test experimentally hypotheses concerning anxiety?

Cognitive Models of Anxiety

The previous section presented cognitive explanations of anxiety and how these might help to account for some of the problems found with traditional models of classical conditioning. This section summarizes the Wells and Matthews (1994) model – the Self-Regulative Executive Function (S-REF) model – which attempts to model the cognitive processes in neurotic reactions. This model gives a flavour of the types of concepts and processes employed in this theoretical perspective.

The mind is seen as a cybernetic system that aims to achieve personal goals in an uncertain environment; this approach is based on the idea of self-regulation of emotion (Carver & Scheier, 1998). The desired state of the world is compared with the actual state of the world, initiating compensatory processes designed to reduce this difference.

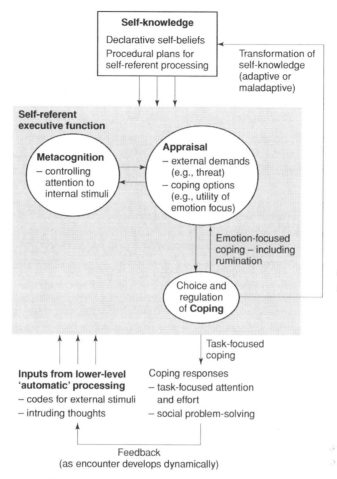

Figure 15.4 Wells and Matthews' (1994) S-REF model. (From Matthews, Deary & Whiteman, 2003; used with permission.)

Cognitive appraisal assesses these two states of the world, and the compensatory mechanisms represent coping mechanisms. The personality factors that predispose people to neurosis (i.e., neuroticism; see chapter 17) are distributed across multiple processes; these processes together form a 'cognitive architecture' (Matthews, Deary & Whiteman, 2003). The separate components and their interactions are shown in figure 15.4.

Self-knowledge concerns the content of self-beliefs, which includes declarative and procedural forms of knowledge (see chapter 7) – such knowledge concerns plans and skills for dealing with challenges. This knowledge can prime the anxious individual to deal with threat in a characteristic manner (e.g., rapid avoidance). As noted above, anxious individuals have overtly negative self-beliefs and tend to overreact to aversive stimuli.

Cognitive stress processes refer to the processes that subserve attempts to understand and manage stressful events, entailing controlled attentional processing that requires cognitive effort. Appraisal of stimuli – *secondary* appraisal involves understanding the significance of the stimuli from the individual's viewpoint – and coping – characteristic ways of dealing with specific situations – are two of the major processes. Also considered important is *metacognition* – loosely speaking, thinking about thinking – which seems distorted in anxious individuals: that is, they tend to have a greater concern for their own thoughts and feelings and as a result are often preoccupied (e.g., *meta-worry* is seen in GAD patients, who worry that their own worries are difficult to control).

Lower-level processes are more automatic, relying less upon controlled effortful processes; these processes tend to fire off when specific threat stimuli are encountered. Neuroticism in general and anxiety in particular seem to be related to these lower-level processes, as well as to self-knowledge processes and conscious strategies.

The S-REF model attempts to account for neuroticism and anxiety in the following manner. Lower-level processing of external stimuli or internal thoughts triggers intrusive ideation, which signals a threat to the individual; this perceived threat then leads to attempts at self-regulation (e.g., minimizing the threat): these attempts are performed by the executive system, which evaluates the threat and selects a coping strategy. These coping efforts may be *emotion-focused* (directed towards thoughts and feelings) or *problem-focused* (directed at behaviours that alter the external reality). When coping is successful the executive system stops its processing.

In the case of anxiety, dysfunctional cognitions tend to *propagate*: appraisals of threat and inappropriate coping strategies lead to enhanced perception of the threat, setting up a vicious circle that serves to maintain and even 'incubate' the emotion. Rumination is seen as a form of emotion-focused coping that only leads to more elaborated representations of negative self-beliefs, making negative self-referent information more accessible. Within the S-REF model, neuroticism is seen as a general property of the system.

Biological *and* Cognitive Accounts

Cognitive accounts of depression and anxiety have tended to replace, or supplement, more traditional theories couched in purely behavioural terms (i.e., stimuli and responses).[7] For example, Seligman's original theory of learned helplessness, which argued that animals, including human beings, instrumentally learn that external uncontrollable aversive events are beyond their behavioural control and thus 'give up' (expressed as depression), has given way to a cognitive theory of attributional style, consisting of explanations (accessible to consciousness) given for good and bad events (Abramson, Seligman & Teasdale, 1978; also see chapter 14 above). Tasks taken from mainstream cognitive psychology (such as the emotional Stroop task) have also been widely used in the study of the disordered cognitive processes in depression and anxiety. This research has been fruitful in identifying a number of perceptual, processing and memory biases.

First, individuals with depressive symptoms tend to show a deficit in explicit memory for positively valenced material; they find it difficult to retrieve happy memories. They also sometimes show a bias in favour of retrieving negative self-referential material – however, few studies show a bias within implicit memory – that is, automatic associative memory, measured by such tasks as stem completion (see chapter 8). Second, individuals with anxiety symptoms do not show explicit memory bias for threat-related material (although panic disorder may be unique in this respect); but there is evidence for an implicit memory bias (McNally, 1995), as well as an attentional bias for threat-related material (Musa et al., 2003).

The S-REF model, summarized above, illustrates the power of models couched in terms of processes common in cognitive psychology to capture some of the main aspects of neurotic thinking, coping and behaviour. Important for such models is their ability to *predict* experimental outcomes rather than simply *describe* what is observed in clinical disorders. In this regard the S-REF model is economical in reducing the variety of clinical symptoms observed to a set of well-delineated functional (cognitive) processes, which hold important implications for understanding the aetiology, maintenance and treatment of such disorders (see Matthews, Deary & Whiteman, 2003).

Biological models tend to focus on *why* cognitive processes are distorted in clinical conditions; for example, why are anxious individuals more sensitive to punishment than non-anxious individuals (Corr, Pickering & Gray, 1997)? This *why* question entails an evolutionary basis, as well as a focus on brain systems that mediate basic behavioural processes of approaching appetitive stimuli and avoiding aversive stimuli (see chapter 17 below). The *why* question and the types of research questions it attempts to answer are compatible with computational models of the structure of cognitive processing.

It is important to bear in mind that cognitive studies and biological studies are *not* alternative theoretical perspectives, as is sometimes suggested and popularized by the flag-waving of the 'cognitive revolution' of the 1950s and 1960s. When the animal constructs an expectation that when it presses a lever a reinforcer follows, then this too can be considered a 'cognitive' process. Certainly modern-day behavioural accounts incorporate a necessary cognitive element.

Now that the dust has begun to settle on this major period of upheaval in psychology, it would seem more appropriate to view these two approaches as complementary ways of describing the same phenomena. This unification of approaches – and the dissolution of the biological–cognitive debate – is seen most clearly in neural network and connectionist approaches, which have an important role for associative links within highly complex 'cognitive' networks of activation patterns and semantic relations.

Neural networks

A number of neural network models have been developed to study classical conditioning in non-human animals (e.g., Grossberg & Schmajuk, 1987; Armony et al., 1995; Salum, Morato & Roque-da-Silva, 2000). These attempt to model behavioural reactions to stimuli in prototypical animal learning situations. They are also being used to model symptoms and treatment responses in patients. For example, Ownby and Carmin (1996) developed a neural network model of panic disorder that is able to simulate both normal and severe levels of anxiety. Manipulations of the network were also able to simulate the effects of 5-HT medication and cognitive-behavioural therapy.

ASK YOURSELF
Why are 'biological' and 'cognitive' theories couched in different languages?

■■□ Molecular Genetics of Neurosis

Now that some of the major features of depression and anxiety have been summarized, let us turn our attention to the molecular aspects of these related disorders. For the present, these disorders are best considered together because, in general, the molecular genetics of psychopathology is still at a very early stage of development, and the specific differences between depressive and anxiety disorders have yet to be elucidated. This literature is still rather confused (and confusing), with positive findings being quickly followed by a failure to replicate – however, these failures to replicate may be due to methodological issues rather than substantive theoretical ones. However, given the importance of this area, this is not a good enough reason to shy away from the considerable advances that are being made. Given the current state of the literature, a picture is painted in broad-brush strokes.

Serotonin genes

Given the importance of SSRIs in treating both depression and anxiety, it should come as little surprise that genes involved in the regulation of 5-HT systems have received considerable research attention. The 5-HT transporter (5-HTT) gene has been extensively studied (for a review of this literature, see Lesch, 2003). This gene is involved in the fine-tuning of 5-HT transmission; also it is an important regulator of morphogenetic activities during early brain development (i.e., cell proliferation, migration, differentiation and synaptogenesis), as well as during adult neurogenesis and plasticity.

The brainstem raphe 5-HT system is the most widely diffused neurotransmitter system in the brain. Raphe neurons project to a number of regions, including the cortex, hippocampus and amygdala. 5-HT neurotransmission is important in emotional behaviour, involved in integrating sensory processing, motor activity, cognition and circadian rhythms, including food intake, sleep and reproductive behaviour. 5-HT orchestrates the activity of several other neurotransmitter systems, and it is one of the major neural modulators in the brain – it is viewed as a master control neurotransmitter, with highly complex functions. Unfortunately for our attempt to understand 5-HT neurotransmission, there are many pre- and postsynaptic receptor subtypes, each of which serves different functions – this fact alone gives us a clue to why the SSRIs are effective in treating so many different neurotic conditions. However, fortunately for us, 5-HT neurotransmission is terminated by reuptake via the 5-HTT receptor complex, and this complex is the initial site of action of widely used 5-HT reuptake inhibitor antidepressants (SSRIs), as well as many anxiolytic drugs.

5-HTTLPR

Human 5-HTT is encoded by a single gene on chromosome 17, composed of 14–15 exons. Expression of this gene is modulated by the 5-HTT gene-linked polymorphism region (5-HTTLPR), in a regulatory region of the transcription site (figure 15.5). In human beings the majority of alleles are composed of either 14 or 16 repeat elements ('short' and 'long' alleles; alleles with up to 22 repeat elements sometimes occur). The short and long 5-

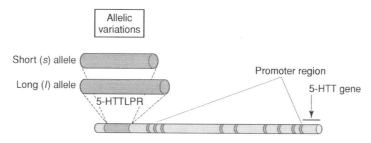

Figure 15.5   5-HT gene and its transcription, showing allelic variation in 5-HTTLPR region, which influences the promoter region, which, in turn, influences the transcription of the 5-HT gene.

HTTLPR variants modulate transcriptional activity of the 5-HTT gene promoter, 5-HTT protein concentration and 5-HT uptake activity. The short (*s*) variant is associated with lower 5-HTT expression and function, and therefore less uptake of 5-HT; the long (*l*) version is associated with higher 5-HTT expression and function, and thus related to increased 5-HT reuptake, and therefore may be a risk for affective disorder (i.e., too low a level of synaptic 5-HT activity).

It may be surprising to see that *less* transcription of the 5-HTT gene is associated with higher neuroticism scores; it might have been thought that less transcription of this gene would result in less reuptake of 5-HT in the synaptic cleft and thus a lower level of neuroticism – after all, do not SSRIs block this reuptake and thus alleviate neurotic symptoms? It is thought that 5-HTT plays a crucial role in brain development that differs from its functions in regulating neurotransmission, thus this inconsistency is more apparent than real (Lesch et al., 2002). It is supposed that chronic low levels of transcription found in the *s*-variant carriers produce a reuptake system that is more active, although the precise mechanism of this process is not known (e.g., by creating supersensitive receptors).

The pattern of evidence relating 5-HTTPLR to mood disorder is mixed. Some evidence has related it to both unipolar and bipolar depression (e.g., Collier et al., 1996), but other studies have failed to replicate these results (see Lesch, 2003). It is difficult to know what to conclude from these initial promising results and subsequent failures to replicate (replication is one of the key criteria in science). There are several reasons for failure to replicate, apart from the obvious one, that the initial findings were due to chance (i.e., a type I statistical error): (a) inadequate statistical power, which leads to a failure to detect a real association present in the population from which the sample is drawn; (b) problems with definitions of affective illness; and (c) difference in the allelic frequencies in the population studies (these vary across ethnic groups), which makes real effects difficult to identify. In addition, there may be important moderating factors, involving other genes: perhaps the final answer involves our knowing: (a) the action of separate genes; and (b) the interaction of these genes in the expression of the phenotype.

In relation to responses to antidepressants, one study reported that 5-HTTPLR genotype was related to response to the SSRI antidepressant fluvoxamine (Smeraldi et al., 1998). Both homozygotes for the long variant (*l/l*) of the 5-HTT promoter and heterozygotes (*l/s*) showed a better response to fluvoxamine than homozygotes for the short variant (*s*/*s*). In a second study (Benedetti et al., 1998), interactions between 5-HTTPLR genotype and responses to the antimania/antibipolar agent lithium and the antipsychotic drug clozapine, both of which are assumed to act through 5-HT mechanisms, have been demonstrated. These studies are examples of pharmacogenetics (see chapter 12) and highlight the importance of genotype for responses to drugs.

Dopamine

Genes involved in dopamine neurotransmission have also been studied in relation to mood disorder (Kalidindi & McGuffin, 2003). This dopamine hypothesis is based on a number of different lines of evidence. First, drugs used in the management of affective disorders often also influence dopaminergic activity. Second, among mood stabilizers, lithium reduces dopaminergic transmission, and the antipsychotics used in the treatment of mania and psychotic depression exert their action mainly through the blocking of dopamine receptors. Third, psychostimulants (e.g., amphetamine), which enhance the activity of dopaminergic transmission, cause a transient elevation of mood in patients with depression. Fourth, a depressive syndrome is frequently observed in Parkinson's patients, which is caused by dopamine depletion. Fifth, dopamine receptor antagonists are sometimes the cause of pharmacologically induced depression. Sixth, there is evidence of reduced levels of the dopamine metabolite *homovanillic acid* in cerebral spinal fluid in depressed patients with motor retardation. Lastly, dopamine has long been associated with appetitive responses (McClure, Daw & Montague, 2003). While these observations in no way prove that dopamine is directly involved in depression, they do, at the very least, raise the possibility of such an involvement. In support of this hypothesis of depression, there is some evidence that dopamine receptor and transporter genes are involved.

For example, Manki et al. (1996) studied the dopamine D_2, D_3 and D_4 receptor and transporter gene polymorphisms and compared bipolar and unipolar patients with controls: they found a significant association between the short allele (the 5-repeat sequence) of the D4 receptor gene and major depression. It was also found that the 4-repeat allele was significantly less frequent in mood-disordered patients than in controls. Benedetti et al. (1998) found that delusional symptoms were significantly associated with long DRD4 variant 7-repeat allele-containing genotype in bipolar and unipolar affective disorder. An association between the DRD4 and unipolar depression was also reported by Macciardi et al. (1994), although there have been failures to report this association in bipolar disorder, suggesting that the association is with unipolar depression only.

Although there may be sound theoretical reasons for suspecting involvement in affective disorder of dopamine receptor genes, the results so far are inconclusive. At best, there seems some support for a small role of functional polymorphisms in the DRD3 and DRD4 genes.

Other neurotransmitter systems

Other studies have examined the role of different classes of neurotransmitters (e.g., norepinephrine, GABA and glutamate) and enzyme systems (especially catecholamine-

O-methyltransferase, COMT), and their respective gene complexes. COMT is an enzyme – much like MAO – that is responsible for the degradation of monoamine neurotransmitters: greater activity of this enzyme leads to less neurotransmitter availability. COMT is involved in both dopamine and norepinephrine pathways. Research in these areas is ongoing, and it will be some time before the roles played by these systems in depression have been fully clarified.

Chapters 2 and 13 indicated that the relationship between genes and the environment is complex – statements of 'genes for' are far too simple-minded. Although family and twin studies point to a substantial genetic contribution to the aetiology of neurotic disorders, identification of the nature of these genetic contributions is difficult. It is possible that genetic heterogeneity (different genes being involved in different families), incomplete penetrance of genes, pleiotropy (i.e., multiple effects of genes), epistasis (i.e., the interaction of genes) and gene–environment interactions all contribute to the final genetic picture.

ASK YOURSELF
How close are we to knowing the genetic basis of anxiety?

Evolutionary Perspectives

Nesse and Williams (1997) discuss the role of evolutionary factors in anxiety. They note that, under certain circumstances, anxiety is beneficial; and this is most evident in the 'fight–flight' reaction highlighted by Cannon (1929): immediate threat elicits a fleeing response; but if the threat is unavoidable (e.g., it is close in proximity) then a fight response is appropriate and the associated negative subjective state serves the function of motivating this response (see chapter 17). Under certain circumstances, fight–flight responses may be *adaptive*, but extreme reactions are *maladaptive* when they are elicited by stimuli that do not present a real threat.[8]

In terms of the anxiety disorders presented above, agoraphobia, specific and social phobias and OCD are clearly maladaptive in the sense that they lead to individual suffering; but a loathing for and avoidance of spiders, snakes, strangers, potentially dangerous places, etc., serves an evolutionary function, namely avoidance of potential danger and hence survival and the increased probability of reproduction (i.e., gene replication). PTSD is termed *maladaptive*, even though it is based on a life-threatening event; but it is adaptive in the sense that it may be an attempt to understand and, therefore, avoid the situation in the future (Marks, 1969; Marks & Nesse, 1997). What would be truly maladaptive in evolutionary terms would be indifference to the experience of life-threatening events.

This discussion shows that there is an important distinction between what is mal(adaptive) in evolutionary terms and in personal terms. In evolutionary terms, the smoke-detector principle of anxiety argues that the cost of getting killed once is much greater than the cost of responding hundreds of times to a false alarm (smoke without the fire): it is obvious which behavioural strategy would be favoured by natural selection. Equally maladaptive in evolutionary terms is the absence of anxiety (*hypophobics*), which leads to injury and compromised reproductive fitness. Seeing adaptive advantage from the gene's-eye view of selfish reproduction helps us to understand why apparently maladaptive traits have evolved, and why they are so often associated with personal suffering: the blind process behind gene replication does not care if we feel terrified, depressed or anxious; it only 'cares' that we avoid life-threatening (and, therefore, replication-limiting) danger, motivated by fear, and develop emotions that promote reproduction (e.g., 'romantic love') and maintenance of the resulting replication machines (i.e., offspring; i.e., 'parental love').

The evolutionary explanation of the anxiety disorders highlights a number of features of fear/anxiety (Marks & Nesse, 1997) that give clues to their ultimate functions: (a) they are not a random set of threatening stimuli, but specific to stimuli and events that played an important part in our evolutionary history (e.g., snakes and spiders, but not electricity, traffic, guns and high-fat food); and (b) they are strongly age-graded (e.g., young children are afraid of strangers). In this sense, fears are said to be 'prepared' (see above), and have an innate power to induce fear or require only a small number of learning trials to be firmly established. Common feared objects/situations highlight the evolutionary basis of anxiety: darkness, being away from home, and strangers; babies and young children show distress when separated from parents or left alone with strangers; toddlers fear heights; etc. In this regard, it is interesting that, in adolescents, fear-potentiated startle is induced in the dark (Grillon et al., 1999); in animals that forage at night and remain behaviourally quiet during the day, exposure to bright light produces fear-potentiated startle (see Grillon & Baas, 2003).

In the case of some anxiety disorders, evolutionary theory provides a strong explanation for the nature of the symptoms. Consider panic attacks. As noted by Nesse (1997), panic may be viewed as an adaptation evolved to facilitate flight from a life-threatening situation; and the sudden increase in heart rate and strength of cardiac contractions sends extra blood to the muscles while the gut feels empty and the skin blanches and becomes cold as blood is moved elsewhere; rapid and deep breathing increases blood oxygen content; cooling sweat is secreted, muscles tighten and tremble; and there is intense mental ability focused on escape: the overwhelming urge to flee the situation provides the emotional drive to escape. These are the type of physiological and psychological reactions that might be expected if we were face to face with a dangerous animal.

Chapter 18 discusses consciousness in terms of a 'what-if' simulation capacity of the external world. This process is especially useful in planning future behaviours: instead of learning how to avoid the lion in the real world, we can instead run through different scenarios 'off-line' and compute the likely consequences – we do this all the time in daily life. Chapter 17 contends that much of our cognitive processing is concerned with negative events – Darwin noted that people are much more affected by punishment than by reward. We need only listen to other people, or to monitor our own thoughts, to realize how much of our cognition is preoccupied with punishment-related ideas. Chapter 14 presented one possible explanation of depression in the form of unavoidable exposure to threatening stimuli (e.g., crowded modern environments). In relation to anxiety (but the same argument applies to depression), the running of 'what-if' simulations of potentially negative events may itself produce pathological levels of anxiety in vulnerable individuals, especially those who generalize these imaginary events to real-world events. Indeed, such off-line processing may sensitize individuals to 'on-line' real negative events. The 'positive thinking' industry is organized around this very idea. It is probable that cognitive biases are of special importance in what-if simulations. Thus, psychopathology may be a price paid for our higher cognitive functions. Other evolutionary explanations are presented in the next chapter.

An evolutionary analysis separates ultimate (distal) functional causes from the proximal (local) mechanisms that tend to dominate psychological and psychiatric approaches. Whereas the social psychiatrist may ask questions about the role of social support in the aetiology of and recovery from depression, the evolutionary psychiatrist is interested in *why* such support is so important. Answers to these questions are reasonably easy to come by in the case of anxiety and, to a lesser extent, depression (see chapter 14); and in the next chapter evolutionary explanations are surveyed for a type of psychopathology that would appear less amenable to analysis in terms of Darwinian fitness, namely schizophrenia.

> **ASK YOURSELF**
> Are there any therapeutic implications of evolutionary explanations of anxiety?

Conclusion

The anxiety disorders comprise a large part of psychiatry and afflict a large number of people to a crippling degree. Most of us experience anxiety at some point, usually in response to some perceived threat. The variety of ways anxiety is manifest poses a challenge to theories that aim to identify a common theme to all the subvarieties – there are important differences between the disorders in terms of pharmacology and psychophysiological findings. However, as discussed in chapter 17, there are reasons for thinking that these different disorders can be understood under a common causal umbrella.

Learning Questions

1. Do all the various anxiety disorders have a single core cause?
2. What does the modulated startle reflex reveal about disordered processes in anxiety?
3. Are biological and cognitive accounts of anxiety incompatible or different sides of the same coin?
4. Describe the 5-HT gene and its importance in understanding the effects of pharmacological treatments.
5. If anxiety serves an evolutionary function, then why does it appear in a 'pathological' form?

NOTES

1 For the moment fear and anxiety are conflated, but as discussed in Chapter 17 there are good reasons for believing that these emotions reflect the operation of two separate, although related, negative emotional systems.

2 Meta-analysis is a procedure used in literature reviews in which data from individual studies are pooled together, weighted by sample size and subjected to statistical analysis. This procedure provides a statistical summary of the whole literature, and can help to explain inconsistencies by examining the effects of moderator variables (gender, age, effects of medication, etc.). In the case of PTSD, moderating variables are length of time of illness (recent patients

show exaggerated startle whether they are medicated or not) and severity (less severe cases do not show exaggerated startle) (Grillon & Baas, 2003).

3   A common confusion concerns the difference between *psychopathology* and *psychopathy*. The two are *not* the same. Psychopathology refers to the science of disease of the mind, or psychiatry, encompassing *all* psychological disorders; psychopathy is only *one* such disorder – in fact only one of the many personality disorders that exist.

4   In this context, 'endo' is used to refer to internal processes that are not directly observable; and measures of endophenotypes consist of laboratory procedures that allow reliability of measurement and appropriate analysis.

5   *Psychophysics* is a branch of psychology concerned with relating psychological sensation and experience to stimuli parameters (e.g., duration, intensity and frequency). Psychophysical functions are then calculated which show for each level of the parameter the probability and intensity of the sensation/experience. In the case of conscious awareness, participants are presented with various combinations of CS duration and mask duration and asked to make a forced choice of some type (e.g., indicate whether the face is emotive or not, or say whether it is male or female).

6   The problem with back-masking experiments is that there are considerable individual differences in forced-choice accuracy, as well as a practice effect in performance: some individuals can reliably and consciously identify faces at very low levels (e.g., 20 ms) and furthermore some types of emotive faces (e.g., fear) are more easy to identify than others (e.g., disgust; P. J. Corr, unpublished data). One option is to reduce CS exposure to levels (e.g., 10 ms) that are below the conscious threshold for all participants, but then there is the problem of showing that such stimuli are processed at all by the brain in sufficient detail to generate a response. An alternative strategy is to use long CS duration intervals (e.g., 170 ms), but to degrade the images with visual noise, thus preventing consciousness awareness.

7   Most theories are somewhere in between on this behavioural–cognitive dimension. More realistically, theories could be positioned in one of the quadrants defined by a two-dimensional framework in which theories can have differing amounts of behavioural and cognitive components.

8   In one interesting study, individuals with higher levels of anxiety were shown to have fewer accidents, suggesting that anxiety serves a protective role by motivating the avoidance of dangerous situations (Lee, Wadsworth & Hotop, 2006).

FURTHER READING

Baron-Cohen, S. (1997). *The Maladapted Mind: Classic Readings in Evolutionary Psychology.* Hove: Psychology Press.

Gray, J. A. & McNaughton, N. (2000). *The Neuropsychology of Anxiety: An Enquiry into the Functions of the Septo-Hippocampal System.* Oxford: Oxford University press.

Toates, F. & Coschug-Toates, O. (2002). *Obsessive–Compulsive Disorder: Practical, Tried-and-Tested Strategies to Overcome OCD.* London: Class Publishing.

Clinical Disorder III: Schizophrenia

Schizophrenia is a severe psychiatric disorder that accounts for a large number of hospital beds; it is one of the most costly disorders in terms of suffering of the individual (and their family) and economic loss to the nation. Schizophrenia poses a major challenge to biological psychology and psychiatry: it is one of the most intensively researched, and least understood, of all the psychiatric disorders. This chapter surveys some of the major approaches to understanding the biological basis of this disorder. (For a brief summary of schizophrenia, see Frangou & Murray, 1996a; for a thorough exposition of its biological bases, see Wong & Van Tol, 2003; for an authoritative resource site, go to: http://www.mentalhealthcare.org.uk/.)

Research has focused on the development of effective treatments for schizophrenia, and much progress has been made. However, schizophrenia research is important for another reason: it highlights the more general scientific problem of understanding the relationship between the physiological and psychological bases of the mind – the altered states of consciousness seen in schizophrenia cast light on some of the fundamental aspects of the mind–body problem (see chapter 1). Therefore, in the account that follows, it should be borne in mind that this chapter is not simply interested in schizophrenia but in what the study of schizophrenia has to say about general psychobiological processes of relevance to all areas of psychology. Indeed, many researchers study schizophrenia because of the scientific problems it highlights: by understanding the biological nature of schizophrenia (an important end in itself), much is learned also about the nature of the mind in general, as well as some of its more exotic manifestations (e.g., consciousness).

▨☐ Schizophrenia: The Split of Fact and Fiction

Although the study of the aetiology, course and treatment has revealed much about its underlying neuropsychological basis, schizophrenia remains a misunderstood disorder – unlike many terms, it is a word worn rough by a million tongues. It may be instructive to consider some of the reasons for this lack of understanding.

The first reason is that this disorder is complex and difficult to understand: it entails what seems like a bewildering number of symptoms, with no clear cause, and, in many patients, a chronic course that impairs family life. A second reason probably relates to the fact that most of us have not experienced the types of disordered states that characterize schizophrenia; in contrast, most of us have experienced, to one degree or another, fear/anxiety and depression sufficient to enable us to have some sense of what it must be like to suffer clinical extremes of these emotions. Thus, schizophrenia is subjectively unknown to many of us; and people tend to fear the unknown. This fear is fuelled by other factors.

One of these factors may be the name itself: 'schizophrenia' is something of an unusual word that does not have an everyday meaning (contrast this with 'depression' and 'anxiety') – indeed, its more common everyday usage refers to 'split personality' and ambivalence (e.g., 'we have a schizophrenic attitude to . . .'). It has a sinister linguistic quality to it. To make matters worse, the behaviour of patients having a diagnosis of schizophrenia (henceforth called 'schizophrenia patients'[1]) can be bizarre and sometimes seem threatening: there is an attributional bias towards blaming individuals for their behaviour – more specifically, people tend to assign internal causes to observed behaviour and underestimate the influence of situational factors (the 'fundamental attribution error': Ross, 1977); in the case of patients, the full range of influences on their behaviour is not appreciated. There is also the fear that one's own family may be affected by this severe disorder – cancer and HIV/AIDS are medical equivalents that similarly arouse fear and misunderstanding. These fears are then fuelled by the widespread promulgation of misunderstandings by the popular media, who have a taste for sensational stories involving violence and murders committed by a small number of schizophrenia patients.[2] Oft-repeated misunderstandings include calling murderers 'psychotic', or 'psychopathic' (which they may be, but usually are not);[3] and there is then the flaw of logic which associates the 'psychotic' with the dangerous: the fact that some murderers are clinically psychotic does not entail the conclusion that all psychotics are murderers.

The term 'schizophrenia' was coined, in 1908, by Bleuler (1950) to describe impairment in associative connections between thoughts and ideas – the loosening of associative threads – these cognitive 'splits' define the meaning of schizophrenia. Thus, the 'schizo' part refers to splits in psychological functions; in other words, a loss of psychological integrity of functioning.[4] One of the founders of the modern science of psychopathology and psychiatric classification, Emil Kraepelin, in 1919 termed this condition *dementia praecox* to highlight what was seen at that time as the progressively deteriorating nature of the illness (it was thought that there could be no return to premorbid functioning). Although this strict prognosis was incorrect and overly pessimistic, it does reflect the reality that most patients (but not all) never return fully to their previous level of psychological, social and occupational functioning.

Before outlining the clinical symptoms seen in schizophrenia, it is first necessary to clarify the difference between schizophrenia and psychosis. First, there are a number of disorders falling under the heading of 'psychosis' that are unrelated to schizophrenia: for example, *substance-induced psychosis* and *delusional* disorder – these disorders all involve a loss of contact with reality and gross distortion in thinking and perception. Psychosis is a defining feature of schizophrenia, but for a diagnosis of schizophrenia to be made there must be other symptoms. Thus, it is important to distinguish psychosis when it is an *associated feature* (e.g., in mania, depression and dementia) and where it is a *necessary feature*.

> **ASK YOURSELF**
> Is the widespread ambivalence towards schizophrenia a result of misunderstanding or a result of more complex factors?

DSM-IV-R Diagnostic Criteria

Schizophrenia patients present with a mixture of signs and symptoms that, for a diagnosis to be made, must have existed for most of the time during a 1-month period, with some signs and symptoms being present for at least 6 months. These signs/symptoms are associated with impaired social and occupational functioning, and are not better accounted for by other disorders (e.g., depression), drug abuse or general medical condition. Typical symptoms of schizophrenia include:

1. Cognitive dysfunctions, involving (a) perceptual aberrations (e.g., objects may look odd in some way; (b) hallucinations (i.e., perceptions without adequate sensory input); and (c) inferential thinking problems (e.g., delusions);
2. Language and communication problems, including impaired fluency, productivity of thought and speech;
3. Impaired behavioural monitoring, with behaviour being inappropriate to the situation;
4. Disrupted affect, including reduced hedonic capacity or inappropriate expression of emotion;
5. Motivational deficits, including lack of volition and drive.

No single symptom is *pathognomonic* of schizophrenia (i.e., absolutely essential); it is the combination of symptoms and their effects on everyday functioning that form the basis of diagnosis.

DSM-IV-R requires that two (or more) of the following symptoms are present for 1 month:

1. delusions;
2. hallucinations;
3. disorganized speech and thinking (e.g., frequent derailment or incoherence);
4. grossly disorganized or catatonic behaviour;
5. negative symptoms (e.g., affective flattening).

However, only one of these symptoms is required if delusions are bizarre or hallucinations consist of a voice keeping up a running commentary on the person's behaviour or thoughts, or two or more voices are conversing with each other. Emphasis is placed on impairment in social and occupational functioning, and not just on the presence of delusions or hallucinations (which are not necessarily seen as pathological in certain social contexts, e.g., religion). Below is a description of some of the major diagnostic signs and symptoms of schizophrenia.

Delusions

Delusions are erroneous beliefs involving a severe misinterpretation of events; they are inconsistent with the patient's educational and cultural background. Holding such a belief is not necessarily a sign of psychosis, for the 'delusion' may be a correct inference (e.g., someone may well be following you, such as a stalker). Truly psychotic beliefs: (a) are immune to reason; and (b) are not held by other people, even those who may be sympathetic to the specific content of the belief (e.g., MI6 / CIA implanting transmitting devices in the brains of critics of the government). Delusions fall into a number of distinct categories.

Persecutory delusions are most common: patients believe they are being tormented, tricked, followed or ridiculed; and that there are people who intend them harm.

Referential delusions are also common: patients believe that gestures, comments, passages from books, newspapers, television, song lyrics or environmental cues (e.g., names on shopfronts) are specifically directed to them. For example, the use of certain words by newsreaders may be interpreted as referring to them specifically. Both of these delusions are nicely epitomized by the case study of Dr Peter Chadwick, described below.

Somatic delusions involve a belief concerning the body (e.g., one's organs have been removed without leaving any physical sign).

Religious delusions entail some belief about one's importance in relation to the supernatural (e.g., God needs the patient to give away all their worldly possessions in order for the world to be saved from divine retribution).

Grandiose delusions involve the belief that one has great things to achieve (e.g., running for political office for the first time with the expectation of *immediate* spectacular success; e.g., being the leader of a new political party and Prime Minister or President within only a few years).

Delusions that are *not* bizarre (i.e., the belief *could* be true), and are not found with the other symptoms of schizophrenia (e.g., marked hallucinations or disorganized speech), are classified as 'delusional disorder'. In contrast to bizarre delusions (e.g., MI6 / CIA-implanted transmitting devices in the brain), non-bizarre delusions involve situations that could *conceivably* happen (e.g., being spied upon; poisoned or infected; loved at a distance; or deceived by spouse or lover).

Other delusions include *thought withdrawal* (i.e., ideas are being taken by an outside force), *thought insertion* (i.e., thoughts are being put into one's mind) and *control delusions* (i.e., one's actions are being manipulated by some outside force).

Hallucinations

Hallucinations are perceptions that occur in the absence of adequate sensory input (also there may be a gross distortion of sensory input). Hallucinations can occur in all sensory modalities, but auditory hallucinations are most common and probably most salient and intrusive. They are usually voices that are perceived as distinct from one's own thoughts ('self-talk'). They may start out as benign and friendly, but then they tend to turn hostile and intimidating. As noted above, certain types of hallucination are seen to be symptomatic of schizophrenia (e.g., several voices conversing with each other and voices maintaining a running commentary on the patient's thought and behaviour).

Chapter 5 highlighted that perceptions are not the direct 'seeing' of stimuli (i.e., there is not a one-to-one correspondence between the physical qualities of sensory stimuli and our subjective experience of them), but are constructed by brain processes. Therefore, the existence of hallucinations is not difficult to comprehend from the sensory processing perspective.

Disordered speech and thinking

Disordered thinking, or 'formal thought disorder', is thought by some psychiatrists to be the most important feature of schizophrenia; this is assessed through disordered speech, comprising: derailment of thought, distraction, loose associations, oblique answers to simple questions; and sometimes severe disorganization making speech incomprehensible, incoherent and a 'word salad' (i.e., words transposed in sentence construction).

Disorganized behaviour

Grossly disorganized behaviour may be shown in various ways: from childlike silliness to unpredictable agitation. Simple actions may be difficult to achieve (e.g., making a meal, maintaining hygiene or dressing appropriately for the weather conditions) or may be clearly inappropriate (e.g., public masturbation).

Catatonic motor behaviour

Catatonic motor behaviour entails a marked decrease in reactivity to the environment, sometimes reaching a degree of total unawareness (*catatonic stupor*), maintaining a rigid posture and resisting efforts to be moved (*catatonic rigidity*), active resistance to instructions or attempts to be moved (*catatonic negativism*), the assumption of inappropriate or bizarre postures (*catatonic posturing*), or purposeless excessive motor activity (*catatonic excitement*).

Negative symptoms

Affective flattening is common. The patient's face may appear immobile and unresponsive, with poor eye contact and reduced body language. *Alogia* is poverty of speech, manifested by brief, laconic, empty replies; there is a diminution of thoughts reflected in decreased fluency and productivity of speech. *Avolition* is an inability to initiate and persist in goal-directed behaviour. Patients may sit for long periods of time and show little interest in participating in work or social activities (negative symptoms can be difficult to evaluate because they are non-specific and found in a variety of disorders).

> **ASK YOURSELF**
> Are the symptoms of schizophrenia different in type or degree from normal processes and behaviours?

Psychiatric Research

For research purposes, schizophrenia is often defined along three main dimensions, but these dimensions are not used for DSM-IV-R diagnosis: (a) *positive symptoms*, involving an excess of normal functions, including delusions and hallucinations, speech and behaviour (these symptoms tend to be the florid symptoms that often accompany the acute phase of the illness and attract medical attention); (b) *negative symptoms*, entailing the absence of normal functions (see above); and (c) *cognitive symptoms*, involving thought disorder, the production and expression of language (e.g., loose and incoherent associations, and neologisms) and impaired attention and information processing, as revealed by neuropsychological testing (see chapter 8).

The diversity and complexity of symptoms pose a real problem to the researcher: reducing this complexity to a much smaller number of fundamental dimensions facilitates research into the dysfunctional processes underlying the disorder. However, researchers taking a more psychological perspective sometimes break down symptoms into finer categories; for example, positive symptoms may be broken down to a number of different types of delusional beliefs and the cognitive processes underlying these false beliefs are analysed in detail (for an overview of this literature, see Bentall et al., 2001).

Prodromal phase

Valuable information concerning the causal factors in schizophrenia comes from the study of the period immediately prior to the active phase of the illness, which is called the 'prodromal phase'. These prodromal symptoms are clinically subthreshold, usually of the positive type: patients may express a variety of unusual or odd beliefs that are not delusional in proportion (e.g., magical thinking); speech may be affected, being vague and digressive; and behaviour may be peculiar but not grossly disorganized. Also, negative symptoms are sometimes found with patients losing interest in previously rewarding activities, becoming socially withdrawn, less talkative and spending much of their day in bed. These are often the early signs of the disorder when parents witness their child 'gradually slipping away', often never fully to return.

Co-morbidity

Very often schizophrenia patients are depressed and/or anxious: they have much to be depressed and anxious about. These neurotic symptoms are often not sufficient to warrant a clinical diagnosis (especially OCD and panic disorder). However, in schizo-affective disorder, there are clinically significant levels of depression or mania. The main symptoms of schizo-affective disorder is an uninterrupted period of illness during which there is a major depression, manic or mixed episode (see chapter 14) concurrent with a diagnosis of schizophrenia. Also there must have been delusions or hallucinations for at least 2 weeks in the presence of prominent mood symptoms. There is also a considerable degree of co-morbidity in schizophrenia (e.g., substance-related disorders); for example, nicotine dependence is especially high (80–90 per cent), with heavy smoking of high-nicotine cigarettes common (see below).

Prevalence, course and risk factors

Schizophrenia typically develops between the late teens and mid-thirties, with onset prior to adolescence quite rare. Whereas for males the modal age of onset is between 18 and 25, for women it is between 25 and 30; and for females there is a second peak later in life (i.e., the female distribution is bimodal). Females tend to have better premorbid functioning than men, and when ill they tend to have positive symptoms that are more affective in nature, whereas for males negative symptoms are relatively more prominent. The prognosis (i.e., expected course and outcome of illness) is also more favourable for females. Many patients attempt suicide (upwards of 50 per cent), with some 10 per cent ending their life by this route.

The lifetime risk of schizophrenia is slightly less than 1 per cent (Gottesman, 1991). It is associated with a number of predictors: pregnancy and delivery complications (Geddes et al., 1999; Hultman et al., 1999; Jones et al., 1998); delayed developmental milestones (Jones et al., 1994); low premorbid IQ (David et al., 1997); and personality characteristics associated with impaired social relations (Malmberg et al., 1998). These predictors suggest that there are neurodevelopmental factors in the aetiology (cause) of schizophrenia.

Other predictors include: urban upbringing (Lewis et al., 1992); immigration (Hutchinson et al., 1996); and cannabis use (Zammit et al., 2002). The significance of these factors is still debated, although there is increasing evidence that cannabis use is a significant factor in the development and maintenance of schizophrenia (Cannon et al., 2003; Grech, Takei & Murray, 1998). Arseneault, Cannon and Murray (2004) reported that, at the individual level, cannabis use confers a twofold increase in the risk for schizophrenia; and that, at the population level, elimination of cannabis use would reduce the incidence of schizophrenia by approximately 8 per cent. Thus cannabis use, although not by itself either a necessary or sufficient cause of schizophrenia, is, none the less, an important *causal* factor that is not, as commonly assumed, a way for patients to alleviate the unpleasant symptoms of schizophrenia. However, these risks are small compared with having an affected first-degree relative (Owen & O'Donovan, 2003). Predictors of schizophrenia are discussed towards the end of this chapter.

ASK YOURSELF
Are clinical symptoms the only, or best, way to understand schizophrenia?

▣ Biological and Phenomenological Explanations

Before reviewing some of the biological approaches to schizophrenia, it is important to address the role that such explanations play in the wider psychological understanding of this disorder: there is more to 'understanding' schizophrenia than compiling a long list of deficits and possible neurochemical causes. In particular, the *content* of psychotic experiences has meaning for the patient, as the content of our experiences have meaning for you and me. These experiences are especially important in regard to treatment interventions, which should take into account the specific psychological states of the individual patient.

There has been much debate concerning the importance of biological explanations of schizophrenia – in the 1960s, the 'antipsychiatry' movement contended that schizophrenia was a normal reaction to a 'mad' world, and it was society that needed changing, not the mind of the schizophrenia patient. This theory is now discounted – however, there are stressors entailed by living in a 'mad' world that may play some part in the development of schizophrenia. There can be little doubt now that biological pathology plays a crucial role in schizophrenia, and the biological mediation of social factors is an important area of research. Throughout this book, it has been stressed that biological processes have an important psychological component, and the interplay between the 'body' and the 'mind' is two-way: drugs can alter the mind, but so too can mind states alter the body. In recognition of this possibility, cognitive-behavioural therapies (for delusions) are available to alter the disordered mind (Liberman, Spaulding & Corrigan, 1995).

This section summarizes these 'software' processes before delving into the 'hardware' of dysfunctional anatomical and neurochemical pathways. These different perspectives are different levels of description and analysis and, therefore, complementary approaches to understanding schizophrenia fully.

Theory of mind and attributional style

Theory of mind (ToM; Premack & Woodruff, 1978) has been widely used to study cognitive deficits in autistic children (see Baron-Cohen, 1995) – it refers to the ability to attribute mental states to the self and others: to 'mind-read'.[5] Frith (1994) suggested that ToM deficits also play an important role in schizophrenia, especially persecutory delusions (Craig et al., 2004). In addition to ToM, attributional style (AS; see chapter 14) may also be important: AS is the individual's habitual way of explaining events. Kaney and Bentall (1989) reported that paranoid patients tend to make excessively external attributions (i.e., blaming other people and circumstances) for negative events. The paranoid patient's avoidance of internal attributions may reflect a dysfunctional strategy for regulating self-esteem; on top of this dysfunctional coping style of external blaming, ToM deficits render patients unable to understand and predict the mind states of others, with the result that they are seen as threatening – as Charles Darwin noted, paranoia may be seen as a diffuse form of fear. These

ASK YOURSELF
What do theory of mind deficits reveal about the everyday function of 'mind-reading'?

cognitive biases can be the subject of cognitive-behavioural therapy, leading the patient to adopt less dysfunctional coping strategies and understanding the intentions and likely actions of other people. For a psychological account of schizophrenia, see Bentall (2003).

Dr Peter Chadwick: Psychologist with 'Psychotic Consciousness'

In order to understand the interplay of biological and psychological factors in psychosis it is appropriate to consider the work of Dr Peter Chadwick, whose (second) Ph.D. was concerned with the cognitive bases of schizophrenia. His account of schizophrenia is informed by the fact that he has experienced psychosis; and his description of his own 'psychotic consciousness' (Chadwick, 1992, 2001), informed by knowledge of the scientific literature, gives a unique insight into this disordered state of mind. In addition, his work highlights the need to make the biological approach relevant to the experiences of patients. As Chadwick (1992, p. xi) wryly noted,

> In their attempt to understand schizophrenia, psychiatrists and clinical psychologists are rather like impotent men writing about the joys of sexual intercourse using verbal reports and physiological recording of their data. Distanced from the phenomenon, their reports often seem contrived and alien.

This perspective has merit because schizophrenia is still not understood, and it should be possible to gain valuable insights into the nature of the disorder by paying attention to the subjective experiences of patients: this phenomenological analysis complements more detailed biological analysis. Not experiencing this state, we may find it difficult, if not impossible, to understand its subjective nature: 'The edges of sanity and the territory beyond turned out to be of a character quite beyond my wildest dreams or nightmares' (Chadwick, 1992, p. xi). Reading the research literature can also not lead to a full understanding; as Chadwick (1992, p. xii) stated,

> The essence and character of the psychotic subject is so easily lost or obscured in the, usually, dry pages of the experimental psychopathology literature – a fact which cannot help researchers and practitioners in this field to relate their conceptual knowledge to the flesh-and-blood people they deal with daily.

These quotations point to an important problem in understanding the psychology of psychiatric disorder: how is it possible to go from a first-hand, subjective perspective to general theories of physiological and psychological dysfunction? In the rest of this chapter the technical aspects of our subject should be seen in the light of the 'flesh and blood' of real people. Keeping in mind real people and their real everyday behaviour helps in this regard: biological psychology is not about abstract and disembodied systems (although they can be useful for exposition), but about real people with integrated systems that produce the states, processes and behaviours witnessed either first-hand or second-hand in others. This fact is nowhere more important than in disordered states of mind, but of course it is equally relevant to *all* states.

Figure 16.1 Dr Peter Chadwick, psychologist, who experienced 'psychotic consciousness' for several years, who obtained a second Ph.D. in schizophrenia research, and who has written a number of books focusing on the positive aspects of schizophrenia and schizotypy. (Photo © Richard Dye.)

Persecuted by 'the Organization': a psychotic day in the life of Dr Chadwick

In order to provide a fine-grained account of the experience of psychosis, sufficient to relate the phenomenon to underlying cognitive, neurochemical and social factors, Chadwick (2001), who received a diagnosis of schizo-affective disorder, recalls the course of a day during his psychosis. (For a full appreciation of Peter Chadwick's 'psychotic consciousness' during that day, you must read the original article; included are quotes to convey some of the subjective nature of the experience.)

'The Organization' is the persecutory group who are conspiring to monitor, mock and destroy. It is demanding he get a job, otherwise they will inflict some severe punishment.

> I *must* get a job.

He takes a bus from his home in Hackney, East London, to central London, to visit an employment agency; but no sooner is he on the bus than he notices that a lot of the shops on the right-hand side of the road are painted green; then he notices that those on the left side of the road are painted red.

> It's red and green again! Always this red and green.

Then the inference is made:

> They must have been painted recently by the Organization. What are they trying to tell me?! It's a clue. It must be. I must work it out. Work out the *meaning*.

Peter senses that people behind him on the bus are watching his every move, waiting to see what choice he takes so they can report back to the Organization.

> I hesitate, dither. I must 'get it right'. I'd written this phrase in a letter to Ivor a week or so ago and a bloke repeated it on the radio yesterday. The letter must have been passed to the Organization. 'Get it right . . . get it right . . . right, right.'

Peter decides to sit on the very edge of the right-hand seat.

> It's uncomfortable sitting like this. Very uncomfortable. It hurts my buttocks. But of course!! That's the whole point! The Organization are laughing at me!! It was all a con, a trick!! I go and sit in a left window seat. I smirk. At least I realized it was a trick. That's something I suppose.

In this bus experience the disordered state of mind, ideas of reference and paranoia are evident. In the following passage is evidence of loose associative thinking, associated with ideas of reference. On the bus Peter remembers someone on the radio talking about 'land' – the tone and emphasis of this radio person were such that Peter thought he must be trying to convey a message. Peter then picked up a newspaper and turned to the jobs section, and there in bold type were the words 'MOORFIELD'S Eye Hospital'.

> Of course! he was priming me for this! 'Moor' and 'fields', they connect with 'land'!! Yes!! It all fits, *this* is the job I must go for!

Once at the hospital, Peter was told that the job was for women only. A female to the left of the women interviewing Peter burst out laughing.

> She must recognise me. Another Organization trick. Very clever this one, very clever indeed. No wonder the girl was laughing. A master prank.

Then back on the street, he looks to see whether other people are looking and laughing at him:

> They are all looking ahead with straight faces. How strange. They must know the prank has worked . . . perhaps they don't agree with what the Organization is doing to me.

Then he notices two women standing on the street corner, and Peter notices that one turns to the other and says:

> 'They don't know who he is but they say he *is* a special person,' nodding as she says the latter words.

The obvious causal inference to Peter was:

> The Organization must, as I thought, be trying to work out *who* I am. Am I an alien? Satan? A prophet? Possessed by the devil? It must be something remarkable to justify all *this* going on!

Further down the road, two other women are talking and one seems to deliberately mouth the word 'BEM', which Peter then assumes must refer to Sandra Bem, the American gender psychologist:

> Is *she* in charge of the Organization. Is she the female King Kong of the whole thing?!! With a gender-bending maverick like me I wouldn't be surprised!! Bem!! *Of course*!

Having had enough of this ridicule, Peter decides to take an irregular route home to confuse 'the Organization'. The he notices that chalked on the pavement is the word 'B ⊕ M':

> . . . this hits me like 'a bomb'. Is this 'Bem the bomb'?! Is it possible that despite all my twists and turns the Organization have modelled my mind so well they can *still* predict me? They must have *known* I'd approach Hackney by walking along the road! Why put the word there otherwise?! They knew what had been said earlier. They probably *told* the women to say what they said. Even all *that* must have been 'set up'! And I walked right into it! As predicted!!

His heart sinks at the thought of this relentless cat-and-mouse game:

> Everything around me is 'orchestrated', orchestrated to the last detail, a set up to influence me. I cannot break free of it, whatever I do the Organization is ahead.

Back at his bedsit, there is no peace for Peter:

> Alas there's no privacy here . . . no privacy anywhere . . . the cracks in the walk plaster . . . hidden microcameras in them . . . the walls, people *listening* through them, like they did in Bristol all the time. The window . . . binoculars on it, cameras with zoom lenses . . . they can see me . . . people watching, watching. [. . .] Are they trying to puncture my pathetic bloated ego by their pranks . . . ? Teach me a lesson? Cure me of my evil sensuous ways? Make me 'come down'? Under observation, always under observation.

While he is listening to the radio, which is the main way the Organization communicates with Peter, some rationality seems to take over:

> After about 10 minutes I decide that the comments and chat, at least with reference to me, are quite random. How strange. This cannot be. It's never happened before.

But then he played with the idea that the word 'random' may hold some special significance:

> 'Random' . . . 'random' . . . does the word 'random' have some special meaning: Is that it? It must have. Is it an *anagram* perhaps?! Of course! It's an anagram of MAD RON . . . But Ron is my friend! Mad Ron! I must *avoid* 'Mad Ron' in future! Well Well. Of course. The Organization are very subtle . . . I must miss nothing . . . use all the hints. Now the people on the radio are laughing . . .' We're doing our best' a bloke says . . . yes, they know I've 'got it', cracked the code, worked it out. Indeed I must miss nothing.

This account of 'psychotic consciousness' reads like the experience of Winston Smith in George Orwell's novel, *1984*, which few of us can hardly appreciate. However, this is the nightmarish world in which many psychotic patients find themselves!

Psychological meaning

Chadwick (2001) provides a detailed psychological analysis of this troubled day in his life. He notes that in a paranoid psychosis there is the bizarre blend of reality and fantasy; all privacy is swept away, with the self and the external environment fused together: thoughts and actions are monitored by others; there is an external locus of control and a diminution in one's own ability, or need, to monitor one's own thoughts. There is an amplification of the speed of thought; and no time to reflect or monitor thoughts, checking for errors or false assumptions. There is increased 'meaning feeling': an increased perceptual sensitivity accompanied by a sense that there is meaning in perception, with colours becoming 'significant', lights brighter, as if they are trying to convey meaning; noises are louder and more threatening. One is surrounded by signs, nothing is mundane or trivial, and the world has hidden meanings. Attentional focus is heightened; and reality becomes reconstructed along delusional lines: 'The delusional system . . . sprawls like a massive magnetic net ready to attract virtually any event, incident or sense impression to it.'

The sections that follow provide scientific evidence to help us understand these disordered psychotic states. It is important to try to keep in mind the *psychological* experience of schizophrenia and how this experience (influenced by social factors) may contribute to the aetiology of schizophrenia (possible social factors are discussed below).

> **ASK YOURSELF**
> Are there aspects of 'psychotic consciousness' in our 'normal', everyday consciousness?

Neuropsychological Assessment

Neuropsychological assessment has shown a number of deficits in schizophrenia, relating to memory, learning, psychomotor abilities, attention and flexible responding. Such data are important in showing the specificity of neuropsychological impairment in schizophrenia, as opposed to psychopathology in general; such information points to the involvement of neurochemical systems and also provides measures by which clinical improvements may be evaluated. Neuropsychological assessment is also important for devising rehabilitation programmes specifically designed to address deficits that impair daily living. A number of major findings emerge from this literature (for a review, see Harvey & Sharma, 2002).

Learning and memory

Learning is a fundamental psychological function (see chapter 7), and its impairment affects many areas of behaviour. It is known that schizophrenia patients have a number of severe problems with memory (Saykin et al., 1991). Even when accounting for the decline in IQ compared with premorbid estimates (Weickert et al., 2000), they typically perform poorly on tests of memory functioning. Premorbid memory is often assessed by measures of reading skill, especially involving irregular words (e.g., yacht), which were learned before the onset of illness.

The most significant memory impairment is seen in declarative, or episodic, memory systems – these systems require conscious, effortful processing at stages of learning and retrieval (see chapter 7). There is a particular problem in encoding (information input): they learn less, and they benefit less from repeated learning trials (Saykin et al., 1991). Accounting for deficits in encoding, schizophrenia patients also recall less in situations in which there are no prompts (i.e., 'free recall'); another form of memory retrieval ('cued recall' and 'recognition' memory) results in less impairment and, sometimes, normal performance. This difference is not simply a result of the fact that free-recall memory tends to be more difficult than cued-recognition memory: these deficits are consistent with hippocampal damage, specifically with the view that the hippocampus resolves conflict between candidate outputs (Gray & McNaughton, 2000): when the output is cued, and therefore the candidate (incorrect) answers are significantly reduced, then performance is markedly improved.

Consistent with other findings in hippocampal-damaged patients, procedural memory is not so impaired in schizophrenia patients. As noted in chapter 7, procedural learning is a form of habit/skill acquisition that does not require conscious, effortless processing at either the learning stage or the retrieval stage; however, medicated patients do show impairments because of the blockade of dopamine receptors in the basal ganglia (Kumari, Soni & Sharma, 1999).

Working memory

Working memory is immediate memory that requires short-term storage and processing; this can be verbal or spatial (Baddeley & Hitch, 1974) – this has been identified as a potential endophenotype in schizophrenia (see Gottesman & Gould, 2003). Working memory consists of (brief) storage ('slave') systems and an attentional central executive that prioritizes tasks. The 'articulatory loop' is specific to verbal information; the 'visuospatial scratchpad' to spatial information (Baddeley, 1986). The central executive is the active processing unit, responsible for the manipulation of information and the system that allocates processing resources to the information in the modality-specific stores. Schizophrenia patients have deficits in these working memory processes. It is thought that working memory deficits are at the core of the cognitive deficits seen in schizophrenia.

Executive functions

Executive functions are required for problem-solving, the allocation of attentional resources and the management of 'on-line' cognitive skills; one particularly vital aspect is the switching between alternate responses and attention, as required by the environment. Speech (e.g., verbal fluency and coherence) is heavily dependent on executive functions.

The 'hypofrontality' (i.e., underactive frontal cortex) associated with negative symptoms should be expected strongly to relate to impairment of executive functioning – sometimes also called 'frontal lobe functions' (e.g., the Wisconsin Card Sorting Test, WCST; see chapter 8) – frontal lobe activation is observed during the performance of these tasks (Callicott et al., 2000), and performance is also impaired by frontal lobe lesions (Stuss & Benson, 1986). Schizophrenia patients have significant impairment on the WCST, and many find it difficult to perform the test at all (e.g., Goldberg & Weinberger, 1994). Importantly, they show reduced prefrontal activation during task performance.

Performance on the Stroop task is also impaired, with increased interference and a higher error rate. For example, in the Tower of London task (see chapter 8), requiring the movement of rings from three pegs in a specific order, executive functioning is required to coordinate short-term memory and planning of moves. Schizophrenia patients need more moves to reach the final solution, and many never achieve this end.

Neuropsychological deficits do not appear to be a result of the duration of the disorder, or a direct result of medication (although some functions are affected by chronicity of illness and medication). These deficits are also observed in first-episode patients prior to medication; and importantly in first-degree unaffected ('normal') biological relatives. For these reasons, it is thought that such deficits may reflect a fundamental vulnerability to schizophrenia, and perhaps may allow identification of vulnerable individuals who may need early intervention to prevent the development of psychosis (Gleeson & McGorry, 2004; see the 'high-risk approach' section below).

> **ASK YOURSELF**
> What underlying deficits in schizophrenia are revealed by neuropsychological tests?

Neuropsychology: Behavioural Tasks

Another way to investigate the neuropsychology of schizophrenia is to use behavioural tasks to measure core cognitive deficits. These tasks are chosen because of their well-defined conceptual (i.e., learning theory) and neurological (i.e., neuroanatomical and neurochemical) foundations – in contrast, many conventional neuropsychological tests are ill-defined in terms of what they measure and which brain processes are implicated. This section presents two such measures: (a) latent inhibition (LI); and (b) the Kamin blocking effect (KBE) (for a description of these tasks, see chapter 8).

The cognitive inhibition hypothesis

The underlying rationale for the use of LI and KBE in schizophrenia research involves the idea that one of the core cognitive deficits is an impairment of cognitive inhibition: both tasks are thought to tap disrupted inhibitory processes and to be related to attentional impairment.

Frith (1979) put forward the *filter deficit* theory, which contends that one of the 'core deficits in schizophrenia is with the mechanism that controls and limits the contents of consciousness' (p. 225), due to deficient inhibitory attentional processing. This theory is closely related to the hypothesis that redundant (unimportant) information is actively inhibited, not simply ignored (Tipper, 1985): this is the *cognitive inhibition hypothesis*. According to this influential model, hallucinations result from incorrect interpretations of input prematurely entering consciousness and attracting attentional processes; awareness of these preconscious thoughts may be misinterpreted as external stimuli, thus giving rise to ideas of reference. Delusions derive from the need to explain perceptions that have prematurely entered consciousness; and thought and speech disorders result from the flood of preconscious material into consciousness (e.g., different word meanings), leading to 'word salad', rapid alterations between different meaning, loose associations between concepts, and general disorganization of thought processes. One way to test the cognitive inhibition hypothesis is to use negative priming (see Peters et al., 2000). LI and KBE provide two behavioural approaches to testing these claims (as noted below, prepulse inhibition is yet another tool available to probe attentional modulation of sensory stimuli).

Latent inhibition (LI)

Latent inhibition (LI) is the impairment of learning a stimulus–stimulus association when one of these stimuli has been previously exposed without any reinforcement or consequence (i.e., passive pre-exposure). The attentional hypothesis of schizophrenia states that psychotic people have impaired cognitive inhibition, therefore they should show less LI. The dopamine hypothesis of schizophrenia (discussed below) leads to the prediction that LI should be impaired in amphetamine-treated normal participants, by virtue of increased dopamine activity. These predictions have been tested in order to provide support for the construct validity of impaired inhibition and attentional dysfunction in dopamine-overactive, normal and psychotic groups (for a review of this literature, see Lubow & Gewirtz, 1995).

In non-human studies, it is indeed found that drugs that facilitate dopamine activity (e.g., amphetamine) impair LI; and drugs that block dopamine activity (antipsychotics, e.g., haloperidol) restore LI deficits and even increase LI. A compelling feature of LI is that it is readily studied in non-human animals; it is, therefore, possible to do the basic pre-clinical science in these animals before moving on to human beings (for a review of this literature, see Swerdlow et al., 1996).

In human beings, LI is absent in acute schizophrenia patients during the first two weeks of medication, but LI is restored following medication. Also, in common with non-human animal studies, the dopamine agonist amphetamine reduces LI, and it is also found to be impaired in individuals who score high on various psychometric measures of 'psychosis-proneness' (see below). However, there is some evidence that, in part, LI is influenced by trait anxiety (Braunstein-Bercovitz et al., 2002) – this anxiety association is also discussed in relation to prepulse inhibition (see below).

One problem with comparing results from non-human and human studies concerns the different types of LI measures employed. Most human LI measures employ a 'masking task' to conceal the to-be-CS in phase I of the experiment (although masking does not seem to be required in children or in tasks using psychophysiological measures, e.g., electrodermal activity). These procedural differences raise questions about the construct validity of LI in a human clinical sample: why is a masking task needed, and does this procedural feature affect the construct validity of the task?

Whatever the precise mechanism of human LI, the failure to inhibit irrelevant information would contribute to unimportant stimuli being given inappropriate attention and processing and, as a result, being assigned undue importance. This bias in processing may also contribute to the development of ideas of reference, delusions, etc. In addition, the cognitive system would be overwhelmed, with irrelevant stimuli, crowding out relevant stimuli; the result would be distraction, incoherence and a loss of touch with reality. From the patient's perspective, though, such stimuli do hold significance and meaning, and nothing seems 'irrelevant'.

Kamin blocking effect (KBE)

Like LI, KBE is found in healthy individuals, but is absent in acute schizophrenia and is sometimes found in chronic medicated schizophrenics, but not always. Also, like LI, the loss of KBE in acute schizophrenic patients is due to faster learning in pre-exposed patients. However, unlike LI, there is only a weak tendency for KBE to differ in magnitude in normal subjects who have high and low schizotypy scores – that is, the normal distribution of 'psychosis-proneness' in the general population (see below). This finding suggests that disrupted KBE is a state marker in schizophrenia, not a trait vulnerability factor or 'endophenotype'.

Endophenotypes

LI and KBE are examples of *endophenotypes*, which refer to behavioural or biological markers that are more closely related to disease processes and the underlying genes than to the clinical phenotype (Gottesman & Gould, 2003; Leboyer et al., 1998) – as noted in chapter 15, endophenotypes can be measured by a wide variety of means. The rationale for this approach is shown in figure 16.2.

LI in particular could be considered an endophenotype, as could disrupted PPI and eye movement deficits (see below). In fact, any such behaviour/biological marker has the potential to be an endophenotype; however, if a measure is to be granted this privileged status, then there needs to be good evidence that it is an underlying trait with a substantial genetic source of variance, which, for example, is observed in (unaffected) first-degree relatives of index patients. In other words, evidence must show that it is a vulnerability *trait*, and not simply a *state* marker of the illness.

The study of endophenotypes is especially useful because of the genetic, clinical and neurobiological heterogeneity of schizophrenia: a set of endophenotypes that reflected dimensions of core dysfunction in schizophrenia and could be related to the complexity of signs and symptoms would provide a powerful way to understand the biology of schizophrenia. Whether they, one day, would replace the clinical phenotype in diagnosis is still open to question, but they play an especially important role in linkage and candidate gene (association) studies (see chapter 13).

ASK YOURSELF

What are the advantages of using LI and KBE to study the causal bases of schizophrenia?

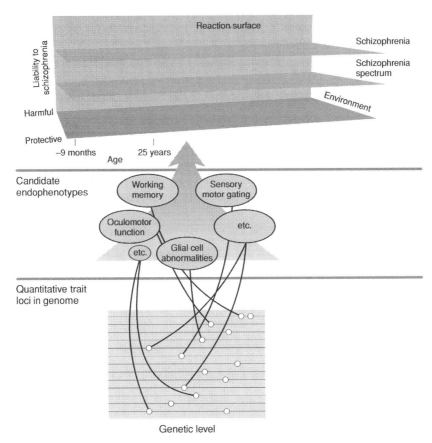

Figure 16.2 Gottesman & Gould's model of endophenotypes. The endophenotype approach suggests that there is a dynamic developmental interplay between genetic and environmental factors that produces a cumulative liability to developing schizophrenia. Measures of endophenotypes can be genetic, physiological (e.g., glial cells) or neuropsychological (e.g., sensory motor gating; PPI). As shown, a protective environment reduces the liability to developing schizophrenia; a harmful (e.g., stressful) one increases the liability to developing schizophrenia.

▭ The Gray et al. (1991) Neuropsychology of Schizophrenia

Data from LI and KBE experiments have been used to test and develop neuropsychological models of schizophrenia. Using such data, Gray et al. (1991) proposed a model to explain the neural dysfunctions that underlie positive symptoms in schizophrenia. It integrates neural and cognitive aspects of these positive symptoms, using evidence from post-mortem neuropathology and neurochemistry, clinical and preclinical studies of dopaminergic neurotransmission, anatomical connections between the limbic system and basal ganglia, attentional and other cognitive abnormalities. The model emphasizes a failure in acute schizophrenia to integrate stored memories of past regularities of perceptual input with ongoing motor programmes (involving the basal ganglia) in the control of current perception. Hyperdopaminergic activity leads to overattention, impaired inhibitory attentional control and a failure to distinguish relevant from irrelevant stimuli. LI was used to test the predictions of the model in schizophrenia samples and healthy non-clinical samples given amphetamine (which is a dopamine agonist; e.g., Thornton et al., 1996).

As noted by Pilowsky and Murray (1991), this model attempts 'to bridge the brainless hypotheses of behavioural psychology and the mindless theories of biological psychiatry' (p. 41). However, such attempts encounter many problems, both theoretical and experimental (e.g., the variety of deficits: which to choose?). Some researchers point to a specific problem with non-human-inspired, lower-level neural models, for example, Claridge and Beech (1991, p. 21):

> The main reason for our doubt is that the model places a heavy explanatory burden on relatively low-level brain structures and brain circuitry, marginalizing the possible influence of the higher nervous system as the *primary* physiological vehicle for schizophrenia.

They go on to suggest,

> Perhaps it is time to admit that schizophrenia is a uniquely human condition. After all, unlike with such 'simpler' mood-based psychopathologies as anxiety, no one has ever demonstrated a convincing example of schizophrenia in an animal, either naturally occurring or experimentally induced. (p. 21)

Claridge and Beech (1991) raise the possibility (but it is only a possibility) that the neural, let alone the psychological, bases of schizophrenia are not to be found in lower-level structures, and that psychophysiological measures of these structures, such as LI, may have limited potential. The complexity of this literature cannot be overstated; as Pilowsky and Murray (1991, p. 42) concluded,

> Some readers may conclude that the authors themselves suffer from a weakened capacity to distinguish between the relevant and the irrelevant, and this has caused them to develop a complex delusion regarding the brain mechanisms underlying schizophrenia.

ASK YOURSELF
What *can't* we learn about schizophrenia from (non-human) animal-based models?

Such theoretical disagreement is the meat and drink of scientific research: theory, counter-theory, empirical test, and finally theoretical resolution.

Psychophysiology

This section summarizes research findings relating to two psychophysiological techniques that have been identified as putative endophenotypes in schizophrenia: prepulse inhibition (PPI) and eye movements (see chapter 9).

Prepulse inhibition (PPI)

Prepulse inhibition (PPI) is thought to provide a simple operational measure of sensorimotor gating, serving to prevent the interruption of ongoing perceptual and early sensory analysis (i.e., pre-attentive stimulus processing) during the time required to analyse new stimuli. It is conveniently measured by eye-blink (EMG) startle: PPI is the (percentage) reduction in amplitude of the startle reflex when the startle-eliciting stimulus (i.e., the pulse) is preceded by a weak stimulus (i.e., the prepulse) at short lead intervals (30–500 ms). Although it is impaired in a number of neuropsychiatric conditions (e.g., obsessive–compulsive disorder, Tourette's syndrome and Huntington's disease), it is notably impaired in schizophrenia and restored following antipsychotic medication (see Swerdlow & Geyer, 1998).

As discussed above, there are severe information-processing problems in schizophrenia, and these may, in part, be due to an inability to gate out sensory information, leading to sensory overload and cognitive fragmentation. Although these information-processing problems may be measured with conventional neuropsychological tests, such tests are limited in the extent to which performance deficits can be related to a specific brain system. In contrast, it is possible to locate precisely the neurobiological basis of attention deficits using PPI in the rat (e.g., microdialysis and lesion studies; see chapter 11); also of importance, it is possible to measure the effects of putative antipsychotics in human and non-human animals – in this regard, PPI, which is known to be sensitive to the neurobiological dysfunctions in schizophrenia, can be used to screen drugs for antipsychotic properties in non-human animals. This approach replaces the hit-and-miss role of serendipity in drug discovery: in its place a rational programme of drug screening can be initiated – for ethical reasons, it would not be possible to conduct such research in human beings. In addition, in human studies, PPI can be shown to be sensitive to controlled attentional processes (Filion, Dawson & Schell, 1993), which itself is a common deficit in schizophrenia (for a summary of this literature, see Corr, Tynan & Kumari, 2002).

It has been possible to develop an animal model of deficient sensory gating using PPI. PPI is reliably disrupted in rodents by injection of psychotomimetic substances (e.g., amphetamine); these effects are reversed by antipsychotics; and the capacity of antipsychotic drugs to restore normal startle inhibition is significantly correlated with their antipsychotic potency (see Swerdlow & Geyer, 1998). It is interesting that nicotine enhances PPI (see Postma & Kumari, 2002), and this may account for the high prevalence of smoking in schizophrenia patients: it may be an attempt to remedy otherwise deficient sensorimotor gating.

PPI and emotion

The use of such psychophysiological techniques can highlight new areas of investigation. For example, it may be asked: are PPI deficits in schizophrenia related specifically to cognitive processes (e.g., disrupted attentional modulation) or emotion? The possible role played by emotion is suggested by such observations as the chronic effects of trauma (e.g., disrupted PPI in PTSD; Grillon & Morgan, 1996).

In an experimental test of this emotion hypothesis, Grillon and Davis (1997) manipulated threat of shock and attention to stimuli in auditory, visual and tactile modalities, and found a gradual decrease in PPI under the threat of shock condition. The authors suggested that this effect was due to a progressive deficit in sensorimotor gating, resulting from the stressful nature of repeated shock anticipation (however, the measure of trait anxiety used in this study was not significantly correlated with PPI).

In two separate samples, Corr, Tynan and Kumari (2002) found that traits of emotionality (especially neuroticism) were negatively correlated with PPI. This finding is important when seen in the light of the finding of higher neuroticism scores in schizophrenia (Van Os & Jones, 2001). These data raise the possibility that some of the variance in PPI seen in psychiatric conditions may be related to emotion (for other accounts of the schizophrenia–PPI connection, see Dahmen & Corr, 2004). Such findings counsel caution when interpreting psychophysiological data in relation to a specific psychiatric disorder. As noted by Hawk and Cook (2000, p. 6),

> if sensorimotor gating is influenced by affective state, then affect would need to be considered in further studies of PPI; otherwise, affective state differences become an alternative explanation of why certain disordered groups (e.g., persons with schizophrenia) show PPI deficits.

Measures such as PPI do not lead to unambiguous data; what they provide is a highly flexible way to probe brain systems and to test experimentally different types of hypotheses. In the spirit of a true scientific approach, the method itself does not limit the range of hypotheses that can be tested: it is a *progressive* method because it highlights new research problems and offers a convenient, yet rigorous, way to put them to the harsh test of experimental method.

Eye movements

In schizophrenia, deficits are observed in smooth-pursuit eye movements (SPEM) and the antisaccade task (see chapter 9). Such measures are sometimes thought to represent an endophenotype (Calkins & Iacono, 2000), reflecting core dysfunctions in the pathophysiology of schizophrenia (see above).

Smooth-pursuit eye movement (SPEM)

Smooth-pursuit eye movement (SPEM) serves to maintain the visual image of a slowly moving object on the fovea; it involves moving the eyes along the trajectory of the visual stimulus. Impaired SPEM occurs in about 50–80 per cent of schizophrenia patients, and between 30 and 40 per cent of their first-degree relatives (this compares with approximately 8 per cent of healthy individuals) (Lencer et al., 2003; Levy et al., 1993). Importantly, SPEM impairments show concordance in MZ twins *discordant* for schizophrenia (Holzman et al., 1980) – that is, eye movement impairment is seen in the identical twin who does not have a diagnosis of schizophrenia.

The antisaccade task

An antisaccade eye movement consists of making a saccade in the mirror opposite direction to the visual stimulus; this eye movement involves inhibition of the prepotent response to follow the stimulus and the ability to move the eyes accurately to the position corresponding to the mirror image of the stimulus. Performance is defined in terms of: (a) error rate (i.e., percentage of incorrect movements in the direction of the stimulus); (b) latency of the correct response; and (c) spatial accuracy (i.e., position of eye in relation to the mirror-image position of the target stimulus).

Schizophrenia patients display increased antisaccade error rate, possibly linked to prefrontal dysfunction (McDowell & Clementz, 2001); and several studies have demonstrated this deficit in relatives of schizophrenia patients (Curtis et al., 2001; Karoumi et al., 2001; Katsanis et al., 1997).

Ettinger et al. (2004) investigated siblings discordant for schizophrenia. SPEM and antisaccade tasks were applied to 24 patients with schizophrenia, 24 of their healthy siblings and 24 healthy controls. The inclusion of siblings and controls without psychiatric illness allowed the isolation of the variable of interest, namely the genetic relatedness to someone with schizophrenia, in the absence of other, potentially confounding, variables. Siblings' SPEM and antisaccade performance levels were predicted to fall in-between those of patients and controls, which was found.

It is also of interest to note that eye movement deficits are correlated with schizotypy in healthy individuals (O'Driscoll et al., 1998). Schizotypal individuals are at increased risk of developing schizophrenia and, therefore, would be expected to display an increased frequency of schizophrenia-related endophenotypes. Importantly, unlike PPI, eye movement deficits in schizotypy are not associated with individual differences in neuroticism (or negative emotionality) (Ettinger et al., 2004). Finally, eye movement impairments in schizophrenia patients are not caused by antipsychotic medication (Ettinger & Kumari, 2003).

Taken together, these findings support the notion that eye movement deficits are not a state marker of the schizophrenic disease process but instead reflect a genetic liability for schizophrenia (as first-degree relatives share about 50 per cent of their genes). Therefore, these deficits may be studied profitably to understand not only the pathophysiology of schizophrenia but also the genetic basis of this disease.

However, it is still possible that eye movement deficits in schizophrenia are the result of a common pathophysiology (i.e., the neural deficits associated with symptoms are also involved in the regulation of eye movements; e.g., frontal areas of the brain), or they are

> **ASK YOURSELF**
> What are the advantages of the endophenotype approach over the conventional symptom-based approach to schizophrenia?

sensitive to the state of the disorder (e.g., attentional problems). However, the finding of a similar pattern of deficits in unaffected ('healthy') relatives of schizophrenia patients argues against these possibilities. In any event, much is to be learned by studying this pattern of impairments in schizophrenia patients, their biological relatives and individuals identified as being at high risk of developing psychosis.

Psychopharmacology

The discovery of drugs effective in the treatment of schizophrenia ('antipsychotics') was revolutionary; within a short time of their discovery patients were relieved of much of their misery, and in some cases patients were restored to their former levels of functioning – as many as 90 per cent of first-episode patients derive a benefit in terms of symptom reduction (Robinson et al., 1999). In recent years, newer classes of antipsychotic drugs have been developed, and these are further improving the clinical picture. The number of affected patients and the costs of long-term treatment have resulted in the psychopharmacology of schizophrenia being one of the most studied topics in psychiatry.

Dopamine has been identified as the key neurotransmitter in the diverse symptoms of schizophrenia. As discussed below, the involvement of the different dopamine pathways explains why there are dysfunctions in so many psychological functions. The 'dopamine hypothesis of schizophrenia' (Carlsson, 1978) is supported by the following observations: (a) antipsychotic drugs (especially the older class of conventional drugs) block dopamine (especially D_2) receptors; and (b) dopaminergic (agonist) drugs (e.g., amphetamine and cocaine) are *psychotomimetic* – that is, they produce symptoms similar to psychotic ones (especially paranoid psychosis) or exaggerate existing symptoms. As shown below, neuroimaging studies support the idea of impairment in dopamine pathways. Before progressing further, it is important to note that not all the symptoms of schizophrenia fit neatly with the dopamine hypothesis, and it is now becoming clear that other neurochemical systems are involved in schizophrenia.

There are two broad classes of antipsychotic drugs, termed 'typicals' and 'atypicals'. These classes have different pharmacological profiles, including adverse side effects.

Typicals: dopamine blockade

The first class of antipsychotics – like the development of many drugs – was based on a serendipitous observation. In the 1950s, the putative antihistamine, chlorpromazine, was found to have antipsychotic properties when used in schizophrenia patients. It was then tested by proper clinical trials (see chapter 12) to confirm its effectiveness as a treatment for schizophrenia. At that time antipsychotic medication caused *neurolepsis*, which is a slowness of motor movements; this behavioural effect was one of the main screening measures to identify putative antipsychotics in non-human animals. For this reason, the early class of antipsychotics are called *neuroleptics* – these dopamine effects are mediated by the nigrostriatal dopamine pathway (other effects, including emotional quieting and affective indifference, are probably mediated by the other dopamine pathways; see below).

By the 1970s, it was known that all neuroleptics with antipsychotic properties blocked dopamine (D_2) receptors, especially in the mesolimbic dopamine pathway. Blockade in the other pathways gives rise to side effects (i.e., mesocortical dopamine pathway and nigrostriatal dopamine pathway: figure 16.3; see below), where blockade of dopamine activity leads to negative symptoms: this is the *neuroleptic-induced deficit syndrome*.

Dr Peter Chadwick (1992, p. 42), who was maintained on a low dose of a typical neuroleptic (haloperidol) to control his psychosis (see above), stated the following,

> there is no way, I think, that I could have regained a clear and conventional rational state of mind . . . without anti-psychotic drugs. [. . .] I would personally confirm that, whatever mavericks may say, they should be the foundation of treatment.

The disadvantages associated with typical antipsychotics relate to their indiscriminate blockade of all D_2 receptors, leading to a variety of undesirable motor disorders; if it

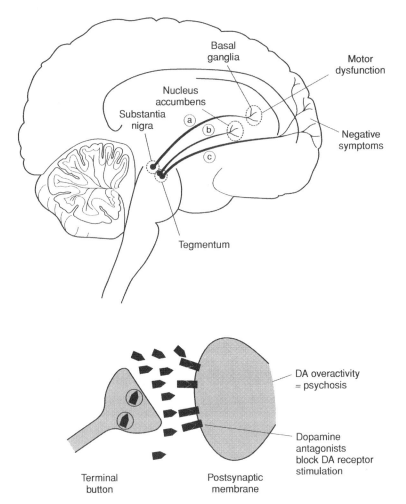

Figure 16.3 Typicals' mode of action. There are three main dopamine pathways in the brain: (a) *nigrostriatal*, axons terminate in the basal ganglia; (b) *mesolimbic*, axons terminate in nucleus accumbens; and (c) *mesocortical*, axons terminate in cortex. (A fourth dopamine pathway is the tuberoinfundibular dopamine pathway, which controls prolactin release – it projects from the hypothalamus to the anterior pituitary gland.) The classic model of action of typical drugs is that they block dopamine receptors which are in a hyperactive state leading to psychosis.

were possible to block only receptors in those dopamine pathways associated with clinical improvement, and not those pathways associated with adverse side effects, then the clinical profile of these drugs would be considerably improved. Also, they are not very effective at reducing negative symptoms and, over time, many patients develop a pattern of non-responsiveness. The newer class of atypical antipsychotics, discussed below, largely overcome these problems.

Smoking and dopamine

It is interesting to note that schizophrenia patients smoke heavily (Margolese et al., 2004). This habit was thought to be motivated by boredom but now it is suspected to be a form of self-medication: nicotine leads to the release of dopamine and thus to a reduction in adverse side effects of D_2 blockade – however, the cost of this habit is a worsening of positive symptoms. This self-medication hypothesis is supported by the finding that smoking patients, compared with controls, have a significantly higher level of nicotine metabolites, suggesting that patients consume higher doses of nicotine, probably by deeper inhalation of cigarettes (Olincy, Young & Freedman, 1997). Some studies suggest that schizophrenia patients smoke in an attempt to self-medicate towards controlling psychotic symptoms (Postma & Kumari, 2002), especially the negative symptoms, cognitive difficulties and sometimes extrapyramidal side effects of antipsychotic drugs (Adler et al., 1993). There is evidence that nicotine reverses some of the adverse cognitive side effects of the typical antipsychotics (Levin et al., 1996).

Atypicals: 5-HT blockade

Recent years have seen the phasing out of the typical antipsychotics in favour of the newer class of antipsychotics known as 'atypicals' – this class is sometimes defined as combined 5-HT–dopamine antagonists (also called, serotonin–dopamine antagonists; SDAs). All SDAs share the same effects: (a) 5-HT–dopamine D_2 antagonism; (b) fewer motor dysfunctions; and (c) efficacy for positive and negative symptoms. The five main atypicals are: clozapine, risperidone, olanzapine, quetiapine and ziprasidone. Due to side effects, the first atypical, clozapine, was initially used only in treatment-resistant patients and for treating negative symptoms; now the atypicals (which vary in the side effects) are used as first-line treatment. Atypicals are also effective as a mood stabilizer in bipolar depression. Unlike typical antipsychotics, there is some suggestion that atypicals improve cognitive functions in patients (Keefe et al., 1999). However, it should be borne in mind that atypical drugs have a range of actions and that putative serotonin–dopamine antagonism remains a hypothesis. It is still not clear precisely how atypicals work.

Unlike the effects of 5-HT in depression and anxiety, in the case of schizophrenia 5-HT works by interacting with dopamine receptors, blocking dopamine release. Specifically, they block dopamine D_2 receptors as well as 5-HT2A receptors (different atypicals have different dopamine and 5-HT profiles in this regard).

Dopamine pathways

5-HT has important effects on the modulation of dopamine activity, but these effects vary depending on the three dopamine pathways. In order to understand the action of atypical drugs it would be helpful to understand the different forms of 5-HT–dopamine antagonism in each of the three main dopamine pathways – but, as noted above, it is not known precisely how atypicals work (this model gives us a way of thinking about possible mechanisms). Importantly, understanding the separate action of these systems explains the diverse cluster of symptoms seen in schizophrenia. Unfortunately, though, these three systems do not map onto the three dimensions of *positive*, *negative* and *cognitive* symptoms discussed above.

Mesolimbic dopamine pathway

The *mesolimbic dopamine pathway* has dopaminergic cell bodies located in the ventral tegmental area (VTA) of the brainstem, and these axons project and terminate in the limbic areas of the brain (e.g., nucleus accumbens). Hyperactivity of this pathway has been associated with emotional behaviour and the positive symptoms observed in schizophrenia, especially auditory hallucinations.

Nigrostriatal dopamine pathway

The *nigrostriatal dopamine pathway* has its cell bodies located in the substantia nigra of the brainstem and its neurons project to the basal ganglia (specifically, the striatum). This system controls motor movements, and is where the primary deficit is found in Parkinson's disease. Hyperactivity in this system is thought to underlie movement disorders such as tics; and chronic blockade of D_2 receptors (e.g., by antipsychotics) often results in motor disorders, mainly drug-induced *tardive dyskinesia* (e.g., tongue protrusions and facial grimacing), as well as jerky movements. It is thought that tardive dyskinesia results from up-regulation (hypersensitivity; increase in number) of dopamine receptors as a form of regulation to compensate for reduced dopamine activity due to the drug-induced D_2 blockade. Some 60 per cent of patients maintained on typical medication develop tardive dyskinesia (Jeste et al., 1999). This is the major system that is affected by typical antipsychotics causing undesirable side effects.

Mesocortical dopamine pathway

The *mesocortical dopamine pathway* has its cell bodies located in the VTA, near the cell bodies for the dopamine neurons of the mesolimbic dopamine pathway. Unlike the mesolimbic pathway, the mesocortical pathway projects to the cerebral cortex. It is thought that the negative symptoms in schizophrenia, as well as some of the cognitive problems, result from a deficit of dopamine in mesocortical projection areas, such as the dorsolateral prefrontal cortex that is involved in a range of cognitive functions. One idea is that this dopamine deficit is a result of burnout of the previously hyperactive dopamine activity giving rise in the first phase of the illness to positive symptoms.

5-HT inhibits dopamine release; therefore, blockade of 5-HT2A stimulates dopamine release. However, atypicals also block D_2 receptors, thus inhibiting dopamine release. Thus SDAs both activate (via 5-HT2A blockade) and inhibit dopamine release (via blockade of D_2 receptors). The net outcome of this tug of war depends on the specific dopamine pathway.

The three dopamine pathways have a different pattern of 5-HT2A–D_2 antagonism. In those systems where blockade of D_2 is less desirable – in the nigrostriatal (motor deficits) and mesocortical (negative symptoms and cognitive deficits) dopamine pathways – the 5-HT2A–D_2 ensures that the blocking of 5-HT2A receptors has more of an effect

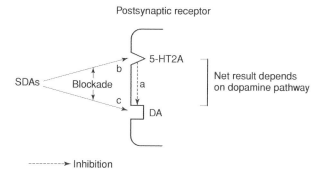

Figure 16.4   Serotonin (5-HT)–dopamine antagonism (SDA) has different effects in the
three main dopamine pathways. First, 5-HT inhibits dopamine (DA) release (a); but SDAs block
the 5-HT2A (postsynaptic) receptor which releases this 5-HT brake on dopamine release (b).
However, SDAs also block dopamine receptors (c) and it is the net result of this 'tug-of-war'
that produces the net reduction in dopamine. The fact that this tug-of-war is different in
each dopamine pathway leads to the favourable profile of atypical drugs: large reduction
in (psychosis-producing) mesolimbic dopamine pathway, and less of a reduction in the
mesocortical and nigrostriatal dopamine pathways, and thus fewer adverse side effects.

on releasing dopamine than blocking D_2 has on reducing dopamine release (in contrast,
in the case of typical antipsychotics, D_2 blockade wins out in all dopamine pathways,
thus leading to adverse side effects). In the mesolimbic system there is a net reduction
in dopamine release, and thereby an improvement in positive symptoms (figure 16.4).

The precise mode of action of atypical drugs is complex: all have different degrees of
5-HT–DA antagonism, and all affect other receptors (D_1, D_3, D_4, as well as numerous
5-HT receptors, not to mention acetylcholine and norepinephrine receptors). It should
also be remembered that the response in the individual patient
may differ markedly from the average type of response. The
therapeutic trick is to balance the positive effects of drugs with
their (largely unpredictable) adverse side effects – once again,
psychopharmacogenetics is important in predicting these side
effects (see chapter 12).

> **ASK YOURSELF**
> Does the effectiveness of
> drugs indicate that schizo-
> phrenia is caused by a neu-
> rochemical dysfunction?

Neurodevelopmental Hypothesis

Chapter 12 discussed the role of early brain development in abnormalities. There has
been a suspicion that such abnormalities are important in schizophrenia. This neurodevelopmental hypothesis (Murray & Lewis, 1987; Weinberger, 1987, 1995), which contends
that neurodevelopmental abnormalities are compensated until early adult life, receives
support from evidence of a higher incidence of schizophrenia in foetuses exposed to
various types of insult (stressful environments; Van Os & Selten, 1998), infections (e.g.,
maternal influenza during pregnancy; Takei et al., 1996), and obstetric complications (see
Gunduz et al., 1999). Although the genetic effects on brain organization start early, it is

hypothesized that symptoms, which typically do not occur until adolescence and early adulthood, develop when the brain prunes its synapses.

Neurodevelopmental deficits could arise from a variety of sources: (a) toxic effects on neurons; (b) inadequate nutrients; (c) inappropriate programmed cell death; (d) poor neuronal migration; and (e) inadequate synaptic connections (see chapter 12). Indeed, any aspects of neuronal functioning, including the support from glial cells, could be involved. This approach helps to explain the neurophysiological processes underlying genetic vulnerability, which correspond to neuronal processes.

If the precise pathological process could be identified, then early psychopharmacological intervention might be effective in blocking the progression of the disorder. However, it would prove necessary to have some diagnostic tool to identify vulnerable individuals (genetic testing may be a good candidate). If the molecular genetic basis of these effects could be identified and the mechanism was relatively straightforward, then it should be possible to moderate the effects of these genes, either by turning them off (i.e., preventing their expression into proteins) or intervening at an appropriate stage during protein synthesis.

> **ASK YOURSELF**
> Why is it suspected that schizophrenia is a neurodevelopmental disorder?

Neuroimaging

There is a large and rapidly growing neuroimaging literature that is providing new insights into the neurobiology of schizophrenia; specifically a number of structural and functional abnormalities have been identified that point to core underlying deficits, especially in first-episode patients and their biological relatives. Neuroimaging is proving especially useful to investigate brain processes in unaffected individuals who are at high risk of developing the full-blown disorder, and it has proved informative to compare these high-risk unaffected groups with both (a) first-episode, acute, patients, and (b) multiple-episode, chronic, patients. Still another approach is to examine MZ (unaffected) twins of schizophrenia patients: they have the same DNA, but different clinical phenotypes; and it is also possible to examine individuals in the general population who score highly on various measures of psychosis-proneness (e.g., schizotypy; see below).

The next section examines the structural (anatomical) and functional neuroimaging literatures. The technical details of the different neuroimaging technologies are described in chapter 10.

Structural neuroimagin

Using CT scanning, Johnstone et al. (1976) performed one of the first brain scans of schizophrenia patients. This research revealed enlargement of lateral and third ventricles and cortical sulci (e.g., Sylvian fissure), findings that have been replicated many times (Whalley et al., 1999). Such findings are important because there are associations between volume of specific brain regions and cognitive functions (Nasrallah et al., 1983). Ventricular enlargement in particular is associated with longer illness duration, more severe negative symptoms and impaired cognitive functions (Kemali et al., 1985); however, not all schizophrenia patients show increased ventricular enlargement over the course of the illness, and those that do seem to have poorer social functioning.

MRI structural studies support these CT findings. It is particularly significant that ventricular and sulci enlargements are found in first-episode patients (e.g., Degreef et al., 1992), suggesting that it may be a morphological marker for the disease and not simply a consequence of the disease itself – this hypothesis is supported by the observation of enlarged ventricles in unaffected adolescents who are at a high risk of developing the disorder (e.g., Cannon et al., 1993). There is also evidence of reduced frontal lobe volume, more specifically prefrontal cortex (some frontal lobe regions may be enlarged, not reduced). Many studies have reported reduced temporal lobe volume, and structures in the limbic system (hippocampus, amygdala and entorhinal cortex) also show reduced volume. Meta-analyses of this literature are given by McCarley et al. (1999) and Wright et al. (2000). An excellent summary is provided by Sharma and Chitnis (2000).

In relation to sensorimotor gating (e.g., PPI) and sensory processing in general, the thalamus has been the focus of interest (see chapter 5). Ettinger et al. (2001) investigated thalamic volumes in a group of patients who were experiencing their first psychotic episode. The results showed that thalamic volumes were smaller in those patients at the early onset of the illness. Such studies show how putative endophenotypes (PPI) can be used to pinpoint possible dysfunctional structures in the psychotic brain, which can then be tested with neuroimaging techniques.

Functional studies

Liddle et al. (1992) compared symptoms and regional cerebral blood flow (rCBF) using PET. A factor of 'psychomotor poverty' was characterized by reduced activity in the left dorsolateral prefrontal cortex (hypofrontality) and anterior cingulate. This provided evidence for the idea that the negative symptoms of schizophrenia are related to underactivation of the frontal lobes. The factor of 'disorganization' was associated with reduced blood flow in the right prefrontal cortex together with reduced activity in the left temporal lobe, which is associated with speech production. A factor of 'reality distortion' was positively correlated with blood flow in the hippocampus region and the left prefrontal cortex. These data point to specific pathways for the three main clusters of symptoms.

In terms of the anterior cingulate cortex, consider the study by Blackwood et al. (2004). They scanned two group of participants: (a) eight men with a diagnosis of schizophrenia who had delusions at the time of scanning, and (b) eight age-matched controls. During scanning, participants were presented with either neutral or threatening statements, some of which were potentially self-referential. This factorial design produced four sets of conditions: (a) threatening/potentially self-referential (e.g., 'He is a liar'); (b) threatening/non-self-referential (e.g., 'Clive is a liar'); (d) neutral/potentially self-referential (e.g., 'He is resting'); and (c) neutral/non self-referential (e.g., 'Clive is resting') (none of the participants were named Clive). After each statement, participants had to decide whether they felt the statement was self-referential or not. In terms of verbal responses, there was little evidence of a systematic difference between the groups. However, in terms of neuroimaging significant differences were found. When reading potentially self- referential statements, deluded participants showed significantly attenuated anterior cingulated cortex activation compared with control participants. On the other hand, the posterior cingulate cortex showed the reverse pattern: greater activation in the deluded participants with self-referential statements. The authors interpret the failure of the anterior cingulate cortex activation in terms of impairment in self-reflection in the deluded state.

Hypofrontality

Spence et al. (1998) conducted a PET study during the acute phase and then again during remission. The dorsolateral prefrontal cortex had reduced activity during the acute phase, but after 4–6 weeks, when symptoms were improving, there was increased blood flow in these regions. This type of data suggests that hypofrontality is a *state*, not a *trait*, of schizophrenia. Weinberger, Berman and Zec (1986) used PET to examine brain activity in schizophrenia patients during the performance of the WCST, a test of executive functioning believed to reflect prefrontal cortical functions.

Using fMRI, Stevens et al. (1998) found that, while healthy controls showed increased activity in the left inferior frontal gyrus during both verbal and non-verbal working memory, this activation pattern was reduced in schizophrenia patients (there was also a reduction of activation in some temporal areas). Given the structural studies of reduced volume in the temporal lobe, such findings implicate this region in the cognitive deficits and symptoms associated with schizophrenia.

Lesion model vs. functional dysconnectivity

Many neuroimaging studies have adopted an implicit 'lesion model' of the pathophysiology of schizophrenia: that is, there are specific regions that are dysfunctional. As a result of more sophisticated neuroimaging techniques, as well as more sophisticated experimental designs and advances in basic neuroscience knowledge, there is now greater emphasis upon 'functional dysconnectivity': that is, the integrated activity across a number of regions is important (Andreasen, Paradiso & O'Leary, 1998). One way to assess such dysconnectivity is to perform structural analysis to look for discrepancies between related brain regions; another way is to assess the integrity of functions associated with interrelated regions. As is often the case, these two areas represent different, though complementary, ways of looking at the same problem.

As an example of the functional dysconnectivity hypothesis, Wiser et al. (1998) used PET to study rCBF during the performance of a memory task. Although performance was equal between schizophrenia patients and controls, the two groups showed different activation patterns. Wiser et al. argued that these data support the idea of 'cognitive dysmetria', which is a disruption of the interaction between cortical (especially frontal) functions. In a test of this hypothesis, Jennings et al. (1998) used PET scanning of regional brain activity during a semantic processing task: in healthy controls, the regions were positively connected (i.e., increased activity in one region led to increased action in the other), but in schizophrenia patients these areas were negatively correlated. Specifically, negative interactions were observed between frontal and temporal regions. Such observations point to a breakdown in the usual connectivity of brain areas.

Functional study of drugs

Because it is possible to scan patients on a number of occasions, MRI technology could be used to determine the optimal drug to use, assessed in terms of the reinstatement of functional brain activation patterns, rather than relying on a hit-and-miss strategy as conventionally used. The targeting of specific pharmacological profiles and specific cognitive functions would also aid the prescription of the most appropriate drug for the specific pattern of symptoms (including cognitive impairment) in patients. Advances in understanding the aetiological basis of schizophrenia would also be greatly helped by scanning patients during remission and relapse in order to tease apart the underlying causal processes from the functional consequences of symptomatology. Several studies have used neuroimaging to examine the effects of antipsychotic drugs.

In one fMRI study, patients were first scanned when they were receiving typical medication; then half of the patients were switched to the atypical risperidone (the other half were maintained on the typical). Six weeks later, patients were scanned once again. The results showed that patients switched to the atypical risperidone showed increased BOLD responses in the right dorsolateral prefrontal cortex and supplementary motor area (SMA) (Honey et al., 1999).

Broich et al. (1998) examined the activity of typical and atypical drugs at dopamine receptors using SPECT. Patients on typical antipsychotics had much higher levels of striatal D_2 receptor blockade, and a higher incidence of motor side effects, as compared with drug-free or clozapine-treated schizophrenia patients.

Kapur et al. (1998) studied dopamine and 5-HT receptor binding characteristics of several antipsychotic drugs, and the relationship between receptor occupancy, symptoms and side effects (different doses of the atypical drug Olanzapine were employed). Even at a low dose, this atypical drug blocked virtually all cortical 5-HT2A receptors; but blockade of dopamine D_2 receptors was related to dose.

Functional study of genetics

The fact that concordance rates for schizophrenia MZ twins is not 100 per cent supports the operation of non-genetic factors in the aetiology of schizophrenia, and indicates that genes may operate by conferring a greater cerebral sensitivity to environmental factors (e.g., infection). Given that MZ twins may have completely separate chorions or amnions (i.e., the membranous sacs enclosing the foetus), there are a number of factors that might account for discordance amongst these twins: (a) changes in chromosomes or gene changes; or (b) differences in blood circulation and oxygenation during gestation and at birth, leading to differential exposure to infectious agents, drugs or chemicals during gestation. There is some evidence to show that concordant twins (i.e., when both twins have a diagnosis of schizophrenia) are more likely to have shared a foetal sac and to have shared a placenta (Davis & Phelps, 1995). Brain imaging has been used to study familial relationships in the hope of identifying genetic risk factors.

A large percentage of genes are expressed directly in the brain (approx. 30 per cent; approx. 10,000 genes); variations in these genes may thus be expected to influence brain development and function. Volumetric studies of MZ and DZ twins show differences in cerebral volume to be strongly genetically influenced (Bartley, Jones & Weinberger, 1997; Pennington et al., 2000). Imaging the brain of affected and unaffected MZ twins thus provides an important way to investigate the relative genetic and environmental contributions to schizophrenia.

Scanning of twins discordant for schizophrenia reveals that the affected twin shows more severe structural abnormalities than the unaffected twin (e.g., Noga et al., 1996). Berman et al. (1992) used PET to study regional blood flow during the performance of the WCST and reported hypofrontality in the affected twin (i.e., reduced activity in the prefrontal areas). Neuropsychological tests also reveal greater impairment in the affected twin, although the unaffected twin is often slightly more impaired than healthy controls. Such data point to a genetic basis to schizophrenia, but also additional factors that lead to the full-blown expression of psychosis.

Presumed obligate carriers

Studies of families with multiple generations affected by schizophrenia offer an insight into its pathogenesis. In these families it is often possible to identify a *presumed obligate carrier*: someone who is assumed to carry the schizophrenia gene(s) but who remained unaffected. Structural and functional imaging studies can then be carried out on the family in an attempt to identify *trait* abnormalities in the obligate carrier. Such findings show that obligate carriers and unaffected siblings have some of the structural abnormalities associated with schizophrenia; interestingly, presumed obligate carriers have increased lateral ventricular volume, a loss of normal cerebral asymmetry (see below) and reduced volume in limbic areas, which may be a genetic predisposition to schizophrenia (Sharma & Chitnis, 2000).

Problems of interpretation

In order to achieve unambiguous mapping of region to function in the normal brain it is first necessary to have a thorough understanding of cognitive functions, but our knowledge is still rudimentary. In the case of disordered brain states, the problem is more difficult. For example, when a schizophrenia patient performs a cognitive task they may use different strategies from those used by a healthy individual. This possibility renders the interpretation of the structure–function relationship problematic. As noted by Fletcher (2004, p. 579),

> A functional neuroimaging study may certainly provide a signpost to pathology but, standing alone, an fMRI observation that, say, an attenuation of language-related temporal lobe activation characterizes schizophrenia is no more proof that the temporal lobe houses a key causative abnormality in schizophrenia than would the observation of a slowed reaction time be indicative that schizophrenia is caused by slow reaction times.

Causal inference is also a problem. A structure–function relation could reflect one of three mechanisms: the brain region identified could be: (a) the cause of the disorder; (b) a consequence of the disorder; or (c) a compensation for the disorder. Thus, caution is needed in interpreting structure–function differences.

> **ASK YOURSELF**
> How is neuroimaging being used to reveal the underlying causal bases of schizophrenia?

Quantitative Genetics

Many studies have confirmed the genetic contribution to schizophrenia. As already noted, concordance rates are significantly higher in MZ twins, as compared with DZ twins. Gottesman and Shields (1982), using data from around 40 family studies spanning the whole of the twentieth century, were able to show that schizophrenia is increased in biological relatives with the disorder. Although the lifetime risk in the general population is around 1 per cent, it is 10 per cent for siblings, and 13 per cent for the offspring of affected parents. In a review of seven methodologically modern studies, the finding of an approximately tenfold increase in risk of schizophrenia in first-degree relatives remains (Kendler & Diehl, 1993). It appears that shared genes rather than shared environment underlie the increased risk in relatives (McGuffin et al., 1994). The proband-wise concordance rate for schizophrenia in MZ twin pairs is 41–65 per cent (mean is approx. 50 per cent) compared with 0–28 per cent (mean is approx. 10 per cent) for DZ twins, corresponding to heritability estimates of 80–85 per cent (Cardno & Gottesman, 2000).

Importantly, adoption studies show that the increased risk of schizophrenia comes from the biological parent, not the adopting parents (Heston, 1966; Kendler, Gruenberg & Kinney, 1994; Kety et al., 1994; Rosenthal et al., 1971; Wender et al., 1974) – this latter finding discounts the possibility that the family environment is primarily responsible for the development of schizophrenia: if you have a parent with the disorder then your chances of also developing the disorder are substantially increased even if you were adopted at an early age.

The first adoption design was carried out by Heston (1966), who compared the incidence of schizophrenia in 47 adult adopted-away offspring of hospitalized schizophrenia women with that of matched adoptees whose birth parents had no known psychiatric illness. This publication is a classic in the field, being credited with single-handedly turning the tide from assuming that schizophrenia was caused by environmental factors to recognizing the importance of genetics (Plomin et al., 2001) – the earlier twin studies, which suggested a substantial genetic influence, were countered with the environmental explanation that this was due to early parental influences.[6]

Set against this substantial genetic liability is the fact that there is also a substantial *discordance* in MZ twins. This observation means that having the same genome is not sufficient to develop the disorder; other factors must also play a role. These range from different foetal environment, chance infections to life stressors. However, even in MZ twins discordant for a diagnosis of schizophrenia, there is often evidence of some related pathology (e.g., schizoaffective disorder and schizotypal personality disorder), which together comprise the *schizophrenia spectrum* (Farmer, McGuffin & Gottesman, 1987; Kendler et al., 1997; see below).

The family inheritance pattern of schizophrenia rules out the possibility of a single major gene effect (recessive or dominant). Whatever the genetic mode of transmission, it is non-Mendelian (McGue & Gottesman, 1989); it is probably oligogenic (a small number of genes of moderate effect) or polygenic (many genes of small effect), or even a combination of these two modes of transmission. The number of susceptibility loci, the disease risk conferred by each loci and the degree of interaction between loci are still unknown. It is possible that there are considerable interactions between genetic loci (i.e., *epistasis*) and complex gene–environment interactions (see chapter 13). Irrespective of the precise mode of transmission, genetic studies also show that the conferred liability is not restricted to schizophrenia, but extends to a spectrum of disorders: schizoaffective disorder, schizotypal personality disorder and manic-depressive psychosis.

ASK YOURSELF
Why are genetically identical twins often discordant for a diagnosis of schizophrenia?

Molecular Genetics

Quantitative genetic studies show conclusively that genetic effects are highly important in schizophrenia. The obvious question then relates to the molecular basis of these effects. Without knowing anything about this complex field, given our knowledge of the psychopharmacology of schizophrenia, it might be suspected that genes coding for dopamine and 5-HT neurotransmission are implicated. These are, indeed, the obvious candidate for molecular work and have been the focus of this research effort. As an example of this research strategy, there is evidence that smooth-pursuit eye movements (SPEM) are related to a locus on chromosome 6 (Arolt et al., 1996).

Linkage studies

There have been a number of linkage studies aimed at identifying major genes. As discussed in chapter 13, linkage is good at identifying genes of large effects in single-gene disorders. However, the results of linkage studies in schizophrenia 'must be viewed as disappointing' (Owen & O'Donovan, 2003, p. 469). There have been positive findings of linkage between genetic loci and family effects, but these were not replicated, although this work is still ongoing. If the genetic liability to schizophrenia is due to the operation of many genes of small effect, which is often suspected, then even those large-scale linkage studies would be unsuccessful: to detect genetic factors of these small magnitudes very large sample sizes are needed. Although linkage results have been largely negative, this outcome is in itself informative, as it indicates that there do not exist a small number of genes each exerting a large effect.

Association studies

Association studies offer a more powerful means of identifying genes of small effect and therefore may be more appropriate for genetic analysis. Screening the whole genome by association presents difficulties because of the large and as yet unknown number of markers required to achieve comprehensive coverage. Most studies have chosen to select specific genes or loci to be tested by association. Because of doubts concerning the robustness of linkage findings in schizophrenia, most studies to date have focused on single candidate genes. However, one problem with association studies is that many of them simply do not have sufficient statistical power to detect or confirm the presence of alleles of small effect. The most obvious candidate genes have been first highlighted in the psychopharmacology literature: genes involved in serotonergic and dopaminergic neurotransmission have been the focus of much attention; attention has also turned to glutamatergic and GABAergic genes.

The genetics of schizophrenia is an enormous field of investigation and many putative loci have been identified. Reviewed below are some of the more robust findings reported in this complex literature.

5-HT2A receptor gene

Novel antipsychotic drugs target serotonergic systems. The first genetic evidence came from an association study of the 5-HTR2A genes that encode the 5-HT2A receptor – there have been a few negative findings, but a large-scale meta-analytical study (Williams et al., 1997) points to this gene being involved.

Dopamine receptor genes

The dominant neurochemical hypothesis of schizophrenia involves dysregulation of the dopaminergic systems, with the dopamine D_2 receptor widely favoured. However, linkage studies examining the gene for this receptor subtype (the dopamine receptor D_2, DRD2) has produced a mixed picture of positive and negative findings. Stronger genetic findings come from study of the DRD3 gene, which encodes the D_3 receptor (see Owen & O'Donovan, 2003).

Neurogulin-1 gene

In the past few years there has been great excitement at the apparent discovery of a specific gene involved in neuronal growth and plasticity, which is also associated with schizophrenia (e.g., Williams et al., 2003). Neurogulin-1 (NRG1), which is found on chromosome 8, is a growth factor that contributes to the formation and maturation of glial cells, as well as neuromuscular and interneuronal synaptic activity, by up-regulating the expression of specific neurotransmitter receptor subunits. Its association with schizophrenia is intriguing when seen in the light of the neurodevelopmental hypothesis, which states that schizophrenia is a late-onset disorder of the nervous system (see above). Deficits in schizophrenia may comprise neuronal migration, neurotransmitter receptor expression and myelination.

One of the receptors of the NRG1 gene shows a deficit in the prefrontal cortex of schizophrenia patients (Corfas, Royman & Buxbaum, 2004; Corvin et al., 2004), which fits in with the neuroimaging evidence showing hypofrontality in such patients (see above). In addition, Hashimoto et al. (2004) measured mRNA expression levels in post-mortem dorsolateral prefrontal cortex (DLPFC) from matched patients and controls, and suggested that subtle abnormalities in expression patterns of NRG1 in DLPFC may be associated with the disorder.

Okada and Corfas (2004) reported that NRG1 also regulates synapse development in the hippocampus (CA1 region, where long-term potentiation effects have been found; see chapter 7). In this brain area, NRG1 seems to reduce the expression of $GABA_A$ receptors, as well as reducing the mean amplitude of GABAergic inhibitory postsynaptic potentials. Okada and Corfas (2004) proposed that the role of NRG1 in the formation and maturation in the hippocampal inhibitory synapse is down-regulation, rather than up-regulation, of receptor subunit expression. Their results suggest that NRG1 may contribute to the reduction in GABAergic synaptic activity in hippocampal CA1 neurons that normally occurs during early postnatal development. It is also known that NRG1 is involved in glutamateric signalling by regulating NMDA receptors, which themselves are involved in neural plasticity (see chapter 7). Thus, neurogulin, as well as other candidate genes associated with a diagnosis of schizophrenia, seem involved in neurotransmitters other than dopamine and 5-HT (principally glutamate and GABA).

There is still much work to be done on the molecular genetics of schizophrenia; this work has been greatly facilitated by the Human Genome Project and significant advances are likely to be made in the years to come. However, given the polygenic nature of most psychiatric disorders, 'psychiatry has had little success in definitively identifying "culprit" genes or gene regions in the development of diseases categorized by using the field's diagnostic classification schemas' (Gottesman & Gould, 2003, p. 636). But then the search for such genes is still very much at an early stage.

Chromosomal abnormalities

In addition to linkage and association strategies, a third way to understand the role of DNA is to investigate chromosomal abnormalities (*cytogenetic abnormalities*), such as translocations and deletions (see chapter 2). These chromosomal abnormalities may be pathogenic in a number of ways: (a) direct disruption of genes; (b) the formation of a new gene comprising a fusion of two or more genes that are normally spatially separated; (c) indirect disruption of the function of neighbouring genes by a so-called position effect; or (d) the alteration of gene dosage in the case of deletions, duplications and unbalanced translocations. It is possible that there is a genetic liability to the development of these abnormalities (Miller, 2000). If true, these alterations, which could happen at multiple sites, may explain why specific loci are difficult to identify and then replicate. In addition, it may explain the schizophrenia spectrum (from full-blown psychosis to subclinical personality aberrations), as well as the genetic overlap of schizophrenia and other disorders (e.g., bipolar depression). This genetic effect might also help us to comprehend why there is a 50 per cent discordance in MZ twins. It is also possible that there are

ASK YOURSELF
How will knowledge of the molecular genetic basis of schizophrenia contribute to revealing its neuropsychological bases?

subtle differences in their genomes, such that, contrary to received wisdom, MZ twins are not genetically identical and, in the course of splitting of the gamete (egg), DNA or chromosomal abnormalities occur.

The 'High-risk' Approach

Is it possible to identify the predisposing neurodevelopmental dysfunction in vulnerable individuals before they develop psychosis? If it were, then this would provide important insight into the trait factors that *predict* subsequent breakdown. This information would show which deficits serve a causal (*trait*) role and which are *states* of the illness. Such information would represent an important advance in scientific knowledge.

Meehl's schizotaxic hypothesis

One highly influential model of schizophrenia was advanced by Meehl (1962), who proposed that, due to a single major gene (the 'schizogene'; aetiology), an epigenetic (developmental) brain process leads to a neural integration defect, resulting in impaired neural transmission and, in consequence, impaired cognitive and social functioning. Especially, there are problems relating to associative loosening and aberrant ideas.

The brains of affected individuals are said to be 'schizotaxic', and in most cases this leads to schizotypy (this concept is described below). Schizotypy is seen as resulting from the interactions of a schizotaxic brain and social influences: schizotaxic individuals reared in an optimal social environment may not develop schizotypy, but according to Meehl such optimal environments are rare, therefore a schizotaxic brain and schizotypy are highly correlated. Whether or not the schizotype goes on to develop clinical signs and symptoms of schizophrenia is, according to Meehl, a function of the presence of *potentiators*, which include personality dispositions (e.g., introversion and anxiety); *depotentiators* reduce the likelihood of the expression of clinical schizophrenia.

Meehl's work set the theoretical infrastructure for the development of measures of schizotypy, calling attention to genetic, brain and social influences on the development of psychosis-proneness and schizophrenia (see Meehl, 2001).

Edinburgh High Risk Study

There has been much interest in attempting to identify predictors of 'schizotaxic' brains. This research employs a 'high-risk strategy': a population of at-risk individuals are identified and a sample of this population is tested on neuropsychological measures *before* the onset of illness. Such a research programme, set up in 1994, is the Edinburgh High Risk Study (EHRS), in Scotland, which aimed to study over a 5-year period the underlying pathogenesis of schizophrenia – similar studies have been conducted in Copenhagen, Israel and New York (see Hodges et al., 1999).

In the EHRS, the sample comprised individuals between 16 and 25 years of age – initial contact and investigation took place around the peak time for the expression of schizophrenia. They were defined as at risk if they had at least two family members with a diagnosis of schizophrenia. In the first report of this sample (Hodges et al., 1999), 100 at-risk individuals and 30 healthy controls were tested. Although no members of these groups had developed schizophrenia, some important differences were apparent: a range of psychiatric problems, including depression, anxiety, OCD and alcohol dependency.

Structural MRIs were carried out on this sample. The results revealed that individuals at risk of developing schizophrenia, but before symptoms appear, have several structural brain abnormalities that are similar to those in schizophrenia patients; specifically, at-risk individuals reveal a relatively small amygdala–hippocampal complex or thalamus. The mean volume of the left amygdala–hippocampal complex in the at-risk group is midway between the mean volumes of the first-episode group and the healthy controls: this pattern of data strongly suggests that structural brain abnormalities in individuals at risk of schizophrenia are genetically mediated (Lawrie et al., 1999).

With a small increase in the sample sizes, Byrne et al. (1999) reported on neuropsychological assessment of the two groups (at-risk n = 104; control n = 33). The at-risk individuals performed more poorly than the control individuals in all measures of intellectual functions, executive function, mental control/encoding and learning and memory.

Seventy-eight at-risk individuals and 22 healthy individuals completed a number of neuropsychological tests 2 years apart. The at-risk group performed worse on verbal memory and executive functions; but of most interest is the fact that those in the at-risk group who went on to develop psychosis had a decline in IQ, verbal memory and executive function before the breakdown. As Cosway et al. (2000, p. 1111) noted,

> The results suggest that the development of psychotic symptoms is preceded by a decline in IQ and memory. This may reflect a general and a more specific disease process respectively.

The outcome of this study revealed neuropsychological differences in many areas of function, and these differences were not accounted for by the presence of psychotic symptoms. As noted by Byrne et al. (2003, p. 38),

ASK YOURSELF
Which research questions can only be addressed by a high-risk approach?

These results suggest that what is inherited is not the disorder itself but a state of vulnerability manifested by neuropsychological impairment, occurring in many more individuals than are predicted to develop the disorder.

The Schizophrenia Spectrum: Schizotypy

The founding fathers of modern-day psychiatry (Kraepelin and Bleuler) were well aware of the distribution of psychosis-like cognitions and behaviours in the general population, and specifically among the relatives of hospitalized psychotic patients. Anecdotal accounts of aberrant cognitions/behaviours in relatives of patients have long been available in the medical profession. It is now recognized that there is a 'schizophrenia spectrum', including, at one end, frank psychosis, and moving through schizotypal personality disorder (SPD) to schizotypy (*schizophrenic phenotype*; a term coined by Rado (1953) to refer to subclinical disordered thinking and impaired interpersonal relations). This spectrum may represent a personality dimension, of the type postulated by Eysenck (1952) and later elaborated by other psychologists.

Schizotypal personality disorder (SPD)

Schizotypal personality disorder (SPD) is defined by DSM-IV as a pervasive pattern of social and interpersonal deficits marked by acute discomfort and a reduced capacity for close relations as well as by cognitive or perceptual distortions and eccentricities of behaviour. SPD individuals may have ideas of reference (e.g., being spied on), hold odd beliefs, be superstitious or preoccupied with paranormal phenomena, and be suspicious and distrustful of others. They may also feel that they have special powers or the ability to foretell the future or to be able to read or influence the thoughts of others. Mild hallucinations may be present, as may unusual or idiosyncratic speech (e.g., loose, digressive and vague). They are usually not able to negotiate the full range of affects and interpersonal cueing required for successful relationships and often appear to act in an inappropriate, stiff or constricted way. Their dress may be unkempt or unusual; they may not maintain eye contact; and they may find it difficult to engage in social banter.

Such aberrant cognitions and behaviour are not restricted to a clinical diagnosis of SPD but also observed, albeit in less marked degree, in the general (non-clinical) population. Various schizotypy measures have been developed to measure these aberrant characteristics. Spitzer, Endicott and Gibbon (1979) listed the following aspects of the schizotypy: magical thinking, ideas of reference, suspiciousness, recurring illusions, social isolation, odd speech, undue social anxiety and hypersensitivity, and inadequate rapport (aloof and cold).

Schizotypy questionnaires

Questionnaire measures of schizotypy have been popular. Some questionnaires are built around the clinical symptoms of SPD (e.g., Raine, 1991); others are single-scale questionnaires which measure everyday examples of schizotypy (e.g., belief in the power of charms; e.g., Rust, 1988); still others are based on a theoretical analysis of schizophrenia and the various syndromes seen in the disorder (e.g., positive and negative symptoms; e.g., Gruzelier, 1996, 1999, 2002); and the final category takes a truly dimensional approach and attempts to uncover the separate factors involved. An example of the latter type of schizotypy questionnaire is the 'Oxford and Liverpool Inventory of Experiences' (OLIFE; Mason, Claridge & Jackson, 1995), which measures four factors (see table 16.1). An excellent overview of schizotypy research is provided by Claridge (1997).

Study of such 'well' populations circumvents the problems associated with the study of schizophrenia patients (e.g., medication effects, chronicity of illness and hospitalization). Importantly, it allows genetic study in large populations, where specific genetic models of inheritance may be tested.

Table 16.1 Sample items from the Oxford and Liverpool Inventory of Experiences (OLIFE; Mason, Claridge & Jackson, 1995)

Unusual experiences:	Do you think you could learn to read other's minds if you wanted to?
	Have you ever felt you have special, almost magical powers?
	Can some people make you aware of them just by thinking about you?
	Do you sometimes feel that accidents are caused by mysterious forces?
Cognitive disorganization:	Do your thoughts ever stop suddenly causing you to interrupt what you are saying?
	No matter how hard you try to concentrate do unrelated thoughts always creep into your mind?
	Are you easily distracted from work by daydreams?
Introvertive anhedonia:	Do you feel that you cannot get 'close' to other people?
	Are you mostly quiet when you are with other people?
	Do you tend to keep in the background on social occasions?
	Is it hard for you to make decisions?
Impulsive non-conformity:	Do you at times have an urge to do something harmful or shocking?
	Do you think people spend too much time safeguarding their future with savings and insurance?
	Do you often have an urge to hit someone?
	Do people who drive carefully annoy you?

Latent inhibition (LI)

Latent inhibition (LI) has already been discussed in this chapter. Given the fact that LI is reduced in schizophrenia patients, and assuming that the normality–abnormality continuum is valid, then LI should also be impaired in 'well' people who score highly on schizotypy measures.

Lubow et al. (1992) found that individuals who had low schizotypy scores had intact LI, whereas those with high scores, as predicted, had impaired or absent LI. It is also interesting that tobacco smokers have a higher propensity to experience perceptual aberrations, magical thinking, impulsiveness and social anhedonia (Williams et al., 1996); and it has been reported that tobacco smokers perform much like schizotypes and schizophrenia patients on LI, even after schizotypy has been controlled – yet another reason to give up the 'demon weed'!

LI research shows how a fruitful exchange between non-human animal and human research can be used to study the neurobiological basis of a normally distributed personality dimension, the results of which hold important implications for our understanding of the vulnerability factors in schizophrenia. More work is needed to clarify the structural relations of general factors of personality and clinically relevant schizotypy scales, especially

ASK YOURSELF
What insights have been gained from the dimensional approach to schizotypy and schizophrenia?

in their relation to experimental measures purportedly measuring disrupted cognitive processes germane to psychopathological conditions. A good summary of this literature is given by Lubow and De La Casa (2002).

Evolutionary Perspectives

Twin and adoption studies point to a substantial genetic contribution to schizophrenia, and advances in molecular genetics are beginning to uncover the DNA bases of this contribution. However, these findings present a puzzle: how did the genes that contribute to schizophrenia survive extinction by natural selection? On the face of it, extinction of the 'schizophrenia gene', because of the reproductive disadvantage (i.e., impaired fecundity; reduced by 50 per cent, particularly in males, in some cultures), should be expected. Given knowledge of genetics and evolution (chapter 2), it may well be suspected that there is some advantage conferred by these genes in the general (non-schizophrenia) population. As noted by Brüne (2004), the persistence of schizophrenia points to a number of possibilities: (a) genes confer an advantage in terms of survival or reproduction; or (b) genes may be linked to other genes that have an advantage. A number of specific hypotheses have been advanced to explore these possibilities.

Huxley et al. (1964) argued that schizophrenia is only one phenotype manifestation of a pleiotropic gene (i.e., a gene that produces more than one phenotype). In biological relatives, this gene might confer fitness advantages, such as resistance to infection (Erlenmeyer-Kimling, 1968), increased fertility (Huxley et al., 1964), superior language skills (Crow, 1995, 2000) or a degree of 'healthy' suspiciousness (Jarvik & Deckard, 1977). These survival and reproduction advantages may compensate for the selective disadvantage of schizophrenia and thus serve to perpetuate the gene. There has also been the long suspected association of creativity and psychosis (Eysenck, 1995, provides a neuropsychological model based on latent inhibition, loose associative processes and dopaminergic functioning). Some of these theories are discussed below.

Social threat perception and paranoia

Charles Darwin made the point that paranoia may be seen as an expression of extreme fear. This line of thought was developed by Green and Phillips (2004) in their theory that paranoia may be seen as an offshoot of social threat perception. Here we see an obvious link between fear/anxiety and psychotic symptoms. They note that rapid detection of threat in the social environment is critical for survival, and the studies of the cognitive biases in schizophrenia have accumulated to implicate biased processing of threat-related information in relation to persecutory delusions. For example, using the Stroop procedure (see chapter 8) to investigate pre-attentive processing of words referring to delusional themes (rather than colour words), schizophrenia patients with persecutory delusions are slower in naming the ink colour of 'paranoid' or threat-related words. These findings suggest that such patients have heightened pre-attentive processing of threatening information. What this conclusion suggests is that the cognitive content of paranoia may have an emotional basis. By their nature, persecutory delusions refer to the intention of others to harm. Seen in an evolutionary context, the development of an ideation dominated by this perceived social threat is not without function.

Imagination and creativity

In relation to creativity, it is interesting to consider the personal perspective of Peter Chadwick (see above). According to Chadwick (1992, 1997), delusions involve the release of an innate fiction-making capacity, but one put to self-destructive ends. Creativity is one product of this fiction-making capacity, which is put to good use in creative scientists and artists who have the heightened capacity to make meaningful connections between stimuli. The creative scientist or writer contains their ideas and can play with them imaginatively; however, the psychotic is contained by them and becomes, as it were, the out-of-control vehicle of imagination. This destructive side of the power of imagination can push aside useful creative work by the preoccupying and emotionally dominating psychotic imagination. The capacity of the brain to generate 'what-if' simulations, which is one of the finest products of evolution, in the form of conscious experience, is discussed in chapter 18. Chadwick's thesis is a version of the 'Devil makes work for idle hands', saying: the mind makes (destructive) work for idle imagination. According to this position, creative work (writing, painting, etc.) can be used as a form of therapy to channel imaginative energy along useful lines.

Early stress adaptation

There is evidence that stressful environments can compromise dopaminergic circuits in the brain. For example, rats reared in social isolation develop brains that are hyper-dopaminergic, and they show patterns of deficits found in acute schizophrenia. For example, Ellenbroek and Riva (2003) reviewed this literature and concluded that maternal deprivation leads to a large variety of behavioural changes (e.g., disruption to PPI and LI); and such deprivation leads to neurochemical changes, predominantly in the hippocampal formation, suggestive of a reduced plasticity.

This early social stress explanation has been used to explain the higher incidence of schizophrenia in immigrant populations. Although these effects may be seen as pathological, they may also be seen as adaptive: an organism reared in such a threatening environment may well become sensitized to potentially life-threatening stimuli. The organism may adapt by being fearful, distrustful of conspecifics, have altered attentional focus on the malign motives of others, and development of the cognitive bias in delusions (e.g., confirmation bias). Clearly, there are many people in society with these traits, albeit at a subthreshold level. These early events and processes may develop the 'lock' into which the 'key' of later events (e.g., starting at university in an unknown city) turn to open the doors of full-blown psychosis. Chadwick (2001) points out that there may be a strong political and social dimension to psychosis, which should not be reduced to neurochemistry or cognitive neuropsychology (although such processes may be implicated); the nature of the modern world (e.g., starvation, war and disease) may quite literally drive some people mad.

Sexual selection

Shaner, Miller and Mintz (2004) proposed that sexual selection plays an important role in the perpetuation of the gene(s) contributing to schizophrenia (see chapter 2) – in other contexts sexual selection has been applied to puzzling traits with high heritability (Andersson, 1994; Darwin, 1871). Take the classic case of the beautiful peacock tail that is genetically influenced and persists despite conferring apparently considerable disadvantages; however, this trait is selected because males with the most beautiful tails do virtually all of the mating and reproducing (Petrie, Halliday & Sanders, 1991): it seems to serve as a *fitness indicator*. However, in peacocks, ugly tails are also found: why? Is it possible to apply the line of reasoning for the peacock tail to understand the evolution of schizophrenia?

Sexual selection relates to differential reproductive success, not survival success; in other words, mate choice. Is it possible that human beings evolved fitness indicators through sexual selection? Some evidence suggests that a number of human body traits evolved through mate choice, including male height, muscularity and facial structure (Perrett, May & Yoshikawa, 1994), and size of female breasts and buttocks (Etcoff, 1999; Miller, 2000). Also, human psychological factors (including language, music and humour) may have evolved as fitness indicators through mutual mate choice (Miller, 2000). The development of language, in particular, would confer a considerable adaptive advantage, in terms of communicating danger, coordinating attacks on enemies and predation.

The Shaner, Miller and Mintz (2004) hypothesis is that schizophrenia is the negative extreme of a mental and behavioural ability that evolved as a fitness indicator through mate choice. In individuals with high genetic fitness and a favourable prenatal and postnatal environment, neurodevelopmental processes should result in an adult brain capable of attractive courtship behaviour; however, at the negative end of this pole, neurodevelopment should result in an aberrant brain prone to unsuccessful courtship behaviour. The existence of a negative pole of this sexual selection dimension is consistent with a polygenic model of transmission: some unfortunate individuals will receive a less than adequate combination of genes leading to inadequate fitness-supporting behaviour.

If it is assumed that the genes underlying this adaptive, sexually selective trait are polygenic and independently assorted in each generation, then the distribution of phenotype values would be normally distributed. The implication of this model is that phenotypes found at the low end of this distribution would be maladaptive. This type of model explains: (a) why schizophrenia persists in the general population; and (b) the adaptive significance of the genes that are involved (see figure 16.5).

Cerebral asymmetries: the language hypothesis

Shaner, Miller and Mintz's (2004) model of the evolutionary factors underlying the persistence of schizophrenia in the population takes a broad perspective from behavioural ecology and evolutionary psychology. Other models have attempted to relate evolutionary factors to the specific symptoms and neurodevelopmental processes in schizophrenia. One of the best-formulated theories of this type was postulated by Crow (1995, 2000),

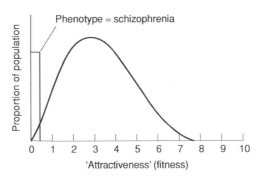

Figure 16.5 Shaner, Miller and Mintz's (2004) model of 'attractiveness' and schizophrenia: hypothetical relationships among fitness, the attractiveness as an indicator trait and the prevalence of schizophrenia. In this normal distribution of phenotypes, a threshold that defines an unattractive extreme (associated with schizophrenia) contains 1 per cent of the total population.

who argued that schizophrenia is linked to the evolution of language: it represents an abnormality of an evolutionarily advantageous phenotype. Crow's theory fits well with the language impairment seen in schizophrenia – this impairment reflects an abnormality in the neurodevelopment of brain systems. This theory helps to explain the structural and functional neuroimaging findings discussed above. Other researchers have also drawn attention to the importance of functional asymmetries in schizophrenia (e.g., Flor-Henry, 1969; for a review of this literature, see Gruzelier, 1999).

Crow's theory argues that there is a failure of the normal process of lateralization and that this failure is manifested by lack of normal hemisphere asymmetries in structures involved in language, and by abnormal connections between them (e.g., abnormalities in the corpus callosum). One of the most studied asymmetries in schizophrenia has been the planum temporale (PT) – a region in the posterior superior portion of the superior temporal gyrus that is heavily involved in language function (Kwon et al., 1999). In right-handed healthy controls, the PT exhibits a normal left larger than right asymmetry. However, in schizophrenia patients, several studies have provided evidence of loss or reversal of this asymmetry (e.g., Barta et al., 1997), as well as other asymmetries (Bilder et al., 1999). There is also some evidence that the inferior parietal lobe may also show this reversal effect – it is intriguing to note that it was this area that was unusual in Albert Einstein's brain (see chapter 3), in whose family schizophrenia is found. There are also asymmetries in the cerebral hemispheres, with the right frontal lobe larger than the left and the left occipital lobe larger than the right (Petty, 1999). As these asymmetries are under genetic control, this may be an important locus of genetic influence in schizophrenia.

Horrobin's cultural explosion thesis

Horrobin (1998, 2001) argues that schizophrenia was probably present at the earliest stages of human development, about 150,000 to 100,000 years ago, around which time there was a cultural explosion with the emergence of art, religion and warfare. It is noted that family members of schizophrenia patients show increased incidence of schizophrenia, bipolar depression, alcoholism and psychopathy, but also creativity, energy and leadership skills. It is argued that these changes are caused by the 'schizophrenia genome'. Horrobin argues that these dramatic changes were induced by mutations in lipid (fatty) metabolism that changed the biochemistry of the brain. Horrobin goes on to argue that the ratio of unsaturated fats to saturated fats in the diet is related to the outcome of schizophrenia; and that phospholipase A2 (PLA2; an enzyme in neurons in the brain) is abnormally high in schizophrenia. Abnormal dopamine activity may be the result of high PLA2 activity, and this may explain why antipsychotics, which affect this enzymatic activity, are effective in treating schizophrenia.

Thus, the price humankind paid for this newly evolved culture was schizophrenia, schizotypy and bipolar depression: the very metabolic and biochemical processes that led to human cultural evolution left us vulnerable to the major psychiatric disorders. Horrobin points out that family studies of the highly creative in society show evidence of the 'schizophrenia genome' – for example, Einstein's son was diagnosed as having this disorder, while Sir Isaac Newton had schizotypal tendencies and, during one period of his life, frank psychotic symptoms. Developmental delays (e.g., dyslexia) are also explained by this same process, with Horrobin noting that Charles Darwin showed delayed development. Crow argues that Horrobin's theory does not account for why so few of us develop schizophrenia or one of the other related disorders.

These intriguing evolutionary explanations are highly speculative and open to criticism as 'just-so' stories. In particular, it is difficult to generate hypotheses that could be put to the empirical test. None the less, these explanations show that it is possible to formulate evolutionary theories of apparently 'pathological' behaviour. As this type of 'evolutionary psychiatry' is still in its infancy, no doubt in the years to come more rigorous theories will be formulated that allow proper empirical tests to be conducted. If nothing else, these theories serve to caution us not to jump to the conclusion that certain forms of behaviour are 'abnormal', 'aberrant' or 'pathological' simply because they do not conform to our (largely socially defined) normative values. Without these behaviours, and their underlying genome, human beings might not have evolved.

> **ASK YOURSELF**
> Is schizophrenia an inevitable consequence of human evolution?

Integrating Causes in Schizophrenia

To conclude this chapter by saying that schizophrenia is a complex psychiatric disorder that is still not understood would be an understatement. This chapter has borne witness to the fundamental biological nature of this disorder; and it has been shown that there may be either positive or negative evolutionary forces[7] behind the development of this phenotype. But it should be remembered that there may be social, political and historical factors implicated too (e.g., stressful early environment, contributing to the aetiology of schizophrenia – a point made by R. D. Laing and the 'antipsychiatry' movement in the 1960s and which is all too easily overlooked). There may also be interactions between genetic vulnerability and these social factors.

One well-researched source of influence is maternal stress (Selten et al., 1999); for example, children born to mothers whose husbands died during the period of pregnancy are at an increased risk of developing schizophrenia, as are children born as a result of an unwanted pregnancy (Myhrman et al., 1996). Even adverse historical events, such as the invasion of the Netherlands by the German army, have been found to be important (Van Os & Selten, 1998; these authors discuss the possible mechanisms of stress-induced schizophrenia). The effects of postnatal stress are more difficult to quantify, but there is evidence of early stress in certain types of schizophrenia (Scheller-Gilkey et al., 2004). As noted by P. K. Chadwick (personal communication, June 2004),

> I think the bottom-up processes you talk about do give a *bias* but it is in a social and political and emotional context that then these biases all come together and are orchestrated by the 'delusional model of the world' – which of course is a brain-wide experienced *mental* event. Without knowing the motivational and social context of the person one can't 'get' from the bottom-up processes *to* the experience of madness. The overall patterns are different in different people. Will we ever know enough about an individual person to do the job properly and well?!

> **ASK YOURSELF**
> Will any adequate neuropsychological model of schizophrenia have to consider social, political and historical factors?

Conclusion

In evaluating the true biological contribution to schizophrenia it should be remembered that estimates of heritability are dependent on environmental factors (see chapter 2); and there is still a long way to go before the molecular genetics of schizophrenia is understood. In addition, the fact that drugs improve many of the symptoms of schizophrenia does not confirm that biology is the *only*, or indeed the important, *causal* factor (but such factors would be mediated by the brain). What is needed are empirical data to support hypotheses: there is so much to clarify in schizophrenia research that reasonable hypotheses should not be discounted without proper study. However, given the research evidence, it is appropriate not to take sides in the so-called 'nature vs. nurture debate': both sides of this coin are important (see chapter 13). Specifically, the temptation to assume that schizophrenia is, in some simple-minded sense, 'biological' should be eschewed. The going from (biological) mechanism to (psychological) meaning, and vice versa, is also highly problematic, yet a complete theory of schizophrenia would need to provide a way to travel back and forth between these bottom-up and top-down levels of explanation.

Learning Questions

1. Why is there misunderstanding surrounding the concept of schizophrenia?
2. What are the diagnostic features of schizophrenia and how do these differ from a diagnosis of psychosis?
3. What do we learn about the psychotic state from considering cognitive theories and personal experiences?
4. Have neuropsychological testing and neuroimaging told us anything new about schizophrenia?
5. What is the 'endophenotype' approach and how is it used in schizotypy research?

NOTES

1   The noun 'schizophrenia patient' is often preferred to the adjective 'schizophrenic patient' because the latter is construed by some researchers and patients as dehumanizing, referring to the person rather than the disease.

2   A small number of murders each year are committed by schizophrenia patients as a result of their disorder (e.g., the Devil's voice telling them to kill their children), usually compounded by refusal to take medication. Some researchers point to the higher incidence of murder and violence among a subgroup of schizophrenia patients (e.g., Stuttaford & Sharma, 1999), who tend to be male, young, have a previous history of violence, and who refuse medication. However, these acts of violence should be seen against the following facts: (a) the vast majority of murders and violent acts in society are committed by non-psychiatric 'normal' people; (b) the vast majority of schizophrenia patients are not violent and do not commit criminal acts; and (c) self-harm and suicide, as well as violent acts against these patients, far outweigh patients' violence. If one were to target and stigmatize violent and dangerous individuals in society, then it would not be to schizophrenia patients that one would look but to the 'normal' drunken young males at bar closing time on Friday/Saturday nights!

3   The confusion of 'psychotic', 'psychopathy' and 'psychopathology' is widespread in society; this is also a common confusion seen in abnormal psychology essays and examination scripts.

4   'Split personality' has nothing to do with schizophrenia disorder, but refers to what used to be called 'multiple personality disorder', now 'dissociative identity disorder' (DSM-IV-R): this disorder consists of the presence of two or more distinct identities or personalities.

5   To illustrate theory of mind, if I took a key from your pocket and placed it under a book, then *I* know, because I have a theory of *your* mind, that you will not look for your key under the book: you will try your pocket first. People with ToM deficits confuse their *own* state of mind with that of *others*.

6   This belief was a consequence of Freudian dogma, which associated 'bad environment' with 'bad mothering'. In a related vein, autism (which at the time was known as 'childhood schizophrenia') too was thought to be a direct consequence of having an emotionally cold mother. Several female psychiatrists (e.g., Lorna Wing) had autistic children and set about challenging this spurious theory.

7   'Positive' evolutionary forces refer to natural and sexual selection of the schizophrenia phenotype (e.g., 'healthy' suspiciousness); 'negative' forces refer to this phenotype being a deficit of some positively selected phenotype (e.g., language).

FURTHER READING

Chadwick, P. K. (1992). *Borderline: A Psychological Study of Paranoia and Delusional Thinking*. London: Routledge.

Claridge, G. & Davis, C. (2003). *Personality and Psychological Disorders*. Oxford: Oxford University Press.

Read, J., Mosher, L. R. & Bentall, R. P. (eds) (2004). *Models of Madness: Psychological, Social and Biological Approaches to Schizophrenia*. London: Routledge.

Personality: Emotion and Motivation

Learning Objectives

To be able to:

1. Define the meaning of individual differences and explain random and systematic sources of variation.
2. Evaluate the main structural models of personality.
3. Discuss how basic emotional and motivational systems have been related to extroversion and neuroticism.
4. Summarize molecular genetics and neuroimaging studies of personality.
5. Evaluate evolutionary approaches to individual differences.

Every person who has ever lived or will ever live is unique. This uniqueness comprises the study of *personality*, which is also known as 'individual differences' or 'differential psychology'. This chapter explores this fascinating topic in terms of how a biological perspective helps to account for variation seen in everyday (normal) behaviour, as well as in psychopathological (abnormal) behaviour: traits writ large.

In addition to summarizing the biological foundations of personality, this chapter has another aim in our understanding of biological psychology: to show how a reductionist approach can be successfully used to explain the emergence of complex phenomena in biological systems from much simpler building blocks – such psychological complexity has already been seen in the construction of sensory experience based upon raw sensory stimulation (see chapter 5).

In recent years, there has been renewed interest in the biology of personality, partly as a result of opportunities opened up by new technologies (e.g., psychogenomics and neuroimaging). But, before the 1980s, there was the widespread belief in psychology that personality was a social construction and, to the extent that personality was a viable concept at all, then biological explanations were, at best, very limited or, at worst, focusing on inappropriate levels of description. Despite recent trends, there is still much confusion over the nature of personality; therefore, our tour of personality begins with a discussion of the conceptual issues surrounding the field. (A rich source of information is available at www.personality-project.org, a site maintained by one of the leading personality psychologists, William Revelle.)

Personality Uniqueness

What is meant by 'uniqueness'? If I ask you to define your uniqueness, you would list a number of characteristics; and when I ask you to think about the reasons for your unique personality you would almost certainly cite your life experiences. It is unlikely that you would define your personality in terms of molecular and cellular brain processes; neither you nor I think of our personalities in terms of AGCT sequences, ion channels, allosteric interactions and Hebbian reverberatory circuits. Yet personality is the product of the brain.

How is this naked scientific pronouncement – which, when attired in the lavish robes of biochemical processes and recursive networks of neurons, *must* be true – compatible with our sense of uniqueness? This is a core problem that has led to a misunderstanding of the scientific account of personality.

Systematic and random differences

There are two important senses in which individuals are unique: (a) *systematic differences*, and (b) *random differences*. To illustrate this distinction, let us consider two identical (MZ) twins. These genetic clones have the same genome, and let us further assume that they are reared in the same environment. Putting aside any prenatal complications or physical trauma (e.g., childhood infections), these two children have similar brains and similar psychological processes and behaviours – it may also be guessed that they would subjectively experience the world in similar ways. But they should not be expected to have identical personalities.

However, when *differences* between twins are compared with differences between other people, then something important is immediately apparent: the *difference* between twins is much less than that between other people. (The study of such differences is, of course, the domain of quantitative genetics; e.g., twin studies; see chapter 13.)

Random (unsystematic) sources of influence on personality are not of interest to the research scientist; but, to *you* and *me*, they represent much that is important: to a large extent, we define ourselves by our 'random' experiences. These influences on our personality development give us our sense of self and the views of the world: they provide our own personalized meaning in life. Therefore, it may seem strange – perhaps even somewhat perverse – to study personality as systematic differences *between* people, but that is what the research scientist must do in their formulation of general models of personality that attempt to provide principles and laws sufficient to describe and explain individual behaviour.

Of course, this uniqueness does not imply the absence of the operation of systematic laws, but it does imply the near impossibility of accounting for each and every personality difference in terms of the precision of scientific tools currently available in psychology. A similar type of 'chaos' is seen in other natural and biological systems, where a perturbation to the initial or ongoing states of the system produces highly complex and unpredictable outcomes (for a discussion of how such processes relate to personality, see Carver & Scheier, 1998). In time, perhaps, these 'random differences' may, with increasing sophistication of measurement and theory, become 'systematic (i.e., predictable) differences', allowing these sources of variation, underlying differences between people, to be accounted for by general laws of behaviour.

ASK YOURSELF
Are there sources of influence on personality that could never be studied by the tools of science?

Conceptual and Real Nervous Systems

This preamble has set the scene for our exploration of the biological basis of personality. Now, it is tempting to list the various (indeed, the many) descriptive models of personality and then present various biological theories that purport to account for these descriptive models – many textbooks follow this well-trodden path. But this chapter takes a more unusual course in its focus on the foundation stones of the biological approach to personality.

Before progressing, the concept of a 'trait' needs defining. Traits are the psychological building-blocks of personality; and their physiological bases are constructed according to 'blueprints' that can be 'read' by behavioural experiments (learning theory). Even in the absence of knowledge of the workings of the real nervous system, learning theory helps to construct a 'conceptual nervous system', which can then be used as scaffolding in our attempt to understand the functioning of the real (physiological) nervous system (Gray, 1975). In this way, there is a two-way dialogue between behavioural data (psychology) and brain data (neurology): these data come together in neuropsychology. According to this Hebbian-inspired approach (see chapter 1), a 'mindless' brain is no better than a 'brainless' mind: both *neuro* and *psychology* are needed.

According to Gray (1972, pp. 372–3),

> both genetic and environmental factors and the interaction between them must act by altering the *physiological* basis of behaviour. In the long run, any account of behaviour which does not agree with knowledge of the neuro-endocrine systems and which has not been gained through the direct study of physiology *must* be wrong.

Thus, knowledge and study of the physiology of behaviour are fundamental to understanding personality. This point is underscored by the existence of numerous competing theoretical and descriptive models of personality: biological study of the foundations of personality is key to the building of more elaborate theoretical superstructures.

The start of the journey into this neuroscience of personality is equipped with a working definition:

ASK YOURSELF
Why is a physiological account an important part of any viable theory of personality?

Personality is composed of structural features (i.e., 'traits') and functional processes (i.e., the 'neuroendocrine system') that organize reactions to environmental stimuli to produce predictable patterns of emotion, cognition and behaviour across time and in different situations.

▢ Darwin's Expression of Emotion in Man and Animals

Current neuropsychological models of personality rest heavily on emotional processes; but this was not always the case. It is, therefore, intriguing that in one of Darwin's (1872) long-forgotten (or at least largely ignored) masterpieces – *The Expression of the Emotions in Man and Animals*[1] – he focused: (a) on the commonality between non-human and human animals' expressive emotions; and (b) the nature of emotion seen in human beings (providing an early descriptive and explanatory structure). Darwin's book is a masterpiece of careful observation and quite brilliant interpretation – a mark of its genius is that if it were published today it would still be fresh and relevant.[2]

In demonstrating the similarities between non-human animal and human facial expressions, Darwin established an evolutionary link across the phylogenetic scale and showed that human emotional expressions are universal, and not culture-specific: this hypothesis has now been firmly established, and is a major driving force in understanding human emotion (Ekman, 1998).[3] Darwin did not deal specifically with personality, but his book is full of examples of individual differences in emotional expressions.

Darwin's three principles of emotional expression

Darwin proposed three principles of the expression of emotion, to answer the 'why' question. (a) *Serviceable associated habits*: some actions and expressions relieve certain sensations and desires when certain states of mind are experienced; and over time these habits become permanent – these expressions often serve physiological functions – there was a clear adherence here to the Lamarckian process of acquired inheritance.[4] (b) *Antithesis*: according to the first principle of associated habits, certain states of mind (e.g., anger) lead to certain habitual actions, but, when the opposite state of mind (e.g., joy) is induced, there is a strong and involuntary tendency to the performance of actions and expressions of a directly opposite nature. These opposite reactions seem to negate the opposing action, and there is opposite exaggeration of action and expression to communicate the opposite state of mind. Darwin showed the postural bodily expressions of a dog ready to attack (body upright, tail erect, hairs bristled, pricked ears directed forwards, fixed stare and lips tight) to be opposite to the same dog when meeting its master (i.e., body sinks downwards, tail lowered and wagged from side to side, hair is smooth, ears depressed, head down and lips hanging). (c) *Direct action of the nervous system*: stimulation of the nervous system gives rise to certain definite forms of action and expression, depending on the connection of the nerve cells and partly as a result of habit (given the limited knowledge of the nervous system at that time this principle was necessarily vague).

Well, what does Darwin's work have to do with personality? First, the importance of cross-species similarities in the expression of emotion was demonstrated: this is important in relation to personality because biological models have relied heavily upon experimental data from non-human animals (e.g., effects of drugs, lesions and selective breeding; see below). Second, the importance of basic emotions in human behaviour was highlighted – during the heyday of behaviourism, the 'emotions' were seen to reflect an outmoded and confused way of thinking about the mind. Lastly, in his book it is evident that complex emotional behaviour can be influenced by learning (principle 1) and genetics/physiology (principle 3). All that is now needed to add to Darwin's account of emotion is the idea of variation in the population – a principle central to the whole concept of evolution (see chapter 2) – for us to see that individual differences in emotional expression are relevant to personality. This line of argument also supports the idea that non-human animals have personalities (see below).

Expression and communication

It is interesting to note that, unlike the majority of work today on the expression of emotion, Darwin's did not focus on its communicative function. As discussed below, recent neuroimaging work has used facial expressions to probe and understand the neural basis of emotion, and now this in turn is being used to explore the neural basis of personality. Indeed, Darwin avoided any discussion of communication until the very end of his book. Was he avoiding this function? According to Ekman (1998), he may well have been. One popular notion current at the time of Darwin's writing was that expressions were given to Man by the Creator to communicate intimate feelings. Darwin was keen to refute the role of the Creator, and may have overcompensated by neglecting it (almost) entirely.

In terms of adaptive value, emotional expressions serve as an important form of communication, conferring advantage in terms of kin fitness – genetic relatives who observed the emotion experienced would know, via observational learning, that a specific stimulus (e.g., snake) was associated with a specific emotional state, as revealed by the expression (observation learning activates many of the neural circuits involved in first-person learning). Inclusive fitness would explain how genes coding for the expression of emotion could be transmitted (see chapter 2) – in this respect, it would be interesting to observe if the detail of expressed emotion varied as a function of genetic relatedness (a hypothesis yet to be tested). From neuroimaging studies, which are discussed below, the perception of emotive faces does not seem to convey pure information, but is able to induce the emotional state – this would be an important survival advantage, as it would provide motivation to approach stimuli that produce positive states and to avoid stimuli that produce negative emotions in others.

Neuroimaging data reveal something else of interest to a Darwinian perspective on emotion: facial expressions are 'contagious' (see Wild, Erb & Bartels, 2001) – in cinema, one common ploy to induce emotion (e.g., horror: terror + sympathy) is to show the emotional expression of the actor looking at some (unseen) stimulus (e.g., approaching monster). This ploy was put to good effect in the 1960 film *Peeping Tom* (directed by Michael Powell), in which the sexual sadist (who had been traumatized by his medical father by being used as a subject in his homespun experiments on fear) induced escalating terror in his victims by having them observe their own facial fear expressions while being attacked – a clever use of the contagion principle of emotion (figure 17.1). On a related point, it is intriguing how fascinated humans are with depictions of horror – the whole horror-film genre is testimony to this fascination: is it possible that humans are disposed to pay close attention to the circumstances of others' horrifying experiences, and thereby safely engage in a potentially useful (sometimes life-saving) vicarious experience?

Figure 17.1 Scene from *Peeping Tom*. The principle of emotion contagion was put to good dramatic effect in the film, in which the sexual sadist generated terror in his victims by having them watch their own fearful faces. (Photo courtesy Kobal Collection.)

Largely upon the basis of Darwin's seminal work, *basic emotions* (anger, happiness, fear, surprise, disgust and sadness) are seen as universal forms of emotion expression (and thus experience) in all human societies (Ekman & Friesen, 1971) – including those societies that have not been influenced by Hollywood. (One unlikely theory was that the apparently universal facial expressions shown by anthropologically interesting societies was the result of mimicking Western expressions as seen on films; see Ekman, 1992.) Considerable work has now been devoted to understanding the neural processing of these basic emotive expressions; see Batty and Taylor, 2003 (figure 17.2).

Personality in animals

This discussion has assumed that non-human animals also have personalities; and, indeed, much of this chapter discusses theories of personality that are based on non-human animal studies of brain and behaviour. At this point it would be sensible for us to pause to consider whether it makes sense to talk of 'animal personality' – for sure, still considered an oxymoron in some quarters of psychology.

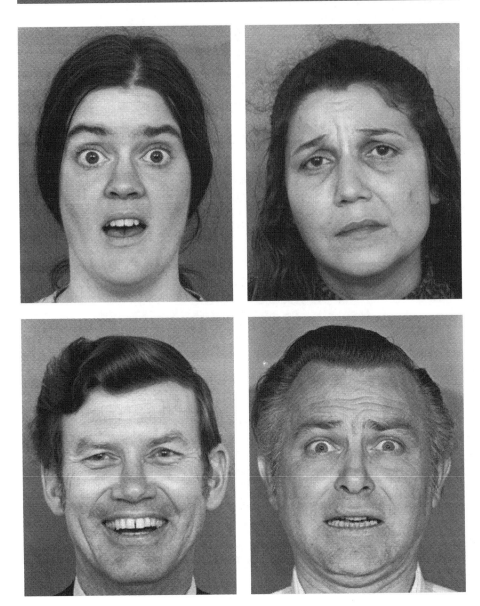

Figure 17.2 Six basic emotional facial expressions: surprise, sadness, happiness, fear, disgust and anger. (© 1988–2005 Paul Ekman.)

From a Cartesian position (see chapter 1), it is a nonsense to talk of animal personality, because only human beings have minds; 'the animals' are little more than clockwork machines, and thus can have no 'personality' – as least none that is comparable to human personality. As Cartesian dualism is now largely out of scientific favour, it might be thought that animal personality is accepted in psychology; but, as noted by Gosling

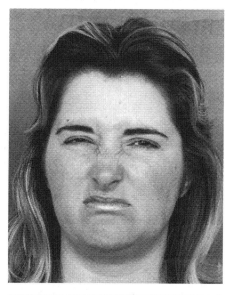

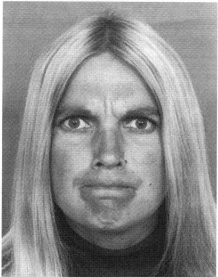

Figure 17.2 *(cont'd)*

(2001, p. 78), 'Even today, the idea of "animal personality" is often treated with scepticism or even ridicule.'

However, some of the pioneers of psychology took this possibility seriously (e.g., Donald Hebb). For example, Robert Yerkes (1939, p. 97) wrote,

> I am assuming that personality is the correct and adequate term for what is now known concerning the integrated behaviour of the chimpanzee. Indeed, in my present thinking there is no question about the reality of chimpanzee mind, individuality, and personality.

ASK YOURSELF
On the basis of Darwin's work, can we infer that non-human animals *experience* emotions in a similar way to humans?

Darwin's work was important in highlighting the continuities between human and non-human expressions (and thus experience) of emotion and, by so doing, bringing an evolutionary analysis to one of the most important functions of the human mind. His groundbreaking work prepared the way for the building of a neuroscience of emotion and individual differences in emotional processes: the foundations of personality.

Emotion as Fiction

Before moving on, let us consider the behaviourist's view of emotion. As noted by Skinner (1953),

> The 'emotions' are excellent examples of the fictional examples of the fictional causes to which we commonly attribute behavior.

Thus, according to Skinner, emotions are fictions that do not drive behaviour; they are constructions of the mind – at best, distracting epiphenomena – of little scientific importance. How the emergence of emotion evolved by Darwinian processes is not discussed by Skinner; nor are the central states of motivation embodied in the emotions considered to be relevant. However, there *is* a problem with emotion, and this shares much with the problem of consciousness discussed in the next chapter, namely, why do we *feel* emotional states, and why doesn't reinforcement (e.g., reward) work without this intermediate state?

Jaak Panksepp: neuroscientist and bereaved father

One of the most influential psychologists in the area of emotion is Jaak Panksepp. His *Affective Neuroscience: The Foundations of Human and Animal Emotion* (1998) defined a new field of psychological enquiry. Here is his account of what happened during the writing of his seminal work:

> during the middle of the present efforts, I underwent the most painful time of my life: My precious daughter . . . died along with three friends, on a dismal Good Friday evening in 1991 when a drunken driver, evading arrest, careered into their car. After the event, my spirit was demoralized, and I could not face the labors of this book for several years. Through the magic of friends and modern psychiatric drugs, my spirits were partially restored. In the fall of 1993, I restarted the project and eventually devoted renewed energy to these labors in loving memory of my daughter. (p. x)

This account reveals some important things about emotion. First, why do we have such intense and painful emotions? If it is assumed that they do not serve a function – which is still a possibility – then neither their origin nor their expression is explained. Second, emotion has behavioural consequences and these consequences serve important ends: emotions are not just free-floating, disembodied 'mental things'. In the case of bereavement, they engage a period of intense re-evaluation and withdrawal from the environment, often leading to depression: this seems an adaptive response to a highly aversive event occurring without warning (i.e., without foresight) – under such circumstances, withdrawing from everyday behaviour offers the chance to assess one's (unsuccessful) behavioural repertoire (see chapter 14) – in Panksepp's case this may be seen an 'non-adaptive', but such a response would be important in our ancestral past when our own behaviour could lead to death (e.g., not making sufficient plans to protect offspring from predators).

Lastly, neurobiologically based emotion psychologists, such as Panksepp (but all such psychologists, for few have escaped bereavement of some kind), develop neural theories in the full light of the subjective nature of emotions. Thus discussion of 'emotions being central states elicited by reinforcers', couched in a rather clinical language, does not deny the subjective nature of emotion – for often it is all too real – but rather is putting this topic into appropriate scientific terms in order that its neuropsychological nature and, ultimately, its essential subjective quality may be understood.

Thus, emotions are facts; they *are* data – this may make them interesting, but it does not, of course, make them scientifically important.[5] However, given what is known about their specificity, their evocation by reinforcers, and their behavioural consequences, it would seem premature – indeed, unjustified – to dismiss them as 'fictions': whether ultimately they will be relegated to this lowly scientific station should be the consequence of adequate scientific examination; such examination should not be stillborn by a (philosophical) assertion of their irrelevance.

Darwin's *Expression* book did much to show that emotion can be measured objectively, and now the behavioural effects of emotion are being rigorously studied – like Panksepp, Darwin also suffered the intense emotion of losing a beloved child.[6] Unlike Skinner's work, this research is showing that the concept of emotion is necessary to make sense of experimental data: for example, why do the presentation of reward and the omission/termination of expected punishment have similar effects? The hypothesis that they both activate a central 'pleasure' pathway in the brain, which can be lesioned, neuroimaged, altered by drugs and measured during rewarded behaviour, provides the scientific foundations for the concept of positive emotion. The necessity of inferring central states in order to understand behaviour in standard conditioning paradigms (e.g., sensory preconditioning; see chapter 7) has already been noted – these central states also need to be invoked to understand the behaviour of non-human animals, which, too, show all the overt signs of emotional experience. The subjective quality of emotion ('qualia'; e.g., the anguish of bereavement) is considered in the next chapter.

> **ASK YOURSELF**
> Would we *really* be better off without negative emotions?

▧ The Economics and Politics of Emotion

What is the function of emotion? Emotion can be viewed as a device that exerts control over the allocation of psychological resources. In high emotionality states, psychological resources are devoted to the demands of the threat (or promise). Emotion opens the affective floodgates and permeates all psychological processes. In the case of high fear, attention is focused on the source of the threat, all ongoing cognitive activity is halted, and resources are allocated to processing the nature of the threat. In such states, intellectual capacity is impaired and resources are recruited – or, more precisely, 'press-ganged' – into the task at hand. Positive emotions, such as love, have a similar effect of swamping the entire psychological system with a certain positive hedonic tone.

In everyday life, the mind may be likened to a 'mixed economy' that has low-level emotion and cognitive activity working together in a flexible manner; but, with the evocation of these processes, the system goes onto a war footing and into a 'command-economy' model with all resources devoted to meeting the immediate challenge (favourable or unfavourable). Affectively disordered patients are in such a command-economy state: their emotions flood the whole system and put it into a negative hedonic state. A 'free-market' state of mind would not be adaptive: emotion and cognition need to be coupled in order for emotion activation, triggered by environmental threats/promises, to influence cognitive processes (e.g., attention, memory and problem-solving).

From this perspective, the function of emotion is to influence all ongoing psychological processes to meet the challenges presented by reinforcement (a special case of feedback from the environment): it serves to bathe the whole system in an emotionally laden tone and, rather like the effects of a filter, the external world is perceived and processed in a highly selective (and, at times, distorted) manner.

The 'cold war' of emotion activation

One important aspect of the emotions is their involuntary nature: they are mandatory. Their involuntary nature is seen in clinical anxiety and depression (chapters 14 and 15), and also in everyday 'normal' emotions. For example, when loved ones die, we feel grief; when we are insulted, we feel anger; when we have to present a talk in front of people, we feel anxious; and, when we see our children succeed, we feel pride. Although some degree of control is possible over our emotions, most emotions, most of the time, just 'fire off'. In many situations, it would be far preferable if emotion could be controlled: who wants to feel the harsh grief of bereavement or the extreme anxiety of preparing for an important talk or examination? But why are emotions involuntary?

The MAD doomsday strategy

From an evolutionary perspective, involuntary emotions make sense. Pinker (1997) likens emotions to the USA–USSR cold war nuclear strategy of the 1950s, 1960s and 1970s: 'mutually assured destruction' (MAD). (This strategy was played to comic effect in the Peter Sellers film *Dr Strangelove*.) Cold war MAD strategy relied upon a Doomsday Machine, which is a device which when it detected incoming ballistic missiles would *automatically* retaliate – there would be no committee or late-night presidential meetings to discuss the next course of action; instead, action would be immediate, deadly and assured. The logic of this MAD strategy was that, as both sides knew this *assured* outcome, neither would be so foolish as to initiate a first strike and thereby guarantee their own destruction. The certainty of mutual destruction was preferable to the uncertainty entailed by voluntary governmental decisions, which introduced second-guessing and the greater likelihood that one side would conclude that they could survive if they launched a first strike. (The comedy in the *Dr Strangelove* film comes when a missile is accidentally fired, triggering activation of the Doomsday Machine in the USSR.)

Emotion may be similar to a Doomsday Machine. When loved ones die, we feel terrible grief. Now, if we had control of our emotion, then we would try to reduce this grief – indeed, this is the very goal of bereavement therapy. The same is true of fear, anxiety, disgust, anger, etc. However, as these emotions motivate behaviours, evolved by natural selection, to avoid threatening and dangerous stimuli, this termination of emotion would reduce fitness (i.e., viability and fecundity). In addition, if other conspecifics knew that you could control your emotions, then they would not necessarily expect a retaliatory strike: it is near certainty of a retaliatory strike that deters their behaviour in the first place. Now, according to evolutionary psychology, in order to convince conspecifics that you would retaliate with equal force you first have to convince not them but *yourself*, hence the involuntary nature of emotional feelings. How many times have we heard people saying 'I couldn't control myself'?

Thus, emotions may represent a general doomsday strategy that is automatically activated when certain events occur (e.g., loss of loved one, or verbal insult). This strategy has two purposes: (a) to ensure that individuals reap the consequences of their own behaviour that reduce genetic fitness; and (b) to signal to others that they will reap the consequences of their behaviour (i.e., mutually assured destruction). This type of approach to emotion goes a long way to helping us understand the automaticity of the generation of emotional states, as well as the variety and severity of emotional experiences, especially ones of the negative variety. If control of emotion were possible then anxiety and depression wouldn't exist.

> **ASK YOURSELF**
> What would be some of the consequences of the ability to suppress emotional states?

Structural Models of Personality

This section considers some of the main structural (descriptive) models of personality; in subsequent sections, these descriptive models are related to causal biological factors. At the outset it should be noted that the development of most structural models of personality has been blind with respect to possible biological foundations, and only in recent years has there been an attempt to develop descriptive models in accordance with known emotional systems within the brain.

Factor analysis

There have been many attempts to classify individual differences into a taxonomic structure by the use of various forms of multivariate analysis. The technique of factor analysis has been widely used for this purpose. This is a complex mathematical procedure, and is used in a variety of ways in personality research. There is insufficient space to do justice to this important technique, but it should be possible to grasp the basic principles without undue effort (for an introduction, see Kline, 1993) – but do not worry if the details of this procedure seem strange at first (it is a tricky technique to understand).

The purpose of factor analysis is to reduce a correlation matrix into a smaller number of 'axes' or 'factors' that help to define, understand and label the principal dimensions

Table 17.1 Hypothetical correlation matrix of ten variables

	V1	V2	V3	V4	V5	V6	V7	V8	V9	V10
V1	1.00	0.40	−0.56	−0.98	0.88	−0.32	−0.23	−0.11	0.63	−0.25
V2		1.00	−0.59	−0.66	0.87	−0.43	−0.22	−0.55	0.74	−0.54
V3			1.00	−0.45	0.37	−0.45	−0.36	−0.45	−0.85	−0.84
V4				1.00	−0.45	−0.37	−0.29	−0.34	−0.923	−0.75
V5					1.00	−0.85	−0.34	0.88	0.45	−0.43
V6						1.00	−0.37	0.88	−0.68	−0.34
V7							1.00	−0.43	−0.76	−0.23
V8								1.00	−0.65	−0.45
V9									1.00	−0.66
V10										1.00

running through the matrix – i.e., the thread that ties sets of items together.[7] Another way of thinking of factor analysis is as a method in which variation in scores is expressed in a smaller number of axes/factors or constructs. For example, in the physical world, there are three dimensions of space; time adds a fourth dimension.

Factor analysis can be 'exploratory', in which case the dimensionality of a correlation matrix is not hypothesized before data collection; or it can be 'confirmatory', in which case a definite dimensional model is specified and the 'observed' correlation matrix is then compared against this 'target' matrix; some form of 'goodness of fit' statistic can then be used to evaluate the observed–target matrices concordance. Let us consider the simpler case of exploratory factor analysis by using an example involving mood ratings.

Imagine a researcher was interested in exploring the dimensionality of mood states. They devise a ten-item psychometric instrument that measures various aspects of mood. On a 1- to 5-point scale (with 1 = 'strongly agree', 5 = 'strongly disagree'), respondents rate statements: for example, 'I am cheerful most of the time' (V1); and 'I usually enjoy meeting new people' (V2). After collecting data from a large number of respondents, the following pattern of correlations was obtained (table 17.1).

Several things can be seen in table 17.1. The variables correlate perfectly with themselves (these are 1.00s on the diagonal), and the lower half of the matrix is empty because it only repeats the top half of the matrix. However, by simply looking at the pattern of correlations, the dimensional structure is not obvious. We therefore submit the correlation matrix to a factor analysis (various methods exist, with different assumptions and aims). Now let us assume that after factor-analysing this correlation matrix two main factors are found[8] – here the factors are defined by their 'factor loadings' (i.e., how each variable 'loads' onto, or correlates with, the factors).

Figure 17.3 shows the spatial position of variables in relation to factors/axes identified by factor analysis (this is a schematic depiction for clarity only). Shown first (F1 and F2) is the 'unrotated solution' – this is determined purely in mathematical terms and has no direct psychological meaning. The position of these factors serves well the task of the statistician (i.e., to summarize mathematical 'space'); however, the psychologist needs to move from description to interpretation: this is why the process of 'rotation' is of such importance. Looking at the pattern of factor loading, it is evident that all the variables load onto both factors.

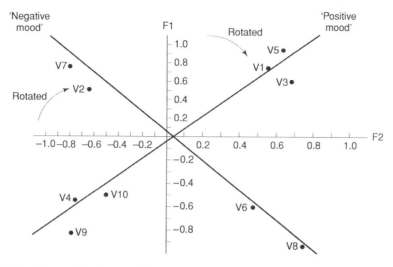

Figure 17.3 Unrotated and rotated factors. Plot of variables in two-dimensional space, showing the unrotated solution (F1 & F2) and rotated solution, simplifying interpretation of the pattern of factor loading (i.e., each variable loads onto only one factor).

Table 17.2 The 'unrotated' and 'rotated' factor matrices, showing 'loadings' of original variables onto factors

	Unrotated solution		Rotated solution	
	Factor 1 'Mood intensity'	Factor 2 'Negative–positive mood'	Factor 1 'Positive mood'	Factor 2 'Negative mood'
V1	0.64	0.53	**0.90**	0.05
V2	0.45	−0.55	−0.15	**0.77**
V3	0.56	0.53	**0.96**	0.03
V4	−0.43	−0.58	**−0.75**	0.17
V5	0.78	0.53	**0.69**	0.23
V6	−0.57	0.47	0.11	**−0.72**
V7	0.62	−0.66	−0.25	**0.59**
V8	−0.78	0.65	0.12	**−0.88**
V9	−0.75	−0.65	**−0.77**	0.09
V10	−0.34	−0.33	**−0.68**	−0.15

Table 17.2 shows the pattern of factor loading in the 'rotated solution'. These rotated loadings are much simplified: each variable loads onto only one factor (highlighted in bold). These factor loadings may be plotted in two-dimensional space to show how they relate to the rotated factors (see figure 17.3).

In the unrotated solution, factor 1 (F1) may be labelled 'Mood intensity' and factor 2 (F2) 'Negative–positive mood'. But in the rotated solution, factor 1 may be labelled 'Positive mood' and factor 2 'Negative mood' (figure 17.3). Although the data shown here are made up, this pattern of loadings reflects what is often found in mood research. 'Mood intensity' is sometimes associated with the personality trait of neuroticism, and 'Negative–positive mood' with introversion/extroversion; and it is often suggested that some alternative rotation of the factors is preferred in order to align them with independent biological sources of influence: for example, Reward system = 'Positive mood', Punishment system = 'Negative mood' (see below).

To recap, structural models of personality have relied upon factor analysis to impose some order on the otherwise chaotic-looking correlations among variables. The details of factor analysis are complex; fortunately, these details are unimportant to understand its use in personality psychology (the mathematical procedures are implemented on statistical programs, and are easily run at the press of a button). The crucial thing to bear in mind is that reductions of correlations to a set of factors that define the 'factor space' do not have psychological meaning; thus, the psychologist is free to move these factors so as to achieve parsimonious interpretation. An example of this procedure is shown below in the case of Gray's rotation of Eysenck's extroversion and neuroticism factors, based on a theory of the brain basis of personality.

Five Factor Model (FFM)

One popular approach to the description of personality has been to search the dictionary for adjectives that describe aspects of behaviour, and then reduce these thousands of adjectives, by the judicious elimination of redundancy, to a few hundred adjectives that can then be administered to a large number of people. The resulting correlation matrix can then be factor-analysed to derive the underlying dimensions of these data. This 'lexical approach' is based on the assumption that important individual differences have been encoded into language and thus into the dictionary.

This approach has led to what is known as the Five Factor Model (FFM), or simply the 'Big-5', comprising: Extroversion, Neuroticism, Agreeableness, Conscientiousness and Openness to Experience (these factors, and their lower-order traits, are shown in table 17.3; Costa & McCrae, 1992). The FFM is in the tradition of an atheoretical exploratory (statistical) approach to personality description. Although there is much debate concerning the reliability, replication and validity of the FFM, of these five factors, Extroversion and Neuroticism, are found, in one form or another, in (almost) all models of personality (see Matthews, Deary & Whiteman, 2003). One of the most popular measures of the FFM is the NEO-PI-R (Costa & McCrae, 1992), which stands for Neuroticism, Extroversion, Openness Personality Inventory Revised (in this revised version, the domains of Conscientiousness and Agreeableness were added).

Dimensions of personality

The most systematic investigation of personality was conducted by Hans Eysenck over a period of 50 years, from the early 1940s to the late 1990s. Eysenck established the reliability and validity of two major dimensions of personality, extroversion and neuroticism,

Table 17.3   Lower-order 'facets' of NEO-PI-R (from Costa & McCrae, 1992)

Extroversion:	Warmth, Gregariousness, Assertiveness, Activity, Excitement-seeking, Positive emotions
Neuroticism:	Anxiety, Anger/hostility, Depression, Self-consciousness, Impulsiveness, Vulnerability
Conscientiousness:	Competence, Order, Dutifulness, Achievement/striving, Self-discipline, Deliberation
Agreeableness:	Trust, Straightforwardness, Altruism, Compliance, Modesty, Tender-mindedness
Openness to experience:	Fantasy, Aesthetics, Feelings, Actions, Ideas, Values

and did more than any other psychologist to establish a biological explanation of the variation seen in these dimensions. It is instructive to see how Eysenck's approach differed from the lexical approach of the FFM.

In contrast to the FFM approach, Eysenck (1944, 1947) based his factor analysis on a medical checklist, under the assumption that neurotic symptoms are at the extreme end of normally distributed personality dimensions – traits writ large. He factor-analysed the content of this medical checklist taken from some 700 'war neurotics', who had been hospitalized for a variety of disorders (these patients typically were not battle traumatized, but simply unable to cope with the rigours of military life). This factor analysis produced two major dimensions that allowed a parsimonious statistical summary of the medical data (i.e., the extreme expressions of personality: neurosis). Eysenck then replicated these two factors/dimensions on a sample of the normal population using a questionnaire.

In 1952, Eysenck postulated a third dimension of personality, 'psychoticism', to account for psychotic conditions (e.g., schizophrenia and bipolar disorder). Along with extroversion and neuroticism, psychoticism carves up factor space in such a way as to account for the relationships seen among psychiatric disorders. These three dimensions are now measured by the Eysenck Personality Questionnaire (EPQ-revised; Eysenck & Eysenck, 1991), which has a yes/no response format. Examples of questionnaire items are shown in table 17.4.

Eysenck used factor analysis to explore the dimensionality of the medical checklist, and the items themselves were analysed because of the theory that in clinical disorders are seen the extreme expressions of normal behaviour. This perspective offers a way to anchor the position of the factors to real-world behaviours.

Affective Neuroscience Personality Scales (ANPS)

Other personality researchers have started from a theory-driven perspective and built descriptive models on the basis of behavioural, pharmacological and neuroscientific theory. Jaak Panksepp (1982, 1998) is a leading advocate of *affective neuroscience*, which is concerned with understanding the neuroscientific basis of emotion systems and individual

Table 17.4 Sample of items from the Eysenck Personality Questionnaire (EPQ-revised)

Extroversion:	Do you have many different hobbies?
	Are you a talkative person?
	Do you enjoy meeting new people?
	Can you get a party going?
Neuroticism:	Do you ever feel 'just miserable' for no reason?
	Do you suffer from your 'nerves'?
	Are you often troubled by feelings of guilt?
	Do you worry about awful things that might happen?
Psychoticism:	Would it upset you a lot to see a child or an animal suffer?
	Can you on the whole trust people to tell the truth?
	Would you take drugs which may have strange or dangerous effects?
	Is (or was) your mother a good woman?
Lie:[9]	Are *all* your habits good and desirable ones?
	As a child, were you ever cheeky to you parents?
	Do you always wash before a meal?
	Do you always practise what you preach?

differences within these systems. Panksepp (2003) provided a useful discussion of the differences between *affective science* and *cognitive science*, the core of which is illustrated in the following quote from Panksepp's paper (p. 12),

> In sum, one guiding premise of 'affective neuroscience' is that a natural neurobiological function of the brain is to generate a menagerie of positively and negatively valenced affect states, of various degrees and types of arousal, that help guide the organism in life-sustaining activities. The basic affects may directly reflect certain types of ancient neuroinstinctual systems in action – yielding wide-scale neurodynamics that permeate the quality of our movements, actions, and higher cognitive activities. Emotions are not simply informationally encapsulated brain processes as some cognitively oriented investigators seem to believe.

Davis, Panksepp and Normansell (2003) developed the Affective Neuroscience Personality Scales (ANPS) to measure variations in a number of basic emotion systems identified in non-human animals. As the authors noted (p. 57),

> One of the more urgent questions of human psychology is how to parse the primary affective states that are subsumed by the temperamental variability that constitutes human personality. . . . It is generally assumed that the effectiveness of therapeutic practice, both psychological and somatic, should be informed by the structure of the clients' personality. Indeed, in the current era of biological psychiatry, it is often suspected that the efficacy of certain psychotropic agents may interact with pre-existing personality strengths and weaknesses, leading to differential efficacy of agents.

Davis et al. (2003) noted that there is no consensus whether personality should be studied with a theoretically-driven strategy or with a purely exploratory, statistical strategy. They (2003, p. 58) argued,

Table 17.5 Description of scales from Affective Neuroscience Personality Scales (ANPS)

Personality factor	Factor description
Positive affect:	
1. Playfulness	Fun vs. seriousness; playing games with physical contact; humour and laughter; and being generally happy and joyful.
2. Seeking	Feeling curious and having the urge to explore; striving for solutions to problems and puzzles; positively anticipating new experiences; and having a sense of being able to accomplish almost anything.
3. Caring	Nurturing and being drawn to children and pets; feeling soft-hearted towards people and animals in need; feeling empathy; liking caring for the sick; wishing to be liked by others.
Negative affect:	
4. Fear	Feelings of anxiety, tension; worrying and struggling with decisions; ruminating about past decisions; losing sleep; and typically not being courageous.
5. Anger	Easily irritated and frustrated, leading to anger; expressing anger verbally or physically, and remaining in this angry state for long periods of time.
6. Sadness	Loneliness; crying frequently; thinking about loved ones and past relationships; feeling distress when not with loved ones.
Human factor:	
7. Spirituality	Feelings of being connected to humanity and 'creation' as a whole; feeling a sense of 'oneness' with creation; striving for inner peace and harmony; relying on spiritual principles; and searching for 'meaning' in life.

> In our estimation, optimal emotional personality evaluation should be based on empirically based viewpoints that attempt to carve personality along the lines of emerging brain systems that help generate the relevant psychological attributes.

Furthermore,

> personality variability that is especially important for understanding some of the foremost, internally experienced psychological dimensions of individuals should be related to the activity level of specific emotion systems.

Davis, Pantsepp and Normansell (2003) constructed a psychometric instrument to measure seven basic affective tendencies: (a) *Playfulness*, (b) *Seeking*, (c) *Caring*, (d) *Fear*, (e) *Anger*, (f) *Sadness*, and (g) *Spirituality*, the last of which the authors contend is a uniquely human attribute of special relevance to psychopathological conditions (see table 17.5). These affective neuroscience scales are based on Pantsepp's (1998) analysis of fundamental animal behaviour, and, although they would not be necessarily accepted by all researchers in this area, they do demonstrate the range of non-human animal behaviours observed that can be extended to human beings.

The ANPS is still at an early stage of development and has yet to be evaluated against psychopathological criteria or against laboratory-based measures of the underlying neuropsychological emotion systems. However, it illustrates the value of considering individual differences in basic emotional systems, found cross-species, especially in the 'higher' mammals, as a foundation for the formulation of personality theory and the development of psychometric instruments to measure personality traits.[10]

Is there an optimal descriptive model of personality?

There is an embarrassingly large number of competing structural models from which to choose; each has its own unique theoretical (or atheoretical) starting point, test construction method and validation evidence. Debate over the optimal structural model of personality has dominated personality psychology for many years, and is still far from being resolved. For example, in reply to a paper by Costa and McCrae (1992), entitled 'Four ways five factors are basic', Eysenck (1992) outlined 'Four ways five factors are *not* basic'. Block (1995, 2001) also takes issue with the apparent 'consensus' of the FFM. Eysenck (1991) provided a very useful list of criteria for an adequate taxonomic model of personality. As discussed below, these debates may not be amenable to resolution without a thoroughgoing biological analysis (Corr, 2004; McNaughton & Corr, 2004); and, indeed, various descriptions of biologically defined factor space may be compatible.

> **ASK YOURSELF**
> How can a biological approach help to resolve the problem of the number and nature of descriptive personality factors?

Fortunately, nearly all descriptive models of personality contain Extroversion and Neuroticism, in one form or another, although these are sometimes subsumed under broader dimensions of Positive Affect (PA) and Negative Affect (NA), respectively (e.g., the ANPS). The basic emotions already discussed similarly fit into this two-system model of personality, although each specific emotion has a separate neural basis.

Causal Theories of Personality

The most comprehensive biological model of human personality was developed by Hans Eysenck. In 1967, Eysenck postulated that introverts and extroverts differ because they have (typically) different states of brain arousal: introverts are typically highly aroused and thus develop typical traits of introversion (comprising stimulus avoidance/shyness); extroverts are typically less aroused and thus develop typical traits of extroversion (i.e., stimulus seeking and gregariousness). These differing (cortical) arousal levels were postulated to result from differences in response thresholds of their ascending reticular activating system (ARAS) in the brainstem – a system that diffusely projects to the cortex (see chapter 3). According to this theory, compared with extroverts, introverts have lower response thresholds and thus are more easily aroused. The notion is that there is a homeostatic balance of level of arousal and hedonic tone: too little and too much arousal is experienced as suboptimal, and behaviour serves the function of modulating arousal to the optimal level. This behavioural regulation constitutes the personality trait of introversion–extroversion: over-aroused introverts shy away from stimulation; under-aroused extroverts seek it out. The second major dimension, Neuroticism, was postulated to relate to emotional (limbic) activation and emotional instability.

Literally hundreds of experimental studies have been performed to test Eysenck's hypotheses, and it is now well established that there is a relationship between level of arousal and introverson–extroversion across a wide range of performance domains (see Eysenck & Eysenck, 1985). However, the precise pattern of effects is not consistent and seems sensitive to many factors, such as time of day of testing and the precise nature of the behavioural or cognitive task (for a review of this literature, see Matthews & Gilliland, 1999). However, Eysenck's (1967) biological theory provides a clear rationale for the personality–psychopathology continuum: this dimensional view of personality–psychopathology is now widely accepted (e.g., Cloninger, Svrakic & Przybeck, 1993). Although the details of Eysenck's theory are problematic, its general scientific approach has proved highly fertile, leading to important advances in our understanding of the brain processes involved in personality.

Eysenck's theory generates a number of important predictions concerning the development of neurotic conditions. Specifically, the theory predicts that neurotic introverts – that is, those who are emotionally reactive and highly cortically arousable – condition more easily to aversive stimuli and thus are more liable to the symptoms of neurotic conditions. The association of Neuroticism and neurotic disorders is not a tautology: it is the neural processes of a reactive (emotional) limbic system, coupled with an active ARAS, that promote classical conditioning and lead to the *development* of neurotic symptoms. In this context, these neural processes represent *trait* factors and the neurotic conditions *state* factors: the development of neurotic states is not an inevitable consequence of possessing trait neuroticism (e.g., drugs can reduce emotional reactivity and thus retard the development of neurotic states in high-trait neurotic individuals).

The problems with Eysenck's theory have been discussed by Gray (1970, 1981; see Corr, 2004). These problems led to the formulation of an alternative biological account of Extroversion and Neuroticism discussed here – the general approach of this theory has been replicated by other researchers in similar models of personality (e.g., Cloninger, Svrakic & Przybeck, 1993; Depue & Collins, 1999).

Reinforcement Sensitivity Theory (RST)

On the basis of a critique of Eysenck's model of personality, Jeffrey Gray (1970, 1981) proposed that Extroversion and Neuroticism should be rotated to align with two major neurobiological systems: (a) a Punishment Mechanism; and (b) a Reward Mechanism (Pickering, Corr & Gray, 1999; see figure 17.9 below). On the basis of several lines of evidence, Gray (1970) argued that the factor of 'Anxiety' (Anx) was associated with a punishment mechanism, and 'Impulsivity' (Imp) with a reward mechanism. According to this theory, individual differences in these punishment and reward mechanisms give rise to characteristic patterns of behaviour: Punishment = Anxiety; Reward = Impulsivity. This theory, now known as Reinforcement Sensitivity Theory (RST; Pickering, Díaz & Gray,

1995), has generated a large and growing experimental literature (this is reviewed by Corr, 2004).

RST states that high impulsivity individuals are most sensitive to signals of reward, relative to low impulsivity individuals; and high anxiety individuals are most sensitive to signals of punishment, relative to low anxiety individuals. According to this formulation, Eysenck's Extroversion and Neuroticism dimensions are derivative factors of the more fundamental Anxiety and Impulsivity: Extroversion reflects the balance of reward and punishment sensitivities (introverts are more punishment sensitive; extroverts more reward sensitive); and Neuroticism reflects their combined strengths (for a revised version of formulation, see figure 17.9 below).

RST can explain why introverts are typically more aroused than extroverts: punishment is more arousing than reward, and as introverts are more punishment sensitive they are accordingly more (typically) aroused. It is interesting to note that Darwin (1872, p. 344) recognized the power of punishment (e.g., criticism) to arouse emotion more easily than reward (e.g., praise): 'Every one feels blame more acutely than praise.'

There is now a consensus concerning the fundamental importance of reinforcement processes in personality; as noted by Pickering et al. (1997, p. 63),

> one cannot but remain impressed by the sheer frequency with which significant relationships nonetheless do emerge between one or other relevant personality trait and one or other relevant change in behaviour due to reinforcement effects. Somewhere in the human brain there clearly are systems which influence individual differences in sensitivity to reinforcement.

Gray's RST model is complex, and in recent years has responded to new empirical evidence with a major revision (Gray & McNaughton, 2000). The next section summarizes the features of the most recent formulation of RST: it serves to provide a general model of defensive (aversive) and approach (appetitive) motivation, and helps to explain how individual differences in the functioning of these systems give rise to everyday (normal) and pathological (abnormal) behaviour – in the nature of a fast-moving area of neuroscience, this 2000 theory has already been refined by McNaughton and Corr (2004).

ASK YOURSELF
Why do some psychologists contend that a biological approach to understanding personality is not only desirable but essential?

A General Model of Defensive and Approach Motivation

Biological models of personality need to explain the two major motivational requirements of any viable organism: (a) there is the need to *avoid* noxious stimuli (especially predators); and (b) there is the need to *approach* appetitive stimuli (e.g., food and sexual partners). Here is discussed a general model of defensive motivation, comprising separate states of fear and anxiety, and approach motivation, comprising reward-mediated behaviours. This model can be used to account for the similarities and differences between the neurotic disorders, already discussed in chapters 14 and 15.

The Gray and McNaughton (2000) theory of anxiety is based on 'etho-experimental' studies in which the rat's natural defensive behaviours are observed in artificially contrived (but, to the rat, realistic) environments in which experimental control of a number of key factors can be achieved. In this type of naturalistic environment, the effects of drugs on ethologically valid defensive behaviours can be studied (i.e., 'ethopharmacology'). These drug effects can then be used to dissect the systems; in other words, separable systems can be identified on the basis of their sensitivity to different classes of drugs. Blanchard and Blanchard (1989) devised a 'Fear/Defensive Test Battery' and an 'Anxiety/Defensive Test Battery' to measure different aspects of defensive behaviour. They showed that some drugs affect fear, but not anxiety; other drugs affect anxiety, but not fear. This observation gave rise to the identification of two separate systems: one mediating fear, the other mediating anxiety. (A special issue of the journal *Neuroscience and Biobehavioral Reviews* has been devoted to this topic; Blanchard, Blanchard & Graeff, 2001.) This fear–anxiety distinction now plays a major part in the Gray and McNaughton approach (2000; also see McNaughton & Corr, 2004).

The Gray and McNaughton (2000) refinement of Gray's (1970, 1981, 1982) RST, already outlined above, has three main systems: (a) the *fight–flight–freeze system* (FFFS); (b) the *behavioural approach system* (BAS); and (c) the *behavioural inhibition system* (BIS). Each system is considered in turn.

Fight–Flight–Freeze System (FFFS)

The *fight–flight–freeze system* (FFFS) mediates reactions to *all* threats (i.e., unconditioned and conditioned punishment). This system is composed of a hierarchical array of modules, each of which controls a specific reaction (see figure 17.4) – such hierarchical models are common in the behavioural architectures, where control is organized at different levels in the nervous system depending on specific environmental demands (see Toates, 2004).

At the bottom of the hierarchy is 'undirected escape', controlled by the *periaqueductal grey* (PAG; a structure located in the midbrain), which represents coarse-grained behaviour to flee the situation (it is a 'panic-like' response). It has long been known that electrical stimulation of the PAG leads to either flight (if the situation allows this response) or fight (if the situation prevents escape) (Flynn, 1967; Panksepp, 1982) – Graeff associated this reaction with panic (the feeling we would have if we suddenly walked in front of an oncoming train). (For a review of this literature, see Graeff, 2004.) In relation to the extremes of fear, terror and panic, Darwin (1872, p. 292) noted that there is:

> a sudden and uncontrollable tendency to headlong flight; and so strong is this, that the boldest soldiers may be seized with a sudden panic.

Moving up the hierarchy leads to more controlled and sophisticated behaviours: 'directed escape', controlled by the *medial hypothalamus*, and still further up, 'active avoidance', controlled by the amygdala; and at the top of the hierarchy, 'discriminated avoidance', controlled by the *anterior cingulate*.[11]

The FFFS is responsible for behaviours designed to avoid/escape aversive stimuli, and is activated when there is a strong motivation to *leave* the environment in which the threat is detected (Gray & McNaughton, 2000). As noted by Darwin (1872, p. 289), 'The word "fear" seems to be derived from what is sudden and dangerous.' Under these circumstances, fleeing the situation is the preferred strategy; but it is not always possible.

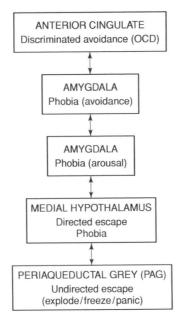

Figure 17.4 The defensive hierarchy. Threats are processed by the *fight–flight–freeze system* (FFFS), which is hierarchically organized, with explosive 'panic' reactions at the lowest level (greatest threat) and discriminated avoidance (potential threat), associated with obsessive–compulsive behaviour (OCD), at the highest level of the hierarchy. Higher levels inhibit lower levels, but all levels prime each other to prepare for rapid action.

One reason for believing that these reactions, and the associated emotional states, do not reflect anxiety per se is that drugs that reduce anxiety in human beings ('anxiolytics') are much less effective in reducing behaviour on the Fear/Defensive Test Battery (but they are affected more by drugs that reduce panic, 'panicolytics') – panicolytics are much less effective at reducing behaviour on the Anxiety/Defensive Test Battery.

A similar dissociation is found in human clinical conditions. In contrast to the majority of anxiety-related disorders classified by the DSM, the risk of specific phobia is not related to neurotic introversion (Marks, 1969); and simple phobia is not relieved by anxiolytic drugs (Sartory, MacDonald & Gray, 1990). For this reason, phobia is seen as a fear response, consisting of simple avoidance of the feared object.

As discussed below, anxiety involves fear, but in environments where fear-mediated (avoidant) behaviours are not adaptive – for example, when the animal is feeding. This desire to leave the situation (to avoid the feared stimulus) and the opposing drive to enter the situation (e.g., to feed) produces conflict and the cognitive and emotional states associated with anxiety (e.g., worry, rumination and vigilance).

Defensive distance

The important parameter in determining which fear response is observed is 'defensive distance' (figure 17.5): the smallest defensive distances result in explosive attack (e.g., a

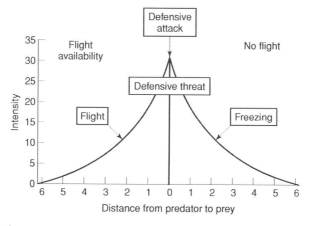

Figure 17.5 Defensive distance and FFFS behaviours. Distance is the important parameter in determining the appropriate reaction to threat. At short defensive distance, explosive attack is appropriate; but at longer distance, depending on the constraints of the situation, either flight or freezing is appropriate. (From McNaughton & Corr, 2004; used with permission.)

rat nose to nose with a cat); intermediate defensive distances result in freezing and flight (depending on where escape is possible); and very great defensive distances result in normal non-defensive behaviour.

In human beings, the psychological state at very small defensive distance would be labelled 'panic'. The commonly associated cognition in panic is, 'I'm going to die.' Intermediate defensive distances can be equated with phobic avoidance (i.e., shying away from perceived threat).

Behavioural Approach System (BAS)

In order to survive and reproduce, animals need to do more than avoid danger; they must also approach appetitive stimuli. The *behavioural approach system* (BAS) – sometimes loosely called the behavioural *activation* system – is the system responsible for achieving this goal (see Pickering & Gray, 1999).

The function of the BAS is to initiate exploratory behaviour that brings the organism closer to final biological reinforcers (food, sexual partners, etc.); its associated neurology involves the basal ganglia (the striatum and pallidum), the dopaminergic fibres that ascend from the cell bodies of the substantia nigra and the ventral tegmental area to innervate the basal ganglia, the thalamic nuclei closely linked to the basal ganglia, and, similarly, the neocortical areas (motor, sensorimotor and prefrontal cortex) closely linked to the basal ganglia. The behavioural functions discharged by the BAS are shown in figure 17.6. The BAS is also sensitive to 'relief of non-punishment', which non-human animal studies show has similar behavioural effects to the presentation of appetitive stimuli – it is interesting to speculate that this emotional state underlies some 'paradoxical' behaviours that involve either actual punishment or the threat of punishment (e.g., potentially dangerous activities such as bungee jumping).

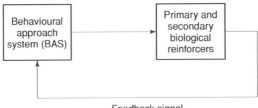

Feedback signal

Figure 17.6 The function of the behavioural approach system (BAS) is to reduce the temporal and spatial gap between biological needs and the source of primary and secondary biological reinforcers (e.g., food).

Behavioural Inhibition System (BIS)

In the revised Gray and McNaughton (2000) theory, the BIS is a *goal conflict* resolution system, instantiated in the septo-hippocampal system and the amygdala (which generates emotional arousal).[12] The BIS is activated when the animal is *entering* an environment where there is either immediate danger (in the case of rats, the sight of a cat), or a potential danger (e.g., smell of cats, or aversive conditioning to the environment).[13] That is, the BIS is activated when there is concurrent activation of the FFFS and the BAS – for example, when the animal is foraging in an open space. When not in goal conflict, the BIS is 'just checking'; when in conflict, it is in 'control mode' and takes charge of ongoing behaviour (Gray, 1982).

Figure 17.7 shows inputs to the FFFS and the BAS, and the resulting outputs of the BIS; these include: (a) behavioural inhibition (i.e., risk assessment and behavioural caution; *not* freezing); (b) an increase in attention; and (c) an increase in arousal. This state of apprehension and uncertainty is 'anxiety'. From an evolutionary standpoint this reformulated view of the BIS makes considerable sense. As noted by the sociobiologist E. O. Wilson (1975, p. 3),

the hypothalamus and the limbic system are engineered to perpetuate DNA.

Specifically, the BIS allows a resolution to the balance of approach–avoidance tendencies: when activated, the BIS scans the external environment and internal (memory) processes to gather information on the potential threat: either the threat is deemed imminent, in which case FFFS behaviour is dominant, or the perception of threat is minimized – threat perception is reduced by anxiolytics.

Defensive systems and psychopathology

It is now time to relate specific defensive reactions, mediated by the FFFS and the BIS, to the main mood disorders, namely anxiety and depressive disorders. As shown in figure 17.8, when the FFFS is active and the animal is motivated to leave the situation, this flight/escape/avoidance response is comparable to a human phobia; but 'panic' is comparable to the fight/freeze response observed when avoidance is not possible at a short defensive distance.

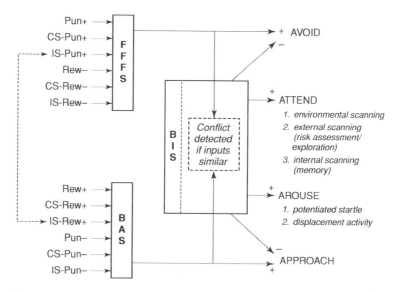

Figure 17.7   FFFS/BAS = BIS activation. The *fight–flight–freeze system* (FFFS) is activated by innate (PUN+) and conditioned signals of punishment (CS-PUN+), as well as by innate stimuli (IS-PUN+; e.g., snakes and blood), and the actual (REW–) or signal of (CS-REW–) omission of reward, as well as the omission of innately rewarding stimuli (IS-REW–; e.g., sexual mate): all of these stimuli comprise punishment (this is the 'fear system'). The behavioural approach system (BAS) mediates all rewarding stimuli, including the omission of actual or signals of punishing stimuli (this is the 'anticipatory pleasure system'). The behavioural inhibition system (BIS) is activated when there is goal conflict between approach and avoidance tendencies (this is the 'anxiety system'): once activated, attention is increased and risk assessment of the situation, including behavioural caution, doubt and rumination, is made before a choice is made between FFFS-dominated or BAS-dominated responding. (From McNaughton & Corr, 2004; used with permission.)

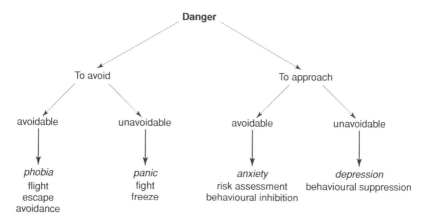

Figure 17.8   Avoid/approach defensive symptoms. The avoidance and approach of danger are related to specific clusters of clinical symptoms. (From McNaughton & Corr, 2004; used with permission.)

In the case of defensive behaviours when entering an appetitive environment, 'anxiety' is experienced when the threat is avoidable; and 'depression' is observed when the threat is unavoidable. In relation to anxiety and depression, it is interesting to note Darwin's (1872, p. 176) observation,

> If we expect to suffer we are anxious; if we have no hope of relief, we despair.

The pharmacological basis of these links between defensive motivation and psychopathology are necessarily complex. Studies of the type developed by the Blanchards have advanced our knowledge of the hierarchical nature of aversive motivational systems and their sensitivity and insensitivity to different classes of drug. This research has greatly helped to clarify the distinction between fear and anxiety, two states of negative emotion that have often been considered as one emotion – but, in some, respects, they are opposing emotions (e.g., fear is evoked when there is motivation to leave the feared situation; anxiety is evoked when there is the motivation to enter the feared situation). The type of model developed by Gray and McNaughton (2000) helps to explain, on the one hand, why there exist different affective clinical conditions.

Chapter 13 discussed the study by Kendler et al. (2003), which provided genetic evidence for two major factors underlying the common psychiatric syndromes: 'internalizing' (depression and anxiety) and 'externalizing' (substance abuse and conduct disorder). These two factors map onto the two major motivational systems discussed above: punishment and reward sensitivity. In support of the fear–anxiety distinction, Kendler et al. (2003) also found that, within the internalizing factor, anxiety and phobia (fear) have separate genetic bases. Thus, it is possible to see the important interplay of quantitative genetics in psychiatry, revealing the underlying genetic–environment architecture of psychopathology, and experimental neuropsychology, which reveals the processes involved in these underlying factors. When these two complementary, but very different, approaches converge on the same conclusion, then it is possible to construct theoretical models with a high degree of confidence.

> **ASK YOURSELF**
> What are the advantages of a 'bottom-up' (causal systems) approach over a 'top-down' (statistical/descriptive) approach to personality?

With these new concepts firmly in mind, let us turn to personality aspects of these motivational systems and the way in which the different clinical categories described in chapters 14 and 15 may be subsumed under a single 'neurosis' umbrella. As shown, normal variation in these personality factors may represent the same underlying vulnerability factors identified in psychopathology.

Defensive/Approach Motivation and Personality

So far only emotion and motivation *states* have been discussed; now our attention turns to their *trait* (personality) components. There are important roles for 5-HT and dopamine genes in personality (see below); according to this general framework, the neurotransmitters that are coded by these genes serve to modulate the broad motivational tendencies: 5-HT in the case of defensive motivation; dopamine in the case of approach motivation. It is at this general level that personality exerts its influence (Gray &

McNaughton, 2000; McNaughton & Corr, 2004). Within these broad motivational systems it may be seen that there exist relatively separate modules in the defensive hierarchy; these separate modules should be expected to have their own neurotransmitter systems and genetic basis, as indeed do the various clinical disorders; however, it is not at this level of specificity that personality is found, but at the broader, more encompassing level. It is, therefore, for this reason, as previously discussed in chapters 14 and 15, that the SSRIs seem to play an important role in many neurotic conditions: what SSRIs influence is the perception of threat – in other words, the *perceived* defensive distance – which affects functioning at all levels of the defensive hierarchy.

Perceived defensive threat thus acts like a magnification factor. For a given individual, defensive distance is directly related to the actual distance from the aversive stimulus; but between individuals and within the same individual at different times (and especially in different drug states) defensive distance is expanded or contracted with respect to actual distance. Defensive distance, then, is in psychological (cognitive) terms the level of *perceived* threat. Its magnification is in psychological (personality) terms fearfulness or sensitivity to threat (see Perkins & Corr, 2006).

The idea of the perception of threat and perceived defensive distance is crucial in understanding the effects of the SSRIs: they do not affect defensive behaviours in a straightforward fashion (i.e., reduce them), but they seem to shift the patient along the defensive distance axis and thus lead to the corresponding defensive behaviour. The concept of defensive distance depends on the fact that different behaviours can be shown at the same actual distance and result in, for example, opposite effects of drugs on behaviour in different individuals; none the less, defensive behaviours change in an orderly sequence as the level of threat changes. An important consequence is that comparison of individuals on a single measure of performance at a single level of threat may produce confusing results (e.g., one person may be in a state of panic and so cease moving; another may actively avoid and so increase their movement). In this regard, it is interesting to note that the experimental literature on the effects of neuroticism is very mixed, with neuroticism being associated with a wide range of behaviours. With the hindsight afforded by the account given here, this confused pattern of effects is explicable. In addition, the basic confusion between fear-related and anxiety-related behaviours adds to this apparent behavioural inconsistency.

The discussion has focused on defensive (aversive) motivation, but a similar 'magnification factor' view of personality may be applied to the role of dopamine and approach motivation. Dopamine reduces appetitive distance, so that, for a given magnitude of an appetitive stimulus, its appetitive value is magnified. Individuals low on reward motivation would need a greater-value appetitive stimulus to produce the same level of approach as seen in individuals high in reward motivation.

Extroversion and neuroticism rotations

Let us now turn to the important issue of the relationship between defensive and approach motivation systems and the well-established personality dimensions of Extroversion and Neuroticism. The precise relations of the FFFS/BIS and BAS to these personality dimensions has still to be fully clarified; however, for present purposes,

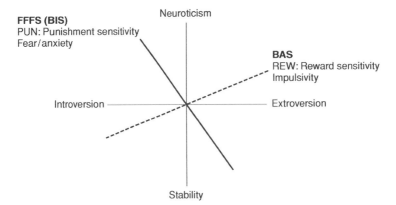

Figure 17.9 Revised E/N rotation. Position in factor space of the fundamental FFFS/BIS (PUN: punishment sensitivity) and BAS (REW: reward sensitivity) and the emergent *surface expressions* of these sensitivities, namely, Extroversion (E) and Neuroticism (N). (Adapted from Corr, 2004; used with permission.)

'Punishment Sensitivity' (PUN; more precisely, perceived defensive distance) may be substituted for 'Anxiety'; and 'Reward Sensitivity' (REW; more precisely, perceived value of appetitive stimulus) for 'Impulsivity'. These relations are shown in figure 17.9. (For simplicity, the FFFS and the BIS are joined together in PUN, but it is possible that separate personality factors are found that preferentially relate to these separate processes and states – for example, it is possible that a low FFFS individual still shows considerable anxiety because of the impairment of their BIS, which fails to resolve the FFFS–BAS conflict.)

It is important to note that our understanding of the biological basis of personality is still in its infancy – perhaps now entering that difficult period of adolescence – and there is much more thinking and data collection needed before a mature theory emerges. This is a typical state of any scientific field: only non-scientific views ('dogma') enjoy the privileged, but false, state of certainty. Specifically, psychometric work is needed to clarify the precise personality factors that correspond separately to the FFFS, BAS and BIS.

According to the theoretical position adopted here, personality may be defined as:

> A long-term (trait) level of sensitivity of a biological system with significant genetically or environmentally induced variance in the population; which, at the broadest level, comprises sensitivities to specific classes of aversive and appetitive stimuli.

It is important to know that this 'trait' is not set in stone; it is a semi-stable process that is amenable to change. On the one hand, traits evident over the lifespan do have a significant impact on reactions to aversive environmental events. Those prone to anxiety disorders are defined as being neurotic introverts, and this trait disposition has been found to be associated, in Australian firefighters, with reactions to traumatic events, leading to the development of post-traumatic stress disorder (PTSD). Even in such a population that is self-selected for low reactivity to stressful events, prior neurotic introversion scores predict the disorder better than the extent of exposure to the event (McFarlane, 1989). However, it is also known that PTSD itself produces a change in personality scores, possibly by virtue of damage to the hippocampus.[14] Thus, there seems to be an interplay of personality (trait) disposition and environmental events, and not an immutable predisposition given at birth.

> **ASK YOURSELF**
> How successful is reinforcement sensitivity theory in accounting for the personality traits of extroversion and neuroticism?

Human Analogues of Defensive Behaviours

Over the years a number of questionnaires have been developed to measure sensitivities to reward and punishment (see Corr, 2004); these various measures are driven by the central postulates of reinforcement sensitivity theory (RST). However, another approach to developing personality measures of RST is demonstrated by the following study, which has extended to human beings the implications of an etho-experimental approach to defensive reactions.

Blanchard et al. (2001) examined human reactions to scenarios modelled on defensive reactions to aversive stimuli seen in rodents. Students read a set of 12 scenarios involving present or potentially threatening conspecifics (see below). Each scenario is modelled on features known to influence defensive responding in rodents: (a) *dangerousness*, (b) *escapability*, (c) *distance*, (d) *ambiguity*, and (e) *place of concealment or protection*. These factors were operationalized as the following human defensive behaviours:

1. Hide
2. Freeze, become immobilized
3. Run away, try to escape, remove self (flight)
4. Threaten to scream or call for help
5. Yell, scream or call for help
6. Threaten to attack
7. Attempt to struggle
8. Check out, approach or investigate (risk assessment)
9. Look for something to use as weapon
10. Beg, plead for mercy or negotiate.

Participants are presented with the 12 scenarios; for example,

> 'You are sleeping in bed during the night, but suddenly wake up thinking you have heard a suspicious noise. It is dark and you are alone.' [Check out, approach or investigate – risk assessment.]

> 'Coming home one day, you find an expected shoe-box-sized package waiting for you by the mailbox. As you sit down to open it, you notice a faint ticking sound that appears to come from inside the package.' [Run away, try to escape, remove self – flight.]

Then they are required to choose a primary defensive reaction to each threat. In this intriguing study, it was found that human reactions to these manipulations resembled those of rodents, although there were differences between males and females which reflect the perceived degree of threat. For example, the scenario,

> 'You are alone as you exit an empty campus building late one night. Just as you get outside, you feel a hand grab your arm.'

Females typically choose, 'Yell, scream or call for help'; males typically choose, 'Check out, approach or investigate.'

In future work it would be valuable to examine individual differences in such reactions and then map these individual differences onto general measures of personality (e.g., Extroversion and Neuroticism), as well as specific measures of reward sensitivity and punishment sensitivity (e.g., the Carver & White, 1994, BIS/BAS scales). This work would help to resolve one major problem in relating causal emotion/motivation systems to the descriptive level of personality: how to relate descriptive factors of personality to biologically causal factors.

Isomorphism: are biological factors and personality factors aligned?

There is some reason to doubt that well-established personality factors such as Extroversion and Neuroticism would be replaced by factors that corresponded more faithfully to the axes of biological causation (e.g., reward sensitivity and punishment sensitivity). Put another way, what are the optimal *descriptive* measures of personality, and are they configured in the same way as the optimal *causal* (biological) factors? This is the problem of *isomorphism*.

In the case of the Gray and McNaughton (2000) neuropsychological theory of personality, the FFFS mediates punishment, and the BAS mediates reward; however, the FFFS and the BAS relate to *both* Extroversion and Neuroticism. Figure 17.10 provides one model of how the interplay of the FFFS and the BAS leads to the development of Extroversion

> **ASK YOURSELF**
> Is it preferable to focus on the biological level of personality or the descriptive level?

and Neuroticism: that is, the joint operation of the two major motivational tendencies in social behaviour (for a more detailed exposition of this approach see Corr, 2004). Although the details of such models can get complicated, their implications for understanding the *causal* level and the *descriptive* level of personality are clear enough.

▢ Neuroimaging

There have been very few neuroimaging studies of personality, but many more of emotion processing – but now personality studies are being conducted, partly in recognition of the considerable individual differences seen in neural responses to emotive stimuli (as already discussed, these individual differences are related in systematic ways to well-established dimensions of personality).

It is now known that particular brain regions are involved in face processing (the fusiform gyrus and superior temporal sulcus); and clinical neuropsychological case studies suggest

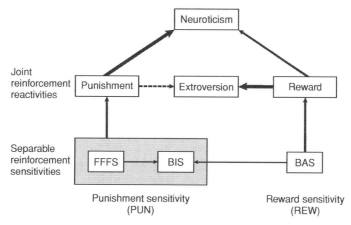

Figure 17.10 FFFS/BIS × BAS model of Extroversion and Neuroticism. A schematic representation of the hypothesized relationship between: (a) FFFS/BIS (punishment sensitivity; PUN) and BAS (reward sensitivity; REW); and (b) their relations to Extroversion (E) and Neuroticism (N). E is shown as the balance of punishment (PUN) and reward (REW) reactivities; N reflects their combined strengths. Inputs from the FFFS/BIS and BAS are excitatory (unbroken line) and inhibitory (broken line). The strength of inputs to E and N reflects the 30-degree rotation of PUN/REW and E/N: relatively strong (thick line) and weak (thin line) relations. The input from punishment reactivity to E is inhibitory (i.e., it reduces E), the input from reward reactivity is excitatory (i.e., it increases E). The BIS is activated by simultaneous activation of the FFFS and the BAS, and its activation increases punishment sensitivity. It is hypothesized that the joint effects of PUN and REW give rise to the surface expression of E and N: PUN and REW represent the underlying biology; E and N represent their joint influences at the level of integrated behaviour. (Adapted from Corr, 2004; used with permission.)

that different aspects of faces are processed in separate neural subsystems (i.e., selective impairments are seen in recognizing facial emotions without a deficit in facial identity). Furthermore, separate neural networks has been demonstrated for processing specific facial emotions, including cortical (prefrontal, frontal and orbitofrontal cortices, occipito-temporal junction, cingulate cortex and secondary somatosensory cortex) and subcortical structures (amygdala, basal ganglia and insula).

Neural correlates of emotion processing

The amygdala, in particular, has often been associated with the processing of fearful and sad faces, while the cingulate gyrus is activated by happy faces, and the orbital frontal regions by angry faces; in contrast, disgust seems to activate preferentially the basal ganglia and insula. (For a summary of this literature, see Batty & Taylor, 2003.)

Using PET, Paradiso et al. (1999) attempted to identify the neural circuits associated with the evaluation of visual stimuli for emotional valence. Regional blood flow was measured during the rating of pictures for their emotive content (pleasant, unpleasant and neutral). Evaluation of pleasant pictures (relative to neutral pictures) was associated with differential activation in the cingulate and visual cortex; and evaluation of the unpleasant pictures (relative to neutral pictures) in the nucleus accumbens and visual cortex (when compared with the pleasant pictures, activation was observed in the amygdala).

Blair et al. (1999) used PET to examine the neural correlates of the processing of sad and angry faces. During scanning, participants performed a sex discrimination task (to engage attention and processing of the faces) using images of faces expressing varying degrees of sadness and anger. The results revealed that increasing intensity of sad facial expression was associated with enhanced activity in the left amygdala; and increasing intensity of angry facial expression was associated with enhanced activity in the orbitofrontal and anterior cingulate cortex – angry expressions did not generate a differential signal in the amygdala.

Morris, Ohman and Dolan (1998) examined conscious (overt) and non-conscious (covert) processing of angry faces – in the covert condition, faces were backward masked with a neutral face (for details of this procedure, see chapter 15). Prior to face presentation, one of the two presented faces had been classically conditioned to a loud noise (UCS) – although participants report not being able to see the angry face, they nevertheless showed a conditioned response (CR), indicating that the face had been processed. A significant neural response was elicited in the right, but not left, amygdala to masked presentations of the conditioned angry face; but unmasked presentations of the same face produced enhanced neural activity in the left, but not right, amygdala. The data show that the human amygdala can discriminate between stimuli solely on the basis of their acquired behavioural significance; and they also suggest that the left and right amygdala may play different roles in the covert and overt processing of aversive stimuli.

One fMRI study showed that, during the presentation of happy facial expressions, BOLD signal increase was observed in the left anterior cingulate gyrus, bilateral posterior cingulate gyri, medial frontal cortex and right supramarginal gyrus, brain regions previously implicated in visuospatial and emotion processing tasks; but no brain regions showed increased signal intensity during presentation of sad facial expressions (Phillips et al., 1998a). The neural correlates of disgust, literally 'bad taste', were studied by Phillips et al. (1997), using fMRI: they, once again, found activation of the amygdala to fearful faces, but disgust faces activated the anterior insular cortex, but not the amygdala (see also Phillips et al., 1998b). This is an example of double dissociation (see chapter 8). Phillips et al. (2004) repeated the above experiment, but this time the faces were presented either above identification threshold (i.e., 170 ms) or below threshold (i.e., 30 ms). Once again the double dissociation was found at above-threshold presentation, but not for below-threshold presentation, suggesting that there are different neural correlates to overt and covert processing of emotive faces.

Whalen et al. (2001), using fMRI, reported greater activation in the dorsal amygdala in a fear vs. anger contrast, and in the ventral amygdala in a fear vs. neutral contrast, suggesting different parts of the amygdala are involved in different negative emotions. Interestingly, Hariri et al. (2002b) found that the amygdala is more activated by fearful faces than by fear-inducing pictures, pointing to the preferential processing of information revealed by the face. This finding supports Darwin's idea that facial expressions of emotion play an important role in evolution – although, as discussed above, he downplayed the communicative function of facial expressions that seems central to the function of facial expressions.

An important factor in the extent of amygdala activation to fearful and angry facial expression is conscious cognitive control. In an fMRI study, Hariri et al. (2003) showed that, whereas perceptual processing of threatening and fear-related slides was associated with a bilateral amygdala response, cognitive evaluation of the same stimuli was associated with the reduction of this amygdala response and a correlated increase in activation in prefrontal cortex and anterior cingulate cortex. (For a thorough review of emotion and amygdala activation, see Zald, 2003.)

5-HTTLPR and amygdala

If the 5-HT promotor polymorphism gene (see below) is involved in individual differences in reactions to emotive stimuli, and such reactions are mediated by the amygdala, then it should be expected that polymorphisms in this gene should be related to activation in the amygdala. Hariri and Weinberger (2003) reported that individuals with the short version of this gene have greater amygdala activity, as assessed by fMRI, in response to the presentation of fearful stimuli.

Neural correlates of personality

In the first fMRI study relating measures of personality to emotion-related brain reactivity, Canli et al. (2001) required female-only participants to watch positive and negative scenes. The results showed that brain reactivity to positive (relative to negative) pictures correlated with extroversion in a number of cortical and subcortical locations, including the amygdala; similarly, brain reactivity to negative (relative to positive) pictures correlated with neuroticism at several sites. However, the study lacked a baseline (neutral) condition, so the BOLD responses represented differences in activation patterns to positive and negative images – thus, it was not possible to distinguish increased activation to positive stimuli from decreased activation to negative stimuli.

In a second study, Canli et al. (2002) tested both males and females (the first study tested only females), and it also included a baseline (neutral) condition. The finding that amygdala activation to happy (vs. neutral) faces correlated with extroversion was replicated. Importantly, this relation was specific to happy faces, because amygdala activation to other emotional facial expressions did not correlate significantly with this trait.

Reuter et al. (2004) tested males and females in an fMRI-emotion task, using slides that depicted facial reactions indicative of fear, disgust, sexual arousal and joy. They also took specific measures of sensitivity to reward and sensitivity to punishment, as measured by the Carver and White (1994) BIS/BAS scales. BIS scores were significantly correlated with brain activity in response to disgust in the anterior cingulate, (right) amygdala and thalamus. Unexpectedly, there was also a significant correlation between BAS score and brain activity induced by disgust in the insula. Significant correlation between BIS scores and fear-induced brain activity was observed in the cingulate and thalamus – the BAS scale was not associated with fear-related brain activation. The BAS scale was associated with brain activation to erotic pictures, and this activation was observed in the hippocampus. Such data show the complexity of FFFS, BIS and BAS reactions to emotive stimuli; and, although the pattern of effects are not highly consistent at this time, they do show that individual differences in sensitivity to reinforcing stimuli are related to differential patterns of emotion-related brain processing: this is the central claim of RST.

The neuroimaging literature on emotion and personality is reviewed by Canli and Amin (2002). It is noteworthy that the degree of neural activation is related to the degree of subjective intensity of stimuli, and furthermore these *state* emotion effects, as induced by external stimuli (e.g., emotive faces), are related to the well-established personality dimensions of Extroversion and Neuroticism. This is an area of intense research interest, and the next few years will witness new knowledge of direct relevance to the neuroscience of personality. There is also now an interest in 'social neuroscience' (Cacioppo et al., 2000; Ochsner & Lieberman, 2001), which aims to uncover the neuroscientific nature of social behaviour – here it is probable that individual differences will be found to be important.

A number of other functional studies of extroversion and neuroticism have been conducted in relation to working memory (WM) and attentional processes. Using fMRI, Gray and Braver (2002) found that BAS-active individuals showed better WM and lower WM-related activation in the caudal anterior cingulate cortex (ACC). Eysenck's arousal theory of personality has been interpreted as suggesting that activation in arousal circuits in the brain, including the dorsolateral prefrontal cortex (DLPFC) and anterior cingulate cortex (ACC), should be correlated with extroversion. Kumari et al. (submitted) tested this hypothesis and reported that, using a working memory task, higher extroversion scores were correlated with task-relevant activity in both the DLPFC and ACC.

Lastly, there may be structural anomalies associated with neuroticism. Knutson et al. (2001) found that this factor of personality was negatively correlated with the ratio of brain to the remainder of intracranial volume, a finding suggesting that individual differences in stress reactivity contribute to reductions in brain volume observed during adulthood. This conclusion was supported by the finding that only two facets of neuroticism, namely anxiety and self-consciousness, were related to brain ratio.

These data show that there are complex patterns of activation in response to emotive faces, and some structures (e.g., the amygdala) seem to be involved in mediating various emotions. Indeed, measures of behavioural inhibition taken at 2 years of age showed that the more inhibited individuals showed a greater fMRI response in the amygdala to novel faces in adulthood (mean age 22 years). Such data show: (a) the existence of fundamental personality differences at a very young age; and (b) the stability of personality over the course of development.

Anxiety: amygdala and/or septo-hippocampal system?

Neuroimaging can be used to resolve theoretical questions. Much research assumes that fear and anxiety are related states, and that classical conditioning paradigms can be used to understand the genesis and maintenance of neurotic behaviour (see chapter 15). However, as noted in this chapter, in some important respects, fear and anxiety are opposing states; and classical conditioning does not explain anxiety, nor, in fact, can it explain fear. Now, one dominant theory argues that the amygdala is the site of action of fear conditioning, and thus fear (see LeDoux, 1996). However, the Gray and McNaughton theory (2000) challenges this theory. They point out several disconcerting findings for this 'amygdalo-centric' view.

First, the amygdala seems to do too much: it is responsible for cue-reinforcer conditioning with aversive *and* appetitive stimuli; and unconditioned responses, such as aggressive and sexual behaviour, also depend on this structure. Thus, the amygdala seems to be involved in controlling the *outputs* of many, if not all, emotion systems: it is responsible for producing *general emotional arousal* (the evidence discussed above shows that it is also involved in mediating emotional reactions to happy faces).

In addition, anxiety is not about fear of pain solely, but also failure or loss of reward. There is evidence that frustrative non-reward (i.e., the non-appearance of an expected reward) is aversive.[15] Certain forms of frustration, particularly those that are anticipatory, are reduced by anxiolytics. However, lesion of the amygdala does not affect frustration-mediated responses – so it seems that there is a problem to be solved: an obviously negative emotional state, which is sensitive to anxiety-reducing drugs, is not affected by destruction of the amygdala 'emotion centre'. Therefore, this negative emotion must be generated somewhere else. Also, there are other behaviours related to anxiety that are not affected by lesions to the amygdala.

The Gray and McNaughton (2000) theory holds that the processing of anxiety-related information is performed by the septum and hippocampus – the 'septo-hippocampal system' (SHS) – and this outputs to the amygdala, which then generates the emotional *arousal* component of anxiety (for an updated version of this theory, see McNaughton & Corr, 2004). Does neuroimaging have the potential to resolve this theoretical conflict?

Ploghaus et al. (2001) presented healthy volunteers with a painful heat stimulus under conditions of either low or high anxiety (high anxiety was induced by the presentation of a stimulus that threatened of an even more painful stimulus). Activation indexed by fMRI was found to be increased in the hippocampal formation, along with correlated activity in a region of the insular cortex specialized for pain perception.

Furmark et al. (2002) tested social phobic patients during a public-speaking task, which generates an approach(BAS)–avoidance(FFFS) conflict. PET activity was measured in a control (no treatment) group and before and after treatment of two kinds: drug and cognitive-behavioural therapy. In those patients who responded to treatment (not all did), and independently of the treatment applied, improvement in symptoms was associated with a decrease in rCBF in the hippocampus and the amygdala. This finding is consistent with the Gray and McNaughton (2000) theory that *social* phobia involves dysfunction in both the hippocampus and the amygdala – in contrast, simple phobia, where avoidance is possible in the absence of an approach–avoidance conflict, the hippocampus is not involved (i.e., simple phobia is fear, not anxiety).

More generally, what this type of analysis indicates for biological psychology is that the search for the 'lesion' (i.e., the site) of any behaviour, but especially complex emotions, is problematic, as is the belief that each site mediates only one major function. In the case of the hippocampus, this has been variously restricted to memory, long-term potentiation or even highly specific functions, such as spatial memory.

> **ASK YOURSELF**
> In what ways can neuroimaging be used to test different causal models of personality?

Non-human Animal Selection Studies

The inheritance of personality has yet to be addressed. Several approaches may be used to explore this issue, including statistical and molecular genetic strategies. There is also the powerful strategy of selective breeding; this strategy has the advantage of allowing a more rigorous analysis of the mode of genetic influence. In particular, it provides *direct* evidence for inheritance.

Selected breeding entails the selection and inbreeding of animals (usually rats and mice) with low and high values on some normally distributed phenotype (e.g., behavioural indicators of fearfulness); an unselected control strain is also maintained to ensure that it is the selective breeding that is producing the differences observed in the phenotype.

It is known that artificial selection has long been practised by human society: its results are evident in domestic pets and farm animals, where preferred phenotypes (e.g., friendly dogs and high-yield milking cows) were selected generation on generation to produce breeds that are very different from the original stock – in the case of dogs, not only are these now very different from the wild wolf, from which they derive, but there is great variety within the domestic dog. The splendid variety of show pigeons derives from the colourless wild variety of pigeon. In an interesting study, in Russia, tame foxes have been interbred for more than 40 generations, with the result that a new breed of fox has evolved which, unlike its feral relatives, which are wary of human contact, are like dogs in their friendliness and eagerness for human contact – so remarkable has been their evolution that they are now kept as house pets (Trut, 1999).

Just as human society has selectively bred for desired traits, so too Nature has select-ively bred from desired (i.e., best-fitting) phenotypes: this was the basic argument of Charles Darwin's theory of natural selection – of course, in Nature's case, selection is a blind process, guided by the invisible hand of 'survival of the fittest' (in terms of the local environment) and reproductive success. However, this theory is core to the idea that personality has evolved, and that artificial 'domestic' selection can be used to under-stand the process of natural selection: the observation that it is possible – indeed, relat-ively easy – to breed separate phenotypes in non-human animals strongly supports the theory that Nature too can naturally select phenotypes – indeed, given the ease of domes-tic breeding, is not evolution by natural selection inevitable?

One of the longest and largest selective breeding programmes selected mice for activ-ity in a bright-lit box (open field). In this open field environment, many animals freeze, defecate and urinate, whereas others explore it: these individual differences are assumed to reflect fearfulness. Selective (in)breeding of the low and high fearful mice produces, over 30 generations (in mice, a generation is only 3 months), two distinct phenotypes: the high-activity line became increasingly more active; and the low-activity line became even more inhibited and fearful (the unselected control line stayed unchanged). In fact, over these 30 generations, there is a 30-fold average difference in activity: the high-activity, bold mice run long distances in the open field; in contrast, the low-activity, timid mice sit quivering in the corner (DeFries, Gervais & Thomas, 1978).

Broadhurst (1960) selectively bred rats on the basis of open-field performance, in which he selected rats with high and low rates of defecation. This procedure led to two strains that differed significantly in their defecation in the open-field test: rats with high defeca-tion rates were called the Maudsley reactive (MR) strain; and rats with low defecation rates were called the Maudsley non-reactive (MNR) strain. These strains have been influen-tial in testing animal models of fear/anxiety. For example, they are used to test drugs for their anti-anxiety properties.

An important result of such experiments is that the difference between low- and high-activity strains increases each generation, implying that the trait being selected is controlled by many genes of relatively small (polygenic) effect, rather than a few genes of major effect (oligogenic). This finding explains why there are individual differences in personality: with unselected (natural) human breeding, genes get recombined, producing a normal distribution of values within a population (see below).

Strains of non-human animals bred for emotionality are used in molecular genetic technologies aimed at identifying sequences of DNA implicated in emotional behaviour. This line of research offers the opportunity to investigate the genetic basis of emotionality using rigorous methodologies not possible in human beings; and it offers the promise of yielding results that are directly applicable to understanding normal and pathological expression of emotions in human beings. As discussed by Flint (2004), this work has been facilitated by Gray's general approach to emotion and personality, which highlights the congruence of animal models of anxiety and human neuroticism.

> **ASK YOURSELF**
> In what ways do selective breeding studies confirm that non-human animals have personalities?

▢ Human Genetics

Genes make a major contribution to individual differences in human personality (Plomin et al., 2001); this is shown by quantitative studies and is now being addressed at the molecular level of explanation. It has also been possible to examine the genetic foundation of individual differences in non-human animals, where considerable work has been directed to understanding such behaviours as fearfulness (e.g., selective breeding studies; see above).

In a large genetic study of personality, Loehlin and Nichols (1976) studied nearly 800 pairs of adolescent twins and reached several conclusions: (a) nearly all personality traits show moderate heritability; and (b) although environmental variance is important, virtually all of this variance makes children growing up in the same family different from one another (i.e., non-shared environment). This last conclusion challenges our intuitive notions of personality; that is, the family environment exerts an important influence on the development of personality. Indeed, many theories of personality (e.g., psychoanalysis) are based upon this flawed assumption. It is often said that parents are environmentalists after the birth of their first child, but geneticists after the birth of their second.

How this effect of non-shared environment comes about is not entirely clear. It is possible that there are simply more sources of influence outside the family environment. In addition, it is possible that children develop a form of 'learned irrelevance' to the family environment, leading to a withdrawal of attention from it (possibly mediated by a process comparable to latent inhibition), which is then allocated to extra-family stimuli (e.g., friends). There is also the possibility that an *active* process of seeking varied and external stimuli is part of growing up and becoming independent outside the family unit – this process would have an obvious adaptive function of learning 'to stand on one's own two feet', necessary to secure a sexual mate and build an independent life sufficient to raise children. Less interesting is the possibility of a methodological factor: when assessing shared (family) and non-shared (extra-family) environments, there is more variance in the latter than in the former, hence it may appear more important in statistical designs that are sensitive to *differences*. There is the added possibility that the influence of these two types of environment is itself influenced by personality, with some types of people being 'home birds' (possibly the shy, retiring types), while the more venturesome types are influenced more by factors outside the family environment. This possibility is supported by the finding that different personality types 'niche pick': if the family environment does not conform to the temperament of the child, then they are more likely to look for their personality–environment fit elsewhere.

Loehlin (1992) summarized the results from a number of large-scale studies, with a total sample size of 24,000 pairs of twins. For extroversion, correlations were about 0.50 for MZ (identical) twins and 0.20 for DZ (fraternal) twins. Studies of twins reared apart appear also to indicate genetic influence, as do adoption studies for Extroversion. However, for Neuroticism, adoption studies point to less genetic influence than twin studies – indeed, the sibling data indicate little or no genetic influence at all. Lower heritability in adoption than in twin studies could be due to special environmental effects that boost identical twin similarity (e.g., gene–environment interaction). Model-fitting analyses across twin and adoption studies produce heritability estimates of about 50 per cent for Extroversion and 40 per cent for Neuroticism. In regard to the other three factors of the FFM model-fitting summary of family, twin and adoption data produce estimates of 45 per cent for Openness to Experience, 38 per cent for Conscientiousness and 35 per cent for Agreeableness.

There is now overwhelming evidence that personality is influenced by *both* genetic and environmental factors, as well as their complex interplay. From a biological perspective this should came as no surprise: the mind (including personality) is a product of the brain; the brain is influenced by both genetic and environmental factors; therefore, the mind (personality) is influenced by the genetics and environmental factors. This point is perhaps now too obvious to mention, but, in the past, personality was deemed to be an environmentally determined variable, with genetics playing little, if any, role.

It is important, once again, to recall the caveats presented in chapter 13 concerning the interpretation of genetic and non-genetic influences. The genetic estimates presented here are group means; it is likely – indeed, given what is known about the personality processes, probable – that there is a wide spread of influences at the individual level of analysis. For example, individuals born with an overactive fear system may well have a higher genetic loading than individuals with an underactive fear system, but adverse environmental experiences can lead to heightened trait fear in low and high genetic-loaded individuals – as always, the outcome is probabilistic.

In order to understand the complex interaction of genetic and environmental factors, it is important to understand the molecular basis of personality as well as the impact of environmental events.

Molecular genetics

Since the 1990s the search has been on for the DNA foundations of personality. Two genes have attracted particular attention: (a) dopamine receptor D_4 (DRD4); and (b) 5-HT (serotonin) transporter promoter region (5-HTTLPR). An excellent summary of this research is provided by Ebstein, Benjamin and Belmaker (2003). As noted by these authors (pp. 370–1),

Although historically the proof of the heritability of complex human traits was based on twin, family and adoption studies, advances in molecular genetics may allow investigators to bypass this classical methodological troika,[16] and by directly demonstrating association of a particular quantitative trait locus . . . with a specific gene, will establish the heritability of the trait.

The whole field is summarized in a book that would have been impossible a few years ago, *Molecular Genetics and the Human Personality* (Benjamin, Ebstein & Belmaker, 2002). Dopamine genes are associated with approach (appetitive) motivation, and 5-HT genes with defensive (aversive) motivation.

Dopamine receptor D$_4$ (DRD4)

Great excitement accompanied the publication in 1996 of two reports showing an association between a dopamine receptor subunit (DRD4) and the personality trait of novelty seeking (Benjamin et al., 1996; Ebstein et al., 1996): individuals who score high on this trait are characterized as being impulsive, exploratory, fickle, excitable, quick tempered and extravagant.

This gene consists of seven alleles involving 2, 3, 4, 5, 6, 7 and 8 repeats on a 48-base-pair sequence on chromosome 11 that codes the D$_4$ receptor of dopamine. It is expressed primarily in the brain's limbic system. The number of repeats alters the receptor's structure, which has been shown to affect the receptor's efficiency. The shorter alleles (2, 3, 4 or 5 repeats) code for receptors that are more efficient in binding dopamine than are the receptors coded for by the longer alleles (6, 7 or 8 repeats). Individuals with a long-repeat DRD4 allele are said to seek novelty to compensate for their less efficient dopamine binding.

DRD4 alleles are usually grouped as *short* (approx. 85 per cent of the population) or *long* (approx. 15 per cent of the population) alleles. In both studies, individuals with long repeats had significantly higher novelty-seeking scores; this genetic variation and its associated behaviours were also found *within* families, a result indicating that the association is not due to ethnic differences: that is, within a family, individuals with the long repeat had significantly higher novelty-seeking scores than did their siblings with the short repeat. Over 12 studies have now reported this effect, although there have also been failures to replicate (perhaps because of the small effect size; Plomin et al., 2001). For a summary of the DRD4 and personality literature, see Prolo & Licinio (2002). This genetic influence on novelty seeking is very modest (only about 4 per cent; Benjamin et al., 1996), a finding that corroborates the idea that personality involves the action of many genes of small effect.

DRD4 also shows an association with hyperactivity: long-repeat alleles are associated with risk-taking, as would be expected on the basis of the novelty-seeking association. In addition, this long repeat has been associated with heroin addiction (see Ebstein & Kotler, 2002), which is interesting given the long-known association of the trait of sensation seeking and drug abuse, including opiate abuse.

Animal studies support these human findings. DRD4 knock-out mice (i.e., the DRD4 gene has been prevented from expressing proteins; see chapter 13) show increased sensitivity to alcohol and reduced behavioural response to novel stimuli. Also, there is evidence that dog breeds with the short version tend to be docile (e.g., golden retrievers) as compared with long-version, more aggressive dogs (see Ebstein, Benjamin & Belmaker, 2003).

5-HT transporter promoter region (5-HTTLPR)

Given the survey of the importance of 5-HT in relation to depression and anxiety (chapters 14 and 15), it should be suspected that genes coding for 5-HT neurotransmitter functions are implicated in neurotic conditions and neurosis in general; and it may also be suspected that the genes specifically involved in the transporter mechanism, which is responsible for the reuptake of excessive 5-HT from the synaptic cleft, play an especially important role. On both counts, these suspicions would be correct.

As discussed in chapter 15, the human 5-HTT is encoded by a single gene on chromosome 17; it is composed of 14 to 15 exons spanning a large area. Transcription activity of the human 5-HTT gene is modulated by a polymorphic repetitive element, the 5-HTT gene-linked region (5-HTTLPR).

The brainstem raphe 5-HT system is the most widely distributed neurotransmitter system in the brain; these neurons diffusely project to a variety of regions (cortex, hippocampus and amygdala). In the brains of adult human and non-human primates and other mammals, 5-HT neurotransmission is a major modulator of emotional behaviour and integrates cognition, sensory processing, motor activity and circadian rhythms, including food intake, sleep and reproductive activity. 5-HT orchestrates the activity and interaction of several other neurotransmitter systems. Although 5-HT may be viewed as a master control neurotransmitter within this highly complex system of control, 5-HT's actions as a chemical messenger are primarily terminated by reuptake via 5-HTT: this transporter plays a critical role in regulating 5-HT neurotransmission in numerous projection sites in the brain.

There have been a number of studies investigating the role of allelic variation in 5-HT transporter (5-HTT) function in various clinical conditions, including mood disorders, panic disorders, obsessive–compulsive disorder, attention deficit disorder, autism, schizophrenia, Alzheimer's disease and substance abuse. There is a substantial body of evidence to indicate that personality traits such as neuroticism (or negative emotionality) are involved in affective spectrum disorders (Kendler et al., 1993). In particular, generalized anxiety disorder and major depression have common genetic origins, and the phenotypic differences between anxiety and depression seem to be dependent on the environment; and it is also known that there is overlap between neuroticism and general vulnerability to anxiety/depression in terms of the genes involved (Kendler, Gruenberg & Kinney, 1994; Kendler et al., 1994; for a brief summary of this literature, see Eley, 2003). These findings suggest that when a QTL, such as 5-HTTLPR, is found for neuroticism, the same QTL should be found to be associated with anxiety and depression. Consistent with the dimensional perspective, anxiety and depression represent the extreme end of variation in negative emotionality. An important implication of this conclusion is that the study of neuroticism in the general population should enable the identification of genes of relevance to clinical disorders.

In one study, individuals with the short and long version of the gene were examined in terms of their reactions to multiple aversive life events, for example losing a job (Caspi et al., 2003). They found that, of the individuals with the long version, only 17 per cent developed depression, but, of those with the short version, 43 per cent developed depression – this supports the finding reported in chapter 15 that low transcription of this gene is related to higher levels of neuroticism, a finding that is apparently inconsistent with the view that high levels of reuptake are related to neurotic conditions (for a resolution to this apparent contradiction, see chapter 15). This gene was also found to be associated with responses to stress during childhood and whether individuals experiencing multiple aversive life events thought about or attempted suicide. Cause and effect here must be treated with caution. For example, it is probable that 'childhood stress' is not due to person-independent external events, but to some extent involves the *perception* and interpretation of the environment. The discussion above highlighted that the perception of threat is an important aspect of the personality dimension of Neuroticism.

Given genetic knowledge, cross-species similarities should come as no surprise (see below). For example, Lesch (1997) compared genes across a range of mammals (including tree shrews, rhesus monkeys, chimpanzees and human beings) and estimated that the 5-HTTLPR gene implicated in Neuroticism was probably introduced into the genome about 40 million years ago! This cross-species similarity is important when seen in the light of the fact that 5-HT reuptake inhibitors, related to the functioning of this gene, are the first-line treatment for a range of human conditions of anxiety and depression.

There have been a large number of studies looking at associations between genes, especially 5-HT and dopamine genes, and personality, but this literature is complex and contains many failures to replicate. Whatever the reasons for these failures, and there are many (the most important ones being inadequate statistical power due to sample size, and homogeneity within the population tested, which restricts the variance and thus the chance of detection and association), they counsel caution. In fact, in a meta-analysis of 46 studies, Munafo et al. (2003, p. 471) concluded that there were significant associations between 5-HTTLPR and DRD4 polymorphisms and personality traits, but when a multivariate analysis was conducted, which included age, sex and ethnicity as covariates (i.e., the contribution to variance of these factors was removed), only the 5-HTTLPR association with harm avoidance (a measure of anxiety) remained significant; but even this association disappeared when unpublished data were included and the data were adjusted for stability of population frequency. Reif and Lesch (2003) provide a summary of the gene–personality literature in their paper on the molecular architecture of personality. Plomin (2002) gives a summary of individual differences research in the 'postgenomic era'.

> **ASK YOURSELF**
> What are the routes by which genes influence personality?

◫ Evolution of Individual Differences

In a similar vein to clinical conditions, personality traits have a polygenic basis: many genes of small effect seem to underlie the approximately normal distribution of scores of the major factors of personality. Also, it is evident that there is a substantial non-genetic (environmental) contribution to personality variance, and there is reason to suspect the existence of complex gene–environment interactions. Given this polygenic nature of personality, it is easy to see why so much variation exists: in each generation genes get reassorted in a random fashion, and this leads to a small number of people having a low value on a particular trait, others having a high value, and most people being bunched around the more frequently occurring centre of the distribution. This generational probabilistic resorting would be sufficient to curtail the elimination of all individual differences.

Variation may also be maintained by several equally successful (good-fitting) evolutionary strategies. For example, for every brave (low-fear) individual who achieves fame and status in battle, and thereby increases his chance of reproduction, there are the fallen soldiers who never get the chance to reproduce; in this environment there may be timid (high-fear) individuals who phobically stay at home and manage to reproduce and protect their offspring. In purely genetic terms, who possessed the most adaptive phenotypes in the Second World War: the brave soldiers who were first into battle or the 'war neurotics' who ended up back home, taking part in Hans Eysenck's factor-analytical studies? Fortune may favour the brave, but natural selection may favour the fearful.

As discussed in chapters 14–16, apparently maladaptive traits may well have an evolutionary advantage, and this alone may maintain the frequency of the underlying genes at a viable level in the population. Indeed, many of the clinical disorders seem to serve fairly obvious evolutionary functions: fear and anxiety, although personally distressing when extreme, keep us out of harm's way; and even the suspicion, hostility and loose cognitive associations seen in schizophrenia/schizotypy are not without their benefits. To live a miserable, suspicious, fear-ridden, cognitively distorted life is better (i.e., more fitness-enhancing; see chapter 2), from the selfish gene's-eye perspective, if it serves the interests of survival and reproduction – a 'balanced' level of happiness, trust and cognitive realism may not be so adaptive. Taking the gene's-eye view of what is adaptive and what is not goes a long way to helping us understand the process of evolutionary forces and the existence of 'pathological', as well as 'normal', phenotypes.

The adaptiveness of traits is usually seen in terms of modern-day environments, where extreme values on some traits appear to confer no survival or reproductive advantage; but the genes underlying traits evolved in the past (sometimes the long past), when environmental conditions were very different from those experienced today. Humans fear harmless snakes and spiders, but are careless when it comes to the much more dangerous inventions of modern society (e.g., electricity, driving and unhealthy food). From an evolutionary viewpoint, humans should be terrified of contraceptives – for they block the very process by which selfish genes replicate (see chapter 2) – but there are probably few condom phobics seen in the psychiatric clinic!

> **ASK YOURSELF**
> If emotional and motivational processes serve important evolutionary functions then why do large individual differences in these processes exist?

Conclusion

It should now be (perhaps too) evident that, although great strides have been taken in understanding the biological basis of personality, there are still many unanswered – indeed, many unasked – questions. The application of powerful new techniques of investigation (e.g., molecular genetics and neuroimaging) will surely change this picture in the years to come, and throw important new light on our very individuality.

But now it is clear that the combination of basic elements can generate much of the complexity of personality; as in the case of colour receptors, a few basic emotion systems combine to produce the full 'colour' of emotional experience that forms the foundations of personality.

Learning Questions

1. In what sense do we each have a unique personality?
2. Why are there so many competing descriptive models of personality?
3. How does reinforcement sensitivity theory (RST) account for extroversion and neuroticism?
4. What do genetics studies tell us about the relationship between personality and clinical depression/anxiety?
5. Can we explain individual differences by reference to genetic and evolutionary processes?

NOTES

1 The entire book can be read at http://etext.lib.virginia.edu/toc/modeng/public/DarExpr.html (other websites also contain the entire text).

2 Boakes (1984) provides a discussion of the influence of Darwin's idea on early psychology, and how the concept of emotion became obsolete with the advent of behaviourism.

3 Ekman's (1998) book contains more complete material than Darwin's first edition, which was published in 1872 (for this reason it is a definitive edition).

4 At that time, when the 'genetics' of inheritance was unknown – indeed, the word had not been coined for the process of inheritance – the Lamarckian idea of evolution by acquired characteristics was a perfectly sensible hypothesis. However, not knowing the precise mechanism obscured the fundamental distinction between 'social inheritance' (wealth, surname, etc.) and 'biological inheritance' (i.e., DNA). Features of some forms of emotional expression, bodily gestures and situational constraints on the expression of emotion show evidence of social inheritance (i.e., learning). For example, several generations of men may show a marked peculiarity of expression (e.g., stroking back of the head), which might be interpreted as biologically transmitted but is simply a learned, social form of inheritance. Without the sophisticated experimental designs of genetics (see chapter 13), it was next to impossible for Darwin to clarify these issues.

5 Evolutionary psychologists find it difficult to believe that the love of one's children, the negative emotions felt when they are threatened and the joy experienced by their success are of no adaptive importance: if true, it would indeed be odd that positive and negative emotions are isomorphic with their survival and fecundity and thus the interests of the 'selfish gene' (see chapter 2).

6 It is thought the death of Darwin's daughter Annie, at the age of 11 years, had a major impact on his thinking, especially in relation to a benign God and the role that emotion plays as a phenomenon of Nature.

7 The 'correlation coefficient' is a statistical measure of the relationship between two variables: the sign (−/+) of the correlation refers to whether variables are negatively or positively related; and the magnitude of the coefficient refers to the strength of the relation (−1 = perfect negative correlation; +1 = perfect positive correlation; 0 = no correlation).

8 At this point in the analysis an important decision must be made: how many factors should be 'extracted' – this decision must be based on some extraction criterion, usually consisting of a distinction being made between important and trivial factors, for example, as defined by the amount of variance explained by each factor or the adequacy of the factors to account for most of the variance in the original variables.

9 The Lie scale measures response distortion due to deliberate faking or social desirability response set (i.e., tendency to endorse only socially acceptable responses).

10 It would be wise to follow Darwin's lead in not assuming that some species are 'lower' or 'higher' than others – all species are equal in terms of evolution – arguably, the 'lower' life forms much more so, as they have been in existence for very much longer than so-called 'higher' life forms (e.g., human beings). The idea that there is a tree of life, with higher, more evolved life forms at the top, may be traced to the great Greek philosopher, Aristotle. The residual notion that human beings are superior to 'the animals' has a theological basis, not a scientific one.

11 Experimental destruction of the amygdala in non-human animals or degeneration in human beings leads to impaired reactions to aversive stimuli, a condition known as *Kluver–Bucy* syndrome – an example of the use of neurophysiology and clinical neuropsychology to arrive at a common conclusion.

12 The 1982 version of the theory postulated that the BIS is activated by *conditioned* stimuli of punishment (and innate fear stimuli); however, even in this theory, it was implicit that there was a goal conflict between approach and avoidance (the effects of a *conditioned* stimulus on ongoing behaviour represent goal conflict; and consistent effects of anxiolytics are found only on punishment tasks that entail some form of conflict).

13 The motivational propensities to *leave* an environment (FFFS-mediated) and *enter* an environment (BIS-mediated) are jointly known as 'defensive direction' (McNaughton & Corr, 2004).

14 Unlike the other anxiety disorders (see chapter 15), PTSD is defined solely by its symptoms and may represent less an anxiety disorder than a permanent pathological change in personality defined in general terms as heightened threat sensitivity.

15 An example of frustrative non-reward would be being told that you have won a large sum of money on a lottery and then some time afterwards being told that this was a mistake (or practical joke). Although financially your situation would not have changed, this lack of expected reward would be a significant psychological event (in one such case, the lottery 'winner' became so depressed that he blew out his brains with a shotgun).

16 A word from Russian, meaning a team of three horses abreast; in this case: time, family and adoption genetic methodologies.

FURTHER READING

Benjamin, J., Ebstein, R. P. & Belmaker, R. H. (eds.) (2002). *Molecular Genetics and the Human Personality*. Washington, DC: American Psychiatric Association.

Matthews, G., Deary, I. J. & Whiteman, M. C. (2003). *Personality Traits*. Cambridge: Cambridge University Press.

Panksepp, J. (1998). *Affective Neuroscience: The Foundations of Human and Animal Emotion*. Oxford: Oxford University Press.

chapter
18
Cognition: Computation and Consciousness

Learning Objectives

To be able to:

1. Describe the 'brain–mind gap problem' and explain its importance in biological psychology.
2. Outline the computational theory of mind and relate it to domain-specific cognitive modules.
3. Explain the importance of consciousness and the problems it poses for biological psychology.
4. Summarize neuropsychological and experimental findings relating to conscious awareness.
5. Evaluate the value of a biological approach to consciousness that attempts to account for its form and function.

Cognition is rightly hailed as the finest product of evolution, providing us with, among other things, the means to reflect upon our own existence. This chapter considers the two main aspects of cognition: computation – *why* and *how* information is processed – and consciousness – experiential awareness of the external world and internal thoughts and feelings: the psychological essence of *self*.

Computation and consciousness are vast areas of study, and this chapter can do little more than highlight some of the problems and possible solutions from a biological perspective. These topics are discussed in a back-to-back manner, and each of the two major sections stands, and may be read, in its own right. It is intended that, by the end of this chapter, you should, at the very least, have a better understanding of these problems; and, it is to be hoped, a better idea of the type of solutions needed. The discussion is challenging: startling research findings shatter our most cherished beliefs of our self and of our understanding of the external world – *understanding*, as opposed to blind faith, is not for the faint-hearted! Despite some of the (necessary) complexity of this material, be reassured that your ideas may be just as good, if not better, than those of philosophers who have reflected upon these topics for millennia.

▣□ Understanding Biological Psychology: *Minding* the Gap

In the Preface it was noted that, in comparison with many textbooks on physiological psychology and biological psychology, the emphasis of this text would be more on biological *psychology* than *biological* psychology. But now a thorny problem must be faced – one steeped in the historical discussion of the 'mind–body problem'. Throughout this book both the physical stuff (brain) and the mental stuff (mind) of biological psychology have been considered, but the way in which these mind–body stuffs were related to one another was rather loose and ill-defined It is, therefore, appropriate that, at the end of a book of this type, the relationship between the brain and mind is considered in some detail – in other words, how to bridge the brain–mind gap signified by the humble hyphen. Our discussion could, of course, continue as if there were no problem; but this expedient strategy would not make the problem go away – it would only allow us to jump over the gap, eyes closed firmly, in the hope that not recognizing it would make it go away.

So let us start with the assumption that computation and consciousness *are* problems for biological psychology. It is assumed that they are a product of natural selection and are instantiated in the physical brain. These modest assumptions are not accepted by those philosophers and psychologists who argue that the mind cannot be 'reduced to', or 'identified with', the brain (at least as currently conceived). Limitation of space prevents adequate consideration of this important literature – fortunately Blackmore (2003) provides an excellent summary.

Mind your language

Before much progress can be made, the use of language in this area of psychology should be mentioned. Perhaps reflecting its deep philosophical roots, the words used to talk about cognition, especially consciousness, are thought by many philosophers and psychologists to betray one's theoretical leanings. For example, Dennett (1991) contends that most people, even those who espouse a materialistic philosophy, find it difficult to break away from a Cartesian mode of thought (termed 'Cartesian materialism'). According to Dennett, this wrong-headed mode of thought is revealed through the use of such terms as 'the product of computation', 'stimuli entering awareness' and 'the contents of consciousness', reflecting a belief that, somehow, consciousness is a place or process that things enter and leave, separate from other brain processes. Dennett has a point: the words used influence how we think about problems; and, as I have stressed throughout this book, *thinking* rigorously about problems is fundamental to clarifying them, and only by clarifying problems may their solution be found. In the Second World War, a common slogan ran, 'Loose Talk Costs Lives'; for our purposes, this may be reworded, 'Loose Thinking Costs Knowledge'.

> *ASK YOURSELF*
> Why are computation and consciousness often considered outside the remit of biological psychology?

▦☐ Cognition: Introduction

Let us start with an introduction to cognition in general before moving on to discussing computation and consciousness. 'Cognition' refers to 'knowing', which is a broad category involving both conscious information that can be recalled and non-conscious information that either is not explicitly known or cannot be verbally articulated.

The cognitive revolution of the 1950s – baptized by Noam Chomsky's (1959) highly critical review of B. F. Skinner's (1957) *Verbal Behavior* – was motivated by the perceived inadequacies of radical behaviourism, which rejected concepts relating to internal processes mediating the link between stimuli and responses (e.g., thought processes). The idea that internal representation (knowledge structures) and processes (e.g., decision-making) were important led to the emergence of a number of related fields (e.g., cognitive science, cognitive neuroscience, artificial intelligence, neural networks) built upon existing fields such as information theory, cybernetics and computer engineering, all underpinned by a general philosophy of mind (see chapter 1). One of the first books to emphasize the cognitive approach was by Miller, Galanter and Pribram (1960), who argued that units of behaviour, and their planning, could be likened to computer programs. As noted by Harnish (2002, p. 4),

> Construed narrowly, cognitive science is not an area but a *doctrine*, and the doctrine is basically that of the computational theory of mind (CTM) – the mind/brain is a type of computer.

Information: the 'bit' brain

The concept of 'information' is key to cognitive science. A useful definition of information derives from the field of cybernetics, which uses engineering principles to specify the key components of the flow of information over a channel. According to this approach, 'information' is the product of processing that reduces possibilities and uncertainty. Formally, using engineering terminology, a 'message' (information) travels from a 'sender' to a 'receiver' over a 'channel' which has a specific 'capacity' and a certain amount of 'noise'.

Within this information-theory framework, the standard measure of information is the 'bit' (i.e., binary digit). One 'bit' of information about a situation reduces uncertainty by one-half – thus, flipping a coin would reduce the uncertainty regarding two possible alternative states (i.e., heads or tails) to just one. Two 'bits' of information reduce the uncertainty about a situation involving four possibilities to one (first bit, 4 to 2; second bit, 2 to 1). Simply acquiring different messages about the same event, which does not reduce uncertainty, does not add 'information'.

Modules of mind

A particularly influential approach in cognitive science is Fodor's (1983) theory of *modules*, which are dedicated cognitive processors called 'input systems'; these are purely functional in nature and defined in terms of their computations. According to Fodor, input systems track the environment; and they represent the character and arrangement of things in the world on the basis of law-like information produced by transducing proximal stimuli (e.g., light energy) that represent the character and arrangement of things in the world that cause them (e.g., reflectance from surfaces). Modules are relatively self-contained processors with specific tasks. Input systems may be contrasted with 'central systems', which draw data from anywhere in the system.

As discussed below, evolutionary psychology has adopted this modular view of mind – although the validity of evolutionary arguments does not rest upon the validity of the modular approach. This perspective argues for the evolution of specialized adaptive modules that deal with *specific* environmental challenges (e.g., how to find and keep a sexual partner). However, there is still considerable debate concerning the nature of modules, especially their degree of domain specificity. Many psychologists prefer to view the brain–mind as a general-purpose processor that can be applied to any problem at hand (avoiding a snake or playing chess), rather than as an innately prepared perception–action system.

Although on the face of it these different perspectives may seem incompatible, they are not necessarily so. Some brain processes do, indeed, seem highly modular, while other processes seem to offer a greater degree of flexibility. It remains a possibility that this general–specific processing dimension is inherent in the hierarchical organization of the brain.

The next section can do little more than skim over the surface of this large and complex literature, focusing on those aspects of computation which may be informed by a biological perspective (Dawson, 1998, provides an excellent introduction to cognitive science). None the less, our brief Cook's tour should provide some insight into the sort of problems facing cognitive science and their implications for biological psychology.

ASK YOURSELF
What are the advantages to viewing the brain–mind as an information processor?

▢ Computation: Overview

Computation is concerned with specifying not only the general problem of information processing – the *why* question – but also with the procedures of information processing – the *how* question. Let us take as an example the very words you are now reading. From the light energy reflected off the page to the semantic understanding of this sentence, a tremendous amount of processing is required. The arbitrary shapes of the visual stimuli entering your eyes quickly get processed into meaning; but there are many intermediate stages in this effortless chain of events, involving feature extraction of individual letters (e.g., the lines and angles of the letter 'A') into words (e.g., APPLE) and phonemic (sound of word), grammatical (how the word modifies, and is modified by, other words in the sentence) and syntactic (formal arrangement of words) processing. An important aspect of this complex information processing is its non-consciousness. These complex computational stages take place without awareness: only the initial visual stimuli and the final product (i.e., what the sentence means) are accessible to the conscious mind.

Computation: algorithms and computers

As noted above, cognitive science and the general computational approach that underpins this science rely upon the type of computation performed by computers: this is more than a mere 'computer metaphor' – it is not saying that brain computation can be *likened* to computer processing; it is saying that cognitive science is based on the same computational ideas as those implemented in a computer (a 'computer' is simply a device that does computation: it computes). Thus, in a fundamental sense, computation is what computers do, and our only understanding of brain computation is from this computational (computer) perspective.

Without this computational *theory*, there would be little idea as to how the brain actually processes information – more precisely, it would be difficult even to start to think about brain processing. Of course, cognitive scientists do not believe that they know all there is to know about computational processes, but similarly they do not believe that there is anything else involved in how the brain computes. Understanding must start somewhere; that is, with *some* computational theory.

The computational algorithm

What is meant by 'computation'? Computers work on the basis of a 'computational algorithm'; this is a mathematical operation that can be performed by a computer. It is important to note that 'computer' in this sense is used to refer to a machine with unlimited memory storage and unlimited time to process (Penrose, 1987) – its failings are thus not due to capacity limitations. The 'Turing machine' (named after the brilliant mathematician Alan Turing) is the basis of the mathematical algorithmic process used by the computer. Computational psychology thus views the mind as a set of formalized mathematical algorithms. As in a machine, the brain's algorithmic process is broken down into elementary steps, where at each step the operation to be carried out is perfectly clear-cut and immediate, and so also is the procedure for moving on to the next elementary step. This computational theory of mind (CTM) emerged first in a 'digital' form, and then in a 'connectionist' form – in its various manifestations it relies on computing procedures (see chapter 7).[1] One of the earliest exponents of the computational approach in psychology was Kenneth Craik (1943), who died at an early age in a bicycle accident.

Software vs. hardware

It is obvious that the computational approach draws a sharp distinction between software and hardware. Indeed, the computational approach to mind would not be possible without this assumption. This computational perspective assumes that one day it may be possible to build a computer (e.g., an artificial brain) that has all the formal properties of the brain and thus all its qualities. This perspective follows the logic of computational science, and forms the most widely held view of the brain–mind: 'functionalism', which contends that once the input–output relations have been (perfectly) simulated then all the qualities of these input–output relations will be obtained (thus, one day, there will be a thinking computer that is conscious – indeed, this logic implies that machines today must have at least some of the qualities of the human mind). This is a highly seductive hypothesis, because it appears that it must be true – otherwise it is necessary to invoke some other entity/process, over and above functional relations, to explain the outputs of the brain (especially consciousness). However, there are reasons for thinking that functionalism is wrong (see Gray, 2004); anyhow, it remains an untested assumption – a rather large, uncashed cheque against an account of unknown funds.

For a start, it must be supposed that it would be possible *perfectly* to match input–output functions: this is a big supposition. Functionalism may be true in principle, but unobtainable in practice. But, as I show below, there are reasons for thinking that the brain may not be a computational device of the type studied by (past and current) computer engineers.

Second, there is a world of difference between input–output relations being *simulated* – where functions are not 'real' (e.g., the lightning and thunder generated by a computer simulation of a weather system is not *real* lightning and thunder) and *instantiated* – where the machine takes on the physical attributes of the formal input and output variables and, therefore, the whole system assumes their intervening (functional) properties (this whole-systems approach would resemble a robot rather than a desktop computer). As discussed below, it is often assumed that for such a robot to be able to carry out the full functions of the human mind then it would need to have some degree of true consciousness (but see the 'zombie problem' below). For such robots to survive and reproduce in a harsh selection environment, they would need to develop central states corresponding to animal emotion and motivation, for the reasons presented in chapter 17. As discussed below, they would also need to construct an internal model of the external world which incorporated the notion of an egocentric 'self'. At this level of sophistication they would not be 'robots' as conventionally conceived: they would start to resemble real animals and behave in ways that adhere to the biological constraints and challenges of their environment. They would start to resemble us. It may be thought that these robots are, after all, only machines, albeit rather sophisticated ones, and whatever they might 'think' is artificial and of no real biological importance: it is all a construction of their wiring and software. However, as discussed at the end of this chapter, there are reasons to believe that this is exactly the nature of biological animals, including human beings.

To instantiate the functions of the brain–mind in an artificial device may require the 'right stuff'. The possibility that there may be something special about the material of the brain and its processes should not be dismissed too prematurely – the history of science is riddled with seemingly 'bizarre' claims that have been rejected, only later to be accepted as conventional science (e.g., the Earth moving around the sun, and quantum mechanics). In other words, a 'wetware' (biological systems) model of the brain–mind may be necessary.

The 'wetware' arguments

What are the reasons for thinking that a 'wetware' view of the brain–mind is important – that is, the indivisible nature of the computational process and the physical machine in which it is run (in this case, the brain)? First, there is the risk of over-applying the hardware–software distinction when discussing the brain–mind – as discussed in chapter 1, this is a convenient distinction only. Our mother tongue cannot be predicted from the structure of our brain – it is a 'software' feature. However, language processing is not solely a feature of software, although its computational processes may be simulated in software.

Broadly speaking, the computer is a general machine (or, at least, it can be designed that way). In contrast, the brain and mind co-evolved and were shaped by Darwinian processes – much of the 'programming' is therefore 'hard-wired', and much more like a specific-purpose robot than a general-purpose computer. Also, the brain is a massively parallel-processing device; although it may be implemented on a computer, this feature of the brain may be especially important.

In addition, there is one way that the brain is quite unlike a digital computer. It is not possible suddenly to reprogram the visual cortex for auditory processing, but it is easy to load Microsoft Word into memory locations that just a moment ago stored Microsoft PowerPoint. The hardware of the computer is indifferent to the software: the brain and mind are very different in this important respect.[2] This difference may not be trivial – the truth is, we don't know. Scientific progress is still at an early stage of development and a good deal is yet to be known. However, there is the suspicion, at least, that brain computations are not merely software-based – and thus cannot be understood from a purely computational perspective – but that they are tied to the underlying neural machinery, especially genetically influenced hardware that imposes constraints and biases on processing (an example is given below). This possibility does not imply that computer simulation is not a valuable approach to modelling psychological processes, but it does suggest that 'innate' (i.e., genetic and hardware architecture) factors may need to be taken into account in such models and *instantiated* in biologically realistic models.

Roger Penrose[3] (1987, p. 263) asserts:

> that 'understanding' is *not* just a question of *software* (that is, programs or algorithms), but that the *hardware* should also be important. By 'hardware' is meant the actual physical construction of the object – either computer or brain.

According to Penrose (1994), the mind (including consciousness) cannot, in principle, be fully understood in computational terms. This conclusion, which comes from the realm of Kurt Gödel's theorem of mathematical logic and quantum mechanics, states that, for any sufficiently powerful logical system, statements can be formulated that can be neither proved nor disproved within that system – in other words, some mathematical statements are *non-computable*, even by the world's biggest computer. It is stated that as brains *can* compute such statements it must follow that brains are not computers – that is, they are not devices that conform to computational algorithms, as conventionally understood. If true, this statement holds fundamental implications for the computational view of the mind.

Less exotically, the brain may not be digital at all; there may be important analogue processes that do not require translation into and from digital form: oscillating brain patterns would be one example of an analogue form. When we look at a clock with a face and hands, the time is represented spatially by the position of the hands: it is in analogue form (sundials that reflect the sun are the most pristine form of analogue clocks). But when we look at a digital watch we lose this spatial representation, and now numbers are used to depict time: this digital form requires a translation into time. Thinking in terms of a digital computer may thus be misleading, producing problems for understanding the brain that might not exist if analogue principles were employed.

> **ASK YOURSELF**
> If the brain–mind is not *some* form of computer, then what is it?

Computation: Evolutionary Psychology

For the moment at least, let us accept that the brain–mind is a computational device of *some kind*. Is it a content-free device, or are its algorithmic processes biased in terms of processing (i.e., what it selects for processing and how it processes)? Evolutionary psychology (EP) has much to say on these questions.

Multimodularity

Evolutionary psychology aims to understand the structure of the human mind: in particular the content and form of processing shaped by Darwinian (natural and sexual) selection. It assumes that the brain–mind is composed of a set of information-processing, Fodor-type modules (or 'programs') to solve adaptive problems faced by our ancestors. These modules are composed of a large number of domain-specific expert systems, containing: inference procedures, regulatory rules, motivational priorities, goal definitions, assumptions that embody knowledge, regulatory structure and value weightings specific to an evolved problem domain. These programs have an obvious advantage in terms of speed and accuracy of response (see Carruthers & Chamberlain, 2000). Accordingly, the 'brain' and 'mind' are alternate terms to refer to the same system; and the mind is what the brain does, described in computational terms (Cosmides & Tooby, 1987; Pinker, 1997). Over evolutionary time, it was the *computational* properties of alternative neural circuits, and their relative ability to solve adaptive information-processing tasks, that resulted in some neural circuits being selected while others were not selected. Thus, 'computation' is what the brain does to solve adaptive problems; it is not the content of mind. In this sense, all aspects of the mind are computational: 'cognitive' (e.g., language) as well as 'emotional' processes.

Over the last two decades, many cognitive researchers have found evidence for the existence of a diverse collection of inference systems, including specializations for reasoning about objects, physical causality, number, language, the biological world, the beliefs and motivations of other individuals, and social interactions (see Barkow, Cosmides & Tooby, 1992).

Computational social reasoning

According to Cosmides (1989; Cosmides & Tooby, 1989, 1992), human beings have two major effects on each other: they can help (bestowing benefits) or hurt (inflicting costs). Importantly, social behaviour is conditional: reciprocity is required – if you expect me to scratch your back, then you will have to scratch mine. (Many families play the annual reciprocity game of who did and did not send a Christmas card – if you do not believe in the principle of reciprocity, then stop sending cards, gifts, etc., and see how many you receive in return!)

From an evolutionary perspective, one challenge of computation is to monitor and calculate the conditional value of social behaviour. Let us consider social exchange, involved in cooperation, reciprocal altruism or reciprocation (for review, see Cosmides & Tooby, 1992; discussed in chapter 2). The giving and taking involved in the process of social exchange are a complex process, entailing the construction of hypotheses about the structure of the exchange. It is thought that social exchange could not have evolved unless there existed the cognitive machinery to detect individuals who cheat (e.g., Axelrod, 1984; Axelrod & Hamilton, 1981; Boyd, 1988; Trivers, 1971; Williams, 1966). In this context, a cheater is an individual who accepts a benefit without satisfying the requirements upon which the provision of the benefit was contingent. Let us now explore the cheater detector in more detail; then experimental evidence for its existence is reviewed.

Cheater detection

Chapter 2 summarized the evolution of reciprocal altruism and cooperation in social animals. These forms of social behaviour were less easy to understand than kin selection, which is based directly on genetic relatedness. However, evolutionary models are now available to account for the widespread cooperation observed between non-genetically related individuals – most of our social life would be impossible without such cooperation. Now, simply being 'nice' to each other – admirable though that may be in an idealistic way – would not lead to the evolution of cooperation: simply imagining cheaters taking advantage of this 'niceness' is sufficient to show that the cheating strategy would quickly come to be dominant (a form of runaway psychopathy). To counter this possibility, cooperating individuals need to keep track of social behaviour: of the giving and receiving of resources. This social tracking is not an easy task; it is a difficult computational problem.

Evolutionary psychology has been successful in accounting for the evolution of 'cheat detectors'; that is, computational procedures dedicated to monitoring the selfish and selfless action of other people. The cheater detector extends to all social relationships.

Wason selection task

The notion that human beings have evolved a specific computational procedure for the detection of cheating is intriguing, and, although it seems demanded by theories of the evolution of social behaviour, is there evidence for it?

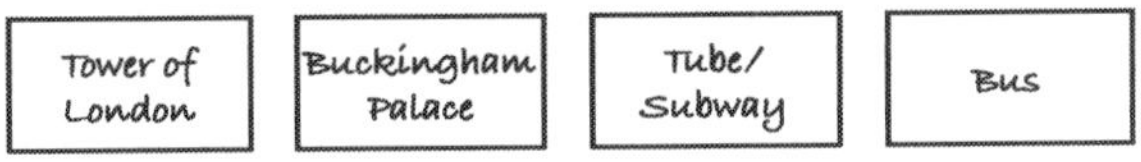

Tower of London	Buckingham Palace	Tube/ Subway	Bus

Figure 18.1 Wason selection task.

The Wason selection task (Wason, 1966; Wason & Johnson-Laird, 1972) is a standard measure of logical reasoning in cognitive psychology. In this task, experimental participants are asked to look for violations of a conditional rule of the form *If P then Q*.

Consider the Wason selection task presented in figure 18.1. Imagine that part of your new job for the Mayor of London was to study the demographics of transportation. You read a report on the habits of London residents that says:

If a person visits the Tower of London, then that person takes the tube [subway].

Four cards show (potential) information about four London residents (each card represents one person). One side of a card tells where a person went, and the other side how that person got there. Your task is to indicate which card(s) you definitely need to turn over to see if any of these people violated the above rule. Without looking at the answer below, now decide which card(s) you must turn over.

Have you made your decision? Now, from a purely logical point of view, the rule has been violated whenever someone goes to the Tower of London without taking the tube/subway. Hence the logically correct answer is to turn over the Tower of London card (to see if this person took the tube/subway) and the Bus card (to see if the person taking the bus went to the Tower of London). More generally, for a rule of the form *If P then Q*, one should turn over the cards that represent the values *P* and *not-Q*. Well, was this your answer?

Do not feel too disappointed if you did not make this logical choice: you are in good company. Many people confronted with this task do not make the logically correct choice. Indeed, fewer than 25 per cent of participants spontaneously make the correct choice; and even formal training in logical reasoning does little to boost performance on tasks of this kind (e.g., Cheng et al. 1986; Wason & Johnson-Laird, 1972). But why do people tend to make the wrong (logically speaking) choice? Put another way, if the brain is a general-purpose computational device, sensitive to mathematical rules (including logical inference), then why does it fail on this task? This 'failure' of logical reasoning suggests the operation of algorithms that are using pre-existing knowledge. Indeed, a large literature exists to show that people are not very good at detecting logical violations of if–then rules in Wason selection tasks, *even when these rules deal with familiar content drawn from everyday life* (e.g., Manktelow & Evans, 1979; Wason, 1983).

The Wason selection task has proved an attractive tool to study social exchange because: (a) it tests reasoning about conditional rules; (b) the task structure remains constant even when the content is changed; (c) content effects are easily elicited; and (d) there is an existing body of evidence against which performance on new content domains may be compared.

However, this task can be modified to show just how *good* people are at reasoning in situations involving cheating (Cosmides, 1989; Cosmides & Tooby, 1989, 1992). This is

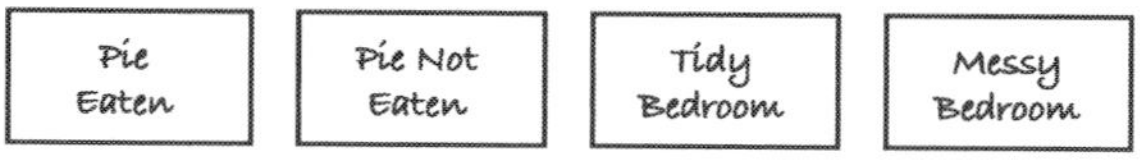

| Pie
Eaten | Pie Not
Eaten | Tidy
Bedroom | Messy
Bedroom |

Figure 18.2 Wason selection task – cheating.

a striking and counter-intuitive result: it strongly implies that the biases people show in cognitive processes (for example, in this case conditional reasoning) reflect built-in dispositions and are not the result of some purely logical computational algorithm.

Let us try our hand at this task again, but this time within a cheating domain (remember the purely logical structure of the task is unchanged). In our new domain, one is entitled to a benefit only if one has fulfilled a requirement (in the general form: 'if you take benefit B, then you must satisfy requirement R'). For example:

If you are to eat the pie, then you must first tidy your bedroom.

Cheating is accepting the benefit (i.e., eating the pie) specified without satisfying the condition (i.e., tidying your room). See figure 18.2.

Here the correct answer 'pops out': people turn over 'Pie Eaten' and 'Messy Bedroom' cards. Turning over the other two cards would not help us decide if the rule had been violated. In fact, when asked to identify violations of a social contract, the (adaptively) correct answer is immediately obvious to the majority of participants (65–80 per cent).

Everywhere it has been tested (in many different counties), people do not treat social exchange problems as equivalent to other kinds of reasoning problems. It seems that, in solving this task, people are using 'representational primitives' (e.g., 'benefit', 'cost', 'obligation', 'entitlement', 'intentional' and 'agent'). The conclusion from such research is that computational procedures activated by social exchange do not engage logical reasoning but track choices made by cheaters. In relation to some forms of psychopathology, it is intriguing to speculate that the cheater detector is overactive, leading to various forms of delusional and paranoid states (e.g., delusional jealousy; see chapter 16).

> **ASK YOURSELF**
> Has evolutionary psychology advanced our understanding of the computational nature of the brain–mind?

▢ The Meme Machine Computational Contagion

Chapter 2 outlined the notion of the 'meme' as the unit of the self-replicating system of cognition (the study of this system is called 'memetics'). It is interesting to consider memetics in the context of the degree of built-in content (or bias towards acquiring such content) of computation. Blackmore (1999) developed the idea of the meme first postulated by Dawkins (1976), who argued that it is the unit of cultural transmission. While we should acknowledge that the concept of the meme is still new and controversial, it does provide an insight into the type of mechanisms that seem to play an important part in our computational processes.

The meme is a unit of imitation and replication; in a comparable manner to Darwinian (genetic) natural selection, replication of memes occurs by 'memetic selection'.[4] Certain memes (e.g., ideas) are preferred by cognition over others; that is, some memes are 'fitter' (in a Darwinian, but non-genetic, sense) than others. An obvious example of a meme is the content of love (or loss of) in many forms of entertainment: our minds seem especially attuned to these stimuli and 'we cannot get them out of our head'. They are rather like a virus, jumping from brain–mind to brain–mind, and once they get in they infect the whole system. Memetics provide a way of thinking about cultural transmission: how ideas get passed from one individual to the next, eventually to form a community of shared ideas.

In principle, memes could be self-replicating entities, genetically unconstrained, with the simple instruction COPY ME; this is the view taken by Dawkins and Blackmore (they state that there is no reason why success in a meme should have any connection with genetic success). This position may be tenable when two competing memes appear which are indifferent to genetic success; but as soon as competition arises then it should be expected that the success of transmission of memes would be strongly influenced by adaptive functions. For example, consider two biblical memes: (a) 'an eye for an eye, a tooth for a tooth'; and (b) 'turn the other cheek'. Do these competing memes have an equal chance of propagating in most societies?

> **ASK YOURSELF**
> What are the similarities and differences between genetic evolution and memetic evolution?

Whatever one thinks of memetics – many researchers think it a problematic concept – the problem addressed by memetics must be faced: how are ideas, thoughts, etc., acquired and how do these get transmitted throughout a community? Memetics presents another challenge to the notion that the brain–mind is a content-free computational algorithmic device.

Consciousness: Overview

Consciousness is often said to be the last remaining mystery in science: it is such a perplexing phenomenon that scientists and non-scientists alike find it difficult to know how to *think* about it. This section examines this mystery from the perspective of biological psychology: that is, from an evolutionary view of the brain–mind. This discussion will put forward a strong case for the potential of the biological approach to provide significant insights into the nature of consciousness. This is not an impartial account; instead, it is aimed at raising some of the important issues and pointing to ways of thinking about these issues within a biological perspective. If this section is successful, it should encourage you to think critically, challenge the conclusions reached and go off to learn more about this fascinating subject.

At this point it is important to make a fundamental distinction. The *processes* involved in consciousness present no real problem when it comes to the functions served (focused attention, selection of salient information, etc.): these can be addressed by the conventional tools of 'normal science'. The real problem is encountered when the 'raw feel' of consciousness is considered: that is, its experiential qualities; this is not easily addressed by normal science approaches. How the brain generates this experience is considered the 'hard problem' of consciousness (Chalmers, 1995, 1996).

Our discussion of this fascinating area of psychology must, of necessity, be brief. None the less, many of the important problems for biological psychology are presented, and some tentative biological explanations are proffered. If this discussion whets your appetite for further study and leads to the conclusion that biological answers are, in principle, possible, then this section has served its purpose. In terms of further reading, Velmans (2000) provides a lucid and detailed account of the problems addressed by studies of consciousness and the many philosophical traditions that have attempted to solve these problems; Cotterill (1998) provides a stimulating exploration of the many conceptual and neuroscientific issues; and Blackmore (2003) provides a highly readable and lively summary of the whole field.

The rediscovery of consciousness

Until the 1990s, when a number of influential articles and books appeared (e.g., Crick, 1994; Dennett, 1991), scientists paid little attention to consciousness. Before this time, talk of 'consciousness' was considered scientifically naive, inappropriate, or worse: the activity of a confused mind. One major turning point was the publication of the edited volume of Blakemore and Greenfield (1987), *Mindwaves*, which still remains essential reading. However, before the heyday of behaviourism, consciousness was considered a central topic in psychology, as demonstrated by William James' *Principles of Psychology* (1890). Despite this recent resurgence of interest, most psychologists do not have a serious research interest in consciousness studies. As noted by Crick and Koch (1998), scientists often consider consciousness (a) to be a philosophical problem and therefore best left to philosophers, or (b) when considered a scientific problem, too premature to study it.

However, this state of affairs is changing, encouraged in part by the widespread availability of technology (e.g., neuroimaging) as well as the adoption of a bullish materialist approach that states that, whatever consciousness *is* and is *for*, it is the product of the brain and therefore to be understood in terms of neuroscience. This neuroscience 'bullishness' is epitomized by the 'neural correlates of consciousness' approach.

Neural correlates of consciousness

One approach to understanding consciousness is to investigate the 'neural correlates of consciousness' (NCC; Crick, 1994; Crick & Koch, 1995, 1998, 2003; for a summary, Koch, 2004), which involves identification of the specific patterns of brain activity that correlate with particular conscious experience. One advantage (or, according to some authors, drawback) of this general approach is that it sidesteps some of the intractable mysteries, in particular how brain processes generate conscious awareness: they just *do*. The search for the neural correlates of consciousness is, therefore, empirical and initially neutral with respect to issues of causality – a pragmatic approach, with no time-wasting, hand-wringing, philosophical debates. According to Crick and Koch (1998, p. 7),

> We think that most of the philosophical aspects of the problem should, for the moment, be left on one side, and that the time to start the scientific attack is now. We can state

bluntly the major question that neuroscience must first answer: It is probable that at any moment some active neuronal processes in your head correlate with consciousness, while others do not; *what is the difference between them?* In particular, are the neurons involved of any particular neuronal type? What is special (if anything) about their connections? And what is special (if anything) about their way of firing? The neuronal correlate of consciousness is often referred to as the NCC. Whenever some information is represented in the NCC it is represented in consciousness.

Crick and Koch (1995) proposed that the key function of consciousness is to produce the best current interpretation of the visual scene in a form that provides usable information to the planning process of the brain. Crick and Koch focused on visual awareness because it is the easiest to study, experiments can be performed in human beings, cross-species comparisons are possible and much is already known about this sensory system. Neuroimaging is the obvious way to explore the neural correlates of consciousness. However, too few studies have been conducted to yield any consistent pattern of findings – no doubt this gap in the literature will become increasingly filled in the years to come.

A major problem with this approach is that the neural correlates of consciousness are exactly that: *correlates*. Correlation (usually) does not entail causation, and it is this causation question that is of most interest (for a discussion of the differences between correlation, causation and identity, see Velmans, 2000, 2002a). But, if the neural correlates were identified, then this would allow causal hypotheses to be formulated and tested – science first describes regularities (correlations) and only then attempts to account for the pattern of correlations (causation). In principle, consciousness is no different in this respect.

> **ASK YOURSELF**
> Is the 'neural correlates of consciousness' approach a sensible place to start the scientific investigation of consciousness?

Defining the Problems of Consciousness

Before much progress can be made in providing a biological understanding of consciousness, the main problems that *any* viable theory of this mysterious phenomenon must address need to be outlined.[5] These problems are divided into (a) the 'easy problems' and (b) the one 'hard problem', by David Chalmers (1995, 1996). The 'easy problems' are ones that it is possible, at least, to think about without getting more confused, and to address using the standard tools of normal science; the one major 'hard problem' is how the brain generates experiential consciousness: this is hard even to think about, let alone try to explain in conventional scientific terms.

The phenomenal problem

The first problem concerns what it is like to be conscious. I know what *my* consciousness is like, but I cannot know what *your* consciousness is like, and there seems no way, *in principle*, I can know what your consciousness is like. It would, however, be possible for us to agree that our conscious states are similar by the exchange of information and the testing of hypotheses based on these putative common states. But there is no way that either you or I, or anyone else, can truly know whether someone else is conscious in the same way as us – intersubjectivity may *suggest* we are consciously aware in the same way, but how could this ever be known for certain?

Zombies

Zombies exist in Hollywood B-movies, but do they exist in reality? The term 'zombie' is a philosophical invention intended to cover the possibility that there may be other people who act just like us (I am assuming you are not a zombie), but who do not have subjective experience (i.e., 'qualia'; the plural of 'quale' – colours, sounds, smells, pain, etc.). Our theories of consciousness are so poor – if our ignorance can be graced with the word 'theory' – that it is not possible to know whether zombies could exist.

This is an important problem for the following reason: a better theory to account for the essential role of qualia is needed; and with this theory it might be possible to theorize on what can and cannot be done in their absence. This would reveal the ways in which zombies would (or would not) be deficient. It is at this crucial juncture that the function of consciousness would be exposed.

The objective vs. subjective problem

Velmans (2000) notes that there are two different perspectives on consciousness. The first is our subjective experience, which only the individual can access: this is the 'subjective' 'first-person perspective'; the second is the 'objective' examination of brain processes, behaviour, etc., from the 'third-person perspective'. These two perspectives are very different and give rise to completely different types of information. Importantly, although they may be seen as compatible, their respective information content is not interchangeable. For example, you could know everything there is to know about my brain processes, but you would still not be able to experience my conscious states; Velmans (2002b) calls this state of affairs 'ontological monism combined with epistemological dualism' – that is, there is one thing to be known (the mono 'brain–mind') but two (dual) ways of knowing it.

The above interrelated problems represent difficulties for integrating information from different perspectives; they do not in themselves imply anything about the causal relationship between the brain and consciousness: they only make it difficult for us to understand these causal processes.

The physical world is 'causally closed' problem

Another problem that is said to bedevil consciousness is the 'causal closure' of the physical world – this problem is seen by none other than Sir Karl Popper (1977; also see Popper & Eccles, 1977) as being of decisive importance. Assuming there exist 'mind' events, which are subjective, which are different from 'brain' (physical) events, which are objective, then it is generally agreed that subjective events cannot influence objective events. This has led Popper – one of the most influential philosophers of the last century – to endorse a dualistic theory of brain–mind. However, this 'problem' may be more apparent than real, because it is a big assumption that two such realms exist. Only when the fundamental distinction between brain/objective and mind/subjective is respected does the problem arise. A biological perspective is especially well placed to cut this particular Gordian knot.

The adaptive problem

Does consciousness serve some adaptive function? This might be expected if it is assumed that it evolved by Darwinian selection. It is possible that it did evolve but does not serve a function – it could be a chance by-product of other cognitive processes. However, even if it is accepted that it serves some adaptive function, then it is very difficult to see why these functions could not be performed non-consciously. What does conscious awareness bring to the adaptive party?

The binding problem

The binding problem concerns how the brain integrates the outputs of processing in separate areas into a seamless experience. In addition to this spatial binding, there is also temporal binding. When we listen to speech we hear the first word, then the second, then the third, and so on, and the meaning of the speech comes with the addition of more words; but this is not how we experience speech: sentences do not seem to start as gobbledegook and then acquire meaning – which they *must* do in real time – but they seem to have meaning throughout. How the brain achieves this feat is not well understood.

The problem with problems

With many 'problems' in the area of consciousness, one's initial theoretical perspective defines what is, and what is not, problematic. Indeed, in a wider context, a 'problem' reflects a perceived fact that does not fit one's *theoretical* framework. Problems are not problems in themselves – they do not dangle in the air – they are problems of *something*, and that something is defined by initial assumptions and the structure of one's argument: some theoretical system (for further discussion see Corr & Perkins, 2006).

The 'causal closure of the physical world' is one such 'problem'. If the brain–mind problem is discussed in terms of objective vs. subjective, then it is indeed a problem to conceive of how subjective mental stuff can influence objective physical stuff. Once objective and subjective stuffs are seen as different aspects of the same brain process, then so-called 'subjective' stuff can influence 'objective' stuff. In this way it is possible to find a way for consciousness to have a causal influence – more precisely, the brain processes underlying what is experienced as consciousness having a brain–brain causal influence.

ASK YOURSELF
Are some problems in consciousness studies simply too difficult even to think about?

◻◻◻ The Lateness of Conscious Experience

This section discusses one set of experimental findings that have crucial implications for any functional theory of consciousness. Since the 1960s, Benjamin Libet (1985) has conducted a series of experiments which seem to show that it takes some 500 ms of brain activity for consciousness to occur: this is the 'lateness' of conscious experience.

Libet has conducted a variety of experiments. In some experiments, the sensory cortex of awake patients was directly stimulated (Libet, 1982) – these patients were undergoing neurosurgery, during which the surgeon stimulates parts of the cortex to localize functions. In one series of studies, the somatosensory cortex was stimulated with trains of pulses – such stimulation leads to sensory perception (e.g., being touched; see chapter 3). What was intriguing about these studies was the finding that there appeared to be a necessary period of 'neuronal adequacy', involving 500 ms of continuous stimulation, before consciousness was experienced.

A number of different types of experiments were conducted to test whether, indeed, conscious awareness lags 500 ms behind the initial sensory stimulation. In one such experiment, Libet stimulated the skin, and then between 200 and 500 ms later stimulated the somatosensory cortex. If skin stimulation takes 500 ms to generate consciousness, then stimulating the cortex after 200 ms should abolish the conscious experience of the touch. This is what was found, supporting the idea that a period of neuronal adequacy is required for consciousness to appear.

The problem with these findings for any adaptive theory of consciousness is that, long before 500 ms, motor actions have already been initiated (e.g., the removal of the hand from a hot stove occurs before awareness of the hand touching the stove). In this specific case, removal of the hand is involuntary and not controlled by conscious processes. However, events are not experienced as if they happened 500 ms ago: consciousness appears to refer to what is happening *now*. Libet suggests that the conscious experience of a stimulus is 'referred back in time' once neuronal adequacy has been achieved, to make it *seem* as if there was no delay. There are many criticisms of Libet's experiments as well as his interpretation of his data (e.g., Libet, 2003; Zhu, 2003; see Blackmore, 2003), but the basic finding of the lateness of conscious awareness seem solid.

Concerning the volition of will, in later experiments, Libet explored absolute timing using conscious intentions. Briefly, the typical experiment required participants to note the instant they experienced the wish to perform a 'voluntary' action (e.g., simple flexion of finger) – that is, the instant they were consciously aware of this wish to act. To record this time, participants remembered the position of a revolving spot on a cathode ray oscilloscope, which swept the periphery of a face like the second hand of a clock. During this time, the 'readiness potential' was recorded by EEG. This procedure allowed Libet to calculate the time at which the participant thought they had decided and then compare this moment with the timing of events in their brains. He found evidence that these 'conscious decisions' lagged between 350 and 400 ms behind the onset of 'readiness potentials' recorded from scalp electrodes – once again, the conscious wish came a long time *after* the brain started to initiate the action.

What is important for us is the puzzling finding that conscious experience comes so late after the initial stimulation, and often long after motor actions.[6] Thus, any theory of consciousness needs to take account of these findings. As noted by Gray (2004, p. 23),

The scandal of Libet's findings is that they show *the conscious awareness of volition to be illusory.*

Velmans (1991) reviewed a large literature to show that conscious awareness comes after the performance of tasks across a wide variety of domains: analysis of sensory input; analysis of emotional content of input; phonological and semantic analysis of heard speech; phonological and semantic preparation of one's own spoken words and sentences; learning; the formation of memory; choice and preparation of voluntary acts; and planning and execution of movements. Lateness of awareness is a real problem; but, as discussed below, it may provide the key to unlocking some of the mysteries of consciousness. From a physicalist point of view, all mind events (e.g., thinking and consciousness) must be *caused* by a physical process in the brain that *preceded* the conscious awareness of these events – it could hardly be otherwise.

Before moving on, one thing about these approaches to consciousness should be noted: the use of experimental methods (e.g., EEG) allows research questions to be answered in a way that is simply not amenable to philosophical (i.e., verbal) debate. As these results show, the experimental approach can reveal findings that run counter to conventional wisdom. Therefore, in the absence of experimental support, it may be prudent to remain agnostic concerning the validity and relevance of philosophical conclusions.

ASK YOURSELF
What could be the possible reason for conscious awareness being 'referred back in time'?

Neuropsychological Disorders

Some of the best evidence relating conscious awareness to brain processing comes from clinical neuropsychology: the psychological effects of various forms of brain damage (see chapter 8). In particular, case studies that show a dissociation of performance from conscious awareness are especially informative.

As noted by Weiskrantz (1997), in every major class of defects in which patients apparently lose some particular cognitive ability through brain damage, examples of preserved capacities can be found of which the patient is unaware – this range extends from perception to meaning and language, with several different subtypes within each of the categories. Indeed, brain damage comes in a wide spectrum, from the globally and severely impaired to the mild and selectively impaired (e.g., being unable to remember names). Often the latter deficits are not obvious to untrained observers and can be accommodated through changes in daily habits / routines.

Performance without awareness

In such cases, the patient is unaware that the capacity remains; in other cases, the patient is actually unaware of the events they can detect and discriminate. Amnesic patients learn and retain information, but have no conscious 'memory' – in some patients there is no experience of remembering an event beyond a minute or so. In 'blindtouch' (also known as 'numbsense'; Weiskrantz, 1997) patients are able to locate the position of a tactile stimulus on the arm that has lost the (conscious) sense of touch (i.e., the associated qualia).

In prosopagnosia there is a loss of specific memory of familiar faces, but the patient demonstrates through indirect means that this information is retained. In unilateral neglect, information can be processed in the left side of the visual space even though the patient not only denies seeing it but also behaviourally ignores it. The patient who has lost the ability to comprehend language can nevertheless demonstrate through reaction time testing that there is intact capacity to process both semantic and syntactic information of which the patient remains unaware and which cannot be used in their discourse. A complementary condition, 'anosognosia', in which the patient denies the existence of a deficit, such as cortical blindness or hemiplegia, is also intriguing in relation to consciousness.

Blindsight

Blindsight (Weiskrantz, 1986, 1997, 2003) is an intriguing neuropsychological condition consisting of impaired visual awareness but preserved visual performance (see chapter 5). For example, a vascular accident (e.g., burst blood vessel) can destroy part of the visual cortex, creating a *scotoma*, or 'blind spot' – that is, a large hole in the visually experienced world on the opposite side of the damage. Such patients claim not to 'see' visual stimuli, but when asked to undertake a performance task they show stimulus discrimination at above-chance levels – in other words, they are processing visual stimuli, but this sensation is not entered into conscious awareness.

> **ASK YOURSELF**
> What do neuropsychological conditions reveal about the apparent unity of conscious experience?

▢▢ Normal States of Blindness, Inattention and Amnesia

It is not necessary to go to the neuropsychological clinic to observe aberrations of consciousness; these can be found in the study of normal behaviour. The highly selective nature of consciousness is demonstrated in three types of experiment: (a) *change blindness*, (b) *inattentional blindness*, and (c) *inattentional amnesia*.

Change blindness

Change blindness experiments show how our experience of a seemingly unchanging visual scene can be wrong. Look at the two pictures in figure 18.3. Do you notice the difference? But now consider the following experiment: you are asked to look at the left-hand picture and then *at the exact moment* you move your eyes (which occurs several times per second; i.e., saccades) the picture is changed for the one on the right. Now, would you notice the difference so easily? The answer is 'No'. This effect can be seen even with large changes in the visual scene (e.g., the clothes worn by someone talking to you). When our eyes are fixated (i.e., stationary), changes in the visual scene are noted without difficulty (e.g., motion detectors pick up movement and focus attention on the location); but, when a change occurs during an eye movement or a blink, 'change blindness' occurs. In other words, during saccades, blindness to the visual scene occurs, yet we do

(a)   (b)

Figure 18.3 Change blindness pictures. The following two pictures, showing Dr Susan Blackmore at her desk, demonstrate change blindness: if one picture (a) were presented and then, during a saccade, picture (b) were shown, then it is highly likely that the difference in the scene would not be noticed: this is change blindness. (From Blackmore, 2003; photos courtesy Susan Blackmore.)

not experience the visual world as a series of discrete scenes interposed with blind moments: visual percepts are uninterrupted and continuous. (For an online paper and visual demonstrations of change blindness, go to: http://nivea.psycho.univ-paris5.fr/.)

Change blindness is observed using a variety of methods, for example: changing images during a saccade, as measured by eye-tracking equipment; moving the whole picture slightly, thus forcing a saccade during the change; presenting brief grey flashes between the images; introducing an image flicker.

Change blindness could be due to saccades wiping out the previous image, or to inattention to specific parts of the visual array. Rensink, O'Regan and Clark (1997) tested these two theoretical positions. They found that, when changes were made in areas of central interest, an average of 7 alterations were required for participants to notice the change; but, when changes were made in areas of low interest, then an average of 17 alterations were needed. For a neuroimaging study of change blindness and awareness, see Beck et al. (2001).

Change blindness implies that the confidence typically placed in the conscious awareness of the external world is not warranted. It appears that perception is much more than just passively 'seeing' the external world; if this is not true then why are not large discrepancies not noticed immediately? It appears that most processing is directed to salient aspects of the visual scene – a change from a spider to a snake would be easily noticed – and when less salient aspects of the scene are changed these are simply not noticed.

This selective processing is consistent with the conditioned attention theory of latent inhibition: experimental data show that unimportant stimuli in our environment receive progressively less attention with continued exposure and are actively inhibited (see chapters 8 and 16). For example, we do not pay attention to, or often even notice, the ticking of the clock, the hum of the computer, the singing of the birds, etc. In relation to the impaired selective attention (e.g., as shown by disrupted latent inhibition) in psychotic states (see chapter 16), these observations suggest a novel hypothesis, yet to be tested: schizophrenia patients should be *better* at detecting changes in the visual scene; that is, they show 'change awareness'. If confirmed, this finding would point to a possible *disadvantage* of non-selective attention, namely paying attention to such stimuli is a waste of processing resources and a (potentially dangerous) distraction from processing salient and important stimuli.

Inattentional blindness

Is attention necessary for consciousness or do perceptual systems just 'take in' what is out there in the visual environment? An amusing and startling demonstration of inattention blindness is shown in the film *Gorillas in our Midst* (Simons & Chabris, 1999). In this film, two teams of students are throwing balls to one another and an observer is told to watch one team very carefully and to count the number of catches they make. After the film the observer is asked to say whether they noticed anything unusual during the film. Most observers say 'No'. Then the film is played back and to the astonishment of the majority of observers they now notice what they did not the first time: a girl in a gorilla suit slowly walks right into camera shot, turns to the camera, thumps her chest and then walks off on the opposite side of the screen. How could the observer have missed *that*? Very easily, is the answer. This film really has to be seen to be believed.

Inattentional amnesia

O'Regan and Noe (2001) discuss the phenomenon of 'inattentional amnesia', first described by Wolfe (1997, 1999; Wolfe, Klempen & Dahlen, 2000). Wolfe, Klempen and Dahlen (2000) employed a visual search paradigm in which participants search for a target symbol among a number of distractor stimuli (figure 18.4). The time it takes to search for each target symbol is recorded. The novel feature of this visual search paradigm is that, on each trial, exactly the same visual display is repeated, but the target symbol changes. Now, if an internal representation of the external world is built up over successive trials, then it should be expected that looking at the same display, which remains visible between 5 and 350 repetitions, would result in a stable internal representation of the display. Wolfe,

Repeated search: Five repetitions

Figure 18.4 Inattentional amnesia experimental set-up. In the repetitive search paradigm, the search display does not change, only the probe changes on each trial, yet reaction time is not facilitated by this repetition. (From J. M. Wolfe, 'Cognitive neuroscience. How do you pay attention?', figure 2, pp. 813–15, from *Nature* 400, 1999. Copyright © 1999 by J. M. Wolfe. Reprinted by permission of
the author and Nature.)

Klempen and Dahlen (2000) found that the efficiency of search rate did not improve over trials, as would be expected if a stable internal representation of the display is indeed built up. In contrast, when the display is memorized (i.e., an internal representation is built up), search times are faster than when it is visually presented.

As discussed by O'Regan and Noe (2001), these results can be interpreted in the following way. Before attention is directed to a region of the visual field, only elementary features (e.g., lines, texture, colour) are analysed; this is done automatically by low-level modules in the visual system. But, once attention has been directed to a particular spatial location, then the features are combined together to form a percept. When visual attention then moves to a different location, the previous percept 'disaggregates' and fades to its elementary features.

Once again, it does not seem to be the case that the human mind builds up a picture-like representation of the external world. O'Regan and Noe (2001) interpret inattentional amnesia as showing that 'seeing' consists in 'having seeking-out routines that allow information to be obtained from the environment'. Importantly, perception is selective, constructive and action-oriented. Of course, some form of representation must exist, otherwise long-term memory would not be possible and nor would imagination; but this does not imply that *all* stimuli, especially those involved in moment-to-moment processing, are represented irrespective of their importance.

> **ASK YOURSELF**
> What are the implications of change and inattentional effects for the apparent unity of consciousness?

⬛☐ 'Online' and 'Offline' Processes

A distinction of particular significance regarding computational processes in consciousness is discussed in this section. Standard psychology textbooks continue to contrast 'learning theories' and 'cognitive theories'; and this approach follows the long-fought territorial battles between stimulus–response (S–R) theorists (e.g., Hull), who argued for automatic bonds between eliciting stimuli and responses, and cognitive theorists (e.g., Tolman), who argued that, intervening between stimuli and responses, knowledge structures and processes are required (see MacPhail, 1998). In a review of the literature, Toates (1998) draws our attention to the fact that both processes are observed in human and non-human animals, and that consideration of both processes may help us to better understand normal and abnormal behaviour in general, and consciousness in particular.

According to Toates' model, a stimulus (S) has a certain strength of tendency to produce a response (R; formerly called 'habit strength'); that is, S has a response-eliciting potential, which varies from zero to some maximum value (this strength depends upon innate factors and learning). 'Cognition' in this context refers to those processes that encode knowledge about the world in a form not tied to particular behaviour (Rs). Where there is uncertainly, novelty or a mismatch of actual against expected outcomes, behavioural control shifts from the S–R (online) processing, which is fast and coarse-grained in its analysis, to cognitive (offline) processing, which is slow and fine-grained in its analysis. The particular circumstances that give rise to the different weightings are shown in figure 18.5.

Toates' model helps us to understand the adaptive value of consciousness. This model contends that some actions that can be organized at a low (online) level can none the less

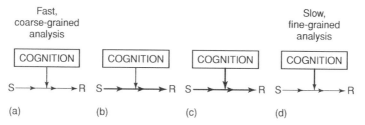

Figure 18.5 Toates' model. Different strengths of relation between stimulus (S) and response (R), as indicated by weights (thickness) of arrows: (a) balanced S–R/cognition weightings; (b) strong S–R weight with weak cognition weight; (c) strong S–R weight with strong cognition weight; and (d) weak S–R link with strong cognition weight.

be affected by conscious (offline) processes: higher-order, conscious processes can modulate the strength of connections controlling behaviour organized at a relatively low level of the control hierarchy. For example, a fear state that is processed consciously may sensitize the whole defensive system and thereby effect fast, automatic responses. Indeed, such a process has already been seen in the case of 'fear-potentiated startle' (see chapters 9 and 15): the conscious processing of affectively laden pictures modulates eye-blink startle to an acoustic stimulus. Thus, Toates emphasizes the weights attached to motor programs, and how cognitive, conscious (offline) processes can modify the weights (i.e., firing potential) of online responses. One advantage of this approach is the avoidance of confusion-making terms such as 'objective' and 'subjective', because both online and offline processes are the product of the brain and both are composed of objective, physical stuff. Thus, problems of the 'causal closure of the physical world' (see above) are not encountered – the related *why* (i.e., function) problem is a different matter.

In the context of visual perception, Milner and Goodale (1995) refer to two streams in visual processing: the 'online' and 'seeing' systems. The 'online' system is the action system, which can be indexed by various performance measures; it is automatic and reflex-like, occurring before the time needed to achieve conscious awareness of the action and the eliciting stimuli. This system seems to use the dorsal processing stream (see chapter 7) – Milner and Goodale propose that rather than being the 'where' stream, as suggested by Ungerleider and Mishkin (1982), it is the 'how' stream. The ventral stream, in contrast, is largely conscious: it is the 'what' stream, and is similar to the 'offline' processes discussed in this section. As discussed above in the context of Crick's 'neural correlates of consciousness' approach, knowledge about the visual system has played an important role in theories of consciousness: it is one rich in qualia, and one amenable to varied and rigorous experimental investigation.

> **ASK YOURSELF**
> What are the evolutionary advantages to having two behavioural systems?

Consciousness: A Tentative Biological Model

Let us now put to work our newly acquired knowledge of the problems of consciousness and online and offline processes. Although there have been a large number of attempts to construct models of consciousness, most have not taken a strictly biological perspective, as to do so would have suggested definite initial assumptions and constraints on the form of the *general* theory. (Space prevents a proper description of these attempts; see Blackmore, 2003.) The biological position is epitomized in the following quote from Francis Crick (1994, p. 7):

> The scientific belief is that our minds – the behavior of our brains – can be explained by the interactions of nerve cells (and other cells) and the molecules associated with them. This is to most people a really surprising concept. It does not come easily to believe that I am the detailed behavior of a set of nerve cells, however many there may be and however intricate their interactions.

This is the 'astonishing hypothesis' – a few moments' reflection reveals just how astonishing it really is. What are the implications of taking this hypothesis seriously? Some of the implications are truly remarkable, serving to challenge our view of the world and of ourselves.

Critically thinking about consciousness

The most difficult aspect of addressing any problem is deciding where to *start* thinking: rarely is this at the place that yields the final answer. The mere act of thinking is self-perpetuating, leading to refinement of assumptions and conclusions. It is important that the starting assumptions are clear and easily refutable; by such refutation, new ideas appear and move along the path to the final answer. In this spirit, the following 'working assumptions' are delineated; each and every one of these assumptions is open to challenge – the scientist does not care about the final truth of working assumptions, so long as they provide a way into thinking about and investigating the problem: it is by *this* route only that the veridical status of assumptions and their related conclusions is decided.

The major assumption of the approach adopted here is that the biological perspective offers sound principles upon which hypotheses may be constructed. These principles certainly allow bold statements of widespread application – such statements are a strength in theory formulation. As noted by Dennett (1991, p. xi),

> we often learn more from bold mistakes than from cautious equivocation.

Theoretical desiderata

Is it yet possible to sketch a model of consciousness that addresses, and maybe even solves, the problems of consciousness, including the *why* (i.e., function) problem? From the outset, the *how* question (i.e., how does the brain generate consciousness) has been avoided because, in common with all theories and despite much speculation, little (if anything) is known about how this feat of nature is achieved – this is not a serious omission because solution of the other problems is not conditional upon solution of this problem. From the biological perspective advanced here, any viable model of consciousness would need to take into account the following factors – these are the 'working assumptions'.

1. Consciousness is the product of evolution;
2. Consciousness is functional – it serves an adaptive purpose, and is not merely epiphenomenal;
3. Consciousness is a product of the brain (physical monism);
4. Consciousness comes too late to have a causal influence *on the processes it represents*;
5. Consciousness, and perception in general, is a construction: the brain does not merely 'represent' the external physical world, it *constructs* it;
6. Consciousness theories must account for the 'causal closure of the physical world';
7. Consciousness theories should be incorporated into an existing nomothetic system, taking into account known neuropsychological processes and findings;
8. Consciousness theories should generate experimental hypotheses that allow the possibility of refutation (i.e., theory *falsification*): the principal criterion of a 'scientific' statement.

> **ASK YOURSELF**
> In what ways are incorrect, but clearly formulated, hypotheses useful in science?

▢ Jeffrey Gray's Neuropsychology of Consciousness

One theory that meets the above theoretical desiderata has been proposed by Jeffrey Gray (2004), who built his model upon the known neuropsychological processes in anxiety and schizophrenia (see Gray, 1995).[7] This model assumes Darwinian evolution, and provides a cogent rationale for this assumption; importantly, it also assigns a specific function to consciousness that conforms to Libet's lateness data (see above). In addition, Gray's model shows potentially important links between consciousness, schizophrenia and anxiety: it forces us to consider the integrity of psychobiological processes and encourages us not to pigeonhole psychological phenomena into arbitrary, if convenient, categories. As shown below, some of the assumptions and postulates of Gray's model are startling, and some of its implications are quite amazing. If nothing else, Gray's model shows that it is possible to pursue a biological approach even to apparent mysteries, in a form that allows testable hypotheses and the falsification of incorrect assumptions and hypotheses.

The construction of consciousness awareness

Chapter 5 highlighted the fact that conscious perception and its associated qualia (e.g., colour) are a product of the brain; indeed, they are a *construction* of the brain. When we look out at the world, we seem just to 'see' a solid, three-dimensional world 'out there'. But what is seen is the product of the internal processing in the brain: this *must* be true (Velmans, 2000). This is a remarkable fact, because the world 'out there' seems so real. Of course, the external world is real, as is confirmed by physics, but its properties are different from those experienced – even if the external properties and the perceived properties were identical, this does not challenge this constructivist argument (selective lesion of the brain leading to specific patterns of lesioned consciousness, e.g., impaired or absent colour qualia, have already been discussed). Dreaming provides impressive proof that our brain has the ability to construct the rich qualia of visual perception *in the absence* of adequate sensory stimulation.

To avoid misunderstanding, 'construction' does not mean that perception is not real; only that the experience of it is not necessarily an accurate reflection of what we feel and think we are 'seeing'. In this sense colour is constructed (and 'illusory'). It looks like a property of the external world – it does look as if it is 'out there' and not solely in our heads – but it is known to be (to some degree, at least) a psychological construction of the brain mapped onto the physical energy emitted by objects in the external world (see chapter 5). Energy from the physical world informs the selection of hypotheses about the world that guides construction (hallucinations seem to reflect the breakdown of this source of influence, resulting in aberrant perceptions). Gray makes the important point that this correspondence is apparently so real because it is necessary to engage with salient parameters of the real 'out there' world in order to survive and reproduce: the organism needs to be sensitive to dimensions, sharp edges, distance, and be able to categorize objects.

Indeed, so good is this correspondence that it is difficult to appreciate that there is any problem at all. Sometimes this construction is evident in the form of 'visual illusions' (see chapter 5): alternative configurations of the same physical stimulus are apparent; backgrounds and foregrounds reverse before our very eyes; and we 'see' lines (in the form of light contrasts; see chapter 5) that simply do not exist in the physical world. Often visual illusions are interpreted as showing that the visual system is not perfect and it can be tricked with ambiguous stimuli. The more general inference is often not drawn: *all* perception is constructed and, in a fundamental sense, illusory.

Conscious experience is constructed in another important sense. Libet's results show that it takes at least some 250 to 350 ms for events impinging on our senses to become conscious; long before this time, the brain has initiated actions related to these sensations (e.g., pulling your hand away from a hot surface; braking hard when driving; returning a ball in competitive tennis). But past events are experienced as if they were happening *now*: this is an illusion.

It could be – and sometimes is – argued, especially by philosophers, that the perception of the external world is not a construction of the brain but, somehow, an adequate representation of what really is 'out there': this is our workaday naive stance. If this theoretical position is accepted, then other problems arise, principally that perception is not a perfect representation of the physical world. There is also the problem of why and how the brain carves up the world into finite categories when no such categories exist in the physical properties of sensory stimuli. For example, there is a continuous range of electromagnetic energy reflected off surfaces, but this light energy is perceived in terms of colour *categories*: categories do not exist in the electromagnetic spectrum; they exist only in our brains. The construction of perception thus seems unavoidable.

There is now ample evidence that the brain can and does construct illusory percepts. A salient example is illusory phantom limb pain, in which the new amputee subjectively experiences pain in the lost limb – sometimes great pain (it is a vivid quale) *in* the limb. The quale is experienced where simple reasoning tells us it cannot be (i.e., in the absent limb), yet it is an experience as real as your experience of reading the words on this page – just a whole lot more painful.

Is conscious awareness a product of evolution?

There has been much debate concerning the possible evolutionary function of consciousness, with some researchers arguing that it is the emergent property of a highly complex brain that appeared at some point in brain–mind evolution – it came, as it were, in the form of a 'free offer', no cost attached – and it is 'epiphenomenal', like the hot air coming out of the engine rather than the engine itself. As noted by Gray, this explanation does not have the ring of truth about it. He presents a cogent argument for challenging this position. For a start, consciousness must have developed *somehow*, and it would seem to be an expensive evolutionary luxury and, indeed, it is difficult to understand how it could be a by-product of some other process. In addition, Gray (2004, p. 90) argues,

> Whatever consciousness is, it is too important to be a mere accidental by-product of other biological forces. A strong reason to suppose that conscious experience has survival value is this. It is only by appeal to evolutionary selection pressures that we can explain the good fit that exists between our perception of the world and our actions in dealing with it, or between my perception and yours. Biological characteristics that are not under strong selection pressure show random drift, which would be expected to destroy the fit.

Thus, if it is not assumed that the evolutionary process is responsible, then why is the internal construction of the world in such good accord with the known physical parameters of the real physical world? This problem could be avoided altogether by the adoption of a naive (and neuropsychologically impoverished) position that the brain is some form of general-purpose perception machine that just 'sees' what is out there. But it is very difficult to conceive of how the brain would achieve this feat. For example, how could the brain just see colour, when colour itself is not a property of the physical world?

However, in the nature-of-consciousness debates, there are always ways to escape such conclusions. Perhaps non-conscious perception and consciousness developed separately, and then, at a later stage, became attached to each other, leading to conscious perception. Or perhaps consciousness is the property of *any* organization of matter of a particular structure; even perhaps the world itself is, in some sense, conscious, and we are all part of this panpsychic experience. Such theoretical positions are difficult to evaluate and next to impossible to test scientifically and, therefore, *falsify*. Clever ideas are not sufficient for understanding. What is needed is some way of deciding between ideas that are veridical and those that are groundless. The only way to do this is to conduct scientific investigations, which demand the formulation of theories in a form that permits the generation of operational hypotheses that are amenable to empirical test. Some thinkers would view this position as being overly restrictive. They would argue that their theories are falsifiable in principle, and may be amenable to empirical test at some time in the future, but not now. Is it not justified to question the value of theories that are formulated in such a way as to make them immune from testing? With enough ingenuity, is it not possible to propose *some* tests of *all* theories?

Evolution has produced the brain to compute a good enough, but not perfect, fit between the physical properties of the external world and the brain construction of the world experienced in the form of awareness and qualia (i.e., sensory properties, such as redness). The imperfection observed supports a Darwinian explanation. For example, as noted above, there is no discontinuity in the wavelengths of light energy impinging on our eyes, yet this energy is carved up into different categorical 'colours'. Why? This categorization makes sense when it is considered that fruits are usually coloured red or orange against a background of green foliage; thus classification of light energy into different colours is shaped by the functional significance (i.e., the meaning) attached to objects in nature (e.g., fruits vs. foliage), not the physical properties of the stimuli. Pain is another good example. As noted in chapter 5, the absence of pain sensation is a serious threat to life, with many patients dying at a relatively early age due to their failure to avoid the noxious stimuli that the experience of pain identifies.

The function of conscious awareness: late error detection

Consciousness and qualia thus seem to be constructed in the brain, and the form of this construction strongly points in the direction of evolution by natural selection. Now the function of consciousness needs to be tackled: if it evolved, then it evolved for some reason, that is, it has an adaptive value. Libet's data show that consciousness comes too late after the processes it represents to influence those represented processes (i.e., effects cannot come before causes). According to Gray (2004, p. 107),

> Conscious experience serves three linked functions. (1) It contains a model of the relatively enduring features of the external world; and the model is experienced as though it *is* the external world; (2) within the framework afforded by this model, features that are particularly relevant to ongoing motor programs or which depart from expectation are monitored and emphasized; (3) within the framework of the model, the controlled variables and setpoints of the brain's unconscious servomechanisms can be juxtaposed, combined and modified; in this way, error can be corrected.

To understand these functions, imagine you are confronted by a dangerous snake and your fear system fires off an automatic (online) motor program (e.g., flight; see chapter 17): all this happens long before (hundreds of milliseconds) you are consciously aware of ('see') the snake. It would now be highly adaptive to 'replay' the immediate past in order to analyse its contents, especially at those times when the online fear behaviour did not achieve its goal (in this instance, increasing defensive distance).

Central to this model is the 'comparator', which was originally developed in the context of the neuropsychology of anxiety (see chapter 17). The comparator compares the *expected* state of the world with the *actual* state of the world. When there is no discrepancy, then 'all is going to plan' and the comparator is said to be in 'just checking mode'. However, when there is a mismatch between the expected and actual states of the world, then the comparator goes into 'control mode'. According to Gray, in this control mode, the *contents* of consciousness are generated (e.g., attention to snake).

The relevance of online and offline systems can now be seen. According to this model, online (non-conscious) processes are modified by offline (conscious) processes; in

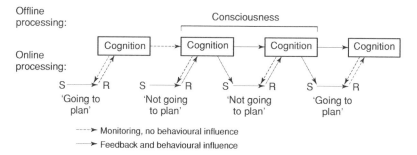

Offline
processing:

Online
processing:

Consciousness

----► Monitoring, no behavioural influence
——► Feedback and behavioural influence

Figure 18.6 Late error detection: online and offline interactions. Offline processes monitor the success of online processes, and, when 'everything is going to plan', online processes are not influenced by cognition; but, when an error signal is detected by cognition, then the salient features of the error signal generate conscious awareness. Although conscious experience lags behind online processes, crucially, *underlying* cognitive processes alter the weight of subsequent online processes (e.g., speed of response), and thus exert a causal effect. Putting your hand in a hot fire *does* alter future online fire-related responses.

Toates' terminology, the weights attached to response propensities in online processes are adjusted on the basis of the fine-grained offline processes. This process is shown in figure 18.6.

Offline processes do have causal effects on *subsequent* online processes; in other words, our behaviour is modified by experience: we *learn*. Before our discussion slides blindly into a dualistic mode of thinking, it needs to be emphasized that both online and offline processes are products of the brain, but they have different functions. Specifically, they differ: (a) in their temporal characteristics; (b) their level of analysis; and (c) their representation in conscious awareness. Online processes are very fast, involving coarse-grained analysis of salient features, and are not represented in conscious awareness; in contrast, offline processes are slow, taking hundreds of milliseconds to generate, entail fine-grained analysis, and are represented in conscious awareness. This dual system serves evolutionary challenges well: a fast 'dirty' response system coupled with a slower 'cleaner' response system for post-action processing, similar to the cutting room in film production: shoot the film first and worry about how it all fits together at the editing stage.[8]

Thus, online behaviour, which *always* comes before the generation of conscious awareness, can be modified by offline processing, which brings to the forefront those salient features (e.g., novelty and mismatch) that require closer analysis. It is intriguing that during the sleep state we experience rich qualia when there is no adequate sensory stimulation; furthermore, sleep facilitates consolidation of memory and enhances problem-solving: here we may also be witnessing the effects of offline processing on online behaviour (e.g., the enhancement of learning following sleep).

Arguably, Gray's theory dissolves the problem posed by Velmans (2002a), 'How could conscious experiences affect brains?' The 'subjective state' of conscious experience is also an 'objective state' of the brain (i.e., it is a product of the brain), and it is this objective state of the brain that is replayed back in the form of conscious experience. Thus, what exists is brain ⇒ brain effects. By this process, it is possible to deal with problems arising from the possibility that the 'physical world is closed'.

The section below addresses the *why* question of conscious awareness – that is, why there *seems* to be a problem entailed by brain ⇒ mind and mind ⇒ brain. However, Velmans' counter-position is that the neural correlates of consciousness would have the same information content as subjective awareness, thereby performing the same functions – in short, conscious phenomenology is not *identical* with the neural correlates of that phenomenology. The position adopted in this chapter is that consciousness *is* identical with these neural events (not simply correlates), but it is still necessary to provide an account for the *experience* of conscious awareness.

In summary of this section, Gray's (2004) theory provides consciousness with an evolutionary function: it facilitates learning (via offline to online influences) by modifying the computational processes (specifically modifying behavioural weights attached to specific stimuli) involved in online processes.

Conscious awareness as an inhibitor of (incorrect) prepotent responses

One important consequence of modifying behavioural weights attached to online processes may be to inhibit prepotent (online) responses. The evolutionary problem is how to ensure that online automatic responses are appropriate. It would be desirable to be able to inhibit the firing off of these automatic behavioural routines in some circumstances (e.g., inhibiting avoidance behaviours when in foraging mode), even if this inhibition takes several hundreds of milliseconds (usually enough time to have important consequences; see chapter 17).

An experimental analysis of the power of conscious awareness to inhibit prepotent (automatic) responses is seen in the 'Jacoby exclusion task'. In this task, words are presented either too fast for conscious recognition (i.e., 50 ms) or slow enough for recognition (i.e., 150 ms); backward masking is used to ensure these precise presentation times (i.e., after 150 ms, a visual mask overwrites the word and removes this word from further processing).

Imagine you are a participant in this experiment. You are presented, either with very fast or slow presentation times, with the prime word:

HOUSE

Then you are given a stem-completion task, for example:

HOU _ _

You could complete the stem with S and E to make 'HOUSE'.

The crucial manipulation in this task is the instruction to participants *not* to complete the word stem with a prime word. In the above example, your might complete it:

HOUND

This is an easy task when the word is presented *above* the threshold of awareness (at 150 ms). But what happens when the word is presented with the prime word *below* the threshold of consciousness? In this case, there is a failure to follow the instruction not to complete the word stem with the presented prime word. In fact, what happens is that the word stem is completed *more often* with the covertly presented prime word.

In other words, covert presentation serves to automatically 'prime' the completion of the word stem, even when the conscious mind does not want this to happen. This result points to something important about conscious awareness: somehow, conscious processing enables the inhibition of prepotent (automatic) responses. This is potentially a fundamental role for consciousness: in unfamiliar or unpredictable environments, being *unable* to stop the running of automatic (online) routines would be a severe disadvantage – instead of being the successful predator with a hearty meal as a result, we might be the meal of some other predator. As discussed in chapter 17, there is a necessary balance of avoidance and approach behaviours; excessive dominance of one system over the other would compromise genetic fitness.

Controlled and automatic performance

There is considerable evidence from experimental psychology to show that conscious awareness, and focused attention in particular, is necessary during the *initial stages* of learning a new task. This position is accepted by many theorists, including Velmans (2000), who asks: what do qualia add to focal attentive processing? When a new skill is learned it is necessary to attend consciously to the task and to consciously control behaviour; but as practice continues performance becomes increasingly automatic and less dependent on conscious control – finally fading from consciousness entirely (e.g., learning to drive a car, riding a bicycle or using a keyboard are all examples of this phenomenon). In the later stages of learning, performance becomes fast, effortless, automatic and (largely) error-free. At this stage, conscious control may even interfere with skilled performance (e.g., when thinking of your steps as you walk down stairs).

As noted by Gray, these observations suggest that conscious control is exerted only at critical junctures, when a definite choice has to be made. But, when in automatic mode, errors can occur: for example, when travelling by car on a route taken each day to work, it is easy to make an error and continue on the work route when we want to go elsewhere). Thus, automatic routines are well suited to fixed tasks, but they are not so good for tasks requiring a departure from fixed routines (e.g., a novel task) or when automatic performance is not going to plan.

Summary of Gray's model of consciousness

The central propositions in Gray's theory are:

1. Perception is a construction of the brain (in this sense, it is illusory);
2. The close match between the physical description of the external world and the brain construction of the external world is strong evidence for the evolution of consciousness;
3. The function of consciousness is to act as a 'late error detector';

4. The contents of consciousness result from the output of the 'comparator', which on a moment-to-moment basis compares the *actual* world with the *expected* world;

5. Conscious awareness consists in selective attention to those parts of the (represented) environment that call for particular processing (e.g., those that contained novelty or where a mismatch was detected);

6. Consciousness allows fine-grained, late (offline) analysis to modify coarse-grained, fast (online) reactions;

7. The behavioural weights attached to online motor programs are affected, via servomechanisms, by offline processing (e.g., this inhibits inappropriate prepotent responses);

8. Consciousness does have a causal influence, not on the processes it represents but on subsequent online behaviours.

Extending the late detection model: what-if simulations

Consistent with the general form of Gray's model is the additional idea that consciousness allows 'what-if' simulations of future behaviour, produced offline in a virtual reality environment that contains the important features of the real physical environment (e.g., imagination). Indeed, this function seems highly important to human beings: much of our time is spent thinking about the likely consequences of our behaviour and making plans for the future. The selection pressure for this dissociated process – which can be equated with consciousness in general – could have been the need to engage in complex, and potentially punishing and rewarding, social interactions. Such behaviours require complex computational processes, specifically involving inferences concerning the likely behaviour of other people. The causal inferences used to detect cheating have already been discussed; added to this is the need to 'read the minds of others' (i.e., theory of mind; see chapter 16), which requires a complex process of simulations to run through the likely outcomes of specific social choices. Humphrey (1986, 1987) advanced this very theory: conscious awareness provides an 'inner eye' – which reflects upon its own processing – allowing the computation of complex problems facing the social animal.

Let us now use our offline, what-if simulation modeller. Compare two phenotypes facing complex social problems: one phenotype simply computes errors in online programs; the second anticipates these errors by running realistic simulations, away from the (potentially punishing) stimuli in the real environment. Which phenotype would be more successful in terms of survival and reproduction? In many environments, it would be the latter. Now, if this same process could be used to solve complex social problems associated with approach motivation (e.g., securing and keeping a mate, influencing other conspecifics, achieving status and privileges in the social structure), then it is possible to conceive of the development of social intelligence. In a relatively short period of time these selection pressures could have easily produced *us*.

Thus, the offline, late error detection mechanism seems to have acquired the capacity to be dissociated from immediately preceding online processes. This additional evolution of offline processing may well necessitate awareness (i.e., the experience of qualia), especially when adequate sensory stimuli are not present, in order to build an *apparently* real-time simulation model encompassing the central features of the external world – this model is reactivated and experienced in dreams, which is dissociated from immediately preceding behaviours and calls upon stimuli held in memory; and it is trivially easy to produce the qualia of imaginary scenes (e.g., what your home looks like). However, has a convincing argument been made for the need for conscious *awareness*? Following Velmans' (2000) pertinent position, maybe all these functions of offline processes and simulation could be achieved non-consciously?

> **ASK YOURSELF**
> How successful is Gray's model in accounting for the evolutionary functions of consciousness?

But Why Conscious *Awareness*?

Gray's theory makes a fundamental contribution to our understanding of the *behavioural consequences* of consciousness that serve a function consistent with an evolutionary account. That is, consciousness serves as a late, offline, comparator of the match or mismatch between online behaviour and its consequences. It is assumed that consciousness allows a late, fine-grained analysis of immediately preceding behaviour.[9] However, there is one remaining problem with this view, which troubles most adaptive theories of consciousness. In principle – but we should always be wary of 'in principle' arguments – late error detection and inhibition of prepotent responses, as well as what-if simulating, could be achieved without conscious awareness (although it may also be said that, 'in principle', the de facto evolution of consciousness shows that these functions could not be achieved non-consciously).

Velmans (2000) poses this pertinent question: why are we conscious? More precisely, why should information processing, even of great sophistication, be conscious? This question deserves a non-evasive answer. What does conscious awareness bring to the party? Is it possible to provide a biological account for the necessity of qualia (e.g., awareness of the redness of red)? But what, precisely, might conscious *awareness* bring to the party? This section presents two possible functions of conscious awareness and qualia: (a) *sensory–perceptual integration* and (b) the *constructed self*.

Sensory–perceptual integration

One promising theory to explain the need for awareness and qualia is Jackendoff's (1987) 'intermediate-level' theory of consciousness, which argues that we are not normally aware of sensation unaffected by conceptual interpretation or of pure conceptual structure, but only of an admixture of the two processes. The conceptual structure results from top-down processing, sensation from bottom-up processing: conscious experience results at the point where these two forms of processing meet. This process solves one of the major computational problems of perception: how to combine (a) the raw sensory input from the environment, with (b) the perceptual–cognitive categorization of the external world (e.g., shapes and colours). At this point (indeed, nearly always) there would be a mismatch, the comparator would go into 'control mode' and generate the qualia of consciousness.

Following Jackendoff's theory, it may be supposed that awareness of only those stimuli which require intermediate-level integration is necessary. The subjective experience of colour is perhaps the best example. Colour is a psychological construction of the brain, influenced by different patterns of reflectance from surfaces: these patterns of electromagnetic energy impinge upon the eye, are transduced into electrical signals and sent on to the brain for higher-level processing (including categorization). This higher level of cortical analysis needs to 'hypothesis-test' incoming (unprocessed) stimuli. This hypothesis-testing is achieved by producing 'offline' subjective awareness that receives post-action analysis, which in turn then fine-tunes future online analysis and response.

A dedicated opponent of these functional accounts may continue to argue that all of these functions could, in principle, be performed non-consciously. This assertion is, of course, no less an uncashed cheque than any functionalist assertion. Might there be a more compelling reason for conscious awareness?

The constructed self

This section considers the egocentric nature of conscious awareness: it seems that *I* am the centre of the action. This egocentricity makes perfect sense in evolutionary terms. If consciousness serves the function of enhancing genetic fitness, then our phenomenal world should revolve around *us*, the gene-replication machine. (Although this line of argument goes beyond Gray's, 2004, theory of consciousness, it is entirely consistent with the construction of the illusory world of conscious experience.)

Evolution had a major problem to resolve. On the one hand, it needed to develop a brain that could extract and abstract physical features of the external world; yet, on the other hand, it also had adaptively to respond to the external world – even though the *experience* of this external world was contained only in the brain. One solution may have been to construct the *experience* of the external world in the gene-replication machine (you and me) as if it were actually out there in the real physical world (of predators, food, shelter, sex, etc.). Thus, the construction of the illusory self may have been a solution to this problem, explaining the egocentric perspective. *Now* when the snake is detected, it is constructed and *experienced* in the same spatio-temporal configuration as it truly is in the physical world. Thus, in the virtual reality of our constructed experience, what is experienced as the world 'out there' involves the self as the central actor. This may not simply be a consequence of perceptual perspective; it is also an emotional, cognitive ad motivational perspective (see chapter 17). But Velmans' (2000) tough question arises once more: what do qualia add to information processing?

Is conscious awareness itself a grand construction?

Once the notion that perception and conscious awareness are a construction of the brain and thus illusory is seriously entertained – that is, they are not what they seem (e.g., colour appears to be but is not a property of the physical world) – a number of seemingly amazing, yet viable, propositions are presented. There is now no reason to believe that our sense of conscious awareness is also not a construction – another trick of the brain. This position would help to account for the mystery of consciousness, which seems to elude our powers of rational thought. The fact that consciousness, the self, etc. *seem* so real does not present a problem for this hypothesis: it would not function if it were otherwise.

Is it possible finally to account for the elusive qualia in biological terms? That is, in terms which put the self in the world 'out there', where it needs to be in order to deal most efficiently with real-world challenges (e.g., avoidance of predators). To illustrate this argument, imagine yourself watching a horror film in which a victim is hunted for sport by aggressive aliens: do *you* really care if the victim is finally hunted down and torn to pieces by the laughing monsters? I assume you do not *really*. Now, imagine that *you* are the victim and *you* are being hunted by the alien monsters. Your horror would now be experienced as terror, and now you *would* care about the outcome. Maybe evolution has produced a construction of the external world in which the self is central: it has an 'intentional stance'; it is motivated; it is emotional; it approaches reward and avoids punishment, and it cares about behavioural consequences. Maybe the trick of evolution has been to produce a gene-replication machine that experiences and cares about those aspects of the physical world that are germane to its survival and reproduction.

According to this highly speculative position, asking further questions about qualia, phenomenal experience, etc. is rather like asking the magician to explain their 'magic' – all they could ever do is to explain how they tricked us, and we would find this news very disappointing. Likewise, with conscious awareness: disappointment should be expected here too. At this point, you may well be left wondering whether or not you have been the subject of a devious sleight of hand. After all, you may say, 'I'm still conscious!' But that *is* the point: if our perception of the external world is a construction of the brain, then it would, of necessity, have to seem real. What happens if this hypothesis is turned on its head, and it is assumed that conscious awareness is *not* a construction of the brain: now all the old philosophical problems that philosophy has struggled with for millennia come rushing back in to confuse the mind.

Maybe you are thinking that *everything* might be a construction, even our brains. Here the argument is saved by our Darwinian perspective. Our 'illusory' construction of the external world is a very close approximation to the real world out there, as it would need to be for evolving organisms to survive in this world. It is also possible to measure the external world in physical terms and see how this physical description corresponds to our perceptual description. A determined critic could argue that everything *is* a construction; but how would she ever be able to know this? With some justification, it may be assumed that there is a physical world out there, and one can get on with the job of understanding it. An important conclusion from the illusory perspective is that only by using the objective methods of science can understanding ever be reached.

Science is still no closer to explaining how the brain actually generates qualia – the 'hard problem' – even if these qualia are merely illusory. However, considerable progress has been made in understanding, and potentially resolving, some of the 'easy' problems of consciousness.

ASK YOURSELF
If the sense of self is not a construction of the brain and a 'grand illusion', then what is it?

▩☐ Conclusion

The Hebbian tradition in psychology emphasizes the importance of physiology for psychology and of psychology for physiology. This *neuropsychological approach* is now widely accepted in mainstream psychology, and many examples of the uses of the conceptual nervous system (cns; e.g., learning theory) and the central nervous system (CNS; e.g., neuronal networks) have been presented. Hebb's seminal influence (see chapters 1 and 7) is now realized in the work of many psychologists. This book has presented the work of one such psychologist, Jeffrey Gray, whose research shows how it is possible to build a unified field of psychology based upon fundamental physiological *and* psychological concepts (see McNaughton, 2004). Gray has produced influential theories in anxiety, personality, schizophrenia, consciousness and neural repair (stem-cell transplantation).

In contrast to this unified approach, many areas of psychology remain divided along 'party-political' lines (social, cognitive, applied, etc. – sometimes with overt 'political' agendas). Indeed, reading articles and books in some of these subdisciplines gives the impression that the other subdisciplines do not exist. This state of affairs is unfortunate and threatens the very existence of psychology as an independent discipline. Scientifically, it is also unfortunate, because all subfields of psychology have much to learn from each other. Without wanting to claim special status, biological psychology along Hebbian lines does force us to consider both the neurological and the psychological – both of which are of equal importance – and thereby does not allow us the false comfort of focusing on only one part of psychology to the exclusion of other equally important parts. Toates (2001) is indeed correct to note that the future of psychology 'lies in reinforcing bridges rather than blowing them up'.

Our journey has come to an end. As should now be clear, science has made a remarkable contribution to understanding the human mind: our perceptions, our thoughts, our emotions, our experiences, our despair, our sense of self. It has also solved some of the problems that have puzzled philosophers for millennia; and now it is even starting to yield rational explanations for some of Nature's deepest mysteries. The science of psychology is unique in its linking of conceptual and real processes (e.g., the processes mediating neurology and overt behaviour), and this is seen clearly in biological psychology, which, though still young, will in its maturing years bring further dazzling developments and daunting challenges.

Learning Questions

1. What are the major problems entailed when explaining the 'mind' in terms of the 'brain'?
2. Has the study of the cheater detection module helped to clarify the computational nature of the brain–mind?
3. What are the 'easy problems' and the 'hard problem' of consciousness, and why are they important?
4. Does Gray's theory of consciousness offer a viable account of the form and function of consciousness?
5. What are the main arguments for assuming that consciousness evolved by Darwinian selection?

NOTES

1   The *type* of processing carried out need not be algorithmic; cognitive processes seem to use short cuts known as 'heuristics' to simplify problems and achieve a 'good enough' solution in the minimum possible time. Also, parallel-distributed processors (see chapter 7) may use non-algorithmic procedures. However, even these types of processing are *implemented* in algorithmic machines (computers). Of course, the assumption that the brain is an algorithmic machine may simply be wrong.

2   The brain has a certain degree of plasticity, and reprogramming is possible on a longer time scale. For example, in those blind from birth, the spatial processing normally driven by vision may acquire auditory input; and, in animals like the blind mole rat, evolutionary rewiring of other inputs to what was visual cortex is complete (Catania, 2002). But this is much more like rebuilding the machine than reprogramming it.

3   Sir Roger Penrose has made a fundamental contribution to the mathematical analysis that led to the hypothesis, and subsequent confirmation, of black holes – points of 'singularity' – of dense matter out of which nothing escapes, including light (hence their blackness).

4   Meme theorists consider memes to represent another form of Darwinian evolution, but by non-genetic means. According to Blackmore, memes can be cooperative, neutral or hostile to genes.

5   Here you might reasonably have expected a definition of consciousness, but these are highly contentious. Some theorists draw a distinction between consciousness and self-consciousness; others view consciousness as being 'about' something (e.g., perceptual stimuli); and still others see it as essentially contentless. Others view it as purely cognitive in nature, but recently there has been a trend to point to its emotional aspects.

6   With Dennett in mind, we are not slipping back into a sloppy Cartesian mode of thinking because this 'late' conscious awareness is itself a product of brain processing, but this brain processing is not the same as that observed during the initiation of the act represented by the conscious experience.

7   I am indebted to Jeffrey Gray for allowing me to see a prepublication draft of his book, which was provisionally titled *Constructing Consciousness*, and, just before his death in April 2004, for email correspondence concerning his ideas.

8   However, where this analogy falls down is in the detail of the visual information processed. Change blindness and inattentional blindness seem to show that we do not capture a veridical image of the whole visual scene, but only those parts to which our attention is directed. In this respect, it is the online process that selects the stimuli for processing – although this can be modified by previous offline processes (e.g., where in the field the snake may now be).

9   If we restrict our discussion of consciousness to its apparently subjective quality, then it could be argued that functional theories of consciousness do not really explain anything about consciousness. However, we are assuming that to understand consciousness is to address one of its problems, namely, what possible function it could serve.

FURTHER READING

Blackmore, S. (2003). *Consciousness: An Introduction*. Abingdon: Hodder & Stoughton.

Gray, J. A. (2004). *Consciousness: Creeping Up on the Hard Problem*. Oxford: Oxford University Press.

Velmans, M. (2000). *Understanding Consciousness*. London: Routledge.

Glossary

Ablation. Surgical removal of part of brain; a form of 'lesion'.

Action. Motor movements defined in terms of their purpose.

Action potential. The all-or-none burst of electrical activity from the axon hillock down the axon to the terminal buttons; one form of 'nerve signal'.

Activational effects. A change in the sensitivity or activity of a system as a result of hormonal effects (e.g., sexual motivation); usually dependent on the availability of the activating hormone.

Acuity. The ability of sensory systems to resolve fine physical detail.

Acute. Early stages in the presentation of an illness.

Adaptation. (a) A change in the organism's functioning to fit the demands of the local environment; (b) a decrease in the activity in a sensory neuron during the presentation of a stimulus.

Adaptive. A characteristic that has evolved by natural or sexual selection that led to the differential transmission of genes related to the adaptive trait.

Addiction. Usually used to refer to the process of 'dependence'; correctly refers to dependence plus repetitive behaviours that have negative personal and social consequences.

Additive genetic variance. Individual differences caused by the independent effects of alleles that 'add up' in their effects (contrast with 'non-additive genetic variance').

Affect. The continuum of pleasure–displeasure in subjective feeling, sometimes described in multidimensional terms.

Afferent nerve. A nerve that conveys information towards a target site; e.g., sensory neuron (from the Latin *affere*, 'to bring to').

After-image. A visual illusion experienced following the termination of a stimulus after prolonged exposure (e.g., due to fatigue of receptors).

Agnosia. A clinical neuropsychological condition entailing impairment of visual object recognition.

Agonist. A chemical molecule that occupies and stimulates a receptor in a similar manner to the naturally occurring neurotransmitter (i.e., ligand).

Algorithm. A mathematical operation performed by a computer, following a set of procedures to achieve some specified goal; a step-by-step logical method for solving a problem or accomplishing a task.

Allele. Variants of genes that occupy the same location on the chromosome.

All-or-none principle. The action potential either fires or does not, and is not graded in magnitude; the magnitude of the action potential is independent of the intensity of the eliciting stimulus.

Allosteric. Interaction of neurotransmitter-binding receptor sites (e.g., activation of one type of receptor may be necessary for the activation of a different receptor type).

Alpha activity. An EEG wave associated with drowsiness.

Altruism. Self-sacrifice for the genetic benefit of genetically related kin.

Alzheimer's disease. A common neurodegenerative disease of the central nervous system; a form of dementia with a particular cellular pathology.

Amino acid. One of the 20 building-blocks of proteins, specified by a codon (triplet) of DNA.

Amnesia. A clinical neuropsychological condition entailing memory disorder, in which either old information cannot be retrieved (retrograde amnesia) or new information cannot be stored (anterograde amnesia).

Amplitude. The height of a wave/cycle; the strength of a response.

Analgesia. The physiological and pharmacological processes of pain reduction.

Androgen. A class of hormones involved in sexual differentiation and activation, and especially important in the development of male sexual characteristics.

Animal model. The use of non-human animals to model important features of human processes (e.g., dopamine processes underlying stimulus salience implicated in schizophrenia).

Antagonist. A chemical molecule that occupies and blocks a receptor so that other molecules (e.g., reverse agonist drugs or naturally occurring neurotransmitter ligands) can no longer bind to and activate the receptor.

Anterior. Towards the front.

Anterograde amnesia. A form of amnesia in which events experienced *after* trauma can no longer be retrieved.

Anxiety. A negative state of rumination and worry concerning potential danger in the future.

Anxiogenics. Any drug that increases anxiety; often reserved for drugs that have specific anxiety effects.

Anxiolytics. Any drug that reduces anxiety; term often reserved for drugs that have specific anti-anxiety effects.

Aphasia. A clinical neuropsychological condition entailing the disruption or loss of language functions (receptive or expressive).

Apoptosis. Process of cell death, vital in the healthy regulation of cells, but when dysregulated can lead to pathological effects (e.g., dementia or cancer).

Appetite. A central state of want relating to some desired stimulus; the motivation to gain access to food and ingest it.

Appetitive. A motivational phase of behaviour comprising the desire to approach and obtain a desired biological reinforcer (e.g., food and mate); the process reducing the spatial and temporal gradient to a biological reinforcer.

ARAS. Ascending reticular activation system; a system of ascending projections from the brainstem that modulate the brain's sensitivity and reactivity to stimuli; involved in the sleep–wake cycle and implicated in arousal-based performance effects.

Arousal. A physiological state of readiness that facilitates subsequent behaviour and which can be measured by psychophysiological means (e.g., EEG).

Association. A methodology used to examine the relationship between allelic frequencies and a phenotype; the correlation may be direct, in which a DNA marker is functional and causes the phenotypic variation, or indirect, in which a DNA marker is near a functional polymorphism that causes the phenotypic variation.

Associative learning. The procedures and processes involved in learning the temporal and spatial association of two stimuli.

Automatic processes. Cognitive processes that occur without conscious awareness and effort.

Autonomic nervous system (ANS). Part of the peripheral nervous system (PNS), which regulates internal processes in the body; divided into sympathetic and non-sympathetic branches.

Autoreceptor. Presynaptic receptor that responds to neurotransmitter released by the presynaptic cell.

Autosomal gene. A gene on any of the chromosomes other than the 23rd X/Y sex-determining pair.

Backward mask. Suppression of the perception of one stimulus by another; method used to achieve very short presentation times.

Behavioural sensitization. A form of Pavlovian conditioning leading to increased activity in a specific environment as a result of drug action in the same environment.

Beta activity. An EEG wave associated with alertness.

Binding. The process of combining separate streams of information into a unified percept; the process involved in combining information to form the (experiental) unity of consciousness.

Biological. The study of living forms, involving their structure, processes and functions.

Blindsight. A clinical neuropsychological condition entailing the preserved ability in subjectively blind people to perform behavioural tasks at above-chance levels.

Bottom-up. A form of data-driven processing that relies on the parameters of physical stimuli; contrasted with 'top-down' processing.

Candidate gene. A gene presumed to be involved in a particular phenotype.

Causality. The logical inference of effects from causes; usually achieved by the experimental manipulation of variables and control groups that constrain the number of possible logical inferences.

Central executive. The supervisory system that regulates subsystems of 'working memory'.

Central nervous system (CNS). The brain and spinal cord.

Central state. The internal set of processes that cannot be directly observed but is inferred from behavioural effects (e.g., sensory preconditioning); a central state (e.g., arousal/emotion) has a broad influence on other processes.

Central sulcus. The large groove separating the frontal and parietal cortices.

Cerebral cortex. The outer layer of the brain, comprising the folds and ridges.

Cerebrospinal fluid (CSF). The fluid that fills the brain's ventricles and the central canal of the spinal cord; serves to reduce pressure on the base of the brain.

Change blindness. The perceptual phenomenon of not noticing important changes when visual scenes are changed; thought to reflect the fact that perception is not simply a progressively built-up representation of the world, in which such gross changes would be quickly noticed.

Chromosome. The structure containing sequences of DNA that form genes; all cells (apart from ova and sperm 'gamete' cells) have 23 pairs of chromosomes, identical in males and females apart from the 23rd sex-influencing pair (X/Y).

Circadian rhythm. A rhythm that has a periodicity of approximately 24 hours, involved in the sleep–wake cycle.

Cistron. Length of DNA spanning a gene region, containing: (a) exons, which are coding sequences, and (b) introns, which are non-coding regions.

Chronic. Long-term duration of illness.

Classical conditioning. The strengthening of an associative bond between two stimuli by virtue of systematic pairing, leading to the initially neutral conditioned stimulus (CS; e.g., light) taking on the response-eliciting properties of the unconditioned stimulus (UCS; e.g., food); also known as Pavlovian conditioning.

Cloning. The common process of making copies of a specific piece of DNA, usually a gene; in genetics cloning does not refer to producing a whole organism.

Coding. The correspondence between physical stimuli parameters and processing in the central nervous system.

Codon. The triplet DNA base pairs that code for an amino acid; the gene is composed of a sequences of codons.

Co-morbidity. The presence of several disorders together.

Compound. A molecule made up of more elementary parts.

Computation. The mathematically defined system of processing of information thought to be fundamental to brain processing (based on the science of computer technology); the view that brain–mind processing is composed of algorithms that compute information.

Computer. A computational device that implements mathematical (algorithmic) procedures for information processing; more generally, any device that computes information irrespective of procedures.

Computerized tomography (CT). An X-ray procedure for neuroimaging the structure of the brain.

Concentration gradient. A difference in the concentration of two or more substances, which produces a biological effect (e.g., sodium/potassium concentrations in neurons).

Concept-driven. The influence of concepts on processing physical stimuli (e.g., categorization in visual perception); also known as 'top-down' processing; often contrasted with 'data-driven'.

Concordance. In genetics the presence of a particular condition in two family members (e.g., twins); discordance refers to the lack of common phenotypes in family members (e.g., schizophrenia in twins).

Conditioned immune suppression. A suppression of the immune system caused by a conditioned stimulus (CS; e.g., smell of hospital) that has been paired with an aversive unconditioned stimulus (nausea-inducing drug).

Conditioned response (CR). The response elicited by a conditioned stimulus (CS) after Pavlovian conditioning/learning; also related to conditioned *emotional* response, which is a conditioned central state that can be indirectly measured by response suppression during operant behaviour.

Conditioned stimulus (CS). A stimulus that acquires its power to elicit a response (CR) following association with a biologically significant stimulus (i.e., an unconditioned stimulus; UCS).

Cones. Colour-coding sensory receptors in the retina of the eye.

Conscious awareness. The subjective awareness of the external world and ongoing psychological processes; often used as a synonym for consciousness, but relating to its perceptual qualities.

Consciousness. The state of subjective awareness of internal and external events; often divided into further categories, but a problematic concept surrounded by considerable controversy and debate.

Consolidation. The process of the strengthening of memory after acquisition.

Constancy. The perception of constant features of visual objects despite changes in size on the retina.

Consummatory. The phase of behaviour involving the consumption of final biological reinforcer (e.g., eating and copulation).

Contralateral. The opposite side of the brain; usually in relation to sensory systems that cross over during the passage to the brain.

Controlled processing. Processing that involves effort and attentional resources, sometimes related to conscious awareness.

Cooperation. Altruistic acts that do not have a reciprocal payback from the recipient of the act.

Cranial nerves. The nerves linking the peripheral sensors and muscles to the brain (e.g., facial muscles) that do not go via the spinal cord.

Craving. The subjective urge for a stimulus (e.g., drug) that preoccupies thoughts and feelings.

Data-driven. The influence of the physical features of stimuli on processing (e.g., motion in visual perception); also known as 'bottom-up' processing'; often contrasted with 'concept-driven'.

Declarative memory. A type of memory involving the conscious knowing of something; that which can be verbally 'declared'.

Delusion. A belief involving a severe misinterpretation of events, which is immune to reasoned argument and opposing fact, and which is inconsistent with the patient's educational or cultural background.

Dementia. Neurodegenerative disease of the brain, cognitive (e.g., involving memory, attention), emotional and personality impairments.

Deoxyribonucleic acid (DNA). The simple molecule that contains genes and whose double-helical structure supports reproduction by dividing and forming complementary base pairs.

Dependence. The technical term for the continued need to administer a drug in order to prevent a withdrawal syndrome.

Depolarization. The change in electrical charge across the membrane of the axon that occurs during an action potential.

Determinism. The philosophical principle that every effect has an identifiable cause.

Development. Alteration in structure and function that occurs over time; often referred to as 'growth'.

Differentiation. The formation of specialized cells from simpler source cells.

Distal cause. Ultimate cause.

Dizygotic. Refers to two zygotes (eggs); 'dizygotic twins' refer to non-identical, or 'fraternal', twins.

DNA marker. A polymorphism in DNA that is used to identify sequences of DNA in narrowing down the search for specific genes on specific chromosomes.

Dominant gene. A gene (allele) which is expressed if present; contrast with 'recessive gene'; an allele that produces a particular phenotype when present in a heterozygous state.

Dopamine hypothesis. A major pharmacological hypothesis of schizophrenia which relates symptoms to an access of dopamine in specific dopamine pathways.

Dorsal. Towards the back or top of head.

Dorsal root ganglion. The structure that contains the cell bodies of sensory neurons.

Dorsal stream. The stream of visual information going to the parietal cortex; involved in the processing of 'where' information.

Double blind. A study in which neither the participant nor the tester/assessor knows which conditions (experimental or control) participants have been allocated; used to eliminate bias in treatment or assessment.

Double dissociation. A form of inference that allows functions to be assigned to specific brain structures: damage to area X_1 impairs function Y_1 but leaves function Y_2 intact, while damage to X_2 impairs function Y_2 but leaves function Y_1 intact.

Down-regulation. The desensitization of receptors, usually produced by a reduction in their number.

Drug. Chemicals that are exogenously derived and not needed for the normal functioning of the cell and which have the capacity to alter the functioning of a cell.

Dualism. A philosophical theory of the relationship between mind and brain which contends that the physical and mental are separate though interacting domains; contrast 'methodological' and 'property' dualism: mind–brain are different ways of thinking about and understanding ('methodological') or fundamentally different 'things' ('property').

Effector. A muscle or gland that carries out some function.

Efferent nerves. A nerve that conveys information away from a target site; for example motor neurons (from the Latin *effere*, 'to bring forth').

Electroencephalography (EEG). The study of the electrical activity of the brain by placing recording electrodes on the scalp.

Element. A substance that cannot be broken down further into small substances.

Emergent properties. The philosophical idea that new properties arise at each level of organizational complexity; the whole is more than the sum of its parts.

Endophenotype. Laboratory or indirect measures that better reflect underlying pathophysiology than the surface phenotype (e.g., signs and symptoms in schizophrenia); also called 'intermediate phenotypes' (e.g., eye movement dysfunctions in schizophrenia).

Environment. A source of influence on a phenotype that cannot be accounted for by genetic variations between individuals or statistical error in measurements; can be analysed into different components to describe the nature of this influence: (a) shared environments are common to children in the same family, and (b) non-shared environments are unique to each child in the same family (e.g., having different friends). The 'environment' is to some extent the result of perceptual bias (e.g., anxious people experiencing their environment as threatening) and selection (i.e., certain genotypes seeking out certain environments); there is considerable interaction between genes and environment, which renders the notion of a fixed environment 'out there' a problematic concept.

Enzyme. A protein that controls the rate of chemical reactions.

Episodic memory. Memory for particular episodes or personal experiences.

Epistasis. The interactive effects of genes (i.e., the function of one gene depends upon levels/alleles of another gene); contrasted with additive genetic effects; the extent and importance of epistasis is unknown.

Ethology. The study of animal behaviour in their natural environments (a branch of zoology).

Evoked potential (EP). The EEG response to an eliciting stimulus or event; when tied to an experimental stimulus, it is known as an 'event-related potential' (ERP); measured by summing over many trials to isolate systematic response from electrical noise.

Evolution. The process of transmutation or transformation in which organisms change through the process of natural selection; a random process in which genetic mutations that confer reproductive advantages are passed on to future generations.

Exon. A DNA sequence that codes for amino acids and which is transcribed in messenger RNA (contrast with 'intron').

Explicit memory. Memory that is accessible to conscious awareness; similar to 'declarative memory'; opposed to 'implicit memory'.

Exploratory behaviour. Information-gathering behaviour that allows assessment of the environment, usually controlled by appetitive motivation.

Extinction. The process of the progressive weakening of a conditioned response (CR) when presentation of the conditioned stimulus (CS; e.g., light) is no longer 'reinforced' by the unconditioned stimulus (UCS; e.g., food).

Factor analysis. A multivariate statistical technique used to reduce a large correlational matrix to a much smaller number of underlying dimensions; widely used to examine the psychological dimensions that underlie complex forms of behaviour.

Fear. A negative state of impending danger relating to aversive stimuli that are close either temporally or spatially; the negative state that motivates immediate avoidance/escape.

Fecundity. Reproductive (fitness) value.

Feedforward. Action that anticipates the appropriate response in the immediately following period of time; contrast with 'feedback'.

Fissure. Long, deep sulcus.

Fitness. The value of an animal's reproductive potential; a parameter used to assess the probability of evolution by natural selection of social behaviour (e.g., spite).

Fovea. The area in the centre of the retina specialized to process fine detail.

Frequency. Number of cycles per second (see 'amplitude').

Frequency coding. Information conveyed by the frequency of action potentials; used in various sensory systems for stimulus discrimination.

Frustration. The negative state experienced when reward is either omitted or terminated; shares many functional properties with fear; a form of disappointment.

Functional neuroimaging. Neuroimaging involving measurement of brain activity during the performance of a task; contrast with 'structural neuroimaging'.

Functional specialization. The processing of functions by specific areas of the cortex (e.g., Broca's area and speech production).

Gamete. Sex cells: ova and sperm.

Ganglion. A collection of cell bodies of neurons in the peripheral nervous system (plural: ganglia).

Gate theory. The theory of Melzack and Wall (e.g., 1965 and 1984), which proposes a sensory 'gate' in the spinal cord controlling the passage of nociceptive (pain) signals.

Gene. A sequence of DNA that codes for polypeptides and proteins.

Gene expression. The turning on and off of genes, leading to the production of proteins.

Genetic code. The mapping of triplet DNA base pairs onto the 20 amino acids that comprise proteins in 'gene expression'.

Genetic marker. Locations in a DNA sequence that cut the sequence at known locations; used to reduce the search region for the specific gene of interest.

Genetic relatedness. The proportion of shared heritability held by common descent; more generally, the overlap in genetic variability between two individuals (e.g., siblings = 0.5).

Genome. The genetic make-up of the species/individual.

Genomic imprinting. The process by which an allele at a given locus is expressed differently, depending on whether it is inherited from the mother or father.

Genotype. The complete genome of the individual; contained in each cell in the body in identical form (save localized mutations resulting from cell divisions).

Genotype–environment correlation. Genetic influence on exposure to environment; experiences that are correlated with genetic propensities.

Genotype–environment interaction. Genetic sensitivity or susceptibility to environments.

Generalization. The observation that a conditioned response (CR) may be elicited by any stimulus on the same sensory dimension as the conditioned stimulus (CS); the form of the response curve is an inverted U, with maximal response to the CS and progressively weaker responses to other stimuli on either side of this maximal stimulus value.

Gland. The site at which hormones are produced and secreted.

Glial cells. Various forms of support cells essential for the maintenance and effective functioning of neurons (e.g., myelin sheath).

Gonads. Male testes and female ovaries.

Graded potential. A nerve signal that varies according to the intensity of the eliciting stimulus (contrast with 'action potential' and 'all-or-none principle').

Grey matter. Areas of nervous systems with a high density of nerve cells and dendrites (contrast with 'white matter').

Group selection hypothesis. The theory that individuals' behaviour evolves because it benefits the reproductive fitness of the species.

Gyrus. Ridges observed along the clefts (sulci) on the cerebrum.

Habituation. The simplest form of learning, which is defined as the weakening of the strength of a response as a result of the stimulus that elicits the response being repeatedly presented without reinforcement; opposite of sensitization.

Hallucination. Perceptions in the absence of adequate sensory input, or a grossly disordered perception in the presence of sensory stimuli.

Hallucinogen. A class of drug that radically alters sensory perceptions.

Hardware. The physical-material device in which software instructions (programs) are implemented (see 'software').

Hard-wired. Neuronal systems and synaptic connections that have little flexibility and have a high degree of consistency across individuals.

Hebb synapse. Structural changes that occur between synapses as a result of learning.

Hebb's rule. The principle that, if a neuron receives an input from another neuron, and if both neurons are highly activated and have the same sign (either excitatory or inhibitory), then the weight between the neurons is strengthened.

Hedonic. The subjective quality of pleasure (positive affect).

Heritability. The *estimate* of the proportion of variance in a phenotype that may be attributed to genetic effects.

Heteroreceptor. Presynaptic receptor that responds to some chemical other than the neurotransmitter released by the same cell.

Heterozygeity. Different versions of genes (alleles) on chromosomes.

Hierarchical control. The ability of (rostal) higher levels in the brain exerting control over (more caudal) levels; important in the cognitive control of basic instincts, motivation, emotion and behaviour.

Holism. The idea that the whole is greater than the sum of the parts; the contention that psychological phenomena need to be understood from the perspective of whole-system processing (e.g., Gestalt perceptions).

Homozygeity. Identical versions of genes (alleles) on chromosomes.

Homunculus. The idea of a 'little man' in the head; used to criticize the notion that images are 'seen' by something in the brain; a caricature showing the degree of cortical processing devoted to sensory and motor systems.

Hormone. A chemical messenger secreted into the blood at one location and acting on sites in other locations; shares some similarities with neurotransmitters, but has a number of distinctive features.

Hyperpolarization. The change in electrical charge across the membrane of the axon to a more negative value than the resting potential; occurs after an action potential.

Identity theory. A philosophical theory that argues that every mind event is accompanied by a brain event.

Illusion. A distortion of perception relative to some objective standard; the perception of something that is real but perceived in a way that does not correspond faithfully to the stimulus or event.

Immune system. The system of defence against pathogens (e.g., viruses) and cancerous cells; has important relations to the central nervous system and the neuroendocrine system.

Implicit memory. Memory that is not accessible to conscious awareness; similar to 'procedural memory'; contrasted with 'explicit memory'.

Inattentional amnesia. The phenomenon that exposure to the same stimulus does not necessarily enhance performance to that stimulus, suggesting that perception is constructive rather than purely representational.

Inattentional blindness. The phenomenon of not noticing features of the environment when attention is directed to other stimuli; most strikingly demonstrated by the film *Gorillas in our Midst*.

Incentive. A stimulus that has the power to elicit appetitive motivation.

Incentive salience. The value of an incentive stimulus, measured in terms of its power to elicit appetitive motivation.

Inclusive fitness. The sum of individual fitness and the effects an individual's actions have on the reproductive success of genetic relatives.

Individual fitness. Individual reproductive success.

Information. A technical term referring to the flow of information in a processing system, concerning the degree to which uncertainty is reduced by the message; often defined in terms of the 'bit' (binary digit), which is the amount of information that reduces uncertainty by one-half.

Instrumental conditioning/learning. A form of associative learning in which the presentation of a stimulus (e.g., food) is depending on a response (e.g., lever press).

Interactionism. The combination of different 'things' (e.g., processes) to produce a higher-order level of complexity; takes different forms with radically different philosophical implications.

Interneuron. A neuron that connects sensory and motor neurons.

Intracranial self-stimulation (ICSS). The electrical stimulation of the 'pleasure centre' of the brain, conducted via implanted electrodes, and which is contingent on an instrumental response.

Intron. DNA sequence *within* a gene that does not code for amino acids.

Ionotrophic receptor. A type of receptor whose binding by a neurotransmitter leads to activation via ion channels; involved in fast action of neurotransmitters.

Ipsilateral. The same side of the brain; usually used in relation to sensory systems.

Kamin blocking effect (KBE). The blocking of the development of a conditioned stimulus (CS), when presented in combination with a second CS that has been previously associated with an unconditioned stimulus (UCS).

Karyotype. The method of defining chromosomes.

Kindling. A process of heightened activation of a system due to prior activation (may be important in psychiatric illness).

Kin selection. Behaviours directed at increasing the survival and fecundity (fitness) of genetically related individuals.

Lamarckian evolution. The plausible but factually incorrect theory that evolution occurs by the inheritance of acquired characteristics (e.g., long necks due to stretching are passed to offspring); contrast with 'natural selection'.

Latent inhibition (LI). The retardation of stimulus–stimulus associability when one of the stimuli has been previously 'pre-exposed' (i.e., presented with any consequence/reinforcement); LI is thought to reflect the conditioned withdrawal of attention from the pre-exposed stimulus.

Latent learning. Learning that occurs 'silently' and is only manifest in behaviour when the animal is motivated to perform.

Lateral. Towards the side; away from the midline.

Lateral inhibition. Inhibition between regions of a sensory surface.

Lateralization. Cortical asymmetry, in which one hemisphere has a larger role in functional processing (e.g., language and the left hemisphere).

Learning. A procedure or process involved in the change (or potential for change) in behaviour as a direct result of exposure to stimuli regularities; psychological change due to experience.

Lesion. Disruption of the functioning of a part of the brain through either experimental damage (e.g., ablation) or accident.

Ligand. A naturally occurring neurotransmitter substance.

Limbic system. A region of the forebrain comprising a number of structures involved in emotion, motivation processes, learning and memory, including: the hippocampus, the fornix and the amygdala.

Linkage. A methodology used to determine the pattern of genetic inheritance underlying a phenotype; the technique used to detect linkage between DNA markers and a phenotype (the close proximity of loci on a chromosome does not independently assort at reproduction so is not lost through the generations).

Locus. The site of a specific gene on a chromosome (Latin for 'place').

Long-term depression (LTD). A structural and functional change in the postsynaptic membrane following learning, supporting the weakening of associative links; see 'long-term potentiation'.

Long-term memory (LTM). Memory held over longer periods of time, from minutes to years.

Long-term potentiation (LTP). A structural and functional change in the postsynaptic membrane following learning, supporting the strengthening of associative links; see 'long-term depression'.

Magnetic resonance imaging (MRI). A neuroimaging technique that produces images of the structure of the brain by measuring differences in oxygen flow; functional MRI (fMRI) is used to image the brain during the performance of tasks, thus revealing which areas of the brain are associated with task performance.

Magnetoencephalogram (MEG). A technique to measure electrical activity in the brain; has a high degree of temporal resolution and combines the temporal advantages of EEG with the spatial advantages of MRI.

Maturation. Changes in the structure and function of the nervous system as a result of development; often contrasted with learning.

Membrane. Structure that surrounds a cell.

Membrane potential. Electrical voltage across cell membrane.

Meme. The unit of self-replication of cognition, first proposed by Dawkins (1976) as the unit of cultural transmission; the study of memes is 'memetics' – still a controversial idea.

Memory. A change in the nervous system as a result of learning that affects subsequent retrieval of information.

Mendelian genetics. Knowledge concerning the 'particulate' nature of the units of inheritance (genes).

Metabotropic receptor. A type of receptor whose binding by a neurotransmitter leads to activation via signal proteins and G proteins; involved in slow action of neurotransmitters.

Microarrays. A technique used to identify activated genes in a tissue sample.

Microelectrode. A tiny electrode that is able to record and stimulate a single neuron.

Mind. An ambiguous term that has many meanings; here used to refer to the products of the computation of the brain, whether conscious or non-conscious.

Module. Dedicated information processing system that is relatively autonomous and devoted to the computation of a specific goal.

Molecular. The fine detail of structure and processes (e.g., molecular genetics).

Molecular genetics. The study of the sequence of DNA and its relation to protein synthesis and structure/function (this is also known as 'qualitative genetics'; contrast with 'quantitative genetics').

Molecule. Smallest possible piece of a compound that retains the property of the compound.

Monism. Philosophical contention that the mind and brain are reflections of a single underlying 'thing' (e.g., physical material).

Monoamine. Class of neurotransmitters, including dopamine, serotonin (5-HT) and norepinephrine.

Monozygotic. Refers to one zygote (egg); monozygotic twins refer to identical twins.

Motor homunculus. A graphic depiction showing the areas and relative size on the motor cortex devoted to motor functions.

Motor neuron. A neuron that conveys a nerve signal to a muscle.

Mutation. A change in the sequence of DNA in a gene that alters protein production; the source of (chance) variation that allows the differential reproduction of individuals that underlies evolution by natural selection.

Myelin. The fatty glial cell that sheaths the neuron's axon to speed nerve conductance.

Natural selection. The selection of favoured phenotypes by Nature, which leads to differential reproduction and the transmission of the genes underlying the phenotype; considered to be the means of evolution; similar process to domestication of animals, but the selector is not the breeder but Nature's challenges, which some phenotypes meet better than others.

Negative feedback. A signal of a deviation of desired and actual state that leads to adjustments in the system designed to reduce the error signal.

Negative reinforcement. The termination or omission of a stimulus (e.g., shock) contingent upon an instrumental response that strengthens the probability of the future emission of that response.

Neglect. A neuropsychological impairment resulting from brain damage that results in the patient ignoring a part of the sensory world (e.g., left visual field).

Nerve. A bundle of axons in the peripheral nervous system.

Nervous system. The total nervous system, including the brain, spinal cord and peripheral nervous system (i.e., the somatic and autonomic nervous system).

Neural network. A computer system of processing units linked together in a highly integrated network that learns the association between input stimuli and target outputs; used for a wide variety of purposes, from pattern recognition to modelling complex psychological processes; in neuroscience, neural networks are used to model real neuronal processes in order to develop simulations sufficient to generate and test hypotheses.

Neural plasticity. The brain's capacity for neuronal and synaptic reorganization, fundamental to the physiological instantiation of learning.

Neuroendocrine system. The system responsible for the action of hormones in the body, including organs and types of hormones.

Neurogenesis. The process of generation and regeneration of neurons.

Neurohormone. A chemical resembling both a neuron and a neurotransmitter, released by neurons and conveyed in the blood.

Neuroimaging. A set of techniques allows the measurement of the volume and functional activity of the brain.

Neuromodulator. A chemical (neurohormone or neurotransmitter) having a diffuse effect on target neurons, influencing the general tone of neurons.

Neuron. A specialized type of cell in the nervous system that conveys information by chemical neurotransmission.

Neurophysiology. The field of study that uses experimental tools of investigation, including such invasive techniques as recording/stimulation from electrodes in the brain and lesion.

Neuropsychological test. Standardized tests designed to assess psychological functions; used to diagnosis brain injury and to design and assess rehabilitation programmes.

Neuropsychology. The relationship between neurophysiological structure and psychological function.

Neuroscientist. A person with advanced knowledge and training in the neurosciences; sometimes also trained as a psychiatrist or a psychologist, especially when in the field of brain–behaviour relations.

Neurosis. A collection of psychological disorders, principally involving some form of anxiety or depression.

Neuroticism. A major trait of personality reflecting increased likelihood of neurosis.

Neurotic paradox. The observation that classically conditioned emotional responses in neurosis do not undergo the expected process of extinction when the unconditioned aversive stimulus has been removed.

Neurotransmitter. A chemical substance that conveys information from one neuron to another (or to a muscle) across the synaptic gap.

Nociceptive neuron. A neuron with a tip that is sensitive to tissue damage, which conveys an action potential that leads to the experience of pain.

Node of Ranvier. Short unmyelinated section of axon.

Non-additive genetic variance. Individual differences due to the effects of alleles (dominance) or loci (epistasis) that interact with other alleles or loci.

Nosology. Classification and description of mental disorders.

Nucleus. The structure inside the cell that contains chromosomes; a cluster of cell bodies in the brain (plural: nuclei).

Oestrogen. A term used to refer to a class of hormones produced by female ovaries.

Offline processing. High-level actions that are slow and rely on controlled attentional processing; contrast with 'online processing'.

Online processing. Low-level reflexive actions that are fast and do not rely on controlled attentional processing; contrast with 'offline processing'.

Ontogeny. The history of the growth of the individual; often contrast with phylogeny.

Operant conditioning. A type of instrumental learning in which reinforcement is linked to behaviour; used to 'shape' complex behaviours from simpler naturally occurring behaviour.

Opioid. A class of drugs with effects that resemble those of morphine and heroin.

Organizational effect. An alteration in structure occurring to development as a result of hormonal influence.

Pangenesis. The (incorrect) theory of the mechanism of inheritance advanced by Darwin before Mendel's work was widely appreciated.

Parasympathetic branch. A branch of the autonomic nervous system (ANS); involved in 'rest–digest' functions; opposite functions to sympathetic branch of ANS.

Pathophysiology. The pathological physiology process underlying a disorder.

Penetrance. The degree of expressivity of a gene; the degree to which the expression of a gene depends on environmental factors; the proportion of individuals with a specific genotype who manifest that genotype at the phenotype level.

Peripheral nervous system. Composed of the somatic nervous system and the autonomic nervous system outside the central nervous system.

Personality. Individual differences in behaviour, cognition, emotion and motivation that reflect the functional activity of important systems (e.g., approach and avoidance motivational systems) that pervade psychological functions and influence a wide range of behaviour; relatively separate clusters of such individual differences are known as 'traits' (contrast with 'state').

Phantom limb pain. The experience of pain in a limb that has been amputated.

Pharmacokinetics. The study of the time course of a drug and its metabolites in the body.

Phenomenology. The subjective experience of a disorder from the patient's perspective.

Phenotype. The expression of biological processes in behaviour that can be observed and measured, but which may have complex genetic and environmental causes; contrasted with 'genotype'.

Pheromone. An airborne chemical that is used as a form of communication between individuals of a species; thought to influence sexual arousal; its role in human beings is controversial.

Phylogeny. The development and history of a species.

Placebo. Effects of a neutral substance on the basis of expectation and belief (e.g., pain relief); precise mechanism unknown but thought to relate to natural healing process.

Plasticity. The flexibility of the central nervous system to alter structure on the basis of learning/experience.

Polymerase chain reaction (PCR). A widely used technique in molecular genetics for the cloning of sequences of DNA to produce a sufficient amount for further analysis of sequence and function.

Polymorphism. A locus with two or more alleles; variation in the population at a specific locus.

Positive reinforcement. The presentation of a stimulus (e.g., food) contingent upon an instrumental response that strengthens the probability of the future emission of that response.

Positron emission tomography (PET). A neuroimaging technique used to measure metabolism and blood flow in the brain; useful in identifying the location of the effects of drugs in the brain.

Posterior. Towards the back.

Postsynaptic. The receiving neuron's dendrites.

Prepotent response. A response with a strong probability of being elicited by adequate stimuli.

Prepulse inhibition. The inhibition of the strength of response to a startling stimulus when the stimulus is preceded very briefly by a weaker stimulus (i.e., the prepulse).

Presynaptic. The releasing neuron's terminal buttons.

Procedural learning. Learning involving the acquisition of habits and motor skills or rule-based routines not involving awareness of material; sensitive to regularities in the structure of stimuli.

Procedural memory. The forms of structural changes involved in the retention of procedural information (e.g., habits and motor skills).

Prosopagnosia. A clinical neuropsychological condition entailing a deficit in face recognition.

Prostheses. The use of artificial devices to replace dysfunctional limbs and organs; now extended to brain structures (e.g., hippocampus).

Protein. Chemical structures that result from gene expression.

Protein synthesis. The building of proteins from gene expression.

Proximal cause. Local or immediate cause (e.g., neurotransmitters).

Psychiatry. A branch of medicine dealing with mental illness; a psychiatrist is a medically trained doctor who specializes in the diagnosis and treatment of mental illness, and who can prescribe drugs and has legal powers to involuntarily hospitalize patients (see 'psychologist' and 'neuroscientist').

Psychogenomics. The study of the genetic basis of psychological processes, including processes that are not readily apparent in behaviour (e.g., sensory preconditioning); also known as behavioural genetics.

Psychologist. A person trained in the study of human cognition, emotion, motivation and behaviour, usually with an advanced taught degree in one of the many specialisms (e.g., Clinical or Forensic Psychology) or a research degree (e.g., doctorate).

Psychology. The study of cognition, emotion, motivation and behaviour, in all their normal and abnormal forms; often used to refer to the study of the 'mind'.

Psychoneuroimmunology. The study of the interaction of psychological, neurological and immunological processes.

Psychopathology. Study of diseases of the mind.

Psychopharmacogenetics. The study of the genetically related individual differences in responses to drugs, especially in relation to psychoactive drugs; 'pharmacogenetics' is the more general term for individual differences in all types of drug effects.

Psychopharmacology. The study of the action and effects of chemicals on psychological processes.

Psychophysiology. The study of psychological processes and states from measurement of the surface of the body.

Psychosis. A number of severe psychiatric disorders that involve a loss of contact with reality (e.g., delusions, schizophrenia).

Qualia. The subjective qualities of consciously experienced percepts (e.g., redness).

Quantitative genetics. The statistical analysis of genetic and non-genetic (environmental) influences on a phenotype; the methodology is also used to analyse different environmental influences (e.g., shared and non-shared environments); also called 'behavioural genetics' or 'statistical genetics'; contrast with qualitative genetics.

Quantitative trait loci. A gene in a multiple gene system that contributes a relatively small but important influence on a phenotype.

Receptive field. The region on the receptive surface (e.g., skin) that can excite or inhibit a given neuron.

Receptor. (a) Structures on cells that are occupied by neurotransmitters which affect the functioning of the cell; (b) the tip of a sensory neuron that is sensitive to a physical stimulus.

Recessive gene. A gene which is expressed only when two alleles are present.

Reciprocal altruism. A form of cooperative social behaviour in which apparently selfless behaviour earns a compensating payback.

Recombination. A reassortment of genes during reproduction, leading to variety in behaviour.

Reductionism. A philosophical theory arguing that behaviour can be explained by the action of low-level biological processes (e.g., neuronal connections).

Reinforcement. The experimental procedure used to strengthen behaviour; the theoretical process involved in the strengthening of response–stimulus associations.

Reinforcement schedule. The relationship between instrumental responses and the delivery of reinforcement; basic schedules are based on 'intervals' of time or 'ratios' of work, and more complex schedules contain some combination of these two basic types of schedules.

Reliability. A measure of the consistency of measurement.

Resting potential. The membrane potential of a neuron when it is not conducting an action potential.

Retrieval. The activation of memory to gain access to stored information.

Retrograde amnesia. A deficit in the retrieval of information stored before the trauma.

Reuptake. Reabsorption of a neurotransmitter by the presynaptic terminal.

Reward. An outcome of a behaviour that leads to the experience of pleasure, leading to the increased probability of behaviour on which the reward is contingent

Rod. A type of sensory receptor in the retina, specialized for non-colour coarse-grained information.

Saltatory conduction. Alternation between action potential at nodes and more rapid conduction by the flow of ions between nodes; to 'jump' across nodes.

Sanger method. A simple and elegant technique used to identify the base pairs of a sequence of DNA, named after its inventor; the workhorse of the Human Genome Project, which allowed high throughput once mechanized.

Schizophrenia spectrum. The continuum from full-blown schizophrenia, to schizotypal personality disorders and subthreshold schizotypy; thought to reflect a genetic continuum of vulnerability.

Schizotypy. A normally distributed measure of schizophrenia-like cognitions and emotions in the general population; from *schizo*phrenia pheno*type*; see 'schizophrenia spectrum'.

Secondary messenger. A chemical activated by a neurotransmitter which initiates processes in several areas of the neuron; the neurotransmitter is the 'first' messenger.

Selfish gene. The idea that genes are the units of inheritance and have only one 'selfish' goal of replication as defined by the mathematics of evolution; vehicles (i.e., organisms) that are constructed for the purpose of replication serve this 'selfish' aim.

Semantic memory. Memory for meaning (e.g., a dog is an animal).

Sensitization. The increase in sensitivity of a system as a result of exposure to a noxious stimulus.

Sensory homunculus. A graphic depiction showing the areas and relative size on the motor cortex devoted to sensory functions.

Sensory neuron. A neuron that is sensitive to information in the external world or internal body.

Sensory preconditioning. A behavioural phenomenon observed when two stimuli are associated without reinforcement, and then one of these stimuli enters into a classical conditioning relationship: sensory preconditioning consists of the fact that now when the stimulus that was not entered into this classical conditioning relationship is presented it is observed also to elicit the conditioned response (CR); thought to reflect a 'silent' form of learning by virtue of mere temporal association.

Sensory receptor. Cell that detects physical stimuli and transduces information into action potentials.

Sensory threshold. The minimum level of sensory stimulation needed for above-chance levels of detection/discrimination.

Sex. The method of reproduction that involves combining DNA from two variants of a species (males and females).

Sexual differentiation. Development of male or female sex organs and neural systems underlying sexual behaviour, including secondary sexual characteristics (e.g., pubic hair).

Sexual selection. A variant of natural selection in which the source of the selection pressure is the preference of sexual mates (e.g., females' preference for strong males).

Short-term memory (STM). A limited capacity store for the retention of material over a brief (seconds to minutes) period of time.

Sodium–potassium pump. Pump that removes sodium (Na^+) from cell and includes potassium (K^+).

Software. The set of instructions comprising a computer program that is independent of the device in which it is implemented (see 'hardware').

Somatic nervous system (SNS). Part of the peripheral nervous system that interacts with the external environment (e.g., sensory receptors).

Somatosenses. Sensory system involved in processing of stimuli in tissue and organs of body (e.g., sense of touch).

Spatial summation. The summation of effects of activity from several neurons on a single neuron (see 'temporal summation').

Spinal cord. The column of neurons within the backbone.

Spite. The lowering of someone else's fitness without an increase or even a decrease in one's own fitness (where there is a decrease, spite could evolve only when inclusive fitness was not also lowered).

Split brain. The surgical separation of the two hemispheres by cutting the corpus callosum.

Standardized test. A carefully constructed test of psychological functions that is 'standardized' in two ways: (a) procedure for administration; and (b) availability of test score data on relevant populations against which patients' scores are compared; test construction and standardization comprise the field of psychometrics.

Startle reflex. A defensive reaction to an intense stimulus (e.g., loud noise), comprising a skeletal-muscular wave that travels down the body; can be conveniently measured by eye-blink reflex in human beings and whole-body startle in rodents.

State. A temporary physiological/psychological level of activation and readiness to respond.

Stem cells. A class of undifferentiated cells that have the potential to develop as any form of cell (e.g., neuron or heart cells); stem cell technology holds great potential for the regeneration of diseased tissue, from brain tissue to heart tissue.

Steroid. A class of hormones, including androgens and oestrogens, that act by affecting gene expression in the nucleus of the cell.

Stress. The state of long-term (chronic) effects of exposure to aversive stimulation in which bodily reactions are maladaptive or inadequate to cope effectively with demands of 'stressors'; physiological/psychological 'strain' is a more descriptive term for this abnormal state of functioning; stress is hypothesized to be induced by the combination of (a) high load (e.g., tight deadlines), (b) unfavourable situation (e.g., unstructured and ambiguous task), and (c) lack of control (e.g., low autonomy) – these factors may be actual or interpreted.

Stressors. Aversive stimuli that produce a state of stress; often not the aversive stimuli themselves but the psychological reaction to aversive stimuli, which is influenced by expectations and coping strategies.

Stroke. Damage to the brain and impaired functioning due to blockage in blood supply or rupture of blood vessel; also called 'brain attack'.

Stroop test. A neuropsychological test measuring attentional interference; the standard test requiring the naming of the ink colour of colour names; the modified Stroop test uses emotional words as the source of distraction.

Structural neuroimaging. Neuroimaging involving measurement of brain structure and volume; contrast with 'functional neuroimaging'.

Sulcus. Clefts (grooves) observed on the cerebrum (also called 'fissures').

Superior. Above another part.

Survival of the fittest. A term coined by Herbert Spencer, adopted by Charles Darwin, to refer to the viability and fecundity values of individuals best fitted to environmental demands.

Sympathetic branch. A branch of the autonomic nervous system (ANS); involved in 'fight–flight' functions; opposite functions to parasympathetic branch of ANS.

Synaesthesia. A condition found in otherwise normal people consisting of an abnormality in sensory processing: input to one modality (e.g., hearing a word) leads to experience in another modality (e.g., colour); can also be within modality (e.g., seeing a word produces colour perception).

Synapse. The gap between neurons across which neurotransmitters diffuse; also known as 'synaptic cleft'.

Temporal summation. Combination of effects of more than one synaptic input at different times (see 'spatial summation')

Terminal button. The section of the presynaptic neuron that releases the neurotransmitter into the synapse.

Therapeutic index. The ratio of (a) the drug dose that produces the desired effect in 50 per cent of cases, and (b) the drug dose that produces toxic effects in 50 per cent of cases; a measure of the safety of a drug.

Theta wave. An EEG wave associated with hippocampal activity.

Threshold. Level of stimulation sufficient to trigger a response (e.g., all-or-none action potential at axon hillock).

Top-down. A form of conceptually driven processing that relies on higher levels of processing to interpret physical stimuli; contrasted with 'bottom-up' processing.

Topographical map. Adjacent areas of sensory surfaces (e.g., retina) are represented by adjacent areas in the brain (e.g., visual cortex).

Transcranial magnetic stimulation (TMS). A technique to stimulate the cortex by magnetic fields; can be used in healthy volunteers to assess the effects of temporary lesions of the cortex, as well as a therapeutic technique in depression.

Transduction. Translation of stimulation by sensory stimuli into an electrical signal.

Transporter. A membrane protein responsible for the reuptake of a neurotransmitter from the synaptic cleft.

Two-point threshold. The minimum distance between two points in the sensory surface that can be detected/discriminated; the shorter the distance, the greater the sensory acuity.

Umani. The fifth type of taste receptor that is sensitive to monosodium glutamate, which is broken down during the cooking of glutamic acid; commonly used as a food additive to provide flavour in food.

Unconditioned response (UCR). An innate response that does not require learning (e.g., salivation).

Unconditioned stimulus (UCS). A stimulus (e.g., food) which has the ability to elicit an unconditioned response (UCR); a primary biological reinforcer.

Up-regulation. The sensitization of receptors, usually produced by an increase in their number.

Validity. The degree to which measurement relates to the construct it purports to measure.

Ventral. Towards the lower part of the brain.

Ventral stream. The stream of visual information going to the temporal cortex; involved in the processing of 'what' information.

Ventricles. Spaces in the brain filled with cerebrospinal fluid.

Vesicle. A packet near the axon terminal filled with neurotransmitter.

Viability. Survival value.

Visual neglect. A clinical neuropsychological condition entailing neglect of one sensory field (e.g., left visual field).

White matter. Area of the nervous system comprising mainly myelinated nerves.

Zombie. A philosophical device to cover the possibility that some people may not be conscious, despite appearances to the contrary; an important device when the functions of consciousness are considered.

References

Abramson, L. Y., Seligman, M. E. P. & Teasdale, J. D. (1978). Learned helplessness in humans: Critique and reformulation. *Journal of Abnormal Psychology*, 87, 49–74.

Adams, D. B., Gold, A. R. & Burt, A. D. (1978). Rise in female-initiated sexual activity at ovulation and its suppression by oral contraceptives. *New England Journal of Medicine*, 299, 1145–50.

Adler, L. E., Hoffer, L. D., Wiser, A. & Freedman, R. (1993). Normalization of auditory physiology by cigarette smoking in schizophrenic patients. *American Journal of Psychiatry*, 150, 1856–61.

Aitchison, K. J. & Gill, M. (2003). Pharmacogenetics in the postgenomic era. In R. Plomin, J. C. DeFries, I. W. Craig & P. McGuffin (eds), *Behavioral Genetics in the Postgenomic Era*. Washington, DC: American Psychiatric Press.

Alcock, J. (2001). *The Triumph of Sociobiology*. Oxford: Oxford University Press.

Aleksander, I. & Morton, H. (1995). *An Introduction to Neural Computing*. London: Thomson Computer Press.

Allen, N. B., Trinder, J. & Brennan, C. (1999). Affective startle modulation in clinical depression: Preliminary findings. *Biological Psychiatry*, 46, 542–50.

American Psychiatric Association. (2000). *Diagnostic and Statistical Manual of Mental Disorders (Fourth edition): DSM-IV-R*. Washington, DC: American Psychiatric Association.

Anderson, B. & Harvey, T. (1996). Alterations in cortical thickness and neuronal density in the frontal cortex of Albert Einstein. *Neuroscience Letters*, 210, 161–4.

Andersson, M. (1994). *Sexual Selection*. Princeton, NJ: Princeton University Press.

Andreasen, N. C., Paradiso, S. & O'Leary, D. S. (1998). 'Cognitive dysmetria' as an integrative theory of schizophrenia: A dysfunction in cortical–subcortical–cerebellar circuitry? *Schizophrenia Bullettin*, 24, 203–18.

Arai, Y., Ijuin, T., Takenawa, T., Becker, L. E. & Takashima, S. (2002). Excessive expression of synaptojanin in brains with Down syndrome. *Brain and Development*, 24, 67–72.

Arancio, C., Perna, G., Caldirola, D., Gabriele, A. & Bellodi, L. (1995). Carbon dioxide-induced panic in twins: Preliminary results. *European Neuropsychopharmacology*, 5, 368.

Araque, A., Parpura, V., Sanzgiri, R. P. & Haydon, P. G. (1999). Tripartite synapses: Glia, the unacknowledged partner. *Trends in Neurosciences*, 22, 208–15.

Armony, J. L., Cohen, J. D., Servan-Schreiber, D. & LeDoux, J. E. (1995). An anatomically constrained neural network model of fear conditioning. *Behavioral Neuroscience*, 190, 246–57.

Arolt, V., Lencer, R., Nolte, A., Muller-Myhsok, B., Purmann, S., Schurmann, M., Leutelt, J., Pinnow, M. & Schwinger, E. (1996). Eye tracking dysfunction is a putative phenotypic susceptibility marker of schizophrenia and maps to a locus on chromosone 6p in families with multiple occurrence of the disease. *American Journal of Medical Genetics*, 67, 564–79.

Arseneault, L., Cannon, M. & Murray, R. M. (2004). Causal association between cannabis and psychosis: Examining the evidence. *British Journal of Psychiatry*, 184, 110–17.

Asfaw, B., Gilbert, W. H., Beyene, Y., Hart, W. K., Renne, P. R., WoldeGabriel, G., Vrba, E. S. & White, T. D. (2002). Remains of *Homo erectus* from Bouri, Middle Awash, Ethiopia. *Nature*, 416, 317–20.

Axelrod, R. (1984). *The Evolution of Cooperation*. New York: Basic Books.

Axelrod, R. & Hamilton, W. D. (1981). The evolution of cooperation. *Science*, 211, 1390–6.

Baddeley, A. (1986). *Working Memory*. Oxford: Clarendon Press.

Baddeley, A. D. & Hitch, G. J. (1974). Working memory. In G. A. Bower (ed.), *Recent Advances in Learning and Motivation* (Vol. 8). New York: Academic Press.

Bain, K. (2004). *What the Best College Teachers Do*. Cambridge, MA: Harvard University Press.

Baker, R. R. & Bellis, M. A. (1995). *Human Sperm Competition*. London: Chapman & Hall.

Balaban, E. (2002). Human correlative behavioral genetics: An alternative viewpoint. In J. Benjamin, R. P. Ebstein & R. H. Belmaker (eds), *Molecular Genetics and the Human Personality*. Washington, DC: American Psychiatric Publishing.

Barkow, J. H., Cosmides, L. & Tooby, J. (1992). *The Adapted Mind: Evolutionary Psychology and the Generation of Culture*. Oxford: Oxford University Press.

Baron-Cohen, S. (1995). *Mindblindness: An Essay on Autism and Theory of Mind*. Cambridge, MA: MIT Press.

Baron-Cohen, S. (1997). *The Maladapted Mind: Classic Readings in Evolutionary Psychopathology*. Hove: Psychology Press.

Barsh, G. S., Farooqi, I. S. & O'Rahilly, S. (2000). Genetics of body-weight regulation. *Nature*, 404, 644–51.

Barta, P. E., Pearlson, G. D., Brill, L. B., Royall, R., McGilchrist, I. K., Pulver, A. E., Powers, R. E., Casanova, M. F., Tien, A. Y., Frangou, S. & Petty, R. G. (1997). Planum temporale asymmetry reversal in schizophrenia: Replication and relationship to gray matter abnormalities. *American Journal of Psychiatry*, 154, 661–7.

Bartley, A. J., Jones, D. W. & Weinberger, D. R. (1997). Genetic variability of human brain size and cortical gyral patterns. *Brain*, 120, 257–69.

Bartoshuk, L. M. (2000). Comparing sensory experiences across individuals: Recent psychophysical advances illuminate genetic variation in taste perception. *Chemical Senses*, 25, 447–60.

Baruch, I., Hemsley, D. R. & Gray, J. A. (1988). Differential performance of acute and chronic schizophrenics in a latent inhibition task. *Journal of Nervous and Mental Disorders*, 176, 598–606.

Batty, M. & Taylor, M. J. (2003). Early processing of the six basic facial emotional expressions. *Cognitive Brain Research*, 17, 613–20.

Bauby, J. D. (1997). *The Diving Bell and the Butterfly: A Memoir of Life in Death*. London: Vintage.

Beck, D. M., Rees, G., Frith, C. D. & Lavie, N. (2001). Neural correlates of change detection and change blindness. *Nature Neuroscience*, 4, 645–50.

Beck, J. G., Ohtake, P. J. & Shipherd, J. C. (1999). Exaggerated anxiety is not unique to CO_2 in panic disorder: A comparison of hypercapnic and hypoxic challenges. *Journal of Abnormal Psychology*, 108, 473–82.

Becker, J. B. et al. (eds) (2002). *Behavioral Endocrinology* (2nd edn). Cambridge, MA: MIT Press.

Benedetti, F., Serretti, A., Colombo, C., Campori, E., Barbini, B., di Bella, D. & Smeraldi, E. (1998). Influence of a functional polymorphism within the promoter of the serotonin transporter gene on the effects of total sleep deprivation in bipolar depression. *American Journal of Psychiatry*, 156, 1450–2.

Benjamin, J., Ebstein, R. P. & Belmaker, R. H. (2002). *Molecular Genetics and the Human Personality*. Washington, DC: American Psychiatric Association.

Benjamin, J., Li, L., Patterson, C., Greenberg, B. D., Murphy, D. L. & Hamer, D. H. (1996). Population and familial association between the D4 dopamine receptor gene and measures of Novelty Seeking. *Nature Genetics*, 12, 81–4.

Bentall, R. P. (2003). *Madness Explained: Psychosis and Human Nature*. London: Allen Lane.

Bentall, R. P., Corcoran, R., Howard, R., Blackwood, N. & Kinderman, P. (2001). Persecutory delusions: A review and theoretical integration. *Clinical Psycholology Review*, 21, 1143–92.

Benton, A. L. (1959). *Right–Left Discrimination and Finger Localization: Development and Pathology*. New York: Hoeber-Harper.

Benton, A. L., Hamsher, K. D., Varney, N. R. & Spreen, O. (1983). *Contributions to Neuropsychological Assessment*. New York: Oxford University Press.

Berenbaum, S. A. & Hines, M. (1992). Early androgens are related to childhood sex-typed type preferences. *Psychological Science*, 3, 203–6.

Berg, E. A. (1948). A simple objective treatment for measuring flexibility in thinking. *Journal of General Psychology*, 39, 15–22.

Berman, K. F., Torrey, E. F., Daniel, D. G. & Weinberger, D. R. (1992). Regional cerebral blood flow in monozygotic twins discordant and concordant for schizophrenia. *Archives of General Psychiatry*, 49, 927–34.

Besson, C. & Louilot, A. (1995). Asymmetrical involvement of mesolimbic dopmaingeric neurons in affective perception. *Neuroscience*, 68, 963–8.

Bilder, R. M., Wu, H., Bogerts, B., Ashtari, M., Robinson, D., Woerner, M., Lieberman, J. A. & Degreef, G. (1999). Cerebral volume asymmetries in schizophrenia and mood disorders: A quantitative magnetic resonance imaging study. *International Journal of Psychophysiology*, 34, 197–205.

Birbaumer, N., Ghanayim, N., Hinterberger, T., Iversen, I., Kotchoubey, B., Kubler, A., Perelmouter, J., Taub, E. & Flor, H. (1999). A spelling device for the paralysed. *Nature*, 398, 297–8.

Birzniece, V., Johansson, I. M., Wang, M. D., Backstrom, T. & Olsson, T. (2002). Ovarian hormone effects on 5-hydroxytryptamine2A and 5-hydroxytryptamine2C receptor mRNA expression in the ventral hippocampus and frontal cortex of female rats. *Neuroscience Letters*, 319, 157–61.

Bishop, D. V. M., Canning, E., Elgar, K., Morris, E., Jacobs, P. A. & Skuse, D. H. (2000). Distinctive patterns of memory function in subgroups of females with Turner syndrome: Evidence for imprinted loci on the X-chromosome affecting neurodevelopment. *Neuropsychologia*, 38, 712–21.

Blackmore, S. (1999). *The Meme Machine*. Oxford: Oxford University Press.

Blackmore, S. (2003). *Consciousness: An Introduction*. London: Hodder & Stoughton.

Blackwood, N. J., Bentall, R. P., Ffytche, D. H., Simmons, A., Murray, R. M. & Howard, R. J. (2004). Persecutory delusions and the determination of self-relevance: An fMRI investigation. *Psychological Medicine*, 34, 591–6.

Blair, R., J. R. (1999). Responsiveness to distress cues in the child with psychopathic tendencies. *Personality and Individual Differences*, 27, 135–45.

Blair, R. J., Morris, J. S., Frith, C. D., Perrett, D. I. & Dolan, R. J. (1999). Dissociable neural responses to facial expressions of sadness and anger. *Brain*, 122, 883–93.

Blakemore, C. & Greenfield, S. (eds) (1987). *Mindwaves: Thoughts on Intelligence, Identity and Consciousness*. Oxford: Blackwell.

Blanchard, C. D., Hynd, A. L., Minke, K. A., Minemoto, T. & Blanchard, R. J. (2001). Human defensive behaviors to threat scenarios show parallels to fear- and anxiety-related defense patterns of non-human mammals. *Neuroscience and Biobehavioral Reviews*, 25, 761–70.

Blanchard, R. J. & Blanchard, D. C. (1989). Attack and defensive behaviors in rodents as etho-experimental models for the study of emotion. *Progress in Neuropsychopharmacological and Biological Psychiatry*, 13, 3–14.

Blanchard, R. J., Blanchard, D. C. & Graeff, F. G. (2001). Foreword. *Neuroscience and Biobehavioral Reviews*, 25, 575–6.

Bleuler, E. (1950). *Dementia Praecox*. New York: International Universities Press.

Bliss, T. V. P. & Lomo, T. (1973). Long-lasting potentiation of synaptic transmission in the dentate area of the anaesthetized rabbit following stimulation of the perforant path. *Journal of Physiology*, 232, 331–56.

Block, J. (1995). A contrarian view of the five-factor approach to personality description. *Psychological Bulletin*, 117, 187–215.

Block, J. (2001). Millennial contrarianism: The five-factor approach to personality description 5 years later. *Journal of Research in Personality*, 35, 98–107.

Boakes, R. (1984). *From Darwin to Behaviourism: Psychology and the Minds of Animals*. Cambridge: Cambridge University Press.

Boaz, T. L., Perry, N. W., Raney, G., Fischler, I. S. & Shuman, D. (1991). Detection of guilty knowledge with event-related potentials. *Journal of Applied Psychology*, 76, 788–95.

Bonneh, Y. S., Cooperman, A. & Sagi, D. (2001). Motion-induced blindness in normal observers. *Nature*, 411, 798–801.

Borella, P., Bargellini, A., Rovesti, S., Pinelli, M., Vivoli, R., Solfrini, V. & Vivilo, G. (1999). Emotional stability, anxiety, and natural killer activity under examination stress. *Psychoneuroendocrinology*, 24, 613–27.

Born, J., Hansen, K., Marshall, L., Molle, M. & Fehm, H. L. (1999). Timing of end of noctoral sleep. *Nature*, 397, 29–30.

Boyd, R. (1988). Is the repeated prisoner's dilemma a good model of reciprocal altruism? *Ethology and Sociobiology*, 9, 211–22.

Braff, D., Stone, C., Callaway, E., Geyer, M., Glick, I. & Bali, L. (1978). Prestimulus effects on human startle reflex in normals and schizophrenics. *Psychophysiology*, 15, 339–43.

Brambilla, P., Nicoletti, M. A., Harenski, K., Sassi, R. B., Mallinger, A. G., Frank, E., Kupfer, D. J., Keshavan, M. & Soares, J. C. (2002). Anatomical MRI study of subgenual prefrontal cortex in bipolar and unipolar subjects. *Neuropsychopharmacology*, 27, 792–9.

Brandstatter, H. & Guth, A. (2000). A psychological approach to individual differences in intertemporal comsumption patterns. *Journal of Economic Psychology*, 21, 465–79.

Braunstein-Bercovitz, H., Rammsayer, T., Gibbons, H. & Lubow, R. E. (2002). Latent inhibition deficits in high-schizotypal normals: Symptom-specific or anxiety-related? *Schizophrenia Research*, 53, 109–21.

Bremner, J. D., Randall, P., Scott, T. M., Bronen, R. A., Seibyl, J. P., Southwick, S. M., Delaney, R. C., McCarthy, G., Charney, D. S. & Innis, R. B. (1995). MRI-based measurement of hippocampal volume in patients with combat-related posttraumatic stress disorder. *American Journal of Psychiatry*, 152, 973–81.

Bremner, J. D., Vythilingam, M., Vermetten, E., Nazeer, A., Adil, J., Khan, S., Staib, L. H. & Charney, D. S. (2002). Reduced volume of orbitofrontal cortex in major depression. *Biological Psychiatry*, 51, 273–9.

Brenner, S. (2001). *My Life in Science*. London: Science Archive Limited.

Broadhurst, P. L. (1960). Applications of biometrical genetics to the inheritance of behaviour. In H. J. Eysenck (ed.), *Experiments in Personality: Psychogenetics and Psychopharmacology*. London: Routledge Kegan Paul.

Brogden, W. J. (1939). Sensory pre-conditioning. *Journal of Experimental Psychology*, 25, 323–32.

Broich, K., Grunwald, F., Kasper, S., Klemm, E., Biersack, H. J. & Moller, H. J. (1998). D2-dopamine receptor occupancy measured by IBZM-SPECT in relation to extrapyramidal side effects. *Pharmacopsychiatry*, 31, 159–62.

Brown, G. W. & Harris, T. (1978). Social origins of depression: A reply. *Psychological Medicine*, 8, 577–88.

Brown, J. S., Kalish, H. I. & Farber, I. E. (1951). Conditioned fear as revealed by magnitude of startle response to an auditory stimulus. *Journal of Experimental Psychology*, 41, 317–28.

Browne, J. (1995). *Charles Darwin: Voyaging*. New York: Alfred A. Knopf.

Browne, J. (2002). *Charles Darwin: The Power of Place*. New York: Alfred A. Knopf.

Bruce, V., Green, P. R. & Georgeson, M. A. (2003). *Visual Perception: Physiology, Psychology, and Ecology* (4th edn). New York: Psychology Press.

Brüne, M. (2004). Schizophrenia: An evolutionary enigma? *Neuroscience and Biobehavioural Reviews*, 28, 41–53.

Brunet, M., Guy, F., Pilbeam, D. & Taisso, H. (2002). A new hominid from the Upper Miocene of Chad, Central Africa. *Nature*, 418, 145–51.

Buckley, T. C., Blanchard, E. B. & Neill, W. T. (2000). Information processing and PTSD: A review of the empirical literature. *Clinical Psychology Review*, 20, 1041–65.

Buss, D. M. (1999). *Evolutionary Psychology: The New Science of the Mind*. London: Allyn and Bacon.

Buxton, R. B. (2002). *Introduction to Functional Magnetic Resonance Imaging: Principles and Techniques*. Cambridge: Cambridge University Press.

Byrne, M., Clafferty, B. A., Cosway, R., Grant, E., Hodges, A., Whalley, H. C., Lawrie, S. M., Cunningham Owens, D. G. & Johnstone, E. C. (2003). Neuropsychology, genetic liability, and psychotic symptoms in those at high risk of schizophrenia. *Journal of Abnormal Psychology*, 112, 38–48.

Byrne, M., Hodges, A., Grant, E., Owens, D. C. & Johnstone, E. C. (1999). Neuropsychological assessment of young people at high risk of developing schizophrenia compared with controls: Preliminary findings of the Edinburgh High Risk Study (EHRS). *Psychological Medicine*, 29, 1161–73.

Byrne, R. W. & Whiten, A. (1988). *Machiavellian Intelligence: Social Intelligence and the Evolution of Intellect in Monkeys, Apes and Humans*. Oxford: Clarendon Press.

Cabeza, R. & Kingstone, A. (eds) (2001). *Handbook of Functional Neuroimaging of Cognition*. Cambridge, MA: MIT Press.

Cacioppo, J. T., Berntson, G. G., Sheridan, J. F. & McClintock, M. K. (2000). Multilevel integrative analyses of human behavior: Social neuroscience and the complementing nature of social and biological approaches. *Psychological Bulletin*, 126, 829–43.

Cacioppo, J. T. & Tassinary, L. G. (1990). *Principles of Psychophysiology: Physical, Social, and Inferential Statistics*. Cambridge: Cambridge University Press.

Calkins, M. E. & Iacono, W. G. (2000). Eye movement dysfunction in schizophrenia: A heritable characteristic for enhancing phenotype definition. *American Journal of Medical Genetics*, 97, 72–6.

Callicott, J. H. (2003). An expanded role for functional neuroimaging in schizophrenia. *Current Opinion in Neurobiolology*, 13, 256–60.

Callicott, J. H., Bertolino, A., Mattay, V. S., Langheim, F. J., Duyn, J., Coppola, R., Goldberg, T. E. & Weinberger, D. R. (2000). Physiological dysfunction of the dorsolateral prefrontal cortex in schizophrenia revisited. *Cerebral Cortex*, 10, 1078–92.

Canli, T. & Amin, Z. (2002). Neuroimaging of emotion and personality: Scientific evidence and ethical considerations. *Brain Cognition*, 50, 414–31.

Canli, T., Sivers, H., Whitfield, S. L., Gotlib, I. H. & Gabrieli, J. D. (2002). Amygdala response to happy faces as a function of extraversion. *Science*, 296, 2191.

Canli, T., Zhao, Z., Desmond, J. E., Kang, E., Gross, J. & Gabrieli, J. D. (2001). An fMRI study of personality influences on brain reactivity to emotional stimuli. *Behavioral Neuroscience*, 115, 33–42.

Cannon, M., Arseneault, L., Poulton, R., Murray, R. M., Caspi, A. & Moffit, T. E. (2003). Cannabis use in adolescence and risk for adult schizophrenia: A birth cohort analysis. *Schizophrenia Research*, 60, 35.

Cannon, T. D., Mednick, S. A., Parnae, J., Schulsinger, F., Praestholm, J. & Vestergaard, A. (1993). Developmental brain abnormalities in the offspring of schizophrenic mothers. I. Contributions of genetic and perinatal factors. *Archives General Psychiatry*, 93, 551–64.

Cannon, W. B. (1929). Organization for physiological homeostasis. *Psychological Review*, 9, 399–41.

Capecchi, M. R. (1994). Targeted gene replacement. *Scientific American*, 270, 52–9.

Cardno, A. G. & Gottesman, I. (2000). Twin studies of schizophrenia: From bow-and-arrow concordances to star wars Mx and functional genomics. *American Journal of Medical Genetics*, 97, 12–17.

Cardno, A. G., Rijsdijk, F. V., Sham, P. C., Murray, R. M. & McGuffin, P. (2002). A twin study of genetic relationships between psychotic symptoms. *American Journal of Psychiatry*, 159, 539–45.

Cardon, L. R. (2003). Practical barriers to identifying complex trait loci. In R. Plomin, J. C. DeFries, I. W. Craig & P. McGuffin (eds), *Behavioral Genetics in the Postgenomic Era*. Washington, DC: American Psychiatric Press.

Carling, A. (1992). *Introducing Neural Networks*. Wilmslow: Sigma Press.

Carlson, N. R. (1998). *Physiology of Behavior* (6th edn). Boston: Allyn & Bacon.

Carlson, N. R. (2000). *Physiology of Behaviour* (7th edn). London: Allyn & Bacon.

Carlsson, A. (1978). Does dopamine have a role in schizophrenia? *Biological Psychiatry*, 13, 3–21.

Carroll, D., Ring, C., Shrimpton, J., Evans, P., Willemsen, G. & Hucklebridge, F. (1996). Secretory immunoglobulin A and acute cardiovascular response to acute psychological challenge. *International Journal of Behavioral Medicine*, 3, 266–79.

Carruthers, P. & Chamberlain, A. (2000). *Evolution and the Human Mind: Modularity, Language, and Meta-Cognition*. New York: Cambridge University Press.

Carver, C. S. & Scheier, M. (1998). *On the Self-Regulation of Behavior*. Cambridge: Cambridge University Press.

Carver, C. S. & White, T. L. (1994). Behavioral inhibition, behavioral activation, and affective responses to impending reward and punishment: The BIS/BAS scales. *Journal of Personality and Social Psychology*, 67, 319–33.

Caspi, A., Sugden, K., Moffitt, T. E., Taylor, A., Craig, I. W., Harrington, H., McClay, J., Mill, J., Martin, J., Braithwaite, A. & Poulton, R. (2003). Influence of life stress on depression: Moderation by a polymorphism in the 5-HTT gene. *Science*, 301, 386–9.

Castellucci, V. F. & Kandel, E. R. (1974). A quantal analysis of the synaptic depression underlying habituation of the gill-withdrawal reflex in Aplysia. *Proceedings of the National Academy of Science*, 71, 5004–8.

Catania, K. C. (2002). The nose takes the starring role. *Scientific American*, 287, 38–43.

Caviness, V. S. J., Lange, N. T., Makris, N., Herbert, M. R. & Kennedy, D. N. (1999). MRI-based brain volumetrics: Emergence of a developmental brain science. *Brain and Development*, 21, 289–95.

Chadwick, P. K. (1992). *Borderline: A Psychological Study of Paranoia and Delusional Thinking*. Florence, KY: Routledge.

Chadwick, P. K. (2001). Psychotic consciousness. *International Journal of Social Psychiatry*, 47, 52–62.

Chalmers, D. J. (1995). Facing up to the problem of consciousness. *Journal of Consciousness Studies*, 2, 200–19.

Chalmers, D. (1996). *The Conscious Mind: In Search of a Fundamental Theory*. Oxford: Oxford University Press.

Chambers, R. (1844/1994). *Vestiges of the Natural History of Creation*. Chicago: University of Chicago Press.

Chang, F. L. & Greenough, W. T. (1982). Lateralized effects of monocular training on dendritic branching in adult split-brain rats. *Brain Research*, 232, 283–92.

Chapin, J. K., Moxon, K. A., Markpwitz, R. S. & Nicolelis, M. A. L. (1999). Real-time control of a robot arm using simultaneously recorded neurons in the motor cortex. *Nature Neuroscience*, 2, 664–70.

Chaudhari, N., Landin, A. M. & Roper, S. D. (2000). A metabotropic glutamate receptor variant functions as a taste receptor. *Nature Neuroscience*, 3, 113–19.

Cheng, P. W., Holyoak, K. J., Nisbett, R. E. & Oliver, L. M. (1986). Pragmatic versus syntactic approaches to training deductive reasoning. *Cognitive Psychology*, 18, 293–328.

Chomsky, N. (1959). A review of B. F. Skinner's *Verbal Behavior. Language*, 35, 26–58.

Churchland, P. S. & Sejnowski, T. (1992). *The Computational Brain.* Cambridge, MA: MIT Press.

Claridge, G. (1997). *Schizotypy: Implications for Illness and Health.* Oxford: Oxford University Press.

Claridge, G. & Beech, T. (1991). Don't leave the psyche out of neuropsychology. *Behavioral and Brain Sciences*, 14, 21.

Claridge, G. & Davis, C. (2003). *Personality and Psychological Disorders.* London: Arnold.

Cleare, A. J., Murray, R. M. & O'Keane, V. (1998). Assessment of serotonergic function in major depression using d-fenfluramine: Relation to clinical variables and antidepressant response. *Biological Psychiatry*, 44, 555–61.

Cloninger, C. R., Svrakic, D. M. & Przybeck, T. R. (1993). A psychobiological model of temperament and character. *Archives of General Psychiatry*, 50, 975–90.

Clow, A., Lambert, S., Evans, P., Hucklebridge, F. & Higuchi, K. (2003). An investigation into asymmetrical regulation of salivary S-IgA in conscious man using transcranial magnetic stimulation. *International Journal of Psychophysiology*, 47, 57–64.

Cohen, D. (1972). Magnetoencephalography: Detection of brain's electric activity with a superconducting magnetometer. *Science*, 175, 664–6.

Conca, A., Koppi, S., Swoboda, E., Krecké, N. & König, P. (1996). Transcranial magnetic stimulation: A new therapeutic approach to the treatment of depressive illness. *European Psychiatry*, 11, 290.

Cook, P. A. & Wedell, N. (1999). Non-fertile sperm delay female remating. *Nature*, 397, 486.

Cooke, D. J. & Michie, C. (2001). Refining the construct of psychopathy: Towards a hierarchical model. *Psychological Assessment*, 13, 171–88.

Cookson, W. (1994). *The Gene Hunters: Adventures in the Genome Jungle.* London: Aurum Press.

Corfas, G., Roy, K. & Buxbaum, J. D. (2004). Neuregulin 1-erbB signaling and the molecular/cellular basis of schizophrenia. *Nature Neuroscience*, 7, 575–80. [Review.]

Corr, P. J. (2002a). J. A. Gray's reinforcement sensitivity theory and frustrative nonreward: A theoretical note on expectancies in reactions to rewarding stimuli. *Personality and Individual Differences*, 32, 1247–53.

Corr, P. J. (2002b). J. A. Gray's reinforcement sensitivity theory: Tests of the joint subsystems hypothesis of anxiety and impulsivity. *Personality and Individual Differences*, 33, 511–32.

Corr, P. J. (2004). Reinforcement sensitivity theory and personality. *Neuroscience and Biobehavioral Reviews*, 28, 317–32.

Corr, P. J. & Gray, J. A. (1995). Attributional style, socialization and cognitive ability as predictors of sales success: A predictive validity study. *Personality and Individual Differences*, 18, 241–52.

Corr, P. J. & Perkins, A. M. (2006). The role of theory in the psychophysiology of personality: From Ivan Pavlov to Jeffrey Gray. *International Journal of Psychophysiology*, in press.

Corr, P. J., Pickering, A. D. & Gray, J. A. (1995). Sociability/impulsivity and caffeine-induced arousal: Critical flicker/fusion frequency and procedural learning. *Personality and Individual Differences*, 18, 713–30.

Corr, P. J., Pickering, A. D. & Gray, J. A. (1997). Personality, punishment, and procedural learning: A test of J. A. Gray's anxiety theory. *Journal of Personality and Social Psychology*, 73, 337–44.

Corr, P. J., Tynan, A. & Kumari, V. (2002). Personality correlates of prepulse inhibition of the startle reflex at three lead intervals. *Journal of Psychophysiology*, 16, 82–91.

Corr, P. J., Wilson, G. D., Fotiadou, M., Kumari, V., Gray, N. S., Checkley, S. & Gray, J. A. (1995). Personality and affective modulation of the startle reflex. *Personality and Individual Differences*, 19, 543–53.

Corvin A. P., Morris, D. W., McGhee, K., Schwaiger, S., Scully, P., Quinn, J., Meagher, D., Clair, D. S., Waddington, J. L. & Gill, M. (2004). Confirmation and refinement of an 'at-risk' haplotype for schizophrenia suggests the EST cluster, Hs.97362, as a potential susceptibility gene at the Neuregulin-1 locus. *Molecular Psychiatry*, 9, 208–13.

Cosmides, L. (1989). The logic of social exchange: Has natural selection shaped how humans reason? Studies with the Wason selection task. *Cognition*, 31, 187–276.

Cosmides, L. & Tooby, J. (1987). From evolution to behavior: Evolutionary psychology as the missing link. In J. Dupre (ed.), *The Latest on the Best: Essays on Evolution and Optimality*. Cambridge, MA: MIT Press.

Cosmides, L. & Tooby, J. (1989). Evolutionary psychology and the generation of culture: II. Case study: A computational theory of social exchange. *Ethology and Sociobiology*, 10, 51–97.

Cosmides, L. & Tooby, J. (1992). Cognitive adaptations for social exchange. In J. Barkow, L. Cosmides & J. Tooby (eds), *The Adapted Mind*. New York: Oxford University Press.

Costa, P. T. & McCrae, R. R. (1992). Four ways five factors are basic. *Personality and Individual Differences*, 13, 653–65.

Costa, P. T., Jr & McRae, R. R. (1992). *Professional Manual of the Revised NEO Personality Inventory (NEO PI-R) and NEO Five-Factor Inventory (NEO FFI)*. Odessa, FL: Psycholgical Assessment Resources.

Cosway, R., Byrne, M., Clafferty, R., Hodges, A., Grant, E., Abukmeil, S. S., Lawrie, S. M., Miller, P. & Johnstone, E. C. (2000). Neuropsychological change in young people at high risk for schizophrenia: Results from the first two neuropsychological assessments of the Edinburgh High Risk Study. *Psychological Medicine*, 30, 1111–21.

Cotterill, R. (1998). *Enchanted Looms: Conscious Networks in Brains and Computers*. New York: Cambridge University Press.

Crabbe, J. C. (2003). Finding genes for complex behaviors: Progress in mouse models of the addictions. In R. Plomin, J. C. DeFries, I. W. Craig & P. McGuffin (eds), *Behavioral Genetics in the Postgenomic Era*. Washington, DC: American Psychological Association.

Craig, I. W. & McClay, J. (2003). The role of molecular genetics in the postgenomic era. In R. Plomin, J. C. DeFries, I. W. Craig & P. McGuffin (eds), *Behavioral Genetics in the Postgenomic Era*. Washington, DC: American Psychiatric Press.

Craig, J. S., Hatton, C., Craig, F. B. & Bentall, R. P. (2004). Persecutory beliefs, attributions and theory of mind: Comparison of patients with paranoid delusions, Asperger's syndrome and healthy controls. *Schizophrenia Research*, 69, 29–33.

Craik, K. J. W. (1943). *The Nature of Explanation*. Cambridge: Cambridge University Press.

Crawford, C. B. & Krebs, D. L. (1998). *Handbook of Evolutionary Psychology: Ideas, Issues, and Applications*. Mahwah, NJ: Lawrence Erlbaum.

Crick, F. (1994). *The Astonishing Hypothesis: The Scientific Search for the Soul*. London: Simon & Schuster.

Crick, F. & Koch, C. (1995). Are we aware of neural activity in primal visual cortex? *Nature*, 375, 121–3.

Crick, F. & Koch, C. (1998). Consciousness and neuroscience. *Cerebral Cortex*, 8, 97–107.

Crick, F. & Koch, C. (2003). A framework for consciousness. *Nature Neuroscience*, 6, 119–26.

Croiset, G., Nijsen, M. J. M. A. & Kamphuis, P. J. G. H. (2000). Role of corticotropin-releasing factor, vasopressin and the autonomic nervous system in learning and memory. *European Journal of Pharmacology*, 405, 225–34.

Crow, J. F. (2003). Was there life before 1953? *Nature Genetics*, 33, 449.

Crow, T. J. (1995). Constraints on concepts of pathogenesis. Language and the speciation process as the key to the etiology of schizophrenia. *Archives of General Psychiatry*, 52, 1011–14.

Crow, T. J. (2000). Schizophrenia as the price that homo sapiens pays for language: A resolution of the central paradox in the origin of the species. *Brain Research Reviews*, 31, 118–29.

Curtis, C. E., Calkins, M. E., Grove, W. M., Feil, K. J. & Iacono, W. G. (2001). Saccadic disinhibition in patients with acute and remitted schizophrenia and their first-degree biological relatives. *American Journal of Psychiatry*, 158, 100–6.

Cuthbert, B. N., Bradley, M. M. & Lang, P. J. (1996). Probing picture perception: Activation and emotion. *Psychophysiology*, 33, 103–11.

Cuthbert, B. N., Patrick, C. J. & Lang, P. J. (1991). Imagery in anxiety disorder patients: Visceral and startle probe responses. *Psychophysiology*, 28, 18.

Dahmen, J. C. & Corr, P. J. (2004). Prepulse-elicited startle in prepulse inhibition. *Biolological Psychiatry*, 55, 98–101.

Dalgleish, T. (1995). Performance on the emotional Stroop task in groups of anxious, expert and control subjects: A comparison of computer and card presentation formats. *Cognition and Emotion*, 9, 341–62.

Damasio, A. (1994). *Descartes' Error: Emotion, Reason, and the Human Brain*. New York: Grosset. Putnam.

Damasio, H., Grabowski, T., Frank, R. G., A. M. & Damasio, A. R. (1994). The return of Phineas Gage: Clues about the brain from the skull of a famous patient. *Science*, 264, 1102–5.

Dannon, P. N., Dolberg, O. T., Schreiber, S. & Grunhaus, L. (2002). Three and six-month outcome following courses of either ECT or rTMS in a population of severely depressed individuals – Preliminary report. *Biological Psychiatry*, 51, 687–90.

Dantendorfer, K., Prayer, D., Kramer, J., Amering, M., Baischer, W., Berger, P., Schoder, M., Steinberger, K., Windhaber, J., Imhof, H. & Katschnig, H. (1996). High frequency of EEG and MRI brain abnormalities in panic disorder. *Psychiatry Research: Neuroimaging*, 68, 41–53.

Daruna, J. H. (1996). Neuroticism predicts normal variability in the number of circulating leuco-cytes. *Personality and Individual Differences*, 20, 103–8.

Darwin, C. (1859/1968). *On the Origin of Species by Means of Natural Selection, or the Preservation of Favoured Races in the Struggle for Life*. Princeton, NJ: Princeton University Press.

Darwin, C. (1868). *The Variation of Animals and Plants under Domestication*. London: J. Murray.

Darwin, C. (1871/1981). *The Descent of Man, and Selection in Relation to Sex*. Reprinted with an introduction by T. J. Bonner & R. M. May. Princeton, NJ: Princeton University Press.

Darwin, C. R. (1872/1998). *The Expression of the Emotions in Man and Animals*. Reprinted with commentary by P. Ekman. Oxford: Oxford University Press.

Darwin, C. (1993). *The Autobiography of Charles Darwin, 1809–1882*. New York: Norton.

Darwin, E. (1794). *Zoonomia; or, The Laws of Organic Life*. London: J. Johnson.

Davey, G. C. L. (1995). Preparedness and phobias: Specific evolved associations or a generalised expectancy bias? *Behavioral and Brain Sciences*, 18, 289–325.

Davey, G. C. L. (1997). A contemporary conditioning model of phobias. In G. C. L. Davey (ed.), *Phobias: A Handbook of Theory, Research and Treatment*. Chichester: Wiley.

Davey, G. C. L., Cavanagh, K. & Lamb, A. (2003). Differential aversive outcome expectancies for high- and low-predation fear-relevant animals. *Journal of Behavior Therapy and Experimental Psychiatry*, 34, 117–28.

David, A. S., Malmberg, A., Brandt, L., Allebeck, P. & Lewis, G. (1997). IQ and risk for schizophrenia: A population-based cohort study. *Psychological Medicine*, 27, 1311–23.

Davidson, R. J. (2002). Anxiety and affective style: Role of prefrontal cortex and amygdala. *Biological Psychiatry*, 51, 68–80.

Davis, J. O. & Phelps, J. A. (1995). Twins with schizophrenia: Genes or germs? *Schizophrenia Bulletin*, 21, 13–18.

Davis, K. L., Buchsbaum, M. S., Shihabuddin, L., Spiegel-Cohen, J., Metzger, M., Frecska, E., Keefe, R. S. & Powchik, P. (1998). Ventricular enlargement in poor-outcome schizophrenia. *Biological Psychiatry*, 43, 783–93.

Davis, K. L., Panksepp, J. & Normansell, L. (2003). The Affective Neuroscience Personality Scales: Normative data and implications. *Neuro-Psychoanalysis*, 5, 57–69.

Davis, M. (1986). Pharmacological and anatomical analysis of fear conditioning using the fear-potentiated startle paradigm. *Behavioral Neuroscience*, 100, 814–24.

Davis, M. (1989). Sensitization of the acoustic startle reflex by footshock. *Behavioral Neuroscience*, 103, 495–503.

Davis, M. (1990). Animal models of anxiety based on classical conditioning: The conditioned emotional response (CER) and the fear-potentiated startle effects. *Pharmacologic Therapy*, 47, 1478–565.

Dawkins, R. (1976). *The Selfish Gene*. Oxford: Oxford University Press.

Dawkins, R. (1986). *The Blind Watchmaker*. London: Longman.

Dawkins, R. (1995). *River out of Eden*. London: Weidenfeld.

Dawkins, R. (2003). *A Devil's Chaplain*. London: Weidenfeld.

Dawson, M. E., Schell, A. M. & Filion, D. L. (1990). The electrodermal system. In J. T. Cacioppo & L. G. Tassinary (eds), *Principles of Psychophysiology: Physical, Social and Inferential Elements*. Cambridge: Cambridge University Press.

Dawson, M. R. W. (1998). *Understanding Cognitive Science*. Oxford: Blackwell.

de Angelis, L. (1995). Effects of valproate and lorazepam on experimental anxiety: Tolerance, withdrawal, and role of clonidine. *Pharmacology Biochemistry and Behavior*, 52, 329–33.

de Bellis, M. D., Keshavan, M. S., Shifflett, H., Iyengar, S., Dahl, R. E., Axelson, D. A., Birmaher, B., Hall, J., Moritz, G. & Ryan, N. D. (2002). Superior temporal gyrus volumes in pediatric generalized anxiety disorder. *Bological Psychiatry*, 51, 553–62.

de Jong, P. & Merckelbach, H. (1991). Covariation bias and electrodermal responding in spider phobics before and after behavioural treatment. *Behaviour Research Therapy*, 29, 307–14.

De La Casa, L. G. & Lubow, R. E. (2001). Latent inhibition with a response time measure from a within-subject design: Effects of number of preexposures, masking task, context change, and delay. *Neuropsychology*, 15, 244–53.

de Waal, F. B. M. (1982). *Chimpanzee Politics*. London: Jonathan Cape.

de Waal, F. (2005). *Our Inner Ape: The Best and Worst of Human Nature*. New York: Riverhead.

DeBruine, L. M. (2002). Facial resemblance enhances trust. *Proceedings of the Royal Society: Biological Sciences*, 269, 1307–12.

Decety, J. (ed.) (1998). *Perception and Action: Recent Advances in Cognitive Neuropsychology*. Hove: Psychology Press.

Deecke, V., Slater, P. J. B. & Ford, J. K. B. (2002). Selective habituation shapes acoustic predator recognition in habour cells. *Nature*, 420, 171–3.

DeFries, J. C., Gervais, M. C. & Thomas, E. A. (1978). Response to 30 generations of selection for open-field activity in laboratory mice. *Behavior Genetics*, 8, 3–13.

Degreef, G., Ashtari, M., Bogerts, B., Bilder, R. M., Jody, D. N., Alvir, J. M. & Lieberman, J. A. (1992). Volumes of ventricular system subdivisions measured from magnetic resonance images in first-episode schizophrenic patients. *Archives of General Psychiatry*, 49, 531–7.

Deinzer, R., Kleineidam, C., Stiller-Winkler, R., Idel, H. & Bach, D. (2000). Prolonged reduction in salivary immunoglobulin A (sIgA) after a major academic exam. *International Journal of Psychophysiology*, 37, 219–32.

DelBello, M. P., Strakowski, S. M., Zimmerman, M. E., Hawkins, J. M. & Sax, K. W. (1999). MRI analysis of the cerebellum in bipolar disorder: A pilot study. *Neuropsychopharmacology*, 21, 63–8.

Dennett, D. C. (1991). *Consciousness Explained*. Boston, MA: Little Brown.

Dennett, D. C. (1996). *Darwin's Dangerous Idea: Evolution and the Meanings of Life*. New York: Simon & Schuster.

Dennett, D. (2003). Interview with Laurie Taylor. *The Times Higher Education Supplement*, 28 February.

Depue, R. A. & Collins, P. F. (1999). Neurobiology of the structure of personality: Dopamine, facilitation of incentive motivation, and extraversion. *Behavioral and Brain Sciences*, 22, 491–517.

Desmond, A. & Moore, J. (1991). *Darwin*. London: Michael Joseph.

Deutch, A. Y. & Roth, R. H. (1999). Neurotransmitter. In M. J. Zigmond, F. E. Bloom, S. C. Landis, J. L. Roberts & L. R. Squire (eds), *Fundamental Neuroscience*. San Diego: Academic Press.

DeValois, R. L. & DeValois, K. K. (1975). Neural coding of colour. In E. C. Carterette & M. P. Freidman (eds), *Handbook of Perception*, vol 5. New York: Academic Press.

Diamond, M. C., Scheibel, A. B., Murphy, G. M., Jr & Harvey, T. (1985). On the brain of a scientist: Albert Einstein. *Experimental Neurology*, 88, 198–204.

Dimberg, U. & Ohman, A. (1982). Facial reactions to facial expressions. *Psychophysiology*, 19, 643–7.

Dimberg, U. & Ohman, A. (1996). Behold the wrath: Psychophysiological responses to facial stimuli. *Motivation and Emotion*, 20, 149–82.

Dominy, N. J. & Lucas, P. W. (2001). Ecological importance of trichromatic vision to primates. *Nature*, 410, 363–6.

Dudek, S. M. & Bear, M. F. (1992). Homosynaptic long-term depression in area CA1 of hippocampus and effects of N-methyl-D-aspartate receptor blockade. *Proceedings of the National Academy of Science*, 89, 4363–7.

Dunn, L. M. & Dunn, L. M. (1981). *Peabody Picture Vocabulary Test-Revised*. Circle Pines, MN: American Guidance Service.

Easton, A. & Emery, N. (2005). *The Cognitive Neuroscience of Social Behaviour*. London: Taylor & Francis.

Ebstein, R. P., Benjamin, J. & Belmaker, R. H. (2003). Behavioral genetics, genomics and personality. In R. Plomin, J. C. DeFries, I. W. Craig & P. McGuffin (eds), *Behavioral Genetics in the Postgenomic Era*. Washington, DC: American Psychological Association.

Ebstein, R. P. & Kotler, M. D. (2002). Personality, substance abuse, and genes. In J. Benjamin, R. P. Ebstein & R. H. Belmaker (eds), *Molecular Genetics and the Human Personality*. Washington, DC: American Psychiatric Publishing.

Ebstein, R. P., Novick, O., Umansky, R., Priel, B., Osher, Y., Blaine, D., Bennett, E. R., Newmanov, L., Katz, M. & Belmaker, R. H. (1996). Dopamine D4 receptor (D4DR) exon III polymorphism associated with the human personality trait of novelty seeking. *Nature Genetics*, 12, 78–80.

Edelman, G. M. (ed.). (1987). *Neural Darwinism: The Theory of Neuronal Group Selection*. New York: Basic Books.

Ehnvall, A. & Ågren, H. (2002). Patterns of sensitisation in the course of affective illness. A life-charting study of treatment-refractory depressed patients. *Journal of Affective Disorders*, 70, 67–75.

Ekman, P. (1992). Are there basic emotions? *Psychological Review*, 99, 550–3.

Ekman, P. (1994). Strong evidence for universals in facial expressions: A reply to Russell's mistaken critique. *Psychological Bulletin*, 115, 268–87.

Ekman, P. (1998). *The Expression of the Emotions in Man and Animals*. A republication of Charles Darwin, 1872, with commentary. Oxford: Oxford University Press.

Ekman, P. (2001). *Telling Lies: Clues to Deceit in the Marketplace, Politics, and Marriage*. New York: W. W. Norton.

Ekman, P. & Friesen, W. V. (1971). Constants across cultures in the face and emotion. *Journal of Personality and Social Psychology*, 17, 124–9.

Eley, T. (2003). Something borrowed, something blue. *The Psychologist: Bulletin of the British Psychological Society*, 16, 626–9.

Ellenbroek, B. A. & Riva, M. A. (2003). Early maternal deprivation as an animal model for schizophrenia. *Clinical Neuroscience Research*, 3, 297–302.

Elliot, R. (1998). The neuropsychological profile in unipolar depression. *Trends in Cognitive Sciences*, 2, 447–54.

Ellis, R. & Humphreys, G. W. (1999). *Connectionist Psychology: A Text with Readings*. Hove: Psychology Press.

Epstein, S. (1979). The stability of behaviour: I. On predicting most of the people much of the time. *Journal of Personality and Social Psychology*, 37, 1097–126.

Erlenmeyer-Kimling, L. (1968). Mortality rates in the offspring of schizophrenic parents and a physiological advantage hypothesis. *Nature*, 220, 798–800.

Esteves, F., Parra, C., Dimberg, U. & Ohman, A. (1994). Nonconscious associative learning: Pavlovian conditioning of skin conductance responses to masked fear-relevant facial stimuli. *Psychophysiology*, 31, 375–85.

Etcoff, N. (1999). *Survival of the Prettiest: The Science of Beauty*. New York: Doubleday.

Ettinger, U., Chitnis, X. A., Kumari, V., Fannon, D. G., Sumich, A. L., O'Ceallaigh, S., Doku, V. C. & Sharma, T. (2001). Magnetic resonance imaging of the thalamus in first-episode psychosis. *American Journal of Psychiatry*, 158, 116–18.

Ettinger, U. & Kumari, V. (2003). Pharmacological studies of smooth pursuit and antisaccade eye movements in schizophrenia: Current status and directions for future research. *Current Neuropharmacology*, 1, 285–300.

Ettinger, U., Kumari, V., Chitnis, X. A., Corr, P. J., Sumich, A. L., Rabe-Hesketh, S., Crawford, T. J. & Sharma, T. (2002). Relationship between brain structure and saccadic movements in healthy humans. *Neuroscience Letters*, 328, 225–8.

Ettinger, U., Kumari, V., Crawford, T. J., Corr, P. J., Das, M., Zachariah, E., Hughes, C., Sumich, A. L., Rabe-Hesketh, S. & Sharma, T. (2004). Smooth pursuit and antisaccade eye movements in siblings discordant for schizophrenia. *Journal of Psychiatric Research*, 38, 177–84.

Ettinger, U., Kumari, V., Crawford, T. J., Flak, V., Sharma, T., Davis, R. E. & Corr, P. J. (2005). Saccadic eye movements, schizotypy and the role of neuroticism. *Biological Psychology*, 68, 61–78.

Evans, D. (2003). *Placebo*. London: Harper Collins.

Evans, J. S. (2003). In two minds: Dual-process accounts of reasoning. *Trends in Cognitive Science*, 7, 454–9.

Exner, S. (1894). *Entwurf zu einer physiologischen Erklarung der psychischen Erscheinungen* (A Design of a Physiological Explanation of Psychic Phenomena). Leipzig, Vienna: FranzDeuticke.

Eysenck, H. J. (1944). Types of personality: A factorial study of 700 neurotics. *Journal of Mental Sciences*, 90, 851–61.

Eysenck, H. J. (1947). *Dimensions of Personality*. London: K. Paul Trench Trubner.

Eysenck, H. J. (1952). *The Scientific Study of Personality*. London: Routledge.

Eysenck, H. J. (1967). *The Biological Basis of Personality*. Springfield, IL.: Thomas.

Eysenck, H. J. (1968). A theory of the incubation of anxiety/fear responses. *Behaviour Research and Therapy*, 6, 309–21.

Eysenck, H. J. (1979). The conditioning model of neurosis. *Behavioral and Brain Sciences*, 2, 155–99.

Eysenck, H. J. (1985). Incubation theory of fear/anxiety. In S. Reiss & R. R. Bootzin (eds), *Theoretical Issues in Behaviour Therapy*. Orlando, FL: Academic Press.

Eysenck, H. J. (1991). Dimensions of personality: 16, 5 or 3? Criteria for a taxonomic paradigm. *Personality and Individual Differences*, 12, 773–90.

Eysenck, H. J. (1992). Four ways five factors are *not* basic. *Personality and Individual Differences*, 13, 667–73.

Eysenck, H. J. (1995). *Genius: The Natural History of Creativity*. Cambridge: Cambridge University Press.

Eysenck, H. J. & Eysenck, M. W. (1985). *Personality and Individual Differences: A Natural Science Approach*. New York: Plenum.

Eysenck, H. J. & Eysenck, S. B. G. (1991). *Manual of the Eysenck Personality Scales*. London: Hodder & Stoughton.

Farmer, A. E., McGuffin, P. & Gottesman, I. (1987). Twin concordance for DSM-III schizophrenia. Scrutinizing the validity of the definition. *Archives of General Psychiatry*, 44, 634–41.

Fehr, E. & Gachter, S. (2002). Altruistic punishment in humans. *Nature*, 415, 137–40.

Ferster, C. B. & Skinner, B. F. (1957). *Schedules of Reinforcement*. New York: Appleton-Century-Crofts.

Fibiger, H. C. & Phillips, A. G. (1988). Mesocorticolimbic dopamine systems and reward. *Annals of the New York Academy of Science*, 537, 206–10.

Filion, D. L., Dawson, M. E. & Schell, A. M. (1993). Modification of the acoustic startle-reflex eyeblink: A tool for investigating early and late attentional processes. *Biological Psychology*, 35, 185–200.

Fisher, R. A. (1918). The correlation between relatives on the supposition of Mendalian inheritance. *Transactions of the Royal Society of Edinburgh*, 222, 309–68.

Fitch, R. H. & Denenberg, V. H. (1998). A role for ovarian hormones in sexual differentiation of the brain. *Behavioral and Brain Sciences*, 21, 311–27.

Fletcher, P. C. (2004). Functional neuroimaging of psychiatric disorders: Exploring hidden behaviour. *Psychological Medicine*, 34, 577–81.

Flint, J. (2004). The genetics of neuroticism. *Neuroscience and Biobehavioral Reviews*, 28, 307–16.

Flint, J., Corley, R., DeFries, J. C., Fulker, D. W., Gray, J. A., Miller, S. & Collins, A. C. (1995). A simple genetic basis for a complex psychological trait in laboratory mice. *Science*, 269, 1432–5.

Flor-Henry, P. (1969). Schizophrenic-like reactions and affective psychoses associated with temporal lobe epilepsy: Etiological factors. *American Journal of Psychiatry*, 126, 400–4.

Flynn, J. P. (1967). The neural basis of aggression in cats. In D. C. Glass (ed.), *Neurophysiology and Emotion*. New York: Rockefeller University Press.

Fodor, J. (1983). *The Modularity of Mind*. Cambridge, MA: MIT Press.

Fossati, P., Harvey, P. O., Le Bastard, G., Ergis, A. M., Jouvent, R. & Allilaire, J. F. (2004). Verbal memory performance of patients with a first depressive episode and patients with unipolar and bipolar recurrent depression. *Journal of Psychiatric Research*, 38, 137–44.

Frangou, S. & Murray, R. M. (1996a). *Schizophrenia*. London: Martin Dunitz.

Frangou, S. & Murray, R. M. (1996b). Imaging as a tool in exploring the neurodevelopment and genetics of schizophrenia. *British Medical Bulletin*, 52, 587–96.

Freeman, W. M., Nader, M. A., Nader, S. H., Robertson, D. J., Gioia, L., Mitchell, S. M., Daunais, J. B., Porrino, L. J., Friedman, D. P. & Vrana, K. E. (2001). Chronic cocaine-mediated changes in non-human primate nucleus accumbens gene expression. *Journal of Neurochemistry*, 77, 542–9.

Friend, S. D. & Stoughton, R. B. (2002). The magic of microarrays. *Scientific American*, February.

Frith, C. D. (1979). Consciousness, information processing and schizophrenia. *British Journal of Psychiatry*, 134, 225–35.

Frith, C. (1994). Theory of mind in schizophrenia. In A. S. Davis & J. C. Cutting (eds), *The Neuropsychology of Schizophrenia*. Hove: Erlbaum.

Frodl, T., Meisenzahl, E. M., Zetzsche, T., Born, C., Jäger, M., Groll, C., Bottlender, R., Leinsinger, G. & Möller, H. J. (2003). Larger amygdala volumes in first depressive episode as compared to recurrent major depression and healthy control subjects. *Biological Psychiatry*, 53, 338–44.

Furmark, T., Tillfors, M., Marteinsdottir, I., Fischer, H., Pissiota, A., Langstrom, B. & Fredrikson, M. (2002). Common changes in cerebral blood flow in patients with social phobia treated with citalopram or cognitive-behavioral therapy. *Archives of General Psychiatry*, 59, 425–33.

Gazzaniga, M. (1970). *The Bisected Brain*. New York: Appleton-Century-Crofts.

Gazzaniga, M. S. & LeDoux, J. E. (1978). *The Integrated Mind*. New York: Plenum Press.

Geddes, J. R., Verdoux, H., Takei, N., Lawrie, S. M., Bovet, P., Eagles, J. M., Heun, R., McCreadie, R. G., McNeil, T. F., O'Callaghan, E., Stober, G., Willinger, U. & Murray, R. M. (1999). Schizophrenia and complications of pregnancy and labor: An individual patient data meta-analysis. *Schizophrenia Bulletin*, 25, 413–23.

Genome International Sequencing Consortium (2001). Initial sequencing and analysis of the human genome. *Nature*, 409, 860–921.

George, M. S. (1996). Rapid transcranial magnetic stimulation (RTMS): A potential new neuro-psychiatric treatment. *Biological Psychiatry*, 39, 512.

George, M. S. (1997). Functional neuroimaging and mood. *Electroencephalography and Clinical Neurophysiology*, 102, 1–2.

George, M. S., Nahas, Z., Molloy, M., Speer, A. M., Oliver, N. C., Li, X. B., Arana, G. W., Risch, S. C. & Ballenger, J. C. (2000). A controlled trial of daily left prefrontal cortex TMS for treating depression. *Biological Psychiatry*, 48, 962–70.

Gleeson, J. F. M. & McGorry, P. D. (2004). *Psychological Interventions in Early Psychosis: A Treatment Approach*. London: Wiley.

Gloor, P. (1969). The work of Hans Berger. *Electroencephalography and Clinical Neurophysiolology*, 27, 649.

Goldberg, T. E. & Weinberger, D. R. (1994). Schizophrenia, training paradigms, and the Wisconsin Card Sorting Test redux. *Schizophrenia Research*, 11, 291–6.

Golden, C. J. (1981). A standardized version of Luria's neuropsychological tests. In S. Filskov & T. J. Boll (eds), *Handbook of Clinical Neuropsychology*. New York: Wiley.

Golden, C. J., Purisch, A. D. & Hammeke, T. A. (1985). Luria-Nebraska Neuropsychological Battery: Theoretical orientation and comment. *Journal of Consulting and Clinical Psychology*, 50, 291–300.

Gosling, S. D. (2001). From mice to men: What can we learn about personality from animal research? *Psychological Bulletin*, 127, 45–86.

Gottesman, I. I. (1991). *Schizophrenia Genesis: The Origins of Madness*. New York: Freeman.

Gottesman, I. I. (2003). A behavioral genetics perspective. In R. Plomin, J. C. DeFries & P. McGuffin (eds), *Behavioral Genetics in the Postgenomic Era*. Washington, DC: American Psychological Association.

Gottesman, I. I. & Bertelsen, A. (1989). Confirming unexpressed genotypes for schizophrenia. Risks in the offspring of Fischer's Danish identical and fraternal discordant twins. *Archives of General Psychiatry*, 46, 867–72.

Gottesman, I. I. & Gould, T. D. (2003). The endophenotype concept in psychiatry: Etymology and strategic intentions. *American Journal of Psychiatry*, 160, 636–45.

Gottesman, I. I. & Shields, J. (1967). A polygenic theory of schizophrenia. *Proceeding of the National Academy of Science*, 58, 199–205.

Gottesman, I. I. & Shields, J. (1972). *Schizophrenia and Genetics: A Twin Study Vantage Point*. New York: Academic Press.

Gottesman, I. I. & Shields, J. (1982). *Schizophrenia: The Epigenetic Puzzle*. Cambridge: Cambridge University Press.

Gould, E., McEwen, B. S., Tanapat, P., Galea, L. A. & Fuchs E. (1997). Neurogenesis in the dentate gyrus of the adult tree shrew is regulated by psychosocial stress and NMDA receptor activation. *Journal of Neuroscience*, 1, 2492–8.

Goy, R. W. & McEwen, B. S. (1980). *Sexual Differentiation of the Brain*. Cambridge: MIT Press.

Goy, R. W., Bercovitch, F. B. & McBrair, M. C. (1988). Behavioral masculinization is independent of genital masculinization in prenatally androgenized female rhesus macaques. *Hormones and Behaviour*, 22, 552–71.

Graeff, F. G. (2004). Serotonin, the periaqueductal gray and panic. *Neuroscience and Biobehavioral Reviews*, 28, 239–59.

Graham, F. K. (1975). The more or less startling effects of weak prestimulation. *Psychophysiology*, 12, 238–48.

Graham-Rowe, D. (2003). World's first brain prosthesis revealed. *New Scientist*, 12 March.

Gray, J. A. (1970). The psychophysiological basis of introversion–extraversion. *Behaviour Research Therapy*, 8, 249–66.

Gray, J. A. (1972). The psychophysiological basis of introversion–extraversion: A modification of Eysenck's theory. In V. D. Nebylitsyn & J. A. Gray (eds), *The Biological Basis of Individual Behavior*. New York: Academic Press.

Gray, J. A. (1975). *Elements of a Two-Process Theory of Learning*. London: Academic Press.

Gray, J. A. (1979). *Pavlov*. London: Fontana.

Gray, J. A. (1981). A critique of Eysenck's theory of personality. In H. J. Eysenck (ed.), *A Model for Personality*. Berlin: Springer.

Gray, J. A. (1982). *The Neuropsychology of Anxiety: An Enquiry into the Functions of the Septo-Hippocampal System* (1st edn). Oxford: Oxford University Press.

Gray, J. A. (1987). *The Psychology of Fear and Stress* (2nd edn). Cambridge: Cambridge University Press.

Gray, J. A. (1995). The contents of consciousness: A neuropsychological conjecture. *Behavioral and Brain Sciences*, 18, 659–722.

Gray, J. A. (2004). *Consciousness: Creeping Up on the Hard Problem*. Oxford: Oxford University Press.

Gray, J. A. & McNaughton, N. (2000). *The Neuropsychology of Anxiety: An Enquiry into the Functions of the Septo-Hippocampal System* (2nd edn). Oxford: Oxford University Press.

Gray, J. A., Feldon, J., Rawlins, J. N. P., Hemsley, D. R. & Smith, A. D. (1991). The neuropsychology of schizophrenia. *Behavioral and Brain Sciences*, 14, 1–84.

Gray, J. R. & Braver, T. S. (2002). Personality predicts working-memory-related activation in the caudal anterior cingulate cortex. *Cognitive and Affective Behavioural Neuroscience*, 2, 64–75.

Gray, J. R. & Thompson, P. M. (2004). Neurobiology of intelligence: science and ethics. *Nature Neuroscience*, 5, 471–82.

Grazzini, E., Guillon, G., Mouillac, B. & Zingg, H. H. (1998). Inhibition of oxytocin receptor function by direct binding of progesterone. *Nature*, 392, 509–12.

Grech, A., Takei, N. & Murray, R. M. (1998). Psychosis and cannabis use. *Schizophrenia Research*, 29, 21.

Green, M. J. & Phillips, M. L. (2004). Social threat perception and the evolution of paranoia. *Neuroscience and Biobehavioral Reviews*, 28, 333–42.

Greenfield, S. (2001). *Brain Story: Unlocking our Inner World of Emotions, Memories, Ideas, and Desires*. New York: Dorling Kindersley.

Greenough, W. T., Juraska, J. M. & Volkmar, F. R. (1979). Maze training effects on dendritic branching in occipital cortex of adult rats. *Behavioral and Neural Biology*, 26, 287–97.

Greist, J. H., Katzelnick, D. J., Jefferson, J. W. & Kobak, K. A. (1996). Treatment of social phobia with SSRIs. *European Neuropsychopharmacology*, 6, 4.

Griez, E. & Schruers, K. (1998). Experimental pathophysiology of fear. *Journal of Psychosomatic Research*, 45, 493–503.

Grigorenko, E. L. (2003). Epistasis and the genetics of complex traits. In R. Plomin, J. C. DeFries, I. W. Craig & P. McGuffin (eds), *Behavioral Genetics in the Postgenomic Era*. Washington, DC: American Psychological Association.

Grigoryan, G. A., Gray, J. A., Rashid, T., Chadwick, A. & Hodges, H. (2000). Conditionally immortal stem cell grafts restore spatial learning in rats with lesions at the source of cholinergic projections. *Restorative Neurology and Neuroscience*, 17, 183–201.

Grillon, C. (2002). Associative learning deficits increase symptoms of anxiety in humans. *Biological Psychiatry* 51, 851–8.

Grillon, C., Ameli, R., Charney, D. S., Krystal, J. & Braff, D. (1992). Startle gating deficits occur across prepulse intensities in schizophrenic patients. *Biological Psychiatry*, 32, 939–43.

Grillon, C. & Baas, J. (2003). A review of the modulation of the startle reflex by affective states and its application in psychiatry. *Clinical Neurophysiology*, 114, 1557–79.

Grillon, C. & Davis, M. (1997). Fear-potentiated startle conditioning in humans: Explicit and contextual cue conditioning following paired versus unpaired training. *Psychophysiology*, 34, 451–8.

Grillon, C., Merikangas, K. R., Dierker, L., Snidman, N., Arriaga, R. I., Kagan, J., Donzella, B., Dikel, T. & Nelson, C. (1999). Startle potentiation by threat of aversive stimuli and darkness in adolescents: A multi-site study. *International Journal of Psychophysiology*, 32, 63–73.

Grillon, C. & Morgan, C. A. (1996). Fear-potentiated startle in Vietnam veterans with PTSD. *Biological Psychiatry*, 39, 555–6.

Groh, J. M., Trause, A. S., Underhill, A. M., Clark, K. R. & Inati, S. (2001). Eye position influences auditory responses in primate inferior colliculus. *Neuron*, 29, 509–18.

Gronwall, D. M. A. (1977). Paced auditory serial-addition task: A measure of recovery from concussion. *Perceptual and Motor Skills*, 44, 367–73.

Grossberg, S. & Schmajuk, N. A. (1987). Neural dynamics of attentionally modulated Pavlovian conditioning: Conditioned reinforcement, inhibition, and opponent processing. *Psychobiology*, 15, 195–240.

Grunhaus, L., Schreiber, S., Dolberg, O. T., Polak, D. & Dannon, P. N. (2003). A randomised controlled comparison of electroconvulsive therapy and repetitive transcranial magnetic stimulation in severe and resistant nonpsychotic major depression. *Biological Psychiatry*, 53, 324–31.

Gruzelier, J. H. (1996). The factorial structure of schizotypy. I. Affinities and contrasts with syndromes of schizophrenia. *Schizophrenia Bulletin*, 22, 611–20.

Gruzelier, J. H. (1999). Functional neuropsychophysiological asymmetry in schizophrenia: A review and reorientation. *Schizophrenia Bulletin*, 25, 91–120.

Gruzelier, J. (2002). A Janusian perspective on the nature, development and structure of schizophrenia and schizotypy. *Schizophrenia Research*, 54, 95–103.

Gunduz, H., Woerner, M. G., Alvir, J. M., Degreef, G. & Lieberman, J. A. (1999). Obstetric complications in schizophrenia, schizoaffective disorder and normal comparison subjects. *Schizophrenia Research*, 40, 237–43.

Haaga, D. A. F. & Beck, A. T. (1995). Perspectives on depressive realism: Implications for cognitive theory of depression. *Behaviour Research and Theory*, 33, 41–8.

Hamilton, W. D. (1963). The evolution of altruistic behaviour. *The American Naturalist*, 97, 354–6.

Hamilton, W. D. (1964a). The genetical evolution of social behaviour, I. *Journal of Theoretical Biology*, 7, 1–16.

Hamilton, W. D. (1964b). The genetical evolution of social behaviour, II. *Journal of Theoretical Biology*, 7, 17–52.

Hamilton, W. D. (1996). *Narrow Roads of Gene Land: The Collected Papers of W.D. Hamilton*. New York: W.H. Freeman/Spektrum.

Hamm, A. O., Greenwald, M. K., Bradley, M. M. & Lang, P. J. (1993). Emotional learning, hedonic change, and the startle probe. *Journal of Abnormal Psychology*, 102, 453–65.

Hamm, A. O., Cuthbert, B. N., Globisch, J. & Vaitl, D. (1997). Fear and the startle reflex: Blink modulation and autonomic response patterns in animal and mutilation fearful subjects. *Psychophysiology*, 34, 97–107.

Hariri, A. R., Mattay, V. S., Tessitore, A., Fera, F. & Weinberger, D. R. (2003). Neocortical modulation of the amygdala response to fear stimuli. *Biological Psychiatry*, 53, 494–501.

Hariri, A. R., Mattay, V. S., Tessitore, A., Kolachana, B., Fera, F., Goldman, D., Egan, M. F. & Weinberger, D. R. (2002a). Serotonin transporter genetic variation and the response of the human amygdala. *Science*, 297, 400–3.

Hariri, A. R., Tessitore, A., Mattay, V. S., Fera, F. & Weinberger, D. R. (2002b). The amygdala response to emotional stimuli: A comparison of faces and scenes. *Neuroimage*, 17, 317–23.

Hariri, A. R. & Weinberger, D. R. (2003). Functional neuroimaging of genetic variation in serotonergic neurotransmission. *Genes, Brain and Behaviour*, 2, 341–9.

Harnish, R. M. (2002). *Minds, Brains, Computers: An Historical Introduction to the Foundations of Cognitive Science*. Oxford: Blackwell.

Harvey, P. D. & Sharma, T. (2002). *Understanding and Treating Cognition in Schizophrenia: A Clinician's Handbook*. London: Martin Dunitz.

Hashimoto, R., Straub, R. E., Weickert, C. S., Hyde, T. M., Kleinman, J. E. & Weinberger, D. R. (2004). Expression analysis of neuregulin-1 in the dorsolateral prefrontal cortex in schizophrenia. *Molecular Psychiatry*, 9, 299–307.

Hawk, L. W. & Cook, E. W. (2000). Independence of valence modulation and prepulse inhibition of startle. *Psychophysiology*, 37, 5–12.

Hawkins, R. D. & Kandel, E. R. (1984). Is there a cell-biological alphabet for simple forms of learning? *Psychological Review*, 91, 375–91.

Haykin, S. (1999). *Neural Networks: A Comprehensive Foundation*. New Jersey: Prentice Hall.

Hebb, D. O. (1949). *The Organization of Behaviour: A Neuropsychological Theory*. London: Wiley.

Hebb, D. O. (1953). On human thought. *Canadian Journal of Psychology*, 7, 99–110.

Hebb, D. O. (1955). Drives and the C.N.S. (Conceptual Nervous System). *Psychological Review*, 62, 243–54.

Hecht-Nielsen, R. (1991). *Neurocomputing*. Reading: Addison-Wesley.

Heim, C., Newport, D. J., Bonsall, R., Miller, A. H. & Nemeroff, C. B. (2001). Altered pituitary–adrenal axis response to provocative challenge tests in adult survivors of childhood abuse. *American Journal of Psychiatry*, 158, 575–81.

Hermann, C., Ziegler, S., Birbaumer, N. & Flor, H. (2002). Psychophysiological and subjective indicators of aversive Pavlovian conditioning in generalised social phobia. *Biological Psychiatry*, 52, 328–37.

Hess, R. A., Bunick, D., Lee, K., Bahr, J., Taylor, J. A., Korach, K. S. & Lubahn, D. B. (1997). A role for oestrogens in the male reproductive system. *Nature*, 390, 509–12.

Heston, L. L. (1966). Psychiatric disorders in foster home reared children of schizophrenic mothers. *British Journal of Psychiatry*, 112, 819–25.

Hines, M., Golombok, S., Rust, J., Johnston, K. J. & Golding, J. (2002). Testosterone during pregnancy and gender role behaviour of preschool children: A longitudinal study. *Child Development*, 73, 1678–87.

Hodges, A., Byrne, M., Grant, E. & Johnstone, E. (1999). People at risk of schizophrenia. Sample characteristics of the first 100 cases in the Edinburgh High-Risk Study. *British Journal of Psychiatry*, 174, 547–53.

Holzman, P. S., Kringlen, E., Levy, D. L. & Haberman, S. J. (1980). Deviant eye tracking in twins discordant for psychosis. A replication. *Archives of General Psychiatry*, 37, 627–31.

Hom, J. & Reitan, R. M. (1990). Generalized cognitive function after stroke. *Journal of Clinical and Experimental Neuropsychology*, 12, 644–54.

Honey, G. D., Bullmore, E. T., Soni, W., Varatheesan, M., Williams, S. C. & Sharma, T. (1999). Differences in frontal cortical activation by a working memory task after substitution of risperidone for typical antipsychotic drugs in patients with schizophrenia. *Proceedings of the National Academy of Sciences*, 96, 13432–7.

Horrobin, D. F. (1998). Schizophrenia: The illness that made us human. *Medical Hypotheses*, 50, 269–88.

Horrobin, D. F. (2001). *The Madness of Adam and Eve: How Schizophrenia Shaped Humanity*. London: Bantam.

Hosokawa, T., Rusakov, D. A., Bliss, T. V. & Fine, A. (1995). Repeated confocal imaging of individual dendritic spines in the living hippocampal slice: Evidence for changes in length and orientation associated with chemically induced LTP. *Journal of Neuroscience*, 15, 5560–73.

Hubel, D. H. & Wiesel, T. N. (1962). Receptive fields, binocular interaction and functional architecture in the cat's visual cortex. *Journal of Physiology*, 160, 106–54.

Hubel, D. H. & Wiesel, T. N. (1977). Ferrier lecture. Functional architecture of macaque monkey visual cortex. *Proceedings of the Royal Society of London: Biological Sciences*, 198, 1–59.

Hubel, D. H. & Wiesel, T. N. (1979). Brain mechanisms of vision. *Scientific American*, 241, 150–62.

Hultman, C. M., Sparen, P., Takei, N., Murray, R. M. & Cnattingius, S. (1999). Prenatal and perinatal risk factors for schizophrenia, affective psychosis, and reactive psychosis of early onset: Case-control study. *British Medical Journal*, 318, 421–6.

Humphrey, N. (1986). *The Inner Eye*. London: Faber & Faber.

Humphrey, N. (1987). The inner eye of consciousness. In C. Blakemore & S. Greenfield (eds), *Mindwaves*. Oxford: Blackwell.

Humphreys, G. W. & Riddoch, M. J. (1987). *To See But Not to See: A Case Study of Visual Agnosia*. Hove: Erlbaum.

Hutchinson, G., Takei, N., Fahy, T. A., Bhugra, D., Gilvarry, C., Moran, P., Mallett, R., Sham, P., Leff, J. & Murray, R. M. (1996). Morbid risk of schizophrenia in first-degree relatives of white and African-Caribbean patients with psychosis. *British Journal of Psychiatry*, 169, 776–80.

Huxley, J., Mayr, E., Osmond, H. & Hoffer, A. (1964). Schizophrenia as a genetic morphism. *Nature*, 204, 220–1.

Issa, A. M. (2000). Ethical considerations in clinical pharmacogenomics research. *Trends in Pharmacological Science*, 21, 247–9.

Jackendoff, R. (1987). *Consciousness and the Computational Mind*. Cambridge, MA: MIT Press.

Jamison, K. R. (1993). *Touched with Fire: Manic-Depressive Illness and the Artistic Temperament*. New York: Free Press.

Jamison, K. R. (1995). *An Unquiet Mind*. New York: Knopf.

Jamison, K. R. (2002). *Manic-Depressive Illness and Creativity*. Scientific American (Mysteries of the Mind special edition), 32–7.

Janszky, J., Szucs, A., Halasz, P., Borbely, C., Hollo, A., Barsi, P. & Mirnics, Z. (2002). Orgasmic aura originates from the right hemisphere. *Neurology*, 58, 302–4.

Jarvik, L. F. & Deckard, B. S. (1977). The Odyssean personality. A survival advantage for carriers of genes predisposing to schizophrenia? *Neuropsychobiology*, 3, 179–91.

Jasper, H. (1958). Report on the committee on methods of clinical examination in electro-encephalography. *Electroencephalography and Clinical Neurophysiology*, 10, 370–5.

Jeffreys, A. J., Wilson, V. & Thein, S. L. (1985). Individual-specific 'fingerprints' of human DNA. *Nature*, 316, 76–9.

Jemmot, J. B. & Magloire, K. (1988). Academic stress, social support, and secretory immunoglobulin A. *Journal of Personality and Social Psychology*, 55, 803–10.

Jennings, J. M., McIntosh, A. R., Kapur, S., Zipursky, R. B. & Houle, S. (1998). Functional network differences in schizophrenia: A rCBF study of semantic processing. *Neuroreport*, 9, 1697–1700.

Jeste, D. V., Lacro, J. P., Bailey, A., Rockwell, E., Harris, M. J. & Caligiuri, M. P. (1999). Lower incidence of tardive dyskinesia with risperidone compared with haloperidol in older patients. *Journal of the American Geriatric Society*, 47, 716–19.

Johnstone, E. C., Abukmeil, S. S., Byrne, M., Clafferty, R., Grant, E., Hodges, A., Lawrie, S. M. & Owens, D. G. C. (2000). Edinburgh high risk study – findings after four years: Demographic, attainment and psychopathological issues. *Schizophrenia Research*, 46, 1–15.

Johnstone, E. C., Crow, T. J., Frith, C. D., Husband, J. and Kreel, L. (1976). Cerebral ventricular size and cognitive impairment in chronic schizophrenia. *Lancet*, 2, 924–6.

Jones, P. B., Rantakallio, P., Hartikainen, A. L., Isohanni, M. & Sipila, P. (1998). Schizophrenia as a long-term outcome of pregnancy, delivery, and perinatal complications: A 28-year follow-up of the 1966 north Finland general population birth cohort. *American Journal of Psychiatry*, 155, 355–64.

Jones, P., Rodgers, B., Murray, R. & Marmot, M. (1994). Child development risk factors for adult schizophrenia in the British 1946 birth cohort. *Lancet*, 344, 1398–402.

Jones, S. (2003). *Y: The Descent of Men*. New York: Houghton Mifflin.

Joseph, M. H., Peters, S. L., Moran, P. M., Grigoryan, G. A., Young, A. M. & Gray, J. A. (2000). Modulation of latent inhibition in the rat by altered dopamine transmission in the nucleus accumbens at the time of conditioning. *Neuroscience*, 101, 921–30.

Kalat, J. W. (1998). *Biological Psychology* (6th edn). Pacific Grove, CA: Brooks/Cole.

Kalidindi, S. & McGuffin, P. (2003). The genetics of affective disorders: Present and future. In R. Plomin, J. C. DeFries, I. W. Craig & P. McGuffin (eds), *Behavioral Genetics in the Postgenonic Era*. Washinton, DC: American Psychological Association.

Kamin, L. J. (1968). 'Attention like' processes in classical conditoning. In M. R. Jones (ed.), *Miami Symposium on the Prediction of Behavior, 1967: Aversive Stimulation*. Coral Gables: University of Miami Press.

Kamin, L. J. (1974). *The Science and Politics of IQ*. Potomac, MD: Erlbaum.

Kandel, E. R. (1991). Cellular mechanisms of learning and the biological basis of individuality. In E. R. Kandel, J. H. Schwartz & T. M. Jessell (eds), *Principles of Neural Science*. Norwalk: Appleton & Lange.

Kaney, S. & Bentall, R. P. (1989). Persecutory delusions and attributional style. *British Journal of Medical Psychology*, 62, 191–8.

Kang, D. H., Davidson, R. J., Coe, C., Wheeler, R. R., Tomarken, A. J. & Erschler, W. B. (1991). Frontal brain asymmetry and immune function. *Behavioural Neuroscience*, 105, 860–9.

Kapitany, T., Schindl, M., Schindler, S. D., Heßelmann, B., Füreder, T., Barnas, C., Sieghart, W. & Kasper, S. (1999). The citalopram challenge test in patients with major depression and in healthy controls. *Psychiatry Research*, 88, 75–88.

Kapur, S., Zipursky, R. B., Remington, G., Jones, C., DaSilva, J., Wilson, A. A. & Houle S. (1998). 5-HT2 and D2 receptor occupancy of olanzapine in schizophrenia: a PET investigation. *American Journal of Psychiatry*, 155, 921–8.

Karoumi, B., Saoud, M., d'Amato, T., Rosenfeld, F., Denise, P., Gutknecht, C., Gaveau, V., Beaulieu, F. E., Dalery, J. & Rochet, T. (2001). Poor performance in smooth pursuit and antisaccadic eye-movement tasks in healthy siblings of patients with schizophrenia. *Psychiatry Research*, 101, 209–19.

Katsanis, J., Kortenkamp, S., Iacono, W. G. & Grove, W. M. (1997). Antisaccade performance in patients with schizophrenia and affective disorder. *Journal of Abnormal Psychology*, 106, 468–72.

Katzman, M. A., Struzik, L., Vijay, N., Coonerty-Femiano, A., Mahamed, S. & Duffin, J. (2002). Central and peripheral chemoreflexes in panic disorder. *Psychiatry Research*, 113, 181–92.

Keck, M. E., Welt, T., Müller, M. B., Erhardt, A., Ohl, F., Toschi, N., Holsboer, F. & Sillaber, I. (2002). Repetitive transcranial magnetic stimulation increases the release of dopamine in the mesolimbic and mesostriatal system. *Neuropharmacology*, 43, 101–9.

Keefe, R. S., Silva, S. G., Perkins, D. O. & Lieberman, J. A. (1999). The effects of atypical antipsychotic drugs on neurocognitive impairment in schizophrenia: A review and meta-analysis. *Schizophrenia Bulletin*, 25, 201–22.

Kelso, S. R. & Brown, T. H. (1986). Differential conditioning of associative synaptic enhancement in hippocampal brain slices. *Science*, 232, 85–7.

Kelso, S. R., Ganong, A. H. & Brown, T. H. (1986). Hebbian synapses in the hippocampus. *Proceedings of the National Academy of Sciences*, 83, 5326–30.

Kemali, D., Maj, M., Galderisi, S., Ariano, M. G., Cesarelli, M., Milici, N., Salvati, A., Valente, A. & Volpe, M. (1985). Clinical and neuropsychological correlates of cerebral ventricular enlargement in schizophrenia. *Journal of Psychiatric Research*, 19, 587–96.

Kendler, K. S. & Diehl, S. R. (1993). The genetics of schizophrenia: A current, genetic-epidemiologic perspective. *Schizophrenia Bulletin*, 19, 261–85.

Kendler, K. S., Gruenberg, A. M. & Kinney, D. K. (1994a). Independent diagnoses of adoptees and relatives as defined by DSM-III in the provincial and national samples of the Danish Adoption Study of Schizophrenia. *Archives of General Psychiatry*, 51, 456–68.

Kendler, K. S., Karkowski-Shuman, L., O'Neill, F. A., Straub, R. E., MacLean, C. J. & Walsh, D. (1997). Resemblance of psychotic symptoms and syndromes in affected sibling pairs from the Irish Study of High-Density Schizophrenia Families: Evidence for possible etiologic heterogeneity. *American Journal of Psychiatry*, 154, 191–8.

Kendler, K. S., Kessler, R. C., Neale, M. C., Heath, A. C. & Eaves, L. J. (1993). The prediction of major depression in women: Toward an integrated etiologic model. *American Journal of Psychiatry*, 150, 1139–48.

Kendler, K. S., Neale, M. C., Kessler, R. C., Heath, A. C. & Eaves, L. J. (1992). Major depression and generalized anxiety disorder: Same genes, (partly) different environments? *Archives General Psychiatry*, 49, 716–22.

Kendler, K. S., Prescott, C. A., Myers, J. & Neale, M. C. (2003). The structure of genetic and environmental risk factors for common psychiatric and substance use disorders in men and women. *Archives of General Psychiatry*, 60, 929–37.

Kendler, K. S., Walters, E. E., Truett, K. R., Heath, A. C., Neale, M. C., Martin, N. G. & Eaves, L. J. (1994). Sources of individual differences in depressive symptoms: Analysis of two samples of twins and their families. *American Journal of Psychiatry*, 151, 1605–14.

Kennedy, J. L., Collier, D. A. & Rietschel, M. (2000). Pharmacogenetics in psychiatry satellite meeting at the American College of Neuropsychopharmacology, 2000. *Neuropsychopharmacology*, 26, 123–7.

Kety, S. S., Wender, P. H., Jacobsen, B., Ingraham, L. J., Jansson, L., Faber, B. & Kinney, D. K. (1994). Mental illness in the biological and adoptive relatives of schizophrenic adoptees. Replication of the Copenhagen Study in the rest of Denmark. *Archives of General Psychiatry*, 51, 442–55.

Khan, A., Leventhal, R. M., Khan, S. & Brown, W. A. (2002). Suicide risk in patients with anxiety disorders: A meta-analysis of the FDA database. *Journal of Affective Disorders*, 68, 183–90.

Kiessling, A. A. & Anderson, S. (2003). *Human Embryonic Stem Cells: An Introduction to the Science and Therapeutic Potential*. Sudbury, MA: Jones & Bartlett.

Klein, D. F. (1993). False suffocation alarms, spontaneous panics, and related conditions. *Archives of General Psychiatry*, 50, 306–17.

Kline, P. (1993). *The Handbook of Psychological Testing*. London: Routledge.

Kmita, M., Fraudeau, N., Herault, Y. & Duboule, D. (2002). Serial deletions and duplications suggest a mechanism for the collinearity of Hoxd genes in limbs. *Nature*, 420, 145–50.

Knutson, B., Momenan, R., Rawlings, R. R., Fong, G. W. & Hommer, D. (2001). Negative association of neuroticism with brain volume ratio in healthy humans. *Biological Psychiatry*, 50, 685–90.

Koch, C. (2004). *The Quest for Consciousness: A Neuro-Biological Approach*. Englewood, CO: Roberts.

Koenig, J. I., Kirkpatrick, B. & Lee, P. (2002). Glucocorticoid hormones and early brain development in schizophrenia. *Neuropsychopharmacology*, 27, 309–18.

Koffka, K. (1935). *Principles of Gestalt Psychology*. New York: Harcourt Brace.

Koh, K. B. (1998). Emotion and immunity: Relation to individual differences in subclinical anxiety. *Journal of Psychosomatic Research*, 45, 107–11.

Kolb, B. & Whishaw, I. Q. (2003). *Fundamentals of Human Neuropsychology* (5th edn). New York: Worth Publishers.

Konsman, J. P., Parnet, P. & Dantzer, R. (2002). Cytokine-induced sickness behaviour: Mechanisms and implications. *Trends in Neuroscience*, 25, 154–9.

Kroto, H. (2002). Opinion. *The Times Higher Education Supplement*, 22 November.

Kubler, A. (2004). 'Locked in': Have psychologists got the key? *The Psychologist: Bulletin of the British Psychological Society*, 17, 128–31.

Kuelz, A. K., Hohagen, F. & Voderholzer, U. (2004). Neuropsychological performance in obsessive-compulsive disorder: A critical review. *Biological Psychology*, 65, 185–236.

Kumar, A., Bilker, W., Lavretsky, H. & Gottlieb, G. (2000). Volumetric asymmetries in late-onset mood disorders: An attenuation of frontal asymmetry with depression severity. *Psychiatry Research: Neuroimaging*, 100, 41–7.

Kumari, V., Soni, W. & Sharma, T. (1999). Normalization of information processing deficits in schizophrenia with clozapine. *American Journal of Psychiatry*, 156, 1046–51.

Kumari, V., ffytche, D. H., Williams, S. C. R. & Gray, J. A. (submitted). Personality predicts fMRI activity during working memory and at rest.

Kwon, J. S., McCarley, R. W., Hirayasu, Y., Anderson, J. E., Fischer, I. A., Kikinis, R., Jolesz, F. A. & Shenton, M. E. (1999). Left planum temporale volume reduction in schizophrenia. *Archives General Psychiatry*, 56, 142–8.

Landis, C. & Hunt, W. A. (1939). *The Startle Pattern*. New York: Farrar.

Lang, P. J., Bradley, M. M., Cuthbert, B. N. & Partrick, C. J. (1992). Emotion and psychopathology: A startle probe analysis. In L. J. Chapman, J. P. Chapman & D. C. Fowles (eds), *Progress in Experimental Personality and Psychopathology Research*. New York: Springer.

Lawrie, S. M., Byrne, M., Miller, P., Hodges, A., Clafferty, R. A., Cunningham Owens, D. G. & Johnstone, E. C. (2001). Neurodevelopmental indices and the development of psychotic symptoms in subjects at high risk of schizophrenia. *British Journal of Psychiatry*, 178, 524–30.

Lawrie, S. M., Whalley, H., Kestelman, J. N., Abukmeil, S. S., Byrne, M., Hodges, A., Rimmington, J. E., Best, J. J. K., Owens, D. G. C. & Johnstone, E. C. (1999). Magnetic resonance imaging of brain in people at high risk of developing schizophrenia. *Lancet*, 353, 30–3.

Lawson, C., MacLeod, C. & Hammond, G. (2002). Interpretation revealed in the blink of an eye: Depressive bias in the resolution of ambiguity. *Journal of Abnormal Psychology*, 111, 321–8.

Lazarou, J., Pomeranz, B. H. & Corey, P. N. (1998). Incidence of adverse drug reactions in hospitalized patients: A meta-analysis of prospective studies. *Journal of the American Medical Association*, 279, 1200–5.

Leboyer, M., Bellivier, F., Nosten-Bertrand, M., Jouvent, R., Pauls, D. & Mallett, J. (1998). Psychiatric genetics: Search for phenotypes. *Trends in Neuroscience*, 21, 102–5.

Leckman, J. F., Mayes, L. C. & Cohen, D. J. (2002). Primary maternal preoccupation revisited: Circuits, genes, and the crucial role of early life experience. *South African Psychiatry Review*, 5, 4–12.

LeDoux, J. E. (1996). *The Emotional Brain: The Mysterious Underpinnings of Emotional Life*. New York: Simon & Schuster.

LeDoux, J. (1996). Emotional networks and motor control: A fearful view. *Progress in Brain Research*, 107, 437–46.

LeDoux, J. E. (2000). Emotion circuits in the brain. *Annual Review of Neuroscience*, 23, 155–84.

LeDoux, J. E. (2002). *Synaptic Self: How Our Brains Become Who We Are*. New York: Viking.

Lee, W. E., Wadsworth, M. E. J. & Hotop, M. (2006). The protective role of trait anxiety: A longitudinal cohort study. *Psychological Medicine*, 36, 345–51.

Leigh, R. J. & Zee, D. S. (1999). *The Neurology of Eye Movements* (3rd edn). New York: Oxford University Press.

Lencer, R., Trillenberg-Krecker, K., Schwinger, E. & Arolt, V. (2003). Schizophrenia spectrum disorders and eye tracking dysfunction in singleton and multiplex schizophrenia families. *Schizophrenia Research*, 60, 33–45.

Leonard, B. E. (2003). *Fundamentals of Psychopharmacology* (3rd edn). Chichester: Wiley.

Lesch, K. P., et al. (1997). Molecular biology, pharmacology, and genetics of the serotonin transporter: Psychobiological and clinical implications. In H. G. Baumgarten & M. Gothert (eds), *Serotonergic Neurons and 5-HT Receptors in the CNS*. New York: Springer.

Lesch, K. P. (2003). Neuroticism and serotonin: A developmental genetic perspective. In R. Plomin, J. C. DeFries, I. W. Craig & P. McGuffin (eds), *Behavioral Genetics in the Postgenomic Era*. Washington, DC: American Psychological Association.

Lesch, K. P., Greenberg, B. D., Higley, J. D., Bennett, A. & Murphy, D. L. (2002). Serotonin transporter, personality, and behavior: Toward dissection of gene–gene and gene–environment interaction. In J. Benjamin, R. P. Ebstein & R. H. Belmaker (eds), *Molecular Genetics and the Human Personality*. Washington, DC: American Psychiatric Publishing.

LeVay, S. (1991). A difference in hypothalamic structure between heterosexual and homosexual men. *Science*, 253, 1034–7.

Levin, E. D., Wilson, W., Rose, J. E. & McEvoy, J. P. (1996). Nicotine–haloperidol interactions and cognitive performance in schizophrenia. *Schizophrenia Research*, 18, 221.

Levy, D. L., Holzman, P. S., Matthysse, S. & Mendell, N. R. (1993). Eye tracking dysfunction and schizophrenia: A critical perspective. *Schizophrenia Bulletin*, 19, 461–536.

Lewis, G., David, A., Andreasson, S. & Allebeck, P. (1992). Schizophrenia and city life. *Lancet*, 340, 137–40.

Lewohl, J. M., Wang, L., Miles, M. F., Zhang, L., Dodd, P. R. & Harris, R. A. (2000). Gene expression in human alcoholism: Microarray analysis of frontal cortex. *Alcohol: Clinical and Experimental Research*, 24, 1873–82.

Lewontin, R. C., Rose, S. & Kamin, L. J. (1984). *Not in our Genes*. New York: Pantheon.

Lezak, M. D. (1995). *Neuropsychological Assessment*. Oxford: Oxford University Press.

Liberman, R. P., Spaulding, W. D. & Corrigan, P. W. (1995). Cognitive behavioural therapies in psychiatric rehabilitation. In S. R. Hirsch & D. R. Weinberger (eds), *Schizophrenia*. Oxford: Oxford University Press.

Libet, B. (1982). Brain stimulation in the study of neuronal functions for conscious sensory experiences. *Human Neurobiology*, 1, 235–42.

Libet, B. (1985). Unconscious cerebral initiative and the role of conscious will in voluntary action. *Behavioral and Brain Sciences*, 8, 529–66.

Libet, B. (2003). Timing of conscious experience: Reply to the 2002 commentaries on Libet's findings. *Consciousness and Cognition*, 12, 321–31.

Liddle, P. F., Friston, K. J., Frith, C. D. & Frackowiak, R. S. (1992). Cerebral blood flow and mental processes in schizophrenia. *Journal of the Royal Society of Medicine*, 85, 224–7.

Lindemann, B. (2001). Receptors and transduction in taste. *Nature*, 413, 219–25.

Livingstone, M. & Hubel, D. (1995). Through the eyes of monkeys and men. In R. Gregory, H. Harris, P. Heard & D. Rose (eds), *The Artifical Eye*. Oxford: Oxford University Press.

Llorca, P. M., Chereau, I., Bayle, F. J. & Lancon, C. (2002). Tardive dyskinesias and antipsychotics: A review. *European Psychiatry*, 17, 129–38.

Loehlin, J. C. (1992). *Genes and Environment in Personality Development*. Newbury Park, CA: Sage.

Loehlin, J. C. & Nichols, R. C. (1976). *Heredity, Environment, and Personality: A Study of 850 Sets of Twins*. Austin: University of Texas Press.

Loewi, O. (1953). *From the Workshop of Discoveries*. Lawrence: University of Kansas Press.

Lopez, J. F., Vazquez, D. M., Chalmers, D. T. & Watson, S. J. (1997). Regulation of 5-HT receptors and the hypothalamic–pituitary–adrenal axis: Implications for the neurobiology of suicide. *Annals of the New York Academy of Sciences*, 836, 106–34.

Lorenz, K. (1965). Preface to the 1965 edition of *The Expression of the Emotions in Man and Animals*. In C. Darwin, *The Expression of the Emotions in Man and Animals*. Chicago: University of Chicago Press.

Lubow, R. E. (1989). *Latent Inhibition and Conditioned Attention Theory*. Cambridge: Cambridge University Press.

Lubow, R. E. & De La Casa, G. (2002). Latent inhibition as a function of schizotypality and gender: Implications for schizophrenia. *Biological Psychology*, 59, 69–86.

Lubow, R. E. & Gewirtz, J. C. (1995). Latent inhibition in humans: Data, theory, and implications for schizophrenia. *Psychological Bulletin*, 117, 87–103.

Lubow, R. E., Ingberg-Sachs, Y., Zalstein-Orda, N. & Gewirtz, J. C. (1992). Latent inhibition in low and high 'psychotic prone' normal subjects. *Personality and Individual Differences*, 13, 563–72.

Lumsden, C. J. & Wilson, E. O. (1981). *Genes, Mind, and Culture: The Coevolutionary Process*. Cambridge, MA: Harvard University Press.

Lundh, L. G., Wikström, J., Westerlund, J. & Öst, L. G. (1999). Preattentive bias for emotional information in panic disorder with agoraphobia. *Journal of Abnormal Psychology*, 108, 222–32.

Luo, M., Fee, M. S. & Katz, L. C. (2003). Encoding pheromonal signals in the accessory olfactory bulb of behaving mice. *Science*, 299, 1196–201.

Lupien, S. J., de Leon, M., de Santi, S., Convit, A., Tarshish, C., Nair, N. P., Thakur, M., McEwen, B. S., Hauger, R. L. & Meaney, M. J. (1998). Cortisol levels during human aging predict hippocampal atrophy and memory deficits. *Nature Neuroscience*, 1, 69–73.

Lykken, D. T. (1982). Presidential Address, 1981. Research with twins: The concept of emergenesis. *Psychophysiology*, 19, 361–73.

Macciardi, F., Verga, M., Kennedy, J. L., Cavallini, M. C., Catalano, M. & Smeraldi, E. (1994). Association between schizophrenia and the dopamine receptor DRD4. *European Neuropsychopharmacology*, 4, 375–6.

Mackintosh, N. J. (ed.). (1994). *Animal Learning and Cognition*. San Diego, CA: Academic Press.

Macmillan, M. B. (2000a). *An Odd Kind of Fame: Stories of Phineas Gage*. Cambridge, MA: MIT Press.

Macmillan, M. B. (2000b). Restoring Phineas Gage: A 150th retrospective. *Journal of the History of the Neurosciences*, 9, 42–62.

MacPhail, E. M. (1998). *The Evolution of Consciousness*. Oxford: Oxford University Press.

Maddox, B. (2002). *Rosalind Franklin: The Dark Lady of DNA*. New York: Harper Collins.

Malmberg, A., Lewis, G., David, A. & Allebeck, P. (1998). Premorbid adjustment and personality in people with schizophrenia. *British Journal of Psychiatry*, 172, 308–13.

Malthus, T. (1798). *An Essay on the Principle of Population*. London: J. Johnson.

Manki, H., Kanba, S., Muramatsu, T., Higuchi, S., Suzuki, E., Matsushita, S., Ono, Y., Chiba, H., Shintani, F., Nakamura, M., Yagi, G. & Asai, M. (1996). Dopamine D2, D3 and D4 receptor and transporter gene polymorphisms and mood disorders. *Journal of Affective Disorders*, 40, 7–13.

Manktelow, K. I. & Evans, J. S. (1979). Facilitation of reasoning by realism: Effect or non-effect? *British Journal of Psychology*, 70, 477–88.

Mann, J. J., Anjilvel, S., Campbell, C. E., Van Heertum, R. L. & Malone, K. M. (1997). PET studies of prefrontal cortical activation by serotonin in major depression. *Biological Psychiatry*, 42, 216.

Maquire, E. A., Frackowiak, R. S. J. & Frith, C. D. (1997). Recalling routes around London: Activation of the right hippocampus in taxis drivers. *Journal of Neuroscience*, 17, 7103–10.

Maquire, E. A., Gadian, D. G., Johnsrude, I. S., Good, C. D., Ashburner, J., Frackowiak, R. S. & Frith, C. D. (2000). Navigation-related structural changes in the hippocampi of taxi drivers. *Proceedings of the National Academy of Science*, 97, 4398–403.

Margolese, H. C., Malchy, L., Negrete, J. C., Tempier, R. & Gill, K. (2004). Drug and alcohol use among patients with schizophrenia and related psychoses: Levels and consequences. *Schizophrenia Research*, 67, 157–66.

Marks, I. M. (1969). *Fears and Phobias*. New York: Academic Press.

Marks, I. M. & Nesse, R. (1997). Fear and fitness: An evolutionary analysis of anxiety disorders. In S. Baron-Cohen (ed.), *The Maladapted Mind: Classic Readings in Evolutionary Psychopathology*. Hove: Psychology Press.

Marr, D. (1982). *Vision: A Computational Investigation into the Human Representation and Processing of Visual Information*. San Francisco, CA: Freeman.

Martin, S. J. & Morris, R. G. M. (2002). New life in an old idea: The synaptic plasticity and memory hypothesis revisited. *Hippocampus*, 12, 609–36.

Mason, O., Claridge, G. & Jackson, M. (1995). New scales for the assessment of schizotypy. *Personality and Individual Differences*, 18, 7–13.

Matchett, G. & Davey, G. C. (1991). A test of a disease-avoidance model of animal phobias. *Behavioral Research Therapy*, 29, 91–4.

Matthews, G., Deary, I. J. & Whiteman, M. C. (2003). *Personality Traits* (2nd edn). Cambridge: Cambridge University Press.

Matthews, G. & Gilliland, K. (1999). The personality theories of H. J. Eysenck and J. A. Gray: A comparative review. *Personality and Individual Differences*, 26, 583–626.

Mawer, S. (2003). DNA and the meaning of life. *Nature Genetics*, 33, 453.

McBride, W. J., Murphy, J. M. & Ikemoto, S. (1999). Localisation of brain reinforcement mechanisms: Intracranial self-adminsitration and intracranial place-conditioning studies. *Behavioral Brain Research*, 101, 129–52.

McCarley, R. W., Wible, C. G., Frumin, M., Hirayasu, Y., Levitt, J. J., Fischer, I. A. & Shenton, M. E. (1999). MRI anatomy of schizophrenia. *Biological Psychiatry*, 45, 1099–119.

McClintock, M. K. (1999). Reply: Reproductive biology: Pheromones and regulation of ovulation. *Nature*, 401, 232–3.

McClure, S. M., Daw, N. D. & Montague, P. R. (2003). A computational substrate for incentive salience. *Trends in Neurosciences*, 26, 423–8.

McCulloch, W. S. & Pitts, W. (1943). A logical calculus of the ideas imminent in nervous activity. 1943. *Bulletin of Mathematical Biophysics*, 9, 127–47.

McDowell, J. E. & Clementz, B. A. (2001). Behavioral and brain imaging studies of saccadic performance in schizophrenia. *Biological Psychology*, 57, 5–22.

McFarlane, A. C. (1989). The aetiology of post-traumatic morbidity: Predisposing, precipitating and perpetuating factors. *British Journal of Psychiatry*, 154, 221–8.

McGorry, P. D. & Gleeson, J. (2003). *Psychological Interventions in Early Psychosis: A Treatment Handbook*. Chichester: Wiley.

McGue, M. & Gottesman, I. I. (1989). A single dominant gene still cannot account for the transmission of schizophrenia. *Archives of General Psychiatry*, 46, 478–80.

McGuffin, P. & Kalidindi, S. (2002). The genetics of affective disorders: Present and future. In R. Plomin, J. C. DeFries, I. W. Craig & P. McGuffin (eds), *Behavioral Genetics in the Postgenomic Era*. Washington, DC: American Psychiatric Press.

McGuffin, P., Owen, M. J., O'Donovan, M. C., Tharpar, A. & Gottesman, I. I. (1994). *Seminars in Psychiatric Genetics*. London: Gaskell Press.

McGuffin, P., Katz, R., Watkins, S. & Rutherford, J. (1996). A hospital-based twin register of the heritability of DSM-IV unipolar depression. *Archives of General Psychiatry*, 53, 129–36.

McGuffin, P., Katz, R. & Bebbington, P. (1988). The Camberwell Collaborative Depression Study. III. Depression and adversity in the relatives of depressed probands. *British Journal of Psychiatry*, 152, 775–82.

McNaughton, N. (2004). The conceptual nervous system of J. A. Gray: Anxiety and neuroticism. *Neuroscience and Biobehavioral Reviews*, 28, 227–8.

McNaughton, N. & Corr, P. J. (2004). A two-dimensional neuropsychology of defense: Fear/anxiety and defensive distance. *Neuroscience and Biobehavioral Reviews*, 28, 285–305.

Meehl, P. E. (1962). Schizotaxia, schizotypy, schizophrenia. *American Psychologist*, 17, 827–38.

Meehl, P. E. (2001). Primary and secondary hypohedonia. *Journal of Abnormal Psychology*, 110, 188–93.

Meeks, J. J., Weiss, J. & Jameson, L. J. (2003). Dax1 is required for testis determination. *Nature Genetics*, 34, 32–3.

Melzack, R. & Wall, P. D. (1965). Pain mechanisms: A new theory. *Science*, 150, 971–9.

Melzack, R. & Wall, P. (1984). *The Challenge of Pain*. Harmondsworth: Penguin.

Mendel, G. (1866). Versuche über Pflanzen-Hybriden (Experiments in Plant Hybridization). *Verhandlungen des naturforschenden Vereines in Brünn* (Proceedings of the Natural History Society of Brünn), 4, 1865, 3–47.

Merikangas, K., Fenton, B., Stolar, M. & Dierker, L. (1998). Familial aggregation and high risk study of social phobia. *European Psychiatry*, 13, 170.

Merikangas, K. R., Avenevoli, S., Dierker, L. & Grillon, C. (1999). Vulnerability factors among children at risk for anxiety disorders. *Biological Psychiatry*, 46, 1523–35.

Mersch, P. P., Middendorp, H. M., Bouhuys, A. L., Beersma, D. G. & van den Hoofdakker, R. H. (1999). Seasonal affective disorder and latitude: A review of the literature. *Journal of Affective Disorders*, 53, 35–48.

Metzger, L. J., Orr, S. P., Lasko, N. B. & Pitman, R. K. (1997). Auditory event-related potentials to tone stimuli in combat-related posttraumatic stress disorder. *Biological Psychiatry*, 42, 1006–15.

Metzger, L. J., Orr, S. P., Berry, N. J., Ahern, C. E., Lasko, N. B. & Pitman, R. K. (1999). Physiologic reactivity to startling tones in women with posttraumatic stress disorder. *Journal of Abnormal Psychology*, 108, 347–52.

Michael, N. & Erfurth, A. (2004). Treatment of bipolar mania with right prefrontal rapid transcranial magnetic stimulation. *Journal of Affective Disorders*, 78, 252–7.

Milinski, M. & Wedekind, C. (2001). Evidence for MHC-correlated perfume preferences in humans. *Behavioral Ecology*, 12, 140–9.

Miller, A. R. & Rosenfeld, J. P. (2004). Response-specific scalp distributions in deception detection and ERP correlates of psychopathic personality traits. *Journal of Psychophysiology*.

Miller, G. A., Galanter, E. & Pribram, K. H. (1960). *Plans and the Structure of Behavior*. New York: Holt.

Miller, G. F. (2000). *The Mating Mind: How Sexual Choice Shaped the Evolution of Human Nature*. New York: Doubleday.

Miller, G. (2000). Mental traits as fitness indicators: Expanding evolutionary psychology's adaptationism. *Annals of the New York Academy of Sciences*, 907, 62–74.

Miller, N. E. (1959). Liberalization of basic S-R concepts: Extensions to conflict behavior, motivation, and social learning. In S. Koch (ed.), *Psychology: A Study of Science*, vol. 2. New York: McGraw-Hill.

Milner, A. D. & Goodale, M. A. (1995). *The Visual Brain in Action*. Oxford: Oxford University Press.

Milner, B. (1966). Amnesia following operations on the temporal lobes. In C. W. M. Whitty & O. L. Zangwill (eds), *Amnesia*. London: Butterworths.

Mogg, K., Bradley, B. P., Millar, N. & White, J. (1995). A follow-up study of cognitive bias in generalised anxiety disorder. *Behaviour Research and Therapy*, 33, 927–35.

Mogg, K., Bradley, B. P., Dixon, C., Fisher, S., Twelftree, H. & McWilliams, A. (2000). Trait anxiety, defensiveness and selective processing of threat: An investigation using two measures of attentional bias. *Personality and Individual Differences*, 28, 1063–77.

Money, J. & Ehrhardt, A. A. (1972). *Man and Woman, Boy and Girl: Gender Identity from Conception to Maturity*. Baltimore, MD: Johns Hopkins University Press.

Money, J. & Ehrhardt, A. A. (1975). Ablation penis: Normal male infant sex-reassigned as a girl. *Archives of Sexual Behavior*, 4, 65–71.

Monti-Bloch, L., Jennings-White, C., Dolberg, D. S. & Berliner, D. L. (1994). The human vomeronasal system. *Psychoneuroendocrinology*, 19, 673–86.

Moore, H., Dvorakova, K., Jenkins, N. & Breed, W. (2002). Exceptional sperm cooperation in the wood mouse. *Nature*, 418, 174–7.

Moran, C. M. W. (1966). *Churchill: The Struggle for Survival, 1940–1965*. Boston: Houghton Mifflin.

Morris, J. S., Ohman, A. & Dolan, R. J. (1998). Conscious and unconscious emotional learning in the human amygdala. *Nature*, 393, 467–70.

Mowrer, O. H. (1960). *Learning Theory and Behavior*. New York: Wiley.

Munafo, M. R., Clark, T. G., Moore, L. R., Payne, E., Walton, R. & Flint, J. (2003). Genetic polymorphisms and personality in healthy adults: A systematic review and meta-analysis. *Molecular Psychiatry*, 8, 471–84.

Murray, C. J. & Lopez, A. D. (1997). Mortality by cause for eight regions of the world: Global Burden of Disease Study. *Lancet*, 349, 1269–76.

Murray, R. M. & Lewis, S. W. (1987). Is schizophrenia a neurodevelopmental disorder? *British Medical Journal*, 295, 681–2.

Musa, C., Lépine, J. P., Clark, D. M., Mansell, W. & Ehlers, A. (2003). Selective attention in social phobia and the moderating effect of a concurrent depressive disorder. *Behaviour Research and Therapy*, 41, 1043–54.

Myhrman, A., Rantakallio, P., Isohanni, M., Jones, P. & Partanen, U. (1996). Unwantedness of a pregnancy and schizophrenia in the child. *British Journal of Psychiatry*, 169, 637–40.

Nadel, L. & Jacobs, W. J. (1996). The role of the hippocampus in PTSD, panic and phobia. In N. Kato (ed.), *The Hippocampus: Functions and Clinical Relevance*. Amsterdam: Elsevier.

Nasrallah, H. A., Kuperman, S., Jacoby, C. G., McCalley-Whitters, M. & Hamra, B. (1983). Clinical correlates of sulcal widening in chronic schizophrenia. *Psychiatry Research*, 10, 237–42.

Nauta, W. J. (1972). Neural associations of the frontal cortex. *Acta Neurobiologiae Experimentalis*, 32, 125–40.

Navon, D. (1977). Forest before trees: The precedence of global features in visual perception. *Cognitive Psychology*, 9, 353–83.

Nelson, H. E. & O'Connell, A. (1978). Dementia: The estimate of premorbid intelligence levels using the National Adult Reading Test. *Cortex*, 14, 234–44.

Neshige, R., Kuroda, Y., Kakigi, R., Fujiyama, F., Matoba, R., Yarita, M., Luders, H. & Shibasaki, H. (1991). Event-related brain potentials as indicators of visual recognition and detection of criminals by their use. *Forensic Science International*, 51, 95–103.

Nesse, R. (1997). An evolutionary perspective on panic disorder and agoraphobia. In S. Baron-Cohen (ed.), *The Maladapted Mind: Classic Readings in Evolutionary Psychopathology*. Hove: Psychology Press.

Nesse, R. M. & Williams, G. (1997). Are mental disorders diseases? In S. Baron-Cohen (ed.), *The Maladpated Mind: Classic Readings in Evolutionary Psychopathology*. Hove: Psychology Press.

Nesse, R. M. & Williams, G. C. (1998). Evolution and the origins of disease. *Scientific American*, 279, 86–93.

Noga, J. T., Bartley, A. J., Jones, D. W., Torrey, E. F. & Weinberger, D. R. (1996). Cortical gyral anatomy and gross brain dimensions in monozygotic twins discordant for schizophrenia. *Schizophrenia Research*, 22, 27–40.

Nowak, M. A. & Sigmund, K. (1998). Evolution of indirect reciprocity by image scoring. *Nature*, 393, 573–7.

Nunn, J. A., Gregory, L. J., Brammer, M., Williams, S. C., Parslow, D. M., Morgan, M. J., Morris, R. G., Bullmore, E. T., Baron-Cohen, S. & Gray, J. A. (2002). Functional magnetic resonance imaging of synesthesia: Activation of V4/V8 by spoken words. *Nature Neuroscience*, 5, 371–5.

Oates, K. & Wilson, M. (2002). Nominal kinship cues facilitate altruism. *Proceedings of the Royal Society: Biological Sciences*, 269, 105–9.

Ochsner, K. N. & Lieberman, M. D. (2001). The emergence of social cognitive neuroscience. *American Psychology*, 56, 717–34.

O'Driscoll, G. A., Lenzenweger, M. F. & Holzman, P. S. (1998). Antisaccades and smooth pursuit eye tracking and schizotypy. *Archives General Psychiatry*, 55, 837–43.

O'Driscoll, G. A., Benkelfat, C., Florencio, P. S., Wolff, A. L., Joober, R., Lal, S. & Evans, A. C. (1999). Neural correlates of eye tracking deficits in first-degree relatives of schizophrenic patients: A positron emission tomography study. *Archives of General Psychiatry*, 56, 1127–34.

Ohman, A. & Soares, J. J. (1993). On the automatic nature of phobic fear: Conditioned electrodermal responses to masked fear-relevant stimuli. *Journal of Abnormal Psychology*, 102, 121–32.

Ohman, A. & Soares, J. J. F. (1998). Emotional conditioning to masked stimuli: expectancies for aversive outcomes following nonrecognized fear-relevant stimuli. *Journal of Experimental Psychology: General*, 127, 69–82.

Okada, M. & Corfas, G. (2004). Neuregulin1 downregulates postsynaptic GABAA receptors at the hippocampal inhibitory synapse. *Hippocampus*, 14, 337–44.

Okulski, P., Hess, G. & Kaczmarek, L. (2002). Anisomycin treatment paradigm affects duration of long-term potentiation in slices of the amygdala. *Neuroscience*, 114, 1–5.

Olds, J. (1962). Hypothalamic substrates of reward. *Physiological Review*, 42, 554–604.

Olds, J. & Milner, P. (1954). Positive reinforcement produced by electrical stimulation of septal area and other regions of rat brain. *Journal of Comparative and Physiological Psychology*, 47, 419–27.

Olincy, A., Young, D. A. & Freedman, R. (1997). Increased levels of the nicotine metabolite cotinine in schizophrenic smokers compared to other smokers. *Biological Psychiatry*, 42, 1–5.

Oquendo, M. A. & Mann, J. J. (2001). Neuroimaging findings in major depression, suicidal behaviour and aggression. *Clinical Neuroscience Research*, 1, 377–80.

O'Regan, J. K. & Noe, A. (2001). A sensorimotor account of vision and visual consciousness. *Behavioral and Brain Sciences*, 24, 883–917.

Orr, S. P. & Roth, W. T. (2000). Psychophysiological assessment: Clinical applications for PTSD. *Journal of Affective Disorders*, 61, 225–40.

Owen, M. J. & O'Donovan, M. C. (2003). Schizophrenia and genetics. In R. Plomin, J. C. DeFries, I. W. Craig & P. McGuffin (eds), *Behavioral Genetics in the Postgenomic Era*. Washington, DC: American Psychological Association.

Ownby, R. L. & Carmin, C. N. (1996). Further development of a neural network for panic disorder. *Biological Psychiatry*, 39, 524.

Padberg, F., di Michele, F., Zwanzger, P., Romeo, E., Bernardi, G., Schule, C., Baghai, T. C., Ella, R., Pasini, A. and Rupprecht, R. (2002). Plasma concentrations of neuroactive steroids before and after repetitive transcranial magnetic stimulation (rTMS) in depression. *Neuropsychopharmacology*, 27, 874–8.

Panksepp, J. (1982). Toward a general psychobiological theory of emotions. *Behavioral and Brain sciences*, 5, 407–68.

Panksepp, J. (1998). *Affective Neuroscience: The Foundations of Human and Animal Emotions*. New York: Oxford University Press.

Panksepp, J. (2003). At the interface of the affective, behavioral, and cognitive neurosciences: Decoding the emotional feelings of the brain. *Brain and Cognition*, 52, 4–14.

Paradiso, S., Johnson, D. L., Andreasen, N. C., O'Leary, D. S., Watkins, G. L., Ponto, L. L. & Hichwa, R. D. (1999). Cerebral blood flow changes associated with attribution of emotional valence to pleasant, unpleasant, and neutral visual stimuli in a PET study of normal subjects. *American Journal of Psychiatry*, 156, 1618–29.

Park, S. B. G. (1998). Neural networks and psychopharmacology. In D. J. Stein & J. Ludik (eds), *Neural Networks and Psychopathology*. Cambridge: Cambridge University Press.

Parr, L. A. & de Waal, B. M. (1999). Visual kin recognition in chimpanzees. *Nature*, 399, 647–8.

Pasini, A. & Rupprecht, R. (2002). Plasma concentrations of neuroactive steroids before and after repetitive transcranial magnetic stimulation (rTMS) in major depression. *Neuropsychopharmacology*, 27, 874–8.

Patrick, C. J., Bradley, M. M. & Lang, P. J. (1993). Emotion in the criminal psychopath: Startle reflex modulation. *Journal of Abnormal Psychology*, 102, 82–92.

Patterson, C. (1999). *Evolution*. London: The Natural History Museum.

Pavlov, I. P. (1927). *Conditioned Reflexes*. Oxford: Oxford University Press.

Pelham, B. W. (1993). The idiographic nature of human personality: Examples of the idiographic self-concept. *Journal of Personality and Social Psychology*, 64, 665–77.

Pennington, B. F., Filipek, P. A., Lefly, D., Chhabildas, N., Kennedy, D. N., Simon, J. H., Filley, C. M., Galaburda, A. & DeFries, J. C. (2000). A twin MRI study of size variations in human brain. *Journal of Cognitive Neuroscience*, 12, 223–32.

Penrose, R. (1987). Minds, machines and mathematics. In C. Blakemore & S. Greenfield (eds), *Mindwaves: Thoughts on Intelligence, Identity and Consciousness*. Oxford: Blackwell.

Penrose, R. (1994). *Shadows of the Mind: A Search for the Missing Science of Consciousness*. Oxford: Oxford University Press.

Perkins, A. M. & Corr, P. J. (2006). Reactions to threat and personality: Psychometric differentiation of intensity and direction dimensions of human defensive behaviour. *Behavioural Brain Research*, 169, 21–8.

Perna, G., Caldirola, D., Arancio, C. & Bellodi, L. (1997). Panic attacks: A twin study. *Psychiatry Research*, 66, 69–71.

Perrett, D. I., May, K. A. & Yoshikawa, S. (1994). Facial shape and judgements of female attractiveness. *Nature*, 368, 239–42.

Persinger, M. A. (2001). The neuropsychiatry of paranormal experiences. *Journal of Neuropsychiatry and Clinical Neuroscience*, 13, 515–24.

Persinger, M. A. & Fisher, S. D. (1990). Elevated, specific temporal lobe signs in a population engaged in psychic studies. *Perceptual and Motor Skills*, 71, 817–18.

Peters, E. R., Pickering, A. D., Kent, A., Glasper, A., Irani, M., David, A. S., Day, S. & Hemsley, D. R. (2000). The relationship between cognitive inhibition and psychotic symptoms. *Journal of Abnormal Psychology*, 109, 386–95.

Peterson, L. R. & Peterson, M. J. (1959). Short-term retention of individual verbal items. *Journal of Experimental Psychology*, 58, 193–8.

Peterson, C., Semmel, A., von Baeyer, C., Abramson, L. Y., Metalsky, G. I. & Seligman, M. E. P. (1982). The attributional style questionnaire. *Cognitive Therapy and Research*, 6, 287–300.

Petrie, M., Halliday, T. & Sanders, C. (1991). Peahens prefer peacocks with elaborate trains. *Animal Behaviour*, 41, 323–31.

Petty, R. G. (1999). Structural asymmetries of the human brain and their disturbance in schizophrenia. *Schizophrenia Bulletin*, 25, 121–39.

Phalipon, A., Cardona, A., Kraehenbuhl, J. P., Edelman, L., Sansonetti, P. J. & Corthesy, B. (2002). Secretory component: A new role in secretory IgA-mediated immune exclusion. *Immunity*, 17, 107–15.

Phillips, M. L., Bullmore, E. T., Howard, R., Woodruff, P. W., Wright, I. C., Williams, S. C., Simmons, A., Andrew, C., Brammer, M. & David, A. S. (1998a). Investigation of facial recognition memory and happy and sad facial expression perception: An fMRI study. *Psychiatry Research*, 83, 127–38.

Phillips, M. L., Williams, L. M., Heining, M., Herba, C. M., Russell, T., Andrew, C., Bullmore, E. T., Brammer, M. J., Williams, S. C. R. & Morgan, M. J. (2004). Differential neural responses to overt and covert presentations of facial expressions of fear and disgust. *Neuroimage*, 21, 1484–96.

Phillips, M. L., Young, A. W., Scott, S. K., Calder, A. J., Andrew, C., Giampietro, V., Williams, S. C. R., Bullmore, E. T., Brammer, M. & Gray, J. A. (1998b). Neural responses to facial and vocal expressions of fear and disgust. *Proceedings of the Royal Society London: Biological Sciences*, 265, 1809–17.

Phillips, M. L., Young, A. W., Senior, C., Brammer, M., Andrew, C., Calder, A. J., Bullmore, E. T., Perrett, D. I., Rowland, D., Williams, S. C., Gray, J. A. & David, A. S. (1997). A specific neural substrate for perceiving facial expressions of disgust. *Nature*, 389, 495–8.

Pickering, A. D., Corr, P. J. & Gray, J. A. (1999). Interactions and reinforcement sensitivity theory: A theoretical analysis of Rusting and Larsen (1997). *Personality and Individual Differences*, 26, 357–65.

Pickering, A. D., Corr, P. J., Powell, J. H., Kumari, V., Thornton, J. C. & Gray, J. A. (1997). Individual differences in reactions to reinforcing stimuli are neither black nor white: To what extent are they Gray? In H. Nyborg (ed.), *The Scientific Study of Human Nature: A Tribute to Hans J. Eysenck at Eighty*. London: Elsevier Science.

Pickering, A. D., Díaz, A. & Gray, J. A. (1995). Personality and reinforcement: An exploration using a maze-learning task. *Personality and Individual Differences*, 18, 541–58.

Pickering, A. D. & Gray, J. A. (1999). The neuroscience of personality. In L. Pervin & O. John (eds), *Handbook of Personality* (2nd edn). New York: Guilford Press.

Picton, T. W., Bentin, S., Berg, P., Donchin, E., Hillyard, S. A., Johnson, J. R., Miller, G. A., Ritter, W., Ruchkin, D. S., Rugg, M. D. & Taylor, M. J. (2000). Guidelines for using human event-related potentials to study cognition: recording standards and publication criteria. *Psychophysiology*, 37, 127–52.

Pilowsky, L. & Murray, R. M. (1991). Why don't preschizophrenic children have delusions and hallucinations? *Behavioural and Brain Sciences*, 14, 41–2.

Pinel, J. P. J. (2000). *Biopsychology* (4th edn). Boston: Allyn & Bacon.

Pinker, S. (1997). *How the Mind Works*. New York: Norton.

Pinker, S. (2002). *The Blank Slate: The Modern Denial of Human Nature*. New York: Viking.

Pirmohamed, M., James, S., Meakin, S., Green, C., Scott, A. K., Walley, T. J., Farrar, K., Park, B. K. & Breckenridge, A. M. (2004). Adverse drug reactions as cause of admission to hospital: Prospective analysis of 18,820 patients. *British Medical Journal*, 329, 15–19.

Pizzari, T. & Birkhead, T. R. (2000). Female feral fowl eject sperm of subdominant males. *Nature*, 405, 787–9.

Ploghaus, A., Narain, C., Beckmann, C. F., Clare, S., Bantick, S., Wise, R., Matthews, P. M., Rawlins, J. N. & Tracey, I. (2001). Exacerbation of pain by anxiety is associated with activity in a hippocampal network. *Journal of Neuroscience*, 21, 9896–903.

Plomin, R. (1994). *Genetics and Experience: The Interplay between Nature and Nurture*. London: Sage.

Plomin, R. (2002). Individual differences research in a postgenomic era. *Personality and Individual Differences*, 33, 909–20.

Plomin, R. P. (2003). General cognitive ability. In R. Plomin, J. C. DeFries, I. W. Craig & P. McGuffin (eds), *Behavioral Genetics in the Postgenomic Era*. Washington, DC: American Psychiatric Press.

Plomin, R., Asbury, K. & Dunn, J. (2001). Why are children in the same family so different? Nonshared environment a decade later. *Canadian Journal of Psychiatry*, 46, 225–33.

Plomin, R. & Bergeman, C. S. (1991). The nature of nurture: Genetic influences on 'environmental' measures. *Behavioral and Brain Sciences*, 14, 373–427.

Plomin, R. & Crabbe, J. (2000). DNA. *Psychological Bulletin*, 126, 806–28.

Plomin, R., DeFries, J. C., Craig, I. W. & McGuffin, P. (2003). Behavioral genetics. In R. Plomin, J. C. DeFries, I. W. Craig & P. McGuffin (eds), *Behavioral Genetics in the Postgenomic Era*. Washington, DC: American Psychiatric Press.

Plomin, R., DeFries, J. C., McClearn, G. E. & McGuffin, P. (2001). *Behavioral Genetics* (4th edn). New York: Worth.

Plomin, R. & McGuffin, P. (2003). Psychopathology in the postgenomic era. *Annual Review of Psychology*, 54, 205–28.

Plomin, R., Owen, M. J. & McGuffin, P. (1994). The genetic basis of complex human behaviors. *Science*, 17, 1733–9.

Plomin, R. & Spinath, F. M. (2004). Intelligence: Genetics, Genes, and Genomics. *Journal of Personality and Social Psychology*, 86, 112–29.

Politi, E., Balduzzi, C., Bussi, R. & Bellodi, L. (1999). Artificial neural networks: A study in clinical psychopharmacology. *Psychiatry Research*, 87, 203–15.

Popper, K. (1977). *The Logic of Scientific Discovery*. London: Routledge.

Popper, K. & Eccles, J. (1977). *The Self and its Brain*. New York: Springer.

Post, R., Ballenger, J. C., Uhde, T. W. & Bunney, W. (1984). Efficacy of carbamazepine in manic-depressive illness: Implications for underlying mechanisms. In R. Post & T. Uhde (eds), *Neurobiology of Mood Disorders*. Baltimore: Williams & Wilkins.

Post, R., Rubinow, D. and Ballenger, J. (1986). Conditioning and sensitization in the longitudinal course of affective illness. *British Journal of Psychiatry*, 149, 191–201.

Postma, P. & Kumari, V. (2002). Tobacco smoking in schizophrenia: The self-medication hypotheses. *Journal of Advances in Schizophrenia and Brain Research*, 4, 81–6.

Premack, D. & Woodruff, G. (1978). Does the chimpanzee have a theory of mind? *Behavioral and Brain Sciences*, 4, 515–26.

Preti, G., Cutler, W. B., Garcia, C. R., Huggins, G. R. & Lawley, H. J. (1986). Human axillary secretions influence women's menstrual cycles: The role of donor extract of females. *Hormones and Behaviour*, 20, 474–82.

Primrose, S. B. & Twyman, R. M. (2004). *Genomics: Applications in Human Biology*. Malden, MA: Blackwell.

Prolo, P. & Licinio, J. (2002). D4DR and novelty seeking. In J. Benjamin, R. Ebstein & R. Belmaker (eds), *Molecular Genetics and the Human Personality*. Washington, DC: American Psychiatric Publishing.

Radant, A., Tsuang, D., Peskind, E. R., McFall, M. & Raskind, W. (2001). Biological markers and diagnostic accuracy in the genetics of posttraumatic stress disorder. *Psychiatry Research*, 102, 203–15.

Rado, S. (1953). Dynamics and classification of disordered behavior. *American Journal of Psychiatry*, 110, 406–16.

Raine, A. (1991). The SPQ: A scale for the assessment of schizotypal personality based on DSM-III-R criteria. *Schizophrenia Bulletin* 17, 555–64.

Rao, D. C. & Gu, C. (2002). Principles and methods in the study of complex phenotypes. In J. Benjamin, R. P. Ebstein & R. H. Belmaker (eds), *Molecular Genetics and the Human Personality*. Washington, DC: American Psychiatric Press.

Rasmussen, L. E. L., Lee, T. D., Roelofs, W. L., Zhang, A. & Daves, G. D. J. (1996). Insect pheromone in elephants. *Nature*, 379, 684.

Rassovsky, Y., Kushner, M. G., Schwarze, N. J. & Wangensteen, O. D. (2000). Psychological and physiological predictors of response to carbon dioxide challenges in individuals with panic disorder. *Journal of Abnormal Psychology*, 109, 616–23.

Rauch, S. L., Whalen, P. J., Shin, L. M., McInerney, S. C., Macklin, M. L., Lasko, N. B., Orr, S. P. & Pitman, R. K. (2000). Exaggerated amygdala response to masked facial stimuli in posttraumatic stress disorder: A functional MRI study. *Biological Psychiatry*, 47, 769–76.

Raven, J. C. (1960). *Guide to the Standard Progressive Matrices*. London: H. K. Lewis.

Read, J., Mosher, L. R. & Bentall, R. P. (eds) (2004). *Models of Madness: Psychological, Social and Biological Approaches to Schizophrenia*. New York: Brunner-Routledge.

Reif, A. & Lesch, K. P. (2003). Toward a molecular architecture of personality. *Behavioural Brain Research*, 139, 1–20.

Reitan, R. M. & Wolfson, D. (1993). *The Halstead–Reitan Neuropsychological Test Battery: Theory and Clinical Interpretation*. Tucson, AZ: Neuropsychology Press.

Rensink, R. A., O'Regan, J. K. & Clark, J. J. (1997). To see or not to see: The need for attention to perceive changes in scenes. *Psychological Science*, 8, 368–73.

Reuter, M., Stark, R., Hennig, J., Walter, B., Kirsch, P., Schienle, A. & Vaitl, D. (2004). Personality and emotion: Test of Gray's personality theory by means of an fMRI study. *Behavioral Neuroscience*, 118, 462–9.

Ridley, M. (1993). *The Red Queen: Sex and the Evolution of Human Nature*. London: Viking.

Ridley, M. (2003). *Evolution* (3rd edn). Oxford: Blackwell.

Riedel, W. J., Klaassen, T. & Schmitt, J. A. J. (2002). Tryptophan, mood, and cognitive function. *Brain, Behavior, and Immunity*, 16, 581–9.

Riola, R. L., Cohen, M. D. & Axelrod, R. (2001). Evolution of cooperation without reciprocity. *Nature*, 414, 441–3.

Rivas-Vazquez, R. A., Mendez, C., Rey, G. J. & Carrazana, E. J. (2004). Mild cognitive impairment: New neuropsychological and pharmacological target. *Archives of Clinical Neuropsychology*, 19, 11–27.

Robert-Guroff, M. (2000). IgG surfaces as an important component in mucosal protection. *Nature Medicine*, 6, 129–30.

Robinson, D. G., Woerner, M. G., Alvir, J. M., Geisler, S., Koreen, A., Sheitman, B., Chakos, M., Mayerhoff, D., Bilder, R., Goldman, R. & Lieberman, J. A. (1999). Predictors of treatment response from a first episode of schizophrenia or schizoaffective disorder. *American Journal of Psychiatry*, 156, 544–9.

Rojas, R. (1996). *Neural Networks: A Systematic Introduction*. Heidelberg: Springer-Verlag.

Rose, H. & Rose, S. (2001). *Alas Poor Darwin*. London: Vintage.

Rose, S. (1997). *Lifelines: Biology, Freedom, Determinism*. London: Allen Lane

Rose, S., Lewontin, R. & Kamin, L. (1984). *Not in our Genes: Biology, Ideology, and Human Nature*. New York: Pantheon.

Rosenthal, D., Wender, P. H., Kety, S. S., Welner, J. & Schulsinger, F. (1971). The adopted-away offspring of schizophrenics. *American Journal of Psychiatry*, 128, 307–11.

Rosenzweig, M. R. & Bennett, E. L. (1996). Psychobiology of plasticity: Effects of training and experience on brain and behavior. *Behavioral and Brain Research*, 78, 57–65.

Ross, L. (1977). The intuitive psychologist and his shortcomings: Distortions in the attribution process. In L. Berkowitz (ed.), *Advances in Experimental Social Psychology*, vol. 10. New York: Academic Press.

Rowe, D. C. (2003). Assessing genotype–environment interactions and correlations in the post-genomic era. In R. Plomin, J. C. DeFries, I. W. Craig & P. McGuffin. (eds), *Behavioral Genetics in the Postgenomic Era*. Washington, DC: American Psychiatric Press.

Rusch, B. D., Abercrombie, H. C., Oakes, T. R., Schaefer, S. M. & Davidson, R. J. (2001). Hippocampal morphometry in depressed patients and control subjects: Relations to anxiety symptoms. *Biological Psychiatry*, 50, 960–4.

Rushton, J. P., Russell, R. J. H. & Wells, P. A. (1984). Genetic Similarity Theory. *Behavior Genetics*, 14, 575–82.

Russell, M. J., Switz, G. M. & Thompson, K. (1980). Olfactory influences on the human menstrual cycle. *Pharmacology, Biochemistry and Behaviour*, 13, 737–8.

Rust, J. (1988). The Rust Inventory of Schizotypal Cognitions (RISC). *Schizophrenia Bulletin*, 14, 217–322.

Rutter, M. & Plomin, R. (1997). Opportunities for psychiatry from genetic findings. *British Journal of Psychiatry*, 171, 209–19.

Sahlins, M. D. (1976). *The Use and Abuse of Biology: An Anthropological Critique of Sociobiology*. Ann Arbor: University of Michigan Press.

Salum, C., Morato, S. & Roque-da-Silva, A. C. (2000). Anxiety-like behavior in rats: A computational model. *Neural Networks*, 13, 21–9.

Sapolsky, R. M. (1989). Hypercortisolism among socially subordinate wild baboons originates at the CNS level. *Archives of General Psychiatry*, 46, 1047–51.

Sapolsky, R. M. (2000). Glucocorticoids and hippocampal atrophy in neuropsychiatric disorders. *Archives of General Psychiatry*, 57, 925–35.

Sartory, G., MacDonald, R. & Gray, J. A. (1990). Effects of diazepam on approach, self-reported fear and psychophysiological responses in snake phobics. *Behaviour Research Therapy*, 28, 273–82.

Saykin, A. J., Gur, R. C., Gur, R. E., Mozley, P. D., Mozley, L. H., Resnick, S. M., Kester, D. B. & Stafiniak, P. (1991). Neuropsychological function in schizophrenia: Selective impairment in memory and learning. *Archives of General Psychiatry*, 48, 618–24.

Scheller-Gilkey, G., Moynes, K., Cooper, I., Kant, C. & Miller, A. (2004). Early life stress and PTSD symptoms in patients with comorbid schizophrenia and substance abuse. *Schizophrenia Research*, 69, 167–74.

Schmidt, M. E., Risinger, R. C., Hauger, R. L., Schouten, J. L., Henry, M. & Potter, W. Z. (1997). Responses to alpha2-adrenoceptor blockade by idazoxan in healthy male and female volunteers. *Psychoneuroendocrinology*, 22, 177–88.

Schott, B., Richardson-Klavehn, A., Heinze, H. J. & Duzel, E. (2003). Perceptual priming versus explicit memory: Dissociable neural correlates at encoding. *Journal of Cognitive Neuroscience*, 55, 578–92.

Schwartz, C. E., Wright, C. I., Shin, L. M., Kagan, J. & Rauch, S. L. (2003). Inhibited and uninhibited infants 'grown up': Adult amygdalar response to novelty. *Science*, 300, 1952–3.

Schwartz, M. W. & Morton, G. J. (2002). Obesity: Keeping hunger at bay. *Nature*, 418, 595–7.

Schwartz, M. W., Woods, S. C., Porte, D., Jr, Seeley, R. J. & Baskin, D. G. (2000). Central nervous system control of food intake. *Nature*, 404, 661–71.

Segal, Z. V., Gemar, M., Truchon, C., Guirguis, M. & Horowitz, L. M. (1995). A priming methodology for studying self-representation in major depressive disorder. *Journal of Abnormal Psychology*, 104, 205–13.

Segerstrom, S. C. & Miller, G. E. (2004). Psychological stress and the human immune system: A meta-analytic study of 30 years of inquiry. *Psychological Bulletin*, 130, 601–30.

Seligman, M. E. P. (1991). *Learned Optimism*. New York: Knopf.

Seligman, M. E., Abramson, L. Y., Semmel, A. & von Baeyer, C. (1979). Depressive attributional style. *Journal of Abnormal Psychology*, 88, 242–7.

Selten, J. P., van Duursen, R., van der Graaf, Y., Gispen-de Wied, C. C. & Kahn, R. S. (1997). Second-trimester exposure to maternal stress is a possible risk factor for psychotic illness in the child. *Schizophrenia Research*, 24, 258.

Selten, J. P., van der Graaf, Y., van Duursen, R., Gispen-de Wied, C. C. & Kahn, R. S. (1999). Psychotic illness after prenatal exposure to the 1953 Dutch flood disaster. *Schizophrenia Research*, 35, 243–5.

Selye, H. (1976). *Stress in Health and Disease*. Reading, MA: Butterworth.

Serra, A., Jones, S. H., Toone, B. & Gray, J. A. (2001). Impaired associative learning in chronic schizophrenics and their first-degree relatives: A study of latent inhibition and the Kamin blocking effect. *Schizophrenia Research*, 48, 273–89.

Shallice, T. (1982). Specific impairments of planning. *Philosophical Transactions of the Royal Society of London*, 298, 199–209.

Sham, P. (2003). Recent developments in quantitative trait loci analysis. In R. Plomin, J. C. DeFries, I. W. Craig & P. McGuffin (eds), *Behavioral Genetics in the Postgenomic Era*. Washington, DC: American Psychiatric Press.

Shaner, A., Miller, G. & Mintz, J. (2004). Schizophrenia as one extreme of a sexually selected fitness indicator. *Schizophrenia Research*, 70, 101–9.

Shanks, D. R. (1995). *The Psychology of Associative Learning*. Cambridge: Cambridge University Press.

Sharma, T. & Chitnis, X. (2000). *Brain Imaging in Schizophrenia: Insights and Applications*. London: Remedica.

Shekhar, A., Katner, J. S., Sajdyk, T. J. & Kohl, R. R. (2002). Role of norepinephrine in the dorsomedial hypothalamic panic response: An in vivo microdialysis study. *Pharmacology, Biochemistry and Behavior*, 71, 493–500.

Sheline, Y. I. (2003). Neuroimaging studies of mood disorder effects on the brain. *Biological Psychiatry*, 54, 338–52.

Sherman, S. L., DeFries, J. C., Gottesman, I. I., Loehlin, J. C., Meyer, J. M., Pelias, M. Z., Rice, J. & Waldman, I. (1997). Behavioral genetics '97: ASHG statement. Recent developments in human behavioral genetics: Past accomplishments and future directions. *American Journal of Human Genetics*, 60, 1265–75.

Shermer, M. (2002). *In Darwin's Shadow. The Life and Science of Alfred Russel Wallace: A Biographical Study on the Psychology of History*. Oxford: Oxford University Press.

Shin, L. M., Whalen, P. J., Pitman, R. K., Bush, G., Macklin, M. L., Lasko, N. B., Orr, S. P., McInerney, S. C. & Rauch, S. L. (2001). An fMRI study of anterior cingulate function in posttraumatic stress disorder. *Biological Psychiatry*, 50, 932–42.

Shoemaker, D. D., Schadt, E. E., Armour, C. D., He, Y. D., Garrett-Engele, P., McDonagh, P. D., Loerch, P. M., Leonardson, A., Lum, P. Y., Cavet, G., Wu, L. F., Altschuler, S. J., Edwards, S., King, J., Tsang, J. S., Schimmack, G., Schelter, J. M., Koch, J., Ziman, M., Marton, M. J., Li, B., Cundiff, P., Ward, T., Castle, J., Krolewski, M., Meyer, M. R., Mao, M., Burchard, J., Kidd, M. J., Dai, H., Phillips, J. W., Linsley, P. S., Stoughton, R., Scherer, S. & Boguski, M. S. (2001). Experimental annotation of the human genome using microarray technology. *Nature*, 409, 922–7.

Simons, D. J. & Chabris, C. F. (1999). Gorillas in our midst: Sustained inattentional blindness for dynamic events. *Perception*, 28, 1059–74.

Skinner, B. F. (1938). *The Behavior of Organisms*. New York: Appleton-Century-Crofts.

Skinner, B. F. (1948). *Walden Two*. New York. Macmillan.

Skinner, B. F. (1953). *Science and Human Behavior*. New York: Macmillan.

Skinner, B. F. (1957). *Verbal Behavior*. New York: Appleton-Century-Crofts.

Skinner, B. F. (1966). *The Behaviour of Organisms*. New York: Appleton-Century-Crofts.

Skinner, B. F. (1971). *Beyond Freedom and Dignity*. Harmondsworth: Penguin.

Skinner, B. F. (1984). Behaviorism at fifty. *Behavioral and Brain Sciences*, 7, 615–67.

Skuse, D. H., James, R. S., Bishop, D. V. M., Coppin, B. Dalton, P., Aamodt-Leeper, G., Bacarese-Hamilton, M., Creswell, C., McGurk, R. & Jacobs, P. A. (1997). Evidence from Turner's syndrome of an imprinted X-linked locus affecting cognitive function. *Nature*, 387, 705–8.

Slobodkin, L. B. (2003). Just before Watson and Crick. *Nature Genetics*, 33, 451.

Smeraldi, E., Zanardi, R., Benedetti, F., Di Bella, D., Perez, J. & Catalano, M. (1998). Polymorphism within the promoter of the serotonin transporter gene and antidepressant efficacy of fluvoxamine. *Molecular Psychiatry*, 3, 508–11.

Smith, B. D., Rypma, C. B. & Wilson, R. J. (1981). Dishabituation and spontaneous recovery of the electrodermal orienting response: Effects of extraversion, impulsivity, sociability, and caffeine. *Journal of Research in Personality*, 15, 233–40.

Spector, I. P., Pecknold, J. C. & Libman, E. (2003). Selective attentional bias related to the noticeability aspect of anxiety symptoms in generalised social phobia. *Journal of Anxiety Disorders*, 17, 517–31.

Spence, K. W. & Runquist, W. N. (1958). Temporal effects of conditioned fear on the eyelid reflex. *Journal of Experimental Psychology*, 55, 613–16.

Spence, S. A., Hirsch, S. R., Brooks, D. J. & Grasby, P. M. (1998). Prefrontal cortex activity in people with schizophrenia and control subjects: Evidence from positron emission tomography for remission of 'hypofrontality' with recovery from acute schizophrenia. *British Journal of Psychiatry*, 172, 316–23.

Sperry, R. W. (1969). A modified concept of consciousness. *Psychological Review*, 76, 532–6.

Sperry, R. W. (1970). An objective approach to subjective experience. *Psychological Review*, 77, 585–90.

Spiegel, E. A., Wycis, H. T. & Marks, M. (1947). Stereotaxic apparatus for operation on the human brain. *Science*, 109, 349–50.

Spitzer, R. L., Endicott, J. & Gibbon, M. (1979). Crossing the border into borderline personality and borderline schizophrenia: The development of criteria. *Archives of General Psychiatry*, 42, 591–6.

Stahl, S. M. (2000). *Essential Psychopharmacology: Neuroscientific Basis and Practical Applications* (2nd edn). Cambridge: Cambridge University Press.

Stein, D. J. & Ludik, J. (1998). *Neural Networks and Psychopathology: Connectionist Models in Practice and Research*. Cambridge: Cambridge University Press.

Stern, J. A. & Dunham, D. N. (1990). The ocular system. In J. T. Cacioppo & L. G. Tassinary (eds), *Principles of Psychophysiology: Physical, Social, and Inferential Elements*. New York: Cambridge University Press.

Stern, K. & McClintock, M. K. (1998). Regulation of ovulation by human pheromones. *Nature*, 392, 177–9.

Stevens, A. A., Goldman-Rakic, P. S., Gore, J. C., Fulbright, R. K. & Wexler, B. E. (1998). Cortical dysfunction in schizophrenia during auditory word and tone: Working memory demonstrated by functional magnetic resonance imaging. *Archives of General Psychiatry*, 55, 1097–103.

Stone, V. E., Cosmides, L., Tooby, J., Kroll, N. & Knight, R. T. (2002). Selective impairment of reasoning about social exchange in a patient with bilateral limbic system damage. *Proceedings of the National Academy of Sciences*, 99, 11531–6.

Storr, A. (1989). *Churchill's Black Dog*. London: Harper Collins.

Stuss, D. T. & Benson, D. F. (1986). *The Frontal Lobes*. New York: Raven Press.

Stuttaford, T. & Sharma, T. (1999). *In Your Right Mind: Everyday Psychological Problems and Psychiatric Conditions Explored and Explained*. London: Faber and Faber.

Sullivan, P. F., Neale, M. C. & Kendler, K. S. (2000). Genetic epidemiology of major depression: Review and meta-analysis. *American Journal of Psychiatry*, 157, 1552–62.

Sulston, J. & Ferry, G. (2002). *The Common Thread: A Story of Science, Politics, Ethics, and the Human Genome*. London: Bantam.

Sutherland, S. (1976). *Breakdown: A Personal Crisis and Medical Dilemma*. London: Weidenfeld & Nicolson.

Swaab, D. F. & Hofman, M. A. (1990). An enlarged suprachiasmatic nucleus in homosexual men. *Brain Research*, 537, 141–8.

Swain, A., Narvaez, V., Burgoyne, P., Camerino, G. & Lovell-Badge, R. (1998). Dax1 antagonizes Sry action in mammalian sex determination. *Nature*, 391, 761–7.

Swerdlow, N. R., Bakshi, V., Waikar, M., Taaid, N. & Geyer, M. A. (1998). Seroquel, clozapine and chlorpromazine restore sensorimotor gating in ketamine-treated rats. *Psychopharmacology*, 140, 75–80.

Swerdlow, N. R., Braff, D. L., Hartston, H., Perry, W. & Geyer, M. A. (1996). Latent inhibition in schizophrenia. *Schizophrenia Research*, 20, 91–103.

Swerdlow, N. R., Caine, S. B. & Geyer, M. A. (1992). Regionally selective effects of intracerebral dopamine infusion on sensorimotor gating of the startle reflex in rats. *Psychopharmacology*, 108, 189–95.

Swerdlow, N. R. & Geyer, M. A. (1998). Using an animal model of deficient sensorimotor gating to study the pathophysiology and new treatments of schizophrenia. *Schizophrenia Bulletin*, 24, 285–301.

Swerdlow, N. R., Varty, G. B. & Geyer, M. A. (1998). Discrepant findings of clozapine effects on prepulse inhibition of startle: Is it the route or the rat? *Neuropsychopharmacology*, 18, 50–6.

Takei, N., Lewis, S., Jones, P., Harvey, I. & Murray, R. M. (1996). Prenatal exposure to influenza and increased cerebrospinal fluid spaces in schizophrenia. *Schizophrenia Bulletin*, 22, 521–34.

Taylor, S. E. & Brown, J. D. (1988). Illusion and well-being: A social psychological perspective on mental health. *Psychological Bulletin*, 103, 193–210.

Temple, S. (2001). The development of neural stem cells. *Nature*, 414, 112–17.

Teuber, H. L. (1955). Phyiological psychology. *Annual Review of Psychology*, 6, 267–96.

Thapar, A., Gottesman, I. I., Owen, M. J., O'Donovan, M. C. & McGuffin, P. (1994). The genetics of mental retardation. *British Journal of Psychiatry*, 164, 747–58.

Thapar, A. & McGuffin, P. (1997). Anxiety and depressive symptoms in childhood: A genetic study of comorbidity. *Journal of Child Psychology and Psychiatry*, 38, 651–6.

Thayer, R. E. (1989). *The Biopsychology of Mood and Arousal*. Oxford: Oxford University Press.

Thorndike, E. L. (1898). *Animal Intelligence: An Experimental Study of the Associative Processes in Animals*. New York: Macmillan.

Thorndike, E. L. (1911). *Animal intelligence: Experimental studies*. New York: Macmillan.

Thornton, J. C., Dawe, S., Lee, C., Capstick, C., Corr, P.J., Cotter, P., Frangou, S., Gray, N.S., Russell, M.A. & Gray, J.A. (1996). Effects of nicotine and amphetamine on latent inhibition in human subjects. *Psychopharmacology*, 127, 164–73.

Tipper, S. P. (1985). The negative priming effect: Inhibitory processing by ignored objects. *Quarterly Journal of Experimental Psychology*, 37A, 571–90.

Tipper, S. P., Weaver, B. & Milliken, B. (1995). Spatial negative priming without mismatching: Comment on Park and Kanwisher (1994). *Journal of Experimental Psychology: Human Perception and Performance*, 25, 1220–9.

Toates, F. (1998). The interaction of cognitive and stimulus–response processes in the control of behaviour. *Neuroscience and Biobehavioral Reviews*, 22, 59–83.

Toates, F. (2001). *Biological Psychology: An Integrative Approach*. Harlow: Pearson.

Toates, F. (2004). Cognition, motivation, emotion and action: A dynamic and vulnerable interdependence. *Applied Animal Behaviour Science*, 86, 173–204.

Toates, F. & Coschug-Toates, O. (2002). *Obsessive Compulsive Disorder: Practical, Tried-and-Tested Strategies to Overcome OCD* (2nd edn). London: Class.

Tomasello, M. (2000). Primate cognition: Introduction to the issue. *Cognitive Science*, 24, 351–61.

Trevarthen, C. B. (1968). Two mechanisms of vision in primates. *Psychologische Forschung*, 31, 299–337.

Trivers, R. (1971). The evolution of reciprocal altruism. *Quarterly Review of Biology*, 46, 35–57.

Trivers, R. L. (1972). Parental investment and sexual selection. In B. Campbell (ed.), *Sexual Selection and the Descent of Man: 1891–1971*. Chicago, IL: Aldine.

Trivers, R. (1974). Parent–offspring conflict. *American Zoologist*, 14, 249–64.

Trivers, R. (1985). *Social Evolution*. Menlo Park, CA: Benjamin/Cummings.

Trut, L. N. (1999). Early canid domestication: The farm-fox experiment. *American Scientist*, 87, 160–9.

Tryon, W. W. (1998). A neural network explanation of posttraumatic stress disorder. *Journal of Anxiety Disorders*, 12, 373–85.

Turchan, J., Przewlocka, B., Toth, G., Lason, W., Borsodi, A. & Przewlocki, R. (1999). The effect of repeated administration of morphine, cocaine and ethanol on mu and delta opioid receptor density in the nucleus accumbens and striatum of the rat. *Neuroscience*, 91, 971–7.

Turner, A. M. & Greenough, W. T. (1985). Differential rearing effects on rat visual cortex synapses. I. Synaptic and neuronal density and synapses per neuron. *Brain Research*, 329, 195–203.

Ungerleider, L. G. & Mishkin, M. (1982). Two cortical vision systems. In D. J. Ingle, M. A. Goodale & R. J. W. Mansfield (eds), *Analysis of Visual Behaviour*. Cambridge, MA: MIT press.

Vakili, K., Pillay, S. S., Lafer, B., Fava, M., Renshaw, P. F., Bonello-Cintron, C. M. & Yurgelun-Todd, D. A. (2000). Hippocampal volume in primary unipolar major depression: A magnetic resonance imaging study. *Biological Psychiatry*, 47, 1087–90.

van Elst, L. T., Woermann, F., Lemieux, L. & Trimble, M. R. (2000a). Increased amygdala volumes in female depressed human. A quantitative magnetic resonance imaging study. *Neuroscience Letters*, 281, 103–6.

van Elst, L. T., Woermann, F. G., Lemieux, L., Thompson, P. J. & Trimble, M. R. (2000b). Affective aggression in patients with temporal lobe epilepsy: a quantitative MRI study of the amygdala. *Brain*, 123, 234–43.

van Hooff, J. C., Brunia, C. H. M. & Allen, J. J. B. (1996). Event-related potentials as indirect measures of recognition memory. *International Journal of Psychophysiology*, 21, 15–31.

Van Os, J. & Jones, P. B. (2001). Neuroticism as a risk factor for schizophrenia. *Psychological Medicine*, 31, 1129–34.

Van Os, J. & Selten, J. P. (1998). Prenatal exposure to maternal stress and subsequent schizophrenia. The May 1940 invasion of The Netherlands. *British Journal of Psychiatry*, 172, 324–6.

van Vreeswijk, M. F. & De Wilde, E. J. (2004). Autobiographical memory specificity, psychopathology, depressed mood and the use of the Autobiographical Memory Test: A meta-analysis. *Behaviour Research Therapy*, 42, 731–43.

Varty, G. B. & Higgins, G. A. (1995). Reversal of dizocilpine-induced disruption of prepulse inhibition of an acoustic startle response by the 5-HT2 receptor antagonist ketanserin. *European Journal of Pharmacology*, 287, 201–5.

Vaswani, M., Linda, F. K. & Ramesh, S. (2003). Role of selective serotonin reuptake inhibitors in psychiatric disorders: A comprehensive review. *Progress in Neuro-Psychopharmacology and Biological Psychiatry*, 27, 85–102.

Velicer, G. J., Kroos, L. & Lenski (2000). Development cheating in the social bacterium *Myxococcus xanthus*. *Nature*, 404, 598.

Velmans, M. (1991). Is human information processing conscious? *Behavioural and Brain Sciences*, 14, 651–726.

Velmans, M. (2000). *Understanding Consciousness*. London: Routledge.

Velmans, M. (2002a). How could conscious experiences affect brains? *Journal of Consciousness Studies*, 9, 3–29.

Velmans, M. (2002b). Making sense of causal interactions between consciousness and brain. *Journal of Consciousness Studies*, 9, 69–95.

Venter, J. C. et al. (2001). The sequence of the human genome. *Science*, 291, 1304–51.

Villringer, A. & Dirnagl, U. (1997). *Optical Imaging of Brain Function and Metabolism 2: Physiological Basis and Comparison to other Functional Neuroimaging Methods*. New York: Plenum Press.

Vingerhoets, G., Berckmoes, C. & Stroobant, N. (2003). Cerebral hemodynamics during discrimination of prosodic and semantic emotion in speech studied by transcranial Doppler ultrasonography. *Neuropsychology*, 17, 93–9.

Vrana, S. R., Roodman, A. & Beckham, J. C. (1995). Selective processing of trauma-relevant words in posttraumatic stress disorder. *Journal of Anxiety Disorders*, 9, 515–30.

Walker, D. L., Toufexis, D. J. & Davis, M. (2003). Role of the bed nucleus of the stria terminalis versus the amygdala in fear, stress, and anxiety. *European Journal of Pharmacology*, 463, 199–216.

Walsh, V. & Pascual-Leone, A. (2003). *Transcranial Magnetic Stimulation: A Neurochronometrics of Mind*. Cambridge, MA: MIT Press.

Wason, P. C. (1966). Reasoning. In B. M. Foss (ed.), *New Horizons in Psychology*. Harmondsworth: Penguin.

Wason, P. C. (1983). Realism and rationality in the selection task. In J. Evans (ed.), *Thinking and Reasoning: Psychological Approaches*. London: Routledge.

Wason, P. C. & Johnson-Laird, P. N. (1972). *Psychology of Reasoning: Structure and Content*. Cambridge. MA: Harvard University Press.

Wassermann, E. M. & Lisanby, S. H. (2001). Therapeutic application of repetitive transcranial magnetic stimulation: A review. *Clinical Neurophysiology*, 112, 1367–77.

Watson, J. B. (1914). *Behavior: An Introduction to Comparative Psychology*. New York: H. Holt.

Watson, J. D. (1968). *The Double Helix: A Personal Account of the Discovery of the Structure of DNA*. Harmondsworth: Penguin.

Watson, J. D. (2003). *DNA: The Secret of Life*. New York: Alfred A. Knopf.

Watson, J. D. & Crick, F. H. C. (1953). Molecular structure of nucleic acids. *Nature*, 171, 737–8.

Weber, W. W. (1997). *Pharmacogenetics*. New York: Oxford University Press.

Webster, S. (2003). *Thinking about Biology*. Cambridge: Cambridge University Press.

Wechsler, D. (1945). A standardized memory scale for clinical use. *Journal of Psychology*, 19, 87–95.

Wechsler, D. (1955). *WAIS Manual*. New York: The Psychological Corporation.

Wedekind, C., Seebeck, T., Bettens, F. & Paepke, A. J. (1995). MHC-dependent mate preferences in humans. *Proceedings of the Royal Society: Biological Sciences*, 260, 245–9.

Weickert, T. W., Goldberg, T. E., Gold, J. M., Bigelow, L. B., Egan, M. F. & Weinberger, D. R. (2000). Cognitive impairments in patients with schizophrenia displaying preserved and compromised intellect. *Archives of General Psychiatry*, 57, 907–13.

Weinberger, D. R. (1987). Implications of normal brain development for the pathogenesis of schizophrenia. *Archives of General Psychiatry*, 44, 660–9.

Weinberger, D. R. (1995). From neuropathology to neurodevelopment. *Lancet*, 346, 552–7.

Weinberger, D. R., Berman, K. F. & Zec, R. F. (1986). Physiologic dysfunction of dorsolateral prefrontal cortex in schizophrenia, I: Regional cerebral blood flow evidence. *Archives of General Psychiatry*, 43, 11–124.

Weinstock, M. (2001). Alterations induced by gestational stress in brain morphology and behaviour of the offspring. *Progress in Neurobiology*, 65, 427–51.

Weiskrantz, L. (1986). *Blindsight: A Case Study and Implications*. Oxford: Oxford University Press.

Weiskrantz, L. (1997). *Consciousness Lost and Found*. Oxford: Oxford University Press.

Weiskrantz, L. (2003). Mind the gap, after 65 years: Visual conditioning in cortical blindness. *Brain*, 126, 265–6.

Weiss, S. (1999). Pathways for neural stem cell biology and repair. *Nature Biotechnology*, 17, 850–1.

Weller, A. (1998). Human pheromones: Communication through body odour. *Nature*, 392, 126–7.

Wells, A. & Matthews, G. (1994). *Attention and Emotion: A Clinical Perspective*. Hove: Erlbaum.

Wender, P. H., Rosenthal, D., Kety, S. S., Schulsinger, F. & Welner, J. (1974). Crossfostering. A research strategy for clarifying the role of genetic and experiential factors in the etiology of schizophrenia. *Archives of General Psychiatry*, 30, 121–8.

Wertheimer, M. (1923). Untersuchungen zur Lehre von der Gestalt II (Laws of organization in perceptual forms). *Psycologische Forschung*, 4, 301–50.

Whalen, P. J., Shin, L. M., McInerney, S. C., Fischer, H., Wright, C. I. & Rauch, S. L. (2001). A functional MRI study of human amygdala responses to facial expressions of fear versus anger. *Emotion*, 1, 70–83.

Whalley, H. C., Kestelman, J. N., Rimmington, J. E., Kelso, A., Abukmeil, S. S., Best, J. J. K., Johnstone, E. C. & Lawrie, S. M. (1999). Methodological issues in volumetric magnetic resonance imaging of the brain in the Edinburgh High Risk Project. *Psychiatry Research: Neuroimaging*, 91, 31–44.

Wild, B., Erb, M. & Bartels, M. (2001). Are emotions contagious? Evoked emotions while viewing emotionally expressive faces: quality, quantity, time course and gender differences. *Psychiatry Research*, 102, 109–24.

Willemsen, G., Ring, C., McKeever, S. & Carroll, D. (2000). Secretory immunoglobulin A and cardiovascular activity during mental arithmetic: Effects of task difficulty and task order. *Biological Psychology*, 52, 127–41.

Williams, G. C. (1966). *Adaptations and Natural Selection*. Princeton, NJ: Princeton University Press.

Williams, J., McGuffin, P., Nothen, M., Owen, M. J. & the EMASS Collaborative Group (1997). Meta-analysis of association between the 5-HT2a receptor T102C polymorphism and schizophrenia. *Lancet*, 349, 1221.

Williams, J. H., Wellman, N. A., Allan, L. M., Taylor, E., Tonin, J., Feldon, J. & Rawlins, J. N. P. (1996). Tobacco smoking correlates with schizotypal and borderline personality traits. *Personality and Individual Differences*, 20, 267–70.

Williams, N. M., Preece, A., Spurlock, G., Norton, H., Williams, H. J., Zammit, S., O'Donovan, M. C. & Owen, M. J. (2003). Support for genetic variation in the neuregulin 1 susceptibility to schizophrenia. *Molecular Psychiatry*, 8, 485–7.

Wilson, B. A. (1999). *Case Studies in Neuropsychological Rehabilitation*. New York: Oxford University Press.

Wilson, E. O. (1975). *Sociobiology: The New Synthesis*. Cambridge, MA: Harvard University Press.

Wilson, G. D. (1990). Personality, time of day and arousal. *Personality and Individual Differences*, 11, 153–68.

Wiser, A. K., Andreasen, N. C., O'Leary, D. S., Watkins, G. L., Boles Ponto, L. L. & Hichwa, R. D. (1998). Dysfunctional cortico-cerebellar circuits cause 'cognitive dysmetria' in schizophrenia. *Neuroreport*, 9, 1895–9.

Witelson, S. F., Kigar, D. L. & Harvey, T. (1999). The exceptional brain of Albert Einstein. *Lancet*, 353, 2149–53.

Wolfe, J. M. (1997). Experimental psychology. In a blink of the mind's eye. *Nature*, 387, 756–7.

Wolfe, J. M. (1999). Cognitive neuroscience. How do you pay attention? *Nature*, 400, 813–15.

Wolfe, J. M., Klempen, N. & Dahlen, K. (2000). Postattentive vision. *Journal of Experimental Psychology: Human Perception and Performance*, 26, 693–716.

Wong, A. H. C. & Van Tol, H. H. M. (2003). Schizophrenia: From phenomenology to neurobiology. *Neuroscience and Biobehavioural Reviews*, 27, 269–306.

Wong, P. S., Shevrin, H. & Williams, W. J. (1994). Conscious and nonconscious processes: An ERP index of an anticipatory response in a conditioning paradigm using visually masked stimuli. *Psychophysiology*, 31, 87–101.

Woodnorth, M.-A., Kyd, R. J., Logan, B. J., Long, M. A. & McNaughton, N. (2003). Multiple hypothalamic sites control the frequency of hippocampal theta rhythm. *Hippocampus*, 13, 319–32.

Woodnorth, M. A. & McNaughton, N. (2002). Similar effects of medial supramammillary or systematic injection of chlordiazepoxide on both theta frequency and fixed-interval responding. *Cognitive, Affective, and Behavioural Neuroscience*, 2, 76–83.

World Health Organization (1992). *International Statistical Classification of Diseases and Related Health Problems, 1989 Revision* (10th edn). Geneva: World Health Organization.

Wright, C. I., Martis, B., McMullin, K., Shin, L. M. & Rauch, S. L. (2003). Amygdala and insular responses to emotionally valenced human faces in small animal specific phobia. *Biological Psychiatry*, 54, 1067–76.

Wright, C. I., Rabe-Hesketh, S., Woodruff, P. W., David, A. S., Murray, R. M. & Bullmore, E. T. (2000). Meta-analysis of regional brain volumes in schizophrenia. *Amercian Journal of Psychiatry*, 157, 16–25.

Wright, S. (1921). Systems of mating. *Genetics*, 6, 111–78.

Wyatt, T. D. (2003). *Pheromones and Animal Behaviour: Communication by Smell and Taste*. Cambridge: Cambridge University Press.

Wynne Edwards, V. C. (1962). *Animal Dispersion in Relation to Social Behaviour*. Edinburgh: Oliver & Boyd.

Yerkes, R. M. (1939). The life history and personality of the chimpanzee. *American Naturalist*, 73, 97–112.

Young, A. M. J., Ahier, R. G., Upton, R. L., Joseph, M. H. & Gray, J. A. (1998). Increased extracellular dopamine in the nucleus accumbens of the rat during associative learning of neurtral stimuli. *Neuroscience*, 83, 1175–83.

Young, A. M. J., Joseph, M. H. & Gray, J. A. (1993). Latent inhibition of conditioned dopamine release in rat nucleus accumbens. *Neuroscience*, 54, 5–9.

Young, T. (1802). On the theory of light and colors. *Philosophical Transactions of the Royal Society*, 91, 12–49.

Zald, D. H. (2003). The human amygdala and the emotional evaluation of sensory stimuli. *Brain Research Reviews*, 41, 88–123.

Zammit, S., Allebeck, P., Andreasson, S., Lundberg, I. & Lewis, G. (2002). Self report cannabis use as a risk factor for schizophrenia in Swedish conscripts of 1969: Historical cohort analysis. *British Medical Journal*, 23, 1183–4.

Zeki, S. (1993). *A Vision of the Brain*. Oxford: Blackwell.

Zhao, M. Z., Momma, S., Delfani, K., Carlen, M., Cassidy, R. M., Johansson, C. B., Brismar, H., Shupliakov, O., Frisen, J. & Janson, A. M. (2003). Evidence for neurogenesis in the adult mammalian substantia nigra. *Proceedings of the National Academy of Sciences*, 100, 7925–30.

Zhu, J. (2003). Reclaiming volition: An alternative interpretation of Libet's experiment. *Journal of Consciousness Studies*, 10, 61–77.

Zyss, T. (1996). Antidepressive effects of transcranial magnetic stimulation-possible substitution for electroconvulsive treatment in psychiatry. *Electroencephalography and Clinical Neurophysiology*, 99, 377.

Index of Authors

Index of Subjects

twin studies, 366, 370, 372, 373–4, 375–6, 380
  adoption studies, 375
  and depression, 430, 431, 467
  and personality, 519, 555, 556
  psychiatric co-morbidity, 377
  and schizophrenia, 491, 498, 501–2, 503–4, 506–7
'two-process model of learning', 221
two-process theory of neurosis, 456
tympanic membrane, 139, 140
Type 1 personalities and stress, 197
typicals, 493, 494, 501
tyrosine, 420

unconditioned response (UCR), 207, 208, 209, 210
  and eye-blink conditioning, 299, 300
unconditioned stimulus (UCS), 180, 207, 208, 209, 210, 211–15, 220
  and anxiety, 456–60
    CS–UCS predictability, 457
  and eye-blink conditioning, 299, 300
  and microdialysis, 329
  and neural plasticity, 235–6
  psychophysiological testing, 285–6
underarm secretions, 186
unilateral neglect, 254, 581
unsaturated fats and schizophrenia, 515
unsupervised training in neural networks, 230
up-regulation, 113–14

vagus nerve experiment, 102–3
validity, 350–1
  of measurements, 280–1
variable interval reinforcement schedules, 219
variable ratio reinforcement schedules, 219
variable reinforcement extinction effect, 220
variance in quantitative genetics, 366, 367–8, 370, 372, 381, 395
  partitioning of variance, 371, 373–4
vas deferens, 187
vasopressin, 173, 175, 180, 185
venlafaxine, 426–7
ventral posterior nuclei, 128, 129
ventral posteromedial thalamic nucleus, 133–4
ventral roots, 71

ventral streams, 154–5, 254, 585
ventral tegmental area (VTA), 76, 332, 333, 334–5, 496
ventricles of brain, 74, 75, 78–9
  ventricular enlargement and schizophrenia, 498–9, 502
vesicles, 93–5
  and ion gates, 98
vicarious learning, 221
violence inhibition mechanism (VIM), 282
visual agnosia, 253
visual association cortex, 154
visual cortex: impairment effects, 253–4
visual field, 144, 145
visual form discrimination test, 262
visual illusions, 588
visual neglect, 253, 254–5
visual object recognition, 156
visual system, 123–4, 143–60
  cognitive deficits, 253–4, 257, 581–4
  and consciousness, 585
  and learning, 203
visuospatial processing, 84, 85–6, 154
vocabulary tests, 264
volition and consciousness, 579–80
volume of distribution, 359
volumetric MRI, 414
vomeronasal system, 137, 186, 326–7
vulnerability traits, 455, 485, 487, 498, 502, 507–8

Wason selection task, 572–3
waveform analysis, 139, 140
wavelengths: light and vision, 143, 144, 157
'weakly penetrant gene effect', 391
Weigert's myelin stain, 338
weight in neural networks, 226–7
Wernicke's aphasia, 86, 253
'wetware' model, 568, 569–70
'what-if' simulations, 468, 512, 594–5
white light, 144
Wisconsin card sorting test (WCST), 265–6
  and schizophrenia, 485, 500, 502
Wolffian ducts, 178, 187
'word–colour synaesthesia', 257
working memory, 263, 484, 552
World Health Organization, 407

zombies, 577
zygomatic major muscle activity, 287, 288

Made in the USA
Lexington, KY
11 September 2016